Forensic Victimology

Forensic Victimology

Examining Violent Crime Victims in Investigative and Legal Contexts

Brent E. Turvey
Wayne Petherick

AMSTERDAM • BOSTON • HEIDELBERG • LONDON
NEW YORK • OXFORD • PARIS • SAN DIEGO
SAN FRANCISCO • SINGAPORE • SYDNEY • TOKYO
Academic Press is an imprint of Elsevier

ELSEVIER

Academic Press is an imprint of Elsevier
30 Corporate Drive, Suite 400, Burlington, MA 01803, USA
525 B Street, Suite 1900, San Diego, California 92101-4495, USA
84 Theobald's Road, London WC1X 8RR, UK
This book is printed on acid-free paper. ∞

Library of Congress Cataloging-in-Publication Data
Application submitted

British Library Cataloguing-in-Publication Data
A catalogue record for this book is available from the British Library.

ISBN: 978-0-12-374089-2

For information on all Academic Press publications
visit our Web site at www.elsevierdirect.com

Printed in the United States of America
09 10 11 9 8 7 6 5 4 3 2 1

Contents

Acknowledgments

It is impossible to accomplish anything of professional merit alone. If you do, it's because you weren't, and were at the very least surrounded by able minds with capable hands. We had the benefit of that and more. And the result reflects it.

We would like to thank our contributors. Without their hard work, undying professionalism, and commitment to the scientific study of crime and criminals, we could not have put together such an exceptional work. We stand together strong in our multidisciplinary commitment to more informed students, more informed investigations, more informed forensic analysis, and sounder legal outcomes. This textbook has moved criminology a step further in that direction.

In particular, we would like to single out Joe Diaz, Claire Ferguson, and Michael McGrath for recognition and praise of their efforts. Apart from being an able writer, Dr. McGrath has tremendous editorial skills. We thank him for lending us his expertise and being part of this project. Joe Diaz and Claire Ferguson were invaluable resources as well. Both furnished critical research and writing to this project, giving of their time and meeting their deadlines despite significant professional workloads and other commitments. We were lucky to have their talents on board.

Wayne Petherick
Brent Turvey

Contributors

Jose Diaz, MCRIM

Jose Diaz recently completed a Master of Criminology degree at Bond University in Australia. His thesis examined the admissibility of case linkage testimony by expert witnesses and the courts interpretation of its probative value against its prejudicial risk. He received his Bachelor of Science in Criminal Justice Administration from San Diego State University in California. During his undergrad study, his primary focus concerned examining the effects of legislative decisions that grant broader police power and the subsequent implications that arise. He has experience with both the prosecution and defense, working with the Ventura County District Attorney's Office and later with the Alternate Public Defender's Office of San Diego. He can be contacted at: jodias805@gmail.com.

Claire E. Ferguson, MCRIM

Claire E. Ferguson holds her Bachelor of Arts Degree in Honours psychology from the University of Western Ontario in Canada, and a Masters of Criminology from Bond University in Queensland, Australia. She is currently a Doctoral Candidate in the Criminology Department at Bond University where she is studying staged crime scenes. Claire worked for St. Leonard's Society in 2006, writing a narrative to be used for training purposes about homicide cases. In 2007, she undertook an internship with Queensland Fire and Rescue in the Fire Investigation Unit. In 2008, she completed a Crime Scene Analysis Internship with Forensic Solutions. She is also currently an Adjunct Teaching Fellow in the Criminology Department at Bond University. Claire can be contacted at clfergus@staff.bond.edu.au.

Charla M. Jamerson, BSN, RN, BC, SANE-A, CMI, III

Charla Jamerson received her Bachelors of Nursing Science from Excelsior College of Nursing in 2002, and her RN Diploma from the Baptist School of Nursing Northwest in 1995. In 2003, she complete the Graduate Certificate Program in Forensic Nursing and Forensic Internship at the University of Colorado, Colorado Springs. She is a registered Nurse in the State of Arkansas. She is also certified as a Sexual Assault Nurse Examiner by the International Association of Forensic Nurses, and as Medical Investigator by the American College of Forensic Examiners. From 2000–2003, she was the Director of Forensic Nursing and Forensic Nurse Examiner at the Children's Safety Center in Springdale, Arkansas. From 2003–2006, she was the owner, Director of Forensic Nursing Services, and head clinician of Jamerson Forensic Nursing & Investigative Services, Inc. in Fayetteville, Arkansas. She is currently in the Nurse Practitioner Program at Stony Brook University, New York, studying to get her Masters, and can be reached at: cjame24152@aol.com.

Michael McGrath, M.D.

Michael McGrath, MD is a Board Certified Forensic Psychiatrist, licensed in the State of New York. He is a Clinical Associate Professor in the Department of Psychiatry, University of Rochester School of Medicine and Dentistry, Rochester, NY, and Medical Director & Chair, Department of Behavioral Health, Unity Health System, Rochester, NY.

Dr. McGrath divides his time among administrative, clinical, research and teaching activities. His areas of expertise include forensic psychiatry and criminal profiling. He has lectured on three continents and is a founding member of the Academy of Behavioral Profiling. He can be contacted at: mmcgrath@profiling.org.

Wayne A. Petherick, PhD

Wayne Petherick, PhD, is Associate Professor of Criminology at Bond University on Australia's Gold Coast. Here Wayne teaches criminal profiling, Behavioral Evidence Analysis, criminal motivations, forensic criminology and crime and deviance, among others. He also consults to private clients on matters of risk and threat, stalking, miscarriages of justice and crime prevention.

Wayne is the author of *Serial Crime: Theoretical and Practical Issues in Behavioural Profiling* (2005) with Elsevier Science, and numerous other articles on profiling and stalking. Wayne is a board member of the Academy of Behavioral Profiling and Assistant Editor of the Journal of Behavioral Profiling. He can be reached via email on wpetheri@staff.bond.edu.au or wpetheri@profiling.org.

Angela N. Torres, PhD

Angela N. Torres, Ph.D. obtained her Master's degree in 2004. She received her Doctorate in 2007, from Sam Houston State University, in Clinical Psychology with a forensic focus. She completed her pre-doctoral internship in clinical psychology at the Federal Medical Center in Rochester, Minnesota. Dr. Torres obtained a forensic postdoctoral fellowship in Forensic Psychology at Central State Hospital in Petersburg, Virginia, and is currently a Forensic Evaluator there. She has experience in clinical assessment and psychotherapy, as well as forensic assessments including competency to stand trial and sanity at the time of the alleged offense. In addition, Dr. Torres has experience conducting sexually violent predator risk assessments, and participated in a multiple year sex offender recidivism research study. She may be contacted by email at Angela. Torres@csh.dmhmrsas.virginia.gov.

Brent E. Turvey, M.S.

Brent E. Turvey spent his first years in college on a pre-med track only to change his course of study once his true interest took hold. He received a Bachelor of Science degree from Portland State University in Psychology, with an emphasis on Forensic Psychology, and an additional Bachelor of Science degree in History. He went on to receive his Masters of Science in Forensic Science after studying at the University of New Haven, in West Haven, Connecticut.

Since graduating in 1996, Brent has consulted with many agencies, attorneys, and police departments in the United States, Australia, China, Canada, Barbados and Korea on a range of rapes, homicides, and serial/ multiple rape/ death cases, as a forensic scientist and criminal profiler. He has also been court qualified as an expert in the areas of criminal profiling, forensic science, victimology, and crime reconstruction.

In August of 2002, he was invited by the Chinese People's Police Security University (CPPSU) in Beijing to lecture before groups of detectives at the Beijing, Wuhan, Hanzou, and Shanghai police bureaus. In 2005, he was invited back to China again, to lecture at the CPPSU, and to the police in Beijing and Xian – after the translation of the 2nd edition of this text into Chinese for the University. In 2007, he was invited to lecture at the 1st Behavioral Sciences Conference at the Home Team (Police) Academy in Singapore, where he also provided training to their Behavioral Science Unit.

He is the author of Criminal Profiling: An Introduction to Behavioral Evidence Analysis, 1st, 2nd, and 3rd Editions (1999, 2002, 2008); co-author of the Rape Investigation Handbook (2004), and Crime Reconstruction (2006) - all with Elsevier Science. He is currently a full partner, Forensic Scientist, Criminal Profiler, and Instructor with Forensic Solutions, LLC, and an Adjunct Professor in Criminology at Oklahoma City University. He can be contacted at bturvey@ forensic-science.com.

Angela J. van der Walt, PSY.D.

Angela van der Walt holds a Masters of Arts in Forensic Psychology (2002), and a Doctorate in Clinical Psychology (2007), both from Graduate School of Professional Psychology at the University of Denver in Denver, Colorado. She is currently a Licensed Professional Counselor and Associate Provider & Evaluator for the Colorado Sex Offender Management Board. Dr. van der Walt has worked in sex offender therapy for several years, in both group and individual contexts. She may be contacted at: ajmuller99@hotmail.com.

Preface

An Argument for Forensic Victimology
Brent E. Turvey

Victimology is a social science regarded as the scientific study of victims. It is a broad subject with many subcategories of research. Some of these are theoretical and some are applied.

The objective of this textbook is to provide readers with the basic principles and practice standards of *forensic victimology:* the scientific study of victims for the purpose of addressing investigative and forensic issues. It is intended to educate the student in an applied fashion and to act as a guide for victimologist practitioners who assist investigators and provide expert testimony in court. It gives readers the means and rationale for examining victims with a scientific mindset, as opposed to the mindset of a police officer, victim's advocate, or treatment professional.

Dr. Petherick and I collaborated on this text for the following reasons: there is really none other like it available; professionals are less and less encouraged to approach victims with the skepticism that science requires; and victimization is not always simple.

On Friday, March 11, 2005, at 9:00 a.m. in Atlanta, Georgia, a suspected rapist named Brian Nichols overpowered a courthouse deputy. As is customary, his handcuffs had been removed so that he could change from jail to civilian clothes for the jury. Nichols took the deputy's keys and gun and made his way to the courtroom where his trial was to be held. He entered at the back, through the private chambers of Judge Rowland Barnes. Nichols then shot Judge Barnes in the head, killing him. During his escape, Nichols also shot and killed Julie Brandau, the court reporter, and deputy sergeant Hoyt Teasley. Sometime later, Nichols shot and killed U.S. Customs Agent David Wilhelm, taking his badge, gun, and vehicle. By that time, a nationally publicized statewide manhunt was already under way.

FIGURE P.1
Rescue personnel speed one of the victims of Brian Nichols' March, 2005 shooting spree into an ambulance waiting outside of the Fulton County Courthouse in Atlanta, Georgia.

According to Ashley Smith's initial statements to police, the following took place on Saturday, March 12, 2005, at around 2:00 a.m. Nichols encountered 26-year-old Smith in the parking lot of an apartment complex where she had just arrived home. He followed her after she parked and forced his way through her apartment door, with Smith at gunpoint. Nichols tied her hands and feet with masking tape and an extension cord. At one point, he forced her to sit in the bathroom with a towel over her head while he took a shower. He told her who he was, and she was afraid for her life.

But something unexpected happened: at 9:50 a.m., after seven hours of holding Smith hostage in her own home, Nichols allowed her to leave. She called 911. Shortly thereafter, Nichols was taken into custody by authorities. As explained in Mattingly (2005):

Smith said Nichols eventually unbound her hands and feet and that he began to relax as they spoke for hours about religion and family—including Smith's 5-year-old daughter and her late husband, who was stabbed four years earlier and died in her arms.

"I basically just talked to him and tried to gain his trust," she said.

Smith said she showed Nichols family photographs and read him passages from Rick Warren's bestselling book, *The Purpose Driven Life: What on Earth Am I Here For?*

After 6:00 a.m., Smith said she followed Nichols so he could hide [Agent] Wilhelm's truck and then took him back to the apartment in her car. She said that Nichols did not bring any weapons on the trip, and that she had her cellular phone but did not call police.

Smith said Nichols was "overwhelmed" when she made him a pancake breakfast and that the two of them watched television coverage of the manhunt.

Smith said Nichols allowed her to leave for a 10:00 a.m. visit with her daughter, who lives with Smith's aunt. Nichols gave her money, saying he was going to stay at her apartment for a "few days."

She dialed 911 about 9:50 a.m. and within minutes a SWAT team converged on building. After several tense minutes, police saw Nichols waving a white T-shirt.

In subsequent interviews, Ashley Smith gave any and all credit for her survival directly to God, saying that among other things she also read to Nichols from the Bible. The religious community enjoined the sensational mainstream coverage of the case. With Smith's assistance, they promoted her successful use of faith to end Nichols' killing spree, save her own life, and demonstrate that even the most horrific among us cannot resist the word of God.

In the months that followed, Ashley Smith was hailed as a hero by the news media and local law enforcement for executing what some have referred to as a textbook hostage negotiation for her own release. She was also given more than $70,000 in reward money for her role in Nichols' capture. She even coauthored a 2005 memoir, *Unlikely Angel: The Untold Story of the Atlanta Hostage Hero.*[1]

However, in that memoir, Smith publicly revealed for the first time that there were crucial details she had withheld from her account. She was actually a methamphetamine addict who had spent time in a psychiatric facility and had given up custody of her child by the time that Nichols took her hostage. Moreover, her captivity by Nichols did not just include reading from religious works to gain his trust and calm him down; it also involved sharing some of her personal meth stash with him. These were details that had been omitted from her interviews with the religious and mainstream media. More importantly, she also failed to mention her meth addiction,

FIGURE P.2
Ashley Smith's coauthored memoir was published in 2005, the same year as her ordeal with Brian Nichols. In it, Smith admits for the first time details about her methamphetamine addiction and how she shared her drug stash with her captor.

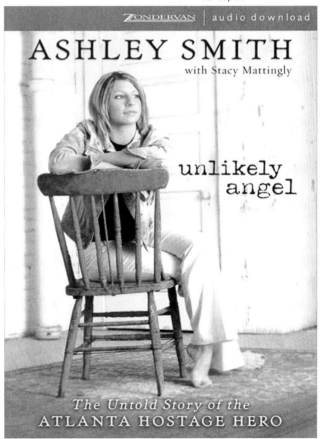

ZONDERVAN | audio download

ASHLEY SMITH
with Stacy Mattingly

unlikely angel

The Untold Story of the
ATLANTA HOSTAGE HERO

---

[1]This was published by Zondervan, which also publishes the *NIV Study Bible*.

possession, and sharing with Nichols to police until giving a supplemental interview to investigators months after the incident. In her memoir, she claims not to have used meth with Nichols and asserts that being held hostage by him was the reason she ultimately decided to stop using altogether.

Despite her deception, the authorities let Smith keep the reward money and did not press charges against her for methamphetamine possession or false reporting. She also turned her story of survival into a credential as an author and motivational speaker. But the story does not end there. Nichols, whose capital murder trial has been postponed four times because of funding issues, has yet to face justice.[2] When the Nichols case gets before a jury, sometime in 2008, it is hoped, there may be a question as to whether Smith can or will be asked to testify against him at trial. If the state does not call her, she may be called by the defense to cast doubt on her version of events as they relate to the charges against him. It's certainly true that in this complex case, the public will not know the full story until Smith takes the stand, raises her right hand, and swears to tell the truth, the whole truth, and nothing but the truth.

Again, victimization is not always simple.

REALISTIC VICTIMOLOGY

The Brian Nichols/Ashley Smith case illustrates how complex victimization can be. Victims are not theoretical, ideological, or archetypal constructs, they are people. They are susceptible to the same frailties and imperfections as the rest of us. Trying to examine victim behavior through any other lens is going to fog the truth and preclude actual understanding. Subsequently, as explained in Fattah (2000), there is a need to move towards what may be referred to as *realistic victimology* (39):

> The current dominant view in victimology of a bad offender and a good victim, of an innocent victim and a guilty criminal, will slowly give way to the more realistic and defensible view of two human beings caught in a web of intricate social relationships and human emotions.

Victimization is not always simple. It does not always happen in a straightforward manner to the innocent, the honest, or even the law-abiding. Nor does it occur in a vacuum under controlled laboratory conditions. Because it involves real people with real lives and real problems, victimization occurs under convoluted circumstances and within or as a result of relationships that are equally complex.

The victimologist is challenged with establishing, examining, and interpreting the features of these complexities. In doing so, she must contend with corrupted and incomplete victim information, the overt falsity of victims and

[2]As of this writing, the defense has reportedly spent around $1.5 million and is out of money; the new judge has stopped jury selection until financial issues have been resolved; and the DA is suing the judge to remove himself from the case for being biased towards the defense.

witnesses, and the unique social-political pressures that arise for and against every victim population imaginable. And that's when things are going well.

Dietrich Dorner, a cognitive psychologist, professor of psychology at the University of Bamberg, and author of *The Logic of Failure: Recognizing and Avoiding Error in Complex Environments* (1996), argues that there are three common features that make problems difficult to solve:

>*Complexity:* When many interdependent features that cannot be understood exist in isolation.
>*Dynamics:* When the environment changes over time, creating pressure.
>*Opacity:* The lack of visibility of certain parameters needed to accurately characterize the situation or problem.

As we will learn throughout this text, it is reasonably safe to argue that victimology suffers from all of these to varying degrees. So how can victimologists make informed and useful examinations and interpretations under these conditions? What Dorner found in his research is that those who were able to solve complex problems gathered information before acting, thought systematically, reviewed their progress, and corrected themselves often. Those who made the most errors tended to cling to preconceived theories, did not correct themselves, and blamed others when things went wrong. The errors made in complex situations, Dorner surmised, were not a feature of human capability; rather they were a feature of poorly conceived reasoning and an overall human tendency for laziness.

Certainly Dorner's findings cannot be irrelevant to the questions posed in victimology. So how does the victimologist apply them in her work? Before we can address that issue, we must first agree what victimology is, and what it is not.

VICTIMOLOGY DEFINED

Victimology is intended to be the scientific study of victims (Drapkin and Viano 1974). Currently, victimologists tend to find themselves operating within one of three main subgroups: general victimology, penal/interactionist victimology, and critical victimology.

General victimology is the study of all those individuals or groups who have suffered harm or loss, whether they are victims of a specific crime, general oppression, or a natural disaster. According to Mendelsohn (1976), this vast landscape includes victims of criminal offenders, the social-political environment, the natural environment, technology, and even those who victimize themselves. General victimologists are concerned with identifying or developing preventative measures, as well as tools for victim assistance. They not only want to study the characteristics and causes of victimization, they also want to determine remedies.

Interactionist victimology, or penal victimology, is the study of the dynamics between victims and their offenders. It is limited, however, to those who have been the victims of a specific crime. Interactionist victimologists study the victim's participation in crime causation through their interaction with the offender, the interaction between the victim and society, and the victim's subsequent role in the criminal justice system. Like the general victimologist, the interactionist intends to examine causes to develop remedies that favor the victim.

Critical victimology has developed in reaction to the way that victimology is defined and studied by the first two subgroups . It seeks to question how criminality and victimity are established, tolerated, and even sanctioned. The basic premise is that any mainstream view of victims perpetuates existing yet inadequate definitions of crime and victimization. This may be observed in the overemphasis in research and policy on certain types of crime and crime victims, because they are clearly defined and easier to grasp. This in turn results in a failure to study—let alone recognize—a host of both victim populations and their related social issues. It may also be observed in the way that a given justice system penalizes those who would elsewhere be viewed as victims, such as prostitutes who are selectively punished in some Western cultures, and victims of rape may be punished in some Islamic cultures.

These victimology subgroups are alike in that they are ultimately oriented towards helping victims, in studying ways of "speeding up a victim's emotional recovery, overcoming adversity, reimbursing financial damages, promoting reconciliation between the injured party and the wrongdoer, and restoring harmony to a strife-torn community" (Karmen 2004, 24). In other words, the professional compass in these subgroups points towards victim betterment. While this is an admirable goal and one well worth serving, it does not always promote an environment where scientific study is welcome.

THE PROBLEM

Contemporary victimologists can be found in many professions, including those associated with academia, the justice system, victim treatment, victim's advocacy, and politics. They routinely have a mandate to help victims above all other considerations, or for political reasons they may need to be perceived as having such a mandate. However, satisfying this ideological imperative often requires uncritical and unconditional regard for those who present themselves, or are presented contextually, as victims. When this political or functional need clashes with the reality of victim imperfection, the results to any given professional can be chilling. The pendulum of bias can swing widely for and against. Consider the effect that this has had on some prosecutors, as described in Pokorak (2007, 710-712):

Although the effect is not often discussed, through the combination of the prosecutor's unique "quasi-judicial" position that is freed from the normal constraints of a fiduciary relationship to an individual client, and the reality of a prosecutor's high volume of cases, the result is that prosecutors have little contact with victims. This dirty open secret starts with the initial years as a young prosecutor. During this period, the thoughtful exercise of prosecutorial discretion may not be developed, but rather it may be constrained by office structures and policies that overload new prosecutors with large case loads of minor matters. In order to prevent serious consequences from mistakes made by inexperienced prosecutors, many prosecution offices regularize plea offers for these less serious, "routine" cases and significantly constrain discretionary decision-making by the new, overloaded members of the office. At this same time, a period of desensitization can occur among the newer members of the prosecution team. This takes the form of two separate, yet interrelated effects of high volume workloads. The first is the objectification of the defendant. Even though the prosecutor has a duty to the defendant as well as to all other members of the public, the reality of human interactions is that it is more difficult to argue that a person should be incarcerated if one knows that individual and sympathizes with his or her plight. Therefore, some prosecutors may be heard to refer to defendants in highly derogatory ways, such as "scumbag," "dirt bag," "animal," and worse.

At the same time this tendency to dehumanize the defendant is being adopted by young prosecutors emulating more experienced attorneys in their office, they begin to realize that the defendants and the victims in cases share many characteristics and sometimes switch roles. Because most crimes are intra-racial and intracommunity, Monday's defendant may also be Wednesday's witness and Friday's victim. Therefore, it is not a difficult leap from demonizing a defendant to treating victims with something less than complete respect.

Additionally, some victims can be very challenging to manage. Work, childcare, or economic constraints may prevent them from being readily available to meet to discuss and prepare the case or even to appear in court when needed. Ongoing relationships between the victim and the defendant also may severely complicate or compromise prosecutions. Certain victims may not present as good witnesses due to their lack of education, language proficiency, or simply because they are not good storytellers. At the same time, victims can be demanding — often calling to get status updates or seeking assistance in other, perhaps unrelated, areas of legal need.

In contrast to the access and communication barriers that might exist between prosecutors and victims, prosecutors, early on, learn to develop close relationships with police witnesses. For example, prosecutors in sexual assault cases have ready access to one or more police officers who help them put together and present their case. Often, these police witnesses interact with the prosecutors on a near-daily basis. Many police officers, in addition to being trained investigators and evidence handlers, are also specifically trained to serve as witnesses. Compared to these helpful professional witnesses, victims can seem to an overworked prosecutor like much more of a problem than an asset to the case development and prosecution strategy.

The result of these two acculturated responses—the dehumanization of defendants and the general impatience with many victims—is that prosecutors tend to rely on the police and investigators to manage victims during the bulk of pre-trial preparation. Simply put, prosecutors all too often would rather hear what a victim has to say from a police officer rather than from the victim herself.

At this point, the problem becomes clear to anyone actually trained as a scientist. Victimology is meant to be a scientific study. But bias that develops for or against victims because of routine contact with them can act as a wall to the mandates of scientific inquiry, namely the requirements of doubt and skepticism.[3] This is a problem because some witnesses lie, some victims lie, and some people lie about being victims. Blind faith in a victim shields them from scientific inquiry; overt mistrust of victims shields others.

It should not take a scientist to put forth the premise that establishing the facts and defining the limits of evidence are preferable to falsity. In the social-political arena of victims and victimology, however, it does. As Goldberg explains (2003, 17-18):

There was a time when you could assume that an intelligent person looking for the truth was guided by the most basic of scientific intuitions: nature will give you a life if only you're going her way....

In social science today we can no longer make this assumption. Even if we continue to assume we are dealing with intelligent people, we find no way to maintain the belief that such people act on an impulse to find the truth. Instead, we find large and increasing numbers of ideologues who act as if nature is not something to be discovered

---

[3] For a useful discussion, see "Science as Falsification" by Karl R. Popper's *Conjectures and Refutations* (1963, 33–39).

no matter what she should turn out to be, but a handmaiden whose purpose is to satisfy one's psychological and ideological needs. Lacking the rudimentary scientific impulse of self-refutation...the ideologue assesses truth not by concordance with reality, but by concordance with psychological and ideological need.

As detailed in Turvey (2006), for more than a century the investigative and forensic science literature has acknowledged the importance of establishing the relationships between the primary components of a crime in order to solve it. These supporting pillars relate directly to evidence that establishes the relationships between *the victim*, *the suspect*, and *the crime scene*. This expansive body of work has given more than a small share of its pages to explaining the necessity of carefully investigating and documenting evidence as it relates to each, and determining the connections that can be reliably demonstrated. Establishing these pillars and the details of their relationships is in fact a threshold goal of all criminal investigation, so that criminal investigators and subsequent forensic examiners may adequately provide the foundation for any related court action.

When these pillars are not investigated, examined, and firmly established, the theories of a case are essentially unsupported. They are at best a weak guess, and at worst, the erroneous result of biasing influences such as politics, emotion, ignorant beliefs, and personal interest. As will be discussed presently, the solution proposed here is the application of *forensic victimology* as a necessary safeguard.

REINFORCING VICTIMITY

Doubt and skepticism are warranted in all realms of victimology, not just because they are mandated by good science, though that should be enough, but because of the manner in which any given system (e.g., school, employer, government, civil or criminal courts), culture (e.g., profession, family, religion, or region), or the general public responds to victims. Victims frequently need and are indeed entitled to counterbalance in the form of compensation for the loss and harm they suffer. However, these counterbalances invite abuse and can be a strong incentive for fraud.

Systemic Reinforcement

We must begin by acknowledging that many systems offer what may be viewed by some as incentives, even rewards, for suffering harm or loss, in the form of various compensations. These range from generally expecting less of victims and removing the barriers that are present in everyday challenges, to protecting them from responsibilities and liabilities, to direct financial reimbursement for a loss. As explained in Holstein and Miller, establishing oneself as a victim is one of the ways that someone can account for personal failures in an acceptable fashion (1990, 11):

> In the course of daily life, we all fall short of our, and others',
> expectations. The ways in which we depict, account for, and
> manage these failures is central to maintaining our public and self
> identities as competent practitioners of everyday life... In addition to
> denying responsibility for particular actions, designating one's self,
> or another, as a victim provides an economical way of telling others
> that the performance at hand should not be taken to exemplify the
> nature, quality, or potential of either the actor engaged in it, or the
> activity itself. Such practices help us maintain a sense of purpose and
> competence in the face of situational demands which might ostensibly
> give little evidence that goals are being accomplished or standards
> being upheld.

Children are trained to think this way the moment they step inside of their first classroom. From grade school to grad school, students who become ill, suffer the death of a close relative, or befall some other personal tragedy are able to miss classes without penalty, skip or retake exams, hand in assignments after their due date, and may even receive some sympathy in their final grade. These lessons are then transferred from the classroom to the workplace. Employees who become ill, suffer the death of a close relative, or befall some other personal tragedy are often able to miss workdays with pay, push back deadlines, and be relieved or even excused from difficult responsibilities without shame or penalty. As further explained in Holstein and Miller (1990, 7):

> Victimization is a method for absolving persons of responsibility.
> When trouble emerges, an "innocent" party—the object of the injury
> or trouble—can be specified by assigning victim status to one or more
> persons, thus exempting them from blame.

In short, whether a student or a professional, one is constantly reinforced with the notion that being a victim freezes the normal course of daily events and thereby shifts responsibility and accountability, if only temporarily.

There are also explicit financial compensations for victimity. Victims can seek or threaten to seek legal remedy in civil court and thereby receive financial or other material remuneration directly from those they believe are responsible for their harm or loss. Additionally, various governments and private organizations have developed victim's assistance programs to provide money for everything from living expenses and lost wages to medical treatment and counseling.

This is a good time to point out that victim compensations are in place for at least two reasons: they are necessary, and they are humane. Compensations are necessary because in most cases when a person falls prey to illness and tragedy it is beyond their control. Furthermore, we often assume that no one would intentionally cause himself or herself harm or loss—or at least we prefer to give people the benefit of the doubt. The subsequent prevailing wisdom is that we should not be penalized for our victimity, even when we fail to guard against it or do things to openly invite it. After all, bad things can happen to anyone. Systemic counterbalances can serve justice, restore a sense of fairness, and give a second chance when one is needed. Compensations are also humane, because victims may be in extreme pain or anguish. They may need time to heal or become whole before they can be expected to resume their life and the responsibilities that come with it.

Just as these systemic compensations are necessary and humane, their existence encourages some individuals to abuse them. Consider the following example:

Case Example: Hurricane Katrina

At 7:10 a.m. EDT on August 29, 2005, Hurricane Katrina made landfall in Louisiana as a Category 3. Maximum winds were clocked at nearly 125 mph. It was the most destructive hurricane in U.S. history, obliterating, rending, and flooding buildings, homes, and lives all along the Gulf Coast. The victims of Katrina are estimated in the millions, including nearly twothousand dead, thousands more wounded, and hundreds of thousands displaced, along with those who also lost property totaling in the billions of dollars.

Attempts to get federal aid to the victims of Katrina ranged from inadequate, to late, to never. They also resulted in one of the largest collective opportunities for victim fraud in recent U.S. history. As explained in a 2006 report by Gregory D. Kutz, Managing Director of Forensic Audits and Special Investigations, and John J. Ryan, Assistant Director Forensic Audits and Special Investigations, both of the United States General Accounting Office (GAO) (Kutz and Ryan 2006, 1):

> We estimate that through February 2006, FEMA made about 16 percent or $1 billion in improper and potentially fraudulent payments to registrants who used invalid information to apply for disaster assistance. Based on our statistical sample, we are 95 percent confident that the range of improper and potentially fraudulent payments is from $600 million to $1.4 billion. In our assessment of whether a payment was improper and potentially fraudulent, we did not test for other evidence of impropriety or potential fraud, such as insurance fraud and bogus damage claims. This means our review potentially understates the magnitude of improper payments made. Examples of fraud and abuse include payments to registrants who used post office boxes, United Parcel Service stores, and cemeteries as their damaged property addresses.
>
> Absent proper verification, it is not surprising that FEMA continued to pay fictitious disaster registrations set up by GAO as part of our ongoing forensic audit. In one case, FEMA paid nearly $6,000 to one

registrant who submitted a vacant lot as a damaged address. Below is a copy of a rental assistance check sent to GAO after FEMA received feedback from its inspector that the GAO undercover registrant did not live at the damaged address, and after a Small Business Administration inspector reported that the damaged property could not be found.

We also found that FEMA provided expedited and housing assistance to individuals who were not displaced. For example, millions of dollars in expedited and housing assistance payments went to registrations containing the names and social security numbers of individuals incarcerated in federal and state prisons during the hurricanes. In addition, FEMA improperly paid individuals twice for their lodging— paying their hotels and rental assistance at the same time. For example, at the same time that FEMA paid $8,000 for an individual to stay in California hotels, this individual also received three rental assistance payments for both hurricane disasters. Finally, we found that FEMA could not establish that 750 debit cards worth $1.5 million went to hurricane Katrina victims. We also found debit cards that were used for a Caribbean vacation, professional football tickets, and adult entertainment.

FIGURE P.3

One of several FEMA debit card designs. Approximately 11,400 were distributed in Houston, Dallas, and San Antonio to those who claimed to be displaced victims of hurricane Katrina.

This example is not proof that everyone is dishonest, or even that most people are dishonest. Rather it demonstrates that a significant percentage of the population is capable of varying levels of dishonesty and opportunism when the circumstances are in place and the appropriate controls are not. This remains true even during times of national crisis, when actual victims will be deprived of the benefits being defrauded. History has taught us that wherever there are sympathetic victims and corresponding efforts to assist them, there will be fraud.

Cultural Reinforcement

As we've already learned, cultural and public responses can be unconditionally warm and accepting for some victims. For others, they can be cold, judgmental, and rebuking. This may have to do with the nature of the crime, the nature of the victim, the nature of the offender, or unrelated elements present in the immediate climate. In their personal estimation of whether responses will be favorable, there are those who will be drawn to embellish, omit, or fabricate some or all of the details of their victimization. There are also those who are compelled to invent their victimization entirely.

Consider the following examples:

Case Example: Tanja J. Morin

On July 17, 2006, 26-year-old Tanja J. Morin of Lancaster, Ohio, called 911 to report that her 2-year-old son, Tyler, was missing. She tearfully explained to the dispatcher: "The only way he could have went is through the back, and the only way you can get the fence open is if somebody kicks it from the outside… Somebody had to come through the yard." The call was made at 10:51 a.m.

Tanja's husband, Michael, immediately came home from work to help in the search for Tyler. He found the couple's youngest child at 11:22 a.m., in a garbage dumpster less than a block away from their home.[4] Had he been left in the dumpster much longer, the heat would have killed him; it was one of the hottest days of the year.

During the initial police investigation, the mother's kidnapping story succumbed to realistic victimology and fell apart. A nearby surveillance camera had captured the activity at and around the dumpster before, during, and after Tyler was reported missing. On the surveillance stills, Tanja can be seen walking hand-in-hand with her youngest son in the alley near the dumpster at 10:35 a.m. A minute later, she can be seen leaving towards her home alone.

Tanja confessed to detectives that she hadn't meant to hurt Tyler, only to create an emergency that would get her husband to come home from work. According to police, she told them, "He wanted to spend money today that we didn't have, and I was trying to think of a way he could come home so he didn't have to spend the money that he had."

Tanja was arrested that day, and charged with attempted murder, child endangerment, and kidnapping. At first, she plead not guilty. The judge subsequently ordered her to submit to a psychiatric evaluation. In November of 2007, she plead guilty to kidnapping, child endangering, and felonious assault charges.

In this case, the mother lived in a severely dysfunctional family where she was apparently convinced that the benefits of creating a false crisis outweighed the potential consequences to her or anyone else. Taken at her word, she was actually a victim of her husband's financial irresponsibility and was acting with good intentions. Certainly her actions were enough to warrant a psychiatric evaluation—something that would not necessarily occur to the court if a man were facing the same charges. In cases of domestic violence and even homicide, women are often treated by the justice system as victims in need of help, and men are viewed as aggressors deserving of punishment. Such distorted views, based on cultural archetypes, can result in diminished responsibility, or at least sympathy, for the mother.

[4]The couple also had a 6-year-old girl and a 4-year-old boy.

Caption: A tearful Tanja Morin is lead away by police. She plead guilty to kidnapping, child endangering, and felonious assault charges in 2007. The dumpster where she placed her child, pictured, was in a gravel parking area less than a block from her home.

The objective, scientific victimologist would restrain from taking this mother or any other alleged victim at their word, as this case and many others demonstrate that the institution of motherhood is not inviolate. Even a mother claiming to have the best intentions can put their child in a garbage dumpster and lie about it, if they think there is something to be gained.

Case Example: D.C. Metro Police Officers Nathan Minor and Peter Snipes

Just after midnight on August 7, 2006, Eugene Radcliff was being treated at Howard University Hospital in Washington, D.C., subsequent to his arrest for possession of cocaine and unlawful entry. Officers Nathan Minor and Peter Snipes had been assigned to guard him. Radcliff escaped, and the two officers called for backup. As Segraves (2007) details:

> A call for help came into police dispatch from Snipes, a 10-year veteran of the force. Snipes said the prisoner had attacked his partner and escaped.

> The officers were giving chase through the Northwest D.C. neighborhood near the hospital and requested backup. A manhunt ensued as police canvassed the area.

> But documents obtained by WTOP reveal a different story....

> In his original statement, Minor, who has been on the force since 2000, wrote: "The defendant kicked me in the midsection knocking me completely to the floor. I then saw the defendant running down the hallway of the hospital. I gave chase...I saw the defendant running northbound on Georgia Avenue."

> But according to an affidavit filed by an agent with the Metropolitan Police Internal Affairs Department, a witness said the prisoner "was not restrained...walked directly out of the hospital with no police officers near, and saw no altercation between the prisoner and police officers."

In other words, witnesses reported that the prisoner simply left the hospital while the officers weren't looking—no fight or chase occurred. After an investigation was conducted into these conflicting accounts, Officers Minor and Snipes changed their story. In October of 2007, they both plead guilty to making false statements, as explained in Alexander (2007, B3):

> Two D.C. police officers pleaded guilty yesterday to making false statements in an official report to cover up an incident in which they allowed a prisoner to escape.

> Officers Nathan Minor, 33, and Peter Snipes, 32, face up to 180 days in prison and $1,000 in fines, prosecutors said. The officers, both assigned to the 1st Police District, resigned from the force as part of their plea agreements and remain free pending sentencing in D.C. Superior Court.

In this case, the officers attempted to establish themselves as victims to account for failure. They were responding to their perceptions of both law enforcement culture and eventual professional accountability. They did not want to appear weak or inept in the eyes of their fellow officers for letting a prisoner walk away, nor did they want to be held accountable for their incompetence by superiors. Rather than admit a mistake and ask for help, they contrived a story with the necessary elements to seem plausible, mitigate responsibility, and deflect scrutiny. They portrayed themselves as victims of a violent criminal made more dangerous by the involvement of drugs. However, they could not control the statements of impartial witnesses to the event.

Case Example: New Hampshire v. Brian Shephard

Work involving victims draws all kinds of people into related professions. Some are balanced and well adjusted, and others are not. The imbalanced and maladjusted seek to please their surroundings, to satisfy the demands of their professional culture against the limits of the facts and evidence. At the far end of the ethical spectrum there are those who actively conceal, obscure, and avert evidence relating to a victim's character, history, or condition. They do so for a variety of reasons. For some, it is a matter of bias in favor of the victim, the police, the prosecution, or against the offender.[5] For others, it is a matter of egoism or narcissism, of needing to be perceived as the hero, the rescuer, or the protector.

In January of 2005, Brian Shepherd was convicted of Aggravated Felonious Sexual Assault.[6] Shepherd and the co-accused, Matt MacDuff, were at a party at the home of the victim, Emily Thompson, on December 2, 2003. Early on at the party, Thompson reportedly advised Shepherd that she would like to have sex with him on the condition that he wore a condom, restating her desire throughout the evening.

Thompson participated in a number of drinking games and smoked marijuana at various times throughout the night. Because of her desire to make friends and fit in, Thompson drank more than she usually would have, and subsequently went into a back bedroom to lay down because of her level of intoxication. She later testified that she had lost interest in sex at this point.

At some point later in the evening, Thompson woke up and two men were engaging in simultaneous sexual penetration with her, though she couldn't identify who these men were. She testified that because of her level of intoxication she could not resist the assault. She noted that she heard MacDuff's voice, but could not make out what she was saying. She then heard an unidentified voice say, "I think she is going to pass out again."

Thompson also testified that the next day she was unsure of what had happened in the bedroom; that she had a sense that something wasn't right but was not

---

[5]This issue will be explored further in Chapter 3 "Constructing Victim Profile," in the section *Examiner Bias*.

[6]Unless otherwise stated, this section is largely adapted from, and all quoted material is taken directly from, *The State of New Hampshire v Brian Shepherd*, Rockingham Superior Court, Docket no. 04-S-1220, March 8, 2007; Court Decision by Justice Tina L. Nadeau.

able to recall specific details. Over the next few days, she heard from friends and other partygoers that she had intercourse with multiple male partners in the back of MacDuff's trailer. Because of these discussions, Thompson reported the assault to the police who interviewed both Shepherd and MacDuff. After initially denying any sexual activity, Shepherd later admitted to the intercourse but maintained that Thompson was both awake and consenting.

At trial, the Shepherd called the co-accused (MacDuff), Detective Mulholland, and toxicologist JoAnn Samson as witnesses. Shepherd presented his theory that Thompson was awake, and that despite passing out several times, she had consented to having sex. The state argued the opposite; that Thompson was heavily under the influence, physically helpless, and therefore not able to resist.

On January 12, 2005, the jury convicted Shepherd. MacDuff was subsequently tried for the same crime, but the court dismissed the case. Shepherd later claimed that new evidence discovered during the MacDuff trial entitled him to a new trial.

After initially bringing the complaint to the attention of police, the victim was subjected to a sexual assault examination, performed by Dr. Wendy Gladstone. By way of introduction to Dr. Gladstone, consider the following background information:[7]

> Dr. Gladstone earned her medical degree from Columbia University before going on to Columbia Presbyterian Medical Center to complete her internship and residency. After residency, she trained for her sub-specialty interest, adolescent medicine, at Children's Hospital Medical Center in Boston. Dr. Gladstone is board certified by the American Board of Pediatrics and is a Fellow of the American Academy of Pediatrics. Dr. Gladstone came to Exeter in 1978 to join the Exeter Clinic. In 1982 she was co-founder of Exeter Pediatric Associates. She is currently an associate at Children's Hospital Medical Center and a member of the teaching staff at Harvard University Medical School. A member of the Society of Adolescent Medicine, the American Public Health Association, the American Professional Society on Abuse of Children, and the [New Hampshire] Attorney General's Task Force on Child Abuse and Neglect. Dr. Gladstone is the Medical Director of Seacoast HealthNet and was the President of the [New Hampshire] Pediatric Society from July 1996 [to] 1999.

---

[7]Biographical material cited from Beansprout Networks at http://www.beansprout.net/, last downloaded July 20, 2007.

As explained in *State v Brian Shepherd* (2007, 3-4):

> MacDuff was tried by a different prosecutor and before a different judge to ensure that MacDuff's testimony, provided under a grant of immunity during the defendant's trial, would not be used against MacDuff in his own trial. On the day of jury selection, the prosecutor learned that Dr. Wendy Gladstone, who had performed a rape kit examination of the victim, had redacted certain portions of her progress notes from the version that she supplied to the State during discovery. Consequently, the State informed the court and MacDuff. As a result, the court conducted an in-camera review of the medical file and released the completed version of Dr. Gladstone's report to the attorney.

> The unprecedented report contained information regarding the victim's history of depression, including a list of counselors and therapists. In addition, the report contained a statement the victim provided during the exam in which she asked Dr. Gladstone not to inform the victim's mother of the sexual assault until after the victim had retrieved her clothing "in order to avoid a confrontation." The victim further explained that she expected her mother to be angry because they did not have a good relationship. The information contained in the complete report lead to the discovery of other mental health records from Seacoast Mental Health and Coastal Counseling. These records revealed that the victim had been diagnosed with a mental health condition which caused her to exercise poor judgment, use impulsive behavior, and engage in dangerous and risky activities that could lead to injury.

Just to recap the situation, Dr. Gladstone performed a sexual assault exam on Thompson. Two men, Shepherd and MacDuff, were subsequently arrested and prosecuted for raping her. Dr. Gladstone, after performing the forensic examination, provided two different reports of her findings. The first report went to the prosecution and included all of the necessary victimological information including the complainant's mental health history and statements to her mother. The second report, a mirror of the first in most ways, did not contain the victimological information regarding the mental health history or the telltale page numbers.

In short, Dr. Gladstone crossed the line between forensic examiner and advocate. She delivered necessary contextual information to the prosecution that was deliberately withheld from the defense in their version of the report. Moreover, one cannot claim that this was a novice mistake, given Dr. Gladstone's background and credentials. As provided by the court (8-9):

In this case, the court finds that Dr. Gladstone was acting as an agent of the State when she examined the victim and collected evidence for an eventual prosecution. Specifically, she is a member of the Attorney General's Task Force regarding Sexual Assault Protocols and she assisted in drafting protocols regarding interview techniques. In addition, she was trained in the proper procedure for evidence collection. Moreover, Dr. Gladstone testified that she examined the victim in this case with the intent to collect forensic evidence during her examination for eventual use at trial. She explained that she collected the evidence in a manner designed to protect the integrity of the chain of custody. Thus, her failure to disclose the complete report of her examination to the police or the County Attorney constituted a breach of the State's duty to the defendant.

The court also finds that Dr. Gladstone knowingly failed to turn over her complete report. She testified at the hearing that she purposely redacted a portion of the first page of the report and the entire second page. In addition, the report she provided to the police was photocopied without page numbers and in a manner that made the document appear complete. As a result, no one involved in the case could have made a request for further discovery because the document the doctor provided contained no indication that any information had been redacted.

As a result of the court's finding that Dr. Gladstone knowingly withheld discoverable material, (material she also admitted was important and relevant to the assault) the court must next consider whether the State can meet its burden to establish beyond a reasonable doubt that the omitted evidence would not have affected the verdict. As stated in its previous analysis, the omitted evidence led to the discovery of mental health records that provided information regarding the victim's state of mind. The defendant could have used the specific diagnoses contained in those records to rebut the victim's claim of non-consensual sexual intercourse. Given that the outcome of the case turned largely on a determination of whether the victim accurately described her level of consciousness and whether the defendant's claim of consensual sex was true, the State cannot meet its burden of establishing beyond a reasonable doubt that the omitted evidence would not have affected the verdict.

This case stands out as an example of intentional concealment of victimology by someone that is supposed to be an impartial forensic examiner. It is an abuse of the court's trust, and ultimately resulted in Brian Shepherd's conviction being overturned.

These examples serve to demonstrate that no victim culture or institution associated with the criminal justice system is wholly immune from the reinforcement that victimity can provide. None are beyond doubt, examination, critique, or redress. Not the institution of motherhood, or the "sacred bond" between a mother and her child; not the culture of law enforcement; and not the "objective" forensic examiner. Within each there are those who are willing to distort or fabricate victimity because they perceive a cultural reward for doing so.

THE SOLUTION

Let's return to our original question: given that victimological evidence can be incomplete, ambiguous, and complex under the best of conditions, and given the possibility of falsity, how can the forensic victimologist make informed examinations and interpretations? How can we apply Dorner's lessons to the problems we face? Answering these questions is the purpose of this text.

As we've already stated, *Forensic Victimology* is the scientific study of victims for the purposes of addressing investigative and forensic issues. The social scientist researching victim-offender relationships; the investigator going though a victim's garbage or cell phone records; the criminal profiler reading a victim's diary or making a "friends and family" list; the forensic nurse taking a victim history or looking for evidence of injury; the reconstructionist examining a victim's toxicology or making a timeline of activities leading up to their demise; the psychiatrist or psychologist performing a mental health assessment; the medical examiner establishing a victim's place of employment or last meal—each collects, examines, and interprets evidence related to forensic victimology. Their work serves criminal investigation and anticipates courtroom testimony. Their findings and interpretations bear directly on determining whether there is a victim, precisely who the victim is, and the potential consequences for those who caused them harm.

Forensic victimology is intended to serve the justice system by educating it. It is aimed at helping to provide more informed investigations, more scientific examinations, and more informed legal outcomes. All of this serves the betterment of society as a whole, if one accepts that truth is better than fiction.

PURPOSE

Forensic victimologists include investigators, criminal profilers, crime reconstructionists, medical examiners, forensic nurses, and testifying academics—anyone who uses their knowledge of victimology to serve investigative or forensic ends. Because of the need for accuracy and reliability in these complementary spheres, the forensic victimologist is best conceived as an objective, dispassionate, and above all scientific examiner. They are critical and skeptical, and they put the establishment of fact before politics or any other consideration. To that end, they take nothing for granted, look for corroboration of any alleged victim's statements, seek out collateral sources of information, and investigate alternate or contributing motives for victim behavior. Most importantly, the forensic victimologist is barred from assuming that alleged victims must have been victimized. For their purposes, victimity must be established unequivocally and may not be asserted simply for ideological purposes. They investigate as scientists, they report as educators, and they understand the gravity of their eventual courtroom testimony.

The purpose of this textbook is to distinguish the investigative and forensic aspects of victim study as a necessary adjunct to the practice of *victimology*. It identifies forensic victimologists in the investigative and forensic communities and provides them with methods and standards of practice needed to be of service. Forensic Victimology is necessary because it provides a scientific balance against the idealization or demonization of victims, a filter for deception and false reporting, and a a means for providing an objective threshold of relevance for victim information and opinions already at work in the criminal justice system.

REFERENCES

Alexander, K. 2007. "2 D.C. Officers Admit Lying About Escape." *Washington Post*, October 19, B3.

Barker, K., and D. Burdick. (eds.) 2000. *New Internatgional Version Study Bible*, Revised. Grand Rapids, MI: Zondervan.

Dorner, D. 1996. *The Logic of Failure: Recognizing and Avoiding Error in Complex Environments*, Cambridge, MA: Perseus Books.

Drapkin, I., and E. Viano. 1974. *Victimology: A New Focus*. Lexington, MA: Lexington Books.

Fattah, E. 2000. "Victimology: Past, Present, and Future." *Criminologie 33*, no. 1: 17–46.

Goldberg, S. 2003. *Fads and Fallacies in the Social Science*: New York: Humanity Books.

Holstein, J., and G. Miller. 1990. "Rethinking Victimization: An Interactional Approach to Victimology." *Symbolic Interaction 13*, no. 1: 103–22.

Karmen, A. 2004. *Crime Victims: An Introduction to Victimology*. 5th ed. Belmont, CA: Thompson/Wadsworth.

Kutz, G., and J. Ryan, 2006. "Hurricanes Katrina and Rita Disaster Relief: Improper and Potentially Fraudulent Individual Assistance Payments Estimated to Be Between $600 Million and $1.4 Billion." GAO-06-844T. Washington, DC: United States Government Accountability Office, June 14.

Mattingly, D. 2005. "Atlanta's 26 Hours of Fear." *CNN.com*, March 15. http://www.cnn.com/2005/LAW/03/14/atlanta.summary/index.html.

Mendelsohn, B. 1976. "Victimology and Contemporary Society's Trends." *Victimology 1*, no. 1: 8–28.

Pokorak, J. 2007. "Rape Victims and Prosecutors: The Inevitable Ethical Conflict of De Facto Client/Attorney Relationships." *South Texas Law Review,* Spring, no. 48: 695–732.

Popper, K. 1963. *Conjectures and Refutations.* London: Routledge and Keagan Paul.

Segraves, M. 2007. "Cops Busted for False Report, Losing Suspect." *WTOP Radio,* September 13. http://www.wtopnews.com/index.php?nid=428&sid=1246487.

Smith, A. 2005. *Unlikely Angel: The Untold Story of the Atlanta Hostage Hero.* Grand Rapids, MI: Zondervan.

Turvey, B. E. 2006. "Beneath the Numbers: Rape and Homicide Clearance Rates in the United States." *Journal of Behavioral Profiling 6*, no. 1.

CHAPTER 1

Victimology: A Brief History with an Introduction to Forensic Victimology

Claire Ferguson and Brent E. Turvey

KEY TERMS

- *Criminal investigation:* the process of gathering facts to be used as evidence and proof in a court of law.
- *The Dark Age:* in victimology, the era after the emergence of written laws and structured governments, where all offenses were viewed as perpetrated against the king or state, not against the victims or their family.
- *Forensic victimology:* the study of violent crime victims for the purposes of addressing investigative and forensic questions. It involves the accurate, critical, and objective outlining of a victim's lifestyles and circumstances, the events leading up to an injury, and the precise nature of any harm or loss suffered.
- *General victimology:* the study of victimity in the broadest sense, including those that have been harmed by accidents, natural disasters, war, and so on.
- *The golden age:* in victimology, the era thought to have occurred before written law, where victims played a direct role in determining the punishment for actions of another committed against them or their property.
- *Interactionist/penal victimology:* an approach to victimology from a criminological or legal perspective, where the scope of study is defined by criminal law.
- *Reemergence of the victim:* the era in the middle of the twentieth century, when a small number of people began to recognize that those who were most affected by criminal acts were rarely involved in the criminal justice process. This led to the realization that victims were also being overlooked as a source of information about crime and criminals.
- *Sanctity of victimhood:* the belief that victims are inherently good, honest, and pure, making those who defend them righteous and morally justified.

CONTENTS

1

Scientific method: a way to investigate how or why something works or how something happened through the development of hypotheses and subsequent attempts at falsification through testing and other accepted means.

Victim: used in the modern criminal justice system to describe any person who has experienced loss, injury, or hardship due to the illegal action of another individual, group, or organization.

Victima: a Latin word used to refer to those who were sacrificed to please a god.

Victimology: the scientific study of victims and victimization, including the relationships between victims and offender, investigators, courts, corrections, media, and social movements.

Victim precipitation: when a crime is caused or partially facilitated by the victim.

Victim prone: individuals who share a capacity for being victimized.

Historically, the Latin term *victima* was used to describe individuals or animals whose lives were destined to be sacrificed to please a deity. It did not necessarily imply pain or suffering, only a sacrificial role. In the nineteenth century, the word *victim* became connected with the notion of harm or loss in general (Spalek 2006). In the modern criminal justice system, the word *victim* has come to describe any person who has experienced injury, loss, or hardship due to the illegal action of another individual, group, or organization (Karmen 2004).

The term *victimology* first appeared in 1949, in a book about murderers written by forensic psychiatrist Fredric Wertham. It was used to describe the study of individuals harmed by criminals (Karmen 2007). Today, as explained in our Preface, *victimology* refers generally to the scientific study of victims and victimization, including the relationships between victims and offenders, investigators, courts, corrections, media, and social movements (Karmen 1990).

According to Ezzat Fattah, PhD, an Egyptian prosecutor turned criminologist, as well as a leading author on the subject of victimology (Fattah 2000, 24):

> the study of victims and victimization has the potential of reshaping the entire discipline of criminology. It might very well be the long awaited paradigm shift that criminology desperately needs given the dismal failure of its traditional paradigms: search for causes of crime, deterrence, rehabilitation, treatment, just desserts, etc.

The authors and contributors of this text concur.

FIGURE 1.1

Dr. Fredric Wertham (1895–1981) reading the first issue of *Shock Illustrated*. A psychiatrist for the New York Department of Hospitals connected with the Court of General Sessions, he is best remembered for his expert testimony in the trial of serial murderer Albert Fish and for his opposition to comic books. In 1954, he wrote a book titled *Seduction of the Innocents*, which argued that comic books were the lowest form of literature and a primary cause of juvenile delinquency, citing their depiction of sex, drugs, and violence. That same year, this book led to an official Congressional Inquiry that ultimately resulted in the "voluntary" creation of the Comics Code Authority (CCA) by the Comics Magazine Association of America. The CCA screened all comic books prior to publication, acting essentially as an industry censor.

Jan Van Dijk, a professor of victimology at Tilburg University, has proposed that there are currently two major types of victimology (1999): general victimology and penal victimology, with major differences stemming from the definitions used to identify victims. General victimology studies victimity in the broadest sense, including those that have been harmed by accidents, natural disasters, war, and so on (Van Dijk 1999). The focus of this type of victimology is the treatment, prevention, and alleviation of the consequences of being victimized, regardless of the cause.

Interactionist (or penal) victimologists, on the other hand, generally approach the subject from a criminological or legal perspective, where the scope of study is defined by criminal law. According to Van Dijk (1999, 2) "the research agenda of this victimological stream combines issues concerning the causation of crimes with those relating to the victim's role in the criminal proceedings," where victims are only those who become such as a result of a crime. Generally speaking, this type of victimology advocates for victims, for their rights or in relation to certain types of prosecutions.

There remains a level of ignorance regarding the nature and even existence of victimology across the professional spectrums that intersect with the subject. Most notably this occurs within the criminal justice system itself, which tends to be populated by those without a scientific, behavioral, or research background. A primer is therefore necessary. The purpose of this chapter is to provide a brief history of victimology as it has evolved in relation to systems of justice until modern times, as a precursor to the development of forensic victimology as a subspecialty. It will then close with discussions on the rationale for the investigative and forensic use of victimology. If readers have not yet studied the Preface, now would be a good time to go back and do so.

HISTORY

It is important to acknowledge where the field of victimology originated and how it has developed. To that end, this section involves a general overview of the victim's role in various systems of justice throughout history. It will conclude with a more specific rendering of the contributions of selected victimologists, subsequent research, and its impact on the discipline.[1]

The concept of victim study as it relates to legal conflict is not new. In fact, it has been around for centuries in various forms. For example, Jerin and Moriarty (1998, 6) contend that there are three distinct historical eras defining the victims' role within justice systems: the *golden age*, the *dark age*, and the *reemergence of the victim*.

The Golden Age
In the so-called *golden age*, which Jerin and Moriarty suggest existed prior to written laws and established governments, tribal law prevailed. In much of tribal law, victims are said to have played a direct role in determining punishments for the unlawful actions that others committed against them or their property. It was reportedly a time when personal retribution was the only resolution for criminal matters. As such, victims actively sought revenge or demanded compensation for their losses directly from those who wronged

---

[1]As will become clear, the victimological literature has often been the product of advocates interested in victim rights, legal reforms, and various liabilities, as opposed to those interested in objective study for the advancement of scientific knowledge. Therefore, some of the terminology used has been less than scientific and even partial. It is presented here purely in an effort to maintain the historical record.

them (Karmen 2007; Shichor and Tibbetts 2002). Doerner and Lab (2002, 2) go so far as to describe this as a *victim justice system* as opposed to a *criminal justice system*, explaining that

> it was up to victims or their survivors to decide what action to take against the offender. Victims who wished to respond to offenses could not turn to judges for assistance or to jails for punishment. These institutions did not exist yet. Instead, victims had to take matters into their own hands.

Clearly, this was not a time of objectivity and critical regard towards victims and their claims. Victims would define the extent of any loss or harm and then seek their own retribution rather than either being investigated or assessed by a disinterested or higher authority. Ostensibly, this could occur without any preestablished burden of proof, with the victim's word set against that of the accused, and judged in an ad hoc fashion within a given community, group, or tribe. In such a system, fault and legal consequence become a matter of character and influence.

Victim-driven approaches to justice became somewhat problematic as populations grew, and as families and groups expanded. This was partly because, in many instances, crimes were not suffered or inflicted against just one person. Depending on the nature of an offense, it might be harmful to an entire family, tribe, or culture. And if the actual offender were not available to be punished, his or her kinsman might bear the responsibility for the harm that had been caused. Worse still, in some instances, successive generations would inherit any insult and injustice committed against the last—wrongfully victimized or wrongfully prosecuted alike. So the commission of a single crime had the potential to draw in many people. Resulting vendettas could lead to longstanding blood feuds between families or tribes for harms that may or may not have actually happened.

Eventually, many came to the realization that although it promoted strong family, clan, and even cultural loyalty, this form of justice did little to resolve conflict. The notion that a crime against one is a crime against many did not serve to alleviate the hardship endured by the individual victims. Neither did holding one kinsman responsible for the crimes of another. Rather, this scheme of justice expanded the harm of the original crime to people that weren't directly involved. It also resulted in cycles of revictimization as groups sought their share of vengeance back and forth (Shichor and Tibbetts 2002). Rather that serving the victim, victim-driven justice actually made matters much worse.

For example, a long-practiced victim-oriented remedy to the problem of crime, debt, and related blood feuds is marriage: the mixing of blood from both sides to vest interests, pay back a loss, or end the need for retaliation. However, even in cultures where tribal law maintains a foothold and such problems are common—as is the case in modern-day Afghanistan—this widely accepted "solution" is known to fail and actually create new victims. As explained in Tang (2007):

> Despite advances in women's rights and at least one tribe's move to outlaw the practice, girls are traded like currency in Afghanistan and forced marriages are common. Antiquated tribal laws authorize the practice known as "bad" in the Afghan language Dari—and girls are used to settle disputes ranging from debts to murder.

> Such exchanges bypass the hefty bride price of a traditional betrothal, which can cost upward of US$1,000. Roughly two out of five Afghan marriages are forced, says the country's Ministry of Women's Affairs.

> Though violence against women remains widespread, Afghanistan has taken significant strides in women's rights since the hard-line Taliban years, when women were virtual prisoners—banned from work, school, or leaving home unaccompanied by a male relative. Millions of girls now attend school and women fill jobs in government and media.

> There are also signs of change for the better inside the largest tribe in eastern Afghanistan—the deeply conservative Shinwaris. Shinwari [tribal] elders from several districts signed a resolution this year outlawing several practices that harm girls and women. These included a ban on using girls to settle so-called blood feuds—when a man commits murder, he must hand over his daughter or sister as a bride for a man in the victim's family. The marriage ostensibly "mixes blood to end the bloodshed." Otherwise, revenge killings often continue between the families for generations....

> About 600 elders from the Shinwar district put their purple thumbprint "signatures" on the handwritten resolution.

> More than 20 Shinwari leaders gathered in the eastern city of Jalalabad, nodding earnestly and muttering their consent as the changes were discussed last week.

> They insisted that women given away for such marriages—including those to settle blood feuds—were treated well in their new families. But the elders declined requests to meet any of the women or their families.

> "Nobody treats them badly," Malik Niaz said confidently, stroking his long white beard. "Everyone respects women."

But Afghan women say this could not be further from the truth. "By establishing a family relationship, we want to bring peace. But in reality, that is not the case," said Hangama Anwari, an independent human rights commissioner and founder of the Women and Children Legal Research Foundation. The group investigated about 500 cases of girls given in marriage to settle blood feuds and found only four or five that ended happily. Much more often, the girl suffered for a crime committed by a male relative, she said. "We punish a person who has done nothing wrong, but the person who has killed someone is free. He can move freely, and he can kill a second person, third person because he will never be punished," Anwari said.

A girl is often beaten and sometimes killed because when the family looks at her, they see the killer. "Because they lost someone, they take it out on her," Naderi said.

There are no reliable statistics on blood-feud marriages, a hidden practice. When it happens, the families and elders often will not reveal details of the crime or the punishment.

Several years ago in nearby Momand Dara district, a taxi driver hit a boy with his car, killing him. The boy's family demanded a girl as compensation, so the driver purchased an 11-year-old named Fawzia from an acquaintance for US$5,000 and gave her to the dead boy's relatives, according to the Afghan Women's Network office in Jalalabad. Three years ago, Fawzia was shot to death, according to a two-page report kept in a black binder of cases of violence against women.

The story of Malia and the nine sheep illustrates the suffering of girls forced into such marriages. Malia listened as her father [Ahmad] described how he was held hostage by his lender, Khaliq Mohammad, because he could not come up with the money to pay for the sheep, which Ahmad had sold to free a relative seized because of another of Ahmad's debts.

Ahmad was released only when he agreed to give Malia's hand in marriage to the lender's 18-year-old son. Asked how she felt about it, Malia shook her head and remained silent. Her face then crumpled in anguish and she wiped away tears. Asked if she was happy, she responded halfheartedly, "Well, my mother and father agreed ..." Her voice trailed off, and she cried again. Does she want to meet her husband-to-be? She clicked her tongue—a firm, yet delicate "tsk"— with a barely perceptible shake of her head. The answer was no.

FIGURE 1.2

"Nazir Ahmad said he was forced to pay a debt of less than $200 by betrothing his [16-year-old] daughter Malia, third from left. From left to right Malia's father, sister, Malia, and her mother, during an interview with Associated Press in their home in Jalalabad, Afghanistan, Sunday, July 1, 2007" (Tang 2007).

The theory is not entirely unsound—join groups or families and their interests to stop the cycle of retaliation and end the need for generational vendettas. However, in reality such marriages can create a whole new set of victims when arranged or coerced in opposition to the desires of those involved. In such cases, the "good news" is different for everyone.

In any event, the notion that this time period or its related practices represents some kind of *golden age* of discretionary justice for any but a favored few seems misplaced, if not entirely mythical. Certainly some victims were free to accuse those who harmed them and seek the vengeance they desired. This would naturally result in increased false reporting. Moreover, there might not be anyone to protect them from the consequences if they did make a report, true or not, let alone protect them from the accused. Consider the following realities of this type of justice:

- The less power or perceived character one had, the less able to report and sustain sympathy for actual victimization;
- The more power or perceived character one had, the more able to abuse the power of accusation (make false allegations for personal gain);

- Given the absence of any standard of evidence, and the known fallibility of eyewitness accounts, the likelihood of being wrong in one's accusations was necessarily high;
- Making an accusation could result in generations of retaliation, including dishonor for children and grandchildren;
- Committing a crime could result in generations of retaliation, including dishonor for children and grandchildren;
- In patriarchal systems, women and children were often forced to pay the price of crimes committed by their adult male kinsman, becoming victims without any voice or recourse.

The list of problems does not end here, but the point is that this was not a golden age for victims or offenders by any stretch of the imagination. Although it might look good to some through the distance of time, the sword of justice swings erratically and irrevocably under such circumstances—and it still favors the favored.

The Dark Age

It has been argued that the so-called *dark ages* of victimology were the result of the emergence of structured local governments and the development of formal legal statutes. These were a byproduct of more stable economic systems, which came about through urbanization and the industrial revolution as well as the rise in power of the Roman Catholic Church (Karmen 2007; Shichor and Tibbetts 2002). As families moved away from their farms and into cities, neighborhoods became depersonalized; the old tribal systems, based on culture and kinship, were no longer viable (Doerner and Lab 2005).

In these emerging criminal-oriented justice systems, offenses were increasingly viewed as perpetrated against the laws of the king or state, not just against a victim or the victim's family. Eventually, focus shifted towards offender punishments and rights, as opposed to victim rights and restoration. Subsequently, as formal systems of criminal justice rose and spread, victim involvement eroded to little more than that of witness for the police and prosecution (Doerner and Lab 2002; Karmen 2007). As Doerner and Lab (2002, 3) explain:

> The development of formal law enforcement, courts, and correctional systems in the past few centuries has reflected an interest in protecting the state. For the most part, the criminal justice system simply forgot about victims and their best interests.

A result of this ongoing evolution is that modern criminal justice systems do not necessarily seek to help the victim in a given case. As subsequent chapters will discuss, those in power invariably create laws to protect cultures, societies, and institutions. In modern Western cultures, for example, society at large is the intended beneficiary: the criminal justice systems seek to separate criminals from society, to deter others from acting criminally via ever-harsher punishments, and ultimately to prevent future victimizations. Whether this is actually being accomplished is a matter of debate, and individual victims are often left by failed law enforcement efforts to seek remedy for the harms they suffer in civil court.

Reemergence of the Victim

A so-called *reemergence of the victim* occurred in the 1950s and 1960s, when a small number of people began to recognize that those who were most affected by criminal acts were rarely involved in the process. Unsettled with the fact that victims' rights and needs had gone by the wayside, they fought to bring this disparity to the public's attention (Karmen 2007). It soon became the consensus amongst various groups, including journalists, social scientists, and those involved directly with the criminal justice system, that "victims were forgotten figures in the criminal justice process whose needs and wants had been systematically overlooked but merited attention" (Karmen 2007, 27).

During the same time, a collection of sociologists, criminologists, and legal scholars came to the same realization—that victims were being overlooked as a source of information about crime and criminals. Their interest in studying victims is what ultimately led to the birth of traditional victimology as a discrete scientific endeavor. While victims' rights were gaining attention, victimology, in its early years, did not seek to address the needs of victims and alleviate their suffering. Rather, it came from a desire to better understand the victim's role in the criminal act, relationship to the offender, and culpability (Doerner and Lab 2002). It is from this research that the field of criminology formally spawned the subspecialty of victimology, and by the early 1970s courses on the subject were being taught at universities across the United States. As announced and described in *Time Magazine* (1971):

> At its last conference, the International Criminological Society included a special session on the behavioral patterns of victims. For the first time in the U.S., three courses in victimology are being offered, one at the University of California, the others at Northeastern University and at Boston University Law School. A major book on the subject is nearing publication, and an international conference devoted solely to victimology has been scheduled for Jerusalem in 1973.

> Most behavioral scientists agree with University of Montreal Criminologist Ezzat Abdel Fattah, who contends that "there are people who attract the criminal as the lamb attracts the wolf." Some of these victims are masochistic or depressed; Criminologist Hans von Hentig described them as longing "lustfully" for injury.

Others, says Northeastern University Victimologist Stephen Schafer, have certain personality traits—for example, the Kennedys' ambition for power—that invite attack by "offending the offender." Israeli Criminologist Menachem Amir, who set up the victimology course at Berkeley, cites cultural factors: to participate in certain lifestyles, such as prostitution and drug addiction, is to court trouble. There are some occupations, too, that are likely to attract violence: cab driver, bank teller, and policeman, among others. The motivation for seeking these jobs sometimes includes an unconscious need to be a victim, or a wish to defy fate.

The type of crime often fits the behavior that provoked it. Theft, for instance, is often stimulated by the victim's negligence, swindles by his greed, and blackmail by his guilt. Murder can be invited by belligerence: in 1969 a national study of bus drivers showed that three who were killed during robberies had vowed not to let "any punk kid" rob them, and had carried and tried to use guns in violation of company rules. In other cases, suicidal wishes have provoked murder—a phenomenon that the mother of Congressional Medal of Honor Winner Dwight Johnson may have recognized when she surmised that her son, shot while committing a holdup, had "tired of life and needed someone else to pull the trigger."

Much of the early research in victimology is foundational to questions that are still being asked today. A brief discussion of the early victimologists and their thinking is warranted.

KEY FIGURES

As mentioned earlier, the origins of scientific victimology can be attributed to a few key figures in criminology, including Hans von Hentig, Benjamin Mendelsohn, Stephen Schafer, and Marvin Wolfgang (Karmen 2007). Their early work involved the first attempts at studying the victim-offender relationship in a systematic fashion, however misguided by generalizations, personal bias, and professional agendas. Each of them will be discussed, as their approaches to victim study are the most relevant to some of the questions posed by modern-day forensic victimologists.

Hans von Hentig

In the first half of the last century, Hans von Hentig was a criminologist from Germany seeking to develop better crime prevention strategies. Having researched the factors that predisposed one to criminality, he began to wonder what might cause a victim to become a victim. He ultimately found that certain victim's characteristics did play a role in shaping the crimes suffered (Doerner and Lab 2005; Meadows 2007).

Specifically, Von Hentig believed that some victims contributed to their own victimization by virtue of many converging factors, not all of which were in their control. Von Hentig described his beliefs to the mainstream media in *Time Magazine* (1948):

> The characteristics and forces that tend to make a man a criminal … are diverse and complicated. A contributing factor may be ugliness, deafness, a physical handicap …

> Victims, Dr. Von Hentig believes, are born or shaped by society much as criminals are … Some types of criminals are attracted to slum areas; so are their victims. Feeblemindedness, common among some types of criminals, is also common among their victims.

> … certain characteristics of law-abiding citizens arouse a counter reaction in the criminal. The inexperienced businessman, for example, invites embezzlement; the nagging wife is flirting with murder; the alcoholic is a natural for robbery. Thus the victim becomes the "tempter."

To his credit, Von Hentig was perhaps the first to systematically study the role victims could play in the crimes committed against them (Van Dijk 1999). He later published *The Criminal and His Victim: Studies in the Sociobiology of Crime* (1948), which contained a chapter devoted solely to discussing these theories. Von Hentig argued for acknowledging the responsibility some victims had in becoming victimized. He even developed a system of categorizing victims along a continuum that depended on their contribution to the criminal act, though currently his terminology may be considered offensive to some.

Von Hentig originally classified victims into one of 13 categories, which could easily be described as a list of characteristics that increase victim vulnerability or exposure to danger (adapted from pages 404–438, with discussion by the authors):

1. *The Young:* Von Hentig was referring to children and infants. From a contemporary point of view, children are physically weaker, have less mental prowess, have fewer legal rights, and are economically dependent on their caretakers (parents, guardians, teachers, and so forth); they also have the potential to be exposed to a wider range of harm than adults. Moreover, they are less able to defend themselves and sometimes less likely to be believed should they seek assistance. This includes children who suffer emotional, physical, and sexual abuse at home because of abusive parents (often under the influence of

drugs and alcohol); children who are bullied at school because of some aspect of their appearance or personality; and children who are forced into acts of prostitution or sold into slavery by impoverished parents. Each suffers different levels and frequencies of exposure to different kinds of harm.

2. *The Female:* Von Hentig was referring to all women. From a contemporary point of view, many women are physically weaker than men. Many have been culturally conditioned, to varying degrees, to accept male authority. And many women are financially dependent on the men in their lives (fathers, husbands, and so forth). To make matters worse, many Western women are conditioned to believe that their value is associated with their bodies, or specifically, their sexuality. In extreme cases, this can lead to low self-esteem, depression, substance abuse, promiscuity, and prostitution, with varying exposure to harm.

3. *The Old:* Von Hentig was referring to the elderly. In a contemporary sense, they have many of the same vulnerabilities as children: they are often physically weaker, mentally less facile, and may be under someone else's care. This can expose them to a range of harms, from the theft of personal property to physical abuse. However, they are also particularly vulnerable to confidence scams, as they can have greater access to money, along with poor memory and a sense of pride that may combine to prevent them from reporting loss.

4. *The Mentally Defective and Deranged:* Von Hentig was referring to the feeble-minded, the "insane," drug addicts, and alcoholics. Those who suffer from any of these conditions have an altered perception of reality. As a consequence, depending on the level of their affliction, personality, and environment, these potential victims may harm themselves and others to varying degrees. They may also suffer many of the same general kinds of exposures as children and the elderly.

5. *Immigrants:* Von Hentig was referring to foreigners unfamiliar with a given culture. Anyone traveling to a culture different from their own is subject to varying gaps in communication and comprehension. This can, depending on where they go and whom they encounter, expose them to all manner of confidence schemes, theft, and abuse, to say nothing of prejudices.

6. *Minorities:* Von Hentig was referring to the "racially disadvantaged," as he put it. What this truly means is prejudice. Groups against which there is some amount of bias or prejudice by another may be exposed to varying levels of abuse and violence.

7. *Dull Normals:* Von Hentig was referring to "simple-minded persons," as he put it. From a contemporary viewpoint, we might consider these as having the same types of exposure to harm as those who are mentally defective and deranged.

8. *The Depressed:* Von Hentig was referring to those with various psychological maladies. From a contemporary viewpoint, those who are depressed may expose themselves to all manner of danger, intentional and otherwise. Additionally, they may take psychotropic medication that alters perception, affects judgment, and impairs reasoning.

9. *The Acquisitive:* Von Hentig was referring to those who are greedy and looking for quick gain. Such individuals may suspend their judgment, or intentionally put themselves in dangerous situations, in order to achieve their goals.

10. *The Wanton:* Von Hentig was referring to promiscuous persons. People who engage in indiscriminate sexual activity with many different partners expose themselves to different levels of disease and varying personalities. Some of these personalities may be healthy and supportive; some may be narcissistic, jealous, and destructive.

11. *The Lonesome or Heartbroken:* Von Hentig was referring to widows, widowers, and those in mourning. From a contemporary standpoint, loneliness is at epidemic proportions, with more than half of marriages ending in divorce, the rise of the culture of narcissism since the late 1970s (see Lasch 1979), and diminishing intimacy skills across all cultures. This category does not apply only to those in mourning; those who are lonely or heartbroken are prone to substance abuse, and can be easy prey for con men, the abusive, and the manipulative.

12. *The Tormentor:* Von Hentig was referring to the abusive parent. In contemporary terms, there are abusive caretakers, intimates, and family members of all kinds. All such abusers expose themselves to the harm they inflict, the resulting angst, and the degree to which their victims fight back. For example, an abusive mother who gets drunk and punches a child exposes herself to the dangers of injuring her hand, of misjudging her strike and even her balance, and of the child punching back.

13. *The Blocked, Exempted, or Fighting:* Von Hentig was referring to victims of blackmail, extortion, and confidence scams. In contemporary times, such victims are still exposed to continual financial loss or physical harm, or must suffer the consequences that come from bringing the police in to assist. In such cases, the attention of law enforcement, and any subsequent publicity, may be the very thing that the victim wishes to avoid.

From a research point of view, these are interesting and even somewhat useful classifications with important theoretical implications, though the terminology is sometimes inappropriate. However, the case-working victimologist must study each victim to determine the extent to which such a classification has a bearing on the harm suffered within a particular crime. Some children are smart and fast; many women are strong and self-assured; some of the elderly are quick and resourceful; immigrants learn languages and customs; and the "blocked" may decide to go to the police. In short, many of the generalizations suggested in this typology may not hold when applied to a specific crime or victim.

Benjamin Mendelsohn

Benjamin Mendelsohn was a French-Israeli lawyer who began studying victims in 1947 (Karmen 2005). While working on the defense of a rape case, he became interested in the correlations between rapists and their victims. He found that there was often a strong interpersonal relationship between the two, and that it could lead some victims to unknowingly invite or even cause their own victimization (Meadows 2007). He referred to this as *victim precipitation*:[2] crime caused or partially facilitated by the victim. He ultimately believed that many victims shared an unconscious capacity for being victimized, and referred to this as being *victim prone*.

Similar to Von Hentig, Mendelsohn developed a typology that categorizes the extent to which a victim is culpable in his or her demise. However, while Von Hentig's typology explains victim contribution based on personal characteristics, Mendelsohn's typology uses situational factors. Mendelsohn's six victim types, as adapted from Meadows (2007, 22) are:

1. *Completely innocent victim:* Exhibits no provocative or contributory behavior prior to the offender's attack.
2. *Victim due to ignorance:* Unwittingly does something that places him or her in a position to be victimized.
3. *Voluntary victim:* Suicides, or those injured while participating in high-risk crimes such as drug abuse or prostitution.
4. *Victim more guilty than the offender:* Victim provokes a criminal act (e.g., throws the first punch in a fight but ends up the loser).
5. *Most guilty victim:* The initial aggressor, but due to circumstances beyond his or her control ends up the victim (e.g., attempts to rob a convenience store but is shot by the storeowner).
6. *Simulating or imaginary victim:* A pretender, or false reporter.

---

[2]According to Doerner and Lab (2002, 9): "Victim precipitation deals with the degree to which the victim is responsible for his or her own victimization."

FIGURE 1.3

A Chinese prostitute is found by authorities in a Guangzhou hotel room with two men. Were she to become the victim of an assault or contract a venereal disease, as do many prostitutes, those using Mendelsohn's typology would likely dismiss her as a *voluntary victim*. This may or may not be accurate. For instance, many prostitutes around the world are sold or tricked into sex work by relatives and brothel owners at a very young age, and then become captive by circumstances that they cannot control.[3] In some cases they are broken in to the trade with beatings, rape, and other forms of torture. Eventually, they can become trapped by fear, shame, poverty, addiction, and disease.

---

[3]The United States is no stranger to the problem of *human trafficking,* which is among the most profitable forms of organized crime in the world. According to Srikantiah (2007, 162–163): "Trafficking is modern-day slavery. Men, women, and children from developing countries are trafficked to industrialized countries for forced prostitution, forced labor, and other forms of exploitation. Increased globalization, including cheaper transportation and communication methods, has resulted in increased migration, including increased trafficking in persons. According to U.S. government estimates, up to 800,000 people are trafficked across international borders annually, and up to 17,500 people are trafficked into the United States each year. These victims include men, women, boys, and girls. The majority of trafficked persons are women and girls, who are more vulnerable to trafficking because of a greater susceptibility to poverty, illiteracy, and lower social status. Individuals are typically trafficked from poor countries, often in the global South, to wealthier countries. Trafficking is an extremely profitable international criminal enterprise, ranking third in profits after the arms and drug markets. The International Labour Organization estimates that human trafficking generates $31.6 billion in organized crime profits annually."

The danger with Mendelsohn's typology is that it doesn't always come with explicit instructions. It does have some important conceptual value, in showing a continuum of possible victim culpability or precipitation. However, if applied broadly, simplistically, and without careful investigation into the facts, it could be misused. Before these descriptors can be applied to a specific case, attention must be paid to the details. This means accepting that not every prostitute or drug user is a voluntary victim; not every bar fight involves a more guilty or most guilty victim; and not everyone who fails to exhibit provocative behavior prior to an attack is completely innocent. While Mendelsohn's typology is interesting in theory, its application to specific cases can be problematic, if not entirely inappropriate, when contextual information is not investigated and considered.

Stephen Schafer, PhD

Dr. Stephen Schafer was a professor of sociology at Northeastern University in Boston, Massachusetts. In 1968, he published what is regarded by some as the first textbook on the subject of victimology, *The Victim and His Criminal: A Study in Functional Responsibility*. According to Van Dijk, this work was significant to the advance of victimology, as it was an "independent study of the relationships and interactions between offender and victim, before, during, and after the crime" (1999, 2). Schafer's study involved interviews with criminals and aimed to build upon the typologies presented in previous works by focusing on victim culpability.

According to Doerner and Lab (2002), Schafer proposed seven types of victim responsibility (or victim precipitation), which are essentially a variation on the work of Von Hentig (2002, 8):

1. *Unrelated victims* (no victim responsibility)
2. *Provocative victims* (victim shares responsibility)
3. *Precipitative victims* (some degree of responsibility)
4. *Biologically weak victims* (no responsibility)
5. *Socially weak victims* (no responsibility)
6. *Self-victimizing* (total victim responsibility)
7. *Political victims* (no responsibility)

In reviewing this typology, we find it to be less of an inclusive measure and more of an incomplete list of circumstances that mitigate victim responsibility because they increase general vulnerability. While it is true that lines are drawn between the *provocative*, the *precipitative*, and the *self-victimizing*, from the examples cited in the literature it is unclear how these categories would be applied to a specific case, as the defining elements are highly subjective. Also, Schafer has inappropriately defined (and therefore presumptively assumed) the specific responsibility of each victim type. There appears to be no room for mitigating circumstances once a victim is put in a particular slot, which is what a pedantic or bureaucratic victimologist could do with this labeling system. *Socially weak victims,* such as immigrants, are regarded as having no responsibility, but what if they are shot while robbing a convenience store? *Biologically weak victims,* such as the elderly, are also regarded as having no responsibility, but what if they are abusing alcohol and become a rancorous precipitative drunk, only to start a physical altercation at home that they lose? As will be discussed throughout this text, the relationships between victims and criminals are far too complex for such rigid presumptions.

However problematic, Dr. Schafer's contribution to the field of victimology must not be dismissed. As Young and Stein explain: "The importation of victimology to the United States was due largely to the work of the scholar Stephen Schafer, whose book *The Victim and His Criminal: A Study in Functional Responsibility* became mandatory reading for anyone interested in the study of crime victims and their behaviors" (2004, 2). Were it not for his efforts, subsequent work leading to our research would not have been possible.

Marvin E. Wolfgang, PhD

Dr. Marvin Wolfgang was a professor of criminology, legal studies, and law at the Wharton School, and founding director of the Sellin Center for Studies in Criminology and Criminal Law, at the University of Pennsylvania. According to Doerner and Lab (2005), Wolfgang was the first to present empirical research findings as support for his theories of victimology. In his work *Patterns of Criminal Homicide* (1958), Wolfgang presented the results of his study of police homicide records, which concluded that over a quarter of the homicides in the city of Philadelphia between 1948 and 1952 involved some element of victim contribution and participation (Doerner and Lab 2005). Wolfgang went so far as to label one type of homicide *victim-precipitated,* where the initial physical violence or threat of physical violence came from the victim, not the offender (Shichor and Tibbetts 2002). This concept of victim precipitation has since been used to study many violent crimes, but it loses some of its validity when property and sex crimes are considered, since provocation by the victim becomes much more subjective in such cases (Shichor and Tibbetts 2002).

FIGURE 1.4

Dr. Marvin Wolfgang, a pioneer of quantitative and theoretical criminology, died in 1998 at the age of 73.

VICTIM STUDY: PAST TO PRESENT

As we have described, the formal discipline of victimology was born out of a desire to study victims for the purpose of answering social and legal questions regarding cause and culpability. Liu explains that "victimologists consider how victims help create the conditions in which they are victimized, how victims contribute to and even provoke their own victimization, and the demographic relationship between victims and offenders" (2006, 175).

On the one hand, victimology began as a preventative issue relating to social health: what can we do to avoid becoming a victim today, and what can we do to reduce the number of victims tomorrow? On the other hand, it was a matter of legal consequence: to what extent did the victim contribute to his or her own demise with respect to circumstances, ignorance, negligence, or intentional provocation? Victimology was the beginning of an attempt, however imperfect, to peel back the layers of the onion and expose the dynamics of the victim-offender relationship. But the political climate has changed how we study victims today.

Modern texts on the subject of victimology, many of them cited in this chapter, have moved away from asking questions that might reveal victim falsity and weaken related advocacy or criminal prosecutions. Rather, they tend to focus on victim statistics, the impact of crime, enhancing victim rights, victim compensation, and developing new victim remedies. Furthermore, they offer broad yet thin reference to victim groups by crime type, in accordance with the Uniform Crime Reports (UCR, to be discussed in Chapter 2). Some texts do not achieve even that level of coverage, being little more than compilations of various writings by authors with diverse views and agendas without organization or theme.

In short, current victimology texts presume victimhood for all of the numbers that apply and provide little that would help inform an objective or critical investigation into the facts and dynamics of a particular victim-offender relationship. In this current perspective, crime is regarded as a social disease with victimology acting as its sociostatistical thermometer—taking the temperature of victim groups and providing a speculative lens for their various maladies. We understand that this is a genuinely important role and one that must not be completely abandoned by the field. Somebody has to look at the numbers and give voice to these groups.

However, it must be acknowledged that despite the collection of victim data, the use of victim statistics, and the promotion of victim sympathy, such approaches to victimology can regularly be found lacking in actual science. In fact, they may even be viewed as biased, or as pandering to victims, advocates, bureaucracies, and their respective agendas. Certainly these voices need the floor, but not the whole floor and not the whole agenda.

Any victim bias is a problem when studying victims of crime: pro-victim and anti-victim alike. However, as discussed in the Preface, a pro-victim bias in victimology is currently being rewarded, because it is socially and politically inoffensive, and maintains the much-needed sanctity of victimhood. Without a presumptive showing regarding the *sanctity of victimhood*,[4] some investigators become lax and apathetic, some prosecutors are loath to go to trial, and some juries are hesitant to convict. As a consequence, anything that gets in the way, whether it be research asking the politically inappropriate questions, investigations that might reveal negative victim information, or forensic examinations that might disprove victim claims, is too often regarded as off-limits to mainstream victimologists.

Victimologists, to achieve any scientific threshold, must be free to remain skeptical, inquisitive, and above all objective. They cannot be attached to a particular sociocultural view or agenda; they cannot be working to achieve satisfaction or remedies for the victim; and they cannot assume the existence of victimhood. Victimologists must be free to question and interpret victim evidence as it is found. As a counterbalance to the victimologists who are in the business of taking temperatures of crime victim populations, often amidst a host of biasing influences including pressure to maintain the sanctity of victimhood, there must be those free to doubt and seek proofs in individual cases. This is the considered role of *forensic victimology*.

FORENSIC VICTIMOLOGY: AN INTRODUCTION

Although many diverse aspects of victim study are encapsulated within general victimology, interactionist victimology, and critical victimology (discussed in this chapter and in the Preface), there is one concept that has been largely overlooked in the related literature to date. *Forensic victimology,*[5] the idiographic and nomothetic study of violent crime victims for the purposes of addressing investigative and forensic issues, has been an implicit feature of the field since its inception. However, forensic victimology has been inappropriately folded in with treatment, punishment, and even advocacy-oriented goals. Expropriated from scientific study and commonly disguised as professional compassion to serve nonscientific agendas, explicit discussions of what may be viewed as forensic victimology by behavioral scientists have been limited.

Forensic victimology is a subdivision of interactionist victimology, in which victims are defined by having suffered harm or loss due to a breach of law.

---

[4]*The sanctity of victimhood* refers to the belief that victims are good, honest, and pure, making those who defend them both righteous and morally justified. Conversely, it suggests that those who doubt them are immoral and unjust in their tasks. Ultimately, it requires victims to meet an unrealistic standard of near perfect victimity. It is anathema to the scientific method.

[5]The term *forensic victimology* was originally defined in Petherick and Turvey (2008). However, the general purpose and practice are as old as criminal investigation itself.

It involves the accurate, critical, and objective outlining of victim lifestyles and circumstances, the events leading up to their injury, and the precise nature of any harm or loss suffered. The purpose of this text is to provide readers with an applied understanding of the principles and practice of forensic victimology; to excavate it from it's current place in the literature as an explicit area of scientific victim study; and to outline its value to investigative and forensic purposes.

Purpose

The primary goals of those involved with other fields of victimology commonly relate to the restoration of victims. They work at empowering the victims; returning the victims to the state they were in prior to suffering harm or loss; or making them feel comfortable again, and satisfied that justice has been served (Williams 2004). Forensic victimology, however, does not seek to assist with victim advocacy or promote victim sympathy. Nor is the forensic victimologist invested in restoring victims and making them whole. However, there is an awareness that the victim evidence gathered, as well as subsequent interpretations, may be used by others for these purposes at a later time.

Forensic victimology is an applied discipline as opposed to a theoretical one. The forensic victimologist seeks to examine, consider, and interpret particular victim evidence in a scientific fashion in order to answer investigative and forensic (i.e., legal) questions. Usually, forensic victimologists serve investigations and court proceedings by endeavoring to

1. Assist with contextualizing allegations of victimization;
2. Help support or refute allegations of victimization;
3. Help establish the nature of victim exposure to harm or loss;
4. Assist with the development of offender modus operandi and motive;
5. Help establish an investigative suspect pool;
6. Assist with the investigative linkage of unsolved cases.

It is understood that investigative and forensic venues are quite different in scope, structure, and function. The questions they need answered are particular to their unique geographical variations. They also represent very different standards of evidence. What may be investigatively useful speculation or theory at one point may lack the sufficiency for subsequent court-worthy opinions. Given the capacity for investigative work to find its way into court, this distinction must be ever-present and crystal clear.[6]

---

[6]This will be discussed shortly and again in Chapter 3.

Philosophy

The unimpeachable philosophy of forensic victimology is that victim facts are preferable to victim fictions; that victim evidence must be gathered and examined in a consistent, thorough, and objective fashion as with any other form of evidence; and that interpretations of victim evidence must comport with the tenets of the scientific method, whether examining the results of a rape kit or assessing victim risk.

The guiding principle for studying victims in investigative and forensic contexts is this: a comprehensive understanding of the victims and their circumstances will allow for an accurate interpretation of the nature of their harm or loss, and it will also teach us about their offender. The less we know about the victim, the less we know about the crime and the criminal. Consequently, the way we collect and develop victim evidence is just as important as our eventual interpretations: they must not be weak, narrow, or based on unproved assumptions.

With this as our standard, it is not possible to avoid the fact that the best way to objectively build knowledge and render valid interpretations is through the scientific method. As Turvey (2008, 47) explains:

> The *scientific method* is a way to investigate how or why something works, or how something happened, through the development of hypotheses and subsequent attempts at falsification through testing and other accepted means. It is a structured process designed to build scientific knowledge by way of answering specific questions about observations through careful analysis and critical thinking. Observations are used to form testable hypotheses, and with sufficient testing hypotheses can become scientific theories. Eventually, over much time, with precise testing marked by a failure to falsify, scientific theories can become scientific principles. The scientific method is the particular approach to knowledge building and problem solving employed by scientists of every kind.
>
> It is important to explain that scientists use the scientific method to build knowledge and solve problems; its use defines them. If one is doing something else, then one is not actually a scientist. As Faigman *et al.* (1997, 48) warns: "Not all knowledge asserted by people who are commonly thought of as scientists is the product of the scientific method."

It follows that in order to meet the definition of scientific study that victimology aspires to, forensic victimology must be conducted with a scientific mindset by those properly educated and trained to employ the scientific method. Any other approach is out of step with this philosophy, serving some other purpose or rationale.

Rationale

Forensic victimology is intended to serve the justice system by educating it. It is aimed at helping provide for informed investigations, requiring scientific examinations of victim evidence presented in court, and more informed legal outcomes. As with any other forensic discipline, it does not take sides and it does not seek to intrude on the ultimate issues of guilt, innocence, or victimity. Further explanation is necessary.

As described in Dienstein (2005, 160) *criminal investigation* is the process of gathering facts to be used as evidence and proof in a court of law. Without an investigation, the facts will be absent and proofs will be impossible to attain. Schultz (2005, 122) explains that prior to being tested in the court-room, a competent investigation will gather or prepare evidence of the follow-ing: "knowledge or proof that a crime has been committed; the existence of a victim(s) … an approved report of the investigation answering the questions of who, what, where, when, why and how; and evidence that has been identified and preserved for the prosecutor." Only then may investigators proceed with their case to the district attorney for prosecutorial consideration.

In the investigative realm, forensic victimology provides for the consistent rec-ognition, collection, preservation, and documentation of victim evidence, all of which will be detailed in subsequent chapters. Questions are asked, context is established, and history is documented. Each piece of victim evidence is scrutinized by investigators and then acted upon again and again until it is an exhausted possibility. This informs the nature, scope, and depth of the inves-tigation. It can also lead to the discovery of additional relevant or dispositive evidence. Ultimately, forensic victimology assists with answering the question of whether and how criminal charges and civil liabilities may be appropriate, which is going to be decided by the court.

More and more, criminal and civil trials alike require the assistance of forensic experts to introduce and explain various kinds of evidence to the jury. In order to do so, a potential witness must first be qualified as an expert by the court. According to Lilly (1987, 483):

> an expert witness possesses knowledge and skill that distinguishes
> him from ordinary witnesses. Presumably, he is in a position superior to
> the other trial participants, including the jury, to draw inferences and
> reach conclusions within his field of expertise.

Significantly different from investigative opinions, which are dynamic and often rendered in haste with incomplete information amidst ongoing efforts to gather facts, forensic opinions are those expert findings regarding the state of the record held to such a level of confidence and certainty that they may be presented in court as best evidence.

In the forensic realm (which necessarily involves and therefore must continuously anticipate the courtroom), forensic victimology is a form of evidence that informs the nature, scope, and depth of any legal proceedings to be decided by the trier of fact (a judge or jury). When presented by a forensic expert, it involves the scientific interpretation of various kinds of victim evidence gathered during the investigation and any subsequent analysis. Ultimately, it assists with demonstrating the actual limits of victim evidence—which criminal or civil theories it supports and which it refutes.

CASE EXAMPLE: INVESTIGATIVE USE OF FORENSIC VICTIMOLOGY

FIGURE 1.5

On December 19, 2007, and partially as the result of media attention by ABC News, Jamie Leigh Jones testified at congressional hearings (the House of Representatives Judiciary Subcommittee on Crime, Terrorism, and Homeland Security Hearing: "Enforcement of Federal Criminal Law to Protect Americans Working for U.S. Contractors in Iraq") regarding her alleged rape and detainment by fellow employees of Kellogg, Brown, and Root (KBR) at Camp Hope, Iraq, in 2005.

Consider the ongoing case of Jamie Leigh Jones, a former administrative assistant with Houston-based Kellogg, Brown, and Root (KBR), a former subsidiary of Halliburton. Jones alleges that she was transferred to Iraq after her supervisor coerced her to perform a sexual favor. As Coady (2007) explains:

> According to the complaint, Jones worked for KBR in Houston as an administrative assistant. She says her supervisor convinced her to have sex with him in exchange for time off to take care of her sick mother. Jones escaped that situation by securing a transfer to another section of KBR, Overseas Administrative Services [OAS] Ltd., also in Houston.
>
> However, her former supervisor made good on his threat to put a negative recommendation in her personnel file if she transferred, the suit says.
>
> Jones transferred again, this time to Iraq as part of OAS. Beginning in July 2005 Jones lived and worked at Camp Hope in Baghdad, where

she was forced to live on a co-ed floor of a male-dominated barracks. Jones says she was constantly subjected to catcalls and partially dressed men as she walked from her second-floor room to the bathroom on the first floor. Although she complained to several Halliburton and KBR managers and other representatives about the sexually hostile living conditions at the barracks and asked to be moved to a safer location, her request went unanswered, Jones says.

After only four days at Camp Hope (which is operated by Halliburton in connection with operations of the U.S. Department of State), Jones alleged that she was drugged and then raped. According to the complaint filed in *Jones and Daigle v. Halliburton Co. DBA Kellogg, Brown, and Root (KBR) et al.* (2007, 8–10):

> Beginning July 25, 2005, Jamie lived and worked at Camp Hope, Baghdad, Iraq. Jamie was housed, during her off-duty hours, in a two-story living quarters which consisted of a room on a co-ed floor in a predominantly male barracks.
>
> … [O]n the evening of July 28, 2005, during her off-duty hours, Jamie was drugged (by what was believed to be Rohypnol) and brutally raped by, on information and belief, several Halliburton/KBR firefighters, including defendant, Charles Boartz, while she was in her room in the barracks. When she awoke the next morning still affected by the drug, she found her body naked and severely bruised, with lacerations to her vagina and anus, blood running down her leg, her breast implants were ruptured, and her pectoral muscles torn—which would later require reconstructive surgery. Upon walking to the rest room, she passed out again. When she returned to the living area, she found Charles Boartz lying in her bottom bed. She asked him what had happened, and he confessed to having unprotected sex with her. Jamie reported the rape to the [sic] Pete Arroyo, one of the operations personnel, who then took her to a KBR medical personnel. The U.S. State Department Diplomatic Security was informed and a rape kit was administered at the combat area surgical hospital run by the U.S. Army.

The complaint goes on to state (23–24):

> a. Immediately following her physical examination, she was placed in a trailer with a bed, a shower and a sink, but without a television, and was refused phone calls to her family despite repeated requests, which amounted to a false imprisonment;
>
> b. She was confronted by KBR supervisors, who gave her two options:
> i. Stay and "get over it"; or
> ii. Return home without the "guarantee" of a job on return.

These options amounted to an unlawful threat to terminate her job for reporting her attack, and dealing with its aftermath.

Jamie was able to convince a guard to let her use his cellular phone. She called her father. Her father was in turn able to enlist congressional assistance to get his daughter home.

Her father immediately called his congressman, Rep. Ted Poe, R-Texas, who ultimately intervened on his daughter's behalf. Her ordeal and congressional testimony are further characterized in Carr (2007):

Appearing before a hearing on the enforcement of laws to protect Americans working in Iraq, Ms. Jones said that on her fourth day in Baghdad some co-workers, who she described as Halliburton-KBR firefighters, invited her for a drink. "I took two sips from the drink and don't remember anything after that," she said.

The next morning she woke up groggy and confused, and with a sore chest and blood between her legs. She reported the incident to KBR and was examined by an army doctor, who said she had been repeatedly raped vaginally and anally.

The doctor took photographs, made notes, and handed all the evidence over to KBR personnel. "The KBR security took me to a trailer and then locked me in a room with two armed guards outside my door," Ms. Jones said. "I was imprisoned in the trailer for approximately a day. One of the guards finally had mercy and let me use a phone."

Ms. Jones called her father in Texas, who called his representative in Congress, Republican Ted Poe. Mr. Poe contacted the State Department, who quickly sent personnel to rescue Ms. Jones and flew her back to Texas.

Ms. Jones said she was still having reconstructive surgery after the brutal rape.

An army doctor collected DNA evidence, including vaginal swabs and scrapings from her fingernails, and placed them in a box for evidence. Ms. Jones said the doctor gave the box to a KBR security officer but it went missing. A State Department diplomatic security agent recovered the kit in May 2007, but the doctor's notes and photographs are now inexplicably missing, undermining any chances of bringing the case through the criminal courts.

Jones filed a lawsuit in May of 2007, nearly two years after the alleged rape, when all other avenues failed to produce criminal charges against those she feels are responsible. The lawsuit led to media coverage, which led to congressional hearings by the House of Representatives Judiciary Subcommittee on Crime, Terrorism, and Homeland Security in December of 2007. As Sauer (2007) explains, KBR has ended its investigation into the matter, and the Department of Justice (DOJ) isn't talking—not even to Congress:

> The Department of Justice refused to send a representative to answer questions from Congress today on the investigations into allegations of rape and sexual assault on female American contractors. "I'm embarrassed that the Department of Justice can't even come forward," said the chairman of the House Judiciary Committee John Conyers, D-Mich. "This is an absolute disgrace," said Conyers. "The least we could do is have people from the Department of Justice and the Defense over here talking about how we're going to straighten out the system right away." . . .

> Jones' congressman, Ted Poe, R-Texas, also testified at the hearing and told the committee how he has not been given any answers as to the status of the investigation by [the] DOJ or the State Department. "The Department of Justice has not informed Jamie or me of the status of a criminal investigation against her rapist, if any investigation exists," Poe said today. "It is interesting to note that the Department of Justice has thousands of lawyers but not one from the barrage of lawyers is here to tell us what if anything they are doing. Their absence and silence speaks volumes about the hidden crimes in Iraq. Their attitude seems to be one of blissful indifference to American workers in Iraq," said Poe.

> Jones told Congress that it wasn't until after she was interviewed by "20/20," that an assistant U.S. attorney in Florida questioned her about her case. "I asked the AUSA, [Association of the United States Army] 'Where should I refer victims to contact me?' and she responded, 'Don't refer them to my office, but you may want to refer them to the office of victims of crime,'" Jones recounted for Congress today.

> But the Department of Justice Crime Victims office, in a letter to Jamie's lawyer, had already said it had closed out her complaint claiming it did not have jurisdiction.

> The Department of Justice, following the hearing, said today that the department is "investigating this matter" but would not elaborate.

As of this writing, no criminal charges have been filed, Congress is awaiting a response from the DOJ, and the lawsuit filed by Jones is ongoing.

Investigative Applications

Forensic victimology is best applied to a case from the very beginning, to provide for the most complete record of victim evidence. However, that is no longer possible in the Jones case. At this late hour, some of the evidence and investigative opportunities may have been lost and some may not. For example, to render the best evidentiary foundation, the forensic victimologist would require or request the following:

1. Investigate and establish a timeline of Jones' activity for at least 24 hours leading up to the time of her alleged attack.

2. Conduct a frame–frame interview with Jones to determine the precise sequence of events leading up to the alleged attack and the period of time involving her alleged captivity.

3. Subpoena all employee records and memorandums related to Jamie Jones, to support or refute her claims regarding her ultimate transfer to Iraq. This would include her e-mail and cell phone records, to determine whom she was talking to in order to establish timeline information and potential suspects.

4. Seal off Jones' quarters at Camp Hope and process it as a potential crime scene. That this was not done at the very outset of her allegations allowed for the loss of valuable evidence that would have either supported or failed to support her allegations, such as biological transfer to her carpet, bedding, towels, rags, clothing, or unknown objects used by the alleged assailants. The current disposition of all of these items would need to be investigated.

5. Investigative interviews of all suspects, floor mates, supervisors, security, and medical personnel involved in or in the vicinity of the alleged rape and detention from start to finish. This would establish a suspect pool, lead to additional evidence, and support or refute her claims of hostility, harassment, rape, and confinement at Camp Hope. This may have been done by the DOJ subsequent to her lawsuit, but there is no indication it had been done prior. For example, suspects should have their e-mail and phone records subpoenaed to see who is communicating during and after the alleged assault. They should also be asked to turn over any digital recording devices to determine whether any recordings were made of the events that evening.

6. Examination and interpretation of the forensic evidence and forensic interview that would have been documented as a part of the sexual assault protocol by medical personnel. While notes and photos may have been lost, there would be a final report, and those medical personnel may still be interviewed about what they documented and observed. This includes submitting recently recovered samples for DNA and toxicology, to establish a potential suspect pool and determine her level of drug and alcohol toxicity. This would also help to objectively support or fail to support her claims of violent rape and drug-related impairment.

7. Subpoena all security records relating to Camp Hope to establish whether, when, and how security personnel may have detained Jones and under whose authority.

8. Examine and document the actual trailer or container where Jones was allegedly held against her will.

9. Subpoena all medical records related to Jones during her time in Iraq and subsequent to her return, to support or refute her claims regarding injury and ongoing reconstructive surgeries.

Obviously a thorough criminal investigation would involve much more than these elements, and these would lead to still further inquiries. However these would be the first things requested by a forensic victimologist seeking to create a solid investigative threshold for later forensic examination and interpretation. Once the forensic victimologist establishes the state of the investigative and forensic evidence—what's been done, what's not been done, and what can yet be done—they may be able to provide further investigative direction or forensic interpretations.

Forensic Applications

In some cases, the forensic victimologist will have an abundance of evidence to work with that provides for opinions that support or refute certain case theories. In this case, given the persistent absence of investigative and forensic efforts with regards to the victim, Jones, and her complaints, that may not be entirely possible. However, failure to render a basic level of investigative care would be evidence of investigative incompetence, if not belligerent ignorance on the part of those responsible. That in itself would be a threshold finding that may be significant in a court of law: that a competent investigation was not performed, that few theories could be supported or refuted in court without this investigation, and that certain evidence should therefore be investigated before anyone becomes certain of anything in court filings, expert reports, or related decisions. It may also be of significance to a governing body seeking to oversee the competence of the DOJ investigation—for example, to use the level of investigative effort as a yardstick when the DOJ steps up to explain under oath before a congressional committee precisely what it has done, what it has not done, and why.

SUMMARY

In the sphere of criminal justice, the word *victim* describes any person who has experienced injury, loss, or hardship due to the illegal action of another individual or organization (Karmen 2004). *Victimology* refers to the scientific study of victimization, including the relationships between victims and offenders, investigators, courts, corrections, media, and social movements

(Karmen 1990). There is a clear gap in the victimology literature, however: little research or attention is paid to the idiographic and nomothetic study of violent crime victims for the purposes of addressing investigative and forensic issues as described in Turvey (2008). This type of analysis may be referred to as *forensic victimology*, which differs markedly from traditional forms of general or interactionist victimology. *Forensic victimology* is the objective study of victims, with a focus on impartially and completely describing all aspects of their life and lifestyle in order to gain a better understanding of how they came to become victimized, how the crime took place, and their relationship with the offender.

The purpose of forensic victimology is aimed at accurately, critically, and objectively describing the victim in order to better understand victims, crime, criminals, and forensic issues. Moreover, forensic victimology does not seek to restore victims to the state they were in prior to being victimized, nor does it wish to assign blame to victims. Forensic victimology is designed to look beneath victim stereotypes, in a scientific manner, in order to improve the understanding of the dynamics of the criminal act as well as the victims themselves.

The purpose of seeking out and presenting information about victims is to help determine whether a crime has been committed, whether the statements made by victims are sufficiently reliable as corroborative evidence, and to determine who committed the crime and in what context. The philosophy behind studying victims in investigative and forensic contexts is that a complete understanding of victims and their circumstances will allow for a comprehensive and correct interpretation of the nature of their suffering, and it will also speak volumes about the person who committed an offense against them. Like all types of evidence, victim information is of much more use if it is developed and interpreted in a consistent and scientific fashion.

The rationale for using forensic victimology in criminal cases is that victim information can serve the justice system by educating it. The aim of forensic victimology is to assist in providing informed investigations, to require scientific examinations of victim evidence that is presented in court, and to result in more informed legal outcomes. Forensic victimology does not take sides, and it does not seek to intrude on the ultimate issues of guilt, innocence, or victimity.

Questions

1. Name three of Hans von Hentig's 13 categories of victims.
2. True or False: Since the end of the "golden age" of victims, there have been no further blood feuds among families and cultures.

3. Choose one: Mendelsohn's typology for categorizing victims is problematic because it relies on
   a. personal characteristics
   b. situational characteristics
   c. demographic characteristics
4. It is difficult to study _____ and _____ crimes through the lens of victim provocation, because they involve more subjectivity.
5. Define *forensic victimology.*
6. Describe how *forensic victimology* differs from other types of victimology.
7. Name three ways that forensic victimologists serve investigations and court proceedings.
8. Describe the scientific method.

REFERENCES

Carr, R. 2007. "Gang-raped then locked in van, Iraq worker says." *The Age*, December 21. http://www.theage.com.au/news/world/gangraped-then-locked-in-van-iraq-worker-says/2007/12/20/1197740465943.html.

Coady, L. 2007. "Ex-Halliburton Worker in Iraq Sues for Rape, Harassment." Andrews Publications, Friday, May 25. http://news.findlaw.com/andrews/em/emp/2007 0525/20070525_jones.html.

Dienstein, W. 2005. "Criminal Investigation." In *The Encyclopedia of Police Science*, 2nd ed., edited by W. Bailey, 160–162. New York: Garland Publishing.

Doerner, W., and S. Lab. 2002. *Victimology*, 4th ed. Cincinnati, Ohio: Andersen Publishing.

———. 2005. *Victimology*, 5th ed. Cincinnati, Ohio: Andersen Publishing.

Faigman, D.L., Kaye, D.H., Saks, M.J., and Sanders, J. (Eds.), 1997. *Modern Scientific Evidence: The Law and Science of Expert Testimony*, Volume 2. St. Paul, MN: West Publishing.

Fattah, E. 2000. "Victimology: Past, Present, and Future." *Criminologie* 331:17–46.

Jerin, A., and L. Moriarty. 1998. *Victims of Crime*. Chicago: Nelson Hall Publishers.

Jones and Daigle v. Halliburton Co. d/b/a Kellogg, Brown, and Root (KBR) et al. 2007. United States District Court, Eastern District of Texas Beaumont Division, Civil Action No. 1: 07CV0295; second amended complaint filed May 30.

———. 2004. *Crime Victims: An Introduction to Victimology*, 5th ed. Toronto: Wadsworth.

Lasch, C. 1979. *The Culture of Narcissism*. New York: W.W. Norton.

Lilly, G. 1987. *An Introduction to the Law of Evidence*, 2nd ed. St. Paul, MN: West Publishing.

Liu, J. 2006 "Victimhood." *Missouri Law Review* 71, Winter: 115–175.

Meadows, R. 2007. *Understand Violence and Victimizations*, 4th ed. Upper Saddle River, NJ: Prentice Hall.

———, and B. Turvey. 2008 "Victimology." In *Criminal Profiling: An Introduction to Behavioral Evidence Analysis*, 3rd ed, edited by B. Turvey. San Diego: Elsevier Science.

Sauer, M. 2007. "DOJ Shuns Hearing on Halliburton/KBR Rape Cases," ABC News, December 19: http://abcnews.go.com/print?id=4027734.

Schultz, D. 2005. "Courtroom Testimony." In *The Encyclopedia of Police Science*, edited by W. Bailey, 122–124. New York: Garland Publishing.

Shichor, D., and S. Tibbetts. 2002. *Victims and Victimizations: Essential Readings.* Illinois: Waveland Press.

Spalek, B. 2006. *Crime Victims: Theory, Policy, and Practice.* New York: Palgrave Macmillan.

Srikantiah, J. 2007. "Perfect Victims and Real Survivors: The Iconic Victim in Domestic Human Trafficking Law." *Boston University Law Review* 87, February: 157–211.

Tang, A. 2007. "Afghan girls traded for debts, blood feuds." *USA Today*, July 9. http://www.usatoday.com/news/world/2007-07-09-afghan-girls_N.htm.

Time Magazine. 1948. "Go Ahead, Hit Me." September 20. http://www.time.com/time/magazine/article/0,9171,799202,00.html.

Time Magazine. 1971. "Is the Victim Guilty?" July 5. http://www.time.com/time/printout/0,8816,905314,00.html.

Turvey, B. 2008. *Criminal Profiling: An Introduction to Behavioral Evidence Analysis,* 3rd ed. San Diego: Elsevier Science.

Van Dijk, J.M. (1999). "Introducing Victimology." Paper on the Ninth Symposium of the World Society of Victimology: http://rechten.uvt.nl/victimology/other/vandijk.pdf.

Von Hentig, H. 1948. *The Criminal and His Victim: Studies in the Sociobiology of Crime.* New Haven: Yale University Press.

Williams, K. 2004. *Textbook on Criminology*, 5th ed. New York: Oxford University Press.

Young, M., and J. Stein 2004. "The History of the Crime Victims' Movement in the United States." National Organization for Victim Assistance, U.S. Department of Justice Grant Number 2002-VF-GX-0009, December. http://www.ojp.usdoj.gov/ovc/ncvrw/2005/pg4c.html.

CHAPTER 2

Victimity: Entering the Criminal Justice System

Brent E. Turvey

KEY TERMS

Availability heuristic: used to judge the commonality, frequency, or likelihood of events; answering a question of probability by asking whether examples come readily to mind.

Bystander apathy: the failure of anyone in a crowd of witnesses to help a victim in unambiguous distress.

Double victimization: the harm and loss suffered by a victim, first from an attacker and second from a criminal justice system that either fails its promise to assist or protect or entirely neglects the victim.

Duty of care: professional obligations to adhere to a reasonable standard of care while performing any acts that could harm others.

Idiographic knowledge: the study of the concrete, or the examination of individuals and their actual qualities; concentrates on specific cases and the unique traits of functioning of individuals.

Mandated reporters: those bound by law to report evidence of crime, abuse, or neglect.

Nomothetic knowledge: the study of the abstract, or the examination of groups and universal laws.

Secondary victimization: the lack of control and subsequent trauma that victims may experience when they are harmed by or dissatisfied with the criminal justice system. Essentially the same as Double Victimization.

Victimity: the state, quality, or fact of being a victim.

Welfare check: police response to a possible call of distress; in some cases involves entering premises to ensure the welfare of those inside.

CONTENTS

Mendelsohn (1963) describes *victimity* as being the opposite of criminality. *Criminality* refers to the state, quality, or fact of being criminal. Therefore, victimity refers to the state, quality, or fact of being a victim. The purpose of this chapter is to describe what this means in an applied sense—what victimity involves as victims enter the criminal justice system and a record of evidence is created.

Understanding this facet of victimity is necessary to the victimologist's efforts for at least two reasons. First, it contextualizes the record of information that is available about or comes directly from victims; it fleshes out victim-related reports and statements. This context helps determine the weight that we place on what may or may not be found in our examinations. The more we know about what is involved in the creation of victim-related documentation, the better our associated judgments will be. Second, unless one has been the victim of a crime or works closely with victims in the justice system, the only frames of reference that come to mind are residual images from film and television. This is a feature of the *availability heuristic.*

As Sunstein (2005, 990–991) explains, people are not always that critical, that deliberate, or that bright. In fact, many are intellectually lazy, reaching only for the explanations and reasons within their immediate cognitive vicinity:

> It is well known that individuals do not always process information well. They use heuristics that lead them to predictable errors; they are also subject to identifiable biases, which produce errors. A growing literature explores the role of these heuristics and biases and their relationship to law and policy. For example, most people follow the representativeness heuristic, in accordance with which judgments of probability are influenced by assessments of resemblance (the extent to which A "looks like" B). The representative heuristic helps explain what Paul Rozin and Carol Nemeroff call "sympathetic magical thinking," including the beliefs that some objects have contagious properties and that causes resemble their effects. The representativeness heuristic often works well, but it can also lead to severe blunders.
>
> People also err because they use the availability heuristic to answer difficult questions about probability. When people use this heuristic, they answer a question of probability by asking whether examples come readily to mind.

The *availability heuristic* is in play when judgments are made based on what one can remember rather than on complete or actual information. We tend to use it for judging the commonality, frequency, or likelihood of events. There is simply no greater influence on the availability heuristic than film and television. The popular media provides false or distorted examples to populate our memory, which are believed to be accurate in the absence of actual knowledge. This may include the notion that victims are weak, helpless, passive, and without flaws. Or it may include the exact opposite.[1]

In our study of victims, we need to move past market-driven archetypes and cultural stereotypes; we need to understand who victims are and what they are actually up against as they enter the justice system. We need to know the hurdles they must clear, how they are perceived and treated, and how information about them is being gathered and disseminated. This chapter will attempt to address some of these issues.[2]

First, we will discuss what it takes to become a victim in the criminal justice system in the most general terms. Then we will touch briefly on the role of law enforcement, of mandated reporters, and the purpose of victim's advocates. Next, there will be a review of the more realistic contact that victims can have with witnesses, emergency services, and the police. The concepts of *bystander apathy, double victimization,* and *duty of care* will be discussed. The chapter will close with an evaluation of the frailty of crime victim data, which is gathered based on documentation subsequent to all of the above.

ON BECOMING A VICTIM

Not everyone who suffers harm or loss reports it to authorities, even if they are able. In fact, the U.S. Bureau of Justice Statistics (BJS 2006) estimates that more than 57% of all crime goes unreported.[3] However, reporting a crime is precisely what must occur before a victim can enter the criminal justice system. This happens in one of several ways:

- A victim suffers harm or loss and reports it to authorities (immediately or eventually);
- A victim suffers harm or loss and someone else reports it to authorities (parent, intimate, doctor, teacher, stranger, witness, etc.);
- A victim suffers harm or loss and the authorities report it themselves.

Primarily, victims report crime to end the harm that is being caused to themselves or others; to prevent future crimes; to help catch and punish the offender; to facilitate the recovery of property; and sometimes because the harm they

---

[1] This is related to the concepts of victim deification and vilification, which will be discussed in Chapter 3, "Constructing a Victim Profile."

[2] The second half of this equation, how victims and victimology are regarded at trial, is covered in Chapter 15, "Victimology at Trial."

[3] This estimate is a reference point only. The true numbers are unknown and widely presumed to be much higher.

suffer requires medical attention. Conversely, victims may decide not to report crime because:

- they consider it a personal matter and don't want the attention;
- they have reported it to someone else of authority and no longer perceive a need to report it to the police;
- they don't think it's important enough to bother the police with;
- they think reporting the crime will take too much time;
- they think the police won't care, won't be competent, or may be biased;
- they feel there is a lack of evidence;
- they feel they may be blamed;
- and in cases involving theft, they may have recovered the property and consider the matter closed.

Consider the perspective of victims of sexual assault, described in Kanter (2005, 277–278):

> At a very fundamental level, the experience of rape defies the ability of the victim to seek help and the ability of those around her, including the legal system, to respond to her needs. Rape, whether seen as a means of gender, race, class, age or other forms of oppression, is also a devastating attack on the physical, psychological and sexual integrity of the individual victim. Furthermore, the most common forms of rape—rape by those known to the victim—involve a betrayal of trust that adds to that devastation. It is not uncommon for victims to be immobilized by the trauma of rape and its psychic aftermath.
>
> Yet few individuals not victimized themselves can comprehend the destructive impact of non-stranger rape, particularly on adolescent girls and college age women. This impact is compounded by the fact that this form of rape is the least acknowledged by society and least punished by the legal system. Except in some cases of stranger rape, victims often fail to acknowledge their own victimization. When they do, they often blame themselves for the assault. In the case of young women, their inexperience in sexual situations combined with a normal adolescent desire to experience sex adds both to their vulnerability to attack and their subsequent feelings of personal responsibility. Feelings of shame, guilt and personal responsibility increase if one adds to this mix the common presence of alcohol and drugs. In these situations, the response of those adults who might offer understanding, support and protection (i.e., parents, teachers, law enforcement) is often quite the opposite, and they too blame the victim just as she blames herself.

Ultimately, victims will make a cost-benefit analysis about reporting crime when the decision is theirs alone. The vast majority "see no benefits to be gained from initiating contact with [criminal justice] system representatives" (Doerner and Lab 2002, 54). The volume of unreported crime makes this clear. However, the decision of whether to report crime is not always entirely up to the victim.

MANDATED REPORTERS

Mandated reporters are those professionals who have regular contact with vulnerable or conversely criminal groups, such as sex offenders, addicts, prisoners, parolees, children, the elderly, and victims of domestic violence, and are furthermore bound by law to report evidence of crime, abuse, or neglect. A short list of mandated reporters would include parole and correction officers, teachers, daycare workers, social workers, women's advocates, children's advocates, police officers, doctors, nurses, and mental health care providers. It bears mentioning that mandated reporters are not simply required to inform the authorities when crimes are disclosed to them by victims. They may also be trained to spot signs of abuse or neglect. And there are legal penalties for failing in that duty.

Typically, mandated reporters are required to report any information and findings to the appropriate law enforcement agency, which will then initiate its own investigation. For example, in cases of child abuse and neglect, they may be required to report any signs or suspicion directly to Child Protective Services (CPS). The process is explained in Lukens (2007, 201–202):

> After a report of suspected child abuse or neglect is made, either anonymously or by a mandated reporter, a social worker from CPS makes an initial determination whether the information provided in the report is sufficient to warrant further investigation. Most reports are screened out at this initial stage. If the CPS worker decides to investigate, the next step is a visit by a CPS investigator to the home where the parent, child, and any other adults who live in the household are interviewed. Based on the results of this investigation, the next phase involves a determination whether there has actually been abuse or neglect. If abuse or neglect is "substantiated," either the family begins CPS supervision while the child remains in the home, or if there is risk of danger to the child, then the child is removed from the family and placed in foster care. Removal can be voluntary or involuntary; unless there is imminent danger to the child, in which case CPS will move for immediate removal on an emergency basis. If abuse or neglect is "unsubstantiated," however, the case will likely be closed in the CPS system.

[handwritten marginal note: gatime panaudoti paperiui part 2]

Ironically, while laws exist to designate mandated reporters and penalties for failing to report, many professionals go about their work unaware of either. However, even when they are informed of a reporting duty as prescribed by law, they may be untrained or unwilling to get involved. These failures are not always a matter of apathy and ignorance, however. For example, as explained in Lukens (2007, 181), some mandated reporters do not report incidents of suspected child abuse or neglect because of concerns that CPS will be associated with the process:

> [T]he chief explanations for under-reporting suspected incidents are the perception by professionals that (1) the child welfare system is overtaxed; (2) intervention by the child welfare system will not resolve the matter satisfactorily; and (3) engagement with the system may be detrimental to the child. Moreover, it is possible that some children simply may not come to the attention of mandated reporters (e.g., very young children not enrolled in school and medical neglect situations where the child is not seen routinely by care specialists), and some may not exhibit any signs of trouble or may be reticent about revealing it (e.g., many of the instances of sexual abuse or emotional neglect). In sum, despite the broad reach of the mandatory reporting system, too many children remain in harm's way because they have not been identified by the child welfare system.

The reality is that CPS workers tend to be jaded, undertrained, and overtaxed. Moreover, there is a lot of subjectivity and caseworker autonomy in the CPS process, at least in practice. Subsequently, professional views regarding CPS may range from too complacent or apathetic in cases of obvious abuse and neglect, and too swift to take children from parents in cases where there are other options. Similar problems exist within other mandated professions, including law enforcement.

THE ROLE OF LAW ENFORCEMENT

The role of law enforcement as it relates to violent crime is oriented towards public safety and upholding the law. As explained in the *Victim's Bill of Rights* of Manitoba, Canada (VBR 2007,):

> The primary role of the police is to enforce the law. The first contact victims have with the police usually happens when they call for help or make a complaint. Complaints, or calls for service, usually result in an incident report. Police may interview victims and any witnesses to see if there is enough evidence to lay a charge.

This is consistent with the perceived role of police in most Western countries, as described generally in Cordner (1995, 11): "The primary objectives of a police department are protection of life and property and maintenance of public order." By and large these objectives are understood and practiced by many law enforcement officers to the best of their ability. However, as will be discussed shortly, there are notable exceptions.

As readers will soon learn, the role of law enforcement is not always in harmony with the needs or desires of the victim. When there is a conflict between the two, the victim will invariably lose all initial skirmishes. Furthermore, we will also learn that police agencies do not necessarily hold, practice, or even perceive a duty of care to the victims of crime, despite conventional public belief to the opposite. This duty, in extreme cases, may need to be compelled with civil litigation.

THE ROLE OF VICTIMS' ADVOCATES

A victims' advocate, when assigned to a case, is intended as a liaison between a victim and/or the victims' family and the criminal justice system. He or she facilitates the arrangement of resources and interviews and the gathering of victim information, and acts as a go-between to help coordinate services from state agencies and private organizations that may be of benefit. The advocate also tends to serve the unhappy role of explaining the peculiarities of the criminal justice system to the victim after entering it.

Victims' advocates can be found in many spheres intersecting with the criminal justice system, including the police department, the prosecutor's office, rape crisis clinics, and various state and nonprofit organizations. Depending on the resources of their particular jurisdiction, police or prosecutors may recommend victims to any one of their own in-house advocates or to outside state and nonprofit agencies, as they perceive the need. However, law enforcement goals may not be entirely benevolent in this effort; they may just want the victim out of the way to avoid the conflicts that can arise, as Goodrum describes (2007, 746):

> For the bereaved victim, the case represents a new and extremely traumatic event, one in which all information and evidence seems critical. For detectives, the case represents one of many. Erez and Rogers (1999) argue that experience desensitizes legal professionals to the horror and tragedy observed in victims. This desensitization when compared to bereaved victims' hypersensitivity may create differences of opinion on the significance of some information, and these differences of opinion may create additional conflict.

As the point of contact, victims' advocates become a source if not the source of details about the case. This is a slippery slope, as the police may or may not be forthcoming with complete or accurate case-related information. A conflict arises when victims and family members need this information to regain their sense of the world, and nobody that knows anything will talk or return phone calls. This is discussed in Goodrum (2007, 747–748) as it relates to cases involving bereaved family members and victims of homicide:

> During the early stages of the murder case, many bereaved victims believed that someone in law enforcement knew (and could tell them) exactly how their loved one died. They wanted to know all of the details surrounding their loved one's last few moments of life and the manner of death. In her advice to mental caregivers of bereaved victims, Rando (1993) explained bereaved victims' compulsive need to understand the specifics of the death and their effort to find meaning in the loss as "related to the need to restore control . . . and a sense of justice and order to the world". (541) Social psychologists relate this type of reaction to the Just World Hypothesis (Lerner 1980), which argues that people will use their belief that the world is a fair and just place to make sense of difficult or harmful situations.

> The search for information represents an attempt to find an explanation for the death that upholds notions of justice. A crime victims' advocate with eleven years of experience counseling victims (primarily bereaved victims) and promoting victims' rights explained:

>> Victims want the truth, no matter how painful it is; they need the truth, instead of going around the truth. They can deal with the truth a lot better than keeping them wondering [about how their loved one was murdered]. (CJ17)

> Detectives and counselors tried to answer bereaved victims' questions as best they could and within the limits of their policies. A victim services counselor with more than five years of experience explained:

>> When the families are wanting information, they meet with the primary detective on the case, and I am also present. Because, of course, he knows all the details, and he knows what he can disclose at the time and what he can't. (CJ01)

> This counselor further explained that she asked detectives not to share any information about the case with her that could not also be shared with the family "because I don't want to be lying to them [about what we know and don't know]". (CJ01)

Victims' advocates are subsequently enlisted to give victims and their families a perceived sense of empowerment, hope, or control in a situation that may in reality offer very little of either. They also provide victims with a human point of contact that has no sensitive case information or authority. Advocates serve primarily to comfort and coordinate logistical details of aid, upcoming interviews, and eventual legal proceedings.

FIRST CONTACT

Initial contact between the victim and the justice system is typically made between a victim and a witness, or a victim and the police. The police are part of the justice system, and witnesses may or may not choose to participate in it. Both are gatekeepers after a fashion, and can present significant hurdles that must be cleared in order for the victim to initiate a criminal investigation, let alone receive aid and comfort. This section will not discuss what happens when things go smoothly, rather it will reveal what can happen in the real world of people and responders when victims are ignored, dismissed, or disbelieved.

Victims and Other People

A rape victim may knock on a stranger's door and ask her to call the police; an assault victim may be found half conscious in an alley by a passerby; or a teacher may be the first to discover a shooting victim at a school. In such cases, initial contact between the victim and the justice system is not through the police but rather fellow citizens who are in the right place at the right time to be of service. These "Good Samaritans" respond to victim peril and injuries, notify the authorities, and become eventual witness when Emergency Medical Services (EMS) or law enforcement arrives. That is, unless they are unwilling to get involved.

In the case of "Bad Samaritans," the failure to help victims may be the result of apathy, distrust, or fear of involvement with respect to the victim or situation as it presents itself.[4] This fear may involve the danger associated with attempting a rescue (e.g., fear of diving into freezing water to rescue a drowning child; fear of pulling a crash victim from a burning vehicle), or it may be related to the consequences for any actions once they get involved (e.g., fear of reprisal from a vengeful offender; fear of litigation from a thankless victim). To be clear, not all of those unwilling to get involved should be viewed as uncaring or selfish.

Case Example: Bystander Apathy, Redux

With situations that involve a group of people, the reluctance of potential Samaritans to get involved with victims of crime is more common. The larger

---

[4] I have worked more than one case involving a naked or partially clothed victim approaching a stranger's home after being sexually assaulted, only to be met by an understandably shocked and distrustful occupant. However, compassion typically wins out in these scenarios.

the group, the more common. The failure of those in a crowd of witnesses to help a victim in unambiguous distress is sometimes referred to as *bystander apathy*. As Scott explains (2003, pp. 39–40):

> On March 13, 1964, Catherine (Kitty) Genovese reached her apartment in Queens, NY, at 3:30 a.m. Suddenly, a man approached with a knife, stabbed her repeatedly, then raped her. When she screamed, "Oh my God, he stabbed me! Please help me!" lights came on and windows opened in nearby buildings. Seeing the lights, the attacker fled; but when no one came to Genovese's aid, he returned to stab her repeatedly and rape her again. The attack lasted more than 30 minutes and was witnessed by 38 neighbors. One couple pulled chairs up to their window and turned off the lights so they could get a better view. No one called police until the attacker departed for good. When the neighbors were questioned about their lack of intervention, they could not explain it.

> The reporter who first publicized this story, and later made it the subject of a book, assumed the bystander apathy was caused by big-city life (Rosenthal). He presumed people's indifference to their neighbors' troubles was a conditioned reflex in crowded cities such as New York. After this incident, many experiments were conducted by social psychologists in an attempt to determine causes of this so-called "bystander apathy" [Latane and Darley(a); (b)]. This research actually discredited the reporter's conclusion, finding that several factors other than big-city life contribute to bystander apathy.

> . . . A key contributor to the bystander effect is a presumption that someone else should assume the responsibility. For example, many observers of the Genovese attack likely assumed that another witness would call police or attempt to scare away the assailant. Perhaps some observers waited for a more capable witness to come to the rescue.

The notion of diffused responsibility as a contributing factor in such cases is further supported in Miller and Clinkinbeard (2006, 12–14):

> Psychological research involving bystander intervention has indicated that individuals are not always willing to help, even when they have the ability to do so.

> In a classic social psychological study, college students witnessed another participant (actually an undercover researcher) in the study suffer from an epileptic seizure. Some students were led to believe that they were the only person aware of the situation, while other students were led to believe that others were also aware of the situation. The investigators found that those who were alone were more likely to

help and to help in a timelier manner than participants who believed that others were aware of the situation. Diffusion of responsibility, the phenomenon in which [the] presence of other individuals lessens the amount of individual responsibility experienced, is used to explain this bystander apathy.

A contemporary example of bystander apathy includes the case of LaShanda Calloway in Wichita, Kansas, as described in Hegeman (2007):

> As stabbing victim LaShanda Calloway lay dying on the floor of a convenience store, five shoppers, including one who stopped to take a picture of her with a cell phone, stepped over the woman, police said.
>
> The June 23 situation, captured on the store's surveillance video, got scant news coverage until a columnist for The Wichita Eagle disclosed the existence of the video and its contents Tuesday.
>
> . . . "It was tragic to watch," police spokesman Gordon Bassham said Tuesday. "The fact that people were more interested in taking a picture with a cell phone and shopping for snacks rather than helping this innocent young woman is, frankly, revolting."
>
> The woman was stabbed during an altercation that was not part of a robbery, Bassham said. It took about two minutes for someone to call 911, he said. Calloway, 27, died later at a hospital.

The Calloway case is markedly different from the Genovese case in that there were no screams for help and no sexual component. In addition, while some bystanders in the market simply ignored the victim, others took photos and video of Calloway that were subsequently posted to www.youtube.com.[5] This particular subset of bystanders was able to emotionally detach from the moment, objectify the victim, and to view her demise as a source of entertainment for themselves and others.

911 and Emergency Personnel

In the United States and Canada, a victim or witness that needs immediate assistance may dial 911 to dispatch police, fire, or medical personnel to his or her location. As the Federal Communications Commission (FCC) explains (2008):

---

[5]The video sharing site www.youtube.com is frequently host to videos posted by victims, witnesses, and offenders alike. The motivations of those posting videos run from public service, to entertainment, to a perpetuation of harm and harassment. However, such posting have also led to more than a few arrests.

The official emergency number in the United States and Canada is 911. Although the first 911 call was placed in Haleyville, Alabama in 1968, it was not until 1999 that the United States Congress directed the FCC to make 911 the universal emergency number in the United States for all telephone services. The 911 network is now a vital part of our nation's emergency response and disaster preparedness system. Emergency personnel and others often learn about emergencies through 911 calls. Dialing 911 quickly connects a caller to a nearby Public Safety Answering Point (PSAP) dispatcher who is trained to route your call to local emergency medical, fire, and law enforcement agencies.

911 lines are designated for emergency calls, such as reporting a crime in progress, reporting a fire, or requesting an ambulance.

As a result of calling 911, a police officer, a firefighter, or a paramedic is meant to respond. In some cases, the 911 dispatcher may decide to send all three. In other cases involving a hang-up, the operator may simply call back or send a patrol car to investigate and perform what is referred to as a *welfare check*.[6]

However, there have been some spectacular and well-publicized failures in the 911 system, including victims being put on hold for extended periods, operators becoming unjustly enraged at emergency callers, operators falling asleep during emergency calls, and operators simply not believing caller's pleas for help—especially those of children. This type of negligent failure has resulted in compounded victim distress, harm, and even death. It has also resulted in civil and criminal liability for the 911 personnel involved.

To contextualize these problems, it should be explained that 911 operators often work long shifts with limited staff and no breaks, and that in some jurisdictions as many as a quarter of all 911 calls may be pranks. However, these problems are not generally sufficient to excuse negligent conduct. Instances of confirmed negligence can result in a 911 operator being reprimanded, transferred, fired, and even criminally prosecuted—all of which occur regularly enough to be a public concern.

One of the more public failures of a 911 system occurred in my home state of Alaska, and involved a recently retired "top cop."

Case Example: Patricia and Glenn Godfrey

In 2002, 53-year-old Glenn Godfrey was former head of the Alaska State Troopers and had just recently stepped down from his position as Alaska

---

[6]A *welfare check* involves police responding to a call that indicates or could indicate that someone is in distress or may need medical attention. Under such circumstances, police may be obliged to enter a locked home in order to determine the health and welfare of those inside.

Commissioner of Public Safety. He and his 52-year-old wife Patricia shared a home together in Eagle River. However, all was not well. They had separated recently and were in the middle of an attempt at reconciliation.

Their separation had been due in no small part to Glenn being in the process of ending an affair with 33-year-old Karen Brand, then vice president of the Alaska State Chamber of Commerce. Brand did not take former Commissioner Godfrey's decision to end their relationship well. According to published accounts, including an official report by the Alaska Office of Victims' Rights (Branchflower and de Luca 2002), Brand entered the Godfreys' Eagle River home on August 2, 2002, while they were away, found Glenn's .44 magnum handgun inside, and waited. When they returned and entered the house, she shot them both. The details of the crime that followed are provided in Mauer (2002):

> Sitting on a pillow in a hallway closet with a protein bar, a bottle of water and a .44 Magnum revolver lifted from the house she'd broken into, Karen Brand apparently passed the time with a Tom Clancy novel. She was awaiting the return of Glenn and Patti Godfrey and, probably more importantly, waiting to hear their reaction to the message she left on their answering machine.

> The message was about her affair with Glenn Godfrey, the retired Alaska public safety commissioner, and it hinted at her growing sense of betrayal.

> . . . The crime scene was the Godfreys' 1980s split-level Eagle River home. It was there that the couple had raised four children while Glenn rose through the ranks of the Alaska State Troopers. In June, at age 53, he retired as the state's top cop.

> Brand, 33, was vice president of the Alaska State Chamber of Commerce and a former legislative aide who had lived in Juneau. She also was married. Police reports show that days before the shooting, on July 30, a person matching Brand's striking description—nearly 6 feet tall, 135 pounds, blond hair, blue eyes—cut through a nearby yard to the Godfreys' home.

> Days later, when police searched Brand's 9-year-old Jeep Cherokee, they found prescription pill bottles for Patti Godfrey. The Godfreys' son Gerad, a private security official, believes Brand entered the house that day and may have stolen the keys to Glenn Godfrey's gun case. Gerad said his father had been searching for the keys for several days. He usually kept them in the door frame above the hallway closet, Gerad said, and with the keys missing—and not wanting to break into the case—he was unarmed on Aug. 3.

> Early Friday, Aug. 2, Brand had shown up at the Godfreys'. According to Patti's just-released statement to police, Godfrey told Brand they were planning to take Patti's father to the doctor that day.

The Godfreys actually planned a family outing to Seward. On the drive south, they kept seeing Brand's car trailing them. At a turnout, Godfrey suddenly got off the road and Brand sped by, according to Patti's statement. Brand got behind them once again until they reached Girdwood.

After the shootings, Brand's car was found parked at the dead-end side of a street near the Godfreys'. No one knows how long Brand was in the Godfreys' house. Police found a window ajar. There was a light in the hall closet, and Brand could have passed the time reading Tom Clancy's "Op-Center" thriller until the Godfreys returned around 11 p.m. Gerad found the book underneath the pillow after police finished their search. A water bottle nearby had Brand's fingerprints.

According to police, Brand left two messages on the answering machine. She talked about having put off buying a house and horse for years at Godfrey's request and suggested Godfrey not keep Patti "in the dark any longer."

She wondered whether he was leading on both women and said she was surprised he lied to her about taking his father-in-law to the doctor that day, because she had thought he never lied to her.

Patti and Glenn moved to the living room, half a flight of steps up from the hall closet, and spent more than an hour talking, she told police. "He admitted he was trying to break off with this person since like January, February."

Patti went to the bathroom. Glenn went downstairs. Patti came back to the couch. She heard two shots. Up the stairs came Brand, who sat down in Patti's pink chair.

"Hello, Patti," Brand said. It was the first time Patti had seen her up close, she told police. Brand had Godfrey's gun in her lap. Patti said Brand was stroking the barrel "like it was a baby or a puppy."

Still believing her husband might be alive, Patti told Brand, "'You just get out of here. Let me go get help for him, please.' She says, 'No.' She says, 'We're all going to burn in hell.'"

As Patti prayed, "she says, 'If I can't have him, nobody can have him.' I'm praying, and she says, 'Hurry up with your prayers.'" After about a minute, Patti decided she'd had enough and rose to call for help.

"I'll see you in hell," Brand said, then started shooting, Patti recalled. After Patti was hit with four shots, the gun stopped firing but Brand kept pulling the trigger. Patti saw Brand reach into her shirt, then watched Brand's expression change dramatically as she picked up the phone. "She's saying: 'No, Patti, no. No, Patti, no.' I totally ignored her."

Patti dialed 911. Brand left in panic. While Patti was talking to police, she heard more shots—several fired into her husband, and then the suicide. When police entered the house about 45 minutes later, the gun was resting on Brand's belly.

Later, during the autopsy, the medical examiner found two unspent rounds in her black sports bra and Patti's credit card in one of her loafers.

(It should also be noted that the autopsy revealed no drugs or alcohol in Brand's system.)

Under most circumstances, calling 911 immediately sets into motion a series of rapidly unfolding events that often can and do save lives. In a case involving someone like Glenn Godfrey, who would be considered law enforcement royalty, one would expect the response to be even more focused, directed, and intense. However, this is not what happened to Patricia Godfrey.

As explained in "Tape of Godfrey's 911 call shows dispatcher's delay" (2002), which is corroborated in the official report prepared by Branchflower and de Luca (2002):

> Anchorage police dispatchers disregarded the address Patti Godfrey gave them during a 911 call, relying instead on inadequate computer information, a tape of the call shows.
>
> A badly injured Godfrey waited 48 minutes for help after she reported that she and her husband, retired public safety commissioner Glenn Godfrey, had been shot inside their Eagle River home. Glenn Godfrey had been killed, although Patti Godfrey didn't know it at the time.
>
> Minutes into the 12:30 a.m. call Aug. 3, Patti Godfrey gave dispatchers the name and phone number of her daughter and repeatedly begged them to call her. Dispatchers didn't make that call, and they didn't ask Godfrey for directions to her house until about 40 minutes into the call.
>
> . . . "I've been shot, please," Godfrey, 52, said in her first words to the 911 dispatcher. Dispatcher Billy Miller, one of two who talked to Godfrey during the call, asked who shot her, where Karen was, what Karen looked like, where the gun was.
>
> Less than two minutes later, Godfrey said, "I . . . she just shot herself, I believe." Godfrey at that point was alert and responsive to questions. She also confirmed the Godfreys' address: 22953 Eagle River Road, at Mile 4.6. But dispatchers did not ask her for directions, which they typically do, Deputy Police Chief Mark Mew said.

Because the address Godfrey gave did not appear in the database, the computer gave similar but incorrect addresses and officers could not find the right house. Several minutes into the call, believing officers were at Godfrey's door, dispatchers assured her help was just outside and told her to hang on.

. . . "I'm begging," she said. "Save Glenn's life. Save Glenn's life. Lord Jesus, please help us. Save Glenn's life. Give us another chance. Lord Jesus. Please God, help him." She described her injuries in detail. One bullet had ripped through her stomach, another through her leg, and her right arm was nearly severed, she said.

. . . As officers failed to show up, Godfrey sounded more angry, telling them they weren't helping her and they were lying about officers being just outside the house. Late in the call, Godfrey hung up on the operators. They called her back immediately and heard the sound of dialing. When Godfrey realized she was on the phone with them, she again killed the connection.

When dispatchers successfully got through again, dispatcher Jeri Wallin told Godfrey they needed her to tell them exactly how to get to her home. "We can't find your house!" Wallin said urgently.

Godfrey gave broken directions, mumbling. By the time officers arrived, it was nearly 1:19 a.m.

In 2003, Patricia Godfrey filed a claim against the estate of Karen Brand for $2 million. In 2004, the city of Anchorage agreed to pay her $700,000 for physical and psychological damage suffered as a result of 911-related failures (Toomey 2004).

VICTIMS AND LAW ENFORCEMENT

As Goodrum (2007) explains, there is an inherent "power struggle" between the victims of crime and law enforcement officers charged with its investigation. Victims come from a personal and emotional context, where they are looking to satisfy needs related to their harm and loss. Law enforcement comes from an objective and professional context, where in the worst instances, behavior can border on dismissive and even apathetic (Goodrum 2007, 753):

Underlying this struggle is the issue of power, and the issue of power emerges repeatedly in research on all types of victims and at all stages of the criminal justice system. In this study, bereaved victims felt powerless because law enforcement workers—as agents of the criminal justice system—controlled the entire investigation process. They determined the bereaved victim's access to the deceased's body;

they also determined the direction and extent of the information flow in the case. Law enforcement workers' control and bereaved victims' relative lack of control in the case frustrated and upset many bereaved victims and hindered their recovery from the crime. Thus, despite the implementation of victims' rights legislation in states across the United States, rights whose purpose is ostensibly to empower victims, the relationship between victims and law enforcement workers remains largely unequal.

Even with the best of intentions, the role of the police is often in direct conflict with the needs of the victim, as Goodrum explains (2007, 729–730):

> Police officers, prosecutors, and judges repeatedly indicate that maintaining an objective and unemotional approach to criminal cases proves important to their work (Erez and Rogers 1999), to upholding the rule of law (Erez and Laster 1999), and to the maintenance of a professional (i.e., stoic) demeanor (Goodrum and Stafford 2003). This approach often means that criminal justice workers see themselves as crime-solvers, not victim helpers, and this definition restricts the amount of time they interact with victims and the types of interaction they choose to take (see Stenross and Kleinman 1989). Prosecutors handling rape cases tend to focus on presenting evidence that will persuade judges and jurors that a rape really happened, not on emotionally preparing victims for their witness testimony (Konradi 1997). Detectives and prosecutors view their role, the victim's role, and criminal cases from a perspective that conflicts with and may even harm victims (see Kondradi 1997; Martin and Powell 1995).

Victims will invariably need different levels of assistance, counseling, advice, logistical information, and comfort. Police and their prosecutorial counterparts may be unable or unwilling to provide any of these. Moreover, many assurances given to the victim by the police in the early stages of an investigation are soon forgotten, having been dispensed for the purpose of comfort only. Whether it is assurances about investigative action or the eventual sentencing of offenders, Doerner and Lab (2002, 55) parse no words when stating, "What it boils down to is that the system is not making good on its promises."

In fact, to keep the justice system moving, prosecutors are apt to plead cases down to avoid going to court, especially if they have large caseloads and competent investigations are not performed at the outset. As will be discussed in Chapter 15, this happens in the majority of cases. With notable exceptions, this will often be in direct conflict with the wishes and even safety of the victim.

Aside from initial promises regarding investigative action and offender sentencing, when police and prosecutors do provide information to the victim it may be incorrect or out of date. This can be the result of miscommunication, bureaucratic snafus, and even personnel turnover. For example, a victim may be assigned a case officer who continually changes without the victim's knowledge as staff are transferred, sent on training, or take extended vacations. Each time the victim calls to inquire about the status of his case, he may need to speak with a new person and explain his circumstances all over again. Additionally, it is not uncommon for a victim to receive a subpoena from the prosecutor's office with no explanation or pretrial interview; to set aside time in her schedule and show up for court; and then sit waiting for several hours before she learns that she wasn't needed at all. Nor is it uncommon for prosecutors to harass victims who are unwilling to be helpful with the power of subpoena, to compel testimony that is favorable to their theories of the case. The effect of these and similar circumstances on a victim's sense of trust, worth, and value in the investigative process can be quite devastating.

Double Victimization

The cumulative ineptness, ignorance, apathy, and even belligerence of those in the criminal justice system can result in what has been referred to as *double victimization*,[7] as Doerner and Lab explain (2002, 55):

> First, they suffer at the hands of their criminals. Then, by participating in the criminal justice system, they risk even more damage. By making a choice to avoid the system, victims are able to minimize their losses.

Goodrum (2007, 7467) goes into further detail, referring to the subsequent lack of control perceived by victims in this context as *secondary victimization:*[8]

> Feeling a lack of control over the criminal justice process can increase victims' feelings of powerlessness and lead to a sense of further victimization (Kilpatrick and Otto 1987). Psychologists refer to this type of further victimization as a secondary victimization or trauma, which may negatively affect well-being (Rando 1993). Social psychologists find that having a sense of personal control over situations positively affects well-being (Mirowsky and Ross 1989), and Amick-McMullan et al. (1989) found a positive association between satisfaction with the criminal justice system's management of the murder case and bereaved victims' psychological well-being. The idea that victims' involvement in the criminal justice system would help restore control and facilitate healing seems like a good one but not if the involvement does not occur in the ways that victims want or expect. Indeed, none of the

---

[7]*Double victimization* refers to the harm and loss that a victim suffers first from the attacker, and second from a criminal justice system that either fails in its promise of assistance or protection, or ignores the victim entirely.

[8]*Secondary victimization* refers to the lack of control and subsequent trauma that victims may experience as they are increasingly harmed by or dissatisfied with the criminal justice system.

eleven victims' rights in this state [state name omitted from study] afford victims the explicit right to give information to the police about their criminal case or to have that information be taken seriously.

It is important to point out that the cumulative harms and losses felt by victims from injuries suffered while in the criminal justice system can be personal, physical, mental, emotional, and financial. And the weight of this loss is not made easier with the passage of time, especially when left unresolved.

Duty of Care

Duty of care refers to obligations imposed on professionals requiring that they adhere to a reasonable standard of care while performing any acts that could foreseeably harm others. It is a legal concept that relates to the liability of agencies and individuals charged with various professional functions, such as doctors and hospitals, mental health professionals and clinics, police officers and departments, security guards and firms, teachers and schools, and others.

Litigation against police agencies across the United States has revealed diverse liability for local law enforcement, and often reduced standards of that must be met—if they may be held accountable at all (not every police agency as a whole may be held civilly liable for their negligence or misconduct, even when it is not in dispute; however, individual officers and governments may). As Miccio discusses (2000, 142–143):

> The modern view of municipal liability for police conduct is narrowly constructed. This doctrine of public duty shapes legal relationships among the police, society, and individual citizens. Under the public duty doctrine, police are not under an affirmative obligation to respond to individual citizen needs. Consequently, because a duty is owed to the public generally, there is no particularized duty of care allocated to individuals.

This issue of liability is a recurrent theme that runs throughout this chapter and the rest of this text. However, some specific examples are warranted at this point.

Case Example: Adela B.

Consider the case of Adela B., taken from Miccio (2000, 137–140):

> Adela and her son Joey lived alone in her home in San Jose, California. They had been a family ever since eleven-year-old Joey could remember. In June of 1993, Adela's boyfriend Richard moved into their home and for about one month, there was relative calm.
>
> In August, however, Richard started his campaign of terror against Adela and Joey. The first attack occurred one August night when Richard came home drunk. Adela refused to allow him into the house,

and when he became loud and abusive, Adela ordered him to leave the property. Richard broke a window and entered the house. Terrified, Adela ran out of the house and onto the street.

Richard chased Adela and, after catching her, dragged her by her hair, pinned her to the ground and began punching her. Adela managed to break from Richard's hold and escape to the car, at which time Richard ran toward the house. Remembering that Joey was still inside, Adela started after Richard, but by that point Joey had also escaped, and the two sought protection in the car. Richard soon found Joey and Adela, and in an attempt to get to them, he started to break the car door. He stopped only when a friend warned him that the police were on their way.

After Richard left with friends, Adela waited for the police to arrive. When officers from the San Jose Police Department responded to the scene, Adela recounted her story of Richard's attack, his intoxication, and his terrorization of her son. The police saw the broken window of her home and the damaged car.

They also saw Joey frightened and crying. Even though the police knew that Richard was on parole, the San Jose Police Department failed to refer the case to either the District Attorney's office for prosecution or to Richard's parole officer. Richard was never arrested for the attack or for violating parole. Three months later, in December of 1993, Richard physically attacked Adela again.

On the evening of December 11, 1993, Richard and Adela went to a dinner party. Richard began drinking and was verbally abusive. By the end of the evening, however, Richard had calmed down. After returning home, Richard again argued with Adela, but this time over her use of the radio. He apparently objected to her listening to the radio in the bedroom and in an act of defiance, took the radio from her and went downstairs to the living room. Adela went after him, and Richard, enraged, chased her. As Adela ran upstairs toward the bedroom, he grabbed her and tried to drag her down the stairs. She held onto the banister but lost her grip when Richard punched her in the back. Richard then threw her down the steps and as she lay at the bottom of the stairs, he punched her with his fists and kicked her with his feet. In spite of his blows, Adela freed herself, ran upstairs to the bedroom, and waited.

Minutes passed. Then, Adela heard Richard retrieve her car keys and, fearing his driving while intoxicated, she ran downstairs to stop him. Richard punched her and left with her car. It was one o'clock in the morning. Adela was alone and frightened that Richard would eventually return. Adela remembered that Richard's parole officer had mentioned that a battered women's shelter in the area might provide help. Adela called the shelter, but the facility would not provide transportation.

Frightened and confused, Adela decided to leave the house. After calling a cab, she picked up Joey at his baby-sitter's house and then proceeded to a motel where the two stayed the night. The following morning, Adela called the house to make sure that Richard was not at home. With the first call, Richard answered and told her that he was leaving. Adela was relieved but doubtful. She waited and called a second time, at which point, there was no answer. Feeling safe, Adela and Joey returned home.

When Adela arrived at the house, she realized that Richard had taken her house and car keys as well as the car. Just as Adela was attempting to break a window to get inside, Richard drove into the carport. Richard got out of the car and walked quickly toward Adela. She backed up, frightened that he would beat her again. As he walked into the house, he muttered that he was living there again. Adela asked Richard for the car keys but before she completed her sentence, Richard began punching her in the head. He then threw her to the ground and continued to punch and kick her. Adela screamed for Joey to call the police.

Terrified by what he was witnessing, Joey ran inside to make the call. Richard chased after the boy with Adela in pursuit. Both she and Joey managed to get into the house. Joey slammed the door shut while Adela held the lock. Then Joey dialed 911.

Once connected to 911, the police dispatcher could hear the terror in Joey's voice as he pleaded for help. The dispatcher could also hear Adela's screams as Richard continued to pound on the door and to break the windows. Richard saw Joey on the phone and heard the boy's screams to the police dispatcher. He now realized that the police were likely on their way to the house. Still holding onto Adela's house and car keys, he fled in her car.

After several minutes, two officers from the San Jose Police Department—a police officer and his sergeant—arrived at the house. Once inside, the officers observed that all of the windows to the house had been broken. They also saw a terrified eleven-year-old boy holding an ax handle to protect his mother, who was vomiting and holding her head as she attempted to answer questions. She was terrified, feeling sick, and hardly able to speak. Nonetheless, she told the officers about the incident the night before and asked them what she should do if Richard returned. The police wanted to know where Richard had gone with her car. Adela speculated that he might have gone to his mother's home. Satisfied with this response, the police left Adela and Joey, but not before advising her that if Richard returned to "well, just call 911."

And Richard did return—just minutes after the two officers left Adela and Joey alone in an unsecured house. Richard entered the house through one of the windows he had broken not minutes before. Taking a shard of glass, he grabbed Adela's head and slashed her over and over again while Joey called 911 screaming for help.

Adela sued the San Jose Police Department, claiming that by leaving her and her son in an unsafe environment, the police negligently performed their duty on December 12, 1993. The trial court, finding that the police did not owe Adela or Joey Benavidez a duty of care, subsequently dismissed her suit. Last May, the California Court of Appeals affirmed.

Readers should understand that when this finding survived the California Court of Appeals, the notion that police do not owe a duty of care to those in Adela's circumstances became a matter of potential legal coverage for police agencies across the entire state, not just in the city of San Jose.

Case Example: Jennifer W.

Consider the case of Jennifer W. in Sparks, Nevada, then a 23-year-old student at the University of Nevada at Reno (see Sonner 2001; "Woman sues police" 1999; "Rape victim" 2001). She called 911 in November of 1998 to report that Timothy Mobly, a man she had met via the Internet after receiving an unsolicited e-mail, had abducted and raped her. As reported in "Woman: Police ignored suspect's earlier assualt" (1999), Jennifer W. told police that after she received the unsolicited e-mail:

she went on to date Mobly several times, but she decided to break off the relationship Nov. 6.

She said she invited Mobly over to her home on that day, and [his roommate Aaron] Cross accompanied him there.

"They kidnapped me at my home," she said. "I was thrown into the trunk of their car like a suitcase" then sexually assaulted.

But she said police did not arrest Mobly or Cross after she reported the incident. Instead, she said, police refused to believe her until after [a] 17-year-old girl was similarly assaulted.

The sexual assault took place in Mobly's home. She threatened to go to the police, but Mobly told her that nobody would believe that a rapist would drive her home; it would be her word against his. He was absolutely right.

Detectives from the Sparks Police Department interviewed Jennifer W. for three hours, accused her of lying, and threatened to prosecute her unless she immediately withdrew her complaint. She continued with the complaint and directed them to look for DNA evidence in his trunk, at which point detectives laughed at her. When she was taken to the hospital for a sexual assault examination, detectives warned her that she would have to pay for laboratory tests if the results came back negative for sexual assault, which they did.

Unfortunately, Mobly and Cross went on to commit another attack in January of 1999. They lured a 17-year-old girl to their apartment using the Internet and raped her in the same manner as Jennifer W. She escaped the next morning.

FIGURE 2.1

Timothy Mobley is extradited back to the United States from Mexico.

In March of 1999, Mobly and Cross pleaded guilty to attacking Jennifer and the 17-year-old girl. After their admissions, Mobly became a fugitive. He skipped bail and failed to appear at his sentencing hearing. He was facing life in prison. He was discovered and detained by Mexican authorities in January of 2002 and extradited back to the United States.

As a result of police conduct, Jennifer W. sued the city of Sparks, the Sparks Police Department, three detectives, and the police chief for damages of more than $900,000. She claimed that she had been humiliated when she tried to report the crime and was shunned by authorities until the second victim surfaced in January, 1999. In August of 2000, she was awarded a $24,999 judgment (Sonner 2001). She also reached an undisclosed settlement with the detectives and the chief of police ("Rape victim" 2001).

Case Example: New Port Richey

Consider also the case of a 41-year-old woman in New Port Richey, Florida, twice raped by the same stranger in her own home between 1998 and 1999, as reported in Davis (2002b):

The first attack occurred in the victim's New Port Richey home on Dec. 5, 1998. The woman, her left eye swollen shut and her mouth bloody with 15 broken teeth, told police she had been brutally beaten, bound, gagged and raped at knifepoint by a stranger.

New Port Richey police detectives, however, did not believe her account and accused her of not telling the truth. "I believe that you were battered," Detective Jackie Pehote told the victim, who had a black eye and 15 broken teeth, "but I do not believe it happened the way you say" (Davis 2002a).

Subsequently, a semen sample taken from the victim sat in a refrigerator at the department instead of being sent to the forensic laboratory for testing. New Port Richey police also failed to test evidence collected from the woman's house. Two weeks later, the police department declared the investigation inactive (Davis 2003b).

Twenty-nine days after the first attack, the same offender raped the victim again, but not before tripping a burglar alarm installed after the first attack, which the police responded to. The rapist hid inside the victim's home until the police left; they did not enter the premises. Once the police were gone, he attacked the victim (Davis 2003a).

While interviewing the victim after this second rape, Detective Pehote asked her: "How could you be so stupid to move back into your house?" Pehote is currently the New Port Richey Police Department's lead detective, having more than ten years with the department but serving as a detective since 1998, when the first rape occurred. Pehote remained in doubt of the victim's rape allegations because of inconsistencies in her statements; he was convinced that a lover had battered the victim after consensual sex (Davis 2003a).

FIGURE 2.2
John Casteel is sentenced to life in prison without parole.

Three days after the second attack, a milk crate filled with items stolen during the rape was delivered back to the victim's house with a note asking her for a date.

Four months after the second rape, the victim recognized her attacker in a convenience store. His name was John A. Casteel, and he lived three blocks from her home. Casteel had recently been released from prison after serving 14 years for a 1983 rape.

In August of 2001, after a four-day trial, a jury convicted John A. Casteel of raping the woman in under an hour. DNA tests linked him to both crimes. He was sentenced to life in prison without parole.

In November of 2002, the victim filed suit against the city of New Port Richey and the two detectives that handled her complaints, alleging that the second rape could have been prevented if police had properly investigated the first. The victim accused them of negligence and intentional infliction of emotional distress. According to reports (Davis 2002a):

> New Port Richey Detective Jackie Pehote was accused by the victim of negligence and gross insensitivity.
>
> "I believe that you were battered," Pehote told the victim, who was left with a black eye and 15 broken teeth after the first attack. "But I do not believe it happened the way you say."

The attorney for the victim argued, among other things, that police failed in their duty to protect the victim (Davis 2003a):

> given the totality of the circumstances, police had a responsibility to protect the woman after the first rape, especially when they responded to the burglar alarm just before the second attack.

The attorney for the city of New Port Richey argued that no such duty exists (Davis 2003a):

> Peter Walsh, the city's attorney for the civil case, argued Thursday that under the law, "there is no duty that New Port Richey owes to a citizen to protect them from a criminal."
>
> The detectives, he said, "owed no special duty to catch this crook and perform a perfect investigation."

Both of the detectives who worked the case were cleared after an internal affairs investigation conducted by Captain Martin Rickus found no wrongdoing (Davis 2002a):

> "Some people may not feel that this approach should be used when dealing with a rape victim," Rickus wrote. "But it is also important that investigators make logical connections between what they are told by victims and what they observe."
>
> The report criticized another detective, William Barrus, for waiting seven months before submitting for testing a semen sample taken from the woman after the first rape.
>
> The report recommends that officers be given clear guidelines outlining the steps to be followed in submitting evidence. It also recommended a sergeant be added to the detective bureau to supervise investigations.

However, Detective Barrus was cited for failing to submit the semen sample from the cases in a timely fashion. He waited seven months. John Casteel's DNA had been in a state database since 1996.

Furthermore, the internal affairs report also uncovered false testimony that Detective Pehote had given in an unrelated death investigation. She claimed under oath that she had not threatened to arrest the wife of the primary suspect in that case during an interrogation. A videotape of the interrogation proved otherwise. Captain Rickus said that she simply became confused under cross-examination and forgot about the threat. When this false testimony from Detective Pehote came to light, the suspect, who had originally been charged with first-degree murder, was allowed to plead guilty to manslaughter (Davis 2002a).

Detective Pehote was also found to have given false testimony in the Casteel case (Davis 2001):

> In the Casteel case, she testified in a deposition that the Police Department at one time had no tape recorders. In fact, the department has never been without tape recorders, [Capt. Darryl] Garman [New Port Richey Police Department spokesman] told the Times for a story last month.

In June of 2003, Pasco-Pinellas Circuit Judge Stanley Mills begrudgingly ruled that no matter how poor any investigation might have been (Davis 2003b),

> the police cannot be held liable for negligence. Florida courts have made it clear, the judge said, that public safety agencies and their employees cannot be sued over discretionary judgments made during the course of an investigation, regardless of the consequences.

As of this writing, the rape victim's case against the city of New Port Richey is proceeding to trial on the victim's remaining claim of intentional infliction of emotional distress.

In summary, it is generally publicized and perceived that law enforcement has a duty to protect life and property. However, its role can actually contribute to double victimization and secondary victimization with no legal requirement of a duty of care to victims of crime or the general public. Victims of crime do not always understand this, nor is it likely to be explained by those guiding them through the criminal justice system.

VICTIM CRIME DATA

In the study of victims and victimity, as for any subject, there are two major approaches of research and knowledge acquisition. The first is *nomothetic knowledge*, or the study of the abstract, which involves the examination of groups and universal laws.[9] The second is *idiographic* knowledge, or the study of the concrete, which involves the examination of individuals and their actual qualities. Idiographic study concentrates on specific cases and the unique traits or functioning of individuals.

According to Hurlburt and Knapp (2006, 287), "Psychologists use the term 'idiographic' to refer to the characteristics of unique individuals and 'nomothetic' to refer to universal characteristics." Moreover, they explain that these terms have been a part of the American psychological landscape since as early as 1898. Consequently, these concepts have a history of application from which we can learn.

Nomothetic studies are those conducted on groups, and idiographic studies are those conducted on individuals. In terms of victimology, it is fair to say that there are nomothetic methods and idiographic methods. A primary goal of idiographic victimology is to study and determine the unique characteristics of the particular victims that have suffered harm or loss as the result of a specific crime. The primary goal of nomothetic victimology studies is to accumulate general, typical, common, or averaged characteristics of victim groups. These characteristics are abstract in the sense that they do not necessarily exist in each individual case—they represent the theoretically possible and at best probable. The problems come when nomothetic methods and results are used inappropriately to make overly confident inferences or conclusive interpretations about individual victims—in other words, applying broad nomothetic knowledge to answer narrow idiographic questions.

Forensic victimology is oriented towards idiographic victim study, however, nomothetic victim data may be used to develop theories or provide a point of fundamental reference with the appropriate caveats. In the absence of actual knowledge about victims, many researchers and some caseworkers invest heavily in the perceived authority of victim statistics. This section will further contextualize the real-world limitations of such nomothetically compiled victim data.

No Numbers

Much of the victim and offender data that is cited in the literature comes from the FBI's Uniform Crime Reports (UCR), which is a compilation of data from reporting law enforcement agencies around the United States. Not every law enforcement agency compiles this information every year, and not every

---

[9]This should go without saying, but not all knowledge derived nomothetically results in universal laws or even useful generalizations. Occasionally, the best we may hope for is to develop a theory or theories about the group under study. Such theories may not apply outside of the study group. Knowing the difference—and saying it out loud—is an indication of scientific honesty.

agency that compiles numbers submits them to the FBI—especially if certain crime rates are high, certain clearance rates are low, or they don't want them made public because the numbers make them appear otherwise ineffectual. So the total number of reporting law enforcement agencies varies from state to state, and from year to year.

Consider the troubles that were experienced in Detroit, Michigan, as reported in Schmitt (2002):

> For the second consecutive year, the FBI's preliminary Uniform Crime Reports, released Monday, don't include numbers from Detroit.
>
> Former Police Chief Benny Napoleon blamed the gaffe on shoddy computer systems.
>
> Chief Jerry Oliver said the problem is deeper.
>
> "This is yet another indication of how broke the systems are within the department," Oliver said Monday. "The only thing I can say is that it did not happen on my watch, and it's mine to fix, and I assure the citizens that it will not happen again."
>
> The statistics are important because people look to the numbers as a barometer of social and economic conditions in the community. In some cases, people use crime numbers—as they use school test results—to help decide where to relocate.
>
> Seven other cities in Michigan with populations of at least 100,000 are included in Monday's report, which lists crime statistics from 2001. The big hole is Detroit.
>
> . . . "Nothing mandates them to submit it," said FBI spokesman Paul Bresson. "Sometimes cities don't have full data available, but are able to get it to us for our annual report, which comes out in October."
>
> . . . Last year, Napoleon declined to give the FBI a letter vouching for the accuracy of Detroit's crime figures for 2000. He explained Monday that the computer system is sketchy. For example, if a car theft is reported and it later turns out to be false, there is no way to purge it from the department's crime data, Napoleon said.

Consider also the statewide problems experienced in Pennsylvania around the same timeframe, as reported in Conti (2002):

> State police trumpeted a 6 percent drop statewide in serious crime for 2001 without mentioning that 127 fewer police departments supplied them with crime data for that year.

The state police system for analyzing the numbers is flawed and paints an inaccurate picture of crime trends in Pennsylvania, said one national expert on crime statistics. State police compared total incidents reported by police in 2000 to total incidents reported by police in 2001, not accounting for a 15 percent decline in the number of police departments submitting reports.

. . . State Sen. Jane Orie, a McCandless Republican and former prosecutor, called the report "deceiving" and said the state police should do what they can to get the most accurate data.

"We need those statistics. We need an accurate account of where crime is increasing so we can send the proper resources there," she said. "And it's not fair to tell people crime is going down if it really isn't."

The number of departments reporting to the state's Uniform Crime Report has dropped steadily since the state police installed a new Internet-based reporting system that was supposed to make the report more accurate. Many local departments say that they do not have the proper computer connections or that their systems are not compatible with the one used by state police.

"The state refused to accept our reports by mail," said West Mifflin police Chief Frank Diener, whose department was one of 16 in Allegheny County and 46 in the five-county southwestern Pennsylvania region that stopped participating in the program last year. "We're trying to get the proper Internet connection to get our reports there again, but that gets costly," he said. "It's another unfunded mandate from the state."

. . . State police Lt. Wes Thurston of the Bureau of Research and Development, which issues the report, said the number of departments participating "fluctuates slightly" year-to-year, so he doesn't see a problem in how the numbers are analyzed. "Some departments just choose not to participate," Thurston said. "And now we have agencies that just don't want to enter some numbers on a screen and press 'submit.'"

Thurston said the new reporting program is set up so that data can be entered only online. As for departments that cannot access the Internet, he said: "They just need to find a place to get online. You don't have to have a computer and Internet connection in the department. You can do it at a library or from home."

The lesson for readers is that it's not just reported crime that matters, but unreported crime as well. One provides a context for the other. What's more, an interpretation of one without an understanding of the other is likely to be misleading.

Bad Numbers

In addition to those providing no crime data, there are also law enforcement agencies reporting creatively to hide increased crime rates, lowered solve rates, and other problems. Consider the following examples, taken from many agencies over the past decade:

Philadelphia, PA

From 1981 to 1999, the Sex Crimes Unit in the Philadelphia Police Department dismissed one-third of victim complaints without investigation, deliberately mislabeled one-fourth of victim complaints to manipulate crime data and make the city appear safer, and managed to maintain one of the worst solve rates in the country (McCoy 2003). In one record-breaking three-year period, the number of sex crimes that went uninvestigated exceeded 2000. According to Fazlollah, McCoy, and Moran (2000):

> The sex-crimes unit, founded in 1981, buried nearly a third of its caseload over the next 17 years. Rapes, attempted rapes and other reported acts were given administrative labels such as "investigation of person" or were rejected as unfounded. Either way, they did not show up in crime statistics. The victims were never told their complaints had been shelved.

> Current and former investigators said they dumped cases to cope with an overwhelming workload and pressure from commanders to generate favorable statistics.

The supervisors and detectives of that unit betrayed their victims both with apathy and for political gain, allowed an untold number of offenders to stay on the streets, and ultimately failed to protect the community they were sworn to serve. In short, it was one of the most publicly documented examples of how *not* to run a major sex-crimes unit in the United States.

Travis County, TX

The Travis Country Medical Examiner's Office (TCMEO) in Austin, Texas, while run by Chief Medical Examiner Robert Bayardo, Doctor of Medicine, was no stranger to errors and controversy. These include a potential impact on homicide statistics and accuracy rates with respect to cause of death. In 2004, an "investigation" was performed that "found no evidence of improprieties" at the TCMEO for numerous instances of death misclassification, among other allegations. This scandal involved the inappropriate labeling of some deaths caused by police officers as *accidental* instead of *homicide*. As reported in Smith (2004):

FIGURE 2.3

Dr. Robert Bayardo, MD, former Chief Medical Examiner, Travis County Medical Examiner's Office. Retired in 2006.

Travis Co. Judge Sam Biscoe on Monday announced the end to a month-long county investigation into allegations that the office of Travis Co. Medical Examiner Roberto Bayardo has improperly handled its investigations into 11 minority Austinites killed by Austin police officers since 1998. "Based on our review of the issues . . . and after our review of the information received from the [ME's] office, we have found no evidence of improprieties that would justify an official investigation at this time," Biscoe said.

Rev. Sterling Lands filed a complaint with Biscoe in July, asking that he investigate 11 "senseless and unprovoked killings" of minorities by APD officers. Lands said he was concerned that in each case Bayardo's office ruled that the deaths were "justified or unrelated to any unjustified actions by law enforcement," he wrote on July 30. Further, Lands said, he was concerned about the "countless numbers of blacks who are incarcerated" based in part on court testimony provided by examiners with the ME's office. Lands also raised questions about whether the doctors had perjured themselves and whether each of the examiners had been "properly accredited and credentialed" over the past two decades.

Biscoe said that upon receiving the complaint, he immediately contacted Bayardo and asked that his office gather the relevant documents for review. Bayardo did that, reviewed the materials, and then met with Biscoe, county Emergency Services Coordinator Danny Hobby, and county commissioners for further review of the cases and to answer questions. In short, Biscoe said, they didn't find anything wrong.

A primary issue of concern for Lands is that several of the 11 cases he cites were adjudged by Bayardo to be not homicides but accidental deaths—thus (arguably) reducing the likelihood of consequences for the police involved. In a memo to Biscoe, Hobby, and the commissioners, Bayardo wrote that his office was able to locate autopsy reports for eight of the 11 individuals Lands referred to, but that he didn't have enough identifying information to locate the other three. Of the eight cases, four deaths were ruled homicide—in each case the victim died from gunshot wounds—and the other four were ruled accidental.

In those four cases, Bayardo said, the underlying cause of the victim's death was the "acute toxic effects" of drugs, which were exacerbated during the struggles with police. "Whenever a person is under the influence of a drug like cocaine, the heart is susceptible" to bursts of adrenaline, he said at a Monday press conference. If the victims hadn't been on drugs, he said, they likely would not have died during their altercations with police. But both Bayardo and Biscoe noted that there is an ongoing national "issue" over whether such deaths should be classified accidental—laying the responsibility for death at the feet of the deceased—or classified as homicide, shifting the blame elsewhere.

The classification of those deaths as homicides does make sense, said Bayardo, "because the direct cause of death is the injury, not the drugs." Indeed, Bayardo pointed to an issue summary prepared this year by the College of American Pathologists that addresses the issue. "[I]f one accepts that the struggle contributes to death, it is difficult to argue against a ruling of homicide," the summary reads. "Such a ruling does not necessarily imply intent, nor is it meant to imply 'murder' or wrongdoing on the part of police." Still, Biscoe said, the justice system provides at least six "checks and balances" for cause of death in addition to the ME's opinion—such as the grand jury process, the district attorney, judges, and juries. That was the only place where Biscoe suggested that Lands' various allegations may be well-founded.

Bayardo and his examiners only testify in murder cases—all told, approximately 38 cases each year—Biscoe said, so they couldn't be responsible for the incarceration of "countless" blacks. Moreover, there is nothing to suggest the MEs have perjured themselves —"this complaint is too general to provide an appropriate response," Biscoe wrote in a press release. "To our knowledge, this claim is untrue and without factual support." Regarding accreditation, for a "short period" of time earlier this year, Deputy Medical Examiner Elizabeth Peacock's state license was "not in good standing," after Peacock let her dues lapse; however, Biscoe said the autopsies she performed during that time period are still good, and there's no indication that she'll be reprimanded for continuing to work during the lapse.

Lands, who was pleased with the timeliness of Biscoe's response to his initial complaint, was nonetheless displeased with the judge's "findings." And, he told KVUE-TV, he is not impressed with Biscoe's decision to let the ME investigate itself. And he said it's "ridiculous to me that anyone would buy" the line that the ME's opinions are "checked" by the grand jury process or by the district attorney. To Lands, the way to ensure fairness and accuracy is to employ a third party to observe autopsy proceedings in cases involving confrontation with police.

The net effect of misclassifying homicides as accidental deaths, which Dr. Bayardo appears to admit was possible, is that overall homicide rates and officer-involved deaths will seem lower. Moreover, any officer involved in deaths that are not classified as homicides are essentially exempt from otherwise mandatory review for negligence or excessive use of force. This is separate from the overt errors that may infect crime data resulting from victim misidentification and inaccurate causes of death.

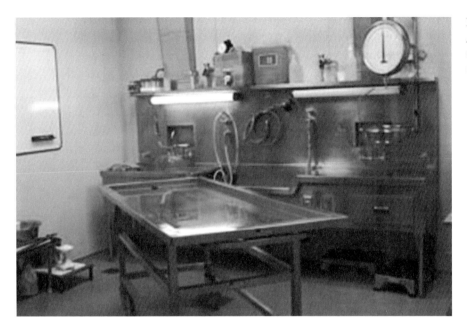

FIGURE 2.4
Autopsy table at the Travis County Medical Examiner's Office.

It also bears noting that in the first half of 2006, all three of the TCMEO's forensic pathologists (including Dr. Bayardo) resigned within a few months of each other (Smith 2006). This mass exodus occurred subsequent to an external audit that was ordered at the tail-end of 2005 because of numerous high profile errors, including the following (Smith 2005):

- In December 2003, the office released the wrong body for cremation. Instead of sending 38-year-old Paul Williams, they released 39-year-old Rayford Floyd, whose family had wanted a burial. Travis Co. Medical Examiner Roberto Bayardo told the *Statesman* Floyd's body had been incorrectly labeled. "We are very sorry this happened," he said. "I had thought we were foolproof."

- In June 2004, the office misidentified the charred remains of an 81-year-old woman as those of a 23-year-old man. In his autopsy report, former Deputy Medical Examiner Vladimir Parungao identified the remains as those of Clayton Wayne Daniels, noting that he'd found a "small segment of penis" and a small amount of urine in the bladder that he matched to Daniels. Unfortunately, the corpse was that of an already dead—and embalmed, buried, and then exhumed—woman, leaving Burnet Co. officials (for whom the ME's office had conducted the examination) wondering if the ME's office actually examined the body. "They've got some serious explaining to do," Burnet Co. attorney Eddie Arredondo told the *Houston Chronicle*.

- In June 2005, the office mistakenly reported that 18-year-old Daniel Rocha, who was shot and killed by police on June 9, was drug-free at the time he was killed. After APD questioned the results, the ME's office performed a second, more discriminating toxicology, which revealed there was a small amount of marijuana in Rocha's bloodstream when he was killed.

- In August 2005, the office reported that Randy "Biscuit" Turner died from cirrhosis caused by alcohol abuse. After learning that Turner didn't drink alcohol, the office reversed its finding to reflect that the cirrhosis was caused by hepatitis C. The alcohol found in Turner's system, the office subsequently reported, was the result of body decomposition.

These types of errors not only affect the quality of the crime data that may be reported to the FBI's UCR, such errors also impact the lives of victims and erode the confidence that the police and community have in the ME's office. It's fair to say that they further diminish victim confidence in the justice system as a whole.

Broward County, FL

As of this writing, two detectives and a deputy have been convicted of criminal charges for their involvement in a crime statistics scandal at the Broward County Sheriff's Office. As reported in "Ex-deputy sentenced to 2 years' probation" (2007):

> He'd just been sentenced to a term of probation for lying on police reports, yet the former Broward sheriff's deputy insisted he was innocent Thursday as he left a Broward courtroom. Shane Campbell said he found no solace [in] escaping a potential jail sentence. "This isn't a relief," Campbell said of his two-year probation sentence. "I didn't do anything wrong."
>
> Circuit Judge Andrew Siegel also ordered Campbell to complete 400 hours of community service.
>
> Campbell, 34, was the second deputy to go to trial in the Sheriff's Office crime statistics scandal and the first to be convicted by a jury. Two other detectives have pleaded guilty to misdemeanors, and a jury acquitted another detective of felony charges in June.
>
> Prosecutors said Campbell fabricated confessions in 2003 and closed cases by pinning property thefts on people who didn't commit them. The closed cases, deemed "exceptional clearances," were classified as solved but didn't result in criminal charges. In April, a jury found the former Weston/Southwest Ranches detective

guilty of two misdemeanor counts of falsifying police reports, each punishable by up to a year in jail. Four days earlier, Siegel had dismissed two felony counts of official misconduct against Campbell. The Sheriff's Office fired Campbell on Monday. He had been suspended without pay.

A third deputy is set to go to trial for related charges in June of 2008.

San Antonio, TX

The San Antonio Police Department has had problems collecting and reporting crime data for years. As reported in Kriel (2008):

> The San Antonio Police Department incorrectly tallied the city's homicide statistics, wrongly calculated how many slayings police solved and failed to update its homicide clearance rates, an audit released Thursday concludes. Some other crimes also were miscounted in the 18-month period evaluated by the report.

> Police Chief William McManus ordered the audit after the San Antonio Express-News published a series of reports questioning the department's homicide clearance rates for 2006.

> In those articles, officials provided three wildly different rates, casting doubt on the department's ability to accurately keep and report its statistics. A clearance rate represents a percentage of cases solved and can be a measure of a police agency's performance.

> The department has had problems with how it submits its crime numbers to the FBI for years. In 2002, the FBI rejected the department's overall clearance numbers because the figures were so low.

> Thursday's report, released by the city auditor's office, evaluated statistics from January 2006 through June 2007.

> It blamed antiquated computer programs, a lack of written procedures, insufficient training and a host of clerical errors. It found the SAPD "has no true central records function in place to ensure accuracy, completeness and compliance" with guidelines set forth by the FBI. "This was embarrassing for us," said Deputy Chief Geraldine Garcia, who oversees the department's handling of records.

> Previous ways of reporting data "obviously weren't very effective," she said.

> The audit did show the reporting of homicide numbers and related clearances "generally" complied with the FBI's Uniform Crime Reporting criteria. But it also highlighted several errors.

Justifiable homicides, such as officer-involved shootings and cases of self-defense, were routinely classified incorrectly, causing the department to tally a lower amount of reported homicides than actually occurred. In 2006, for example, eight justifiable homicides weren't included in the department's figures. Neither was one negligent homicide and another homicide in which the cause of death was undetermined. That would have increased the reported homicides to 129.

. . . The audit also found some officers were counting an offense as cleared when an arrest warrant was issued, rather than when an arrest was made. In addition, officials failed to routinely update their clearance rates. SAPD's Web site originally reported only 36.1 percent of slayings were solved in 2006. When reporters questioned this figure, officials hastily ordered a hand count, which determined 50.4 percent of the homicides had been cleared.

Around the same time, however, the Department of Public Safety released a 40 percent clearance rate for SAPD—a number DPS said was based on the Police Department's own figures. According to the audit, 50.8 percent of homicides were solved in 2006.

The department also over-reported the number of homicides cleared in 2006 and 2007, by two and three homicides, respectively. Though the discrepancies are small, they underline the larger issue of correctly reporting crime statistics. One homicide, for example, was counted in two subsequent years and another was considered solved when it wasn't.

Michael Gilbert, a University of Texas at San Antonio criminologist, said the audit reflects a data-entry problem rather than an attempt to willfully manipulate the figures. "These are things you want the Police Department to know and you want them to fix," he said. However, he added that having perfect data is almost impossible.

The problems in this department echo some of the improper classification practices investigated at the Travis County Medical Examiner's Office, with respect to officer-involved deaths.

The over-reliance on victim crime data from the FBI as meaningful or conclusive has reached near fetishistic levels in victimology texts and related research. While such data provides useful reference points for the purpose of generating theory, fixation on nomothetic crime data is rarely helpful in answering specific questions about the characteristics and qualities of specific victims. It is hoped that examples in this chapter leave readers with a genuinely informed sense of how fallible—or at least vulnerable—crime data can be.

SUMMARY

Victims face many challenges as they enter the criminal justice system. Not everyone that can help them will. Not everyone that is supposed to help them is able, willing, or even technically required to do so. And not everyone that claims to be helping is making things better. As a result of the cumulative effects of an overburdened justice system, apathy from professionals and bystanders alike, and double victimization, victims are often reluctant to report crime or even request the help of authorities. In addition, these limitations and the other contextual problems discussed should prevent victimologists from relying too heavily on any victim-related crime data that may be gathered and submitted by law enforcement.

Questions

1. What are some of the problems with the crime rate and victimological literature to date?
2. Explain the availability heuristic.
3. Why might victims choose not to report crime? Give four reasons.
4. What are some examples of mandated reporters?
5. True or False: The primary role of law enforcement is to enforce the law, not to protect the public.
6. Explain the role of the victim advocate.
7. What is bystander apathy?
8. Explain the difference between double victimization and secondary victimization.

REFERENCES

Amick-McMullan, Angelynne Dean, Kilpatrick, Lois J. Veronen, and Susan Smith. 1989. Family Survivors of Homicide Victims: Theoretical Perspectives and an Exploratory Study. *Journal of Traumatic Stress* 2 (1): 21–35.

BJS (U.S. Bureau of Justice Statistics). 2006. *Criminal Victimization in the United States, 2005.* NCJ 215244. Washington, DC: Bureau of Justice Statistics, December.

Branchflower, S. and de Luca, T. *"Investigative Report Regarding The Anchorage Police Department's E-911 Emergency Response To The Patricia Godfrey Residence"* Alaska Office Of Victims' Rights, OCR Complaint no. 02–004, APD report number 02–039245, November 26, 2002.

Conti, D. 2002. "More than 100 agencies unable to report crime." *The Tribune Review,* September 3.

Cordner, G. 1995. "Administration." In *The Encyclopedia of Police Science,* 2nd ed., edited by W. Bailey, 9–14. New York: Garland Publishing.

Davis, C. 2001. "Detective's actions face inquiry." *St. Petersburg Times,* October 2.

Davis, C. 2002. "Handling of rape cases is upheld." *St. Petersburg Times,* February 7.

Davis, C. 2002. "Victim sues in handling of rape." *St. Petersburg Times,* November 19.

Davis, C. 2003. "Judge may toss suit in rape." *St. Petersburg Times,* May 30.

Davis, C. 2003. "Victim of rape dealt setback in court." *St. Petersburg Times*, June 26.

Doerner, W., and S. Lab. 2002. *Victimology*, 3rd ed. Cincinnati, OH: Andersen Publishing.

Erez, Edna, and Kathy Laster. 1999. Neutralizing Victim Reform: Legal Professionals' Perspectives on Victims and Impact Statements. *Crime and Delinquency* 45: 530–553.

Erez, Edna, and Linda Rogers. 1999. Victim Impact Statements and Sentencing Outcomes and Processes. *British Journal of Criminology* 39 (2): 216–239.

2007. "Ex-deputy sentenced to 2 years' probation." *South Florida Sun-Sentinel*, May 11.

Fazlollah, M., C. McCoy, and R. Moran. 2000. "Timoney to allow sex-case oversight." *Philadelphia Inquirer*, March 21.

FCC (Federal Communications Commission). 2008. "Consumer Information." U.S. Federal Communications Commission: Public Safety and Homeland Security Bureau. http://www.fcc.gov/pshs/services/911-services/consumer.html.

Goodrum, S. 2007. "Victims' Rights, Victims' Expectations, and Law Enforcement Workers' Constraints in Cases of Murder." *Law and Social Inquiry* 32, Summer: 725–757.

Goodrum, Sarah, and Mark C. Stafford. 2003. The Management of Emotions in the Criminal Justice System. *Sociological Focus* 36 (3): 179–196.

Hegeman, R. 2007. "Police: Shoppers stepped over victim." *Associated Press*, July 4. http://abcnews.go.com/US/wireStory?id=3342724.

Hurlburt, R.T., and T.J. Knapp. 2006. "Munsterberg in 1898, Not Allport in 1937, Introduced the Terms 'Idiographic' and 'Nomothetic' to American Psychology." *Theory and Psychology* 16, no. 2: 287–293.

Kanter, L. 2005. "Invisible Clients: Exploring Our Failure to Provide Civil Legal Services to Rape Victims." *Suffolk University Law Review* 38: 253–289.

Kilpatrick, Dean G., and Randy K. Otto. 1987. Constitutionally Guaranteed Participation in Criminal Proceeding for Victims: Potential Effects on Psychological Functioning. *Wayne Law Review* 34: 17–28.

Konradi, Amanda. 1997. Too Little, Too Late: Prosecutors' Precourt Preparation of Rape Survivors. *Law & Social Inquiry* 22: 1–54.

Kriel, L. 2008. "Audit raps SAPD death stats." *San Antonio Express-News*, February 1.

Latane, B. and J.M. Darley(b). *The Unresponsible Bystander: Why Doesn't He Help?* New York: Appleton-Century-Crofts, 1970.

Lerner, Melvin. 1980. *The Belief in a Just World: A Fundamental Delusion*. New York: Plenum Press.

Lukens, R. 2007. "The Impact of Mandatory Reporting Requirements on the Child Welfare System." *Rutgers Journal of Law and Public Policy* 5, no. 1: 177–233.

Martin, Patricia Yancey, and R. Marlene Powell. 1995. Accounting for the "Second Assault": Legal Organizations' Framing of Rape Victims. *Law & Social Inquiry* 19: 853–890.

Mauer, R. 2002. "'I'll see you in hell,' Brand told Godfrey." *Anchorage Daily News*, October 1. http://www.juneauempire.com/stories/100102/sta_godfreyshooting.shtml.

McCoy, C. 2003. "Rape unit reborn out of disgrace." *Philadelphia Inquirer*, June 22.

Mendelsohn, B. 1963. "The Origin of the Doctrine of Victimology." In *Victimology,* edited by I. Drapkin and E. Viano. Lexington, MA: D.C. Heath.

Miccio, G.K. 2000. "Notes from the Underground: Battered Women, the State, and Conceptions of Accountability." *Harvard Women's Law Journal* 23, Spring: 154–171.

Mirowsky, John, and Catherine E. Ross. 1989. *Social Causes of Psychological Distress.* Hawthorne, NY: Aldine de Gruyter.

Rando, Therese A. 1993. *Treatment of Complicated Mourning.* Champaign, IL: Research Press.

"Rape victim looks to move on after sentencing," Associated Press, February 20, 2001.

Rosenthal, A.M. *Thirty-Eight Witnesses.* New York: McGraw-Hill, 1964.

Schmitt, B. 2002. "Detroit bungles data for crime report." *The Detroit Free Press,* June 25.

Scott, G. 2003. "People-Based Safety." *Professional Safety* 48, no. 12, December 1: 33–43.

Smith, J. 2004. "Biscoe defends the M.E." *The Austin Chronicle,* September 3.

Smith, J. "Trouble at the ME's Office" *The Austin Chronicle,* December 2, 2005; url: http://www.austinchronicle.com/gyrobase/Issue/story?oid=oid:315716

Sonner, S. 2001. "Fugitive in jail on $5 million bond for Sparks rapes." *Las Vegas Review Journal,* January 12.

Stenross, Barbara, and Sherryl Kleinman. 1989. The Highs and Lows of Emotional Labor: Detectives' Encounters with Criminals and Victims. *Journal of Contemporary Ethnography* 17: 435–452.

Sunstein, C. 2005. "Group Judgments: Statistical Means, Deliberation, and Information Markets." *New York University Law Review* 80, June: 962–1049.

2002. "Tape of Godfrey's 911 call shows dispatcher's delay." *The Associated Press,* August 25. http://www.juneauempire.com/stories/082502/sta_shooting.shtml.

Toomey, S. 2004. "City to pay Godfrey $700,000." *Anchorage Daily News,* August 14.

VBR (The Victim's Bill of Rights). 2007. *The Role of Law Enforcement Agencies.* Manitoba, CA: Manitoba Justice, May. http://www.gov.mb.ca/justice/victims/services/vrss.html.

1999. "Woman: Police ignored suspects' earlier assault." *Las Vegas Review Journal,* January 17.

1999. "Woman sues police who disbelieved rape charge." *The Holland Sentinel,* March 24.

CHAPTER 3

Constructing a Victim Profile

Brent E. Turvey[1]

KEY TERMS

- *Confirmation bias:* a form of observer bias, it is the conscious or unconscious tendency to seek only evidence which affirms preexisting theories, opinions, or findings.
- *Critical thinking:* indiscriminately questioning all evidence and assumptions, no matter what their source.
- *Falsification:* the act of refuting or disproving a hypothesis or theory. The extent to which any theory is scientific is a function of whether and how attempts at falsification have been made. Theories that have survived repeated vigorous attempts at falsification are considered more scientific, and more reliable, than those that have not. Falsification is the cornerstone of the scientific method.
- *Identification (or Classification):* the placement of any item into a specific category of items with similar characteristics. Identification does not require or imply uniqueness.
- *Idiographic:* the study of the concrete: examining individuals and their actual qualities. Idiographic study concentrates on specific cases and the unique traits or functioning of individuals.
- *Individuation:* the assignment of uniqueness to an item; describing it in such a manner as to separate it from all other items in the universe.
- *Nomothetic:* refers to the study of the abstract: examining groups and universal laws.
- *Observer bias:* the conscious or unconscious tendency to see or find what one expects to see or find.
- *Science:* an orderly body of knowledge with principles that are clearly enunciated and reality-oriented, with principles and conclusions that are reality-oriented and susceptible to testing.
- *Scientific knowledge:* any knowledge, enlightenment, or awareness that comes from examining events or problems through the lens of the scientific method.

CONTENTS

[1]Parts of this chapter have been adapted from material originally published in Turvey (2008).

As discussed in Chapter 2, in the study of crime, criminals, and victims, as for any subject, there are two major approaches to research and knowledge building. The first is *nomothetic,* or the study of the abstract: examining groups and universal laws.[2] The second is *idiographic,* referring to the study of the concrete: examining individuals and their actual qualities. Idiographic study concentrates on specific cases and the unique traits or functioning of individuals.

In terms of victimology in general, it is fair to say that there are nomothetic methods and idiographic methods alike. The primary goal of nomothetic victim studies is to accumulate general, typical, common, or averaged characteristics of victim groups. These characteristics are abstract in the sense that they do not necessarily exist in each individual case—they represent the theoretically possible and at best probable.

The problems come when nomothetic methods or information is used inappropriately to make overly confident inferences or conclusive interpretations about individual victims—in other words, applying broad nomothetic knowledge to answer narrow idiographic questions.

At its very best, nomothetic study will yield general knowledge about victim groups that may or may not be applicable to a particular victim. It will certainly assist researchers who need to discuss and describe group trends that may be found. However, in the face of conclusively answering questions about a specific problem or victim separate from the group, nomothetic knowledge fails. It may be used appropriately to help generate theories, but nomothetic study is not fit for rendering conclusions that are victim specific.

For example, if we study 20 victims as a group (nomothetically), looking for common or recurrent patterns and characteristics, we will learn little about the uniquely integrated characteristics and expressions of each individual victim. The result of our study will be averaged, diluted, and abstract—with group findings that are true for some victims but not others. Moreover, there is the often incorrect assumption that victims, crimes, or offenders are sufficiently similar to be lumped together for aggregate study. In such cases, the resulting nomothetic knowledge is not just average and abstract, it is also inaccurate and ultimately misleading.[3]

---

[2] As noted in Chapter 2, this should go without saying, but not all knowledge derived nomothetically results in universal laws or even useful generalizations. Occasionally, the best we may hope for is to develop general theories about the group under study—which may not apply outside of the study group. Knowing and acknowledging this are indications of scientific honesty.

[3] The limitations of nomothetic research when applied to individual cases are not completely foreign to the criminological literature. One didactic example is Meloy (1998, 8), who was discussing stalkers and threat assessment in specific when he wrote "nomothetic (group) studies on threats and their relationship to behavior are not necessarily helpful in idiographic (single) case research or risk management beyond the making of risk probability statements if the stalker fits closely into the reference groups."

If we study the traits and circumstances of individual victims (idiographically, separate from all others), then we may learn specifics not only about the crimes they suffered but also about the person or persons responsible.

Nomothetic victim profiles, therefore, are characteristics developed by studying groups of victims. Furthermore, nomothetic victim profiles are abstract: they do not represent an actual victim that exists in the real world, they represent varying degrees of theory and possibility.

It should be clear from this discussion that if we want to know the actual nature of a thing we must study it, not just those things we suspect may be similar. Unfortunately, the vast majority of victim research is concerned primarily with, or based primarily on, nomothetic study. Consequently, much of the victim research that exists is inappropriate for rendering *conclusions* about individual victims.[4]

Forensic victimology is concerned with the investigation and examination of particular victims alleged to have suffered specific crimes, that is to say, idiographic victim study. For our purposes, an *ideographic victim profile* is just what it sounds like: a list of the characteristics possessed by a specific victim. It should include physical, biological, mental, social, educational, occupational, and personality descriptors, among others. It is best conceptualized as open-ended, rather than a pedantic checklist—the more information and subsequent descriptors available the better.

The purpose of this chapter is to explain the purpose of constructing victim profiles, in concert with the necessary mindset of the forensic victimologist. It will also provide general standards of practice for forensic victimologists in the rendering and interpretation of victim profiles. The chapter will close with the basic information that a forensic victimologist must gather and examine to construct an informed profile.

THE PURPOSE OF VICTIM PROFILES

As discussed in the first chapter, the forensic victimologist seeks to examine, consider, and interpret particular victim evidence in a scientific fashion in order to answer investigative and forensic (i.e., legal) questions. Most commonly, forensic victimologists serve investigations and court proceedings in the following ways:

---

[4]The term *conclusions* has been italicized because this statement does not refer to theories. Again, nomothetic knowledge is important in the development of theories, but when these theories are presented as conclusions—and without mention of their limitations—nomothetic victimologists cross the line.

1. Assist with contextualizing allegations of victimization;
2. Help support or refute allegations of victimization;
3. Help establish the nature of victim exposure to harm or loss;
4. Assist with the development of offender modus operandi and motive;
5. Help establish an investigative suspect pool;
6. Assist with the investigative linkage of unsolved cases.

Inherent in these considerations is the service of two very separate goals—the *investigative* and the *forensic*. Forensic victimology in the service of investigative goals gathers everything and considers everything. It takes on all information and theories until they are exhausted possibilities. However, as will be discussed in Chapter 15, the court decides actual admissibility of victim evidence (victimology) based on collective issues of precedent, prejudice, and relevance in each case. Part of that equation is the sufficiency and reliability of any expert findings. Forensic victimology in the service of specific forensic (legal) goals must therefore meet a high standard: victimological conclusions and the evidence upon which they rest must be sufficiently reliable to form the basis for courtroom testimony.

Consider the case of Tamara Anne Moonier, of Orange County, California. The "victim" evidence in her criminal complaint, specifically video documentation of an alleged gang rape and her conduct, was crucial with respect to establishing whether or not a crime actually occurred. In other words, a video of the incident, documenting everyone's actions and words, helped to refute allegations of victimization.

FIGURE 3.1

In 2004, Tamara Anne Moonier filed a rape complaint implicating six men in a gang rape. In 2006, she pleaded guilty to felony grand theft, perjury, and presenting a false claim to the state, as well as a misdemeanor count of making a false police report. If any of the accused had been prosecuted and convicted, they faced the possibility of life in prison.

The following is taken from the public record, as presented in Moxley (2006):

> You'll never convince six lucky Orange County guys that porn is bad: a single raunchy sex video is keeping them out of prison. Of course, these 20-year-olds couldn't have foreseen this fate when they filmed their wild gangbang after a night of drinking at a Fullerton bar.
>
> This tale begins in the wee hours of June 6, 2004, when a distraught Tamara Anne Moonier entered a Fullerton police station. She said she'd been kidnapped a few hours earlier from a parking lot at Heroes Bar & Grill, hooded and driven to an unknown residence. Moonier, then 28, told police that a group of men brutally raped her at gunpoint for more than an hour, forced her to perform numerous degrading sex acts on film, demanded her silence and then released her.
>
> "She said she feared for her safety," a law-enforcement officer told the *Weekly*.
>
> With money from a victims' assistance program, Moonier immediately moved from her Fullerton apartment to Dana Point. Meanwhile, alarmed police detectives used her descriptions to launch a manhunt. Within about a week of the alleged crime, Moonier had picked one of the suspects out of a photographic lineup. Eventually all of the men were identified.
>
> But Fullerton police refused to file charges. The suspects had voluntarily turned over the sex video Moonier had described. It showed no gun, no threats of violence and no force.
>
> In fact, the woman not only directed action at times but complimented penis sizes, complained about the lighting, nonchalantly took a cell phone call during the gangbang, yelled, "Get it up!" when some of the men lost their erections, called herself a slut and demanded ejaculations—in her mouth.
>
> She also laughed at least 27 times during the sex, moaned intensely when she wasn't laughing and cheered the men to sexual heroics with, "Yeah! Yeah! Yeah! Yeah!" "I just like sex," Moonier said at one point on the tape. "I can't help it."
>
> Deputy District Attorney Paul J. Chrisopoulos will use the homemade video as Exhibit 1 in his case against Moonier. Last summer, the Orange County grand jury, mostly retired folks, had the thrill (if you want to call it that) of watching the exploits of this petite mother of two children, then toddlers. They indicted her for filing false police reports, committing perjury and stealing funds from a taxpayer-funded victims' program.

If Moonier and her public defender don't gain their senses and seek a plea deal, a judge and jury will soon view the tape. They'll hear more than the following excerpts:

MALE: I took your fucking pants down and started fucking you.

MOONIER: You sure did!

MALE: You liked it, didn't you?

MOONIER: Of course! [Laughs.] Did you?

MALE: Fuck, yeah!

MOONIER: All right then.

MALE: You give good head.

MOONIER: Thank you. I told you I've watched lots of movies.

To one guy unable to get an erection, Moonier said, "You're fucking pathetic. You can't get it up. Forget it."

MALES: She loves this shit [sex].

MOONIER: Yeah, I do. Uhhhhh. Very nice!

When one guy complained that Moonier's teeth hurt his penis during a blowjob, somebody slapped her butt. She responded, "Ouch! Fuck! That's gonna leave a mark. You're gonna kill my game. Now I'm not going to be able to have sex tomorrow night. Damn you." [Laughs.]

MALE: How's my dick feeling?

MOONIER: Your dick goes great, babe!

During the gangbang, a cell phone rang, and one of the guys answered it and calmly talked to a buddy. While Moonier had sex in the doggie-style position, the guy handed her the phone. She didn't scream for help. She said, "Hello? This is Tammy. Yes. He's fucking me from behind!" The guy took the phone back and gave directions to the residence. Moonier simultaneously complimented one man's penis: "Big and nice!" Later, she said, "How many people are we calling?"

MALE: You know I'm a slut?

MOONIER: Among other things.

MALE: Right.

MOONIER: Well, you obviously knew I was!

MALE: Fuck, yeah!

MOONIER: How could you tell?

During intercourse, Moonier said, "I have some work to do. Shut the fuck up. Shhhhhhh. Are you the only one who can perform in front of an audience? The rest of them can't fucking perform. [Moans.] Nice! Much better. Goes in deeper from this angle. [Moans again.]"

A male observer said to the guy having sex, "We can't hear your balls slapping, come on!" [The guy increased the speed of his penetration and Moonier moaned more.] The men cheered their pal on: "Hit harder!" Moonier said, "Shut the fuck up so he can finish. At least somebody will get off tonight."

While performing in the reverse cowgirl position (use your imagination), Moonier turned to the camera and said, "This better not fucking end up on the Internet unless you're gonna give me some of the money!" Minutes later, she yelled at the guys, "Get it up!" And, "That guy can't ejaculate.... Yeah, you fucking gave up on me.... And this one can't even finish either. I'm getting kind of pissed. I just want somebody to finish."

MALE: I want to slap your ass.

MOONIER: I don't need any more marks. You know what's gonna happen the next time I hook up with the fucking cops? They're gonna want to know who the fuck I was with.... I'm fucking three cops!"

MOONIER: You gonna finish this time?

MALE: I really believe she really wants to swallow [the semen].

MOONIER: I always swallow. What's the point? You're gonna get some of it in your mouth anyway. You might as well swallow. I'd be really pissed if somebody was going down on me and fucking turned around to spit. That's just not right. You have to swallow. That's just how it is!"

In November of 2006, Moonier pleaded guilty to felony grand theft, perjury, and presenting a false claim to the state, as well as a misdemeanor count of making a false police report. She accepted a one-year jail sentence. According to "O.C. woman who lied about rape gets time in jail" (2006):

She told police on June 6, 2004, that she had been kidnapped at gunpoint by one man a few hours earlier outside a Fullerton bar, taken to an unknown location and raped repeatedly by six men. She claimed she had never seen the men prior to the attack but was able to identify them through a photo lineup, Schroeder said.

While the case was under investigation, she collected received [sic] a victim assistance check, signing under penalty of perjury that her claims were true, Schroeder said. But one of the accused men provided a videotape of the encounter, which showed Moonier actively participating and orchestrating the sexual encounters, and she was indicted by a grand jury, Schroeder said.

"Moonier could have put six innocent men in prison for the rest of their lives for a crime that they did not commit," said Deputy District Attorney Paul Chrisopoulos. "The funds that Ms. Moonier received are reserved for the victims of crimes to be used for emergency relocation, hospital bills and counseling. When the funds are used fraudulently, it hurts the availability of resources for true victims."

Moonier, who has been diagnosed with bi-polar illness and depression, tearfully apologized to Orange County Judge Carla Singer before the sentencing. "I've changed my life," Moonier said. "I take my medicine. I never believed I had an illness until this happened. I'm very, very sorry."

This case serves a number of purposes. First, it demonstrates that without video documentation of victim conduct, this case would have pitted the word of the complainant against the words of each accused. Had they been arrested, tried, and convicted, each would have been given extensive prison sentences and subsequently required to register as a sex offender. Second, it graphically dispels any preconception that this type of random consensual group activity does not occur. Victimologists must be objective students of human sexual activity, and accept that some people can and will engage in this kind of behavior by choice—whether it is impelled by drugs, alcohol, sexual preference, or any combination of these. Third, and because of this, forensic victimologists must become accustomed to examining a wide variety of sexual activity; they must accept that victim evidence is necessarily graphic; and that alleged victims will make false statements even when they are aware of evidence that can utterly refute their claims. Therefore, basing any conclusion simply on the statements of a victim, without corroboration, is not a legitimate forensic practice. Though victim statements are a very reasonable foundation for the development of initial investigative theory.

STANDARDS OF PRACTICE FOR FORENSIC VICTIMOLOGISTS

In any discipline, practice standards are the fundamental rules that set the limits of evidentiary interpretation. They offer a mechanism for evaluating acceptable work habits and application of methods. Consistent with the general practice standards described in Thornton (1997b, 18), for all forensic examiners, such standards are designed to help reduce bias, encourage the employment of analytical logic and the scientific method, and require the formation of hypotheses and conclusions in accordance with known evidence alone.

It should go without saying that all forensic examiners have a duty to strive for objectivity, competence, and professionalism in their work. They should want their findings to be accurate and their methods to be reliable. To that end, practice standards must define a minimum threshold of competency. They must also help define a practitioner's role and outline a mechanism for demonstrating their facility. They are a compass for diligent practitioners to follow and a reference point to slow down and educate for those who have lost their way.

As this suggests, the purpose of defining practice standards is not only to help professionals achieve a level of competency but also to provide independent reviewers with a basis for checking work that purports to be competent. Practice standards set the bar and are a safeguard against ignorance, incapacity, and incomprehension masquerading as science and reason.

1. Forensic Examiners Must Strive Diligently to Avoid Bias

Dr. Paul Kirk wrote of forensic examination, "Physical evidence cannot be wrong; it cannot be perjured; it cannot be wholly absent. *Only in its interpretation can there be error*" (Kirk and Thornton 1970, 4). With this simple observation, Kirk was referring to the influences of examiner ignorance, imprecision, and bias on the reconstruction of physical evidence and its meaning. The evidence is always there, waiting to be understood. The forensic examiner is the imprecise lens through which a form of understanding comes.

Specifically, there are at least two kinds of bias that objective forensic examiners need to be aware of and mitigate in their casework in order to maintain their professional lens: observer bias and confirmation bias.

Observer bias is the conscious or unconscious tendency to see or find what one expects to see or find. Practically, this means that the forensic examiner might develop an expectation of findings based on information and opinions learned from the popular media, witnesses, and the opinions and findings of others. These influences are particularly insidious because, unlike overt fraud, they can be subconscious. Unless intentionally screened or recognized by the examiner in some fashion, influences can nudge, push, or drag examiner findings in a particular direction.

Confirmation bias is the conscious or unconscious tendency to seek only evidence which affirms preexisting theories, opinions, or findings. It is a specific kind of observer bias in which information and evidence are screened to include those things that confirm a position and to actively ignore, not look for, or undervalue the relevance of anything that contradicts that position. It commonly manifests itself in the form of looking only for particular kinds of evidence that support a given case theory (i.e., suspect guilt or innocence) and actively explaining away evidence or findings that are undesirable without reasonable logic or consideration. This includes filtering of the evidence provided to the victimologist by persons advocating a particular theory or by persons interested in "watching the budget" so that potentially exculpatory evidence is not selected for analysis because it would cost more money or require too much time.

Wrestling with confirmation bias is extremely difficult, often because it is institutional. Many forensic examiners work in systems in which they are rewarded with praise and promotion for successfully advocating their employer's side when true science is about objectively explaining the limits of available evidence. Consequently, the majority of forensic examiners suffering from confirmation bias has no idea what it is or that it is even a problem.

What forensic examiners must understand is their primary value to the justice system: their adherence to the scientific method, and its demands as much objectivity and intellectual honesty as can be brought to bear. Success in the forensic community must be measured by the diligent elimination of possibilities through the scientific method and peer review, not through securing convictions. In other words, the objective forensic examiner is not out to get the bad guy, or to prove that there is a bad guy, but rather to help determine what actually happened and under what circumstances, using the available evidence.

2. Forensic Examiners Are Responsible for Requesting All Relevant Evidence and Information in Order to Render an Adequate Victim Profile and Form Related Opinions

Forensic examiners must define the scope of evidence and information they need in order to perform an adequate examination, partial or otherwise, by making a formal request of their client, employer, or the requesting agency. This includes reports and documentation regarding the crime scene, any evidence collected and tested, investigative efforts and interviews, and forensic examinations performed on the victim. Upon receiving that evidence, they must determine what has been made available and what is missing. This basic task is incumbent upon every forensic examiner.

When forensic examiners are not able to base their findings on complete information as they define or understand it, this must be made clear as part of their conclusions. The reason must also be made clear (evidence was not collected; evidence was lost; evidence was not requested; etc.) A list of victim-related evidence to be gathered and examined is provided in the next section of this chapter.

3. Forensic Examiners Are Responsible for Determining Whether the Evidence They Are Examining Is of Sufficient Quality to Provide the Basis for an Adequate Examination

The harsh reality is that crime scene investigation efforts in the United States are often abysmal, if not completely absent, and in need of major reform (see DeForest 2005). Crime scenes throughout the United States are commonly processed by police-employed technicians or sworn personnel with little or no formal education, to say nothing of training in the forensic sciences and crime scene processing techniques. The in-service forensic training available to law enforcement typically exists in the form of half-day seminars or video courses and taught by nonscientists which, on their own, in no way impart the discipline and expertise necessary to examine crime scenes adequately for the purposes of an objective forensic examination.

In addition, general victim information is often afforded even less attention and consideration. Rather, investigators tend to focus heavily on gathering victim evidence that they deem relevant to the crimes they suspect. Anything beyond the charges they are responding to is a luxury item.

Consequently, if the forensic victimologist requests victim information it may not be immediately available. This should not come as a surprise. However, the mere act of requesting victim information, and explaining why it is important, is in itself a benefit to most investigative efforts.

Once victim information is received, the forensic victimologist must determine whether it comes from a sufficiently reliable source. Is it an objective archive like a security log, or is it a subjective opinion by a coworker? Or is it somewhere in between, containing both objective and subjective information, like an e-mail from the victim written out of anger?

If the forensic victimologist does not receive sufficient victim evidence of sufficient quality, either because it does not exist or it was not gathered, then this is also an important finding with a high degree of relevance to the case. The lack of victim evidence will set limits on what may or may not be inferred.

4. Forensic Examiners Must, Whenever Possible, Visit the Crime Scene

It is highly preferable that any forensic examiner visit the crime scene. The following are examples of the kind of information that may be learned:

- the sights, smells, and sounds of the crime scene, as the victim and the offender may have experienced them;
- spatial relationships within the scene;

- direct observation and experience with potential transfer evidence (vegetation, soil, glass, fibers, and any other material that may have transferred onto the victim or suspects may become evident or may transfer onto the examiner, providing examples of what to look for on victim clothing or in victim vehicles);
- discovery of items of evidence previously missed and subsequently uncollected by investigative efforts, which is far more common than many care to admit, and is one of the most important reasons for visiting the crime scene.

In many cases, it will not be possible for the forensic victimologist to visit the crime scene. This occurs for a variety of practical reasons, including time limitations, budgetary limitations, legal restrictions, the alteration of the scene by forces of nature, or the obliteration of the scene by land or property development. If the forensic victimologist is unable to visit the crime scene for whatever reason, this must be clearly reflected in his or her findings.

It is not disputed that the primary reason for investigating a crime and documenting a crime scene is to provide for later reconstruction and behavioral analysis efforts. Therefore, the inability of the forensic victimologist to visit the scene does not preclude his or her efforts across the board. Competent crime investigation and scene documentation may be sufficient to address the issues in question, or they may not. Each case is different and must be considered separately and carefully with regard to this issue.

5. Forensic Conclusions and Their Basis Must Be Provided in a Written Format

Dr. Hans Gross, a pioneer in criminal investigation and forensic science, referred to the critical role that exact, deliberate, and patient efforts play in the investigation and resolution of crime. Specifically, he stated that just looking at a crime scene and the evidence is not enough. He argued that there is utility in reducing one's opinions to the form of a report in order to identify problems in the logic of one's theories (Gross 1924, 439):

> So long as one only looks on the scene, it is impossible, whatever the care, time, and attention bestowed, to detect all the details, and especially note the incongruities: but these strike us at once when we set ourselves to describe the picture on paper as exactly and clearly as possible....
>
> The "defects of the situation" are just those contradictions, those improbabilities, which occur when one desires to represent the situation as something quite different from what it really is, and

this with the very best intentions and the purest belief that one has worked with all of the forethought, craft, and consideration imaginable.

Moreover, the forensic examiner, not the recipient of the report (i.e., investigators, attorneys, and the court), bears the burden of ensuring that conclusions are effectively communicated. This means writing them down. It also means that the forensic examiner must be competent in intelligible writing, and that reports must be comprehensive with regard to examinations performed, findings, and conclusions.

Verbal conclusions should be viewed as a form of substandard work product. They are susceptible to conversions, alterations, and misrepresentations. They may also become lost to time. Written conclusions are fixed in time, easy to reproduce, and less susceptible to accidental or intentional conversion, alteration, and misrepresentation.

Any forensic examiner who prefers verbal conclusions to written ones reveals a preference for conclusive mobility. Apart from their relative permanence, written conclusions also provide the examiner with the best chance to memorialize methods, conclusions, arguments, and the underlying facts of the case. This includes a list of the evidence examined, when it was examined, and under what circumstances. Generally, a written report should include, but need not be limited to, the following information:

- A preliminary background section, describing the examiner's involvement in the case.
- A section on the chain of custody, describing and detailing the evidence that was examined or included.
- A descriptive section, in which the examiner thoroughly describes the examinations performed (e.g., forensic analysis, victimology, crime scene analysis), with consideration of the facts and evidence.
- A results section, in which the examiner lists any results and conclusions, including their significance and limitations.

The intended users of the end result include detectives, judges, and jurors. The report should be worded so that there is no question in the mind of the reader as to what is being said. If a report cannot be written down in a logical form and easily understood by its intended user, then apart from having no value it is also probably wrong.

Above all else, the written report should not be rendered in such a manner as to leave a false impression in the mind of anyone who might read it—not about what was done, when, how, or what it means. It is the responsibility of the forensic examiner to achieve this level of scientific honesty up front, regardless of what questions may or may not be asked by lawyers at some future date.

6. Forensic Examiners Must Demonstrate an Understanding of Behavioral Science, Forensic Science, and the Scientific Method

Victimology is a multidisciplinary field, based on the principles of the forensic and behavioral sciences. Given the advanced level of knowledge required, it is unclear how a forensic victimologist could perform examinations competently without receiving a baseline of formal education and ongoing training in these areas from non–law enforcement forensic and behavioral scientists.

Consequently, any purported expert in the area of forensic victimology should satisfy the following minimum criteria:

1. At least an undergraduate education in a behavioral science (psychology, sociology, social work, criminology, etc.). Graduate-level education in these areas is preferable. This criterion disqualifies those with undergraduate degrees in unrelated areas such as music, police administration, public administration, and education. It should be noted that there are some online university programs that offer graduate degrees in behavioral science–related areas, without an undergraduate degree requirement, without a thesis requirement, and without actual class time. These programs have limited value to the task of establishing scientific expertise, as they are often designed for professional advancement and résumé enhancement as opposed to imparting research skills and discipline, and facilitating the guided discovery of knowledge and methods.
2. Advanced study, and a working knowledge of the published victimology and criminal profiling literature, covering the areas of behavioral evidence analysis, criminal investigative analysis, and investigative psychology—including the limitations and weaknesses of each.
3. Advanced study and a working knowledge of the published literature in the forensic sciences, specifically those related to evidence analysis and crime reconstruction.
4. Advanced study and a working knowledge of the methods, procedures, and requirements of a criminal investigation.
5. An approach to casework in accordance with objective forensic examination and interpretation, as opposed to a pro–law enforcement mindset.

Having achieved these basic requirements, it is more likely that the forensic examiner will sufficiently appreciate the behavioral sciences, the forensic science, and how they intersect with the scientific method in application to forensic victimology.

7. All Conclusions Must Be Based on Established Facts, Which May Not Be Assumed for the Purpose of Analysis

Many forensic examiners are willing to provide a certain interpretation of offense-related behavior based on experiential comparisons to unnamed cases, factual guesses and assumptions, or nonexistent physical evidence. If the underlying facts have not been established through investigative documentation, crime scene documentation, the examination of physical evidence, or corroborating eyewitness testimony, then any reconstruction of those facts is not a reliable or valid inference of events. This includes hypothetical scenarios.

8. Conclusions Must Be Valid Inferences Based on Logical Arguments and Analytical Reasoning

In the process of establishing the facts that are fit for analysis, facts must be sifted and distinguished from opinions, conjectures, and theories. Inductive hypotheses must further be delineated from deductive conclusions, and conclusions must flow naturally from the facts provided. Furthermore, any opinions or conclusions must be reasonably free from logical fallacies and incorrect statements of fact.

THE SCIENTIFIC METHOD

A strict adherence to and full embrace of the scientific method are the first in a series of steps that can blunt the effects of even the most pervasive forms of bias. Unfortunately, the forensic community as a whole remains uninformed when it comes to defining let alone applying the scientific method. Faigman, Saks, and Sanders (1997, 47) are rather unforgiving but honest when they observe:

> The subject of the scientific method . . . has been described innumerable times, in a multitude of works on manifold subjects, from elementary school textbooks to post-graduate treatises. And yet it remains a subject that is foreign to most lawyers and judges.

Thornton (1997b, 14) goes further and includes most forensic practitioners in the mix of those who do not understand what the scientific method is or how to apply it correctly:

> Those individuals engaged in "scientific" work rarely study the scientific method. To be sure, those engaged

in research are expected to pick up the scientific method somewhere along the way; for the most part scientists don't study the implementation of the scientific method.

On the same subject, Thornton also writes (1997a, 485):

> Many, perhaps even most, forensic scientists are not just inattentive to the scientific method, but ignorant . . . I don't believe that forensic scientists lack the wit to be able to defend their use of the scientific method, but rather that the necessity to do so has not generally been thrust upon them.

The relationship between scientists, the scientific method, and science may be described as follows: Scientists employing the scientific method can work within a particular discipline to help create and build a body of scientific knowledge to the point where its theories become principles and the discipline as a whole eventually becomes a science. The discipline remains a science through the continued building of scientific knowledge, as this is regarded as a process rather than a result.

(Continued)

THE SCIENTIFIC METHOD —CONT'D

Scientific knowledge is any knowledge, enlightenment, or awareness that comes from examining events or problems through the lens of the scientific method. The accumulation of scientific knowledge in a particular subject or discipline leads to its development as a science. The classic definition of a science, as provided by Thornton (1997b, 12), is "an orderly body of knowledge with principles that are clearly enunciated," as well as being reality-oriented with conclusions susceptible to testing.

A strong caution is needed here. The use of statistics does not make something scientific. The use of a computer does not make something scientific. The use of chemicals does not make something scientific. The use of technology does not make something scientific. Wearing a lab coat does not make one's conclusions scientific.

Science is found in the interpretations, or inferences, made by the scientific examiner. The question is this: was the scientific method used to synthesize the knowledge at hand, and has that knowledge been applied correctly to render subsequent interpretations, with the necessary humility? If forensic examiners are not scientific in their methods of examination, then it does not matter how many books, research studies, or agreeable colleagues they are able to cite in defense of their positions.

The scientific method is a way to investigate how or why something works, or how something happened, through the development of hypotheses and subsequent attempts at falsification via testing and other accepted means. It is a structured process designed to build scientific knowledge by way of answering specific questions about observations through careful analysis and critical thinking. Observations are used to form testable hypotheses, and with sufficient testing hypotheses can become scientific theories. Eventually, over much time, with precise testing marked by a failure to falsify, scientific theories can become scientific principles. The scientific method is the particular approach to knowledge building and problem solving employed by scientists of every kind.

The first step in the scientific method is observation. An observation is made regarding some event, fact, or object. This observation then leads to a specific question regarding the event, fact, or object, such as where or when an object originated or how an object came to possess certain traits.

The second step in the scientific method is attempting to answer the question that has been asked by forming a hypothesis, or an educated estimate, regarding the possible answer. Often, there is more than one possible answer. These must be developed and investigated.

The third step in the scientific method is experimentation. Of all the steps in the scientific method, this is the one that separates scientific inquiry from others. Scientific analysts design experiments intended to disprove their hypotheses. Once again, *scientific analysts design experiments intended to disprove their hypotheses, not to prove them.*

Inferences regarding crime-related actions or events are not intended to verify, confirm, or prove investigative theories. Rather, they are meant to support or refute investigative theories. The terms *support* and *confirm* are worlds apart. One suggests assistance and the other finality. This difference may sound semantic to some, but it is not. If the job of the forensic examiner were merely to work toward confirming law enforcement theories, then there would be no point in performing an in-depth analysis of any offense or related behavior. Confirmation is easy to find if that is what one looks for—all one needs to do is ignore everything that works against a prevailing theory and embrace anything that even remotely supports it. But that is not what the scientific method is about. The absolute cornerstone of the scientific method is falsification.

If a hypothesis remains standing after a succession of tests or experiments fails to disprove it, then it may become a scientific theory, which may be stated or presented with a reasonable degree of scientific certainty.

Scientific theories that withstand the test of time and study eventually become scientific principles. Although there is no universal agreement as to whether and when a scientific theory crosses this line to become a scientific principle, it is accepted that a scientific theory, developed with the assistance of the scientific method, has a greater degree of reliability and acceptance than mere observation, intuition, or speculation.

The correct use of the scientific method is impossible without critical thinking and the science of logic to accurately synthesize, interpret, and apply the results.

9. Conclusions Must Be Reached with the Assistance of the Scientific Method

The scientific method demands that careful observations of the evidence be made, and then hypotheses generated and ultimately tested against all of the known evidence and accepted facts. Subsequently, the forensic examiner must provide not just conclusions but all other postulated theories that have been falsified through examinations, tests, and experiments. Falsification, not validation, is the cornerstone of the scientific method. Theories that have not been put to any test or that appear in a report or in courtroom testimony based on rumination and imagination alone (i.e., experience and intuition) should not be considered inherently valid or reliable.

10. Conclusions Must Demonstrate an Understanding of, and Clearly Distinguish between, Individuating Findings and All Others

The concept of identification and individuation is often misunderstood. *Identification* (or *classification*) is the placement of any item into a specific category of items with similar characteristics. Identification does not require or imply uniqueness. *Individuation* is the assignment of uniqueness to an item. To individuate an item, it must be described in such a manner as to separate it from all other items in the universe (Thornton 1997b, 7).

In the presentation of findings, forensic examiners will find themselves using statements that suggest varying degrees of confidence. Vague terms or terms of art, such as *probably, likely, identify, match, consistent with,* and *reasonable degree of scientific certainty,* are among those used to qualify the certainty of findings. Unchecked, this language can be misleading to those it is intended to assist. Confidence statements must be qualified and discussed to the point of absolute clarity.

Without clarification, findings may be misunderstood, misrepresented, and misapplied. When the forensic examiner has given findings, there must remain no question as to whether the findings are individuating and no question as to how this was determined.

If the forensic examiner provides individuating findings of any sort, the nature of the uniqueness and how it was established must be clearly presented. The purpose of presenting findings is to clarify the evidence, not to muddle it.

11. Forensic Examiners Must Demonstrate an Understanding of the Conditions of Transfer (Locard's Exchange Principle and Evidence Dynamics)

It is important to establish the source of any physical evidence relied upon and the conditions under which it was transferred to where it was ultimately found. Forensic examiners must avoid being quick to oversimplify complex issues, such as the examination and interpretation of physical evidence, or to disregard those circumstances that can move, alter, or obliterate that evidence. (These concepts will be discussed further in the next chapter.)

12. Any Evidence, Data, or Findings on Which Conclusions Are Based Must Be Made Available through Presentation or Citation

It is not acceptable for the forensic examiner to provide conclusions based on phantom databases, phantom data, phantom research, phantom evidence, or unseen comparisons. Data, research, and evidence must be detailed to the point where others reviewing the work may easily locate or identify them, in the same way we cite the endeavors of others in written work. Data, research, and evidence that cannot be duplicated or identified by the court in some fashion should not find their way into forensic conclusions.

These minimum practice standards should be applied to the evaluation of any method of forensic examination, both the general and the specialized, in order to show due diligence. If a forensic examiner is able to meet these standards, then a minimum threshold level of professional competency has indeed been achieved. Subsequently, the recipients of the conclusions may be assured that whatever the findings, they can be independently investigated and reviewed for reliability, accuracy, and validity. It bears pointing out that forensic examiners who fail to climb even one of the rungs prescribed will not have reached this threshold. In failing, their findings should be questioned and their subsequent reports and testimony viewed with disfavor.

It is important to clarify that these practice standards do not leave anyone behind, but they do require everyone to show their work. Forensic examinations are not easy and must not be rote. Conclusions must be earned, and that means competency must be demonstrated and peer review embraced. Each forensic examiner has a duty to formulate conclusions with the full reach of everything that forensic science, the scientific method, and analytical logic have to offer. Without these tools, forensic examiners are at risk of not being able to recognize forensic and methodological illiteracy in themselves or others.

These practice standards may also raise the ire of some forensic examiners who have been doing their work based on intuition and experience, perhaps for years, and are unaccustomed to explaining themselves or their methods apart from stating their alleged vast experience. If peer review and criticism are not welcome at a conclusion's doorstep, and instead such visitors are met with hostility and derision, then something other than competency dwells within. To be clearer, the absence of the scientific method and logical inference in any behavioral analysis should not be a point of pride, because it is ultimately evidence of ignorance. Any forensic examination conducted in the absence of the scientific method, analytical logic, and critical thinking is called a guess. The justice system is no place for ignorance or guessing. Consequently, it is not unreasonable to expect that anyone interpreting evidence in such a manner be prepared to explain why.

VICTIMOLOGY: GENERAL GUIDELINES

In terms of what is required for a thorough victimology, the national guidelines *Death Investigation* the National Institute of Justice (NIJ), Section E, "Establishing and Recording Decedent Profile Information," is a good place to start. However, I do not recommend that readers confine themselves to any single victimology checklist. Rather, a victimologist should treat nothing about a victim as trivial. This means analyzing each characteristic that presents itself until it is an exhausted possibility, to see how it relates to the rest of the victim information.

Weston and Wells (1974, 97) provide a quick checklist of preliminary victimological queries that have proven to be most useful in eliciting investigative information. This is the kind of information that should be gathered immediately, ideally before the investigator arrives at a given crime scene:

1. Did the victim know the perpetrator?
2. Does the victim suspect any person? Why?
3. Has the victim a history of crime? A history of reporting crimes?
4. Did the victim have a weapon?
5. Has the victim an aggressive personality?
6. Has the victim been the subject of any field [police] reports?

The following are some basic victimological inquiries that I have found useful when applied to actual casework. Gathering this information, along with the careful examination of physical evidence, provides the starting point for investigative activity. Again, no one checklist can suffice; the victimologist must be willing to sift through each victim's history carefully, with no preconceived theories. This list is inclusive of items found in the National Institute of Justice (1999):

1. Determine the victim's hard physical characteristics (race, weight, height, hair color, eye color, etc.).
2. Determine the victim's occupation or place of work, and shift schedule.
3. Compile the victim's criminal history.
4. Compile a list of the victim's daily routines, habits, and activities.

5. Compile a complete list of victim family members with contact information. Interview each of them.
6. Compile a complete list of victim friends with contact information. Interview each of them.
7. Compile a complete list of victim coworkers with contact information. Interview each of them.
8. Compile the victim's medical history.
9. Compile the victim's psychiatric history—interview all of the victim's mental health care providers.
10. Compile a list of the victim's medications. Compare this with known victim toxicology.
11. Compile the victim's financial history (credit card usage, tax returns, insurance policies, etc.).
12. Compile the victim's educational history.
13. Compile a residence history of the victim (where he or she has lived, when, and with whom, etc.).
14. Spend time, when possible, with the victim's personal items, in the personal environments (hangouts, work, school, home/bedroom, etc.). Examine any available photo albums, diaries, or journals. Make note of music and literature preferences. Do this to find out who victims seemed to believe they were, what they wanted everyone to perceive, and how they seemed to feel about their life in general.
15. Compile all available information regarding the victim's mobile phone, computer, and Internet usage. When available, at least the following should be attempted:
    - Determine the victim's service providers
    - Determine the victim's e-mail addresses
    - Examine the victim's address books or contact databases
    - Examine the victim's incoming and outgoing e-mail
    - Examine all documents on the victim's computer
    - Determine the last known usage of the victim's computer and various software applications
16. Create a timeline of the victim's last known activities, factoring in all witness statements and physical evidence.
17. Travel the last known route taken by the victim in whatever manner the victim used. Try to see that route from the victim's perspective and then from the potential perspective of the offender. Keep these perspectives separate.
18. Look for security video cameras along the victim's route, or potential route, that may have documented the victim's activities or even the actual crime.

CREATING A TIMELINE: THE LAST 24 HOURS

Retracing a victim's last known actions and creating a timeline are critical to understanding the victim as a person, understanding the victim's relationship to the environment, understanding the victim's relationship to other events, and understanding how the victim came to be acquired by an offender.

The general purpose here is to familiarize the forensic victimologist with the last known activities of the victim and subsequently determine, if possible, how a given victim got to a place and time where an offender was able to access him or her. This picture needs to be built from the ground up. It is a rewarding and illuminating process that should not to be overlooked.

A good approach to creating this timeline of locations and events includes at least the following steps:

- Compile all available forensic and factual data.
- Compile all of the crime scene photographs.
- Compile all witness data.
- Create a linear timeline of events and locations.
- Create a map of the victim's route for the 24 hours before the attack, as detailed as possible.
- Physically walk through the victim's last 24 hours using the map and forensic evidence as a guide.
- Document expected background elements of the route in terms of vehicles, people, activities, professionals, and so on for the time leading up to, during, and after the victim was acquired. It is possible that the offender is, or was masquerading as, one of those expected elements.

Attempt to determine the following:

- The point at which the offender acquired the victim.
- The place where the offender attacked the victim.
- How well the attack location can be seen from any surrounding locations.
- Whether or not the offender would need to be familiar with the area to know of this specific location or get to it.
- Whether or not the acquisition of the victim was dependent on some sort of routine or schedule and who could be aware of that schedule.
- Whether or not knowledge of the route would require or indicate presurveillance.
- Whether or not this route placed the victim at higher or lower exposure to an attack.
- Whether or not the acquisition of the victim on that route placed the offender at higher or lower exposure to identification or apprehension.

Investigate the Obvious

It is important to investigate the obvious. Offenders of any kind may know, be acquainted with, or have some type of uninvestigated connection with their victims. These connections exist far more often than we have been led to believe by the published research, especially in the first crimes committed by an offender. Investigate the obvious connections between all victims and potential suspects. Proceed by questioning all investigative assumptions related to the established victimology when first presented with the facts of any case. If a fact cannot be established, then it should not be assumed.

SUMMARY

Forensic victimology is concerned with the investigation and examination of particular victims alleged to have suffered specific crimes, which is an idiographic form of knowledge building. It is intended to serve both investigative and forensic goals, which are very different in scope and reliability with respect to findings. In order to reduce bias and achieve a minimum threshold of reliability, the forensic victimologist must request a sufficient amount of victim information, determine its reliability, and perform examinations in accordance with the practice standards provided. A key feature of this is an applied understanding of the scientific method and an emphasis on theory falsification.

Questions

1. Describe the goals of nomothetic as well as idiographic research.
2. What can nomothetic research best be used for when constructing a victim profile?
3. The vast majority of victim research is concerned primarily with or based primarily on _____ (idiographic/nomothetic) study.
4. What are practice standards?
5. True or False: Physical evidence cannot be wrong. It is the interpretation of this evidence that may err due to ignorance, imprecision, or bias on the part of the examiner.
6. Describe the difference between observer bias and confirmation bias.
7. Name and explain five practice standards for forensic victimologists outlined in this chapter.
8. Why are verbal conclusions viewed as a form of substandard work product?
9. What are the steps of the scientific method?
10. Describe five basic victimological inquiries that should be made in a forensic victimology.

REFERENCES

DeForest, P.R. 2005. "Crime Scene Investigation." In *Encyclopedia of Law Enforcement*, edited by L.E. Sullivan and M.S. Rosen, 111–116. New York: Sage Publications.

Faigman, D., D. Kaye, M. Saks, and J. Sanders, eds. 1997. *Modern Scientific Evidence: The Law and Science of Expert Testimony*, vol. 1. St. Paul, MN: West Publishing.

Gross, H. 1924. *Criminal Investigation*. London: Sweet and Maxwell.

Kirk, P., and J. Thornton. 1970. *Crime Investigation*, 2nd ed. New York: John Wiley and Sons.

Meloy, J.R. 1998. "The Psychology of Stalking." In *The Psychology of Stalking: Clinical and Forensic Perspectives*, edited by J.R. Meloy. London: Academic Press.

Moxley, R.S. 2006. "Great dick, babe: Gang rape or orgy? Let's go to the video." *Orange County Weekly*, February 9.

National Institute of Justice (NIJ). 1999. *Death Investigation: A Guide for the Scene Investigator*. Research Report NCJ 167568. Washington, DC: NIJ.

"O.C. woman who lied about rape gets time in jail." 2006. *CBS2.com News*, November 9. http://cbs2.com/local/Dana.Point.Men.2.524133.html.

———. 1997b. "The General Assumptions and Rationale of Forensic Identification." In *Modern Scientific Evidence: The Law and Science of Expert Testimony*, vol. 2, edited by D. Faigman, D. Kaye, M. Saks, and J. Sanders, . St. Paul, MN: West Publishing.

Turvey, B. 2008. *Criminal Profiling*, 3rd ed. Boston: Elsevier Science.

von Hentig, H. 1948. *The Criminal and His Victim: Studies in the Sociobiology of Crime*. New Haven: Yale University Press.

Weston, P., and K. Wells. 1974. *Criminal Investigation: Basic Perspectives*, 2nd ed. Englewood Cliffs, NJ: Prentice-Hall.

CHAPTER 4

Forensic Nursing: Approaching the Victim as a Crime Scene

Charla M. Jamerson

KEY TERMS

- *Colposcope:* a lighted magnifying instrument used by a gynecologist to examine the tissues of the vagina and the cervix.
- *Colposcopy:* the process of using a colposcope during a vaginal and cervical examination.
- *Contact dermatitis:* a reaction caused by the skin coming into contact with allergens or irritants (e.g., poison ivy, poison oak, and poison sumac).
- *Differential diagnosis:* the possibility that there is more than one cause of any set of injuries, conditions, or symptoms presented by a patient.
- *Forensic medical examination:* the entire examination performed by the forensic examiner, including initial contact, intake assessment, obtaining victim history, physical examination, evidence documentation and collection, and the interpretation of findings, including any related treatment.
- *Forensic nursing:* a subspecialty of forensic science and nursing where the science of nursing is applied to the resolution of legal matters.
- *Locard's Exchange Principle:* when there is contact between two objects there will be an exchange of microscopic material.
- *Medical history:* information about a patient gathered by a health care professional for the purposes of making examinations, providing treatment, and rendering a diagnosis.
- *Negative documentation:* recording of areas of the body where there is no evidence of defect, disease, injury, or potential transfer.
- *Physical examination:* the act of examination of the body by auscultation, palpation, percussion, inspection, and smelling. Also includes the act of investigating the victim and his or her clothing for signs of defect, disease, injury, and potential transfer evidence from a location, weapon, or suspect.
- *Seborrhea* (also *seborrheic dermatitis):* a condition commonly known as dandruff, which can present with rashes that itch intensely and become infected due to breaks in the skin.

CONTENTS

Urethral meatus: the urethra is a tube leading from the bladder that discharges urine outside of the body. In females the urethra is significantly shorter than in males, and the female urethral meatus (or opening) is above the vaginal opening.

Forensic nursing is a subspecialty of forensic science and nursing where the science of nursing is applied to the resolution of legal matters. It involves patient care in the context of evidence documentation, collection, and preservation efforts. Consequently, *forensic nurses* are registered nurses with additional education and training in forensic science and evidence collection. As explained in Nelson (1998):

> The term forensic nursing was officially coined in 1992 when about 70 nurses gathered in Minneapolis for what was billed as the first national convention for sexual assault nurses. It was thrilling to meet with others doing the same work and enlightening to learn about the issues they were grappling with, [Patty Seneski, ENP, RN, president of the International Association of Forensic Nurses (IAFN)] said. That led to the founding of the IAFN.
>
> Six years later, the New Jersey-based group has 1,500 members, who practice in diverse fields. They range from sexual assault nurse examiners (SANEs)—often an entry point into forensic nursing—to nurses who specialize in such areas as domestic violence, child and elder abuse, and emergency trauma. Forensic nurses may also serve as legal nurse consultants or attorneys, Seneski said.
>
> Forensic nurses' responsibilities vary. For example, they may perform death investigations, work with criminals in prison, or counsel schoolchildren who fire guns, said Seneski, a SANE who works in emergency nursing and does consulting.

Under typical circumstances, a forensic nurse will have only one opportunity to examine a patient, an alleged victim. Often this will occur while law enforcement investigators are waiting in the hallway. Additionally, the more time that passes before the examination, the more likely evidence will be lost or biologically degraded. These circumstances and constraints can put considerable pressure on even the most experienced professionals.

The purpose of this chapter is to discuss the roles and responsibilities of forensic nurses, as well as the rationale behind their methods. At the outset, they are required to understand that the victim's body is a crime scene, that victimity must be established and not assumed, and that time is a limiting factor. In the context of forensic victimology, their work also involves understanding the need to develop an appreciation for thoroughness and attention to detail in all aspects of the *forensic medical examination.*

This chapter was not written for the advanced forensic nurse practitioner. However, it is a good place to start for those just entering the profession.[1] It is one professional's primer to the field. It is also written for those professionals who need a basic understanding of what forensic nurses do, and how and why.

ROLES AND RESPONSIBILITIES

The role of the forensic nurse is to function as an objective and scientific finder of fact; to utilize scientific principles and methodology in the recognition, documentation, collection, and interpretation of physical evidence related to diseases, injuries, and crimes that may be suffered by all manner of victims. In doing so, the forensic nurse operates with the understanding that those examined in a forensic context are the potential extension of a crime scene. Subsequently, the forensic nurse must serve as a forensic investigator; as an educator to victims and the community; and as an expert witness within the legal system.

Registered nurses wishing to practice forensic nursing are generally required to obtain specialty training and certification. This training includes theoretical instruction as well as a clinical component that allow them to work with an experienced forensic nurse on the front lines, examining and providing care for crime victims. The importance of this specialty training, as well as continuing education in the specific area of practice, cannot be emphasized enough. It is critical to have both a solid theoretical and clinical background, as it is this foundation that prepares the forensic nurse to understand and appropriately deal with the victim's body as a crime scene.

Because time, the environment, and individual body chemistry all conspire to degrade the physical evidence, the sooner that a forensic examination can be performed on the victim the better. In fact, most jurisdictions allow no more than 72 hours between the alleged crime and any evidence collection efforts performed. Consequently, forensic nurses must be available to work when crime occurs and to respond to a case within approximately an hour. This means being on call essentially 24 hours a day, 7 days a week. Occasionally there will be extenuating circumstances—such as a victim being held in captivity by a perpetrator or delayed reporting under some circumstances—that make a longer interval between crime and examination acceptable. These time constraints vary from state to state and are often determined by the state office of the attorney general.

These concerns are echoed in the National Institute of Justice (NIJ) published guidelines, *A National Protocol for Sexual Assault Medical Forensic Examinations* (2004, 67), which offers the following recommendations regarding evidence collection and its context:

[1] For a complete guide and practice standards, see NIJ (2004).

Recognize the importance of gathering information for the medical forensic history, examining patients, and documenting exam findings, separate from collecting evidence. Examiners should obtain the medical forensic history as appropriate, examine patients, and document findings when patients are willing, whether or not evidence is gathered for the sexual assault evidence collection kit. The history and documentation of exam findings can help in determining if and where there may be evidence to collect and in addressing patients' medical needs. In addition, they can be invaluable in and of themselves to an investigation and prosecution if a report is made. It is also important to document patients' demeanor during the exam process (e.g., crying, shaking, or showing signs of upset) and their statements made related to the assault, because if the case is reported, this information could be admitted as evidence at trial.

Examine patients promptly to minimize the loss of evidence. Evidence can be lost from the body and clothing through a number of mechanisms. For example, degradation of some seminal fluid components can occur within body orifices, semen can drain from the vagina or wash from the mouth, sperm can lose motility, bodily fluids can get washed away, and dried secretions and foreign materials can fall from the body and clothing. Prompt examination also helps to quickly identify patients' medical needs and concerns.

Recognize that evidence may be available beyond 72 hours after the assault. In recent history, 72 hours after a sexual assault has been considered a guideline to use as an outside limit for obtaining evidence for the evidence collection kit. Research and evidence analyses indicate that some evidence may be available beyond this time period. For instance, sperm might be found inside the cervix after 72 hours and urine may reveal traces of certain drugs up to 96 hours after ingestion. Some examples of situations where evidence may be found even after considerable periods of time include when patients complain of pain or bleeding, have visible injuries, or have not washed themselves since the assault, or where there is a history of significant trauma from the assault. Some jurisdictions have extended their standard cutoff time beyond 72 hours (e.g., to 5 days or 1 week).

Due to the stability of DNA and sensitivity of tests, advancing DNA technologies also continue to extend time limits. These technologies are even enabling forensic scientists to analyze stored evidence from crimes that occurred years before. Such breakthroughs demonstrate the importance of collecting all possible evidence.

As suggested, forensic nurses are often a "frontline" professional with respect to making victim contact subsequent to the commission of a violent crime. This is primarily because of how victims enter the justice system. In many cases, victims will report their assault directly to the police. Or they may show up at a local emergency room or medical clinic seeking treatment for their injuries. When law enforcement is involved at the outset, it will take an initial report from victims and then immediately refer them to a clinic or hospital emergency room that performs forensic examinations.

Bear in mind that not every situation is the same, not all victims are able to move under their own power, and each department may have its own policies and procedures to follow. So not everyone arrives at their forensic examination the same way. Subsequent to their initial report to law enforcement or presentation to medical personnel, some victims are transported by the police or emergency medical services; some are transported by friends and family; and some drive themselves.

Once the report to the police has been made and the alleged victim arrives, the forensic nurse should begin the examination. It starts with obtaining consents, biographical intake information, a medical history, and finally a history of events leading up to and surrounding the crime.

CONSENT FORMS

Once the patient arrives at the exam location and the forensic nurse has made his or her introductions, along with any additional staff that may be assisting, it is necessary to obtain the patient's informed consent. Forensic examiners are best off if they begin by explaining the entire forensic medical examination procedure, along with the necessity of evidence collection, to patients, no matter what their age. This will empower patients, involve them in the process, and give them an opportunity to think of and ask questions.

Consent to treat must be obtained before any evidence collection or treatment takes place. This is in keeping with the NIJ (2004, 4), which stipulates:

> Prior to starting the exam and before each procedure, describe what is entailed and its purpose to patients. Be sure that communication/language needs are met and information is conveyed in a manner that patients will understand. After providing this information, seek patients' permission to proceed and respect their right to decline any part of the exam. However, follow exam facility and jurisdictional policy regarding minors and adults who are incompetent to give consent. . . .

Patients should understand the full nature of their consent to each exam procedure. By presenting them with relevant information, they are in a position to make an informed decision about whether to accept or decline a procedure. However, they should be aware of the impact of declining a particular procedure, as it may negatively affect the quality of care, the usefulness of evidence collection, and, ultimately, any criminal investigation and/or prosecution. They should understand that declining a particular procedure might also be used to discredit them in court. If a procedure is declined, reasons why should be documented if the patient provides such information.

Consent forms may vary from one institution to another, but often include consent to conduct a forensic medical examination, including the collection of evidence, urine specimen with drug testing as needed, collection of blood for lab work as needed, use of a colposcope to assist with injury identification, forensic photography (colposcope and digital photography), use of recording equipment, and consent for emergency contraception. If the victim is a minor, then the parent or guardian will need to sign in his or her place.

This is a good time to take stock of the fact that not every victim will react the same way to the procedures involved in the forensic medical exam, let alone the prospect. As explained in the NIJ (2004, 28), victims' perceptions and reactions may be influenced by a variety of circumstances:

Recognize that the medical forensic exam is an interactive process that must be adapted to the needs and circumstances of each patient. Patients' experiences during the crime and the exam process, as well as their postassault needs, may be affected by multiple factors, such as:

- Age;
- Gender and/or gender identity;
- Physical health history and current status;
- Mental health history and current status;
- Disability;
- Language needs and communication modalities;
- Ethnic and cultural beliefs and practices;
- Religious and spiritual beliefs and practices;
- Economic status, including homelessness;
- Immigration and refugee status;
- Sexual orientation;
- Military status;
- History of previous victimization;
- Past experience with the criminal justice system;
- Whether the assault involved drugs and/or alcohol;
- Prior relationship with the suspect, if any;

JAMERSON
Forensic Nursing &
Investigative Services, Inc.

Patient: _____   **Case:** _____

Date: _____   **Age:** _____

1. I hereby authorize Charla Jamerson, BSN, RN, BC, SANE-A, CMI III, Erin Morin, RN, SANE Nurse, Andrea Hudson, RN and/or Alieca Sipes, RN to perform upon _____ the following special procedure: Forensic Sexual Assault Medical Examination with colposcope.

2. I have been completely informed as to and understand the nature and purpose of these procedures: if needed the possible methods of treatment prescribed and risks and hazards involved. I acknowledge that no guarantee or assurance has been made as to the results obtained, and I have knowingly and voluntarily consented to these procedures.

3. I certify that I have read and fully understand this consent; that the explanations referred to were actually made; that I consent to the above services.

_____   _____

Signature of person legally   **Date**
authorized to consent for a minor

_____   _____

Witness Signature   **Date**

FIGURE 4.1

Consent to conduct forensic medical exam with colposcope; form developed by the author and used at Jamerson Forensic Nursing and Investigative Services, Inc.

JAMERSON
Forensic Nursing &
Investigative Services, Inc.

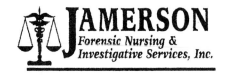

Case #______

CONSENT FOR URINE SPECIMEN COLLECTION

I, ______________________________________, give my consent for Jamerson Forensic Nursing & Investigative Services, Inc. to collect a urine specimen for the purpose of a forensic assessment and investigative information. The purposes may include but are not limited to:

1. **Urine Drug Screen**
2. **Rohypnol and/or GHB screening**
3. **Urinalysis**
4. **ABS 5**
5. **ABS 10**
6. **Any other tests deemed forensically/medically necessary for the purpose of health promotion and/or investigation.**

____ ________________

Signature **Date**

____ ________________

Witness signature **Date**

FIGURE 4.2

Consent to collect urine specimen; form developed by the author and used at Jamerson Forensic Nursing and Investigative Services, Inc.

I, _____, GIVE consent at this time to having Plan B administered to

_____ for the purpose of pregnancy prophylaxis. I have
<u>(Patient Name)</u>
received information on the uses of Plan B as well as the side effects associated with

Plan B.

_____   _____
      Signature   Date

_____   _____
      Signature   Date

I, _____, DECLINE consent at this time to having Plan B administered
to _____ for the purpose of pregnancy prophylaxis. I have received
information on the uses of Plan B as well as the side effects associated with Plan B.

_____   _____
Signature   Date

_____   _____
Witness   Date

FIGURE 4.3

Consent to administer Plan B, emergency contraception taken no more than three days after unprotected sex, which reduces chance of pregnancy by 89 percent; form developed by the author and used at Jamerson Forensic Nursing and Investigative Services, Inc.

I, _____, give my consent for Charla M. Jamerson, BSN, RN, BC, SANE-A, CMI III, Erin Morin, RN, SANE nurse, Andrea Hudson, RN, and/or Alieca Sipes, RN, to conduct a forensic interview. I further understand that I may withdraw my consent at any time for any portion of the remaining interview.

_____
Initials and Signature

Conditions:

1. I understand that this forensic interview is being performed for the purpose of evidentiary information that may be relevant to the case.

_____
Initials and Signature

2. Compact disks, video tapes, and audio recording tapes will be taken during the forensic interview. These can be used for legal purposes if the need arises.

_____
Initials and Signature

3. I understand that the compact disks, video tapes, and audio recording tapes may be used for educational purposes and if so the identity will remain confidential.

_____
Initials and Signature

4. I understand that the forensic interview compact disks, video tapes, and audio recordings will be released to the appropriate agencies, which may include but is not limited to law enforcement.

_____
Initials and Signature

I HEREBY RELEASE JFN AND ITS OWNERS AND EMPLOYEES FROM ANY LIABILITY THAT MAY RESULT FROM THE RELEASE OF THE INFORMATION.

FIGURE 4.4

Consent to conduct forensic interview; form developed by the author and used at Jamerson Forensic Nursing and Investigative Services, Inc.

Statement of Understanding Regarding Videotapes, Records, and Billing

Child: _____

Birth date: _____   Case: _____

    I understand that Jamerson Forensic Nursing may make DVD recordings and audio recordings of child(ren) who is are identified subjects of this document.

    I understand that Jamerson Forensic Nursing will provide the DVD recording and the audio recordings produced in association with any forensic interview and/or medical examination to governmental agencies that are required by law to act in connections with allegedly abused children related to criminal or civil investigations.

    I understand that I have no right to request a copy of the full detailed statement, to view the DVD/audio recordings, or the medical records without the consent and signed release of the appropriate investigative agencies. I agree to accept a verbal summary of the child's interview and/or medical examination in lieu of inspection of the actual DVD recordings or the medical records.

    I understand that Jamerson Forensic Nursing is legally obligated to report suspected child abuse to the Child Abuse Hotline even if I do not give permission.

    It is my understanding that this these child(ren) is are being served by Jamerson Forensic Nursing staff and I further understand that the medical records and the DVD/audio recordings o produced may be used for the Jamerson Forensic Nursing professional training and in house educational programs, research, as well as legal purposes.

    I understand that the protection of my privacy is an important goal of Jamerson Forensic Nursing and that its staff will make every effort to ensure such privacy, including the distorting of facial features and deletion of names.

    I understand that Jamerson Forensic Nursing will make every effort possible to arrange for the Crime Victim's Reparations Fund to pay for bills arising from medical examinations performed at Jamerson Forensic Nursing; however, this in no way obligates Jamerson Forensic Nursing to guarantee the payment of such bills.

Signature of Legal Guardian: _____ Date: _____

Witness: _____ Date: _____

FIGURE 4.5

Statement of Understanding Regarding Videotapes, Records, and Billing; form developed by the author and used at Jamerson Forensic Nursing and Investigative Services, Inc.

- Whether they were assaulted by an assailant who was in an authority position over them;
- Whether the assault was part of a broader continuum of violence and/or oppression (e.g., intimate partner and family violence, gang violence, hate crimes, war crimes, and trafficking);
- Where the assault occurred;
- Whether they sustained physical injuries from the assault and the severity of the injuries;
- Whether they were engaged in illegal activities at the time of the assault (e.g., voluntary use of illegal drugs or underage drinking) or have outstanding criminal charges;
- Whether they were involved in activities prior to the assault that traditionally generate victim blaming or self-blaming (e.g., drinking alcohol prior to the assault or agreeing to go to the assailant's home);
- Whether birth control was used during the assault (e.g., victims may already have been on a form of birth control or the assailant may have used a condom);
- Capacity to cope with trauma and the level of support available from families and friends;
- The importance they place on the needs of their extended families in the aftermath of the assault;
- Whether they have dependents who require care during the exam, were traumatized by the assault, or who may be affected by decisions patients make during the exam process;
- Community/cultural attitudes about sexual assault, its victims, and offenders; and
- Frequency of sexual assault and other violence in the community and historical responsiveness of the local justice system, health care systems, and community service agencies.

Forensic nurses and other assisting staff are admonished to be sensitive about these factors in the process of obtaining consent, as well as during the exam itself. A judgmental, coercive, or inflexible approach is not advised, nor is it professional.

THE INTAKE FORM

The intake form establishes the informational foundation upon which to start prioritizing different aspects of an eventual forensic medical exam. It also acts as a valuable face sheet, giving case basics at a glance for future reference. Intake information includes biographical data about the patient, those involved in the case, and a thumbnail sketch of the crime and the alleged perpetrator. Additional in-depth information is gathered during the forensic interview process or during the medicolegal examination.

Specifically, the intake form establishes the following baseline information:

1. The time and date of the exam.
2. The name of the forensic nurse examiner and anyone who assisted.
3. The patient's name and other identifying information.
4. How to reach the patient if needed, including contact numbers and mailing address.
5. The patient's family and/or guardian information.
6. The patient's insurance information.
7. Date of referral and referral source (hospital, clinic, law enforcement, department of health, etc.).
8. Collaborating law enforcement agencies responsible for investigating the case.
9. Suspect information; this may or may not be available.
10. Brief history of sexual assault exams; some victims receive more than one medical examination related to their injuries, the forensic medical exam being secondary.

It is also necessary that the intake form document the name of the person providing the patient's history to the examiner, and his or her relationship to the patient (such as a mother or father if the patient is a minor). With this information documented, anyone reviewing the file at a later time will be aware of whether the history came directly from the victim. This may go to the credibility of the information provided at some later date.

These guidelines are consistent with the NIJ (2004, 77–78), which offers the following guidelines relating to patient intake:

> **Respond to acute injury, trauma care, and safety needs before collecting evidence.** In addition to promoting physical health, sensitive and timely medical care can help reduce the likelihood of acute psychological trauma and its aftereffects, support patients' existing and emerging coping skills, and set the tone for patients' resumption of normal functioning.
>
> Acute medical needs take precedence over forensic needs. Patients should be instructed to not wash, change clothes, urinate, defecate, smoke, drink, or eat until initially evaluated by examiners, unless necessary for treating acute medical injuries. If drug-facilitated sexual assault is suspected, and patients need to urinate prior to the arrival of examiners, ensure that the urine sample is collected properly while maintaining the chain of custody.
>
> As soon as possible after the initial medical evaluation, management, and stabilization of acute problems and before treating nonacute injuries, the medical forensic exam can be conducted (with patients'

permission). In circumstances in which patients are seriously injured, examiners must be prepared to work alongside other health care providers who are stabilizing and treating them. In such cases, examiners may need to perform exams in settings such as a health care facility's emergency department, an operating room, a recovery room, or an intensive care unit....

Assess safety needs upon arrival of the patient at the exam site. The facility should have procedures to assess safety concerns at the exam site, such as a threat to patients or staff, and to respond to such threats or dangerous situations....

Assess patients' needs for immediate medical or mental health intervention prior to the medical forensic exam, following facility policy. Seek informed consent of patients before providing treatment.... Also, inform them that they have a right to receive medical care regardless of whether the assault is reported to law enforcement, and if and how their reporting decision will affect payment for medical care and exam.

Figure 4.6 is an intake form that can be helpful in establishing baseline data and for starting the evidentiary process.

If the information on this form seems overly basic, that's because it is intended to be. It is precisely the kind of information that is easily misplaced or forgotten, and can result in hours of wasted time when needed but missing at some later point. Getting this information down up front saves time and effort, and limits confusion.

There is flexibility in the sequence that historical information may be gathered, but a good place to start after the initial intake information is with the Review of Systems (ROS). As argued in Billings and Stoeckle (1999), the purpose and clinical importance of the ROS protocol is to screen for potential disease processes that have not as yet been discovered. Furthermore, and from a forensic perspective, it's an excellent filter that keys the examiner in to important areas that may need further investigation. Patients are well known for failing to report everything, and forgetting to mention even vital details of their medical history. Because the ROS goes over each area of anatomy, it may remind them about current conditions or past ailments. It may even help them recall details involving specific areas of their bodies related to the assault. It is also a formal mechanism that allows the forensic examiner to probe for more information.

When eliciting information during the ROS, it is most useful to start with general questions and then move towards the specific. This helps to get the patient focused on thinking about their health. Initial questions might include "How

JAMERSON
Forensic Nursing &
Investigative Services, Inc.

Case # _____

Date of Exam _____ Time of Exam _____

Forensic Nurse Examiner_____

Assistant(s) _____

Collaborating Physician _____

Client's Name _____

Client's Address _____

Race _____ DOB _____ SS# _____

Home Phone # _____ Cell # _____ Pager # _____

Bio-Mom Name _____ Bio-Dad Name _____

Legal Guardian if not Mom/Dad _____

DHS Caseworker _____ Phone _____

County _____ Insurance _____ Policy _____

PCP _____ Phone # _____

Address _____

Referral Source _____ Date of Referral _____

Has client been interviewed? Yes _____ No _____ # of Interviews _____

Has client been seen for a sexual/physical abuse exam in the past: _____

If yes, where, when, and by whom: _____

Alleged Perpetrator _____ Relationship to client _____

Age _____ Alleged Perpetrator still in home? Yes _____ No _____

Date of last contact _____

When contact(s) began _____ # of suspected contacts _____

Client in protective custody if needed _____

Agencies involved: ( ) ASP/CACD   ( ) Law Enforcement   ( ) Medical Personnel

                   ( ) DHS   ( ) Therapist

Name of person providing history to examiner _____

Relationship of historian to client _____

Was guardian notified of appointment date/time prior to appointment date? _____

Signature: _____ Date: _____

FIGURE 4.6

Intake form developed by the author and used at Jamerson Forensic Nursing and Investigative Services, Inc.

is your breathing?" "Are you having any problems with your lungs?" "Have you had any problems with your heart?" "How about your bowels?"

It is helpful to proceed with the interview in a head-to-toe format, as this facilitates a methodical sequence and keeps the interview on track. The Medical History and ROS form in Figure 4.7 is a useful format.

Medical Intake   Case # _____

Current Medications _____   _____

                                                _____   _____

                                                _____   _____

Allergies _____

School Performance/Development _____

Hospitalizations _____

Surgeries _____

Immunizations _____

Family History

Hereditary Diseases: _____

History of mental illness/suicide attempts: _____

History of family violence: _____

Substance Abuse: **Alcohol:** _____

                                        Cannabis: _____

System Review

HEENT: _____   **Cardiac:** _____

Respiratory: _____   **Liver:** _____

Bone, joints, extremities: _____

Skin: _____   **GI:** _____

Neurological: _____

Endocrine: _____

Hematology: _____

_____   _____   _____

    Examiner   *Assistant(s)*   *Date*

FIGURE 4.7

Medical History/Review of Systems (ROS) section of Forensic Medical Exam form; developed by the author and used at Jamerson Forensic Nursing and Investigative Service, Inc.

JAMERSON
Forensic Nursing &
Investigative Services, Inc.

Abdominal/Pelvic Pain: _____

Vulvular/Penile discomfort: _____

Dysuria: _____

UTI: _____

Bowel Changes: _____

Bladder Changes: _____

Vaginal/Penile itching, bleeding, or DC: _____

Rectal itching, bleeding, or DC _____

Constipation: _____

Vomiting / Chronic viruses: _____

BEHAVIOR/EMOTIONAL SYMPTOMS

Sleep pattern: _____

Eating pattern: _____

School problems: _____

Sexual Acting Out/Last Consensual sex: _____

History of STD's: _____

Recent Mood: _____

MENSTRUATION HISTORY

Menarchal age: _____

LMP: _____

Cycle: _____

Tampons _____ **Pads** _____ **Both** _____

History of Vaginitis: _____

Past history of sexual/physical abuse: _____

_____   _____   _____
Examiner   *Assistant(s)*   *Date*

FIGURE 4.7
(Continued)

THE FORENSIC INTERVIEW AND MEDICAL HISTORY

Depending upon the consideration of multiple and less than constant variables such as state law, institutional policies, the condition of the patient, and the availability of qualified staff, the forensic examiner may choose to conduct either the *forensic interview* or the *forensic medical examination* first. It must be noted, however, that the intake and history information is necessary to competently inform and prioritize the physical examination. For example, the clinician may obtain information in the history that indicates a physical injury, or source of pain or discomfort, that needs to be assessed right away; in other cases it is appropriate to start the forensic interview first, followed by the physical examination and subsequent evidence collection. Each patient is unique; any treatment and forensic efforts should be individually crafted to his or her particular condition and history.

Medical history[2] is a significant component of the evaluation in the context of any suspected sexual assault, child molestation, or domestic assault. It provides a baseline of information for the examiner so that recent trauma and injury can be discriminated from past conditions and events. Therefore, it must cover all body systems. In this way, the examiner can identify any acute or chronic problems, as well as any history of past injury or surgeries. It also informs the nature, extent, and sequence of the forensic medical exam. A failure to document and report medical background information prevents informed medical treatment and leaves the forensic examiner without the proper context for accurate interpretations. Ultimately, conducting an accurate forensic medical examination in the absence of a patient medical history is not possible.

These recommendations are consistent with the NIJ (2004, 81–84), which offers the following guidelines regarding medical history:

Coordinate medical forensic history taking and investigative interviewing. Examiners typically ask patients to provide a medical forensic history after initial medical care for acute problems and before the examination and evidence collection. This history, obtained by asking patients detailed forensic and medical questions related to the assault, is intended to guide the exam, evidence collection, and crime lab analysis of findings. Law enforcement representatives also collect information from patients to help in the apprehension of suspects and

---

[2]*Medical history* is the information about a patient gathered by a health care professional for the purposes of making examinations, providing treatment, and rendering a diagnosis. It commonly involves asking patients questions regarding the current and former state of their physical and mental health. Without this background information, examinations, treatments, and diagnoses are at best uninformed, and at worst potentially lethal.

in case investigation. Prosecutors familiar with the legal requirements of the criminal statutes may also need certain specific information.

Gathering information from patients often takes place soon after they have experienced the assault. Not only can discussing the assault cause patients to feel re-violated, but their emotional and physical condition may make communication difficult. They may also be uncomfortable discussing personal matters with involved responders. Those seeking information about the assault should work collaboratively to create an information-gathering process that is as respectful to patients as possible and minimizes repetition of questions.

Promote a streamlined, victim-centered information-gathering process. Jurisdictions employ several methods, including the following:

- Communication and coordination among responding officers, examiners, investigators, and prosecutors as they go about their separate information-gathering processes.
- Examiners, investigators, and prosecutors together ask patients basic questions. One asks questions while the others listen. They then speak to patients separately to gather remaining information required.
- The medical forensic history and investigative interviews are conducted simultaneously to the extent feasible. The SART should determine the information-gathering process, reflecting the best use of resources and needs and consent of patients. The team may agree that a particular person or agency will be the main questioner, resulting in one end document.

Whatever the method selected, jurisdictions should carefully plan how they will coordinate the logistics of medical forensic history taking and investigative interviewing.

Advocates should be able to provide support and advocacy during the history,[3] if desired by patients. The presence of an advocate may help patients feel more comfortable answering questions. Advocates may also assist patients in voicing their concerns about questions being asked and clarifying their needs during this time. Advocates should not answer questions asked of patients or otherwise influence their statements.

---

[3] I have found in my own performance of victim interviews that they are best performed outside the presence of friends, family members, or advocates. They should also be taped to ensure a complete record. The presence of anyone other than forensic personnel during the formal collection of complete patient history can discredit the forensic value of this information at a later time. Rather than making victims more comfortable, the presence of an advocate at this stage can actually make them less likely to be forthcoming and also encourages a sense of individual powerlessness with regard to the process. In the case of remorseful false reporters, the presence of an advocate might also prevent them from recanting.

Presence of family members, friends, and other personal support persons. Prior to taking the history, patients should be informed that the presence of personal support persons (other than advocates) may influence or be perceived as influencing their statements. These individuals could be subpoenaed as witnesses in their case. If, after receiving this information, patients choose to have personal support persons present during the history, these individuals should be advised not to actively participate in the process. For example, they should not answer questions for patients, comment on patients' answers, interrupt patients, or make facial expressions in response to patients' answers.

Consider patients' needs prior to and during information gathering. Pressing issues (e.g., for treatment of serious injuries, crisis intervention and support, and childcare during the exam process) should be addressed before commencing with information gathering. Be mindful of patients' capacity to answer questions during a lengthy information-gathering process, and take breaks as needed.

The facility should have procedures in place and examiners should be educated to accommodate patients' communication skill level and preferred mode of communicating. This is particularly important for patients with communication-related disabilities and non–English speaking patients. If interpreters are necessary, they should be present prior to questioning and there should be space for them in the exam room and rooms where information is gathered. Patients with communication disabilities may wish to use wordboards, speech synthesizers, or other assistive communication devices to help them communicate. The use of cards with pictures (e.g., of medical procedures and human anatomy) may facilitate communications with patients with some types of cognitive disabilities or limited vocabularies.

It is important that examiners are aware of and responsive to verbal and nonverbal cues from patients. For example, patients may react negatively as they recall experiences during the assault or are reminded of previous violence committed upon them. (It is important to document this information.) What they may need most at this point is a break, the understanding of examiners, and opportunities to talk about what they are experiencing. Advocates can be particularly helpful to patients who are dealing with these emotions.

Use a private and quiet setting for information gathering. Ideally, there should be no interruptions and no time constraints for questioners or for use of the room where the information is being gathered. Although some facilities may lack space, an effort should be made to secure a private and quiet setting for this purpose. In many jurisdictions, history taking takes place in the exam room prior to the exam.

Obtain the medical forensic history. The specific questions asked of patients by examiners for the medical forensic history vary from one jurisdiction to the next, as do forms used to record the history. However, the following information should be sought routinely from patients:

1. Date and time of the sexual assault(s): It is essential to know the period of time that has elapsed between the assault and the collection of evidence. Evidence collection may be directed by the time interval since the assault. Interpretation of both the physical exam and evidence analysis may be influenced by the time interval between the assault and the exam.

2. Pertinent patient medical history: The interpretation of physical findings may be affected by medical data related to menstruation, recent anal-genital injuries, surgeries, or diagnostic procedures, blood-clotting history, and other pertinent medical conditions or treatment.

3. Recent consensual sexual activity: The sensitivity of DNA analysis makes it important to gather information about recent consensual intercourse, whether it was anal, vaginal, and/or oral, and whether a condom was used. A trace amount of semen or other bodily fluid may be identified that is not associated with the crime. Once identified, it may need to be associated with a consensual partner, and then used for elimination purposes to aid in interpreting evidence.

4. Postassault activities of patients: The quality of evidence is affected both by actions taken by patients and the passage of time. It is critical to know what, if any, activities were performed prior to the examination (e.g., have patients urinated, defecated, wiped genitals or the body, douched, removed/inserted a tampon/sanitary pad/diaphragm, used oral rinse/gargled, washed, brushed teeth, ate or drank, smoked, used drugs, or changed clothing?).

5. Assault-related patient history: Information such as whether there was memory loss, lapse of consciousness, vomiting, nongenital injury, pain and/or bleeding, and anal-genital injury, pain, and/or bleeding can direct evidence collection and medical care. Collecting toxicology samples is recommended if there was either loss of memory or lapse of consciousness, according to jurisdictional policy.

6. Suspect information (if known): Forensic scientists seek evidence on cross-transfer of evidence among patients, suspects, and crime scenes. The gender and number of suspects may offer guidance to types and amounts of foreign materials that might be found on patients' bodies and clothing. Suspect information gathered during this history should be limited to

that which will guide the exam and forensic evidence collection. Detailed questions about suspects are asked during the investigative interview.

7. Nature of the physical assault(s): Information about the physical surroundings of the assault(s) (e.g., indoors, outdoors, car, alley, room, rug, dirt, mud, or grass) and methods employed by suspects is crucial to the detection, collection, and analysis of physical evidence. Methods may include, but are not limited to, use of weapons (threatened and/or injuries inflicted), physical blows, grabbing, holding, pinching, biting, using physical restraints, strangulation, burns (thermal and/or chemical), threat(s) of harm, and involuntary ingestion of alcohol/drugs. Knowing whether suspects may have been injured during the assault may be useful when recovering evidence from patients (e.g., blood) or from suspects (e.g., bruising, fingernail marks, or bite marks).

8. Description of the sexual assault(s): An accurate but brief description is crucial to detecting, collecting, and analyzing physical evidence. The description should include any:

   - Penetration of genitalia (e.g., vulva, hymen, and/or vagina of female patient), however slight;
   - Penetration of the anal opening, however slight;
   - Oral contact with genitals (of patients by suspects or of suspects by patients);
   - Other contact with genitals (of patients by suspects or of suspects by patients);
   - Oral contact with the anus (of patients by suspects or of suspects by patients);
   - Nongenital act(s) (e.g., licking, kissing, suction injury, and biting);
   - Other act(s) including use of objects;
   - If known, whether ejaculation occurred and location(s) of ejaculation (e.g., mouth, vagina, genitals, anus/rectum, body surface, on clothing, on bedding, or other); and
   - Use of contraception or lubricants.

   These questions require specific and sometimes detailed answers. Some may be difficult for patients to answer. Examiners should explain that these questions are asked during every sexual assault medical forensic exam. They should also explain why each question is being asked.

This information is essential for the forensic nurse to gather before starting the forensic medical examination, as some preexisting conditions can mimic or be confused for abuse (i.e., skin conditions, nonviolent or sports-related injuries unrelated to assault, etc.) and will need to be clearly differentiated. Also, having an awareness of the medical history guides the clinician in making necessary referrals for other problems that may be assessed during the examination.

History of Drug Abuse

It is important to ask the patient if he or she has a history of substance abuse. If the answer is yes, then immediate follow-up questions must include which substances, when was the last use, and how much was taken. Here, it is critical that the forensic examiner explain to the patient the importance of being honest.

The patient needs to fully understand that if he or she has recently ingested a substance such as alcohol, marijuana, cocaine, heroine, methamphetamine—or any other illicit drug—that it will likely show up on the lab tests submitted for analysis. Therefore it is better for patients' health and overall credibility to be up front about drug use. Patients need to know that if they deny drug use and test "hot" for the presence of something illicit, this will make them look intentionally deceitful, as though they are trying to hide information. The forensic examiner should explain that it is better to establish a pattern of honesty during the forensic medical examination, so that any other information provided may be trusted if trust is required.

Ultimately, victim toxicology will be used to inform estimates of the patient's physical and mental capabilities, as well as to assist with addressing the issue of consent. This is discussed in Pittel and Spina (2004, 151–152):

> In contrast to the vast majority of rapes in which an unwilling victim is forced to engage in sexual acts by threats of bodily harm, the alleged victim of drug-facilitated rape may or may not have been a willing and active participant in previous acts of consensual sex, may or may not have voluntarily consented to use drugs with the alleged perpetrator, or may engage in sexual acts in situations where they had sought to obtain drugs from the alleged perpetrator.
>
> With the growing popularity of GHB and Ecstasy (MDMA) as "club drugs" that are commonly used by members of both sexes to enhance energy and to produce euphoria at all-night dances or "raves," it is also likely that at least some alleged victims of drug-facilitated rape were not drugged involuntarily, and that they may have encouraged or initiated sexual intimacies that they later regret or that they perceive to have been forced upon them.
>
> In other cases, the victim may have met the perpetrator at a bar or party and had been willingly talking, dancing, and drinking with him before he slipped something into her drink. At this point, she may become noticeably more flirtatious and amorous, and most people would just assume that she is drunk. People who observe her may believe that her increased sexual behavior is an indication of her interest in the person she is with.

However, it is important to note that if she had ingested Rohypnol, MDMA, or especially GHB, such behavior is very much part of the effect of the drug. It is also possible that during her intoxicated and disinhibited state, she will "voluntarily" ingest other recreational drugs. Such behaviors may appear to be "consensual" to others and in such cases, interviewing waitresses, and other witnesses may be important in determining if the victim was behaving uncharacteristically, even though her behavior appeared to be voluntary. In addition, an indication of a drug being slipped in a drink is that the alleged victim will notice that she feels far more "drunk" than expected, given the amount of alcohol she has ingested, particularly if she had a drink she usually consumes.

In cases involving recreational use or abuse of drugs and alcohol by the patient, it may be necessary to obtain collateral descriptions of the patient's typical behavior while under the influence from friends and family members. In this way, the forensic examiner will have a more complete understanding of how particular drugs affect a particular patient to inform subsequent interpretations—though not necessarily his or her own. That is to say, there are happy drunks, loud drunks, "amorous" drunks, forgetful drunks, and angry drunks. It helps to know which the patient is.

History of Behavioral or Emotional Symptoms and Menstruation

When obtaining history under the behavioral/emotional category, it is important to gather information regarding the patient's mental health, usual sleep patterns, eating patterns, any behavioral problems at school or work, recent mood, as well as any history of sexually transmitted diseases (STDs) and treatment or lack thereof. Most of this information should be easy enough to answer. However, patients may or may not know whether or not they suffer from certain STDs, as more than a few can be present without distinctive or even obvious symptoms.

In addition, it is important to ask about and document the last time the patient had consensual sex. If the patient had consensual sex the same day, or even a few days prior to any reported attack, biological material may still be present. It is therefore necessary to establish the precise nature of the sexual activity, and the potential location of any ejaculate—where it may have landed and where it may have transferred if the patient has continued with his or her daily routine or activities. This can help to explain any mixed samples of biological material that might occur in any subsequent DNA testing of patient samples.

Additionally, this may be important in cases involving older or elderly female patients that have not been sexually active for a number of years. They experience decreased estrogen effect to the vaginal tissue due to menopause and hormonal changes. This is important to establish during the physical examination, and within the context of evidence collection efforts, because oftentimes vaginal tissue that undergoes such changes is more susceptible to injury.

On a related subject, the forensic examiner needs to ask all female patients at what age they started their menstrual cycle; when was their last menstrual period; what their menstrual cycle is normally like (many females experience irregular bleeding patterns with their menses, and this is important data to collect). The examiner also needs to establish their use of pads, tampons, or both during menses.

Each category within the history is important to ask about and document. The forensic examiner should take care and be cognizant to mark every item in each category as it is accomplished. If something doesn't apply to a particular patient, just mark it as not-applicable (n/a). Then review the form to ensure that nothing has been missed.

The purpose of taking a history is not to help give the forensic nurse excuses to hurry through the forensic medical exam and cut corners because of a subjective victim trait. The purpose is to inform collection efforts and eventual interpretations of findings. As stated in the NIJ (2004, 8), forensic examiners must "avoid basing decisions about whether to collect evidence on a patient's characteristics or circumstances (e.g., the patient has used illegal drugs)."

All of these considerations are part of treating the patient's body, including his or her clothing, as a physical extension of a potential crime scene. This will be discussed further in subsequent sections.

THE BODY AS THE CRIME SCENE: PHYSICAL EXAMINATION AND EVIDENCE COLLECTION

The physical examination of the patient's body is one of the most important components in a criminal investigation. According to Turvey (2008, 188) a crime scene is "an area where a criminal act has taken place." Therefore, a victim's body is by definition a physical extension of the crime scene. As explained in LeDray (2004, 120–121), specific to sexual assault but true for all forms of interpersonal violence:

> In addition to the location where the sexual assault occurred, the victim is an important crime scene. With the advances in DNA evidence collection ... the victim may in fact be the most important crime scene in a sexual assault investigation. It is thus important that as a part of your initial investigation you take every step possible to ensure that the medical evidence is not missed or lost.
>
> To help determine whether the patient at hand is indeed a victim, and to establish what actually happened to them, physical evidence of the

crime (or its absence) must be recognized, documented, and collected in accordance with Locard's Exchange Principle—for later examination and interpretation.

Locard's Exchange Principle is the cornerstone of forensic science in general and crime reconstruction specifically. It has come to refer to the belief that every contact between two objects leaves a trace. One explanation from Locard himself, found in *La Police et Les Methodes Scientifiques*, helps us understand what he actually meant (Locard 1934, 7–8):

> Searching for traces is not, as much as one could believe it, an innovation of modern criminal jurists. It is an occupation probably as old as humanity.

> The principle is this one. Any action of an individual, and obviously, the violent action constituting a crime, cannot occur without leaving a mark. What is admirable is the variety of these marks. Sometimes they will be prints, sometimes simple traces, and sometimes stains.

Additionally, a useful discussion regarding Locard's Exchange Principle is provided in Chisum and Turvey (2006, 23–24):

> [Dr. Edmond] Locard is most famous for the forensic axiom that bears his name: Locard's Exchange Principle. It has been misstated, misrepresented, and misattributed over the years by those lecturing and writing authoritatively on the subject. Confusion in the forensic science community and among students has resulted....

> The principle has been adapted and adopted in its English translation by the forensic science community in the United States. As stated by Dr. John Thornton, a practicing criminalist and a former professor of forensic science at the University of California (UC) at Berkeley (Thornton 1997, 29):

> > Forensic scientists have almost universally accepted the Locard Exchange Principle. This doctrine was enunciated early in the 20th century by Edmund Locard, the director of the first crime laboratory, in Lyon, France. Locard's Exchange Principle states that with contact between two items, there will be an exchange of microscopic material. This certainly includes fibers, but extends to other microscopic materials such as hair, pollen, paint, and soil.

By recognizing, documenting, and examining the nature and extent of evidentiary traces and exchanges in a crime scene, Locard postulated that criminals could be tracked down and then later associated with particular locations, items of evidence, and persons (i.e., victims). He regarded this postulation as both obvious and ancient, and he likened the recognition and examination of trace evidence to hunting behavior as old as mankind (Locard 1934, 7).

In terms of applying this to the examination of a victim, the forensic examiner must remember that the body is one of the places where the crime took place. If the patient came into contact with an offender, there will have been a transfer of material between them (and their clothes). It may be microscopic; it may be biological; it may be synthetic; it may be a visible or invisible stain; or it may simply be an impression. As explained by Peterson and Thornton (2002, 147):

> physical evidence is without scope or dimension. Physical evidence runs the gamut from the commonplace to the virtually unique, and the forensic scientist is expected to deal with it all. At one time or another, virtually anything can represent a form of physical evidence, from badger hairs to billiard balls, from bloodstains to bullets. This diversity in the form of physical evidence makes forensic science a necessarily messy, disheveled sort of thing. The forensic scientist has no control over what constitutes physical evidence—it is thrust upon him by the vagaries of life itself.

From any forensic perspective, physical evidence can only achieve its ultimate value and aid in an investigation when the forensic examiner fully appreciates that a victim's body is a crime scene. Physical evidence must be recognized, documented, preserved, and collected accordingly. This is something that was perhaps expressed best more than 50 years ago by Dr. Paul L. Kirk, a father of modern forensic science (Kirk and Thornton 1974, 33):

> The utilization of physical evidence is critical to the solution of most crime. No longer may the police depend upon the confession, as they have done to a large extent in the past. The eyewitness has never been dependable, as any experienced investigator or attorney knows quite well. Only physical evidence is infallible, and then only when it is properly recognized, studied, and interpreted.

The actual search for physical evidence begins with the physical examination of the victim.

The Physical Examination: A Primer

The *physical examination* of the patient is the act of examination of the body by auscultation, palpation, percussion, inspection, and smelling. It also includes the act of investigating the victim and his or her clothing for signs of defect, disease, injury, and potential transfer evidence from a location, weapon, or suspect. The resultant findings (or the absence of findings) are referred to as *physical evidence*. The most informed physical examination follows a process and direction dictated in part by the medical history and forensic interview. According to Giardino and Giardino (2003) the physical examination generally involves the following efforts:

1. Search for and identify any physical injuries or conditions that require treatment.

2. Document physical findings at the time of examination. This may include utilizing photographs, notes, and/or drawings.
3. Obtain laboratory specimens and diagnostic studies when indicated.
4. Collect and preserve forensic evidence.
5. Provide appropriate treatments directed at restoring health when findings or conditions are present.
6. Reassure patient and family of ways to attain or restore health and well-being.
7. Provide appropriate health education and teaching to promote health and wellness.

Each case is different, but most require between two and four hours to complete. However, more complex cases can take six to seven hours, depending on the amount of injury and evidence collection efforts required. A rape case with limited evidence and injury will require less time than a domestic violence case where there is extensive bruising, scratching, and other injuries that must each be carefully measured, photographed, and examined for potential evidence transfer.

Full Body Photos

It is helpful to begin the physical examination by taking full body photographs of the patient: front, back, and sides. Such documentation is very helpful to have in the patient's chart, or in the patient database, as it provides a pictorial view of the patient's presentation at the time of assessment. It also provides for *negative documentation*—recording of areas of the body where there is no evidence of defect, disease, injury, or potential transfer.

Vital Signs

As with the ROS (Review of Symptoms) at intake, the physical examination is best conducted in a head-to-toe format with the comprehensive investigation and documentation of all systems. At the outset, it is best to obtain a full set of vital signs, which should include the patient's height, weight, body mass index (BMI), blood pressure, pulse, temperature, and respiration. The forensic examiner needs to know the patient's general status and vital signs upon presentation. From this information, she or he can determine if the patient is within normal limits (WNL) and physiologically stable, or if the patient is in distress and needs additional care before or during the forensic evaluation.

Mental Status

Next, the forensic examiner needs to assess and document the patient's mental status: whether the patient is alert and cooperative; lethargic, uncooperative, and irritable; or unconscious. It is also important to document if the patient denies or refuses to have the examination, as well as his or her stated reason for refusal. Such information may become contextually important at a later time, as the reason may be factual or fictitious.

Evidence and Injury

In proceeding with the head-to-toe physical assessment, the next areas to examine are the patient's general appearance, skin, head, face, ears, throat, neck, lymph nodes, chest, lungs, heart, abdomen, breasts, extremities, back, and circulation status.

JAMERSON
Forensic Nursing &
Investigative Services, Inc.

Physical Exam   Case # _____

BP: _____   P: _____   T: _____   R: _____

Height: Feet _____   Inches _____

Weight: _____

Mental Status: Alert   Lethargic   Unconscious

                       Cooperative   Uncooperative   Irritable

                       Denied Exam

General Appearance:

_____ Patient is well-developed, well-nourished who does not appear ill. Appropriate posture

     with no visible pain.

_____ Specify otherwise: _____

Skin:

_____ Warm, moist, elastic

_____ Specify otherwise: _____

Head:

_____ Scalp is clean. Hair is of normal texture and distribution.

_____ Specify otherwise: _____

Face:

_____ Facial contour, mobility, and expression are normal. No asymmetry noted

_____ Specify otherwise: _____

Ears:

_____ Canals are clear. Tympanic membranes visible. Hearing adequate for normal

     conversation.

_____ Specify otherwise: _____

Throat:

_____ Tonsils present and not enlarged. No redness or swelling present.

_____ Specify otherwise: _____

Neck:

_____ Trachea midline

_____ Specify otherwise: _____

FIGURE 4.8

Physical Exam form developed by the author and used at Jamerson Forensic Nursing and Investigative Services, Inc.

FIGURE 4.8

(Continued)

Lymph Nodes:

_____ There is no significant lymph node enlargement.

_____ Specify otherwise: _____

Chest:

_____ Normal contour and movement on inspiration and expiration

_____ Specify otherwise: _____

Lungs:

_____ Breath sounds are audible bilaterally. No abnormal breath sounds noted.

_____ Specify otherwise: _____

Heart:

_____ Heart sounds are regular in rhythm and of normal rate.

_____ Specify otherwise: _____

Abdomen:

_____ Normal contour and no tenderness or guarding. Peristaltic sounds audible in four

quadrants.

_____ Specify otherwise: _____

Breasts:

_____ Free from masses, tenderness, discharge, dimpling, or discoloration of skin.

_____ Specify otherwise: _____

Extremities:

_____ Full ROM of joints. No discoloration, tenderness, or edema noted.

_____ Specify otherwise: _____

Back:

_____ There is a normal curvature of the spine. Able to bend from waist.

_____ Specify otherwise: _____

Circulation:

_____ Pulses are palpable and regular.

_____ Specify otherwise: _____

In each category of the physical examination form there is an area that describes findings that are within normal limits (WNL), and then there is another referred to as "specify otherwise" to document findings that are abnormal. In addition to assessing whether each system is within normal limits, the clinician is also focusing on identifying any injuries including bruises, abrasions, lacerations,

FIGURE 4.8
(Continued)

Photographs taken: _____ **Yes**

_____ **No**

_____ _____ _____

Examiner *Assistant* *Date*

TRAUMAGRAM

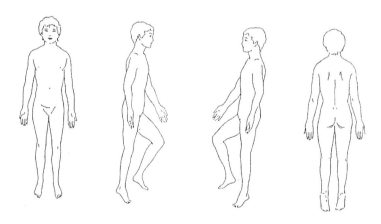

patterned injuries, burns, and any signs of skeletal trauma and/or head trauma. Each case varies. Some cases involve allegations of domestic or physical abuse, while other cases involve allegations of sexual abuse/molestation, however, the head-to-toe physical examination should be conducted in every case.

Specifically, the evaluation of a patient who may have been physically abused or injured also tends to focus on any injuries present. This is best accomplished in a methodical manner, so that any external and/or internal injuries consistent with assault or abuse can be identified and thoroughly documented. However, forensic examiners must be mindful not to focus solely on areas of obvious injury. They must be thorough in their search for evidence and documentation of all other areas of the body.

As already suggested, forensic evidentiary findings may include biological substances such as saliva, semen, bodily debris, hair, or debris from clothing. It is important to note that in many cases of actual assault there are no physical findings. There may be legitimate reasons for this. For example, the victim may have bathed or taken a shower and washed away vital evidence. In cases involving children, the evidence found greatly depends on the time the child disclosed the suspected abuse versus the time the forensic evaluation takes place. In adult victims, this also depends on whether or not the victim was capable, physically or emotionally, of resisting, as well as other contextual variables. Consider the cautionaries offered by LeDray (2004, 134–135):

> It is always important to remember that the absence of injuries does not prove the lack of force or coercion and does not prove consent. Most sexual assault victims are *not* injured. Significant physical injury from a sexual assault is rare and occurs in only 3% to 5% of rape survivors across studies. Fewer than 1% of rape victims have been found to need hospitalization. Even minor injury is usually documented in only about one-third of the reported rapes. Injuries, when they do occur, are, however, more common in stranger rapes and rapes by someone the victim knows intimately, such as a domestic partner, rather than in date rape or acquaintance rape situations (Kilpatrick, Edmunds, and Seymour 1992; Ledray 1999; Bownes, O'Gorman, and Saters 1991; Marchbanks, Lui, and Mercy 1990; Tucker, Ledray, and Stehle Werner 1990).

> In one study of 355 cases, nongenital traumatic injuries were identified in a total of 45% of the cases examined (Gray-Eurom et al. 2002).In another study of 351 rape victims, the overall injury rate was somewhat lower; however, the rate of physical injury for male rape victims (40%) was found to be higher than for female victims (26%). Although 25% of the men and 38% of the women in this study sought medical care after the rape for their physical injuries, only 61% of those seeking treatment told the treating physician they had been raped. The women expressed a strong preference for medical treatment and counseling by a woman. The male victims were, however, less likely to express a gender preference (Petrak and Claydon, 1995). A more recent study of 1076 sexual assault victims found nongenital trauma even more often, 67% of the time (Riggs, Houry, Gayle, Markovchick,

and Feldhaus 2000). It is important that the forensic examiner be aware of the likely pattern of injuries from violence so that she knows the appropriate questions to ask and where to look for injuries on the basis of the history given. Intentional injuries tend to be more central, and accidental injuries more toward the extremities. Especially if domestic violence is involved, injuries are most often inflicted where the victim can easily hide them. The most common injuries are broken eardrums from slapping, neck bruising from choking, punch bruising to the upper arm, and "defensive posturing" injuries to the outer mid-ulnar areas of the arms. Also common are whip or cordlike injuries to the back; punch or bite injuries to the breasts and nipples; punch injuries to the abdomen, especially in pregnant women; punch and kick injuries to the lateral thighs; and facial bruising, abrasions, and lacerations (Sheridan, 1993).

The lesson here is that no injury, or its absence, may be interpreted outside of patient history, event history, and context.

Rapport Building

The head-to-toe physical examination also provides an opportunity for the forensic examiner to establish rapport with the patient. This is possible and helpful no matter what the patient's age. However, examiners must adjust the complexity of their questions and their demeanor in accordance with the patient's age, developmental level, and individual needs based on the intake assessment.

If the patients are children or adolescents, the forensic examiner can take time during the physical exam to teach them about their bodies. The examiner can instruct them regarding their heart and lungs while auscultating their heart and breath sounds. Conversely, the forensic examiner can inquire about their favorite foods and find out about nutritional patterns while listening to the abdomen for bowel sounds. If patients are older, they may remember things about their body that they want to mention or events associated with the crime that involved a particular body part. Each part of the examination is an opportunity to both learn and teach. Rapport building makes this exchange more possible, and more comfortable for everyone.

For example, when examining a child patient's abdomen for any potential abnormalities, she might disclose that the offender ejaculated on her abdomen during the assault. That is crucial information about the crime with forensic implications: there may be dried semen present on the abdomen or within the navel area that needs to be appropriately swabbed, packaged, and submitted for forensic analysis. Absent the attention to the patient's abdomen, the child could easily forget to mention it.

In another example, when examining an adult female patient's breasts, she may recall and disclose that the offender actually licked her breast. Or during the examination the forensic examiner may assess a scratch or abrasion to the breast, or possibly even a bite mark. This type of information and subsequent evidence must be documented, photographed, swabbed, packaged, or submitted for forensic analysis.

Sexual Assault Examination

After the head-to-toe portion of the physical examination, the forensic nurse examiner will explain to the patient that it is time to examine the genitalia or "private parts." It is often helpful to ask the patient what he or she calls those areas of the body, and then refer to those parts with both the patient's terminology and professional terminology. In this way, the forensic examiner provides education by explaining the correct anatomical term, which patients may or may not have heard. However, this approach also works to make patients feel more comfortable by utilizing their language, so as not to speak down to them or appear cold and clinical.

Forensic examiners will need to explain the position they need the patient to be in so that they can examine him or her most effectively. The positioning utilized depends on whether the patient is a child or an adult. Typically, the patient is in one of the following positions:

1. Supine frog-leg (feet and heels together and knees relaxed out and down).
2. Supine/knees to chest or supine with feet in stirrups.
3. Prone knee-chest.
4. Lateral side lying (lateral decubitus).

Forensic examiners need to be sure to explain that this positioning helps them to see the patient's genital area. They must use terminology that the patient can understand and take the time to explain each part of the exam process. Telling patients what is going on each step the way educates them and helps them to feel safe. It is also important throughout the exam process to ask patients how they are doing. If they are physically uncomfortable, help them get comfortable; if they are nervous, ask them to explain, and try to help put them at ease.

Once the patient is properly positioned, the clinician can begin a general survey of the genitalia. This includes inspection of the genitalia with the use of a *colposcope*, which is a lighted magnifying instrument used by a gynecologist to examine the tissues of the vagina and the cervix. The process of using a colposcope during a vaginal and cervical examination is called *colposcopy*. A colposcope allows the forensic examiner to assess for, and record, the presence or absence of genital injury. It's like a camera, flashlight, and microscope all in one that allows visualization of genital tissue

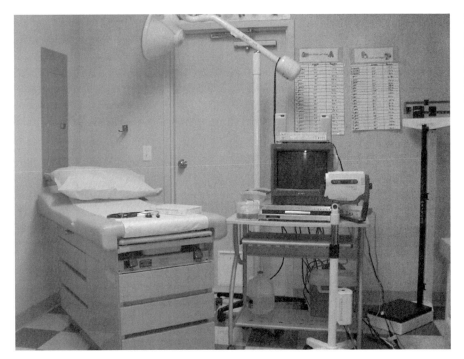

FIGURE 4.9

Adult examination room with videocolposcope and monitor, at Jamerson Forensic Nursing and Investigative Services, Inc.

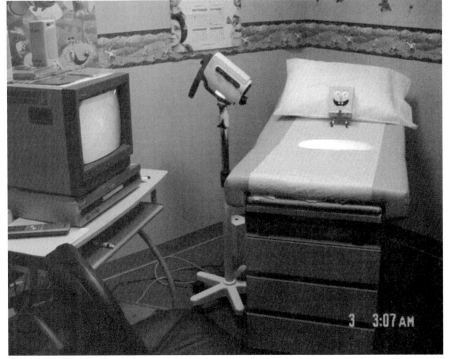

FIGURE 4.10

Child-friendly examination room with videocolposcope and monitor, at Jamerson Forensic Nursing and Investigative Services, Inc.

areas that may be missed with the naked eye or poor lighting. As asserted by Finkel (2002) the colposcope provides not only excellent magnification of the genital tissue, but also an excellent light source that identifies and captures any potential injury or abnormalities on tape or film. Furthermore, it provides a noninvasive method for examining the genitalia—and because the examination is on a screen or monitor, it actually makes the process less intimidating. Patients can observe their own bodies and may even feel more in control.

Again, this can be a time to educate child patients about their genitalia and allows them to ask questions if needed. According to Palusci and Cyrus (2001), a study of children who underwent videocolposcopy found that children generally watched their evaluation and were cooperative and enthusiastic throughout the examination. I have found this to be true as well.

The specifics of the complete physical examination and evidence collection procedures are detailed in the NIJ guidelines.

NIJ Guidelines: Forensic Medical Examination and Evidence Collection Procedures

The NIJ (2004, 89–99) guidelines regarding the Forensic Medical Examination and Evidence Collection Procedures are as follows:

6. Exam and Evidence Collection Procedures

Recommendations at a glance for health care providers to facilitate the exam and evidence collection:

...

Recognize the forensic purpose of the exam. During the exam, examiners methodically document physical findings and facilitate the collection of evidence from patients' bodies and clothing. The findings in the exam and collected evidence often provide information to help reconstruct the details about the events in question in an objective and scientific manner. Of course, health care needs and concerns of patients may be presented in the course of the exam that should be addressed prior to discharge. However, patients must understand that the exam does not provide routine medical care. For example, a pap smear will not be done during the female pelvic exam. (This chapter focuses on forensic components of the exam. Other chapters in the protocol discuss more fully medical and other related needs and concerns of patients.)

Collect as much evidence from patients as possible, guided by the scope of informed consent, the medical forensic history, exam findings, and instructions in the evidence collection kit. Evidence collected during the exam mainly includes biological and trace evidence. To reconstruct the events in question, evidence collected is used in two potential ways in sexual assault cases:

- Transfer or associative evidence can provide information about contact between patients and suspects, patients and crime scenes, and suspects and crime scenes. The type of evidence recovered and its location can provide details about the nature of the contact.
- Identification evidence can give scientific data about the source of a specific piece of evidence.

Be aware of evidence that may be pertinent to the issue of whether the patient consented to the sexual contact with the suspect. In the majority of sexual assaults, patients know the suspects. For example, according to the National Crime Victimization Survey, in 2002, 66.1 percent of rapes/sexual assaults involved offenders who were nonstrangers. Most nonstranger suspects and many stranger suspects (if confronted by the criminal justice system) will claim that the patient consented to the sexual contact. Consent claims typically stem from a lack of evidence and documentation concerning force and coercion. Thus, evidence and documentation of physical findings related to whether force or coercion was used against patients (e.g., findings that reveal injuries, drugs taken involuntarily, or signs of a struggle) are important in these types of cases. However, the absence of physical trauma does not mean that coercion/force was not used or prove that patients consented to sexual contact. Also, some physical findings that suggest force are not necessarily indicative of a sexual assault. It is important to remember that if an investigation takes place, law enforcement officials will look for additional crime scene evidence that may help to overcome a claim of consent.

Understand how biological evidence is tested. Semen, blood, vaginal secretions, saliva, vaginal epithelial cells, and other biological evidence may be identified and genetically typed by a crime lab. The information derived from the analysis can often help determine whether sexual contact occurred, provide information regarding the circumstances of the incident, and be compared to reference samples collected from patients and suspects. A primary method used by crime labs for testing biological evidence is DNA (deoxyribonucleic acid) analysis. The most common form of DNA analysis used in crime labs for identification is called polymerase chain reaction (PCR). PCR allows the analysis of evidence samples of limited quality and quantity by making millions of copies of very small amounts of DNA. Using an advanced form of PCR testing called "short tandem repeats" (STR), the laboratory is able to generate a DNA profile, which can be compared to DNA from a suspect or a crime scene.

Distinguish patients' DNA from suspects' DNA. Blood, buccal (inner cheek) swabbings, or saliva should be collected from patients for DNA analysis to distinguish their DNA from that of suspects. (Procedures for collecting these samples are provided later in this chapter.) If the case is reported, patients' biological samples and DNA profiles should be used only for investigation of the sexual assault, and their DNA profiles should not be inputted into CODIS [Combined DNA Index System]. Neither biological samples nor DNA profiles should be provided to law enforcement or prosecution for another case in which patients may be suspects, inadvertently given to health insurance carriers, or used for research purposes without patients' consent. Criminal justice agency policies should be in place and followed for the secure storage of biological samples and appropriate disposal of these samples and DNA profiles.

Reduce exposure to infectious materials and risk of contamination of evidence. Examiners should take precautions during the exam to prevent exposure (to both patients and health care staff) to blood-born pathogens and other potentially infectious materials. For example, it is important to follow facility policies on washing hands, handling contaminated needles and other contaminated sharps, wearing protective equipment, and minimizing splashing, spraying, and spattering of these materials. (For more information on this topic, see *B.1. Sexual Assault Forensic Examiners.*)

With the ever-increasing sensitivity of DNA analysis, there is a greater chance that accidental contamination can be detected. Forensic evidence, which is usually small in volume, can be contaminated and diluted by foreign DNA. Every precaution should be taken by all first responders to reduce outside contamination and dilution of evidence. For example, examiners should wear nonlubricated gloves and change them throughout the exam/evidence collection whenever cross-contamination could occur. Examiners and other responders should seek guidance from their crime labs on procedures to follow to prevent contamination.

Understand the importance of semen evidence. The relevance of semen evidence in cases involving male suspects covers the spectrum, depending upon case facts. Semen is composed of cellular and liquid components known as spermatozoa (sperm) and seminal fluid. Semen evidence can be useful because it is positive identification that ejaculation occurred, and it can be used to positively identify suspects. However, it is critical to note that failure to recover semen is not an indication that a sexual assault did not occur. There are a number of reasons why semen might not be recovered in these cases: Assailants may have used condoms, ejaculated somewhere other than in an orifice or on patients' clothes or bodies, or not ejaculated at all. Semen may have been depleted by frequent ejaculation prior to the sample in question. [FN193] Chronic alcohol or drug abuse, chemotherapy, cancer, infection (e.g., mumps or tuberculosis), or congenital abnormalities also may suppress semen production. Other factors may contribute to the absence of detectable amounts of semen evidence. For example, significant time delays between the assault and collection of evidence may cause loss of semen evidence, semen may be washed away prior to the exam or improperly collected, and an object other than a penis may have been used for penetration.

Modify the exam and evidence collection to address patients' needs and concerns. . . . In addition, examiners should be aware that patients' beliefs might affect whether and how certain evidence is collected. For example, patients from certain cultures or religious backgrounds may view hair as sacred and decline collection of hair evidence.

Explain exam and evidence collection procedures to patients. Whatever the methods used for seeking informed consent from patients for the exam and evidence collection, the full nature of procedures and options should be explained. Examiners may provide some basic information prior to starting the exam and additional information as the exam proceeds. For example, if the colposcope is used, examiners can explain to patients, at some point prior to its use, what the colposcope is, how it will be used, for what purpose, and how long the procedure will take. Encourage patients to ask questions and to inform examiners if they need a break or do not want a particular part of the exam or evidence collection done. . . .

Conduct the exam. In addition to instructions included in the evidence collection kit, the exam should be guided by the scope of informed consent and the medical forensic history.

In the course of the exam, examiners may question patients about trauma related to the assault. These questions should be specific enough to yield clinically relevant information. For example, simply asking if patients are injured or hurt anywhere is not focused enough— they may not know where they are injured until examined or asked questions such as if they hurt in specific body locations.

General physical examination. Obtain patients' vital signs, note the date and time of the exam, physical appearance, general demeanor, behavior, and orientation, and condition of clothing on arrival. Record all physical findings (which include observable or palpable tissue injuries; physiologic changes; and foreign materials such as grass, sand, stains, dried or moist secretions, or positive fluorescence) on body diagram forms. Use an alternate light source to assist in identifying findings. Be observant for redness, abrasions, bruises, swelling, lacerations, fractures, bites, burns, and other forms of physical trauma. Note areas of tenderness and induration. On dark-skinned individuals, it may be difficult to identify these areas and they may need to be sought out specifically.

Anogenital examination. During the female genital exam, examine the external genitalia and perineal area for injury, foreign materials, and other findings in the following areas: abdomen, thighs, perineum, labia majora, labia minora, clitoral hood and surrounding area, periurethral tissue/urethral meatus, hymen, fossa navicularis, and posterior fourchette. The use of a colposcope during the external genital exam enhances viewing microscopic trauma and may provide photographic documentation.

Then examine the vagina and cervix for injury, foreign materials, and foreign bodies. Use a colposcope or other magnifying device if available. In some jurisdictions, toluidine blue dye may be used to detect trauma, either with or without the use of a colposcope. Examine the buttocks, perianal skin, and anal folds for injury, foreign materials, and other findings. If rectal injury is suspected, an anoscope can be used as a tool to identify and evaluate trauma (it may also be used to help obtain anal swabs and trace evidence).

For male patients, examine the external and perineal area for injury, foreign materials, and other findings, including from the abdomen, buttocks, thighs, foreskin, urethral meatus, shaft, scrotum, perineum, glans, and testes. Document whether patients are circumcised.

Documentation of findings. Record findings from the general physical and anogenital exam on appropriate body diagram forms. Detailed descriptions of findings should be provided as required. During the exam, collect evidence as specified in the evidence collection kit and photograph anatomy involved in the assault according to jurisdictional policy. Follow jurisdictional policy regarding documentation, photography, and collection of bite mark evidence.

Collect evidence to submit to the crime lab for analysis, according to jurisdictional policy. The following evidence from patients, along with completed documentation forms, typically is submitted to the crime lab designated by the jurisdiction. [FN203] Jurisdictions may require collection of additional or different specimens. Instructions on evidence collection are usually contained in the evidence collection kit. If any requested evidence is not collected, examiners should note reasons on documentation forms.

Collect clothing evidence. Clothing frequently contains important evidence in sexual assault cases. It provides a surface upon which traces of foreign materials, such as semen, saliva, blood, hairs, fibers, and debris from the crime scene, may be found. While foreign matter can be washed off or worn off the body, the same substances often can be found intact on clothing for a considerable length of time following an assault. Damaged or torn clothing may be significant, as damage may be evidence of force (do not cut through any existing holes, rips, or stains on clothing). Evidence on patients' clothing can be compared with evidence collected from suspects and crime scenes. Common items collected from patients include underwear, hosiery, blouses, shirts, and pants. Coats and shoes are collected less frequently.

Procedures for collecting clothing, underwear, and foreign material dislodged while undressing:

- Place a clean hospital sheet on the floor as a barrier. Then place the collection paper on the barrier sheet. Be careful to prevent evidence transfer. Document all findings. Ask patients to disrobe (assisting them as requested and then draping them appropriately). When disrobing, have patients remove shoes and then undress over the collection paper to catch any foreign material that is dislodged. If someone assists, she/he should wear gloves.

- Collect clothing pertinent to the assault. First determine if patients are wearing the same clothes worn during or immediately following the assault. If so, the clothing should be examined for any apparent foreign material, stains, or damage. When the determination has been made that items may contain possible evidence, those items should be collected. If it is determined that patients are not wearing the same clothing, examiners should inquire as to the location of the original clothing. If original clothing has not been brought to the exam site, information on clothing location should be provided to law enforcement (if involved) so that clothing can be retrieved before any potential evidence is destroyed. In addition to collecting underwear worn at the time of or immediately after the assault, collect underwear patients are wearing at the time of the exam (if relevant to the case).

- Be sensitive about how much clothing to take as evidence. For example, take patients' coats or shoes only if it is determined that there may be evidence on them. The exam site can coordinate with advocacy programs to ensure that replacement clothing is available for patients in a range of sizes. This clothing is critical in some instances (e.g., a patient may own only the clothing that is being collected).

- If female patients are menstruating, collect tampons and sanitary napkins. Air-dry them as much as possible and then place them in a separate paper collection bag.

- Follow jurisdictional policy for handling and transporting wet evidence that cannot be dried thoroughly at the exam site (e.g., wet clothing, tampons, and sanitary napkins). Ensure that it is packaged in leak-proof containers and separated from other evidence when being transported. It is critical to alert involved law enforcement representatives and crime lab personnel about the presence of wet evidence and the need for its immediate analysis or further drying.

- After drying items according to jurisdictional policy, place each piece of clothing and collection paper in a separate paper bag, label, seal, and initial seal. If additional bags are needed, use new grocery-style paper bags only. The barrier sheet is not submitted as evidence.

- Tape/seal bags closed; label, seal, and initial the seal.

Collect debris.

- Collect obvious debris on patients' bodies (e.g., dirt, leaves, fibers, and hair) on a collection sheet—package, label, seal, and initial seal.

- Fingernail evidence: ask patients whether or not they scratched the suspects' face, body, or clothing. If so, or if fibers of other materials are observed under patients' fingernails, collect fingernail clippings, scrapings, and/or swabbings, according to jurisdictional policy. If fingernail scrapings are collected, package fingernail scrapings and tools used to obtain the sample, label, seal, and initial seal. Cut broken fingernails at the remaining jagged edge for later comparison. Collect a fake nail as a known sample if one is missing. Package, label, seal, and initial the seals.

- If requested, assist patients in putting on exam gowns after clothing and debris are collected.

Collect foreign materials and swabs from the surface of the body. Carefully inspect the body, including head, hair, and scalp, for dried or moist secretions and stains (e.g., blood, seminal fluid, sweat, and saliva) and other foreign material. Use an alternate light source to assist in identifying evidence. Obtain swabs from any suspicious area that may be a dry secretion or stain, any moist secretion, any area that fluoresces with longwave ultraviolet light, and any area for which patients relate a history or suspicion of bodily fluid transfer (e.g., licking, kissing, biting, splashed semen, or suction injury). Also collect swabs from potentially high-yield areas (e.g., neck, breasts, or external genitalia) if the history is absent or incomplete.

- Flake off dried secretions and/or swab dried secretions with a swab moistened with one drop of water. Swab moist secretions with a dry swab. Separate swabs should be used for every sample area collected. Follow jurisdictional policies regarding the number of swabs required to collect each specimen.

- Swab bite marks.

- Optional—smear swabs onto microscope slides, according to jurisdictional policy.

- Cut matted head, facial, or pubic hairs bearing crusted material (or flake off material if possible) and place in an envelope.

- According to jurisdictional policy, air-dry all specimens, package swabs and slides separately, label, seal, and initial seals. Note that coding of evidence must allow the crime lab to know which swab was used to prepare which slide.

- If teeth are flossed prior to oral swab collection, package used floss, label, seal, and initial the seal.

Collect hair combings. Follow jurisdictional policy for collecting hair combings. The purpose of this procedure is to collect hair shed by suspects that may have been transferred to patients' hair. Hair combings may also reveal other foreign materials. Some jurisdictions collect head hair combings only if indicated. Whether or not head combings are collected, it is important to examine head, facial, and pubic hair for secretions, foreign materials, and/or debris and collect as appropriate (see above for collection of debris and foreign materials). Pubic hair combings are typically collected if the assault involved the genital area of patients.

Head hair combings

- Use the comb and collection paper provided for this procedure.
- Place the unfolded paper under patients' heads. Comb head hair towards paper (patients may comb).
- Fold comb with debris/hair into paper. Package paper, label, seal, and initial the seal.

Pubic hair combings

- Use the comb and collection paper provided for this procedure.
- Place the unfolded paper under patients' buttocks and comb hair toward paper (patients may comb).
- Fold comb with debris/hair into paper. Package paper, label, seal, and initial the seal.

Collect hair reference samples as needed. Follow jurisdictional policy for collection of hair reference samples. Many jurisdictions do not collect pubic hair reference samples routinely and some do not collect head hair reference samples routinely during the exam. In other jurisdictions, both samples are collected routinely unless otherwise indicated or declined by patients. Whatever the jurisdictional policy, patients should always be informed about the purpose of collection, procedures used to collect samples, discomfort that may be involved, and how these samples may be used during the investigation and prosecution. If hair reference samples are not collected at the initial exam, it is important to inform patients that there might be a need to collect these samples for crime lab analysis at a later date. They should be aware that hair evidence collected at a later date may not be as conclusive as if it is collected at the time of the initial exam (e.g., due to the fact that hair characteristics can change over time).

When these samples are collected, the indications, timing, and techniques vary. Jurisdictional policies should be in place and followed. Give patients the option of collecting samples themselves.

Collect oral and anogenital swabs and smears. Patients' consent, the medical forensic history, and exam findings should guide collection of oral and anogenital specimens. In general, specimens should be collected only from orifices and areas surrounding the orifices that patients report to be involved in the assault. Keep in mind that some patients may be vague about the type(s) of sexual contact that occurred. Examiners can help clarify which orifices were involved by asking appropriate questions. If there is uncertainty about involved orifices (e.g., because patients have little memory of the assault, were unconscious or incoherent, or do not understand what occurred), collection from oral, vaginal, and anal orifices (with patients' permission) may be appropriate. In some jurisdictions, policy calls for collection from all three orifices. Again, patients' consent is needed to collect these samples. Things to note when collecting these swabs and smears:

- Caution patients who use a bathroom prior to the exam that evidence may be present in pubic, genital, and anal areas and urge them not to wash or wipe away secretions until after evidence collection.

- When taking a swab, examiners should take care not to contaminate the collection with secretions or materials from other areas, such as vaginal to rectal or penile to rectal.

- Follow jurisdictional policy for collecting swabs (and the number of swabs used to collect a sample), smearing swabs on slides, and drying and packaging swabs and slides. Also, follow jurisdictional policy for timeframes in which samples should be collected (e.g., oral and penile samples are only collected within 24 hours of the assault in one jurisdiction) unless otherwise indicated.

- Do not stain or chemically fix swabs or smears.

- When preparing slides, note that coding of evidence material must allow the crime lab to know which swab was used to prepare which slide.

- Document any foreign substance or material introduced by health care providers (e.g., lubricating jelly on a speculum or betadine prior to introduction of a catheter).

Oral sample

- Place swabs together to collect specimen from oral cavity between gums and cheeks and under tongue. Remove dentures and swab with same swabs.
- Optional—smear swabs onto two microscopic slides.
- Air-dry swabs and slides.
- Package slides and swabs, place in envelope, label, seal, and initial the seal.

External genital sample

- Swab external genital dry-skin areas with swabs (blind swabbing by protocol or history), at least one dry and one moistened with a drop of sterile, distilled, or deionized water, according to jurisdictional policy.
- Optional—smear swabs on two microscope slides.
- Air-dry swabs and slides.
- Package slides and swabs, place in envelope, label, seal, and initial the seal.

Vaginal/cervical sample

- Use swabs together to collect a sample from vaginal pool. It is prudent to collect swabs from both the vagina and cervix, regardless of time between assault and exam.
- Optional—smear swabs onto microscope slides.
- Air-dry swabs and slides.
- Package slides and swabs, place in envelope, label (specifically indicating sampling site), seal, and initial the seal.

Wet-mount evaluation. Some jurisdictions require examiners to conduct wet-mount examinations of vaginal/cervical secretions for motile and nonmotile sperm in cases in which a male suspect may have ejaculated in a patient's vagina. Because sperm motility decreases quickly with time and removal from the vagina/cervix, wet-mount evaluation during the exam can provide the only opportunity to see sperm motility. The presence of motile sperm may help narrow the timeframe that the crime could have occurred. In other jurisdictions, however, the crime lab is responsible for all analysis of evidence and examiners do not do the wet-mount evaluation for sperm. Follow jurisdictional policy on whether wet-mount evaluation for sperm is needed and methods of evaluation. If it is required, examiners should be educated on use of the microscope, identification of sperm, and reporting their findings.

- Prepare a wet-mount slide according to jurisdictional policy. Smear one swab collected from the vaginal pool on a slide. Typically, the slide is prepared by placing one drop of normal saline onto the slide. Roll the swab into the drop and place a cover slip on the slide.
- View for presence of sperm under a microscope at 400× or by using a phase contrast or other optically staining microscope (within 10 minutes of preparing slide).
- Air-dry this swab and slide (not removing the cover slip).
- Package swab and slide, place in envelope, label as "wet mount" (specifically indicating sampling site), seal, and initial the seal.

Immediately following collection of vaginal/cervical samples and any necessary wet-mount evaluation, the pelvic examination should be performed and any necessary medical cultures taken.

Penile sample

- Slightly moisten swabs with distilled water and thoroughly swab the external surface of the penile shaft and glans. Swab all outer areas of the penis and scrotum where contact is suspected.
- Gently roll the swabs over one of the microscope slides, according to jurisdictional policy.
- Air-dry swabs and slides.
- Package slides and swabs, place in envelope, label, seal, and initial the seals.

Immediately following this procedure, any necessary medical cultures should be taken.

Perineal area sample

- If there was vaginal/anal contact, there may be leakage of semen in the perineal area. Use an alternate light source on the anal area and flake off or swab areas of dried secretions.
- Optional—smear swabs on microscopic slides, according to jurisdictional policy.
- Flaked dried secretions should be placed into the provided container. Air-dry swabs and slides and package them separately. Place in envelope, label, seal, and initial the seal.
- Avoid contaminating anal/rectal samples by cleansing the perianal area after external secretions and foreign materials have been collected.

Anal/rectal sample

- Collect swabs from the anal cavity. Avoid contact with external skin surfaces.
- Optional—smear swabs on microscopic slides, according to jurisdictional policy.
- Air-dry swabs and slides.
- Package swabs and slides, place in envelope, label, seal, and initial the seal.

At this time, any additional examinations or tests involving the anus should be conducted.

Known blood or saliva sample or buccal swab for DNA analysis and comparison. Many samples collected during the exam contain a mixture of secretions. To interpret genetic typing results obtained from these swabs, it is essential to know the genetic profile of patients. Patients' DNA reference samples are used for this purpose. Follow jurisdictional policy regarding the type of samples accepted by the crime lab. Collection of a buccal swab or saliva sample is encouraged unless it is medically or forensically necessary to take blood. If a blood sample is collected, the most noninvasive method of collection should be used.

Buccal swabs: Decide on a case-by-case basis whether it is appropriate to collect a buccal (inner cheek) swab reference sample for DNA typing rather than a blood sample. For example, a blood sample may not be needed or patients might not allow blood to be drawn. A saliva sample is an alternative to the buccal swab. (Note that buccal swabs and saliva samples are not suitable for blood typing and serology.) If oral copulation is asserted or suspected, a buccal swab or saliva sample for patients' DNA reference may be contaminated. In those cases, blood is usually the better reference sample.

- Buccal swab: Have patients rinse their mouths with tap water and then expose the inner cheek area. Swab this area with gentle pressure. Air-dry the swab, package, place in envelope, label, seal, and initial the seal.

- Saliva sample: Have patients saturate with saliva the inner circle of a folded piece of absorbent paper (e.g., filter paper). Allow the paper to air-dry according to jurisdictional policy. Without touching the inner circle, package the paper, place in envelope, label, seal, and initial the seal. (Patients should not eat, drink, or smoke for at least 15 minutes prior to the saliva sample collection.)

Dry blood

- If drawn blood is not being collected for medical or toxicological purposes, consider dry blood collection because it is a less invasive method of blood collection.

- Using a betadine swab, wipe the tip of the left or right ring finger.
- Using a sterile lancet, prick the finger.
- While holding the finger over one of four circles on the blood collection card, milk the finger, allowing two drops of blood to fall in a circle. Repeat procedure for the remaining circles as required by jurisdictional policy (it may not be necessary to fill all four circles).
- Allow blood to air-dry according to jurisdictional policy. Fill out the patient's name on the first line. Package according to jurisdictional policy, then place in envelope, label, seal, and initial the seal.

Drawn blood

- In order to minimize patients' discomfort, collect drawn blood needed for the reference sample at the same time blood is collected for medical or toxicological purposes.

- Blood for the reference sample may be collected in lavender-top and/ or yellow-top blood drawing tubes. These colored tubes contain preservatives suitable for forensic blood typing. The color to use is typically specified by the designated crime lab. If tubes are included in the evidence collection kit, check expiration dates and replace if expired. Mix according to jurisdictional policy.

- Write the patient's name, date and time of collection, and the collector's initial on the tube. Package according to jurisdictional policy, then place in envelope, label, seal, and initial the seal.

Collect other evidence. Other evidence may be collected beyond what is needed for the sexual assault evidence collection kit.

Toxicology samples. Make the decision about whether to collect toxicology samples for forensic purposes, what to collect, and collection methods according to jurisdictional policy. Do not put toxicology samples in the sexual assault evidence collection kit, unless otherwise indicated. Identify which forensic labs the jurisdiction has selected to analyze these samples, choose a lab, and follow transfer policies....

Keep medical specimens separate from forensic specimens obtained during the exam. Specimens collected for medical purposes should be kept and processed at the medical facility, and specimens collected for forensic analysis should be transferred to the crime laboratory or other specified laboratories for analysis (with patients' consent). It is not necessary to maintain the chain of custody on medical specimens—instead, follow exam facility policy for documenting medical care and storing medical records.

It is important to bear in mind that while these guidelines are thorough, they cannot and will not apply in every case. Forensic examiners must know them well enough to know when they don't apply, and why. It is the spirit of these guidelines, and not the pedantic letter, that matters.

False Positives: Conditions That Mimic Abuse

There are numerous conditions and circumstances that can cause injury consistent with assault or abuse. Therefore, the forensic nurse must be fully aware of the *differential diagnosis*[4] for any finding before making firm conclusions

FIGURE 4.11

Female and Male Sexual Assault Examination forms developed by the author and used at Jamerson Forensic Nursing and Investigative Services, Inc.

Female Examination Case # _____

Tanner Stages	WNL	ABN	DESCRIBE
Breast 1 2 3 4 5			
Genital 1 2 3 4 5			
Perineum			
Medial aspects of thighs			
Buttocks			
Perianal			
Anal folds			
Dentate line			
Tone			
Anal Spasm			
Anal Laxity			
Inguinal Adenopathy			
Vulvovaginal / DC			
Condyloma acuminatum			
Stool in rectal ampulla			

Method of exam for anal tone

( ) Observation   ( ) Digital Exam

( ) Supine   ( ) Knee to Chest

( ) Supine/knee to chest ( ) Colposcope

---

[4]*Differential diagnosis* is strictly defined as the process of weighing the probability of one disease versus that of other diseases possibly accounting for a patient's condition. It considers that symptoms can have multiple causes.

JAMERSON
Forensic Nursing &
Investigative Services, Inc.

	WNL	ABN	DESCRIBE
Posterior fourchette			
Labia minora			
Hymenal ring			
Fossa navicularis			
Rectum			
Labia majora			

Genital exam done with photograph/video   ( ) **Supine**   ( ) **Knee to Chest**

( ) **Colposcope**   ( ) **Direct Visualization**

( ) **Supine/Knee to Chest**

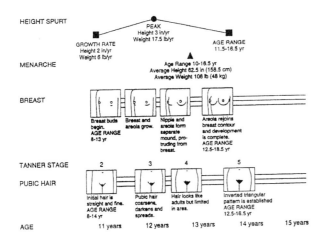

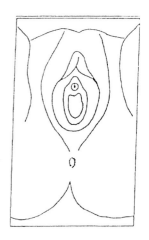

_____   _____   _____

Examiner   *Assistant(s)*   *Date*

FIGURE 4.11
(Continued)

Male Examination   **Case #** _____

Tanner Stages	WNL	ABN	DESCRIBE
Breast 1 2 3 4 5			
Genital 1 2 3 4 5			
Medial aspects of thighs			
Perineum			
Male Anus			
Buttocks			
Perianal Skin			
Dentate line			
Folds, rugae			
Tone			
Anal Spasm			
Anal Laxity			
Urethral D/C			
Condyloma acuminatum			
Stool in rectal ampulla			
Other Lesions			

Method of exam for anal tone   ( ) Observation   ( ) Digital Exam

( ) Supine   ( ) Knee to Chest

( ) Supine/knee to chest ( ) Colposcope

FIGURE 4.11

(Continued)

	WNL	ABN	DESCRIBE
Penis			
Circumcised			
Urethral Meatus			
Scrotum			
Testes			

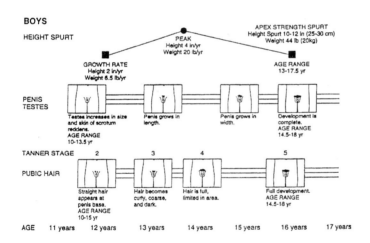

Examiner _____   Assistant(s) _____   Date _____

FIGURE 4.11

(Continued)

JAMERSON
Forensic Nursing &
Investigative Services, Inc.

Case # _____

Cultures	Oral	Rectal	Vaginal	Penile	Lesion
GC					
Chlamydia					
Predominant Organism					

OTHER TESTS ORDERED: to be completed at Washington Regional Medical Center if necessary.

RPR/VDRL	
HIV	
Urine Pregnancy	
Rape Kit (Crime Lab)	
Serum Pregnancy	
Herpes	
Hep B	
Wet Prep:	
Vaginal	
Penile	
Candida	
Trich	

TREATMENT:

SUMMARY:

FIGURE 4.11
(Continued)

Case #_____

Post Assault Symptoms

Urinated	**YES**	**NO**	
Defecated	**YES**	**NO**	
Genital Wipe/Wash	**YES**	**NO**	
Bath/Shower	**YES**	**NO**	
Douche	**YES**	**NO**	
Insert/Remove Tampon	**YES**	**NO**	
Brushed Teeth	**YES**	**NO**	
Oral Rinse	**YES**	**NO**	
Changed Clothes	**YES**	**NO**	

FIGURE 4.11
(Continued)

about its origins. This involves taking into account the possibility that injuries and symptoms may have more than one cause, or a cause unrelated to an assault.

Unfortunately, this basic medical assessment concept can be lost or ignored in a forensic context, where examiners are presented with law enforcement officers or victims insisting that injuries are indeed the result of an assault. The forensic nurse may not make this assumption. Absence of differential diagnosis considerations in any forensic medical exam is the absence of science and the scientific method.

Specific to eliminating false positives in child abuse, but just as important in all other patient examinations, is the advice provided in Burns and Mayer (2000):

Case # _____

_____
_____
_____
_____
_____
_____
_____
_____
_____
_____
_____
_____
_____
_____
_____
_____
_____
_____
_____
_____
_____
_____
_____
_____
_____
_____
_____
_____
_____
_____
_____
_____
_____
_____
_____
_____

Signature: _____ Date: _____

FIGURE 4.11

(Continued)

Case # _____

_____
_____
_____
_____
_____
_____
_____
_____
_____
_____
_____
_____
_____
_____
_____
_____
_____
_____
_____
_____
_____
_____
_____
_____
_____
_____
_____
_____
_____
_____
_____

Signature: _____ Date: _____

FIGURE 4.11
(Continued)

When assessing injuries, the clinician must obtain a complete history, including present illness, review of systems, past medical and psychosocial history, family history (particularly bleeding disorders), and history of injury-related disorders. The caregiver should be permitted to lead the interview with a narrative of the injury. Child abuse should always be suspected when marks or injuries do not match the given history.

Salient clues to child abuse include a history of minor trauma with extensive physical injury, a history of no trauma with evidence of injury, a history of self inflicted trauma that is incompatible with the child's developmental stage, a history of injury that changes with time, and delays in seeking treatment. Caregivers may blame siblings or playmates for serious injuries. When a third party, especially a sibling, is blamed, the clinician should determine if that sibling is developmentally capable of performing the alleged act. Additionally, the description of the injury mechanism must be consistent with injury type, severity, pain history, and developmental age of the injured child.

Burns and Mayer (2000) specifically discuss the interpretation of *bruises,* which can also mislead the forensic examiner if differentials are not considered:

Soft tissue trauma, combined with other trauma findings, may be the most common manifestation of physical abuse. Bruises result from blunt force to the skin surface, which disrupts capillaries and other larger blood vessels. The bruise size and depth are indicative of the force of impact, the size of disrupted blood vessels, the vascularity and connective tissue density, and the fragility of blood vessels. For example, the periorbital area is well vascularized and rapidly shows a black-eye syndrome when impacted.

Toddlers and young children may have some minor bruising caused by rough play; however, these frequent and minor injuries usually overlay bony prominences such as shins, knees, elbows, forehead, and the dorsum of the hands. Lacerations and scrapes usually accompany rough-play bruises.

Underlying body organs influence the pattern of the bruise. Flat objects that strike underlying bony processes may leave marks as a result of the underlying soft tissue compressed against the unyielding bone. Therefore, bruises on relatively protected skin sites, such as cheeks, neck, trunk, genitals, and upper legs, should be considered suspicious for abuse.

On a young infant, multiple bruises of different ages, bruises and marks with geometric shapes, or severe bruising are not consistent with any acceptable history. Deep injuries to an area such as the thigh may not be apparent for hours or days. For example, when examining bruises, the caregiver may state that the child fell down the stairs. Common sense indicates that a fall down nonpadded stairs causes a series of bruises the size and shape of the stair edge; however, bruises would rarely exist on one body area.

The clinician should measure the bruise, describe the color, and draw pictures of the injury on the patient's chart. Based on the informed consent protocols of the individual institution, standard or instant photographs are made and labeled for placement in the patient's record. Instant photographs allow the clinician to verify the quality of the photo before the child leaves the office.

Although the color of a bruise changes with time, a definitive means of dating bruises by color does not exist. On impact, a lesion commonly becomes deep red, blue, or purple. Swelling may last for approximately 2 days until the serum is reabsorbed. Localized or diffuse bleeding into tissue creates extensive bruising in children, especially loose tissue with poorly supported blood vessels such as around the periorbital area and genitals. Generally, the color changes from greenish to yellowish-brown before hemoglobin in the clot degenerates and is absorbed.

Apart from misleading injuries, such as old bruises, unintentional burns, and broken bones from known accidents, there are also misleading infections and skin conditions. For example, an adult female patient may reveal during her history that she has suffered from chronic urinary tract infections since the age of 5, due to the fact that she was born with an anatomical abnormality of the *urethral meatus*.[5] A female with a shorter than normal urethral meatus may be prone to a higher incidence of urinary tract infections. This is because when the tube leading from the bladder to the opening where urine exits the body (also known as the "pee hole," urethral meatus, urethral opening) is short, general bacteria and bacteria from poor hygiene practices, improper wiping, and feces are more likely to migrate up the tube and cause bladder infections. On the other hand, if the patient reports that she has been experiencing burning upon urination, itching, and discharge only since the alleged assault, then these symptoms are more likely related to it.

---

[5]The urethra is the tube leading from the bladder that discharges urine outside of the body. In females the urethra is significantly shorter than in males. The female urethral meatus (i.e., opening) is above the vaginal opening.

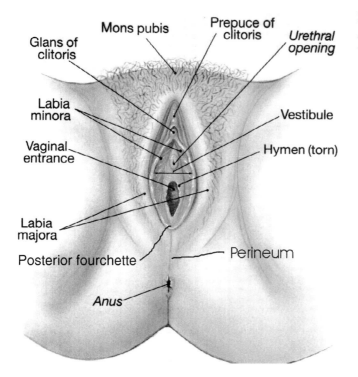

FIGURE 4.12
Anatomy of the external female genitalia.

Mons pubis

Prepuce of clitoris

Urethral opening

Glans of clitoris

Labia minora

Vestibule

Vaginal entrance

Hymen (torn)

Labia majora

Posterior fourchette

Perineum

Anus

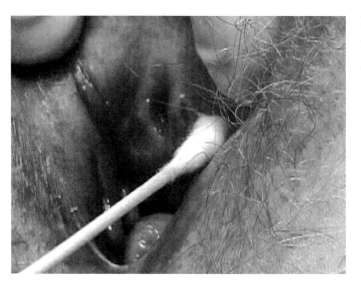

FIGURE 4.13
A forensic examination involves swabbing inside the labia minora for potential biological transfer evidence.

When the ROS reaches the urogenital and anogenital areas of the body, it is therefore important to inquire if the patient has a history of urinary tract infections. If so, at what age did they start and what was going on during the time of the infection? The history may reveal that the patient has had a series of urinary tract and/or vaginal infections with a pattern that coincides with the history of abuse or assault. Failing to document this history at the time of the forensic medical exam can lead to misinterpretations of findings and the inability to make the appropriate referrals for additional medical care.

Let's consider some further examples to illustrate the importance of obtaining patient history regarding hereditary diseases or existing medical conditions, in the context of considering a differential diagnosis.

A patient may reveal in either her medical history or ROS that she has a skin condition known as *contact dermatitis*. This is a reaction caused by the skin coming into contact with allergens or irritants. Examples include poison ivy, poison oak, and poison sumac.

Another example is a skin condition known as *seborrhea*. Also known as seborrheic dermatitis or dandruff, this presents with rashes that can be pruritic (itch intensely) and become infected due to breaks in the skin. Seborrhea in the genital area may be seen more often in infancy, especially in skin folds in the diaper area and between the labia minora and labia majora (Giardino and Giardino 2003).

Furthermore, a seborrheic lesion in the genitalia often presents itself as raised and erythemic (red in color). It may also display as yellowish, slightly moist greasy scales in the perigenital (around the genitalia) areas. Such findings are not the result of abuse, but may be misinterpreted by examiners without sufficient patient history.

Another skin condition that must be eliminated as a cause of symptoms is *lichen sclerosus* (LS), which affects the vulva (or penis) and anus. The symptoms of LS include thinning skin, white patches of skin, itching and/or burning, pain during sexual intercourse, and sores or lesions resulting from scratching. However, not all of the symptoms will necessarily be present. According to the National Institutes of Health (NIH 2005):

> Early in the disease, small white spots appear on the skin. The spots are usually shiny and smooth. Later, the spots grow into bigger patches. The skin on the patches becomes thin and crinkled. Then the skin tears easily, and bright red or purple bruises are common. Sometimes, the skin becomes scarred. If the disease is a mild case, there may be no symptoms.

Other symptoms are:

- Itching (very common)
- Discomfort or pain
- Bleeding
- Blisters.

. . .

Doctors don't know the exact cause of lichen sclerosus. Some doctors think a too active immune system and hormone problems may play a role. It is also thought that people inherit the likelihood of getting the disease. Sometimes, lichen sclerosus appears on skin that has been damaged or scarred from some other previous injury.

Lichen sclerosus is not contagious (it can't be caught from another person).

Differential diagnosis considers the possibility that there is more than one cause for any set of injuries, conditions, or symptoms presented by a patient. The objective forensic examiner embraces this medical reality, and works to eliminate causes rather than to prove a relationship between injuries, conditions, and crime. At the very least, this requires the forensic examiner to document each symptom, condition, and injury present with the patient, as well as to establish any specific history that is relevant.

Documentation

A final word is necessary on proper documentation. It is advised that the entire physical examination be at the very least audiotaped and transcribed for investigative, reconstructive, and court purposes—after all, this is a forensic procedure, and the resulting findings are intended to be used as evidence. Less information is not better. Additionally, it will protect the forensic examiner should the patient claim to have been mistreated during the examination at some later date.

With respect to photographs, take more not less. But be sensitive and professional. As provided in the NIJ (2004, 85–87) guidelines regarding "Photography":

Consider patient comfort and privacy. Minimize patients' discomfort while they are being photographed and respect their need for modesty and privacy. Drape them appropriately while taking photographs.

Also, consider how to best provide support to patients during this time. Patients may want an advocate and/or a personal support person to be present. Take measures to avoid allegations of impropriety when photographing patients. For instance, if for some reason a male photographer is photographing a female patient, another woman should be present at this time.

Explain forensic photography procedures to patients. Taking photographs of patients in the aftermath of an assault can be retraumatizing. To help reduce the chances of retraumatization, help patients understand the purpose of photography in forensic evidence collection, the extent to which photographs will be taken and procedures that will be used, potential uses of photographs during investigation and prosecution (especially anogenital images if taken), and the possible need to obtain additional photographs following the exam. (Also see *A.3. Informed Consent.*)

Take initial and follow-up photographs as appropriate, according to jurisdictional policy. Strive to control every element in the photograph to produce a clear, powerful statement. Photographs should be taken prior to evidence collection.

Patient identification. Link patients' identity and the date to the photographs, according to jurisdictional policy. For example, print the patient's name, date of exam, and the photographer's name/initials on a plain sheet of paper. Photograph this sheet at the beginning and end of the roll of film for identification. Some jurisdictions also photograph the face of patients for identification purposes. Some cameras offer the option of imprinting the date and/or time on the negative, and some have the ability to enter a case number so the face or name of a patient is not on the film.

Mechanisms should be in place (e.g., at law enforcement agencies and exam facilities) to protect patients' privacy and confidentiality related to the photographs.

Clear and accurate photographs. Use the shutter speed and lens aperture to control exposure (automated cameras and flash units can give incorrect exposures). Use adequate lighting whether the source is natural, flood, or flash. Use of flashes and lighting in the exam room can change the color of evidence; a filter may help adjust lighting so that the photograph is truer to color (noting in records any alterations to the environment to enhance photographs). Include a color bar in the photograph to ensure accurate color reproduction.

Strive for undistorted photographs with good perspective (whenever possible, use a normal focal length lens, keep the camera level, and photograph the subject at eye level). Maintain sharp focus (keep the camera steady, focus carefully, use maximum depth of field, and look at the frame of the scene).

A good-quality macros lens with a ring strobe flash offers the best quality and most flexibility for forensic photography involving sexual assault.

Scale. Use an inch scale or ruler for size reference in photographs. In addition to those photographs that identify patients and anatomical locations being photographed, take at least two photographs of each area—one with and one without scale. Taking two photographs in this manner demonstrates that the scale was not concealing anything important. Photograph evidence in place before moving it or collecting it. Do not alter or move evidence when photographing, and make every effort to minimize distraction in photographs while maintaining the focus of areas being photographed.

Orientation of shots. Take at least two shots at three orientations:

1. Take full-body images (anterior, posterior, and lateral) with the patient's face visible and clearly identifiable. Position patients approximately two feet from the corner of the room, using walls to reflect and diffuse flash illumination. When photographing the backs of patients, turn their faces toward the camera so that they can be recognized.

2. Take medium-range photographs of each separate injury, including cuts, bruises, swelling, lacerations, and abrasions. Work from one side to the other and then top to bottom, or design a workable method. Be consistent. Take "regional" shots to show injuries in the context and orientation of a body region; these photographs should include easily identifiable anatomical landmarks.

3. Take close-up images of particular injuries, using the scale. When photographing a wound, show its relationship to another part of the body. Take at least three photographs involving a wound area. Shield uninvolved breast or genital areas when possible; highly graphic photos may be deemed inadmissible in court and make the case less credible. All injuries should be recorded with a close-up attachment. Try to capture subtleties in texture and color. Document pattern injuries caused by an object. Do not use an external light source around an injured eye as it can cause retinal damage.

Photographing skin. Close-up photographs of hands and fingernails may show traces of blood, skin, or hair. Be sure to look for damage to nails or missing nails. Photograph marks of restraint or bondage around wrists, ankles, or neck; they may be compared later with the object in question that made the marks. Photograph transfer evidence present on the body or clothing, such as dirt, gravel, or vegetation.

Bite mark evidence. Photograph bite marks, according to jurisdictional policy.

Accountability. All photographs should be clearly labeled and the chain of custody maintained. Follow jurisdictional policy for development of film, transfer, duplication or additional prints, and storage of photographs. Do not include photographs in the evidence collection kit sent to the crime lab.

Follow-up photographs. Photography should be repeated as new or different evidence on patients' bodies is found following the exam (e.g., bruising may appear days later). Create procedures that examiners, law enforcement investigators, and patients follow to ensure this evidence is documented. In addition to documenting emerging or evolving injuries, follow-up photographs provide documentation of healing or resolving injuries and clarify findings of stable, normal variants in anatomy that could be confused with acute injuries.

For want of a photo not taken, an entire case may be misinterpreted, or left without resolution.

FINDINGS

As explained in the NIJ (2004) guidelines, forensic nurses must conduct and document every examination they perform thoroughly, as though it will go to trial, even though many will not. This is part of maintaining a forensic mindset. The purpose of any forensic examination is to educate the court system. Examination reports that do not provide interpretations about whether and how findings may be consistent with sexual assault, abuse, or the patient's account as provided in the forensic interview are unfortunately common. Such reports are, however, unprofessional—too often they allow forensic examiners latitude in their ultimate interpretations; too often they leave a false or confused impression in the minds of those who read them; and too often they allow attorneys to characterize findings with their own adventitious interpretations.

Additionally, forensic interpretations of exam findings must be made in light of the known victim history and the most current advances in relevant research, methods, and other changes in the field. This places the burden of thorough forensic interviewing squarely on the forensic examiner, as well as the requirement of continuing education. The court should treat forensic interpretations made in the absence of these considerations with skepticism.

To be clear, all forensic examiners' reports should say what they did, what they found, and what it means—not in general, not in part, and not in collusion with a particular side. In other words, the forensic examiner's report should be the truth, the WHOLE truth, and nothing but the truth.

SUMMARY

Forensic nurses are a particular kind of forensic examiner who provide patient care in the context of evidence recognition, documentation, collection, and preservation efforts. They are consequently objective and scientific finders of fact, utilizing scientific principles and medical knowledge to discover evidence related to diseases, injuries, and crimes that may be suffered by all manner of victims. Their job is to perform a forensic medical examination of alleged victims, which includes initial contact, intake assessment, obtaining victim history, physical examination, evidence documentation and collection, and the interpretation of findings, including any related treatment.

After obtaining the proper consents from the victim, the forensic nurse collects intake information from her or his patient to govern the nature and sequence of subsequent examination and treatment efforts. Prior to any physical examination or evidence collection efforts, a forensic interview should be conducted to obtain complete victim history information. Conducting an accurate forensic medical examination in the absence of patient medical history is not possible.

Throughout the entire forensic medical examination, forensic nurses must consider and treat the victim's body as a physical extension of the crime scene. They must approach their task methodically and in a thorough, head-to-toe fashion. This will provide the best opportunity for the recognition, documentation, and collection of potential injuries and evidence transfer.

Interpretations by the forensic nurse should be grounded in an objective consideration of complete victim history, the results of the physical examination, and the consideration of differential diagnoses.

Questions

1. What are forensic nurses required to understand first and foremost?
2. True or False: The medical forensic exam is an interactive process that must be adapted to the needs and circumstances of each patient
3. According to the NIJ what are three pieces of information that must be sought for a medical forensic history?
4. Explain how Locard's Exchange Principle applies to the practice of forensic nursing.
5. Explain the importance of negative documentation.
6. True or False: In an alleged sexual assault, lack of injury to the victim proves consent.
7. Why is it important to properly document a physical examination?

REFERENCES

Billings, J.A., and J. Stoeckle. 1999. *The Clinical Encounter: A Guide to the Medical Interview and Case Presentation*, 2nd ed. St. Louis: Mosby.

Bownes, I., O'Gorman, E., and Saters, A. 1991. A rape comparison of stranger and acquaintance assaults. *MedSciLaw*, Vol. 31, No. 2, pp. 102–109.

Burns, P., and B. Mayer. 2000. "Differential Diagnosis of Abuse Injuries in Infants and Young Children." *Nurse Practitioner*, 25: 15–37, October: http://findarticles .com/p/articles/mi_qa3958/is_200010/ai_n8913928.

Chisum, W.J., and B.E. Turvey. 2006. *Crime Reconstruction*. Boston: Elsevier Science.

Finkel, M. 2002. "The Evaluation." In *Medical Evaluation of Child Sexual Abuse: A Practical Guide*, 2nd ed., edited by M. Finkel and A. Giardino, 23–37. Thousand Oaks, CA: Sage Publications.

Giardino, E.R., and A.P. Giardino. 2003. *Nursing Approach to the Evaluation of Child Maltreatment*. St. Louis, MO: G.W. Publishing.

Gray-Eurom, K., Seaberg, D., and Wears, R. 2002. The prosecution of sexual assault cases: correlation with forensic evidence. *Annals of Emergency Medicine*, Vol. 39, No. 1, pp. 39–46.

Kilpatrick, D., Edmunds, C., and Seymour, A. 1992. *Rape in America: A report to the nation*. Arlington, VA: National Victim Center.

Kirk, P. and Thornton, J.I. 1974. *Crime Investigation*, 2nd ed., New York: John Wiley & Sons.

LeDray, L. 1999. *Sexual Assault Nurse Examiner (SANE) Development and Operation Guide*. U.S. Department of Justice, Office of Victims of Crime.

LeDray, L. 2004. "Forensic Medical Evidence: The Contributions of the Sexual Assault Nurse Examiner SANE." Chapter 6 in *Rape Investigation Handbook*, edited by J. Savino and B. Turvey,. Boston: Elsevier Science.

Locard, E. 1934. *La Police et Les Methodes Scientifiques*. Paris: Les Editions Rieder.

Marchbanks, P.J., Lui, K.J., and Mercy, J.A. 1990. Risk of injury from resisting rape. *American Journal of Epidemiology*, Vol. 132, No. 3, pp. 540–549.

Nelson, V. 1998. "Shattering the Myths about Forensic Nursing." *Nurseweek*, July 13. http://www.nurseweek.com/features/98-7/forensic.html.

NIH (National Institutes of Health). 2005. "Lichen Sclerosus." Bethesda, MD: National Institute of Arthritis and Musculoskeletal and Skin Diseases NIAMS, National Institutes of Health, October. http://www.niams.nih.gov/Health_Info/ Lichen_Sclerosus/lichen_sclerosus_ff.asp.

NIJ (National Institute of Justice). 2004. *A National Protocol for Sexual Assault Medical Forensic Examinations*. Washington, DC: U.S. Department of Justice, Office on Violence Against Women, NCJ 206554, September.

Palusci, V.J., and T.A. Cyrus. 2001. "Reaction to Videocolposcopy in the Assessment of Child Sexual Abuse." *Child Abuse and Neglect* 25, 11: 1535–1546.

Peterson, J., and J. Thornton. 2002. "General Assumptions and Rationale of Forensic Identification." In *Modern Scientific Evidence: The Law and Science of Expert Testimony*, Vol. 3, edited by D. Faigman, D. Kaye, M. Saks, and J. Sanders, 145–. St. Paul, MN: West Publishing.

Petrak, J., and Claydon, E. 1995. The prevalence of sexual assault in a genitourinary medicine clinic: Service implications. *Genitourinary Medicine*, Vol. 71, pp. 98–102.

Riggs, N., Houry, D., Long, G., Markovchick, V., and Feldhaus, K. 2000. Analysis of 1,076 cases of sexual assault. *Annals of Emergency Medicine*, Vol. 35, No. 4, pp. 358–362.

Sheridan, D.J. 1993. The role of the battered woman specialist. *Journal of Psychosocial Nursing*, Vol. 31, No. 11, pp. 31–37.

Thornton, J.I. 1997. "The General Assumptions and Rationale of Forensic Identification," in Faigman, D., Kaye, D., Saks, M., and Sanders, J. (Eds.), *Modern Scientific Evidence: The Law and Science of Expert Testimony*, Vol. 2, St. Paul, MN: West.

Tucker, S., Claire, E., Ledray, L., and Werner, J. 1990. Sexual assault evidence collection. *Wisconsin Medical Journal*, Vol. 89, No. 7, pp. 407–411.

Turvey, B. 2008. *Criminal Profiling: An Introduction to Behavioral Evidence Analysis*, 3rd ed., San Diego: Elsevier Science.

CHAPTER 5

Victim Lifestyle Exposure

Joe M. Diaz, Wayne A. Petherick, and Brent E. Turvey

KEY TERMS

Active precipitation: situations in which the victim directly provokes the offender.

Capable guardians: individuals whose presence or proximity discourages offenders from committing crime. These can be police, security, family members, or regular citizens.

Deification of the victim: the tendency to view the victim as lacking flaws. This can happen after a violent crime, when investigators are given reports that victims were saintly in every aspect of their lives.

High-exposure victims: people routinely exposed to the possibility of suffering harm or loss.

Lifestyle theory: argues that some people are more prone to victimization because their behavior, habits, or customs expose them to a greater frequency of contact with crime and criminals.

Likely offender: one who is motivated to offend due to a variety of factors, including availability and vulnerability of victims, fantasy, and so on.

Low-exposure victims: people infrequently exposed to the possibility of suffering harm or loss.

Medium-exposure victims: people sometimes exposed to the possibility of suffering harm or loss.

Suitable targets: victims or objects that offenders perceive to be susceptible to their modus operandi.

Passive precipitation: when a victim exhibits some personal characteristic that unknowingly threatens or encourages the attacker.

Principle of homogamy: suggests that individuals are more exposed to the possibility of victimization if they frequently associate, or come into contact with, members of demographic groups containing high numbers of criminals.

CONTENTS

Victim Selection - pg 175

General Traits - pg 181

> *Prostitute:* any person who engages in sexual activity for payment.
>
> *Routine activity theory:* examination of victim-offender interaction by considering the spatial and temporal structure of routine legal activities.
>
> *Situational exposure:* harmful elements experienced by the victim resulting from the environment and personal traits at the time of the victimization.
>
> *Victim exposure:* amount of contact or vulnerability to harmful elements experienced by a victim in everyday life as a consequence of biological and environmental factors.
>
> *Victim precipitation:* the extent to which a victim plays a role, either knowingly or unknowingly, in his or her own victimization. Precipitation can be passive or active.
>
> *Vilification of the victim:* viewing or casting certain victim populations as worthless or disposable by their very nature.

It has been said that for every crime there is at least one victim. However, victimity may not be assumed or otherwise presupposed. First, the existence of crime must be established; if there is no crime, there can be no victim. Then it is necessary to establish which participant is the victim. This cannot be assumed either as explained by von Hentig (cited in Wolfgang 1959, 245):

> Here are two human beings. As soon as they draw near to one another, male or female, young or old, rich or poor, ugly or attractive—a wide range of interactions, repulsions as well as attractions, is set in motion. What the law does is to watch the one who acts and the one who is acted upon. By this external criterion a subject and object, a perpetrator and a victim are distinguished. In sociological and psychological quality the situation may be completely different. It may happen that the two distinct categories merge. There are cases in which they are reversed and in the long chain of causative forces the victim assumes the role of a determinant.

Unravelling the causative forces and interactions that comprise a given victim-offender relationship is often not a simple task. Victims may be specifically targeted; a function of opportunity related to place, time, or crime; or they may be random. Forensic victimologists understand that exploring this dynamic can be key to answering any number of investigative and forensic questions. This requires examining the true and precise role that the victim played in his or her own demise—if any at all. In each case there will be multiple possibilities to consider and eliminate, and the dispositive evidence will not always be immediately apparent.

As explained in Petherick and Turvey (2008), one of the many lenses that may be used to examine the victim-offender relationship is the level of *exposure* involved. Generally, *victim exposure* refers to the amount of contact or vulnerability to harmful elements that is experienced by a victim. It is determined by examining *lifestyle exposure* and *situational exposure*. We will begin our explicit coverage of this subject by studying the victim's general lifestyle choices.[1]

EXAMINING VICTIM LIFESTYLE EXPOSURE: PURPOSE AND RATIONALE

It is the aim of this chapter to explore how lifestyle factors can generally provide for victim exposure to harm and influence the subsequent dynamics of victimization. The first section will explore the concept of victim lifestyle exposure—what it is and what it is not. The second section will describe how these lifestyle factors and subsequent exposures may shape the spatial or temporal occurrence of a criminal offense by reference to the theoretical constructs present in the literature. The final section will demonstrate how lifestyle exposure is interpreted through victimology, with reference to established investigative guidelines. Case studies will be provided throughout to illustrate these concepts.

At this point, it is necessary to remind ourselves that studying different aspects of victimology to identify harm and causative influence is not about blaming a victim for his or her demise. Or more precisely, it is not the explicit purpose of forensic victimology to determine whether victims are necessarily to blame for the crimes that are committed against them. There are two very important reasons for this. First, from the perspective of forensic victimology, this type of determination is ultimately a matter for the trier of fact. While the victimologist may assist with this determination by providing relevant information and analysis, it is a judge or jury that decides whether and how a victim may have engaged in some form of contributory negligence. Second, in many cases, as stressed in Turvey (2002, 141), "victims are not responsible for the predatory acts of offenders." This is further explained in Petherick and Turvey (2008, 380):

> The choices victims make to ensure personal safety, despite their best efforts, are only going to be sufficient for an offender of a certain skill level. Put another way, whether or not a victim is going to fall prey to an offender is not exclusively a function of the victim's efforts to maintain personal safety. It is also a function of the amount of skill and time a particular offender is willing to put into his or her method of approach and method of attack.

> Detectives might blame a prostitute, in whole or in part, for being the victim of a violent crime. The same detective might view a student in a similar situation as an unfortunate victim of circumstance. However,

[1]This coverage will continue in Chapter 6, "Victim Situational Exposure."

establishing victim "blame" does not add anything to the investigative effort. All citizens have moments of vulnerability, no matter what level of harm their lifestyle and circumstances expose them too. Criminals are not entitled to commit crimes just because citizens have these moments of vulnerability.

Consequently, the terms and definitions provided in this chapter are designed to help the forensic victimologist examine and depict the relationship of a victim to lifestyle and environment, and subsequently of a given offender to that victim. They provide a language to characterize the facts of a case as established by the corresponding victim evidence. Th e end results are intended to provide insight into the kinds of defenses that a given offender is willing and able to defeat in order to achieve his or her goals with the victim.

It is not the place of any victimologist to make personal or moral judgments about any victim, only to examine the totality of facts and circumstances objectively. This will be discussed further at the end of the chapter, in the section regarding victim vilification and deification.

WHAT IS LIFESTYLE EXPOSURE?

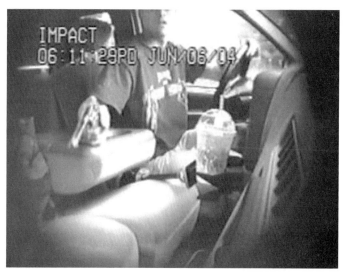

FIGURE 5.1

A car thief in Canada is captured in a police "bait car": first by the hidden camera, then by police as sensors lock the vehicle's door lock and kill the engine. (Courtesy baitcar.com.)

Victim *lifestyle exposure* is concerned with studying the potentially harmful elements that exist in a victim's everyday life as a consequence of biological and environmental factors, as well as past choices. As defined in Petherick and Turvey (2008, 383), victim lifestyle exposure is "the amount of exposure to harmful elements experienced by the victim and resulting from the victim's usual environment and personal traits." It requires an investigation and assessment of the victim's personality, and his or her personal, professional, and social environment (Turvey 2008).

A victim's general *lifestyle exposure* to harm or loss should not be confused with *situational exposure*, which refers to harmful elements experienced by the victim resulting from his or her environment and personal traits at the time of victimization. One analogy to differentiate these concepts is to consider lifestyle exposure as a "weather forecast," anticipating what harmful elements may be present by virtue of what has been present in the past under similar conditions and given various indicators;

incident exposure can then be considered the "daily weather report," identifying the actual cloud coverage, temperature, and precipitation on a given day. An example that more clearly illustrates these concepts involves car keys.

Case Example: Car Keys and Car Thieves

Consider the recent vehicle theft situation on Staten Island, New York (*Newsday* 2008):

> Lt. John Peruffo of the N-Y-P-D's Auto Larceny Unit on Staten Island says more than a third of the vehicles stolen in the borough so far this year had keys in the ignition.
>
> Peruffo says 76 vehicles were reported stolen as of Sunday, 13 more than within the same time frame last year. He says 24 of those had the keys in the ignition.
>
> Another 10 vehicles were stolen with keys found nearby—in a glovebox, on the ground of a parking lot or discovered inside a jacket left behind at a restaurant.

On Staten Island, and other places with similar crime trends, greater lifestyle exposure to vehicle theft would be associated with a habit of leaving car keys unattended or in the ignition. Incident exposure, on the other hand, is a question of whether or not the victim actually left keys in the ignition immediately prior to an actual vehicle theft. In either case, the closer a victim leaves unattended the keys to the vehicle's ignition, the greater the exposure to vehicle theft. It is therefore possible for a victim to have a high lifestyle exposure to vehicle theft by virtue of habitually leaving the keys in the ignition with the engine running when entering a convenience store; and subsequently a low incident exposure by virtue of having the car stolen on a day when it was locked up with the keys safely pocketed.

LIFESTYLE EXPOSURE: THEORETICAL FRAMEWORK

The causal link between a victim's lifestyle and his or her victimization is not always clear. This is because it is difficult to reconcile just how much influence any one lifestyle factor has on the criminal situation. Generally, lifestyle factors can influence harm to the victim in three ways: by creating a perceived conflict with an offender; by increasing the victim's presence around offenders or those predisposed towards criminality; or by enhancing an offender's perception of victim vulnerability. To better understand the influence of lifestyle, it would be beneficial to examine the theoretical arguments behind victim lifestyle exposure.

The following theories are useful in identifying how a victim's lifestyle may contribute to his or her own victimization. They are not exhaustive of the literature but are the most applicable for our discussion. Although general in explaining how lifestyle affects exposure, each theory provides a unique perspective in understanding the role of the victim in the crime.

Victim Precipitation

The relevance of lifestyle exposure to explaining how a victim influences the occurrence of a particular crime is primarily founded on the theoretical arguments of victim precipitation. Victim precipitation theorists first introduced the argument that the dynamics of a criminal act cannot be fully understood solely by looking at the characteristics of the perpetrator but rather must also encompass an examination of the role of the victim. First coined by Marvin Wolfgang (1959) for classifying homicides, the concept was applied where victims had first initiated physical force against their perpetrators.

Deviating significantly from the work of Wolfgang (1959), Menachim Amir later applied a more radical application of victim precipitation. His definition included acts in which victims did not initiate physical force first but rather inadvertently influenced their own harm by way of offender interpreted provocation. Still, in its liberal application, victim precipitation theory has been primarily concerned with explaining the context of victimization as a two-person act. As Rock explains (2007, 42):

> Victim precipitation was propounded first by Mendelsohn, and it
> alludes to the criminally provocative, collusive or causal impact of
> the victim in a dyadic relation variously called the "penal couple"
> (Mendelsohn 1963, 241); the "reciprocal action between perpetrator
> and victim" (von Hentig 1948, 303); the "duet theory of crime" (von
> Hentig 1948, 397); a "situated transaction" (Luckenbill 1977); "the
> functional responsibility for crime" (Schafer 1968, 55), or simply, "the
> victim-offender relationship" (Wolfgang 1957, 1).

Rock (2007, 42) goes on to state that "victim-precipitation portrays crime somewhat neutrally as an interactive process or evolving relation between victim and offender, in which each influences not only the conduct of the other but also the form and content of any crime that may ensue." The major premise of victim precipitation is that victims knowingly and unknowingly contribute to their victimization. According to Siegel (2007), this precipitation can be either passive or active.

Passive precipitation occurs when the victim exhibits some personal characteristic that unknowingly threatens or encourages the attacker. The victim is more exposed to harm because of an offender's perception of conflict during personal interaction. This conflict need not be actual; it may be the result of misperception, misunderstanding, or subconscious influence.

Consider the murder of two patent attorneys and the attempted murder of their paralegal by truck driver Joe Jackson, in Chicago, Illinois. As Maxwell explains (2006):

> On Friday, consumed by his obsession, Jackson gunned down patent attorney Michael McKenna and two others on the 38th floor of a West Loop high-rise before he was shot and killed by police.
>
> The sad motive behind a seemingly inexplicable tragedy comes clear in Jackson's words.
>
> "I need help because I am very upset," he wrote. "I paid my hard earn money to a unmoral man. Pleased help me. He took this because of greed."
>
> The document, which begins "A portable toilet for truck driver which I am one," says Jackson first met McKenna on Feb. 18, 2002:
>
> "He wrote down every detail and ask me every last question about my project he said cause when he submit it to them patent people he needs to know everything about it...He told me this was so kind of joke and he told me it would not work or it was already on the market. I told him absolutely not I drive a truck for almost 25 years off and on and it did not exist."
>
> Material provided by Rev. C.L. Sparks, Jackson's pastor at New Pleasant Valley International Cathedral, includes Jackson's handwritten letter documenting his interaction with McKenna as well as a rough sketch—nothing more than a doodle—of the portable truck-cab toilet.

Passive precipitation also includes those situations where the victim and offender have prior interaction, yet the offender perceives a conflict because of the victim's association with a particular group. In such instances, offenders do not care about the specific identity of the victim. Rather, they see the victim as a reasonable object, or target, for their retributive or anger-retaliatory acts.[2]

As Fletcher describs (1998), the murder of Dr. Barnette Slepian is a good example of how a victim's professional lifestyle choices can influence his exposure to harm through passive precipitation:

> A sniper wielding a high-powered rifle from the cover of darkness shot and killed a well-known abortion doctor Friday night just days after U.S. and Canadian police warned of such an attack, citing four previous shootings against abortion doctors at this time of year in Canada and upstate New York.

[2]As Turvey explains (2008, 285): "Anger retaliatory motive is evidence by crime scene behaviors that indicate a great deal of rage, either toward a specific person, group, institution, or a symbol of either. These types of behaviors are commonly evidenced in stranger-to-stranger sexual assaults, domestic homicides, work-related homicides, and cases involving political or religious terrorists."

> Barnett Slepian, 52, was killed by a single shot fired through a window as he stood in the kitchen of his home about 10 p.m. in this Buffalo suburb, police said today. Slepian, for years a defiant target of antiabortion protesters here, had just returned from a synagogue with his wife and four sons, aged 7 to 15, Amherst police said.
>
> Police said the fatal shot was fired from a wooded area behind Slepian's home and crashed through a kitchen window before mortally wounding him. His wife called emergency personnel, who took Slepian to nearby Millard Fillmore Suburban Hospital, where he was pronounced dead at 11:30 p.m.
>
> The murder shocked activists on both sides of the volatile abortion issue, not only because of its cold-blooded execution, but also because it bore eerie similarities to a series of sniper attacks that have wounded four abortion doctors here in the border region over the past four years. In each of those cases, the doctors were fired on with high-powered rifles through the windows of their homes at approximately this time of year.

In this case, the doctor chose a medical practice that involved performing abortions. Subsequently, he was targeted by extremists who view such abortion as murder, so consequently immoral and, ironically, punishable by death. He did not seek out direct conflict with these extremists, nor was he working at the time of his murder; rather he was executed in his home, in front of his family.

Active precipitation refers to those situations in which the victim directly provokes the offender. These provocations can range from insults to physical assault. Whatever the case, an actively precipitating victim is one who strikes first and ultimately loses the most. Active precipitation is more commonly associated with incident exposure, as precipitation is most apparent in cases where the response towards the victim is immediate. However, it can also be associated with victim lifestyle factors and choices that intentionally seek to trigger a response from a particular group or individual.

Examples of active precipitation may be found in the work of extreme activists who seek out situations where they can put themselves between the object of their cause and danger. This would include riding an inflatable skiff in the path of a whaling ship, chaining oneself to a tree to prevent it from being cut down, or lying down in front of a tank in an act of protest. This extreme activism may be an ongoing lifestyle choice reflective of a particular kind of character, or a once-in-a-lifetime event in response to unacceptable circumstances.

Lifestyle Theory

Lifestyle theory (Hindelang, Gottfredson, and Garofalo 1986) argues that some people are more prone to victimization because their behavior, habits, or customs expose them to a greater frequency of contact with crime and criminals.

As Siegal (2007, 75) explains, "the basis for lifestyle theory is that crime is not a random occurrence but rather a reflection of a person's lifestyle." This is consistent with the *principle of homogamy* (Hindelang, Gottfredson, and Garofalo 1978), which suggests that individuals are more exposed to the possibility of victimization if they frequently associate with, or come into contact with, members of demographic groups containing a disproportionate amount of criminals.

We agree that a victim history of interaction or involvement with criminals can increase exposure to certain kinds of harm and therefore makes harm more likely. For the forensic victimologist, identifying this history and examining it are a necessary part of any assessment, as they may provide both investigative leads and viable suspects. Take, for example, the homicide of Genna Gamble, discussed in Turvey (2002, 152–154) and presented here in near entirety. This case thoroughly highlights the need for an extensive investigation into the background of the victim and exemplifies the increased exposure that arises from interaction with offenders:

> In this case, Douglas S. Mouser was tried for the murder of 14-year-old Genna Lynn Gamble, his stepdaughter. Her nude body was found on the hillside along Dry Creek near Waterford, California, on October 14, 1995. She had been strangled to death.
>
> The state theorized, based on the speculations of detectives and an FBI trained DOJ [Department of Justice] criminal profiler, Michael J. Prodan, that Doug Mouser first killed Genna Gamble at their home in Modesto and then drove her body 20–30 minutes away to dispose of it. They felt that this likely occurred during or after she had taken a shower, explaining her nudity.
>
> The criminal profilers in this case were ultimately allowed to testify on several pertinent issues, including victimology. The DOJ criminal profiler testified to the following, as an expert in crime analysis and victimology (this list is not exclusive):
>
> - He is not a forensic scientist, nor does he know what Locard's Exchange Principle is.
> - Crime scene evidence and victimology are important parts of crime analysis.
> - He did not review much of the available victim information in forming his opinions. He was unaware of the fact that her brother had dealt drugs out of the home, and that she had been spending time with and dating known sex offenders.

FIGURE 5.2

Hillside disposal scene in the murder of Genna Gamble. Note the drag trail leading up from the river bottoms and the position of the body. Source: author's case files.

- He did not visit the crime scene in forming his opinions.
- He reviewed only 15 of the several hundred crime scene and autopsy photos in forming his opinions.
- He did not review Dr. John Thornton's crime reconstruction of the case in forming his opinions.
- Genna Gamble was a low risk victim.
- Genna Gamble was most likely killed by someone who knew her.
- Genna Gamble likely first encountered her attacker in her home.

No relevant case facts were offered to support any of the opinions provided by Special Agent Prodan. In fact, he admitted, rather surprisingly, to reading very little of the available relevant victimology in the case, blaming detectives for not providing the material to him. Ultimately, the basis for his opinions was stated simply as being derived from his education, training, and experience.

The author [Turvey] then testified to the following, as an expert in crime analysis and victimology, for the defense (this list is not exclusive):

- Examined all the material related to the victim provided by discovery.
- Examined all the forensic examinations and reports generated by both defense and prosecution criminalists.
- Reviewed all of the crime scene and autopsy photographs, as well as the crime scene video.
- Visited the crime scene twice—with Dr. John Thornton.
...
- Genna Gamble was at high risk of being a victim of violent crime, owing to the following:
  1. The victim was diagnosed with Oppositional Defiant Disorder. She was characterized by her therapist as exhibiting behavior that included the sudden loss of temper, deliberate antagonizing of others, refusal to obey parental instruction, and impulsivity.
  2. The victim was known to have a low self-image, which would make her particularly susceptible to the approaches of certain types of sex offenders (those that use a con that involves flattery or the suggestion of acceptance).
  3. The victim often spent time at locations socializing with age inappropriate males, unsupervised by adults (Mall, Camelot, and Funworks).
  4. The victim was known to have socialized with a sex offender whose victim of choice included girls in Genna Gamble's age range, that were acquired at locations similar to the types that Genna Gamble frequented when unsupervised.

5. The victim was thought to have been likely to get into a car with someone that she knew from Camelot.
6. The victim's brother, Gerran Gamble, was known to have been dealing drugs, which he stored at their home.

There are many unexplained sexual aspects to the circumstances of Genna Gamble's death, and no evidence of profit or anger motivation in the crime scene.

Genna Gamble was a teenage girl who, among other influences, lived with a drug dealer and was involved with a convicted sex offender. One was an environmental factor; the other was an ignorant choice. Each increased her exposure to harm from the dangers of a particular world of criminal activity. She was also seeking treatment and taking medication for Oppositional Defiant Disorder. She would ignore treatment advice, run away, and discontinue medication when angry—to intentionally create discord with her parents. Whether the actual offender was her stepfather or the sex offender she was seeing, it is hard to imagine that a harmful synergy between her home life, her mental health, and her self-destructive personal habits played no role in her death.

Routine Activity Theory

Developed from the principles of lifestyle theory, *routine activity theory* (Cohen and Felson 1979) examines victim-offender interaction by considering the spatial and temporal structure of routine legal activities. Cohen and Felson (1979, 593) define routine activities as "recurrent and prevalent activities that provide for basic population and individual needs ... formalized work, as well as the provision of standard food, shelter, sexual outlet, leisure, social interaction, learning, and childbearing." Routine activity is directly related to a victim's lifestyle, as both are concerned with the individual's daily routine and habits. The primary argument of routine activities theory is that crime will occur when there is a convergence of what has been termed likely offenders, suitable targets, and the absence of capable guardians (Cohen and Felson 1979). As these three elements in a victim's routine activities are present during the criminal act, each plays a unique role in influencing exposure and can contribute to the dynamics of the victim's situational harm.

From the victimologist's perspective, a *likely offender* is classified as one who is motivated to offend (Cohen and Felson 1979). This motivation may come from a variety of factors, with each case dependent on the surrounding circumstances. Turvey (2008, 204–205) describes six factors that can influence victim selection, all of which are related to offender motivation:

Victim selection is a term that refers to the process by which an offender intentionally chooses or targets a victim. Each offender has their own selection criteria, which satisfies their specific needs. The need for a victim can be primary to the purpose of the offense (the offender's motive) or it can be ancillary. Put another way, a particular victim can be the whole reason for the offense, or the victim may be chosen by other criteria as an object, selected for verbal and behavioral scripting into an offender fantasy. The major factors that can influence this decision-making process (which are not mutually exclusive) include the following.

Availability

This refers to a particular victim's accessibility to the offender. It is related to the concept of *offender exposure*.

Location

This refers to the victim's particular locality in contrast to the offender's. It is often a function of both offender and victim activities and schedules and is also related to the concept of *offender exposure*.

Vulnerability

This refers to the offender's perception of how susceptible a particular victim is to their method of approach and attack. It is also related to the concept of *offender exposure*.

Relationships

This refers to victims who are selected by virtue of being in a relationship with the offender (spouse, parent, family member, coworker, friend, roommate, therapist, teacher, etc.).

Symbolic Criteria

This refers to victims who are selected by virtue of sharing characteristics of those in a relationship with the offender (spouse, parent, family member, coworker, friend, roommate, therapist, teacher, etc.).

Fantasy Criteria

This refers to victims who are selected by virtue of having traits that a particular offender views as desirable or necessary for the satisfaction of a particular fantasy. The nature of those desirable or necessary traits will be borne out in the victimology and the offender signature behavior.

Remember that each of these can be, but is not required to be, an influence on the offender's decision to choose or target a victim.

The criminal profiler must determine what selection criteria are at work for the offender at hand, as evidenced by a convergence of the behavioral evidence. This is best borne out in a thorough comparison of victimology and offender motive (determining who the victim really was, in light of what the offender believed he or she was doing with that victim in that crime scene).

In mining each of these variables from the behavioral evidence, it is important to understand that they are the basis for the questions that will necessarily follow. Why this victim, in this location? And then why this level of force with this weapon? Is there planning or skill in the entire crime or just the method of approach and subsequent attack? Why was the victim killed or left alive?

From this list of influences and motivations, it is evident that as a given victim increasingly satisfies particular offenders' criteria, the more likely it becomes that they will choose to commit an offense against that victim.

From the offender's perspective, *suitable targets* are victims or objects that he or she perceives to be vulnerable (Cohen and Felson 1979). Vulnerability, as suggested earlier, is the offender's perception of how susceptible a particular victim is to his or her modus operandi.[3] An offender's perception that his MO is sufficient to successfully complete a particular criminal act results in an increased exposure towards the victim. Suitable targets may be a function of either incident or lifestyle exposure factors. For example, an offender may generally perceive that intoxicated victims are more easily overpowered, and therefore troll related outlets such as bars and nightclubs for targets. However, the victim must actually be intoxicated at the outset of an attack for this perception to be accurate, and the victim must also be a particular kind of drinker—in other words, not the violent kind. So it is possible under such circumstances for an offender to perceive that a particular type of victim is suitable based on general circumstances, while a particular victim in those circumstances is anything but.

Capable guardians are those individuals whose presence or proximity discourages offenders from committing crime. They can take the form of persons, including police officers, private security, family members, or ordinary citizens. They may also take institutional forms, such as proximity to a building that houses capable guardians, including police stations, secured facilities, government offices, or courthouses. Whatever the case, these individuals or institutions

---

[3] *Modus operandi* (MO) is a term used to describe any offender actions that are intended to perpetrate a crime successfully. These include actions that protect the offender's identity, ensure criminal success, or facilitate escape (Turvey 2008).

must possess the actual ability to respond if criminal behavior is observed.[4] Simply by having capable guardians present, crime may be reduced by discouragement, as there exists a greater chance for outside intervention and ultimate apprehension.

The underlying argument within routine activity theory is that crime occurs where there is an opportunity to commit it. This opportunity is dictated by the motivation of the offender, the vulnerability of the victim, and the lack of capable guardians. As these three elements converge, victimization is more likely to occur.

NOTABLE LIFESTYLE FACTORS

There are many lifestyle factors that are commonly known to increase victim exposure and vulnerability to harm. However, we find even the most experienced investigators and examiners can fail to consider them in their individual assessments—especially when it suits their purposes. The following is a short list of factors (careers and circumstances) with some discussion of their victimological relevance.

Attorneys

It is true that attorneys do have regular contact with criminals, which provides a high lifestyle exposure to violence and the possibility of retaliation. However, these crimes tend to be underreported by attorneys and the media, leading to a lack of general awareness outside of the legal community. This is explained in Kelson (2006, 19):

> Aside from the extensively reported acts of violence in Chicago and Atlanta, numerous acts of violence have occurred against the legal profession throughout 2005. For example, in Montezuma County, Colorado, a man with a history of domestic violence burst into his ex-wife's lawyer's office and shot and killed the 62-year-old attorney. In San Fernando, California, a defendant accused of killing two fellow gang members lunged at his defense attorney during his trial, and slashed her right arm with a jail issues razor, requiring five stitches. In Middletown, Connecticut, a former state trooper shot and killed his ex-wife, her attorney, then himself. In Detroit, Michigan, a former client

---

[4]Young children, for example, are not generally considered to be capable guardians, as they may fail to intervene against the criminal act and may not be able to get help for the victim. However, inanimate objects such as a security camera can be considered capable guardians, as offenders may believe that they are being watched in real time and therefore at risk of both identification and apprehension.

entered his attorney's office building, loitered for fifty minutes on the stairs, and when asked to leave, punched his attorney three times, hit him with a plant stand, and threatened to kill him. Recently, in Provo, Utah, a sex offender was charged for paying an undercover officer to kill the deputy county attorney, prior to his sentencing.

These examples reflect only a sampling of reported incidents of violence against the legal profession in 2005, and represent only a small fraction of those against the legal profession throughout the 2000s. Additionally, numerous incidents of violence regularly occur against the legal profession, but go unnoticed or unreported by the media, or are never disclosed by legal professionals because they do not take them seriously or consider reporting such events as "bad publicity."

Kelson (2006, 20) goes on to discuss findings from one of the few studies related to violence against attorneys, conducted in 2006 by the Utah Bar Association:

in January and February, 2006, the Utah Bar Association conducted a survey of its 8,737 members. Although the results of this survey have not yet been published, they present surprising details of violence experienced by the legal profession. In total, 984 members, representing 11.3% of the bar, responded to the survey. 452 or 45.9% of the respondents reported that they had been threatened or physically assaulted at least once. Only 15.7% of those threatened or physically assaulted considered it serious enough to report the incidents to police authorities.

Four hundred and fifty-two incidents of violence reported in the Utah Bar Association survey, 68 incidents were perpetrated against lawyers by their own clients, and 201 incidents of violence were perpetrated against lawyers by the opposing party in a case. Many of these threats and acts of violence include death threats, assaults, and vandalism to the attorney's property. For example, an opposing party in a divorce action pulled papers from the attorney's hands, threw them on the floor then pushed him backwards. Another member of the Utah Bar reported that an opposing party was arrested and subsequently charged for attempting to hire a hitman to kill him. In yet another incident, a client's husband tried to hit her attorney with golf balls while playing golf at a country club. Two hundred and eighty-four respondents identified that they had been threatened more than once. Interestingly enough, the results of the survey also reveal that at least 27 threats and physical assaults were perpetrated by opposing counsel.

It should be noted that we present the findings here only to show that despite an absence of media attention, violence against attorneys is actual, varied, and ongoing. From an investigative standpoint, this means that the suspect pool for crimes against attorneys may be larger than some might perceive, and largely comprised of non-strangers.

Law Enforcement

Law enforcement officers have regular contact with a wide variety of criminals and controlled substances. This results in a high lifestyle exposure to violence and the possibility of retaliation for simply showing up to work on any given day. They also suffer higher rates of divorce, depression, alcoholism, domestic violence, and suicide than regular citizens. Law enforcement officers are therefore exposed to dangers on the job, at home, and at every place in between, from themselves, their cases, and those they love. From an investigative standpoint, the victimologist cannot be shy about investigating and eliminating any of these as contributory factors when dealing with crimes against or involving the police.

Prostitutes

A *prostitute* is any person who engages in sexual activity for payment. Because prostitution is often illegal and therefore unregulated, prostitutes are often defined by their willingness to get into vehicles or go into hotel rooms with men they don't know, to perform sex acts without being seen by others. This increases their exposure to potential assault, rape, robbery, kidnapping, and even homicide, to say nothing of the risks related to drug abuse and venereal disease, both of which form a crime and criminal nexus with prostitution.

Drug Dealers

Drug dealing is among the most violent and dangerous criminal occupations that exist, no matter the community or the culture. It commonly involves the presence of drugs, cash, and firearms—each of which attracts crime and may be used in the perpetuation of violence of just about every kind. It creates, as with prostitution, a nexus of crime and criminals.

Alcoholism and Drug Addiction

Drug addiction involves a steady progression of drug use, increased dosages, and decreased dosage intervals. Each drug affects the addict differently, depending upon the amount taken, personal chemistry, and the other drugs in the system. The one universal consequence of drug use is the inability to think rationally.

Drug addiction can also be associated with progressively violent and criminal drug-seeking behavior. This behavior is characterized by an intense focus on supporting a drug habit regardless of the cost or consequences. Drug addicts

FIGURE 5.3

Drug investigation task force seizures commonly include evidence that perfectly characterizes the dangers of the drug dealing world: drugs, cash, and weapons. Pictured are the fruits of a State Police/ New Haven Initiative Task Force Investigation carried out in 2007: $102,040 in cash; 588 pounds of marijuana (estimated value of $1.8 million); 1.7 grams of cocaine; 13.8 grams of mushrooms; various items of drug paraphernalia; 3 handguns and 1 shotgun; and assorted vehicles (Source: DPS 2007).

engaged in drug-seeking behavior exist on a continuum that includes falsifying the symptoms of illness to get prescription medications; stealing medication from neighbors under a false pretext; stealing items of value for cash to buy drugs; engaging in prostitution to support a drug habit; to robbing a pharmacy. Whatever they believe will get them their drug is what they do. Period. This essentially completes the nexus of crime and criminals associated with drugs and prostitution.

Alcoholism is a particular kind of drug addiction that is not necessarily illegal—though it can result in illegal activity because of the lack of inhibition and absence of rational thought that necessarily result. Additionally, alcoholics may be very difficult to identify if they develop high functioning, coping, rationalization, and concealment skills. These combine to increase their vulnerability to harm from themselves and others with respect to a persistent lack of judgment, memory, and dexterity.

Additionally, Petherick and Turvey (2008, 384) provide a list of general traits that can influence victim lifestyle exposure and argue that "the more prevalent or intense the trait in the victim's history, the greater the overall lifestyle exposure." This adaptation of Petherick and Turvey's original list is not meant to be all-inclusive but rather to provide the forensic victimologist with a starting point.

1. *Aggressiveness:* People who are more aggressive and confrontational in their behavior are more likely to evoke aggressive behavior in others (see Singer 1981).

2. *Anger:* Angry individuals are less able to think rationally and restrain their impulses. They may also exhibit aggressive behavior.

3. *Emotional Outbursts:* Those who are prone to emotional outbursts—whether angry, sad, or depressed—are vulnerable to lapses of judgment, awareness, and rational thought. This can cause them to engage in behavior that they might otherwise consider unacceptable.

4. *Hyperactivity:* Hyperactive individuals are easily excited and distracted, exhibiting intense emotions and impulsivity. They are consequently vulnerable to lapses in judgment, awareness, and rational thought.

5. *Impulsivity:* Impulsive behavior is done without planning or forethought. As a consequence, impulsive individuals are generally unprepared to meet the challenges that they face, as well as fail to consider the actual consequences of their actions.

6. *Anxiety:* Anxiety is characterized by feelings of fear and apprehension. It is also commonly associated with a broad spectrum of physical symptoms, such as increased heart rate, nausea, erratic breathing, stomachaches, and headaches. If pathological, anxiety can cause irrational fear that results in irrational decisions that increase vulnerability.

7. *Addiction and Substance Abuse:* As previously discussed, addicts often engage in dangerous drug-seeking behavior and are vulnerable to lapses of judgment, awareness, and rational thought.

8. *Self-Destructive Behavior:* Some individuals engage in reckless or self-destructive behavior that routinely puts them in harm's way. Such behaviors exist on a continuum from reckless to overtly self-destructive. They can include driving too fast, binge drinking or eating, overmedicating, and spending beyond one's means.

9. *Passivity:* Passive individuals are those who allow or accept the actions and choices of others without question or defiance. This can remain true even when they are put in situations that expose them to harm or loss, and is especially problematic if they are known to be passive, as others might see them as excellent targets.

10 *Low Self-Esteem:* Those with low self-esteem are more apt to be depressed, to engage in self-destructive behaviors, and to be taken advantage of or otherwise victimized. Depression can create a strong desire to gain and maintain the approval of others—a tendency that is ripe for abuse by those with bad intentions. Low self-esteem can also foster the belief that one deserves to be victimized.

11 *Depression or Hopelessness:* Depression is a deep and persistent sadness or grief; hopelessness is the belief that nothing can be done about it. These are characterized by negative thoughts, moods, and behaviors, as well as irregular eating, sleeping, crying, and reduced sex drive. Depression and hopelessness are also the key ingredients for a suicidal mindset.

12 *Negativity:* Emotional negativity involves the endless indulgence of pessimism and cynicism to nurture feelings of frustration, anger, depression, dissatisfaction, and anxiety. It creates a perceptual bias where almost anything is cause for doubt, suspicion, sadness, or despair. Intense forms of emotional negativity can lead to chronic depression.

13 *Emotional Withdrawal:* This refers to those who have withdrawn from interaction with others; becoming aloof and inaccessible even when physically present. This creates indifference to the problems and emotions of others, and can even lead to their objectification and dehumanization. In extreme cases, a complete emotional shutdown is possible.

14 *Need for Attention or Sympathy:* The need for reassurance from others via their attention or sympathy is closely associated with low self-esteem. Such individuals are more apt to be quick tempered, to engage in self-destructive behaviors, and to be taken advantage of or otherwise victimized.

15 *History of Self-Injury:* This suggests low self-esteem, depression, and may be indicative of mental health problems related to physical, sexual, or emotional abuse.

16 *Aberrant Sexual Behavior:* Sexual promiscuity can lead to increased exposure to sexually transmitted disease and jealous or possessive lovers. Extreme sexual behavior can actually be physically dangerous, depending upon the types of behaviors involved.

ASSESSING LIFESTYLE EXPOSURE

The interpretation of a particular victim's lifestyle exposure is not just a function of compiling abstract group statistics for application to nonexistent victim stereotypes, though this is an unfortunate victimological tradition. Much more is required to achieve a concrete and actual understanding.

To accurately determine a specific victim's lifestyle exposure, his harm needs to be assessed in the context of his specific lifestyle and personality traits. For investigative purposes, lifestyle factors must be questioned as to how, specifically, they contributed to harm. By utilizing the concept of victim *risk*, one may infer a conclusion based upon statistical analyses of the potential to be harmed as being part of a demographic group. However, these conclusions often do not account for the victim's particular characteristics and context, or how they interacted with the offender. For example, statistics indicate that college students are at higher risk of victimization (Fisher et al. 1998). One might assume that the mere situation of being a college student increases exposure to harm. This is not necessarily correct; not all college students are identical. Some expose themselves to more harm than others through their drug and alcohol use, routine, sexual activity, and a number of other factors. Making conclusions about the victim's level of harm based on statistical analyses or probability estimates of risk do not accurately reflect how a specific victim's lifestyle contributed to his harm, nor does it necessarily provide investigative relevance.

In contrast, the concept of *victim exposure* examines how a lifestyle factor specifically increased a victim's contact with harm. Taking the example of Fisher et al. (1998) again, an investigator can discover that the victim was a college student and acknowledge that college students are at an increased exposure to harm; however, the specific interaction of *this* college student with her environment will dictate the *actual* level of potential for harm. One particular student who does not consume alcohol or drugs, lives at home with her parents, does not engage in high-risk sexual activity, and takes self-defense classes will represent a very different level of exposure than the student who does consume alcohol and drugs, lives in a bad part of town, engages in high-risk sexual practices, and does not take self-defense classes. Certain lifestyle traits such as interacting with potential offenders, drug use, and a high frequency of casual sex with strangers may also increase a victim's exposure to harm. Only by looking at the specific interactions of the variables can one sufficiently argue that a victim was exposed to harm.

It should also be noted that, generally speaking, not all lifestyle factors can be said to have the potential to increase harm to a victim. It cannot be reasonably argued that the habit of collecting baseball cards played a significant role in the sexual assault of a male at a nightclub. Nor can it be easily argued that a victim's depression solely increased her exposure to gang-related homicide. Thus, to argue that a lifestyle factor influenced victim-offender dynamics, it needs to be both potentially harmful, in the sense that its presence could be argued to influence opportunity for harm to occur, and also relevant, within the context of who the particular victim was and the criminal behavior that occurred.

THE VICTIM AS A REAL PERSON

Victimology is all about getting to know the victim as a real person. An important facet is realizing that everyone leads multiple lives. At the very least there is a professional or public life that is shown to all. Then there is the private life that is shared only with close friends and family. There is also a sexual life, one that each person lives as a function of his or her sexual relationships and related preferences. In all of a person's lives there will be variations and contradictions. Some will be narrow and focused; others will be broad and scattered. Some will be safe; others will be risky. Some will be open; others will be closed. Unless we know who a victim is, or was, and how the person lived and connected with other people, we cannot say that we truly know the context of the victim's demise or the events leading up to it. And we will most certainly fail to see where the person was exposed to harm.

Unfortunately, the culture within which an investigator or forensic victimologist operates may openly encourage the marginalization, vilification, or deification of a given victim population.

Victim Deification

Deification involves idealizing victims, who are perhaps young schoolchildren, missing adolescents, or those who arrive "predeified" by the press and public opinion. Because of the political or public culture of a certain area or region, certain victim populations tend to be more politically or publicly sympathetic. This view facilitates rationalizations about time expended on the deified case while other investigations suffer; it does not allow for an unbiased victimology because it deprives the investigation of the crime and the true victim context. Deification has the capacity to accomplish the following:

- Cause an incomplete victimology;
- Remove good suspects from the suspect pool;
- Provide coverage for the false reporter;
- Provide coverage for suspects who are family or household members.

Case Example: Victim Deification

This case involves the sexual homicide of a white, blonde, female child victim; the desire to get fast justice for a high-profile crime with horrific and sensational aspects; police refusal to investigate or accept the home as a source of bad things; and the concealment of important victimological information by a zealous prosecutor.

Cynthia Allinger, 9, was last seen on Thursday afternoon, July 4, 1996, near her family's apartment. She was reportedly going to visit some friends that lived nearby. She did not arrive. According to police reports, she was not reported missing to the Pierce County Sheriff's Department until 10:53 p.m. by her mother, Rhonda Plank.

An extensive search began the next day, and police quickly focused their investigation on 30-year-old Guy Rasmussen, a neighborhood man with a past who had been friendly with Cynthia. They put him under surveillance almost immediately to track his movements. By July 7, search efforts had been exhaustive but fruitless. As Reid and Working (1996) describe:

> As the FBI [Federal Bureau of Investigation] joined the search for a missing Lakewood girl, the Pierce County Sheriff's Department said Saturday it assumes that Cindy Allinger was abducted.
>
> Deputies late Saturday were talking with "a person of interest" in the case.
>
> Because a widespread search has turned up no sign of the 9-year-old, officials doubt she simply got lost when she disappeared Thursday evening, said Sheriff's Capt. Nik Dunbar.
>
> "We are assuming she is no longer missing," Dunbar said. "If that were the case, she would've been found. We are assuming there is an abduction that has taken place."
>
> The FBI is helping to draw up a psychological profile of anyone who would commit such a crime, Dunbar said. And the FBI has broad resources to draw on in kidnapping cases....
>
> Deputies late Saturday were interviewing a 30-year-old former neighbor whom they described as a "person of interest" in the case. They found him at a music festival south of Olympia and were bringing him back to Pierce County.
>
> The man was not under arrest.
>
> He had moved out of the girl's neighborhood two weeks ago, Dunbar said.
>
> Cindy had been told to stay away from the man, a drummer, though she might have visited anyway, neighbors have said....
>
> Nearly 70 volunteers fanned out in neighborhoods around her house for a second day Saturday, handing out fliers and looking for signs of her. A Pierce County Explorer Search and Rescue unit went door to door, peering behind fences and under bushes....
>
> Deputies brought in bloodhounds and German shepherds to search for Cindy. German shepherds, often used for sniffing out drugs, are trained

to smell odors hanging in the air, while bloodhounds are used for tracking after whiffing an article of a person's clothing.

"We're going back to some of the areas that the dogs worked but people were not able to get to because of the brush," Dunbar said. "We're cutting down the brush."

Joe Brentin, an Explorer Scout team leader, led a group through the narrow streets among the apartment buildings that crowd the area. He said his group was not finding much.

On July 14, a week later, authorities made another sweep of the same areas with more dogs and search teams, and still nothing (Dunham and Working 1996).

Nearly two weeks after extensive search efforts failed to yield any clues in her disappearance, with no arrests having been made, Cynthia's body was finally discovered. As Turvey describes (1998):

> The body of Cynthia Allinger was discovered at an outdoor crime scene on July 17th, 1996 at 8:30 p.m., by Detective Robert Floberg of the Pierce County Sheriff's Department, in an area of foliage approximately 150 feet behind the unoccupied residence at 4905 SW 123rd Street in Lakewood, WA. It had been placed in a piece of recently discarded carpeting (according to a report by Steven Verhey), beneath a heavy metal water tank, and covered by several layers of older discarded carpeting. This location is approximately 800 yards from her residence, and less than 50 yards from the Bridgeport Way North Interstate 5 onramp.

That her body was found in an area that had been repeatedly searched on previous occasions is interesting, but there's more. The discovery of her body involves the supernatural, apparently. As it turns out, a psychic had written a lengthy letter to Detective Floberg, detailing her role as a prophet for God, stating the precise location where Cynthia's body could be found. The detective, in an unusual breach of investigative protocol, went out alone on the night of July 17 and found her body. Despite orders and forensic training, he moved the body around quite a bit before anyone else could arrive to document the scene the next morning. And he didn't make that last fact known until he testified during the trial of Guy Rasmussen, who was subsequently arrested and charged with the crime. As Gillie (1999a) describes:

> No one is sure of exactly where Allinger's body was found because Pierce County detective Robert Floberg never wrote a report noting he moved the body several feet when he discovered it the night of July 17, 1996.

And Floberg is unsure even today how far or in what direction he moved the body before he called in forensic investigators.

The time and place of Allinger's death is critical to the prosecution's case. Prosecutors contend Rasmussen, a former rock band musician, raped and killed Allinger on July 4, 1996. Rasmussen then hid the body under a pile of carpeting near an abandoned Lakewood house, they contend. Defense attorneys contend Allinger died several days later. They say Rasmussen couldn't have murdered her because he was under police surveillance or out of town during the time defense experts say the young girl died.

Defense attorneys Fred Leatherman and Linda Sullivan said they didn't learn that Floberg had moved the body until he testified last month in Rasmussen's murder trial. Deputy prosecutor Barbara Corey-Boulet, however, said the detective disclosed the information at a hearing in January 1998.

Floberg testified last month that, following up on a letter from a psychic, he went to the site late on July 17, smelled the odor of decaying flesh and found Allinger's body covered with carpeting.

Floberg told attorneys recently that he moved the body several feet and might have rotated the pile of carpeting in another direction in the process of discovering the body.

Curiously, the psychic who wrote the letter to Detective Floberg was also the spiritual guide of Gilbert Bauschman—the father of David Bauschman, who was Rhonda Plank's live-in boyfriend at the time. Rhonda Plank, of course, was Cynthia Allinger's mother.

To recap—a police detective (not the lead investigator) gets a "tip" from a psychic friend of the victim's family. It states precisely where they can find Cynthia's body. And the detective goes out alone to find it, moves everything around, and doesn't tell anybody until he has to on the stand. Now, if one believes in psychics, then one would not think to investigate this version of events or potential connections back to family or household members. If one does not believe in psychics, then one must consider that only the person or persons who killed Cynthia, or those connected to them, would know where to find her body.

After Cynthia's body was found, Guy Rasmussen was again questioned about his possible involvement in her death and asked to give a sample of his DNA, which he did. Going on the assumption that the person responsible must be a stranger, Rasmussen was a perfect suspect because of his history and because he apparently fit the FBI's profile. To our knowledge, however, having carefully examined the investigative record in this case, no effort was made to investigate or eliminate family or household members as suspects. "Stranger crime" was the operational assumption from the very beginning. As Albert (1996) describes:

> 30-year-old [Guy Rasmussen] had been considered a "person of interest" in the case since shortly after the girl's disappearance July 4.
>
> Friday, Pierce County sheriff's detectives received the DNA evidence they had been waiting for since Cindy's body was found July 17.
>
> The evidence matched a blood sample provided by the man, said Curt Benson, sheriff's spokesman.
>
> Friday evening, detectives armed with an arrest warrant took the man into custody at the Java Jump, an all-ages nightspot in Fife where he had been assisting a band.
>
> The man is expected to be arraigned Monday on charges of aggravated first-degree murder, kidnapping in the first degree and rape of a child in the first degree....
>
> Cindy, a slender 4-foot-tall girl who wore a floral-pattern dress, was last seen July 4 when she left her family's home in the Garden Court Apartments near McChord Air Force Base to play outside.
>
> In the following days, hundreds of searchers checked lakes and woods and went door to door, looking for the child. The Federal Bureau of Investigation offered a $5,000 reward and drew a psychological profile.
>
> But Cindy's body was found July 17 in a wooded area near Bridgeport Way Southwest and Interstate 5. The area is just three blocks northeast of Clover Creek, where searchers had concentrated their efforts.
>
> Investigators became interested in the 30-year-old man because witnesses had seen him with the girl the day she vanished. He lived just down the street from her family.
>
> At that time, the man insisted he had nothing to do with the girl's disappearance and was not in the neighborhood July 4.
>
> He claimed detectives were focusing on him only because of his criminal record.
>
> "It's my past coming up to haunt me," the man said last summer.
>
> As a teenager, he was convicted in 1982 in Pierce County of sexual assault against a 16-year-old girl and served five years in prison. In 1990, he served five months after he pleaded guilty to assaulting a 10-year-old Olympia girl.

An important fact to note at this point is that if Guy Rasmussen had killed Cynthia, he would have had to dump her body within a day of her disappearance. If he dumped it anytime after that, the authorities would have seen him do it—because they were already watching him by then. If the evidence demonstrated that her body was dumped after he was put under surveillance, then that would effectively destroy the prosecution's theory of the case.

When the trial started, things went from strange to stranger. The lead prosecutor, Barbara Corey-Boulet, seemed to be under enormous pressure to get a conviction. She was openly harassing defense experts; jailed an 11-year-old honor student to frighten her into giving prosecution-friendly testimony (Gillie 1998a); withheld discovery material; and may have been complicit in evidence tampering. All the while, she and her husband Francis were under investigation for charges stemming from theft and fraud at his former place of work.

Eleven-year-old Cierra Hull had originally told investigators that she saw Cynthia with Guy Rasmussen on the day that she disappeared. Later, she and her family wanted nothing to do with the case. However, this was a witness that the prosecution desperately needed. Her ordeal is described in Hucks (2003):

> Two Pierce County deputy prosecutors say they had no choice in 1998 but to jail an 11-year-old girl as a witness in a murder trial, and Monday asked a judge to dismiss the girl's family's lawsuit against them. Prosecutors Barbara Corey-Boulet and Lisa Wagner said Cierra Hull was vital to the case against child rapist and murderer Guy Rasmussen, but hadn't shown up for a required interview.
>
> Also, they said, her grandmother planned to move her out of state and her family had told police they no longer wanted her involved in the trial....
>
> But attorney Brian Ladenburg, representing Hull's family, said they had been cooperative, and detectives knew by the time they arrested the girl that she simply hadn't had transportation to the missed interview....
>
> On May 28, 1998, after Hull didn't show up for a court-ordered pretrial interview with defense lawyers, Corey-Boulet and Wagner—with the blessing of the prosecutor—asked a judge to detain her as a material witness.
>
> Lawyers for the county and the prosecutors say they had hoped the girl would be held for no more than 12 to 18 hours.
>
> Detectives arrested Hull at Edison Elementary School the next day, just before she was to be named "student of the month."

But Superior Court Judge Karen Strombom wasn't available that Friday afternoon, so Hull spent the weekend at Remann Hall juvenile jail.

"Instead of receiving her student-of-the-month award and being lauded by her peers," Ladenburg said Monday, "she's arrested, thrown in a sheriff's car, taken to Remann Hall for the weekend and then mocked by her peers when she gets out. And she did nothing wrong."

While locked up, Hull was afraid, her lawsuit contends. An older girl spit on her in a fight and she wasn't able to talk to her grandmother as often as she wanted, her lawyer said.

And on that Monday, prosecutors let her go and scheduled the interview for later, he said.

Attorneys for the state and county counter that Hull watched television with the guards and received daily visits from her mother.

Outside the courtroom Monday, attorneys bickered over whether the girl had been unfairly treated. "She came into court in chains," Ladenburg said.

"That's standard procedure" for handling material witnesses, county attorney Dan Hamilton said, noting they feared Hull would flee. "For criminals," Ladenburg shot back.

In an unfortunate decision Hull's lawsuit was dismissed. Her arrest, detention, and placement in jail were determined to be lawful acts by the civil court. Other misconduct and evidence tampering issues in the Rasmussen case are described in Gillie (1998b):

The conduct of prosecutors has been so unethical in the case of a man accused of killing a 9-year-old Lakewood girl that the case should be dismissed, a Seattle defense lawyer claims. In a motion filed in Pierce County Superior Court, Fred Leatherman Jr. contends deputy prosecutors Barbara Corey-Boulet and Lisa Wagner "have intimidated defense witnesses, abused the material witness warrant procedure, hampered the defense investigation, hidden exculpatory evidence, (and) demonized the defendant."…

The Seattle attorney, known for his ardent opposition to the death penalty, listed several specific complaints about the deputy prosecutors' conduct:

The two attorneys used material witness warrants to harass defense witnesses who could provide an alibi for Rasmussen. Leatherman alleges that the prosecutors had those two witnesses, one an 11-year-old girl, the other an Idaho construction worker, arrested on suspicion of not cooperating with prosecutors.

But the two witnesses would have willingly talked to investigators if they had only asked, Leatherman said. The girl, who committed no crime, was held over a weekend at Pierce County's juvenile jail at Remann Hall. The man was arrested in Idaho while on a construction job, returned to Pierce County and held in jail for a week, Leatherman claims.

Wagner said the 11-year-old was arrested only after she failed to show up for a court-ordered deposition, and prosecutors had to track the construction worker through several states before finding him.

Leatherman contends the prosecution failed to provide the defense with complete surveillance logs kept by law enforcement officers who followed Rasmussen.

The prosecutors countered they had turned over all existing logs to the defense. Leatherman said the logs are important because they will show Rasmussen couldn't have dumped Allinger's body in a field where she was found.

Wagner posted a caricature of Rasmussen in her office that showed him with horns drawn on his head. Such a caricature prejudiced defense witnesses called to her office, Leatherman claims. Wagner acknowledged she briefly displayed such a picture in her office.

"When I added the horns to the defendant's mug shot, I was exercising my First Amendment right of free expression," she said. She added that no defense witnesses saw the picture.

Leatherman wants the judge to remove Corey-Boulet from the case because she and her husband have been named as defendants in a civil lawsuit over her husband's management of funds at a medical clinic he managed....

Leatherman contends that if Barbara Corey-Boulet is charged in the clinic investigation, she will have to leave the Rasmussen case, delaying the trial.

Furthermore, defense attorneys argued that key evidence linking Rasmussen to the victim's death was likely planted, as described in Gillie (1999b):

Leatherman also claimed that detectives, desperate to pin charges on Rasmussen, planted DNA evidence on a pair of cutoff shorts and a T-shirt that police seized. That evidence showed blood that matched Allinger's on both pieces of clothing.

Both a specimen of Allinger's spleen and the clothing were stored in a sheriff's property room where detectives could inspect the items unobserved, he said.

He suggested DNA experts in California, who tested the DNA found on the clothing spots, noted a strong odor of chemicals when they opened the bags containing the clothing. Leatherman said that chemical odor came from the preservative used to treat the girl's spleen for storage.

Normally, we are particularly skeptical of any claims that evidence has been planted. However, in this case, we find the theory plausible, given the nature of the evidence, the missing chain of custody for the items involved, and the record of misconduct in the Pierce County prosecutor's office.

At the trial, forensic entomologist Neil Haskell testified that "based on the age and kind of insects present in Allinger's body, she died no earlier than July 7 and as late as July 10, 1996" (Gillie 1999a). Furthermore, plant physiologist Dr. Stephen Verhey testified that the body could not have been at the disposal site for more than six days (Gillie 1999a).

Based on the work of these forensic scientists and others, one of us provided a report to the defense that determined the dumpsite was not the location where the victim was killed—as the prosecution contended (Turvey 2002):

> The physical evidence does not suggest that the location where her body was found is the Primary crime scene, which is a term used to describe a location where an offender engaged in the majority of their attack/assault upon a victim. The reasons for this are as follows:

> The entomological evidence provided by Dr. Haskell suggests that the victim's dead body had been in an indoor crime scene at some point.

> The entomological evidence provided by Dr. Haskell suggests that death may have occurred between July 7 and July 9, several days after the victim's disappearance.

> The entomological evidence provided by Dr. Haskell suggests that the victim's deceased body may have been stored in an intermediate crime scene (a crime scene between the primary scene and the disposal site, where there may be evidence transfer). This location, it is suggested, was more thoroughly protected from insect colonization than the disposal site.

> Dr. Vale has opined that the teeth missing from the victim's mouth were dislodged as the result of physical blows. At least two teeth have not yet been accounted for in this investigation. If the tooth associated with the line of fracture was knocked out at the time of that attack, it is reasonable to conclude that this tooth would be found at the primary crime scene. To this examiner's knowledge, this tooth has not been recovered from the location where the victim's body was discovered.

The nature and extent of the behavior that the offender engaged in with the victim, especially on a day where many people would be outside, would have drawn a great deal of attention if done out in the open.

As an adjunct to performing a crime scene analysis, and out of an abundance of suspicion regarding the true context of the murder, Turvey prepared a written memo requesting victim history, including any reports that might have been prepared by Child Protective Services (CPS). The known victimology made such a request mandatory. The prosecutors met the request with open hostility and denied that CPS reports were relevant to the homicide. In doing so, the prosecutors acknowledged that CPS reports actually existed.

At the end of the trial, the relationship between David Bauschman and Rhonda Plank unraveled. Bauschman landed in Pierce County Jail on a first-degree assault charge that he beat Plank on January 21, 1999. According to Rhonda Plank, this was not the first time Bauschman had choked and beaten her. Subsequently, Bauschman's lawyer sent a letter to the prosecutors in the Rasmussen case with the revelation that Rhonda Plank killed her own daughter. Bauschman initially told investigators with the prosecutor's office that Plank told him she struck Allinger in the face with a 14-inch-long plywood paddle, which the mother used to discipline her three daughters. Bauschman further claimed that Plank said she stuffed something in the girl's mouth to keep her from crying out. This version of events is consistent with the known facts of the case. It would also explain the psychic's letter. Gillie (1999c) details these revelations:

> The twist involved an 11th-hour allegation—since recanted—that the murder victim, 9-year-old Cynthia Allinger, died at her mother's hand, not Rasmussen's.
>
> The contention came to prosecutors' attention Thursday. A lawyer for the boyfriend of Allinger's mother, Rhonda Plank, sent a letter saying the boyfriend claimed Plank killed the girl. The boyfriend, David Bauschman, is in Pierce County Jail on a first-degree assault charge that he beat [and choked] Plank on Jan. 21.
>
> Prosecutors sent a letter to defense attorneys about the allegations Friday.
>
> Tuesday afternoon, Rasmussen's lead defense counsel asked Pierce County Superior Court Judge Karen Strombom, who has presided over the nearly six-month-long trial, to delay the trial for three weeks while the defense investigates the claims.
>
> But Strombom denied defense attorney Fred Leatherman's motion, saying the allegations weren't relevant in the penalty phase of the trial.

Strombom also denied a motion to allow defense lawyers to tell the jury Plank had failed two lie detector tests.

The jury convicted Rasmussen on Jan. 28 of aggravated first-degree murder, kidnapping and rape and now is charged with deciding how he will be punished: by life imprisonment or by death. Before final arguments began in the penalty phase Tuesday, Leatherman left the courtroom to appeal Strombom's rulings to the Washington State Supreme Court.

Pierce County deputy prosecutor Lisa Wagner argued Tuesday that Bauschman's allegations had been proved baseless. She said he failed a lie detector test Thursday and the next day admitted he had lied about Allinger's death because he was upset about what Plank was saying about him in the community and in court.

Bauschman initially told investigators with the prosecutor's office that Plank told him she struck Allinger in the face with a 14-inch-long plywood paddle which the mother used to discipline her three daughters. Bauschman claimed Plank said she stuffed cloth in the girl's mouth to keep her from crying out.

Allinger's body was found beneath carpeting near her Lakewood home two weeks after she disappeared July 4, 1996. An autopsy showed she had a broken jaw and a pair of underwear stuffed down her throat. That same autopsy showed vaginal damage but no sperm on her body. Prosecutor Wagner said Plank had taken lie detector tests about the girl's killing, but Wagner contended the test results were invalid.

Not surprisingly, given the tone of previous rulings, the judge in this case agreed with the prosecution. She found that the allegations weren't relevant in the penalty phase of the trial. As Rasmussen had already been found guilty, this was now a matter to be brought up in the appeals process—which remain ongoing.

Victim Vilification

Vilification involves viewing or casting certain victim populations as worthless or disposable by their very nature. This view presumes that it is okay, or not as bad, to commit crimes against people of certain lifestyles, races, religions, or creeds. This can include people of a particular ethnic origin, people of a certain social class, prostitutes, drug dealers, drug addicts, and runaways. Ultimately, this tends to be guided by an investigator's subjective sense of personal morality—or that of a like-minded community. Ultimately, it facilitates investigative apathy.

Examples of vilified groups, or groups toward which there is no lack of apathy, commonly include the following:

- The homeless or mentally ill
- Homosexuals
- Minority populations within a particular region, such as immigrants and Native Americans
- Prostitutes
- Drug dealers
- Drug addicts
- Teen runaways who become prostitutes or drug addicts
- Individuals of particular religious beliefs

These groups are marginalized either because of prejudice, because they are committing crimes, or because they are viewed as contributing to their demise in some fashion. An extreme example of this level of investigative apathy, or perhaps outright hostility, can be found in Geberth (1996, 850), who defines the term *misdemeanor murders:*

> A "Geberthism" which suggests that when two "shit-birds" (less than productive citizens) kill each other in some sort of drug-related homicide that the crime might actually be considered less than a felony offense. The author obviously uses the term in a facetious manner.

While this is certainly inappropriate humor, as Geberth admits, Geberth has put the term in the glossary of a professional textbook. This would suggest that it is a term that he sanctions as appropriate for use by professionals. This type of thinking is very much in line with the vilification of victims by some serial murderers.

Detectives and investigators who hold negative views toward certain victim populations may not feel the need to investigate the crimes committed against them thoroughly, if at all. The irony being that some of the most skillful serial offenders exploit these attitudes, which can be prevalent in law enforcement and the media alike. They choose their next victim, in part, based on whether or not the community perceives them as disposable. And they thrive in environments where such attitudes persist.

The reality is that victims of crime are human beings. They are not the fictional constructs of our prejudices and biases born of our own morality, true crime novels, or films. As we have always secretly feared and must be willing to admit, they are not unlike our own daughters, sons, mothers, fathers, sisters, brothers, wives, husbands, or friends. They are precious, and they are flawed. They are no more or less deserving of our attention because of their lifestyle choices or situations. If we idealize them, or vilify them, we will not learn who they were. We will not have the context for a complete profile and will not be able to provide investigative direction based on victim-victim and victim-offender connections. Subsequently, if we proceed with the mindset that any victims are more or less deserving of our attention, then we do so at the risk of failing to serve justice. And we will most certainly speed ourselves away from the precious flaws in our own humanity.

CATEGORIZING VICTIM LIFESTYLE EXPOSURE

Many victimologists have developed typologies that attempt to categorize the characteristics and interactions of the victim with the offender (Barnes and Teeters 1943; Fattah 1976; Karmen 1980; Lamborn 1968; Mendelsohn 1963; Schafer 1968; Sheley 1979; Silverman 1974; von Hentig 1948). This is useful, as victim exposure classification provides for reporting and discussion of victim traits. One of the more common typologies referenced was created by Hans von Hentig (1948), who suggested that differences in a victim's psychological, social, and biological factors contribute to differing exposures of vulnerability. His nomothetic classification of "the Young," for example, attempts to describe a young person's inherent exposure to harm. As reiterated by Petherick and Turvey (2008, 381):

> von Hentig was referring to children and infants. From a contemporary view, children are physically weaker, have less mental prowess, have fewer legal rights, and are economically dependant on their caretakers (parents, guardians, teachers, and so forth); therefore, children have the same potential to be exposed to a wider range of harm than do adults. Moreover, they are less able to defend themselves and sometimes are less likely to be believed should they seek assistance. This includes children who suffer emotional, physical, and sexual abuse at home because of abusive parents (often under the influence of drugs and alcohol), children who are bullied at school because of some aspect of their appearance or personality, or children who are forced into acts of prostitution or sold into slavery by impoverished parents. Each suffers different levels and frequencies of exposure to different kinds of harm.

Although this classification does not accurately deduce any specific victim's lifestyle or incident exposure, it does provide the victimologist with a basic understanding of some vulnerabilities to consider in child victims. By this we mean to suggest that these typologies may be useful guides for the victimologist, but not inflexible classifications from which to generalize conclusively.

The main purpose of classifying victim lifestyle exposure is to "arrive at an understanding of the victims lifestyle and conditions, in order that exposure may be fully understood and described to others" (Petherick and Turvey 2008, 383). The following categories of victim lifestyle exposure are derived from Petherick and Turvey (2008, 383), who have been influenced by similar classifications from Hazelwood (1995).

With respect to lifestyle exposure, *low-exposure victims* are those who are infrequently exposed to the possibility of suffering harm or loss; *medium-exposure victims* are those who are sometimes exposed to the possibility of suffering harm or loss; and *high-exposure victims* are those who are routinely exposed to the possibility of suffering harm or loss.

As these definitions suggest, it is important that lifestyle exposure and incident exposure be assessed independently. The forensic victimologist should avoid blanket characterizations of victim risk or exposure that merely combine an assessment of the two. This practice can lead and has led to misrepresentation of actual victim exposure and victim evidence, by virtue of focusing on one area or the other. Making a regular habit of examining and characterizing lifestyle and incident exposure as separate features allows for reporting that avoids imprecision, misrepresentation, and eventual misunderstanding.

In assessing a particular victim's level of lifestyle exposure, the victimologist is also admonished not to confuse relatively stable lifestyle factors with dynamic incident factors. One case involving this type of confusion was the abduction of Gordana Kotevski in Charlestown, New South Wales, Australia. Then New South Wales police profiler Detective Sergeant Kris Illingsworth testified at a Coroner's Court hearing into the alleged abduction. The following extract is taken directly from the transcript (Coroner's Court 2003):

> Q: And it would appear that she didn't have any problems on the information provided to you at home?
>
> A: No there didn't appear to be any issues at all in her background in her victimology.
>
> Q: You were also advised, however, that there were incidents involving her whereby it appeared that she was being stalked by a person?
>
> A: Yes.
>
> Q: In particular one person comes to mind that we've heard about in the inquest and that's a person referred to as a "scary guy" [sic].
>
> A: Yes.
>
> Q: And in forming whatever your ultimate opinion was, no doubt you took that into account, that is a knowledge of her being stalked in the period prior to her abduction?
>
> A: Yes it formed part of her victimology.

Q: Now in terms of coming to your opinion, did you make an assessment of what the victim risk level was in relation to Gordana Kotevski?

A: Yes I did.

Q: Firstly can you tell me what her victim risk level is?

A: Yes, there are low, medium, and high risk levels, and this relates to how much at risk a person was at becoming the victim of a violent crime. Low risk victims are considered to be people who have no real reason to be the victim of a violent crime. They may be particularly security conscious and be very aware of their surroundings and generally not be available to an offender for a violent crime. Medium risk people are generally those with a low risk background but their circumstances tend to elevate the risk factors, and when you get a high risk level then it's someone who's particularly vulnerable and available at the time due to their victimology and/or circumstances.

Q: In the case of Gordana, you assessed her as being in the low victim risk level, generally?

A: Generally, yes.

Q: However, in particular having regard to the circumstances on the night of her abduction you elevated her status to that of a high risk victim?

A: Yes she was a young female walking home late at night or in the late evening, in a darkened unlit part of the street where there were no immediate witnesses in that part, she was in between where witnesses could be located.

It should be clear how the profiler in this case is confusing lifestyle exposure with incident exposure. The point should be clear, but will be restated for the purposes of this discussion: if a victim is a low lifestyle exposure, then one, two, several, or many types of risky behaviors at the time of the crime *do not* increase their lifestyle exposure unless these behaviors are related to lifestyle factors. None of the factors presented by this profiler was related specifically to lifestyle exposure. Separating the two as independent examinations makes this clear.

Ultimately it is the victimologist who determines what lifestyle factors may have affected the victim's exposure to harm or loss based on the unique constellation of facts in a given case. As discussed previously, a lifestyle factor can influence victim lifestyle exposure by creating a perceived conflict with an offender, increasing the victim's presence around offenders, or increasing a victim's perceived vulnerability. Furthermore, in order to argue objectively that a lifestyle factor influenced victim-offender dynamics, it needs to be both potentially harmful, in the sense that its presence could be argued to influence opportunity for harm to occur, and also relevant, within the context of who the particular victim was and the criminal behavior that occurred. Only by utilizing the processes of critical thinking, analytical logic, and the scientific method can an investigator objectively and deductively assess lifestyle exposure.

SUMMARY

Exploring the dynamic between a given victim and offender is key to answering a number of important investigative and forensic questions. This involves examining the role that victims played in their own victimization. One of the ways this role can be examined is by looking at the level of victim exposure, which may provide insight into the kinds of defenses that a given offender is willing and able to defeat in order to achieve his or her goal with the victim.

Lifestyle factors can influence harm to the victim in three ways, as we have discussed: by creating a perceived conflict with an offender; by increasing the victim's presence around offenders or those predisposed towards criminality; or by enhancing an offenders perception of victim vulnerability. According to routine activities theory, crime will occur when there is a convergence of likely offenders (someone motivated to offend), suitable targets (victims perceived to be vulnerable), and the absence of capable guardians (police, witness, etc.). This theory is important because it works on the premise that crime occurs when, where, and against whom there is an opportunity to commit it.

Attorneys and law enforcement have regular contact with a wide variety of criminals. According to the principle of homogamy, this results in high lifestyle exposure to violence and the possibility of retaliation. Prostitutes and drug dealers also have increased exposure to violence because of their occupations' nexus with crime and criminal activity. There are several other factors that, depending on their prevalence and intensity, can increase an individual's lifestyle exposure, including substance abuse, impulsivity, anger, depression, and so on. These factors may increase a person's exposure to harm, by increasing lapses in judgment, awareness, and rational thought, amongst other factors.

In order to assess lifestyle exposure of a specific victim, lifestyle factors must be examined as to how, specifically, they contributed to harm. To determine that a lifestyle factor influenced the offense, it needs to be both potentially harmful and relevant. To categorize victim lifestyle exposure as a guide to the victimologist, it may be helpful to classify victims as high, low, or medium exposure.

Questions

1. The tendency to view a victim as worthless or disposable is known as _____.
2. True or False: The terms *lifestyle exposure* and *situational exposure* can be used interchangeably.

3. According to *routine activities theory* there are three factors that converge to determine whether a crime will occur. Name and describe the three factors.
4. Name and describe two factors that may influence victim selection.
5. List two occupations that may increase victim lifestyle exposure.
6. Name and describe two general traits that can influence victim lifestyle exposure due to their potential to decrease an individual's ability to think rationally.
7. True or False: An important facet of victimology is realizing that everyone leads multiple lives.

REFERENCES

Albert, A. 1996. "Arrest made in girl's killing: 'person of interest' jailed on DNA evidence." *Tacoma News Tribune*, November 16.

Barnes, H., and N. Teeters. 1943. *New Horizons in Criminology*. New York: Prentice Hall.

Cohen, L., and M. Felson. 1979. "Social Change and Crime Trends: A Routine Activity Approach." *American Sociological Review* 44, no. 4: 588–608.

Coroner's Court. 2003. Transcript of Evidence: K. Illingsworth. New South Wales, Australia: March 5.

DPS (Department of Public Safety). 2007. "State Police/New Haven Initiative Task Force investigation leads to large drug/weapons/vehicle seizure and 3 arrests in Woodbridge." Press release. State of Connecticut, Department of Public Safety, May 18.

Dunham, S., and R. Working. 1996. "The area briefly: Lakewood: Dogs fail to find sign of missing girl, 9." *Tacoma News Tribune*, July 14.

Fattah, E.A. 1976. "The Use of the Victim as an Agent of Self-Legitimization: Toward a Dynamic Explanation of Criminal Behavior." In *Victims and Society*, edited by E. Viano, 105–129. Washington, DC: Visage.

Fisher, B., J. Sloan, F. Cullen, C. Lu. 1998. "Crime in the Ivory Tower: The Level and Sources of Student Victimization." *Criminology* 36, 3: 671–710.

Fletcher, M. 1998. "Sniper kills abortion doctor near Buffalo." *Washington Post*, Oct. 25. http://www.washingtonpost.com/wp-srv/national/longterm/abortviolence/stories/sniper.htm.

Geberth, V. 1996. *Practical Homicide Investigation*. Boca Raton, FL: CRC Press.

Gillie, J. 1998a. "11-year-old murder case witness spent weekend locked up: Prosecutors say they feared that her family was leaving the state." *Tacoma News Tribune*, June 3.

———. 1998b. "Murder suspect's lawyer assails prosecutors: Allinger case attorney alleges unethical conduct, wants charges dropped." *Tacoma News Tribune*, July 24.

———. 1999a. "Error pivotal in Rasmussen trial: Detective's failure to record he moved victim's body used by prosecution to attack defense." *Tacoma News Tribune*, January 8.

———. 1999b. "Accused's alibi 'airtight,' defense says: Jurors in Rasmussen murder trial begin deliberations." *Tacoma News Tribune*, January 21.

———. 1999c. "Late allegation arises in Rasmussen case: Lawyers for man found guilty of killing girl raise questions about her mother's role." *Tacoma News Tribune*, February 17.

Hazelwood, R. 1995. "Analyzing the Rape and Profiling the Offender." In *Practical Aspects of Rape Investigation: A Multidisciplinary Approach*, 2nd ed., edited by A. Burgess and R. Hazelwood. New York: CRC Press.

Hindelang, M., Gottfredson, M., and J. Garofalo. 1978. *Victims of Personal Crime: An Empirical Foundation for a Theory of Personal Victimization*. Cambridge, MA: Ballinger.

Hucks, K. 2003. "Officials defend jailing of 11-year-old." *Tacoma News Tribune*, April 22. http://www.corpus-delicti.com/Tribune_042203.html.

Karmen, A. 1980. "Auto Theft: Beyond Victim Blaming." *Victimology* 5, (2-4): 161–174.

Kelson, S. 2006. "Violence in the Legal Profession: Methods of Protection and Prevention." *Advocate* 49 (May): 19–22.

Lamborn, L. 1968. "Toward a Victim Orientation in Criminal Theory." *Rutgers Law Review* 22: 733–768

Luckenbill, D.F. 1977. Criminal homicide as a situated transaction. *Social Problems*, 25: 176–186.

Maxwell, T. 2006. "Letter reveals shooter's anger." *Chicago Tribune*, December 12. http://www.chicagotribune.com/news/local/chi-0612120322dec12,1,3695003.story.

Mendelsohn, B. 1963. "The Origin of the Doctrine of Victimology." *Excerpta Criminologica* 3, May-June : 239–245.

Newsday. 2008. "One third of stolen vehicles on Staten Island had keys in them." February 28. http://www.newsday.com/news/local/wire/newyork/ny-bc-ny—auto-thefts0228feb28,0,4891329.story.

Petherick, W., and B. Turvey. 2008. "Victimology." In *Criminal Profiling: An Introduction to Behavioral Evidence Analysis*, 3rd ed., edited by B. Turvey, . San Diego: Elsevier Science.

Reid, C., and R. Working. 1996. "Sheriff's department believes girl abducted; man questioned." *Tacoma News Tribune*, July 7.

Rock, P. 2007. "Theoretical Perspectives on Victimization." In *Handbook on Victims and Victimology*, edited by S. Walklate, 37–61. Portland, OR: Willian Publishing.

Schafer S. 1968. *The Victim and His Criminal: A Study in Functional Responsibility*. New York: Random House.

Sheley, J. 1979. *Understanding Crime: Concepts, Issues, Decisions*. Belmont, CA: Wadsworth.

Siegel, L. 2005. *Criminology: The Core*, 3rd ed., Florence, KY: Wadsworth Publishing.

Siegal, L. 2007. *Criminology: Theories, Patterns, and Typologies*. Belmont, CA: Thomson Wadsworth.

Silverman, R. 1974. "Victim Precipitation: An Examination of the Concept." In *Victimology: A New Focus*, edited by I. Drapkin and E. Viano, 99–110. Lexington, MA: Heath.

Singer, S. 1981. "Homogeneous Victim-Offender Population: A Review and Some Research Implications." *Journal of Criminal Law and Criminology* 72: 779–788.

Turvey, B. 1998. "Crime Scene Analysis." *Washington v. Guy Rasmussen*, October 12.

———. 2002. *Criminal Profiling: An Introduction to Behavioral Evidence Analysis*, 2nd ed. London: Elsevier Science.

———. 2008. *Criminal Profiling: An Introduction to Behavioral Evidence Analysis*, 3rd ed. San Diego: Elsevier Science.

von Hentig, H. 1948. *The Criminal and His Victim*. Hamden, CT: Archon Books.

Wolfgang, M. 1957. "Victim Precipitated Criminal Homicide." In *Journal of Criminal Law, Criminology, and Police Science*, edited by , 481–.

———. 1959. *Patterns in Criminal Homicide*. New York: Science Editions.

Victim Situational Exposure

Brent E. Turvey

KEY TERMS

Cherry picking: the assignment of greater value to a particular circumstance or finding despite contradictory or equivocal evidence, often because it suits a preferred theory.

Concurrent victims: those who have suffered two or more crimes during the same period of time, sometimes during the same incident.

Consecutive victims: those who have suffered multiple incidents of victimization during different timeframes.

High-exposure victims: those who are routinely exposed to the possibility of suffering harm or loss.

Learned helplessness: the psychological condition in which a person comes to believe that he or she has no control over a given situation, and that any effort to change it is futile. The result is often passive, listless behavior, despite suffering continued harm from something that can in fact change.

Low-exposure victims: those who are exposed to little or no actual harm or loss immediately prior to victimization.

Medium-exposure victims: those who are sometimes, and predictably, exposed to the possibility of suffering harm or loss.

Victim situational exposure: the amount of exposure to harmful elements experienced by the victim that results and from his or her environment and personal traits at the time of victimization.

Before the turn of the century, I was a frequent visitor to the office of Dr. Stephen Pittel in Berkeley, California. Dr. Pittel, still a friend and trusted colleague, is also a forensic psychologist who specializes in cases that involve interpreting the effects of drugs and alcohol. During one of my visits I noticed, taped to the wall above his desk, a photocopied piece of paper that read:

HOMICIDE PREVENTION GUIDELINES

EVERYONE KNOWS THE USUAL WAYS TO KEEP YOURSELF FROM HARM IN CALIFORNIA: STAY OUT OF OAKLAND, LOS ANGELES, SACRAMENTO, FRESNO AND CHICO, DON'T WORK FOR THE POSTAL SERVICE, DON'T DRIVE IN RUSH-HOUR TRAFFIC, DON'T BEGIN OR END INTIMATE RELATIONSHIPS, DON'T MAKE YOUR KIDS CLEAN THEIR ROOMS, NEVER LEAVE HOME, ETC.

IF YOU TRULY VALUE YOUR LIFE, YOU MAY ALSO WANT TO OBSERVE THE FOLLOWING PRECAUTIONS:

1. Don't run out of gas in the foothills.
2. Avoid biker bars.
3. Avoid bikers.
4. Avoid bars.
5. Don't cheat on your Latin lover.
6. Stay out of convenience stores after dark.
7. Don't hire or fire teenagers who wear red, blue, black or white clothing.
8. Avoid men named Billy Joe, Bobby Ray, etc.
9. Beware strangers carrying duct tape.
10. Avoid people who doodle pentagrams or swastikas.

To this list, I would add the following to prevent homicide and domestic violence:

11. Avoid people that bring their own drinks to a party—from the party they just left.
12. Avoid drinking at parties.
13. Avoid parties.
14. Don't date anyone who touts the use of methamphetamine as an aphrodisiac.
15. Don't date anyone who isn't willing to introduce you to his or her parole officer.
16. Don't date anyone who wants to introduce you to his or her parole officer.

Clearly intended as a form of dark humor, this list is also a didactic expression of precisely how one's immediate circumstances can influence direct exposure to harm. Being at the wrong end of a loaded gun exposes one to the harm of being shot; driving anything while intoxicated exposes one to the harm of crashing; and crossing the street, even while sober, exposes one to the harm of being struck by a moving vehicle. That is to say, it is reasonable to suggest there are people, places, and circumstances inherently fraught with harm. Some are easily recognized and avoidable. Some are not.

The purpose of this chapter is to discuss how situational factors can expose individuals to harm. First we will define the concept of *victim situational exposure*. Second, we will discuss the more notable or common situational factors that contribute to victim situational exposure—people, places, and circumstances that position anyone directly in the path of actual harm. This will involve illustrative case examples. Third, and finally, we will explain how victim situational exposure is best interpreted in the context of forensic victimology.

WHAT IS SITUATIONAL EXPOSURE?

Victim situational exposure is the amount of actual exposure or vulnerability experienced by the victim to harm, resulting from the environment and personal traits, *at the time of victimization* (Petherick and Turvey 2008). This is distinct from *lifestyle exposure*, discussed in Chapter 5, which refers to harmful elements that exist, generally, in a victim's everyday life. A few useful analogies are in order.

Consider the issue of alcohol. Being a person who routinely becomes intoxicated increases one's lifestyle exposure to the many harmful effects of alcohol, which will be mentioned shortly. However, unless a victim is actually intoxicated at the time of victimization, it does not necessarily raise situational exposure. It is possible to have a high lifestyle exposure related to alcohol abuse, but a low situational exposure from lack of alcohol use or abuse at the time of victimization. The opposite is also true.

Consider also the issue of firearms. Being a person who does not own a firearm, use a firearm, have one in one's home, or live with or interact with those that do, decreases one's overall lifestyle exposure to the harmful effects of firearms. However, if a victim is at a shooting range for the first time with a new friend or romantic interest and is accidentally shot, it must be recognized that his incident exposure to harm from firearms was quite high at the time of victimization. This is true even if he was not participating or holding a gun, given his situational proximity to multiple loaded firearms being discharged by multiple persons of varying skill levels.

However, not all immediately harmful exposure is as transparent and easy to recognize from the victim's perspective as these basic examples might suggest. Harmful exposure may not even be apparent to investigators, owing to investigative apathy, or the reliance on false investigative assumptions about who and what was present during the crime. The situational harm coming from persons, environments, and circumstances relating to a particular crime must be thoroughly investigated, carefully established, and never assumed.

NOTABLE SITUATIONAL FACTORS

There are many situational factors commonly understood to increase victim exposure and vulnerability to various forms of harm. The following sections provide a short list of such factors, with some discussion of their relevance.

Victim Lifestyle Exposure

As outlined in Chapter 5, victim lifestyle exposure must be established to help place the crime in context from the victim's perspective. Specifically, it assists with establishing victims' physical and mental faculties, as well as their disposition, coping mechanisms, and perception of reality. Some victims are strong, self-assured, and self-aware; others are cynical, untrusting, and quick to fight back; while still others are unsure, submissive, and easy to manipulate. Each will perceive threats and respond to them quite differently.

Circumstances to consider include but are not limited to:

- *Persons involved in an abusive relationship (i.e., intimate partner violence, physical abuse, or sexual abuse).* This involves shame, self-blame, and social isolation. Such individuals tend to have low self-esteem, an inability to invest in genuine trust, and a need to keep to themselves, and they may suffer from *learned helplessness* with respect to their victimization. This in addition to the physical harm they are suffering on a regular basis.

- *Multiple sexual partners.* This refers to individuals who engage in multiple sexual relationships over the same period of time, or numerous sexual relationships over a brief period of time. Such individuals are often eager to please others, and they tend to have problems with self-esteem, trust (trusting too much or not enough), emotional commitment, and intimacy. Additionally, there is the issue of venereal disease, which can be transmitted unknowingly, used as a weapon by the infected, and provide victims with a motive for retaliation. As Pollard discusses (2007, 807–808):

    According to the scientific data, a small subgroup of Americans is choosing to engage in promiscuous sexual activity, leading to a sexual disease epidemic that is costing the American public billions of dollars annually. The statistically few persons who choose to have sex with a large number of partners are creating a high risk of serious bodily harm or even death to others that cannot be completely eliminated by exercising reasonable care.

- All of these variables can significantly color victims' view of other people, the precautions that they take, and their understanding of the dangers that might be present in a given situation. Promiscuity compounds these potentials.[1]

- *Chronic drug and alcohol abuse.* According to Mersy (2003), those engaged in chronic substance abuse often can be identified by red flags such as frequent absences from school or work; a history of frequent trauma or accidental injuries; suffering from depression or anxiety; labile hypertension (blood pressure fluctuations that are sudden and often); gastrointestinal symptoms, such as epigastric distress, diarrhea, or weight changes; sexual dysfunction; and sleep disorders. In short, the body of a substance abuser is in distress, and so is the mind—even when not immediately under the influence. This affects not just how substance abusers feel, but how they reason and react.

- *Mental illness.* This refers to individuals who suffer from any disease or condition affecting the brain, influencing the way they think, feel, act, or relate towards others and their environment. Often this involves diminished coping and problem-solving skills, and even altered perceptions of reality. This may be counteracted by medication, however. Therefore, it is important to establish not only the existence of mental illness, but any medications prescribed, and whether or not victims with mental illness were actually taking them.

It should also be noted that any combination of these elements could have a synergistic effect. In other words, two or more of these or similar circumstances is likely to enhance the frequency and impact of the others. Chronic drugs abuse can lead to multiple sexual partners; abusive relationships can lead to and enhance chronic drug abuse; mental illness can lead to and exacerbate abusive relationships. These types of self-destructive behaviors and circumstances do not typically occur in a vacuum, and those afflicted are not always able to self-correct.

There is, unfortunately, a university-fostered tendency to believe and embrace crime statistics when considering these issues. When done properly, such confidence is not entirely wrong. Without question, looking at things like Uniform Crime Report data can be helpful and even necessary when contextualizing a given crime event. However, an interpretation of situational exposure is not about the statistics or the math. It is about whether the victims were standing in front of the gun or behind it, so to speak. Either the harm is pointed at them, or traveling toward them, or it is not. Learning to examine and interpret this, irrespective of the crime data, is at the heart of understanding situational exposure.

---

[1] Some investigators hold the unfortunate and erroneous belief that evidence of sexual promiscuity is a sufficient basis for unfounded claims of rape (Bryden 1997). That is not the intended or suggested use of such information as provided in this work. We recommend documenting sexual habits in general, whether a victim is promiscuous or selective.

Consecutive and Concurrent Victims

Consecutive victims are those who have suffered multiple incidents of victimization during different timeframes. These successive events may or may not be related. One example would be an adult female victim of domestic violence. She is physically beaten for a period of years, and ultimately leaves her husband or boyfriend. Several months later, while living on her own, she is raped and killed. This involves two separate crimes; two separate timeframes. The crimes might be connected, but only a thorough investigation will reveal whether or not they are.

It is important for victimologists to look for consecutive victimization and to identify it as such for all to know. However, they must also require that it be investigated to determine what connections exist, if any, to the immediate case. For example, there may be personality or dispositional issues that contributed to the first victimization that can help us understand the second. Knowing this and having it available for reference can provide a necessary understanding for the context of victimity that might otherwise be absent.

Concurrent victims are those who have suffered two or more crimes during the same period of time—sometimes during the same incident. This may be at the hands of one or multiple offenders. While under some circumstances the crimes will be related, it is also possible that they are not. Consider again our adult female victim of domestic violence. In this version of the case, instead of leaving her husband or boyfriend, she stays and remains a constant victim. While still suffering from this crime and its effects on a daily basis, she is raped and killed. Two separate crimes; one timeframe. The relationship between them is a possibility to be investigated, not a fact to be assumed.

As with consecutive victimization, it is important for the victimologist to recognize the possibility of concurrent victimization, and to clearly identify it as such when found. The victimologist must also require that it be investigated to establish connections rather than merely assume they exist because of temporal or proximal association. I have found such assumptions all too common, used to form inappropriate conclusions when evidence of an actual connection is weak or even nonexistent.

To illustrate these concepts, consider the case of a 12-year-old girl from Berkeley, California, who suffered two separate incidents of rape, at two separate schools, in two separate months (May and Lee 2000):

> A 12-year-old Berkeley girl who was sexually assaulted by classmates last month was attacked last week at another Berkeley school where she had transferred after the first assault, police said yesterday.
>
> The girl was moved to Martin Luther King Jr. Middle School after last month's reported attack at Willard Middle School, school officials

said. They acknowledged that the girl, who has learning disabilities, received no special protection.

Police said school officials did not tell them that the girl had been transferred until they were called to King after the attack there on Nov. 8, said Berkeley Police Lt. Russ Lopes.

The girl was "conned into going with a young man into a secluded area that she was unfamiliar with—she's not a regular student there, of course—and she was raped by him," Lopes said.

Lopes confirmed last week's reported attack after an anonymous tipster called *The Chronicle* yesterday to report it.

A 13-year-old boy who is a student at King was arrested the day after the incident, on suspicion of rape and penetration with a foreign object, police said. He was released to his parents and has not been charged....

Although Lopes said the girl was raped last week, Berkeley Superintendent Jack McLaughlin said yesterday that the King incident was not similar to what happened at Willard last month.

Police say as many as nine boys molested the girl during a five-hour ordeal on Oct. 25 that began at school and continued in a southwest Berkeley backyard, a vacant lot, an abandoned shed, an underground parking garage and seven other locations throughout the city. One of the boys allegedly assaulted the girl the previous day.

Three of the boys were charged this week with oral copulation, false imprisonment, misdemeanor battery and threatening a witness for reportedly telling the girl on Oct. 26 not to tell anyone about the assault.

It was not known whether the 13-year-old boy in the King assault knew the youths involved in the Willard attack, some of whom were part of a group calling itself the "Mini-mob," Lopes said....

The incidents have created ill will between the school district and the Police Department, and each is blaming the other for mishandling the situation.

McLaughlin said police never indicated the girl who was attacked at Willard needed security after she enrolled at King. "We weren't told she was enrolled at King," said Lopes.

After the second attack, police and school officials met and decided the girl must either be schooled at home or attend school with constant supervision from an aide or some type of guard, Lopes said. She is not attending King....

And new details emerged about the Willard incident. A parent volunteer who discovered the girl near the unlocked shed where the assault reportedly began said three to four boys outside the shed ran away when he asked them what they were doing. Several other boys ran out of the shed, he said.

The girl then walked out of the shed, fully clothed, said the parent, Lee Berry. She said she was "just passing by." Berry said he told her, "child, go home," and reported the incident to the vice principal....

A father of one of the seven boys reportedly involved in the Willard attack also apologized for what happened to the girl, but he said the community is unfairly rushing to judgment. The father said his 12-year-old son told him he watched the boys and the girl during the incident but did not have sex with the girl. "He said, 'Daddy, I was scared. I didn't want the other kids to think I was a punk.'"

The victim in this case suffered multiple concurrent attacks during the timeframe of the first incident. Subsequently, the victim was moved to a new school and attacked a second time weeks later; this separate incident meets the criteria for consecutive victimization. Some of the constant variables between these incidents at different schools include the victim's learning disability, the failure of each school to adequately provide supervision of its students, and the propensity for young boys at both schools to regard kidnapping, sexual assault, and violence as acceptable expressions of any kind. These constant variables, and others like them, raised this victim's lifestyle exposure and incident exposure in tandem—and her learning disability prevented her from recognizing any of the inherent danger.

It should be noted that these concepts are the flip side of *consecutive* and *concurrent offenders*. The *consecutive offender* is a true serial offender that tracks or pursues two or more victims at different times, one right after the other. The *concurrent offender* tracks or pursues two or more victims at the same time.[2]

---

[2]This is specifically referenced in Petherick (2006, 145) with respect to stalkers:

[T]he "consecutive" stalker pursues two or more victims in generally different timeframes, that is, they move from one victim to another. This may occur where a pursuit is thwarted for some reason (the victim moves away or seeks assistance with threat management or from the police, or someone else "catches the stalker's fancy") and the stalker moves onto another victim. . . . [T]he "concurrent" stalker pursues two or more victims at the same time. Neither type is mutually exclusive but does describe an overall victim targeting strategy. For example, one stalker may identify and pursue a new target before moving on from a current victim.

Time of Occurrence

Certain times of day can result in more exposure to various kinds of harm than others. However, any interpretation of the impact of this factor is highly dependent on the location of occurrence as well as other converging circumstances. Time of day cannot be considered in a vacuum. Some examples may help to illustrate.

Bank robberies, for instance, occur most frequently between the hours of 9:00 a.m. and 6:00 p.m. This is primarily because that's when banks are open for business. When they are closed, banks are more difficult to rob and consequently require a far more developed criminal skill set. It is easier to rob a bank when the front door is unlocked and bank personnel can assist with locating and gathering money.

Similarly, most police officers are killed during felonious attacks between the hours of 10:00 p.m. and 12:00 a.m. This is related to the fact that many officers die on patrol while responding to disturbance calls, such as domestic arguments and bar fights. Many others are killed while making arrests or are simply ambushed. These circumstances all trend upwards during this timeframe (UCR 2007).

With respect to sexual assault, the research is very clear that time of day varies as an exposure factor based on the age of the victim. This is detailed in the research conducted by Snyder (2000, 7):

> The time of day when sexual assaults occurred was related primarily to the age of the victim.... For adult victims, sexual assaults were most common between midnight and 2 a.m. From morning through 7 p.m. the number of adult sexual assaults committed in each 1-hour period was essentially constant. The number of adult assaults began to increase in the 8 p.m. hour and increased consistently until the peak in the 2 a.m. hour.
>
> The temporal pattern for the sexual assaults of very young victims, children under age 6, was quite different. For these young victims, the temporal distribution appears to be a combination of two separate distributions. The primary temporal pattern for these crimes has a peak in the 3 p.m. hour. This is also the hour other research has found to be the period when juveniles are most likely to be the victims of violent crime in general (Snyder and Sickmund 1999). This primary temporal pattern shows a consistent increase in the frequency of sexual assaults of very young victims before 3 p.m. and a consistent decline in the hours after 3 p.m. The secondary temporal pattern for the sexual assaults of very young children shows the hours of 8 a.m., noon, and 6 p.m. (traditional meal times) to be periods when the number of sexual

assaults of very young victims spike. The temporal patterns of sexual assault of youth ages 6 through 11, and juveniles ages 12 through 17, appear to be a combination of the patterns of the very young, and the adult victims. These temporal distributions combine the after-school and mealtime hour patterns of very young victims and the temporal patterns of sexual assault for adults.

As this research makes clear, time of day is a factor heavily influenced by the regular activities of the victim, their proximity to abusers, and subsequent supervision—all of which is very often a function of victim age.

Location of Occurrence

Location is one of the most important factors to consider in terms of victim situational exposure. Certain environments contain a great deal of criminal activity; others may place a victim outside the immediate reach of assistance; and still others may physically isolate or confine the victim. A starter list of environmental circumstances to be considered in any forensic victimology should include at least the following:

- *Ownership:* Who owns the location, if anyone, and is it insured? Does the victim know this?

- *Relationship to victim:* What is the relationship of victims to the location? Do they live there, work there, or are they a frequent visitor? Establish how they got there, if it was by choice, and why (if they were attacked at a store, what did they go there to buy; if they were attacked on the street, where did they come from and where were they going). Then establish whether they were familiar with the location or not. Could they anticipate changes in the environment and get around in the dark, or would they have needed light to see?

- *Security:* How hard is it to get in and out undetected; what security measures are in place (doors, locks, cameras, roaming patrols); and are they apparent or concealed? Could security from nearby locations have recorded any crime-related activity? Make a list of security features, their recording capacity, and direct their immediate collection.

- *Ambient lighting:* How much was there, what was its coverage, what was the visibility where the attack occurred, and was it on or available during the attack?

- *Adjacent residences and businesses:* What was the nature of nearby locations? Could the harm from those locations have spilled over into the present location? Make a list of neighboring homes and businesses for interviews and canvassing.

- *Witnesses:* Which vantage points, if any, provided line of sight to the points of entry, points of exit, and activity in the scene? And by whom? Was it an outdoor scene easily viewed by those walking by, or was it an indoor scene in a soundproofed room with no windows? Make a list of potential witnesses for interviews and canvassing.

- *Criminal history:* What is the criminal history of the location? If it's a home, get the 911-dispatch history (dates, times, and reasons for any emergency responses to the residence); what are the criminal histories of the residents, friends, and other family members. If it's a business, same things. Also determine what kind of business; what are the criminal histories of the owners and employees? Has anyone used the location for criminal enterprise, either presently or in the past? Make a list.

In forensic victimology, less information means less certain findings. The inability to account for these or other significant environmental circumstances must be noted in any final report that relies on victimology-related interpretations, and the impact of their absence explained. This provides for changes to interpretations should more information be gathered or otherwise come to light.

Proximity to Criminal Activity

As already suggested, nearness in space, time, or relationship to criminal activity increases one's incident exposure. This can include victim nearness to crime and criminals, or direct victim participation and involvement in criminal activity. The more violence associated with a proximal crime, the greater subsequent victim exposure to harm.

This includes consideration of the victim's profession: drug dealers, drug addicts, and prostitutes are among the highest exposure with respect to violent crime proximity. However (and this is easy to forget), so are those who live with them and those who seek their services—to say nothing of the police who by profession will have regular contact with all manner of offenders and offenses. Some profilers have been known to forget the reality that it is not possible for someone to be a police officer and also have a low lifestyle or incident exposure, unless duties do not bring him or her into contact with criminals of any kind, such as may be found for those officers who work compiling intelligence reports or others who engage in wholly administrative duties. Forensic victimologists can ill afford to repeat the same mistake.

Case Example: Steven Wright, Serial Murderer

Between October and December of 2006, former cruise line steward Steven Wright murdered at least five prostitutes and dumped their bodies around the city of Ipswich in the United Kingdom. He was working as a forklift driver at the time of his arrest. He went on trial in January of 2008. As detailed in *The Telegraph* (2008):

> The bodies of all five women were found dumped in remote locations around Ipswich in Suffolk within 10 days of each other in December 2006, sparking a massive police investigation.

FIGURE 6.1
Stephen Wright was arrested, tried, and convicted for the murders of five prostitutes in the city of Ipswich in the United Kingdom.

Wright, from Ipswich, was arrested on December 19, charged two days later and remanded in custody. He entered five not guilty pleas at Ipswich Crown Court in May 2007....

Detectives in Suffolk launched an inquiry after Miss Nicol vanished on October 30. Just over two weeks later, Miss Adams was reported missing after going to work in Ipswich's red light district.

Her body was discovered in a brook at Hintlesham on December 2, and six days after that Miss Nicol's body was found in water in nearby Copdock.

The body of Miss Alderton, who had not been reported missing, was found in woodland at Nacton on December 10. And on December 12 the bodies of Miss Clennell and Miss Nicholls were found in woods at Levington.

Wright, a former forklift truck driver who will be 50 in April, was arrested seven days later at the home he shared with partner Pam Goodman, a call centre worker.

The charges:

The murder of Gemma Adams, 25, between November 13 and December 3, 2006

The murder of Tania Nicol, 19, between October 29 and December 9, 2006

The murder of Anneli Alderton, 24, between December 7 and December 11, 2006

The murder of Annette Nicholls, 29, between December 7 and December 13, 2006

The murder of Paula Clennell, 24, between December 9 and December 13, 2006.

Stephen Wright admitted to police that he had known at least four of the victims and had also visited them on occasion for sex. However, he denied any involvement in their deaths. In February of 2008, Stephen Wright was convicted on all five counts listed above. The judge, in deciding his sentence, made specific comments about the victims' exposure to harm owing to their drug use and chosen profession, as described in BBC (2008a):

> The victims were working as prostitutes when they were murdered and Mr Justice Gross said Wright had targeted vulnerable women.

FIGURE 6.2

Victims of serial murderer Stephen Wright, clockwise from top left: Annelli Alderton, Gemma Adams, Tania Nicol, Paula Clennell, and Annette Nicholls. Their nude bodies were dumped in isolated areas around Ipswich.

He said: "Drugs and prostitution meant they were at risk. But neither drugs nor prostitution killed them. You did. You killed them, stripped them and left them . . . why you did it may never be known."

The judge said the case met the legal requirements for a whole life sentence because the murders involved a "substantial degree of pre-meditation and planning."

Further detail is provided in BBC (2008b):

Wright, 49, of Ipswich, said during his trial that he had had sex with four of the five women, who were working as prostitutes, but denied killing them. Ipswich Crown Court jurors unanimously found him guilty of all five murders and he will be sentenced on Friday.

"Crucifix pose"

The trial heard the bodies of Miss Alderton and Miss Nicholls were found arranged with their arms outstretched in a crucifix pose....

Suffolk police began an inquiry after Miss Nicol, 19, vanished in late October 2006.

Two weeks later, Miss Adams, 25, vanished and detectives began a "major inquiry," saying there were "obvious similarities."

This was followed by the disappearance of Miss Alderton, 24, Miss Clennell, 24, and 29-year-old Miss Nicholls.

Their bodies were eventually found in isolated locations around Ipswich.

In 2001, Wright worked as a barman at the Brook Hotel in Felixstowe before being sacked for stealing hundreds of pounds from the till, for which he was ordered to carry out 100 hours community service.

It was a DNA sample taken at the time of that conviction which led to police matching samples taken from the dead women.

He was put under surveillance by police before being arrested on 19 December and charged two days later.

Peter Wright QC, prosecuting, said the decision by the women to turn to prostitution "was ultimately to prove fatal."...

Michael Crimp, from the Crown Prosecution Service, said from outside the court: "Steve Wright is the factor that links all five women.

"He was [the] last person to see them alive and the scientific evidence proved that he was responsible for their deaths." One telling piece of evidence was a carpet fibre from the footwell of Steve Wright's car found in Tania Nicol's hair. "This was despite her body being found in water. Her killer failed to destroy this significant piece of evidence."...

"Depraved crime"

Robert Sadd, Crown Advocate for the CPS in Suffolk, said Wright's motive for the killing may never be known. "Quite often in a murder case we do not know the motive or understand it if we do. The evidence leads us to who did it, and that's more important."

Scientific evidence was a crucial factor in the case and Home Office Minister Vernon Coaker said it demonstrated the great strides made in DNA profiling. He said: "This was an evil and depraved crime that caused immense suffering to the families and friends of the victims as well as bringing fear to the local community. All of those affected have my deepest sympathy."

Stephen Wright was ultimately given the maximum penalty—life in prison. As of this writing, police are investigating his possible connection to the deaths and disappearances of several other victims in the same area.

Proximity to Criminal, Violent, or Aggressive Individuals

This type of proximity involves the issue of proximity to criminal behavior. However, it focuses specifically on individuals in the immediate environment, with their particular history of crime, violence, and aggression, or lack thereof. That is to say, one can be around such individuals at a given moment while they are not engaged in violent, aggressive, or criminal activity. Yet the reality of increased victim exposure remains. Such individuals have their history of violent associations, associates, and coping mechanisms, all of which they carry around like so much harmful luggage. Proximity of victims to such individuals is one level of exposure; proximity to individuals engaged in criminal activity is another of greater exposure still.

Number of Potential Victims

It is generally true that there is safety in numbers; in other words, the buddy system can remove one from the path of harm, or speed one from harmful circumstances. Hikers know it; divers know it; and joggers know it. If you get hurt, your buddy can go get help. If you get lost, your buddy can share resources and help find the way home. If you are walking alone at night, however, you are more preferable as a target because there are no witnesses and the odds are even for any offender: one to one.

This all tends to be true as long as the people one is with are not at an increased lifestyle or situational exposure. If your buddy is intoxicated, rather than being an asset he becomes a liability. The same is true if your buddy has a temper, just got in a fight with his significant other and is distressed, or has a mental illness and is not taking his medication.

Also, some more competent and confident offenders prefer to select victims in pairs in order to use one to control the other, such as a mother and a child. This situation is one of the exceptions that proves the rule. Examples include an abusive parent who threatens the life of other family members should anyone tell the police; or the rapist who selects mothers with small children to gain total compliance by threatening harm to the child.

Consider the recent case of 24-year-old David Welker in Orlando, Florida, as described in Prieto (2008):

FIGURE 6.3
Mug shot of 24-year-old
David Welker.

FIGURE 6.4
Welker using the victim's
ATM card at a nearby bank
to withdraw money.

The choice was clear: Either she [would] comply or he would shoot her baby girl.

Her attacker already had pulled a gun and forced her back into her car in the nearly deserted Wal-Mart parking lot. He reclined the front passenger seat and ordered her to lie facedown. He then raped her while she looked at her child in the car seat behind her.

All the while, the victim said, he pressed a .25-caliber pistol against the 15-month-old toddler.

When he was done, he told her to sit in the driver's seat and dump the contents of her purse. He robbed her and ordered her to get into the trunk, leaving her baby alone in the car.

Those details emerged Thursday in an arrest affidavit released by the Orange County Sheriff's Office. Numerous tips and surveillance video led deputies to their suspect, 24-year-old David Welker of Orlando, a felon caught Wednesday afternoon while riding in a car on Orange Center Boulevard.

"It's one of the most heinous rapes I've heard of in a long time," said Carol Wick, chief executive officer of Harbor House, an Orange County domestic-violence agency. "It's horribly traumatic for a woman."

The 35-year-old victim pulled into the Wal-Mart parking lot on South John Young Parkway about 6:15 a.m. Tuesday to pick up milk and supplies for her baby before heading to day care and work, the document said.

She noticed Welker, a skinny man with a long nose and brown hair, waiting near the front door of the store but assumed he was an employee, she told deputies. Security video shows Welker had been loitering there since 5:22 a.m., more than 45 minutes before the attack. He watched others go in and out of the store, the document said.

The victim parked her car and got out, then reached back inside to grab her daughter's sippy cup and pacifier from the center console.

When she turned around, Welker was behind her, ordering her back into the car at gunpoint, the report said. He told her to drive to the back of the store and park.

Fearing for her child's life, she complied, she told detectives.

Taking his time, Welker rummaged through the glove compartment looking for something to steal, according to the affidavit.

Then an unimaginable 20 minutes of terror began. Holding his gun against the toddler, who was awake, Welker began raping the mother, sheriff's reports said. . . .

When it was over, the naked woman climbed back into the driver's seat. Welker picked through the contents of her spilled purse, taking her cell phone, a debit card and $70 in cash, the report said.

Before fleeing, Welker made the woman climb inside the trunk but didn't close it all the way because her daughter was still inside the car. When she determined he was gone, she drove away, seeking help.

According to police records, Welker had been arrested at least 27 times prior to this incident, and had completed a work-release program only a few weeks prior for convictions relating to illegal possession of firearms and grand-theft. When he was arrested for rape and car-jacking in the case at hand, he had at least $200 in twenty-dollar bills on his person, as well as a small amount of marijuana.

Availability of Weapons

Generally speaking, rifles, handguns, knives, saws, crow-bars, screwdrivers, rope, telephone cards, and pantyhose are all tools created to serve a particular function. However, all have been put to use in the crimes of assault, rape, and homicide. This is because many criminal cases involve violent decisions made at the last minute affected by a victim or offender using available materials.

The availability of any weapon or material in a given environment increases the likelihood that it will be used in a physical altercation, should one ensue, or that someone will accidentally injure him or herself or others while handling it for any number of legitimate or illegitimate purposes. The availability of a shotgun in an environment increases victim exposure to shotgun injury or fatality; the availability of knives in an environment increases victim exposure to sharp force injury or fatality; the availability of coat hangers in an environment increases victim exposure to related ligature injury or fatality. However, a weapon's availability does not cause its use.

Care and Supervision

As previously suggested, individuals become more willing to engage in criminal activity when they are not being watched. That is to say, criminal propensity can increase as supervision and accountability decrease. This is why so many offenders choose professions that put them in positions where they are supervising or caring for their preferred victim type (for some, their preferred victim type is teenage boys; for others it is dollar bills). They want to get their victims alone, they want to have their way, and they want deniability. However, if they are being supervised or monitored to any degree, this may not be possible. They may subsequently move their activities to a location or venue where supervision and personal accountability are diminished or entirely absent.

The advent of the Internet, and a false perception of anonymity by some users, has helped to enable waves of criminal conduct—from those violating copyright, to those stealing identities, to those soliciting minors for sex in chat rooms. Consider the number of individuals snared in sting operations such as those set up by programs like *Dateline NBC's* "To Catch a Predator."[3] First, an adult working with the show poses as an underage teen in an online chat room. Once an adult male has made contact for private chat sessions that become sexually explicit, a meeting is arranged at a location that has been surreptitiously rigged with cameras and sound equipment. When the adult male shows up on the premises, having brought items requested by the decoy minor such as sexual lubricants and alcohol, the police literally rush in and make an arrest. The sheer volume of men routinely operating in a criminal fashion on the Internet with respect to grooming minors for sex, simply because they believe their identities are safe, is telling.

Consider the representative case of a 56-year-old rabbi from Maryland, who was stung by "To Catch a Predator," as described in Makron (2006):

> A Maryland rabbi caught in a television sting operation was sentenced to 6 1/2 years in prison yesterday for trying to solicit sex from a 13-year-old boy over the Internet.
>
> David A. Kaye, 56, told the judge that he traveled to Herndon for what he thought would be sex with a boy "as a cry out for help to fight my personal demons." Sobbing as he acknowledged his father, who sat in the courtroom in a wheelchair, Kaye said his conviction had made him face "the reality of who I am. . . . I know I need help. I pray that God allows me to get that help."
>
> Kaye's attorney, Peter D. Greenspun, said the rabbi, who was featured last year on the "To Catch a Predator" series on "Dateline NBC," kept his sexuality secret and spent thousands of hours chatting online in search of liaisons.

[3]See http://www.msnbc.msn.com/id/10912603/.

Kaye thought that he was chatting online with a young adult, Greenspun said. He said Kaye, who is divorced, is in therapy, and he urged a sentence on the low end of federal guidelines, which recommended a term of 63 to 78 months in prison.

"There is a very decent core to this man," Greenspun said.

But U.S. District Judge James C. Cacheris in Alexandria settled on 78 months and said Kaye would then face 10 years of supervised release. The judge said that during that time, Kaye will be forbidden to accept any job involving children, and he ordered him to never be around children younger than 18 without an adult present. . . .

Kaye, of Potomac, is the former vice president of programs at Rockville-based PANIM: The Institute for Jewish Leaders and Values, an educational foundation that trains Jewish leaders. He resigned last year after informing the organization that he would be on "Dateline."

Kaye was convicted in September after a two-day bench trial in which prosecutors presented evidence of sexually graphic chats between him and the boy. In reality, the boy was a 26-year-old man working for Perverted Justice, a group that tries to expose adults who use the Internet for sexual activity with children.

Perverted Justice was working with "Dateline," which paid the watchdog group to create a pedophile sting that ran as a series of TV reports. When Kaye arrived at the Herndon house that the group had set up, he was confronted on camera by NBC correspondent Chris Hansen.

"You know I'm in trouble. I know I'm in trouble," Kaye told Hansen, according to Cacheris's opinion. The judge convicted Kaye on one count of coercion and enticement and one count of travel with intent to engage in illicit sexual conduct. . . .

During the trial, prosecutors presented outtakes from the NBC show and a log of Kaye's chats with the person posing as a 13-year-old. Using the screen name "REDBD," Kaye initiated the chats, Cacheris wrote.

FIGURE 6.5

Part of one of the nude pictures sent by Rabbi David Kaye to someone he thought was a 13-year-old boy but was in fact a man working for the watchdog group Perverted Justice.

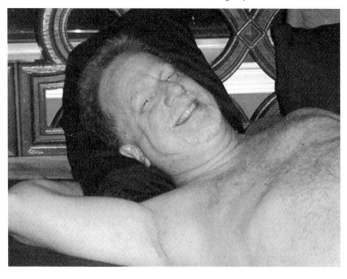

In this particular case, the offender was already in a position of trust within a religious community in Maryland, working for PANIM, which teaches leadership and values to teenagers. However, with the anonymity of the Internet and without the supervision of others, his fantasies found expression. On the day that he was arrested, 18 other men showed up and were arrested as part of the same sting operation.

Victim State of Mind or Perception

This factor refers to the victim's emotional state before, during, and following an attack as evidenced by convergent patterns of behavior and any reliable witness accounts. An agitated or distressed emotional state, for example, may increase victim incident exposure. Additionally, a victim who feels safe in a particular environment or situation will act differently from a victim who does not. Many variables, including the presence of drugs, alcohol, mental illness, or a heightened emotional state such as anger or sadness, affect this directly.

Drug and Alcohol Use

The use of mind-altering substances may decrease physical reaction time, impair judgment, and alter one's perception of reality. In either drug or alcohol use, victim situational exposure is increased dramatically, even for otherwise low-exposure victims. One thing that a person cannot do under the influence of drugs or alcohol is think rationally. This issue is so pervasive across the spectrum of crime and criminal victimization that it is a feature of almost every chapter in this text.

Engaging in Violent or Aggressive Behavior

If the victim engages in violent or aggressive behavior, this can evoke or even provoke a violent response from others. Whether or not this results in legal culpability or diminished culpability is a legal matter for a jury to decide. However, pretending that this doesn't happen is the sort of avoidant victim deification that forensic victimology is intended to prevent.

Violent and aggressive behavior can also distract a victim from matters of personal safety. For example, if victims are driving, they could crash; if they're on a boat, they could lose their balance and fall in; or if they're working with heavy machinery, they could cause an accident.

These factors and many others inform the overall context of the crime, and each one on its own has meaning only when placed against the backdrop of the other known facts in a case. The examination of one factor cannot in itself be used to gauge victim situational exposure. Nor is it acceptable to cherry-pick multiple factors out of context and suppress information that might suggest an unpopular or undesirable level of exposure. This will be discussed further at the end of the chapter.

Furthermore, the existence of any one circumstance is not necessarily enough to cause the tipping point of victim harm, unless direct harm is inherent (such as with drug and alcohol use, or consecutive and concurrent victimization). Having a gun in a home will not cause someone to use it for violence; having drugs in the home will not make someone use them; leaving a child unsupervised at school will not cause the child to be raped. As we've demonstrated here, it is the synergy of corresponding factors and circumstances that exposes victims to ever-increasing levels of harm until their demise becomes almost unavoidable.

INTERPRETING SITUATIONAL EXPOSURE

The interpretation of a particular victim's situational exposure is not just a function of compiling crime statistics, comparing them to the victim's presumed state of being when attacked, and making a general risk assessment. Much more is required to achieve a concrete and actual understanding. The nature, depth, and character of each victim's harm must be investigated, examined, and explained in its context. This means scrupulous examination of the information gathered regarding associated persons and locations. Barring this level of information and effort, the forensic victimologist must have the scientific courage to admit what is known and what is not. He or she must understand the scope and limits of the evidence. This is not too much to ask of any competent forensic examiner.

Categorizing Victim Situational Exposure

The main purpose of classifying victim incident exposure is, as discussed Chapter 5, to "arrive at an understanding of the victim's lifestyle and conditions, in order that exposure may be fully understood and described to others" (Petherick and Turvey 2008, 383). The following categories of victim lifestyle exposure are derived from Petherick and Turvey (2008, 383), which have been influenced by similar classifications from Hazelwood (1995).

With respect to incident exposure, the following classifications may be useful:

Low-exposure victims are those who are exposed to little or no actual harm or loss immediately prior to victimization. For example, an accountant is at home, in the middle of the day, in an upper-class neighborhood with low or no crime and a good security system; no alcohol is involved, and no drugs; there have been no affairs or animosity; and there is no history of crime, violence, or mental illness. A sex offender recently released from prison and visiting a relative who lives nearby invades the accountant's home and ties him to a chair, hoping to find a female victim in the house. Finding no females, the sex offender becomes enraged and robs and kills the accountant.

Medium-exposure victims are those who are sometimes, and predictably, exposed to the possibility of suffering harm or loss. For example, this time the accountant lives in a middle-class neighborhood with a lot of domestic violence calls and a recent series of break-ins. He's also had a few drinks because he's depressed over the fact that his girlfriend won't leave her husband. And when he drinks, he gets angry, which is how he lost his first wife. When the sex offender breaks in, the accountant attacks him and is killed defending his home and property.

High-exposure victims are those who are routinely exposed to the possibility of suffering harm or loss. For example, now the accountant works for an organized crime syndicate and has been embezzling money to support his $5,000/day cocaine and prostitute habit. When he is killed in his bedroom by agents of a crime boss, it is staged to look like a home invasion gone wrong.

Cherry Picking

In forensic interpretations, *cherry picking* involves the assignment of greater value to a particular circumstance or finding despite contradictory or equivocal evidence, often because it suits a preferred theory. This can occur due to ignorance, but it is most commonly associated with examiner bias (see Cooley and Turvey 2006). Forensic examiners are strongly warned against the practice of cherry picking evidence or results to suit their purposes, and then presenting only those findings that cast themselves, the victims, or their clients in the best light. As will be discussed frequently in this text, the forensic examiner's report of findings should be the truth, the WHOLE truth, and nothing but the truth, in strict accordance with the scientific method.

SUMMARY

As the definitions in this and the previous chapter recommend, it is important that lifestyle exposure and incident exposure be assessed independently. The forensic victimologist should avoid blanket characterizations of victim risk or exposure that merely combine an assessment of the two. This practice can lead to misrepresentation of actual victim exposure and victim evidence by focusing on one area or the other. Making a regular habit of examining and characterizing lifestyle and incident exposure as separate features allows for reporting that avoids imprecision, misrepresentation, and eventual misunderstanding.

Additionally, forensic victimologists have a great responsibility to ensure that victim situational exposure factors are established in context, before any conclusive interpretations are made. If they are biased in their examinations or report of findings, or if they are incomplete in their methods, then the actual circumstances of a crime will not be revealed. In an investigative context, the suspect pool will not be properly drawn; in a forensic context, the victimology may be misused to support a weak or circumstantial theory. It is the role of forensic victimologists to educate their clients and prevent such abuses by means of thoroughness and objectivity.

Questions

1. True or False: The situational harm coming from persons, environments, and circumstances relating to a particular crime must be thoroughly investigated, carefully established, and never assumed.
2. Describe the difference between consecutive and concurrent victims.
3. What are three important things to consider when determining a victim's situational exposure?
4. True or False: In forensic victimology less information means less certain findings.
5. The more violence associated with a proximal crime the _____ (greater/lesser) subsequent victim exposure to harm.
6. True or False: The interpretation of a particular victim's situational exposure is a function of compiling crime stats, comparing them to the victim's presumed state of being when attacked, and making a general risk assessment.
7. What is cherry picking? Why is it dangerous?

REFERENCES

BBC (British Broadcasting Corporation). 2008a. "Suffolk killer will die in prison." *BBC News*, February 22. http://news.bbc.co.uk/2/hi/uk_news/england/suffolk/7258115.stm.

———. 2008b. "Wright guilty of Suffolk murders." *BBC News*, February 12. http://news.bbc.co.uk/1/hi/england/suffolk/7256402.stm.

Bryden, D. 1997. "Rape in the Criminal Justice System." *Journal of Criminal Law and Criminology* 87, Summer: 1194–1384.

Cooley, C., and B. Turvey. 2006. "Observer Effects and Examiner Bias: Psychological Influences on the Forensic Examiner." In *Crime Reconstruction*, edited by W.J. Chisum and B. Turvey. Boston: Elsevier Science.

Hazelwood, R. 1995. "Analyzing the Rape and Profiling the Offender." In *Practical Aspects of Rape Investigation: A Multidisciplinary Approach*, 2nd ed., edited by R.R. Hazelwood and A.W. Burgess. New York: CRC Press.

Makron, J. 2006. "Rabbi sentenced in Internet sex sting." *Washington Post*, December 2. http://www.washingtonpost.com/wp-dyn/content/article/2006/12/01/AR2006120100898.html.

May, M., and H. Lee. 2000. "Sexual assault victim attacked again, police say." *San Francisco Chronicle*, November 17.

Mersy, D. 2003. "Recognition of Alcohol and Substance Abuse." *American Family Physician*, April 1. http://www.aafp.org/afp/20030401/1529.html.

Petherick, W.A. 2006. *Serial Crime: Theoretical and Practical Issues in Behavioral Profiling*. Boston: Academic Press.

Petherick, W., and B. Turvey. 2008. "Victimology." In *Criminal Profiling: An Introduction to Behavioral Evidence Analysis*, 3rd ed., edited by B. Turvey. San Diego: Elsevier Science.

Pollard, D. 2007. "Sex Torts." *Minnesota Law Review* 91, February: 769–824.

Prieto, B. 2008. "Man held gun to baby as he raped her mother, Orange Sheriff's Office says." *Orlando Sentinel*, April 11. http://www.orlandosentinel.com/orl-rape1108apr11,0,7462514.story.

Snyder, H. 2000. "Sexual Assault of Young Children as Reported to Law Enforcement: Victim, Incident, and Offender Characteristics." U.S. Department of Justice, Office of Justice Programs, Bureau of Justice Statistics, NCJ 182990, July.

Snyder, H. and Sickmund, M. Juvenile Offenders and Victims: 1999 National Report. Washington, DC: U.S. Department of Justice, Office of Juvenile Justice and Delinquency Prevention, 1999.

The Telegraph. 2008. "Ipswich prostitutes murder trial: Prosecution outlines case against Steve Wright." January 17.

UCR (Uniform Crime Report). 2007. "Law Enforcement Officers Killed and Assaulted, 2006." U.S. Department of Justice, Federal Bureau of Investigation, Uniform Crime Report, October.

CHAPTER 7

Psychological Aspects of Victimology

Michael McGrath

KEY TERMS

Acute Stress Disorder (ASD): a diagnosable mental disorder characterized by the emergence of at least three dissociative symptoms within one month of suffering a traumatic event and lasting at least two days.

Battered Woman Syndrome (BWS): a proposed mental disorder suggested to affect woman who have been involved in long-term violent relationships; the victim learns no longer to try to affect the course of the abuse, as she believes it will not change the outcome.

Blaming the victim: how some perceive any suggestion that a victim may have contributed to his or her own victimization. It should be noted that pointing out how a victim has exposed him- or herself to being victimized is not the same as claiming that he or she deserved to be victimized.

Collateral victims: the spouses, children, other family, and friends of the assaulted individual. They may suffer to varying degrees depending on their insight, age, and relationship to the victim. They may be helpful or unhelpful to the case.

Deification of the victim: the tendency to view the victim as lacking flaws. This can happen after a violent crime, when investigators are given reports that victims were saintly in every aspect of their lives.

Hypnosis: the art of putting someone in an altered state of consciousness, wherein critical thinking tends to be relaxed and the subject is more suggestible than normal. Those undergoing hypnosis may be susceptible to suggestions made by the hypnotist and may make things up or believe their recalled memories to be more accurate than they actually are.

Post-Traumatic Stress Disorder (PTSD): a mental disorder with symptoms similar to ASD (Acute Stress Disorder) but more chronic.

CONTENTS

- *Rape Trauma Syndrome (RTS):*   a syndrome claimed to be developed by victims of rape or attempted rape, which consists of a phase of acute disorganization followed by a phase of long-term reorganization. During both phases various lifestyle factors may be affected, including physical, psychological, social, and sexual. This syndrome has no criteria for accurate diagnosis other than a person having been subjected to the rape itself.
- *Stalking:*   a repetitive act usually undertaken to cause distress to the victim, it may be perpetrated both in the real world and in cyberspace. Behaviors can range from unwanted communications with the victim to sexual assault, kidnapping, and homicide.
- *Stalking Trauma Syndrome (STS):*   involves a cycle of crisis, recovery, and anticipation, as the harassment is ongoing.
- *Victim toxicology:*   the presence or absence of various substances in the system of a victim at a time that is related to the criminal event or the reporting of that event.

Victimology is one of the most important aspects of an investigation, following only the physical evidence found at a crime scene. Knowledge of the victim, including his or her habits, vulnerabilities, and strengths, as well as many other facets of his or her life, may offer investigators insight into the offender who acted against the victim. Some crimes are solved quickly while others are not. Failure to adequately delve into the life of the victim of a serious, unsolved crime (such as a homicide) is inexplicable but not uncommon. This should not be surprising, considering that victimology as a field of study and research is rather young, beginning sometime in the 1940s and gaining momentum on the heels of the civil rights movement, the feminist movement, and a general increasing conservatism about crime in general and a fear of being a victim of violent crime in particular (Wallace 2007).

Having a grasp of the psychological aspects of victimization can be very helpful to the investigator, prosecutor, and defense attorney. Not only will investigators review psychological information related to a deceased victim, but also they will collect information from and interact with live victims. Understanding how the role of victim affects an individual is important, as victims of crime are often victimized twice: once by the offender and again by the criminal justice system. Uncooperative witnesses may be assumed to have filed a false report, when in fact they may be responding to perceived secondary victimization by law enforcement. Very cooperative victims may be perceived as exaggerating the offense, as they do not appear to be as affected as expected. Myths regarding victim behavior, as well as poorly validated victim "syndromes" add to the problem. This chapter will deal with the psychological aspects of victimology including the victim's response to violent crime, several victim syndromes found in the literature, and victim toxicology—the effect of medications and drugs on the victim.

When a violent crime occurs there is often more than one victim. There is the victim or victims involved in the actual assault. Then there are what is best described as *collateral victims:* the spouses, children, other family, and friends of the assaulted individual. All suffer to varying degrees depending on their insight, age, and relationship. Sometimes they are helpful; sometimes they are not. Some support networks assist the victim in recovering and reintegrating into a former lifestyle, to varying degrees. Other support networks either initially doubt the victim's version of events, or at some later time tire of the victim's response and wish that he or she would "just move on." This chapter deals only with the victim who was assaulted, but investigators must keep the collateral victims in mind, as they may be interacting with the victim during an investigation. Certain victim populations requiring specialized knowledge are beyond the scope of this chapter. Such populations include children, the developmentally disabled, and the elderly.

CAUTIONARY NOTES

There are two features of victimology that interfere with its function as a body of knowledge and as an investigative tool: "deification of the victim" and fear of being accused of "blaming the victim." Deification of the victim is the tendency to view a victim as lacking flaws. This is sometimes exhibited after a violent crime (often a homicide) has occurred. Investigators are told by family, friends, and colleagues that the victim was essentially a saint and would never have done this or that. Lacking vital victimology information, investigators are unable to adjust the investigative strategy quickly. I recall one investigation where a sixteen-year-old female was missing. Her family reported to police that the missing girl had never failed to come home in the past. Later it was learned that on many occasions the missing teen had stayed away from home overnight, often attending parties where alcohol and sexual activity were commonplace. Apparently the family was embarrassed that they were unable to control the teen. The inaccurate information delayed law enforcement pursuing appropriate avenues of investigation.

William Ryan (Kennedy and Sacco 1998, 15) is credited with coining the term *blaming the victim.* The term was initially presented in Ryan's book *Blaming the Victim* (1971) as a social construct related to the middle-class blaming the poor for their poverty. The boundaries of "blaming the victim" expanded, and it has since become a method of attack on anyone who dares to intimate that victims may have in some way cooperated with their victimization or placed themselves in the position of being victimized. Pointing out how victims have exposed themselves to risk is different from implying that the victim "deserved" to be victimized. In fact, unwillingness to identify how victims placed themselves in a vulnerable position does nothing to help a deceased victim and is a disservice to a living victim (and potential future victims) who could be educated as to how to minimize exposure to risk in the future. It is well known that rape victims have often been blamed for being raped and that it has taken much education and social pressure to attempt to reverse this attitude.

In the spring of 2004, a twenty-four-year-old female graduate student was found dead in Brooklyn, New York. She had been sexually assaulted and tortured before being killed. Investigation revealed she had been out drinking with a friend in Lower Manhattan. Her friend wanted to go home and the victim wanted to stay out. The friend left her in a bar at about 2:30 in the morning. The friend, likely recognizing that the victim was at risk, called her later on her cell phone to check on her. The victim had gone to another bar and stayed until closing at 4:00 a.m. It is believed she was intoxicated when she left, alone. Her body was discovered around sixteen hours later in Brooklyn (Wilson 2006). Did this young woman deserve what happened to her? Of course not. Did she place herself at risk of an assault by being alone and intoxicated in Manhattan at four in the morning? Absolutely. Yet it was almost verboten for that reality to be mentioned in the media during discussions of the case. My best guess is that the same media commentators who were scrupulously avoiding "blaming the victim" went home and told their daughters not to go out drinking alone late at night, anywhere, let alone Manhattan.

Unfortunately, several months later, an eighteen-year-old recent high school graduate out drinking with a friend in Manhattan was murdered after wandering off by herself, after their car was towed (CBS News 2006). Again, did this young woman deserve to be killed? Of course not. Did she make choices that placed her at significant risk of assault? Absolutely. Would other potential victims benefit from knowing that being female (or male, for that matter), alone, and intoxicated at 3:00 a.m. in Manhattan is a dangerous situation? Should parents tell their children such things? I would only hope so. Is this blaming the victim? No, but it brings the issue of personal responsibility front and center.

A last note of caution pertains to input from experts. There may be times when obtaining professional input from a psychologist or a psychiatrist could be helpful in addressing victim characteristics and response to crime. However, the clinician would be limited to general commentary, as he or she will likely not have evaluated the victim, in which case confidentiality issues may be present. Occasionally, a psychological autopsy is helpful in assessing victimology, or if a crime has occurred at all. This would be the case when it is uncertain whether a death should be ruled a suicide or accidental death, as opposed to a homicide. It should be highlighted that psychological autopsies should be performed by qualified individuals, that is, a forensic psychologist or psychiatrist. Changing the title of a report from a "psychological autopsy" to an "equivocal death analysis," when the review essentially relies on assessing the psychological state of a victim or offender, does not relieve the examiner from the need to be qualified.[1]

VICTIM RESPONSE TO VIOLENT CRIME

Victim response to violent crime is highly variable, making any prediction of how a crime victim should behave problematic, if not impossible. It is reasonable to frame the general response of a victim into three broad stages or phases: the *impact stage*, the *recoil stage*, and the *reorganization stage* (Wallace 2007).

The impact stage is the initial response to the assault. The intensity and length will vary according to the intensity of the assault, the level of physical injury, and the perceived threat to life. The event will be filtered through the age, personality, and general mental health and life experience of the victim. Some victims will weather a vicious assault fairly well, while others will be functionally paralyzed by seemingly minor assaults.

During the recoil stage, victims attempt to deal with the effect of the crime on themselves and their lives. Emotions will be varied and include: sadness, anger, self-pity, fear, and even guilt. At this stage, the victim is attempting to reconstitute his or her former self (Wallace 2007). Denial often develops, and emotional detachment is sometimes evident. To a degree this is healthy, allowing the victim time to slowly come to grips with what has happened. The length of time and the psychological depth of this stage will vary depending on the person.

The third phase or stage involves reorganization. The emotional intensity of the recoil stage is expected to lessen, and the victim is more energized to deal with life's daily activities (Wallace 2007). Some people pass through the three stages fairly quickly, while others never finish the process. Completing the three stages does not mean that the victim no longer thinks about the crime or is not at times reminded of it to varying degrees. Depending on the nature and intensity of the assault, some victims never truly get over it.

---

[1]An excellent example of this is the FBI Equivocal Death Analysis of Clayton Hartwig, accusing him of purposely causing the explosion in the gun turret of the USS Iowa in 1989. The entire botched investigation is described in detail in *A Glimpse of Hell* (London: W.W. Norton, 1999) by Charles Thompson. A critique of the FBI's methodology was presented in R. Otto, N. Poythress, L. Starr, and Darkes (1993), "An Empirical Study of the Reports of APA's Peer Review Panel in the Congressional Review of the U.S.S. Iowa Incident," *Journal of Personality Assessment* 61, no. 3: 425–442; and "The U.S.S. Iowa: Guilt by Gestalt" (1991), Congressional Testimony, *Harper's Magazine*, March 1990, 24–28.

Just as grief and mourning following the death of a loved one is a natural process, reacting to being a violent crime victim with a disruption of one's usual state of mind and daily function is normal and expected. It is the extent of disorganization and the length of time involved that will alert others to the need for formal intervention. Pathologizing normal reactions of victims by mental health professionals can occur.

Acute Stress Disorder

Acute Stress Disorder (ASD) is a diagnosable mental disorder that was introduced in the fourth edition of the *Diagnostic and Statistical Manual of Mental Disorders* (DSM-IV 1994). In the DSM-IV-Text Revision (DSM-IV-TR 2000), the disorder is characterized by the emergence of at least three dissociative[2] symptoms (emotional numbing, feeling "dazed," derealization, depersonalization, dissociative amnesia) within one month after suffering a traumatic event and lasting at least two days. As part of the response to the event, the victim experiences intense fear, helplessness, or horror. The condition resolves within a month, or the diagnosis is changed to reflect the chronicity of symptoms. The traumatic event must be of a severe nature, for example, being exposed to possible death or serious injury, although diagnostic criteria allow for the diagnosis to be made for someone who witnesses such an event or only hears about such an event happening to a loved one or close associate. The traumatic event is persistently reexperienced in some manner, such as in flashbacks and avoiding reminders of the trauma. There is evidence of hyperarousal or anxiety, and the disorder causes significant distress or interferes with the ability to function (DSM-IV-TR 2000). A victim of a violent crime may meet criteria for this disorder, or may suffer some but not all the necessary criteria. Other victims may suffer depression, anxiety, or both.

ASD is well correlated with the later diagnosis of post-traumatic stress disorder (PTSD) in one prospective study (Brewin et al. 1999), with ASD being diagnosed in 19% of victims of violent crime and PTSD at six months being diagnosed in 20%. This might lead to the question of whether they are really two different disorders. It would appear that there is a high level of overlap. Some researchers (Brewin, Andrews, and Rose 2003; Marshall, Spitzer, and Liebowitz 1999) critiqued ASD, questioning the requirement for dissociative symptoms soon after the trauma as a core feature. Theoretically, a person could be diagnosed at day 28 post-trauma with PTSD, but not have met the criteria for ASD during the preceding 28 days. This seems odd. Although the likely goal of the 30-day wait for a PTSD diagnosis is to avoid pathologizing normal reactions to trauma, it seems there should be some leeway to diagnose a post traumatic stress disorder without dissociative symptoms.

[2]The DSM-IV-TR (2000, 822) defines *dissociation* as a disruption in the usually integrated functions of consciousness, memory, identity, or perception of the environment.

Post-Traumatic Stress Disorder

The most well-known mental disorder related to trauma is Post-Traumatic Stress Disorder (PTSD). This is a response very similar to the Acute Stress Disorder, but is more chronic. It can be "acute" if less than three months, "chronic" if greater than three months, and "delayed" if the onset is six months or after the traumatic event. The diagnostic criteria include exposure to a traumatic event with a response including intense fear, helplessness, or horror. The event is reexperienced in a persistent manner in various ways, including one or more of the following: intrusive thoughts of the event; dreams; flashbacks; and psychological and/or physical reactions (rapid heartbeat, sweating) on exposure to cues connected to the event. An example would be a Vietnam veteran having a flashback when hearing something resembling helicopter rotors. In addition, there is emotional numbing and avoidance of stimuli associated with the event, as well as persistent symptoms of arousal, such as poor sleep, anger outbursts, hypervigilance, and an exaggerated startle response (DSM-IV-TR 2000). The stereotypical example is the war veteran who attacks his wife when she wakes him. A victim of a serious assault, including rape, could develop PTSD.

As military conflict includes much opportunity to engender a stress response, PTSD (although not called that) was first recognized during the Civil War. It was called "shell shock" during World War I and "operational fatigue" and "combat neurosis" during World War II. A similar "concentration camp syndrome" was noted in many Holocaust survivors, highlighting that it was the trauma not the person that led to the disorder (Davidson 1995). When initially formulated, the disorder was conceptualized in the context of the events one endures or witnesses during wartime. It is one of the most politicized diagnoses in the *Diagnostic and Statistical Manual,* being a result (at least to some degree) of the victims' rights movement (Gold 2004). The present criteria are broader than when the diagnosis first appeared and include many scenarios that would not have qualified in the past. One of the criticisms of the PTSD diagnosis in a forensic context is the subjective nature of the diagnosis, that is, the victim reports the symptoms he or she claims to have (Miller 2003a). But this critique could be applied to most psychiatric diagnoses. Others claim objective tests, such as the Minnesota Multiphasic Personality Inventory (MMPI), can identify malingerers (Fairbank, McCaffrey, and Keane 1985) with over 90% accuracy, but not all agree, as one study (Perconte and Goreczney 1990) found that the MMPI identified malingerers less than half the time.

The diagnosis of PTSD as a sequelae of rape varies, with one researcher reporting 94% of rape victims showing symptoms of PTSD within a week of being raped (Rothbaum et al. 1992), although the rate drops as time passes. Rothbaum et al. (1992) included 95 victims of rape or attempted rape (which is arguably two different populations) in their study. As is common in studies of rape, there is no mention of the possibility of false reports. Subjects were recruited from an emergency room, as well as other referrals, and later contacted by researchers for the study. We know nothing of the women who chose not to participate. It is possible that they contained a cohort of women who would not develop PTSD, potentially skewing the sample and therefore the results. Of 95 women who entered the 12-week study, 64 completed. This means one-third did not complete. The researchers assumed, since the noncompleters (women who missed at least two of the 12 sessions and were dropped from the study) did not appear to differ from completers at the initiation of the study, that it could be inferred they were representative of the entire study. Arguably they could have been more symptomatic, or less. At the first session, 94% of the women met the criteria (except the 30-day rule) for PTSD. By the fourth session, 65% of the women met the criteria for PTSD, and at 12 weeks 47% (463). The study was prospective, had no control group, mixed victims of rape with victims of attempted rape, and was apparently unaware of the occurrence of false allegations of sexual assault.[3]

Regardless of the actual percentages, rape is a horrible thing to experience, and it should not be surprising that victims exhibit PTSD symptomatology to a considerable degree at some point in their recovery. Interestingly, Rothbaum et al. (1992, 472) suggest that not all rape victims require treatment, because half recover spontaneously. I would argue that timely intervention to support rape victims is crucial in helping to decrease the incidence of psychological sequelae, including PTSD. As Rothbaum et al. (1992, 473) note at the end of their paper: "It is clear that PTSD is a prominent response following rape, although not a universal one."

PTSD has the imprimatur of a DSM-IV-TR (2000) diagnostic entity, but it is not without controversy (Faigman et al. 2006). Some (Summerfield 2001) argue that PTSD is more a social construct than a mental health disorder. Others (Mezey and Robbins 2001) believe the diagnosis has some validity but needs further refinement. And one group of researchers (Yehuda and McFarlane 1995) have come to the conclusion that PTSD may be a distinct clinical entity but not for the reasons proffered by psychosocial theory and stress research. One recent study (Bodkin et al. 2006) raises the real possibility that the PTSD symptom picture (ignoring Criterion A, the trauma) is not necessarily trauma related, as there is so much overlap between PTSD symptoms and symptoms of other psychiatric disorders. In the study of 103 patients enrolled in a depression medication trial, the study found that symptomatic criteria, including one-month duration and functional impairment, "occurred commonly, regardless of trauma history" (180).

---

[3]If the reader thinks false allegations of sexual assault could not possibly skew the findings of such a study, that would be naïve. False allegations of sexual assault vary but can be as high as 50%, depending on the population. False victims included in such a study could be motivated to cooperate with the study to lend validity to their false allegations, reporting expected symptoms to researchers to gain or maintain their victim status.

If one presumes that the DSM is infallible and above politics, only relying on solid science to make its diagnostic category decisions, one would be surprised. We can turn to two examples. Regarding homosexuality, first it was a mental disorder, and then it was not.[4] Regardless of disclaimers, this diagnostic change was in response to pressure from gay rights groups, although the decision is easily supported both socially and medically. Self-defeating personality disorder, which began its life in 1984 as masochistic personality disorder, was introduced as a possible diagnosis. Feminist activists attacked the diagnosis, arguing it was unscientific and would be used against women (Tavis 1992), and they were very likely right on both counts. Self-defeating personality disorder cannot be found in the current DSM (DSM-IV-TR 2000) This commentary is not meant to disparage the DSM to the point of doing away with it, but rather to put the reliability and validity of the DSM in context.

Other Trauma Syndromes in the Literature

Many trauma syndromes have been described that have sparse research to validate their actual diagnostic validity. While literature may exist purporting to support the syndromes, examination of this literature leaves one asking: "Where's the beef?" While PTSD (for better or worse) is the legal gold standard for "proof" that a victim suffered a major trauma, this fails to take into account that victims of violent crime can exhibit symptoms of mental disorders requiring treatment that do not meet criteria for PTSD. Victims can suffer depression, anxiety, dissociative episodes, and other symptoms as independent diagnoses. Obsessive-compulsive traits can emerge or worsen. Avoidance behaviors alone can be debilitative. All deserve attention in the victim of a violent crime. Victims should not be expected to have PTSD as a sine qua non of victimization. Also, the fact that a victim has been diagnosed as having PTSD should not be introduced into the courtroom as proof that the subject suffered a particular trauma, as the symptom picture is not trauma specific.

BATTERED WOMAN SYNDROME

In 1979, Lenore Walker published *The Battered Woman*. After interviewing over 100 women, Walker formulated her theory of the cycle of violence and her adaptation of learned helplessness. Later, she described the Battered Woman Syndrome (BWS) in her seminal work *The Battered Woman Syndrome* (1984). This was a study of 435 women who were involved at some point in a relationship that included domestic violence. Walker raised consciousness regarding the problem, confirming that "battered women come from every walk of life and no particular characteristic in a woman leads her to become an abuse

[4]Currently, unless the subject finds his or her sexual orientation distressing (which is now better seen as a response to a societal expectation), a diagnosis can no longer be made.

victim" (Walker 2000, 17). Regarding one aspect of the research, Walker uses the syndrome to attempt to explain why a woman would remain in a violent relationship, in spite of the physical or psychological violence perpetrated against her. This syndrome has been used at times as a defense after a woman killed her alleged batterer at a time when the victim was not deemed to be in actual peril (e.g., while the batterer was sleeping), or as a reason a woman acted in concert to commit a crime with the alleged batterer.

Walker (1979) described her theory that there was a cycle of violence inherent in domestic violence. There are three phases to the abuse. First there is a tension-building phase. This is followed by the actual physical assault. The third phase is the loving-contrition phase where the batterer often apologizes, begs forgiveness, and promises not to repeat the abuse. Walker (2000, 127) suggests that the third phase "provides the positive reinforcement for remaining in the relationship, for the woman." Walker states (128) that as the domestic violence progresses, the tension-building phase becomes more common and the loving-contrition phase declines. The cycle theory is helpful in describing domestic violence, but it fails to explain why the battered partner does not end the relationship. As the loving-contrition phase is the purported reason the woman remains in the relationship, as it dissipates in time and quality, there would appear to be less of an incentive for the battered woman to stay.

Walker introduced the concept of "learned helplessness" to meet that need. Originally conceptualized by Seligman, Maier, and Geer (1968) after Seligman's experiments with dogs, learned helplessness was the result of administering a noxious stimulus with no means of escape. Eventually the animal stopped trying to evade the stimulus. Walker used this concept for battered women (1979, 47):

> Once we believe we cannot control what happens to us, it is difficult to believe we can ever influence it, even if we later experience a favorable outcome. This concept is important for understanding why battered women do not attempt to free themselves from a battering relationship. Once the women are operating from a belief of helplessness, the perception becomes reality and they become passive, submissive, "helpless."

[5]Walker's original intent was to portray the battered woman as helpless. This new parsing of the word adds little, if anything. The battered woman has apparently gone from being helpless because she believed she could not control something to being helpless because she cannot predict something.

Later, Walker takes pains to explain that: "**Learned helplessness** was confused with being helpless, and not its original intended meaning *of having lost the ability to predict that what you do will make a particular outcome occur*" (Walker 2000, 116; emphasis in original).[5] In other words, the victim adopts a mindset where she no longer tries to affect the course of abuse, as it will make no difference in the outcome. Therefore learned helplessness is not helplessness. But it is the helplessness factor that is presented in court when BWS is presented as a defense or mitigating factor. The revised helplessness in learned helplessness was in response to criticisms of the syndrome, specifically the learned help-lessness issue, where some suggested that battered women were masochistic or had personality traits that led them to provoke the violence. Interestingly, while the theory is meant to explain why women remain with their batterers, it does not explain why women leave their batterers.

In addition, while the syndrome has been used as an explanation or defense for women who kill their batterers, it is these very women whose behavior potentially refutes the syndrome. Browne (1987, 128–130) refers to a "turning point" or change in the domestic violence paradigm for a particular couple. As Blackman (1989, 188) frames it:

> Thus, they may strike back at times that sound less dangerous than previous episodes of abuse, or that may not sound life-threatening at all. Nonetheless, they may reasonably believe that their lives are at risk because of the changes in the abuser's routine style of assault, or because the abuser says or does something, that in the past, has signaled great danger.

The presence of a "turning point" that causes the battered victim to take a new course of action, that is, kill the batterer when he is not posing an imminent threat, "is arguably incongruous with both a learned helplessness response and Walker's cyclical theory of violence because it involves a diversion from, and not a continuation of, existing cognitive and behavioral patterns" (Craven 2003). Walker (2000, 116) frames criticism of her helplessness paradigm as "a good lesson in battered women's feminist politics." She then advises (117) that "even those colleagues who understood the concept of learned helplessness began to reject it in favor of post-traumatic stress theory."

Walker earlier spelled out the relationship between BWS and PTSD, in *Terrifying Love* (1984), Walker's book on battered women who kill, where she advises on how to diagnose BWS ("Making a Diagnosis," 178–179):

> The proper application of Battered Woman Syndrome can make many things clear in cases in which the sanity of a battered woman defendant is in question. Because it is a subcategory of Post-Traumatic Stress Disorder, four specific criteria must be met, clinically measured, and evaluated for Battered Woman Syndrome to be assigned as a psychological diagnosis.

The criteria are the four criteria for diagnosing PTSD, except the duration of at least one month for meeting the symptom criteria. There is a footnote after the last sentence quoted above, indicating that the authority for the claim that BWS is a subcategory of PTSD is "According to section 309.81 of the *American Psychiatric Association's Diagnostic and Statistical Manual of Mental Disorders,* 3rd ed., revised (DSM-III-R)." I was not aware that BWS was a subcategory of PTSD.

In reviewing the cited source, I found first that there is no section 309.81. Presumably this is a typographical error, as the section for PTSD is 309.89 (DSM-III-TR 1987, 247–251). Nevertheless, I could not find where in the DSM-III-TR Walker reads BWS as a subcategory of PTSD.

One would hope that Walker was given enough time to correct this error, but in her second edition of *The Battered Woman Syndrome* (2000, 117) Walker writes:

> And while Battered Woman Syndrome has been similarly criticized for making it easier to pathologize battered woman, it is my opinion that as a subcategory of PTSD, it is the most useful diagnostic category to use for battered women when it is necessary to use a diagnostic formulation.

This quote is difficult to interpret as to what is fact and what is opinion. Walker appears to be stating that BWS is a subcategory of PTSD, and that it is her opinion a diagnosis of PTSD (with BWS as a subcategory) is most useful for diagnostic purposes. But nowhere in the DSM can one find the term Battered Woman Syndrome. As the DSM-III is discussed in relation to "post traumatic stress theory" in the prior paragraph (Walker 2000, 117), a reader would be forgiven if he or she assumed the quote referred to PTSD as defined by the DSM.

I have two comments regarding this last quote. First, it would appear that Walker is suggesting that if you have identified someone as a battered woman and you need a diagnostic category for her (whether for treatment or for court), then PTSD is the most useful diagnosis. I would suggest that the most useful diagnosis would be the one that best encapsulates the symptoms the person suffers from, be it PTSD, depression, anxiety, and so on.

Second, BWS is not a formal subcategory of PTSD, although some may refer to it as such. These kinds of statements are factually incorrect and misleading to those unfamiliar with the various DSMs. In fact, the DSM-III, DSM-III-R, DSM-IV, and the DSM-IV-TR do not list any subcategories of PTSD, other than allowing specification of acute, chronic, or delayed onset. While repeated physical, psychological, and/or sexual assault in a domestic violence situation could very well result in diagnosable PTSD in the victim, the diagnosis would be PTSD, not BSW or PTSD-BSW. These types of comments, claiming or inferring that a particular syndrome is a subcategory of PTSD (see below regarding rape trauma syndrome), seem to imply approval of the purported syndrome by the DSM-IV-TR (and by extension the American Psychiatric Association, which publishes the DSM series) when no such approval or endorsement exists. Motor vehicle accidents can lead to PTSD, and the DSM-IV-TR (2000, 464) notes this, but no one describes a Motor Vehicle Accident (MVA) subcategory of PTSD that can be used as an alternative diagnosis to an MVA Syndrome, because no such subcategory exists. The DSM-IV-TR does not have subcategories related to specific traumas because the symptoms are not trauma specific, despite the wishes of some.

The often-cited[6] four general characteristics of BWS are: (1) the woman believes that the violence was her fault; (2) the woman has an inability to place the responsibility for the violence elsewhere; (3) the woman fears for her life and/ or her children's lives; and (4) the woman has an irrational belief that the abuser is omnipresent and omniscient. The citation offered in such instances is Walker's *The Battered Woman Syndrome* (1984, 95–97), but no such four characteristics can be found on pages 95, 96, and 97.

Battered Woman Syndrome testimony has been offered in the courtroom, usually as a way of educating a jury as to why a woman would kill her domestic partner when not actually in imminent danger, or when the credibility of a domestic violence victim has been attacked. For example, in *State v. Haines* (2006) "limited" expert testimony on Battered Woman Syndrome was upheld when it helped the judge or jury determine the victim's state of mind when she returns to or remains in an abusive relationship despite the alleged abuse. In this case, the victim claimed she had endured an 18-day episode of confinement and abuse, yet remained in the relationship and made conflicting statements when finally reporting the events.

Patricia Johnson spent 15 years in prison in California for shooting her husband. Her conviction was overturned in 2004 because the trial judge would not allow expert testimony on BWS. Ms. Johnson had alleged psychological abuse from her husband (Figueroa 2006). She was convicted again at her second trial. Also in California, Ny Nourn, 18 years old at the time of the crime, was convicted of murder for the December 1993 killing of her boss (Roth 2003). Her boyfriend had become jealous after finding out that she had sex with the victim. She was accused of luring him to his death, with her boyfriend committing the actual murder. Several years after the murder, Nourn came forward to authorities, claiming she had been abused by her boyfriend and felt she had to appease him. Her murder conviction was overturned due to her not being able to present Battered Woman Syndrome evidence to the jury.

As of 1996, the National Institute of Justice guidelines regarding expert testimony related to battering and its effects have been admitted to some degree in every state and the District of Columbia, as well as 16 of 19 federal courts that considered the issue. Some courts have allowed testimony on BWS and some have not. Often a court's review of the situation skirts the issue that the

---

[6]See, for example, http://www.divorcenet.com/states/oregon/or_art02 and http://www.rainn.org/effects-of-rape/battered-woman-syndrome.html.

scientific basis for the syndrome is limited.[7] Some states, such as Ohio, allow testimony on BWS as a matter of legislation. This circumvents the court's gate-keeper function regarding the validity of scientific evidence. Faigman et al. (2006, 266–267) comment in a footnote that this sends the wrong message to researchers, among others: "legislation does not solve the problems associated with poor research methodology or advocacy masquerading as science."

There has been significant criticism of BWS, especially in regard to its use in court. Dixon and Dixon (2003) point out that Walker's research has limitations, including the lack of replication by others and lack of control groups. But Walker argues that such criticism is unfair (2000, 146):

> In conducting this research design, certain decisions were made that were appropriately influenced by the feminist perspective. For example, given the finite resources available, it was decided to sacrifice the traditional empirical experimental model, with a control group, for the quasiexperimental model using survey-type data collection. It was seen as more important to compare battered women to themselves than to a nonbattered control group. Comparing battered and nonbattered women implies looking for some deficit in the battered group, which can be interpreted as a perpetuation of the victim-blaming model.[8] Our data indicate that the differences within the group of battered women studied ranged across the continuum expected for all women. From this, it is possible to hypothesize that whatever differences exist between groups are so minimal that they serve to confuse rather than gain additional knowledge about spouse abuse.

This explanation of why the study parameters were used appears to be a retrospective justification. Walker, rather than accepting valid criticism of her work, is asking for a scientific pass.[9] McMahon (1999, 31) was quite critical of BWS and the science behind it: "the key empirical basis for battered woman syndrome is … characterized by methodological flaws, conceptual imprecision and internal inconsistency." McMahon (1999) noted that Walker's major research consisted of two self-report studies from a nonrandom, self-referred sample. Neither study had a control group. To try and overcome this limitation, in one study

---

[7]Dixon and Dixon (2003) is a good critique of gender-based syndromes from both a scientific and a legal perspective.

[8]Note here how "blaming the victim" is used, as anyone who criticizes this research on the lack of control groups runs the risk of being accused of blaming the victim. This line of defense by Dr. Walker would seem to show she is unable to justify her decisions on standard research grounds.

[9]This is reminiscent of the FBI study that resulted in the Organized-Disorganized Dichotomy of serial offenders: an inadequate study design using flawed questionnaire data resulted in a criminal profiling paradigm that was inherently flawed and never validated. Yet to this day the FBI continues to use (with occasional denials) the Organized-Disorganized profiling paradigm.

Walker (1984) used some of the subjects as their own controls, "by obtaining information from them about non-battering relationships in which they had been involved" (McMahon 1999, 31). The two principal studies Walker relies on for BWS were a preliminary study of "more than 120" battered women and a later study of 403 battered women. These samples were from women who sought help of some nature. The larger study sample (McMahon 1999, 31) "was skewed towards professionally employed women who, after experiencing moderate levels of violence, left their abusive partner: 'self-selected survivors' (Walker 1984, 229)." As McMahon (1999, 31) points out, there is no way to know how reliable the data is, or how representative the sample was of women in general who are battered—a point acknowledged, then dismissed, by Walker (1984). The lack of control groups leaves us not knowing "whether levels of depressions and self-esteem reported by Walker's (1984) respondents are significantly different to those of a comparable sample of women in intimate, heterosexual, nonbattering relationships" (McMahon 1999, 31).

McMahon (1999) cites discrepancies in Walker's study data, giving as an example that while Walker reported that the percentage of battered women who were themselves violent toward the abusive partner was "small,"[10] her own data showed almost one-quarter (24%) of women in a violent relationship reported "occasionally" or "frequently" using physical force (174), hardly a "small" proportion. As Walker provides in the Appendix to the second edition of *The Battered Woman Syndrome* (2000, Appendix A: Table 13, 237), in response to the question, "Did you ever threaten to leave to get something you wanted?" (n = 400) seventy three percentage answered occasionally (52%) or frequently (21%) during a violent relationship. It would appear that (at least for this sample) the battered women had little problem threatening to leave as a form of manipulation. As to using actual physical violence to get what they wanted (n = 397), 23% answered occasionally and 1% answered frequently, which is the data noted by McMahon above. The 1% (2 of 397 subjects) figure for frequent use of violence is simply too low to be believed; and even more so when one realizes that the math is off. Two divided by 397 is 0.5%. While this may be the percentage of battered women who admit in Walker's study to frequently using physical force themselves, it is not likely to be the percentage of battered women who actually engage frequently in physical violence against the batterer.

Compared to other research (Straus 1999), the finding that women assaulted men in marital, cohabiting, and dating relationships on an almost 50–50 basis as men assault women, the percentage proffered (1%, but corrected to 0.5%) for frequent

---

[10]Walker (1984, 150) reports: "Still the percentage was small, with 15% of those in a violent relationship and 5% in a nonbattering relationship reporting the use of violence." This 15% figure is at odds with Walker's Table 13 (174), which give 24% for combined, 23% for occasional, and 1% for frequent use of physical violence.

violence by the female partner could not be accurate. There has been little interest in exploring violence used by women in general, let alone those involved in domestic violence, and pursuing such research is often interpreted as antifeminist (Straus 1999). One meta-analysis (Archer 2000) of physical aggression in heterosexual relationships found that men were more likely to inflict an injury and 62% of those injured were women, but the flip side is that 38% of men were injured by the female partner and women were slightly more likely than men to use physical aggression, "and to use such acts frequently" (651). Walker should have been alarmed by the low levels of occasional violence and the almost nonexistent level of frequent violence suggested by her sample, as an indication that something was seriously amiss with her sample, research methodology, or both.

Additionally, while Walker has described the batterer in her studies, all data on the batterer has been derived from the battered women, a "secondary sampling" approach that tells us about the victim's perceptions of the batterer rather than reliably defining the batterer. Such "secondary sampling" obviously has limited utility.

The Battered Woman (Walker 1979), along with other media chosen by Walker (including one film, four books, and three articles, two authored by Walker [2000, 277]) on the subject of battered women were part of the training for the interviewers who were responsible for day-long interviews and subsequent coding, including coding of subjective data into "usable categories" (Walker 2000, 273). This curriculum on the subject of battered women, which was the basis for the study's hypothesis, ensured that the interviewers were very familiar with not only the area of battered women in general, but Walker's views and theories, specifically the cycle of violence and learned helplessness theory, which was the basis for the research. One cannot help but wonder if bias crept into this study.

Walker identified the issue and then moved past it (2000, 280): "Ideally, of course, those who collect data should be unaware of the hypotheses being tested." Since she felt it was unrealistic to find interviewers who had no knowledge of the subject (which may have been a realistic situation), Walker apparently decided to formalize any potential bias (280):

> First, we attempted to "standardize" [quote marks in original] the amount of information about battering that each interviewer had, by making sure they received the same, though minimal, information about the project. Although the specific hypotheses were not discussed, a general outline of some major explanations for battering relationships was given. Aside from this, there was no control over how much information an interviewer obtained.

It could be argued that the curriculum imposed on interviewers was not small, but that may be in the eye of the beholder. Regardless, Walker made sure that her data collectors were very familiar with what she was looking for, even if unwittingly. As noted by McMahon (1999), many of the questions used were open-ended. With the interviewer's familiarity with the research hypotheses (in general, if not specifically), this is cause for concern. One is left wondering if, having recognized the problem of potential interviewer bias, Walker attempted to standardize it or to maximize it.

Further, the "structured" interview changed during the course of the second larger study. McMahon (1999, 33) notes that "the format of important items relating to sexual assault were varied from open ended questions to closed questions employing forced-choice response categories during the course of the research study." Faigman (1986) criticized Walker's use of leading questions in her research and the fact that her research does not support her three-stage cycle of violence paradigm. For example, in Walker's data (1984, 96–97), the tension-building phase was present in only 65% of the subject relationships, and only 58% had a contrition phase. Faigman (1986) reviewed Walker's data and determined that only about 38% of her cases would have been likely to have experienced the three stages of the cycle of violence. This means that a little over a third of the affected parties met the criteria for the paradigm that their data was used to create or support. Not surprisingly, there is no good empirical research supporting Walker's cycle of violence or BWS-learned helplessness, no matter what version is offered. Studies finding higher-than-average levels of psychopathology in battered women, such as Gleason (1993), do not correlate this directly with a "battered woman syndrome."

In contrast to helplessness and paralysis, some researchers have viewed battered women as survivors who actively seek help. A Texas study of 6,612 women who entered a shelter for battered women (Gondolf and Fisher 1988, 91–93), during an 18-month period in 1984–1985, noted:

> The most outstanding of these [the study's] findings is that the battered women are active helpseekers. The woman's helpseeking appears to increase as the batterer becomes more apparently dangerous and incorrigible. The women, in sum, are not the passive victims that notions of learned helplessness would imply. They are in fact "survivors," in that they assertively and persistently attempt to do something about their abuse.

The study also notes that the help sources to which the women turn have limited ability to intervene, which explains to some degree why some battered women stay in an abusive relationship. Even Walker noted (1984, 27) that her BWS sample sought help: "As the violence escalated, so did the probability that the battered woman would seek help. While only 14% sought help after the first battering incident, 22% did after the second, 31% after one of the worst, and 49% sought help after the last incident."

Relating the helplessness of BWS to a homicide, Walker was prepared to testify to BWS as a diminished capacity part of a self-defense strategy in a case where a woman had hired a hit man to kill her husband (Walker 1989, 293). Helen Martin and her husband Ronald were separated after five years of an allegedly abusive marriage. The husband did not live with Ms. Martin and had made threats to burn down her house. She hired a man to kill her husband, and in December of 1980 the hit man shot the husband as he left Ms. Martin's house after he had signed some legal papers to avoid foreclosure on the house. The court (*State v. Martin* 1984, 897) quotes her as having said, after the first shot, "He's not dying fast enough—hit him again." Ms. Martin then celebrated a friend's birthday. The next day she reported the husband missing, and the day after that she paid the life insurance premiums for her husband's life insurance policies (897–898). The trial judge refused to allow Walker to give BWS testimony. Ms. Martin was convicted of murder and appealed, at least in part, on the basis of being denied the opportunity to present BWS testimony to the jury. The Missouri Court of Appeals upheld the trial judge's ruling. Feigman (1986, 632) found "Walker's intended role in *Martin* deeply disturbing. That the leading theoretician of battered woman syndrome would be willing to characterize Martin as a case of legitimate self-defense seems to call into question the credibility of her testimony in other cases."

Other cases where women hired hit men to kill a spouse then attempted to use a BWS defense include *State v. Leaphart* (1983), where the testimony was not allowed; *State v. Anderson* (1990); and *Anderson* (the same Anderson, now in federal court) *v. Goeke* (1995), where BWS was allowed but a self-defense instruction to the jury was not made; *People v. Yaklich* (1992), where BWS testimony was allowed but not self-defense instruction.

A neglected topic is malingering, or perhaps more likely, false reporting in total or in part. The subject is usually ignored, yet it exists. In a letter to the editor of the *American Journal of Psychiatry,* Neil Blumberg (1992) mentions that he had identified a woman malingering BWS in his forensic practice. But he takes great pains to indicate that his letter "is not intended to criticize the legitimacy or importance of recognizing the battered woman syndrome" (715). If only the doctor had done his homework, he might not have felt the need to be so cautious.

Walker (2000, 161), in describing how one evaluates a battered woman, presents the assumptions she works with: "The first one is to believe a woman when she claims to be battered. It is rare that a woman would make up such ghastly stories." I do not fault Walker for wanting to believe her study subjects; I do, however, fault her for not being realistic regarding the possibility of false reports of victimization in general, and for exaggerating one actor's role while minimizing that of another. Interestingly, Walker further comments (161):

Many of the new strategies for detecting malingering and deception have not been normed on a population of battered women, who may have self-interest in claiming to be battered when they are not, but also may be telling as much of the truth as they can given their long history of lying and manipulating to cover up for the abuser.

So, according to Walker, we can't use any of the non-battered-women–normed methods of detecting malingering, and we should accept at face value any information presented by Walker to us that is drawn from a population that she advises is skilled in deception.

As Dixon and Dixon (2003, 36) point out:

There is neither scientific evidence that such a distinct syndrome truly exists nor consistency of effects across individuals. In addition, as long as researchers only study pre-identified groups of women who all have a battering history, rates of accuracy and error in diagnosing the syndrome will remain unavailable....The paucity of research establishing BSW as a bona fide reliable condition egregiously undercuts the claim that the condition exists as a distinct diagnostic entity. Though the battering of women is likely epidemic, experts cannot reliably diagnose a related "Syndrome."

Dutton (1996) critiques BWS with the following points: (1) there is no single profile of a battered woman; (2) the term "battered woman syndrome" is vague; (3) PTSD, compared to other psychological reactions to battering, is not uniquely relevant for understanding legal (or other) domestic violence–related issues; (4) relevant information for expert testimony, advocacy, and treatment involving battered victims extends beyond the psychological effects of battering; and (5) the term "battered woman syndrome" creates an image of pathology. The 1996 National Institute of Justice (viii) report on the validity of BWS stated: "The term 'battered woman syndrome' portrays a stereotypic image of battered women as helpless, passive, or psychologically impaired, and battering relationships as matching a single pattern, which might not apply in individual cases."

In Walker's most recent study (2006, 148) of 76 battered women conducted in 2002, she used the "definition of PTSD plus additional BWS criteria." "The initial results indicate that PTSD does exist in battered women." No one will argue with this statement. The next sentence is: "BWS has been empirically shown to be a subcategory of PTSD" (150). Once again we are presented with a nonrandomized, self-selected study (n = "the first 76"), without a control group, that is making unsupportable conclusions. The BWS definition is now (147) PTSD (reexperiencing the event, numbing of responsiveness, hyperarousal) plus three additional "effects": disrupted interpersonal relationships; difficulties with body image/somatic concerns; and sexual and intimacy problems.

It would appear that, as the three additional "effects" are what now separates BWS from non–BWS-PTSD, this is what we will use in the future to make the diagnosis of the purported BSW-PTSD subcategory. But there is nothing to tell us what the prevalence of these three "effects" are in women in general and in women who suffer trauma of types other than domestic violence. There is nothing to convince us that these three "effects" are selective for BWS. Once again, we are left with problematic research defining diagnostic syndromes that may be offered in court as part of a mitigating or self-defense presentation.

It is important for the reader and investigator to understand that although I am quite critical of BWS as a "diagnosis" or as a basis for expert testimony, it is my opinion that in individual cases there is room for the expert to evaluate a case and present to a court opinions regarding the state of mind of a victim of domestic violence during the commission of an act, potential reasons for remaining in a violent relationship, and even reasons for participating in a crime. So long as the available evidence warrants the opinions offered, there is no problem. Walker's description of BWS helps describe some victims of domestic violence, but not all, and likely not the majority. Having said this, Walker deserves credit for bringing the social problem of domestic violence to public awareness.

RAPE TRAUMA SYNDROME

Rape is both a sexual act and a violent act. It is about control and anger. Different rapists have different motivations for the crime, and this will play out with the victim. Some rapists need reassurance of their masculinity and actually fantasize that they and the victim have a relationship, apologizing after the crime, even, incredibly, sometimes contacting the victim after the rape.[11] Others seek to punish the victim and can be unnecessarily brutal during the crime. Different levels of violence will be present from different rapists, and sometimes between different rapes by the same rapist. How victims respond to an assault depends on several factors, including the level of violence, fear for their lives, and whether or not they were able to demonstrate some mastery over the situation, either by thwarting the rape entirely or by controlling the rapist in some manner, such as trying to avoid pregnancy and sexually transmitted diseases by getting the rapist to use a condom (*New York Times* 1993).

It is hard to imagine another crime that could be expected to damage or destroy someone's sense of personal security and ability to trust others, except, perhaps, prolonged and intense stalking. Rape is a crime that leads to humiliation, shame, self-doubt, distrust, and anger, among other things. As noted, victims' responses to rape will vary. Unfortunately, sexual assault victims often feel retraumatized by the criminal justice response to them (Koss 2006). Victims

[11]In one case (Massic 2002) a victim had given her cell phone to an alleged rapist, advising him that since he knew her number she would not contact the police about the rape. He called her days later and was arrested after arranging a second meeting.

of rape or attempted rape can suffer from the same symptoms as victims of violent crime in general, but there is an expectation that on average their course may be more intense and prolonged due to the very nature of the assault, physically as well as culturally.

Rape Trauma Syndrome (RTS) was first described by Burgess and Holmstrom (1974a). The syndrome reportedly consists of symptoms exhibited by victims of forcible rape or attempted forcible rape. Data was collected from interviews with all women (146) presenting to the emergency room of a Boston hospital from July 1972 to July 1973 who stated that they had been raped, with later follow-up interviews up to 6 years later (Burgess and Hazelwood 2001). There was no control group. All the subjects of the study were interviewed either by Burgess or Holmstrom. Burgess and Holmstrom (1974a) correctly noted that while the literature on rape as a crime was "voluminous," it had essentially ignored the victim. They divided the 146 subjects into three groups (981): (1) victims of forcible rape or attempted rape, "usually the former"; (2) victims who were an "accessory" due to inability to consent; (3) and "victims of sexually stressful situations," that is, the victim initially consented, but the event went further than she wanted. There is no mention of any attempt to take false allegations of sexual assault into account, or even an awareness of their existence. Therefore it is difficult to know to what extent, if any, the data was in any way affected by this phenomenon.[12]

The syndrome was based on the findings related to the sample cohort (92 women) that reported being forcibly raped (Burgess and Holmstrom 1974a, 981). RTS is formulated to consist of an acute phase and a long-term reorganization phase (982) "that occurs as a result of forcible rape or attempted forcible rape." It is not clear how the attempted forcible rape cohort factored in, as Burgess and Holmstrom clearly state the syndrome was based on the data from the 92 women who reported forcible rape, not those who reported attempted forcible rape (981). We are not given the number of subjects in any cohort other than the forcible rape group. It would appear, without further explanation from the authors of the study, that they used data from the cohort who suffered the most egregious assault and extrapolated it to a second cohort (attempted forcible rape) that, while certainly at risk for a physical and psychological reaction, clearly underwent a different experience. It would seem obvious that an argument could be made that the attempted forcible rape cohort may be expected to, on average, fare better than those who had been forcibly raped, possibly making the data seem less compelling. Burgess and Holmstrom give no explanation for this decision.

Burgess and Hazelwood (2001, 30–33) describe the acute phase of the syndrome as *disorganization*. This phase consists of an *immediate impact phase* and physical and psychological responses to the assault. In the immediate impact

[12]See Chapter 8 of this text for a discussion of false allegations of crime, including sexual assault.

phase the (30) "emotional demeanor of the victim may be one of two types—expressive or guarded." Expressive victims shows their emotions, whereas a guarded victim does not. There is a further admonition that the victim can change from one type to another and even interchange between the two depending on several parameters. This should alert the reader to the fact that the response of the victim is varied and unpredictable.

Burgess and Hazelwood (2001) and Burgess and Holmstrom (1974a) suggest that the victim will have physical and psychological reactions to the sexual assault. There will be disturbances of sleep and appetite as well as various physical complaints. The victim will suffer feelings of fear, humiliation, shame, guilt, and embarrassment, among others. Intrusive thoughts of the trauma may occur. All of these symptoms are found in conditions other than rape trauma. Burgess and Holmstrom (1974b) state that RTS is further complicated by a "compound reaction," wherein the victim has a recrudescence of prior psychiatric problems, and a "silent reaction," wherein the victim suffers from RTS but has not reported a rape. Both scenarios are known reactions to rape and offer nothing to support the validity of RTS.

The long-term reorganization process (Burgess and Hazelwood 2001) can take weeks to years and likely never ends. Various lifestyle aspects are affected: physical, psychological, social, and sexual. Resumption of sexual activity after a rape is affected by the victim's pre-trauma sexual framework and by a post-trauma sense of self, as well as partner reactions to the assault, both conscious and unconscious. Some men, as well as some cultures as a whole, view a rape victim as having been sullied and no longer worthwhile or desirable. Some cannot accept that the victim did not invite the attack in some way or should have died rather that give in to the assault.

Although RTS was presented as a newly discovered syndrome, nowhere in the original paper (Burgess and Holmstrom 1974a) are we given the expected diagnostic criteria to diagnose it. It is surprising to find that a syndrome that has gained significant acceptance in the courts has no criteria for accurate diagnosis other than having been subjected to a specific trauma. It becomes clear that the diagnosis is expected to come from the specific trauma, not from the symptoms. The danger in this is obvious, for when RTS is introduced into a court proceeding as proof that a sexual assault has occurred, the opining expert is indulging in circular reasoning. Also, the acute and long-term phase description of RTS does little, if anything, to differentiate it from other victim responses to violent crime, or other catastrophic events that could potentially lead to a diagnosis of PTSD. As Boeschen, Sales, and Koss observe (1998, 426): "Although still commonly found in the forensic setting, RTS is a phrase no longer used in the clinical setting and thus should no longer be used by a mental health expert." They more forcefully state (428): "Although RTS has historical importance, it makes for confusing and potentially unscientific expert testimony and should no longer be used in the courtroom"; they go on to note that PTSD itself is not without problems when brought into the legal arena.

RTS suffers from the same criticism about BWS. Both are gender-specific syndromes based on single or few studies without follow-up validation by others, drawn from a preselected convenience sample (battered women presenting themselves for help for BWS, and rape victims who came to an emergency room for RTS) with no control group. The "syndromes" consist of symptoms that are not specific to the syndromes and that are exhibited by people who were never battered or raped. Also, both BWS and RTS have been offered in court as proof that the event (battering or rape) occurred, in spite of the lack of an underlying scientific basis. As Dixon and Dixon note (2003, 41): "As with BWS, no evidence exists to differentiate rape victims who develop the syndrome from those who do not develop it, or to differentiate the associated symptoms among women who have and have not experienced rape."

It is hard at times to sort out good science from bad. Cling (2004), a psychologist and lawyer, gives a ringing endorsement to RTS, giving, more than once, proof of the validity and acceptance of RTS the American Psychiatric Association's endorsement of RTS, because (20):

> Their [Burgess and Holmstrom] formulation [of RTS] was accepted and included in the DSM, published by the American Psychiatric Association. Ultimately … RTS was included as a form of PTSD where the stressor is rape.

One is at a loss to explain how Cling has confused the DSM's listing of rape as a possible trauma leading to PTSD with an endorsement of RTS, yet she goes on (21): "It seems clear…that RTS, as PTSD…is recognized as a verifiable disorder with specific symptomology, which can be distinguished from other disorders and is included in the DSM as a subset of PTSD," including the DSM-IV-TR (2000). This was quite a surprise to me. A search of the electronic version (DSM-IV-TR Plus, Version 1.0, 2000) fails to find any mention of RTS, nor can it be found in any prior version of DSM. The word "rape" appears in relation to a trauma that could lead to PTSD, but there is no endorsement (or mention) of RTS, as Cling claims. It is clear that the DSM is accepting rape as a trauma that could lead to PTSD. Nowhere does the American Psychiatric Association or the DSM endorse RTS, regardless of Cling's assertions. RTS has no place either in the vocabulary of mental health practitioners, or in the opinions of experts.

STALKING

Stalking is a repetitive act usually undertaken to cause distress to the victim. It is often a dysfunctional manner of dealing with anger, designed to harass and control the object of the anger, which can be a lover who has rejected the stalker or someone the stalker does not even know. There are cases where the stalker is delusional, believing the victim wants to have a relationship with him or her, and the stalking is an attempt to complete the relationship, but the vast majority of stalking incidents is related to nonpsychotic individuals who know the victim and for some reason are angry at the victim and cannot accept that the relationship is over. The style of harassment increases a victim's feelings of impotence and vulnerability, especially when attempts to involve law enforcement are ineffective. That victims might suffer from psychological symptoms is expected rather than unusual. Anxiety, depression, difficulty sleeping, a heightened startle response, reactive paranoia, and other symptoms or emotions such as anger and rage at the stalker are not uncommon. At times a victim may meet criteria for PTSD.

Stalking is perpetrated both in the real world and in cyberspace, where some stalkers feel empowered by the false sense of anonymity the Internet engenders (McGrath and Casey 2002). Regardless of the method of stalking, the behavior takes a toll on the victim. Respondents in one study (Hall 1998, 133) generally described stalking as "akin to psychological terrorism." Yet one person's stalking may be another's dysfunctional courting (Dennison 2007), with the most common type of stalking due to an obsessional male stalking a female with whom he has had a prior relationship (Meloy 1998).

A victim's response to the perceived threat can include moving to another city, changing jobs and phone numbers, and other measures. Stalkers will sometimes harass victims at work (Logan et al. 2007), affecting job performance and employability, and removing another perceived safe haven.

Rebecca Griego, 26, had ended a relationship with a boyfriend, but he continued to pursue her, causing her to move and change her phone number. She distributed his photo to coworkers and advised them to look out for him. She took out a restraining order in March 2007, after he called her job and threatened to kill her. The only way she was aware he could locate her was at her sister's home or at her job at the University of Washington. In early April 2007 he came to Rebecca's work site, where he shot and killed her then turned the gun on himself (Frey, McNerthney, and Castro 2007).

While stalking behaviors can range from annoying up to sexual assault and kidnapping, and even homicide, the vast majority of stalking behaviors in Hall's (1998) nonrandomized study tended to be unwanted communications (letters, phone calls),[13] with the stalker following the victim at times and driving by his or her home. In domestic violence scenarios, there is a risk that the controlling offender will stalk the spouse or intimate once he or she has finally decided to end the relationship. This must be taken seriously by law enforcement, as victims may be at significant risk of assault if they are confronted by their stalkers and refuse to reengage in the relationship.

[13]The study was done prior to 1998. Today, e-mail communications would be included.

Stalking Trauma Syndrome

Colins and Wilkas (2001, 319) proposed a new syndrome, specifically **Stalking Trauma Syndrome** (STS), to describe what they believe is a diagnosable condition: "STS is a theory that can be related to **post-traumatic-stress disorder** (PTSD), battered woman syndrome, and rape trauma syndrome; yet STS is a unique condition." They compare and contrast STS to BWS and RTS. Regarding STS there is actual helplessness (as opposed to learned helplessness), where the victim is unable to influence the situation. Compared to RTS, STS has an ongoing stressor as opposed to a single incident. While both rape and stalking are about control, the stalker's pursuit of control is ongoing, and, finally, in RTS the syndrome is experienced after the trauma, whereas in STS the victim experiences the syndrome during the trauma (stalking) and afterward (Colins and Wilkas 2001, 320–321).

Colins and Wilkas (2001, 324) present the "Cycle of Crisis" to describe the stalking phenomenon. It consists of three phases: a crisis phase; a recovery phase; and an anticipation phase. Due to the ongoing nature of stalking and the anticipation of further harassment, the victim is unable to recover. No guidance is offered as to how a victim of STS would differ from a victim of RTS who has anxiety and other symptoms on an ongoing basis, with continued fear of sexual assault, or, for that matter, a battered woman still in a violent relationship. The recovery phase is "brief or nonexistent" (323), so in time we have only the crisis phase and the anticipatory phase.

Colins and Wilkas (2001, 324) argue that in the "Cycle of Violence" (there are several elements that affect the duration of the stalking: length of stalking; criminal justice system response; victim support system; and the presence of implied and/or direct threats. Their postulation that the length of the stalking episode is related to the length of the cycle of violence would be hard to argue with, first, because it is simply circular reasoning. Second, the response of the criminal justice system to the stalking would certainly be expected to affect the course of the stalking and therefore its effect on the victim, but this would be true of just about any crime. Colins and Wilkas claim (2001, 325) that "[u]nlike other types of crime, it often seems like a victim of stalking assumes the role of proving his/her case against the stalker." While victims of stalking may need to be proactive in building a case against a stalker, there are many crimes (rape, for one) where a victim sometimes feels the need to prove that a crime has been committed. The claimed exclusivity Colins and Wilkas strive for (presumably to bolster the claim that STS is a unique entity) does not exist.

The victim's support system would be expected to affect the victim's response to the stalking, as it would be expected to affect almost every victim of any crime. It is not clear how this differentiates stalking victims from other victims. The last element in the cycle of violence is the presence of implied versus direct threats, but it is not clear how this affects the length of the cycle of violence, or whether it would shorten or lengthen it.

Colins and Wilkas (2001, 326) then list the "most common psychological effects suffered by victims to be helplessness, hopelessness, anxiety, desperation, and loss of control," with helplessness and hopelessness being the "two key elements" of the syndrome. How this differentiates victims of stalking from other victims of crime or even seriously depressed people in general is not explained. Obviously, the fact that the victim was stalked will guide us, but again, this is a so-called syndrome where the diagnosis is actually the trauma and not the specific symptom set exhibited by the typical stalking victim.

STS is a theory, based on the expectation (unproven) that specific types of trauma lead to specific diagnosable syndromes, either aside from PTSD or as a "subcategory" of PTSD. PTSD allows a broad definition for the instigating trauma, and its diagnosis is made from the symptoms not the trauma. STS suffers from similar problems as BWS and RTS, except that it does not even have a methodologically flawed, nonrandomized, non–control group study to support it.

I want to be very clear regarding STS, BWS, and RTS. Although I am critical of the research (or lack of it) supporting these syndromes, this should not be interpreted as dismissing the suffering of the victims of related crimes. Crime victims may suffer many psychological problems and symptoms. When they meet criteria for a DSM-IV diagnosis, they should be diagnosed and treated. Even if they are not suffering from a diagnosable mental condition, they may benefit from support and information. However, attempting to create trauma-specific syndromes does nothing for the victim and entices attorneys and expert witnesses to bring such syndromes into the courtroom, when the bases for the syndromes have more in common with politics than science.

HYPNOSIS

Occasionally investigators get the idea of using hypnosis to refresh or clarify memories of a crime victim. The use of hypnosis in these cases is to some degree based on the belief that the mind records memories like a camcorder and with help a victim can play back the movie. This memory analogy is faulty, and using hypnosis in this manner has been problematic and is just as likely to hinder an investigation as to help it.

Hypnosis is the art of putting someone in a "trance," which is simply an altered state of consciousness in which the subject will likely be more suggestible than usual, as critical aspects of thinking tend to be relaxed.[14] It is not uncommon for an individual to have the experience of driving somewhere familiar (e.g., home from work) and suddenly realize that he or she is at such and such an

[14]Sadly, I would suggest that critical aspects of thinking tend to be fairly relaxed in many individuals at baseline.

intersection but cannot recall driving for the past few minutes. Yet the driving was negotiated safely. The explanation is that the driver was in a trance state, unconsciously aware of the environment and even responding to it.

Many are surprised to learn, though, that the hypnotic trance is actually a state of focused attention; the subject is focused strongly on something, be it the voice of the hypnotist, or some other stimulus. Hypnosis can be a useful technique in helping someone quit smoking cigarettes, lose weight, or simply as a relaxation technique. It is also an amusing entertainment in a variety of settings. But it can be a dangerous modality to use in trying to elicit or refresh memories, or to prove a fact, as the whole repressed memory industry has shown.

As noted by Webert (2003, 1304) there are three general problems with using hypnosis in legal contexts: (1) the subject is more suggestible than he or she would be otherwise, subject to many influences, including verbal and non-verbal cues from the hypnotist and a possible desire to please the hypnotist; (2) the subject may unintentionally confabulate (i.e., make things up) so that the memories presented are more complete and comprehensible; and (3) the subject may have an enhanced belief in the veracity of his or her hypnotically recalled memories, regardless of their actual truthfulness. There is no way to know how accurate hypnotically recalled memories are, unless they can be independently corroborated through other sources.

Interestingly, there is a famous case where hypnosis resulted in the solving of a crime. In 1976 near Chowchilla, California, three masked men hijacked a school bus full of children and their driver. The victims were left hidden in a moving van buried in a quarry. While the kidnappers were planning ransom demands, the driver and some of the children were able to dig their way out. The driver remembered seeing a license plate from a vehicle used in the hijacking but could not remember the plate number. Under hypnosis he produced several numbers that led to one of the vehicles used in the crime and broke the case (Turco and Scott 1982).

Various jurisdictions have taken different approaches to hypnotic testimony, with courts in Illinois, Virginia, California, and the military courts martial system barring testimony from witnesses who have been hypnotized, while courts in Wyoming, Louisiana, North Dakota, and the federal Ninth Circuit have allowed testimony from witnesses who have undergone hypnosis. Some courts, for example, Wisconsin. Colorado, and the federal Fourth and Fifth Circuit, will allow such testimony if it can be shown to be reliable. Other courts in Minnesota, Arizona, Nebraska, New York, North Carolina, Washington, Michigan, Missouri, Massachusetts, Hawaii, Georgia, Alaska, Delaware, and Illinois have allowed witnesses who have been hypnotized to testify to recollections from prior to the hypnosis. The U.S. Supreme Court has held (*Rock v. Arkansas* 1987) that a defendant (note: the defendant, not just a witness) who has been hypnotized cannot be barred from testifying on the grounds of the Fifth (self-incrimination), Sixth (compulsory process),[15] and Fourteenth (due process) Amendments (Miller 2003b).

Newman and Thompson summarized the status of forensic hypnosis as (2001, 83–84):

> Investigatory forensic hypnosis was based on a well-intentioned but scientifically untenable position: that detailed memories could be accurately retrieved and utilized in criminal investigations. Although anecdotally helpful in some cases, courts recognized the risk hypnotically elicited memories could pose to the rights of a defendant in a criminal case...based on untested theories of repression and misdirected conclusions...[R]esearchers have identified the pitfalls associated with relying on hypnotically retrieved memories, influencing many courts to follow suit in denying the admissibility of such memories.

Any investigator considering using hypnosis as part of an investigation should check with his or her legal department as to the status of hypnotic testimony in the jurisdiction where the case will be prosecuted. Even in jurisdictions that allow hypnotically refreshed testimony, the court will expect that certain protocols have been followed.

VICTIM TOXICOLOGY

Victim toxicology is an important aspect of any investigation. Victims' ability to accurately recount what has occurred during a violent crime can be affected by many factors, including their level of fear; whether or not they were fully conscious during an attack; whether they subsequently were rendered unconscious due to a blunt trauma with potential amnesic effects; and so on.

The reliability of eyewitness memory is notoriously poor in some aspects, as evidenced by many wrongful convictions based on victim eyewitness identification. In addition to potential identification, victims will need to give a detailed account of the crime to assist an investigation. The ability to recall accurately can also be affected by prescribed medications, alcohol, cocaine, and other street drugs. The investigator needs to be aware of this in order to question victims as to medication or drug use.

---

[15]Compulsory process is the ability of a defendant to force a witness to appear (e.g., by subpoena) who can testify favorably to his or her case. An offshoot of this is that the defendant, as his or her own witness, cannot be barred from testifying on a per se ruling.

Consensual alcohol and drug use is a common precursor to rape (Hurley, Parker, and Wells 2006), and alcohol-related rape is more likely to involve acquaintances and strangers than intimates (Horvath and Brown 2006). Rape is already a vastly underreported crime. It is very likely that a rape victim who had consensually used drugs or alcohol with the rapist will think twice before going to the police to press a complaint. This is unfortunate as, regardless of how law enforcement will view the victim as a potential witness, a crime has been committed, and the police should have a record of the complaint and an ID of the alleged perpetrator, if possible. Should other victims later make similar complaints, the fact that a pattern has developed implicating a particular individual is important. Some rapists count on a victim's fear of not being believed due to having drunk alcohol with the rapist or having used an illicit drug such as cocaine. While some may infer a victim's use of alcohol implies poor judgment and likely consent, others understand that the same situation makes the victim vulnerable to a sexual assault. Whether or not a victim presents a good case for prosecution or not, he or she deserves to be treated with dignity and not victimized a second time.

Memory consists of several steps. Described simply, a stimulus (something the victim heard, saw, or felt), such as the sound of a gunshot, must first be perceived by a person. Once perceived, the stimulus can be mentally recorded. Once recorded, at some future date a memory of the stimulus can be retrieved. There can be difficulties with any step in the process. It is even possible, under the right conditions, for false memories to be reported; with the reporter not realizing that what he or she is reporting is false. Drugs can potentially affect all three processes, with difficulties in retrieving memories often related to the effects of chronic drug use. Any drug that obtunds a person can affect perception and the "laying down" of the memory. Drugs known to affect memory include alcohol, benzodiazepines, and marijuana, among others.

Alcohol suppresses many activities in the brain. One effect is to interfere with the recording of a stimulus, or the laying down of memory. It is well known that people intoxicated with alcohol may suffer a blackout, a period of time for which they cannot recall anything. This not because they fell asleep; in fact, others who were with them may have to tell them what they did during the period of blackout. In less extreme forms of memory impairment, it is common for persons intoxicated on alcohol the night before not to be able to recall accurately what they observed or did. Impairment in laying down new memories accurately can start to occur after relatively low doses of alcohol (Kuhn, Swartzwelder, and Wilson 2003).

Investigators should also keep in mind that they may be interviewing a victim who is hung-over, or withdrawing from a drug other than alcohol, when faced with poor recollection of facts, irritability, and fatigue in a victim. Long-term effects of regular alcohol abuse can include actual dementia. A known sequela of severe alcohol dependence is a condition known as Korsakoff's Psychosis. In this condition afflicted individuals cannot lay down new memories. They literally cannot remember anything for but a few seconds. Quite notably, such individuals confabulate to cover this deficit. They will make up any response, no matter how bizarre, to attempt to hide the problem. People with Korsakoff's are easily spotted, because they cannot recall if they met you a few moments before.

Marijuana, like alcohol, inhibits new memory formation, probably due to its effect on cells in the hippocampal region of the brain. A victim who was high on marijuana during an assault may have difficulty remembering things. The psychoactive chemical in marijuana is known as THC (delta-9-tetrahydrocannabinol). Due to its affinity for fat tissues, it can be detected for up to two months in a urine toxicology screen. Therefore, a positive qualitative toxicology screen (indicates if present, not the amount) for marijuana does not necessarily mean that a victim has smoked marijuana in the recent past.

Benzodiazepines are sedatives and affect memory. Drugs in this class include Valium, Xanax, Ativan, and so on. They are known as sedatives, and it is their sedating effect that interferes with the recording of new memories. Many sleeping pills are benzodiazepines (e.g., Restoril) and can affect memory. Keep in mind that many people dangerously ingest more than one drug, such as Valium and alcohol, to get high, and the effects on memory impairment can be enhanced. Rohypnol, also known as "roofies," is a potent benzodiazepine sometimes used as a "rape drug." It is easily concealed in an alcoholic beverage. However, reports of its widespread use may be exaggerated.

Other sedatives such as GHB (gamma-hydroxybutyrate) are known to inhibit memory formation. This is also known as a "date rape drug" due to its rapid onset, which leads to confusion, obtundation, and recall inhibition. GHB is difficult to detect and can easily be "hidden" in an alcoholic drink. If there is timely suspicion that a victim was subjected to a "rape drug," collection of evidence should be a consideration, including a urine sample and any glass the victim drank from (as well glasses used by the suspect for fingerprints or DNA). Emergency room toxicology testing does not routinely test for GHB, or for hallucinogens such as ketamine ("Special K"), phencyclidine (PCP), LSD, mescaline, Ecstasy, and so on, all of which can affect one's perceptions and level of consciousness. Ecstasy (MDMA) has both stimulant and hallucinogenic effects. While there are no controlled studies in humans regarding the effects of Ecstasy on memory (thank goodness), impaired memory is a frequently noted effect of the drug. In fact, users have coined the term "E-tard" (Kuhn, Swartzwelder, and Wilson 2003, 82) to describe heavy users.

Stimulants, such as cocaine and amphetamine, do not impair memory per se. Use must be considered in the context of dosage level and combination with other drugs. Stimulants actually improve concentration, which is why they work in attention deficit disorders. Use can lead to physiological arousal and even psychosis, so faulty memory related to these drugs is more likely a result of misperception of stimuli, as opposed to inability to record the stimuli. Opiates, such as heroin, are sedative in nature and would be expected to affect the ability to perceive. On the other hand, if a person has become tolerant to opiates, the effect might be minor, if at all. For example, 140 milligrams of methadone may have no demonstrable effect on a person who has taken that daily dose for some time.

Some prescription medications, as mentioned earlier, can affect memory. There are many reports regarding such medications, and it is difficult to know how reliable they are. For example, there are reports that statins (cholesterol lowering drugs) such as Lipitor affect memory. Sleeping pills, such as Ambien, are known to cause memory impairment. Some antidepressants, such as Zoloft and other SSRIs (selective serotonin reuptake inhibitors), have a reputation for causing memory problems, but the issue is poorly researched and reliable scientific facts are limited. The number of medications is far too numerous to address here. The side effects of many medications, including some antihypertensives and anticonvulsants, list confusion or memory impairment as potential side effects. In fact, there has been some work on using a beta-blocker as a way of blocking the laying down of traumatic memories post-trauma, if given quickly enough (ClinicalTrials.gov 2007).

It is not possible to predict the level of impairment in a particular person. If an investigator has concerns about a victim's ability to recall events related to a crime, it would be wise to have a full medical history, including any prescribed or illicit medications and drugs and/or alcohol use. While toxicology screens are helpful, it must be kept in mind that they only screen for a limited number of drugs. This information can be assessed by a physician with expertise in pharmacology. It is important to understand that while many things can affect memory, it is quite possible for someone who was intoxicated or affected by a medication to provide accurate information.

CONCLUSION

Victimology is an important facet of any investigation. Victim response to violent crime is varied. It is not possible to predict how a particular person will respond to a particular traumatic event. Victims of violent crime can benefit from appropriate behavioral health interventions when needed, as well as a supportive network of family, friends, and agencies. Battered Woman Syndrome and Rape Trauma Syndrome are gender-based paradigms that have failed, despite commentary to the opposite, to meet the requirements of scientific validity and should not be used as a mental health diagnosis or introduced in a courtroom. Stalking

Trauma Syndrome has yet to have even bad science to support it. Alcohol, drugs, and prescription medications can affect a victim's ability to recall accurately the details investigators need to further an investigation. This should not be interpreted as meaning that all victims who take medication or have used alcohol or drugs are unreliable witnesses. It is paramount that investigators and examiners are aware of these issues in their preparation of an informed victimology.

SUMMARY

A victim's response to violent crime is variable from person to person, making it very difficult if not impossible to predict how a crime victim should or will behave. A victim's response usually involves three stages of recovery: (1) dealing with the initial impact of the attack; (2) attempting to reconstitute his or her former self; and (3) reorganizing him- or herself to attend to life's daily activities.

There have been several attempts to pathologize the normal reactions of victims. The syndromes that have been used to describe these pathologies are Acute Stress Disorder, Post-Traumatic Stress Disorder, Battered Woman Syndrome, Rape Trauma Syndrome, and Stalking Trauma Syndrome. Although there is much overlap between these syndromes, the first two (ASD and PTSD) are the only ones that are recognized by the American Psychiatric Association and that have specific diagnostic criteria within the DSM. The remaining three (BWS, RTS, and STS) have been criticized on many levels.

There is limited research to support the validity of RTS and BWS, and what exists suffers from methodological flaws, including lack of control groups, lack of replication, sample selection, etc. There is no literature to support STS. Furthermore, some argue that RTS and BWS are a result of advocacy or political pressures, rather than having a solid scientific basis. Clearly, this would affect the utility of these diagnoses.

These syndromes are often misrepresented as a subcategory of the recognized disorder PTSD. It should be noted that they are not subsets of this syndrome, although the traumatic event they are the result of may very well cause the emergence of PTSD. The difference is that within these claimed syndromes the diagnosis is actually the trauma and not a specified symptom set exhibited by the victim. It should also be noted that although used in court for these purposes, evidence of these so-called mental disorders should not be used as proof that the victim suffered a particular trauma. When presented in court this argument is not only circular in logic, it is inherently legally unfair, as the syndromes have failed scientific scrutiny and have not been validated.

The ability for victims to recall correctly in a forensics context is affected by hypnosis, medication, alcohol, and street drugs. The investigator needs to be aware of the effects these processes and substances may have on the memory of a victim or witness. It is believed that alcohol, benzodiazepines (as well as other sedatives), and marijuana inhibit new memory formation. On the other hand, stimulants such as cocaine and amphetamines are more likely to affect the perception of a stimulus as opposed to the actual memory formation itself. This being said, it is impossible to predict the level of impairment that these factors will cause in any individual.

Questions

1. The tendency to view a victim as lacking flaws is known as _____.
2. True or False: There is a standard and acceptable way in which a victim of a violent crime should behave.
3. According to Wallace (2007) there are three broad stages or phases that describe the general response of victims of violent crime. Name and describe all three.
4. Acute Stress Disorder is characterized by dissociative symptoms such as _____.
5. Post-Traumatic Stress Disorder was previously known as _____.
6. Name the two syndromes discussed in this chapter that are legitimate mental disorders recognized by the American Psychological Association and present in the DSM.
7. Describe three criticisms of Battered Woman Syndrome.

REFERENCES

American Psychiatric Association. (2000). DSM-IV-TR Plus, Version 1.0, American Psychiatric Publishing Inc.

Anderson v. Goeke. 1995. 44 F3rd 675. 8th Cir.

Archer. 2000. "Sex Differences in Aggression between Heterosexual Partners: A Meta-Analytic Review." *Psychological Bulletin* 126, no. 5: 651–680.

Blackman, J. 1989. *Intimate Violence.* New York: Columbia University Press.

Blumberg, N. 1992. Letter to the Editor: "Battered Woman Syndrome," *American Journal of Psychiatry* 149, no. 5: 714–715.

Bodkin, J.A., H.G. Pope, M.J. Detke, and J.I. Hudson. 2006. "Is PTSD Caused by Traumatic Stress?" *Journal of Anxiety Disorders* 21, no. 2: 176–182.

Boeschen, L.E., B.D. Sales, and M. Koss. 1998. "Rape Trauma Experts in the Courtroom." *Psychology, Public Policy and the Law* 4, no. 1/2: 414–432.

Brewin, C.R., B. Andrews, and S. Rose. 2003. "Diagnostic Overlap between Acute Stress Disorder and PTSD in Victims of Violent Crime." *American Journal of Psychiatry* 160, no. 4: 783–785.

Brewin, C.R., B. Andrews, S. Rose, and M. Kirk. 1999. "Acute Stress Disorder and Posttraumatic Stress Disorder in Victims of Violent Crime." *American Journal of Psychiatry* 156, no. 3: 360–366.

Browne, A. 1987. *When Battered Women Kill.* New York: The Free Press.

Burgess, A., and R. Hazelwood. 2001. "The Victim's Perspective.," In *Practical Aspects of Rape Investigation: A Multidisciplinary Approach*, 3rd ed., edited by R. Hazelwood and A. Burgess, 29–46. Boca Raton, FL: CRC Press.

Burgess, A., and L. Holmstrom. 1974a. "Rape Trauma Syndrome." *American Journal of Psychiatry* 131, no. 9: 981–986.

———. 1974b. *Rape: Victims of Crisis.* Bowie, MD: Robert J. Brady.

CBS News. 2006. "Nightmare Murder in Big Apple." July 26. http://www.cbsnews.com/stories/2006/07/28/national/main1844264.shtml.

Cling, B.J. 2004. "Rape and Rape Trauma Syndrome." In *Sexualized Violence against Women and Children,* edited by B.J. Cling, 13–34. New York: Guilford Press.

ClinicalTrials.gov. 2007. "Effect of Propranolol on Preventing Post-Traumatic Stress Disorder." U.S. National Institutes of Health. http://clinicaltrials.gov/ct/show/NCT00158262.

Colins, M.J., and M.B. Wilkas. 2001. "Stalking Trauma Syndrome." In *Stalking Crimes and Victim Protection,* edited by J.A. Davis, 317–334. Boca Raton: CRC Press.

Craven, Z. 2003. "Battered Woman Syndrome." Australian Domestic and Family Violence Clearinghouse. http://www.austdvclearinghouse.unsw.edu.au/topics/topics_pdf_files/battered%20woman_syndrome.pdf.

Davidson, J.R. 1995. "Posttraumatic Stress Disorder and Acute Stress Disorder." In *Textbook of Psychiatry,* 6th ed., edited by H.I. Kaplan and B.J. Saddock, 1227–1236. Philadelphia: Williams and Wilkins.

Dennison, S. 2007. "Interpersonal Relationships and Stalking: Identifying When to Intervene." *Law and Human Behavior* 31, no. 4: 353–367.

Dixon, J.W., and K.E. Dixon. 2003. "Gender-Specific Clinical Syndromes and Their Admissibility under the Federal Rules of Evidence." *American Journal of Trial Advocacy* 27, June: 25–65.

DSM-III-TR. 1987. *Diagnostic and Statistical Manual of Mental Disorders,* 3rd ed. Text Revised. Washington, DC: American Psychiatric Association.

DSM-IV. 1994. *Diagnostic and Statistical Manual of Mental Disorders,* 4th ed. Washington, DC: American Psychiatric Association.

DSM-IV-TR. 2000. *Diagnostic and Statistical Manual of Mental Disorders,* 4th ed. Text Revised. Washington, DC: American Psychiatric Association.

Dutton, M.A. 1996. "Critique of the 'Battered Woman Syndrome' Model." Applied Research Forum. http://new.vawnet.org/category/Documents.php?docid=375&category_id=695.

Faigman, D.L. 1986. "The Battered Woman Syndrome and Self–Defense: A Legal and Empirical Dissent." *Virginia Law Review* 72, no. 3: 619–647.

———, D.H. Kaye, M.J. Saks, J. Sanders, and E.K. Cheng. 2006. *Modern Scientific Evidence: The Law and Science of Expert Testimony,* vol. 2. Danvers, MA: Thompson/West.

Fairbank, J.A., R.J. McCaffrey, and T.M. Keane. 1985. "Psychometric Detection of Fabricated Symptoms of PTSD." *American Journal of Psychiatry* 142, no. 4: 501–503.

Figueroa, T. 2006. "Jury finds wife guilty of second-degree murder." *North Country Times,* April 12. http://www.nctimes.com/articles/2006/04/13/news/coastal/15_02_514_12_06.txt.

Frey, C., C. McNerthney, and H. Castro. 2007. "Stalker finds victim at UW, kills her." Seattle. pi.com, April 3. http://seattlepi.nwsource.com/local/310031_uwshooting03.html.

Gleason, W.J. 1993. "Mental Disorders in Battered Women: An Empirical Study." *Violence and Victims* 8, no. 1: 53–68.

Gold, L.H. 2004. *Sexual Harassment: Psychiatric Assessment in Employment Litigation.* Washington, DC: American Psychiatric Publishing.

Gondolf, E.W., and E.R. Fisher. 1988. *Battered Women as Survivors: An Alternative to Treating Learned Helplessness.* Lexington, MA: Lexington Books.

Hall, D.M. 1998. "The Victims of Stalking." In *The Psychology of Stalking: Clinical and Forensic Perspectives,* edited by J.R. Meloy, 113–137. San Diego: Academic Press.

Horvath, M., and J. Brown. 2006. "The Role of Drugs and Alcohol in Rape." *Medicine, Science, and the Law* 46, no. 3: 219–228.

Hurley, M., H. Parker, and D. Wells. 2006. "The Epidemiology of Drug Facilitated Sexual Assault." *Journal of Clinical Forensic Medicine* 13, no. 4: 181–185.

Kennedy, L.W., and V.F. Sacco. 1998. *Crime Victims in Context.* Los Angeles: Roxbury Publishing.

Koss, M.P. 2006. "Restoring Rape Survivors: Justice, Advocacy, and a Call to Action." *Annals of the New York Academy of Sciences* 1087, no. 1: 206–234.

Kuhn, C., S. Swartzwelder, and W. Wilson. 2003. *Buzzed: The Straight Facts about the Most Used and Abused Drugs,* 2nd ed. New York: W.W. Norton.

Logan, T.K., L. Shannon, J. Cole, and J. Swanberg. 2007. "Partner Stalking and Implications for Women's Employment." *Journal of Interpersonal Violence* 22, no. 3: 268–291.

Marshall, R.D., R. Spitzer, and M.R. Liebowitz. 1999. "Review and Critique of the New DSM–IV Diagnosis of Acute Stress Disorder." *American Journal of Psychiatry* 156, no. 11: 1677–1685.

Massic, D. 2002. "BU student helps police nab her rapist." *The Digital Voice,* November 21. http://media.www.buvoice.com/media/storage/paper227/news/2002/11/21/News/Bu.Student.Helps.Police.Nab.Her.Rapist-330557.shtml.

McGrath, M., and E. Casey. 2002. "Forensic Psychiatry and the Internet: Practical Perspectives on Sexual Predators and Obsessional Harassers in Cyberspace." *Journal of the Academy of Psychiatry and the Law* 30, no. 1: 81–94.

McMahon, M. 1999. "Battered Women and Bad Science: The Limited Validity and Utility of Battered Woman Syndrome." *Psychiatry, Psychology and Law* 6, no. 1: 23–49.

Meloy, J.R. 1998. "The Psychology of Stalking." In *The Psychology of Stalking: Clinical and Forensic Perspectives,* edited by J.R. Meloy, 1–23. San Diego: Academic Press.

Mezey, G., and I. Robbins. 2001. "Usefulness and Validity of Post-Traumatic Stress Disorder as a Psychiatric Category." *British Medical Journal* 323, no. 7312: 561–563.

Miller, R.D. 2003a. "Novel Mental Disorders." In *Principles and Practice of Forensic Psychiatry,* edited by R. Rosner, 2nd ed., 233–238. London: Hodder Arnold.

———. 2003b. "Criminal competence." In *Principles and Practice of Forensic Psychiatry,* edited by R. Rosner, 2nd ed., 212. London: Hodder Arnold.

National Institute of Justice. 1996. "Validity and Use of Evidence Concerning Battering and Its Effects in Criminal Trials: Report Responding to Section 40507 of the Violence against Women Act." NCJ 160972. http://www.ncjrs.gov/App/Publications/abstract.aspx?ID=160972.

Newman, A.W., and A.W. Thompson. 2001. "The Rise and Fall of Forensic Hypnosis in Criminal Investigation." *Journal of the American Academy of Psychiatry and the Law* 29, no. 1: 75–81.

The New York Times. 1993. "Rapist who agreed to use condom gets 40 years." May 15. http://query.nytimes.com/gst/fullpage.html?res=9F0CE2DF173FF936A25756C0A965958260.

Otto, R., Poythress, N., Starr, L. & Darkes, (1993): An Empirical Study of the Reports of APA's Peer Review Panel in the Congressional Review of the U.S.S. IOWA Incident, *Journal of Personality Assessment* 61, no. 3: 425–442.

People v. Yaklich. 1992. 833 P.2nd, 758. Co. Ct.

Perconte, S.T., and A.J. Goreczny. 1990. "Failure to Detect Fabricated PTSD with the Use of the MMPI in a Clinical Population." *American Journal of Psychiatry* 147, no. 8: 1057–1060.

Rock v. Arkansas. 1987. 107 S. Ct. 2704.

Roth, A. 2003. "Woman convicted in love-triangle murder." *Union Tribune,* January 28. http://www.signonsandiego.com/news/metro/20030128-9999_1m28nourn.html.

Rothbaum, B.O., E.B. Foa, T. Murdock, D.S. Riggs, and W. Walsh. 1992. "A Prospective Examination of Posttraumatic Stress Disorder in Rape Victims." *Journal of Traumatic Stress* 5, no. 3: 455–475.

Ryan, W. 1971. *Blaming the Victim.* New York: Vintage Books.

Seligman, M.E.P., S.F. Maier, and J. Geer. 1968. "The Alleviation of Learned Helplessness in Dogs." *Journal of Abnormal Psychology* 73, no. 3: 256–262.

State v. Anderson. 1990. 785 S.W.2nd 596. Mo. Ct.

State v. Haines. 2006. 112 Ohio St.3d 393, 2006–Ohio–6711. http://www.sconet.state .oh.us/Communications_Office/summaries/2006/1228/050853_050959.asp.

State v. Leaphart. 1983. 673 S.W.2nd 870, 872. Tenn. Crim.

State v. Martin. 1984. 666 S.W.2nd 895. Mo. Ct.

Straus, M.A. 1999. "The Controversy over Domestic Violence by Women: A Methodological, Theoretical, and Sociology of Science Analysis." In *Violence in Intimate Relationships,* edited by X.B. Arriaga and S. Oskamp, 17–44. Thousand Oaks, CA: Sage.

Summerfield, D. 2001. "The Invention of Post-Traumatic Stress Disorder and the Social Usefulness of a Psychiatric Category." *British Medical Journal* 322, no. 7278: 95–98.

Tavis, C. 1992. *Mismeasure of Women.* New York: Touchstone

Turco, R.N., and E.M. Scott. 1982. "Hypnosis: Complications—An Illustrative Clinical Example." *International Journal of Offender Therapy and Comparative Criminology* 26, no. 2: 133–137

"The U.S.S. Iowa: Guilt by Gestalt," Congressional Testimony, *Harper's Magazine,* March, 1990, pp. 24–28.

Walker, L.E. 1979. *The Battered Woman.* New York: Harper Row.

———. 1984. *The Battered Woman Syndrome.* New York: Springer.

———. 2000. *The Battered Woman Syndrome.* 2nd ed. New York: Springer.

———. 2006. "Battered Woman Syndrome: Empirical findings." *Annals of the New York Academy of Science* 1087: 142–157.

Wallace, H. 2007. *Victimology: Legal, Psychological, and Social Perspectives,* 2nd ed. Boston: Pearson.

Webert, D.R. 2003. "Are the Courts in a Trance? Approaches to the Admissibility of Hypnotically Enhanced Witness Testimony in Light of Empirical Evidence." *American Criminal Law Review* 40, June: 1301–1327.

Wilson, M. 2006. "Being alone raises perils in a night on the town." *New York Times,* Late Edition, July 28.

Yehuda, R., and A.C. McFarlane. 1995. "Conflict between Current Knowledge about PTSD and Its Original Conceptual Basis." *American Journal of Psychiatry* 152, no. 12: 1705–1713.

CHAPTER 8

False Allegations of Crime[1]

Brent E. Turvey and Michael McGrath

CONTENTS

Having gathered data on the subject of false allegations of crime for more than a decade, we have observed that false allegations are not only commonplace but also a significant drain on law enforcement resources. Ignorance on the subject abounds, as does political motivation. Consequently, it remains a tremendous problem that few have sought to define, let alone solve.

There are many reasons for false reports. A partial list of motives would include financial gain; to garner sympathy; revenge; to cover up another crime; and to excuse behavior, that is, provide an alibi. Mentally ill individuals sometimes make false reports of crime, but these are often identified by the fact that they are not reality based. Unfortunately, having a serious mental illness also makes one vulnerable to being victimized. Others make false reports due to underlying (nonpsychotic) psychological needs, and these may be harder to ferret out.

While the potential categories of false reports are quite large, this chapter will briefly discuss false allegations of abduction and spend the majority of the discussion on false allegations of sexual assault, although the two will often overlap. These types of crime represent the majority of false reports—and are overwhelmingly committed by females.

[1]Parts of this chapter have been adapted from material originally published in Baeza and Turvey (2002); McGrath (2000); and McGrath (2005).

FALSE ALLEGATIONS OF ABDUCTION

False allegations of abduction serve the same purposes as other false reports, including alibi, sympathy, profit, deflection of responsibility, and others. Consider the following examples, taken from many in just the past few years.

Audrey Seiler

On March 27, 2004, Audrey Seiler, a 20-year-old sophomore at the University of Wisconsin, disappeared from her apartment and was found four days later lying in a marsh. She claimed a man had abducted her at knifepoint. As described in a CNN report (2004a):

FIGURE 8.1

Audrey Seiler, a 20-year-old college student from the University of Wisconsin at Madison, staged her own abduction and falsely reported it to police. She later blamed it on depression.

> Audrey Seiler, a 20-year-old honor student at the University of Wisconsin in Madison, disappeared early Saturday.
>
> She was found Wednesday about two miles from campus in a marshy area of Madison shortly after someone spotted her and called police, authorities said. Seiler was treated at a hospital and released about five hours later.
>
> Blackamore said Seiler told police she was taken at knifepoint and held in captivity, but not harmed. She said she did not know the man....
>
> Seiler described the suspect as a white male in his late 20s or early 30s and about 6 feet tall, police said. He was last seen wearing a black sweatshirt, black hat and jeans, police said.

One of us (Turvey) was asked to examine details of the case for the media. Based on available police reports, there was reason to question Seiler's story despite national press effort that initially sought to deify her. As Rosario describes (2004):

> Brent Turvey, an [Alaskan]-based criminal profiler and forensic scientist with expertise in false reports, said police investigators in Madison will probably wait until the time is appropriate to grill Seiler on specific details on the alleged abduction.
>
> Turvey sees signs of serious doubts in the Seiler case, including the self-reported incident in February in which she claimed she was

knocked unconscious and dragged into a bushy area two blocks from her home. There was no evidence that she was robbed or sexually assaulted.

"That's extremely bizarre behavior, whether you live in Madison or L.A.," Turvey said.[2]

Police soon obtained video surveillance tape of Seiler buying the items used to bind her at a store. It appears she was having difficulty in her relationship with her boyfriend and may have staged the abduction for attention. She was charged with two misdemeanor counts of obstructing officers. As explained in a CNN report (2004b):

Seiler said a man had abducted her from her apartment and taken her to the marsh, where he tied her, bound her and forced her to take cold tablets.

The woman's claim that an abductor was lurking nearby led police to initiate a search, which turned up no suspects.

Police decided Seiler's claim was false after they reviewed videotape from a surveillance camera in an area store that showed the woman buying a knife, duct tape, rope and cold medication a day before she was reported missing.

In addition, police interviewed a man who said he had seen the woman in the marsh on days that she was being sought and that she appeared to be alone and unthreatened.

Interviewed by police during the search, Heather Thue, the student's roommate, said that Seiler "had been very depressed recently, coming out of her bedroom crying all the time."

Thue said that Seiler "had seemed kind of depressed lately and was 'confused' about her relationship" with her boyfriend, who did not pay as much attention to her as she wanted.

Seiler was given three years' probation after pleading guilty to two misdemeanor counts of obstructing police. She was also ordered to make monthly payments to the Madison Police Department to reimburse their investigative expenses. Their efforts cost about $96,000. She ultimately blamed the entire incident on depression.

---

[2]This statement refers to the failure of an alleged offender to rape or rob the victim in such a context; to go to all the trouble of acquiring the victim without any evidence of a motive.

FIGURE 8.2
A 2005 billboard in Duluth, Georgia, evidences the dual public perceptions of Jennifer Wilbanks: missing fiancé and "runaway bride."

Jennifer Wilbanks

Jennifer Wilbanks, a 32-year-old medical assistant (later nicknamed the "runaway bride") disappeared while out jogging on April 26, 2005, four days before her 600-guest wedding. She was immediately declared missing by her family and fiancé. A national media frenzy ensued, during which some in the psychic community declared her dead or in danger, as described in Radford (2005, 7):

> One self-proclaimed psychic in Buffalo, New York, reportedly had a vision that Wilbanks was dead and would be found near some bushes. Another psychic, Christopher Scott, described his involvement in the case at the Blogger News Network Web site: "I am a psychic with experience in this type of investigations [sic] and have offered my

help to Duluth police. I left my number two days ago and I haven't heard a word from them. I was involved in the murder of Robert Crane (from Hogan's Heroes) many years ago. I have participated in other investigation as well.... I have told police that it's vital that I examine her personal articles before they 'cool down....' I fear Wilbanks is in dire straights [sic].... If her parents can afford to offer $100,000 reward, they can afford to fly me in and at least allow me to examine evidence."

A police investigation revealed that she had bought a bus ticket days before her "disappearance." It turned out that she was overwhelmed with her upcoming wedding and got "cold feet." She traveled to Las Vegas, then to Albuquerque, and then called the police—falsely reporting she had been abducted. Later, after questioning, she admitted she had run away on her own (CNN 2005). She eventually pleaded guilty to making a false report and was sentenced to probation, community service, and continuation of mental health treatment (*CBS News* 2005).

Sasha Abney and Bryshada Ward

A 17-year-old girl from San Benito, Texas, was charged with filing a false report after claiming she had been abducted from her home, when in fact she had run away. As Abshire (2007) explains:

The Lampasas County Sheriff's Department issued arrest warrants Thursday for two Terrell women who spun a tale of abduction and returned home three days later to say their disappearance was a hoax.

Sheriff's investigator David Thorp said warrants were issued for both women on charges of making a false report to a peace officer, a Class B misdemeanor punishable by up to six months in jail and a $2,000 fine....

Sasha Abney and Bryshada Ward showed up at a Central Texas gas station Tuesday night after disappearing Saturday night in Mesquite.

"I'm angry, but I'm glad they're safe," Richard Abney, father of Ms. Abney, 20, and uncle of her 17-year-old cousin Ms. Ward, said at a news conference Wednesday outside Mesquite police headquarters.

"We found out this was a hoax," Mr. Abney said. "They missed their curfew, got in deeper and deeper and decided they were going to drive south. They ran out of money and ran out of gas, and they were afraid to call us. We are apologizing to everyone."

Mr. Abney said Ms. Ward hit his daughter with a shoe to cause a minor injury in an attempt to make the Terrell women's story more believable. As for reports that Ms. Abney was unresponsive when found, that was just an act, he said.

This case not only shows the kinds of motives involved in false abduction reports (curfew violations; fear of parental punishment), but the complexity of evidence that even teenagers are capable of staging evidence to back up their story.

We have observed that there appears to be more community and professional willingness to prosecute false reports of abduction than of rape. This may be due to the nature of the crime of rape, because of the nature of media attention and an angry public that feels it has been duped, or because of the type of victims involved. Specifically, alleged rape victims are often examined less carefully than any other type, because some investigators are unable to accept that false reports of rape are possible, to say nothing of being common. Still other investigators are unwilling to go down that investigative road for fear of political sanctions, inside and outside of their department. They may have an activist prosecutor, or an intimidating rape advocacy system, for example, that will step in to defend all alleged victims regardless of the evidence. Rape is a sensitive issue for many, and is more likely to get media attention and a community response in favor of the alleged victim up front than any other. All of these factors and more come bear on an investigation, and eventual prosecution, when a rape is reported. This is an area that requires further discussion and study.

FALSE ALLEGATIONS OF SEXUAL ASSAULT

Rape is one of the most ruinous of crimes, potentially destroying a victim's sense of safety and leading to significant psychological and functional sequela. In the past, unless a woman was significantly injured, claims of rape were often met with distrust. A calm presentation of events was also seen as evidence of a lack of injury, while a hysterical presentation of events was seen as lacking credibility (Aiken, Burgess, and Hazelwood 1995) and more indicative of hypersensitivity than a reaction to a crime. Thus a victim of rape was in a "no win" situation and was as likely to be victimized by the criminal justice system as by the rapist. Rape is also an underreported crime for many reasons, not the least of which is the victim's fear of not being believed and personal embarrassment. It is subsequently all the more surprising that such a large proportion of reported rapes are false.

Rape myths are varied and far from dead (Johnson, Kuck, and Schander 1997). As suggested by Herman (1990), one result of the feminist movement has been a redefinition of rape from a crime to a trait of the human male. In this paradigm, all males are rapists, and due to the inherent inequality between the sexes, any sexual interaction between a male and a female is, by definition, rape (Johnson, Kuck, and Schander 1997). Although this stance is clearly extreme, it has raised consciousness in America related to the crime of rape and the treatment of rape victims. For example, Rape Trauma Syndrome[3] (Burgess and Holmstrom 1974) and testimony related to it have been both barred and introduced at trial in various states (Block 1990). Rape Shield Laws have been introduced in an effort to protect the prior sex life of the rape victim from becoming the focus of inquiry at trial (Bryden and Lengnick 1997). Prior to such statutes, a defense attorney had free reign to delve into the past of the victim. When immaterial to the crime, this invited a jury to come to the conclusion that because the victim had been, or was currently, sexually active, that either she "asked for it," or the damage could not have been too great.

In his seminal work on criminal investigation, in a section dedicated to a discussion of the dangers of preconceived investigative theories, Hans Gross provides one of the earliest and arguably most informed segments on the subject of those who make false allegations of sexual assault (1924, 13–14). His discussion includes topics such as the various motivations for filing false reports, the occurrence of self-injury, and the related responsibilities of the investigating officer. In a more recent text on the history of rape, a discussion of the conceptualization and consequences of such false reports provides little more insight into these and associated problems (Palmer and Thornhill 2000, 159–161). Here the topic is couched in a general discussion of deceitfulness and sex differences, with some statistics. Their conclusion is that there are social factors and sex differences that may contribute to a general reluctance to believe female rape allegations (Palmer and Thornhill 2000, 160).

Jonna Spilbor, a prosecutor who became a defense attorney and then a news commentator, had the following to say regarding false allegations of sexual assault during a discussion of the rape allegation against popular sports figure Kobe Bryant of the NBA (Spilbor 2003):

> The statistics on false rape reports in the U.S. are widely divergent, and often too outdated to be meaningful. Not surprisingly, the numbers also depend on whom you ask. Organizations that tout a feminist agenda claim the number of false rape reports to be nearly non-existent—about two percent. But other organizations, taking the side of men, claim that false reports are actually very common—citing numbers ranging from forty-one to sixty percent.
>
> Amid the statistics, the truth is impossible to ascertain—but it's plain that false reports are indeed made, and that they can ruin the life of the accused, whether or not a conviction follows.
>
> Falsely reporting any crime is shameful. Falsely reporting a rape is especially heinous. The liar who files the false claim dishonors—and makes life all the more difficult for—the many true victims who file

[3]See Chapter 7 for a review of Rape Trauma Syndrome.

genuine rape claims because they have been terribly violated, and seek justice for it. At the same time, and perhaps even more seriously, the false report begins to destroy the reputation, and sometimes the life, of the accused from the very moment it is made—a fact of which many accusers are keenly aware.

A point Spilbor (2003) made very strongly is that it is common for the false reporter to suffer no legal consequences from having made a false report. This is reflective of the social and political context of some false allegations, which often includes the agendas of those involved. For example, in Burgess and Hazlewood's *Practical Aspects of Rape Investigation* (2001) one can read the entire chapter "False Rape Allegations" (Burgess, Hazelwood, and Burgess 2001) and never learn that making a false report of rape to a police officer is a crime, let alone that the false reporter should be held criminally responsible. This would be an example of the politics of victimhood precluding the notion that a "victim" should be held responsible for his or her behavior. This is evident when the chapter ends (195) with the following two sentences:

> Basic principles of police professionalism require that officers who investigate rapes remain objective and compassionate. If they do not, the veracity of the allegation may never be known; and the victim—for she is a victim in either case [i.e., whether the report of sexual assault is true or not]—may never receive the help or support she needs.

There is no mention of what, if anything, should be done for the person (not a victim?) against whom the false allegation was made.

As a counterbalance, we suggest readers consider the representative summary of potential consequences for false allegations provided in Martin (2005, 271):

> In Virginia, "[a]ny person fourteen years of age or older who makes or causes to be made a report of child abuse or neglect that he knows to be false shall be guilty of a Class 1 misdemeanor." Washington applies a similar misdemeanor punishment but does not include the age limit, "[a] person who, intentionally and in bad faith or maliciously, knowingly makes a false report of [alleged] abuse or neglect shall be guilty of a misdemeanor."

> In Indiana, a person who intentionally makes a false report has committed a Class A misdemeanor which is upgraded to a Class D misdemeanor if they have a prior conviction of false reporting. In addition, they may also be liable in damages to the person accused of abuse.

We would add that while it is true that sometimes people who have made a false report may benefit from some form of mental health intervention, this in no way changes the fact that they have committed a crime.

THE LITERATURE

Every so often false reports will be mentioned in the press, and unofficial false report rates crafted outside the realm of formal scientific research will be disclosed to the public.[4] However, the professional literature on the subject of false reports remains scarce. There have, for example, been very few scientific studies conducted to ascertain false report rates or percentages. Further still, there is a dearth in the published literature on even the subject of false reports in general. Put another way, those studying rape and sexual assault do not typically discuss false reports, let alone research the issue. This is due in no small part to the fact that many researchers fear being maligned, blacklisted, or threatened with sanctions should their findings not be politically acceptable.[5]

MacDonald

MacDonald (1973) found that, in 1968, the national average for forcible rapes was 18%. He further found that in a one-year period in Denver, Colorado, 25% of all forcible rapes were unfounded. He felt this was a conservative figure, as the police in Denver did not record as false reports any cases where there was a doubt as to the veracity of the complaint. Referring to the same study, MacDonald (1973) states that 20% of the forcible rape complaints were actually in doubt. MacDonald (1973) does not footnote or otherwise reference this information.

2% False Report Rate

There is no shortage of politicians, victim's advocates, and news articles claiming that the nationwide false report rate for rape and sexual assault is almost nonexistent, citing a figure of around 2%. This figure is not accurate, and attempts to find the original source are elusive.

---

[4]An editorial in the *New York Post* on the now-infamous Oliver Jovanovic false report case (Dunleavy 1999) quoted District Attorney Linda Fairstein from an interview in *Penthouse* magazine where she stated, "There are about 4,000 reports of rape each year in Manhattan, of these half of them didn't happen." In a more recent article, it was stated that out of 2000 uninvestigated cases in Philadelphia, Pennsylvania, from 1995–1997, investigators determined that "600 were false reports or allegations that did not amount to crimes" (Inquirer Staff 2000).

[5]This opinion is based on discussions with fellow investigators and forensic examiners. It is also based on the fact that a number of the articles reviewed for this paper received scathing commentary from the professional community unrelated to reliability and validity. A common complaint was that the identification and prosecution of false reporters cause legitimate victims to fear reporting their crime to law enforcement. As such, it has been argued that presenting any false report numbers is harmful to victims and casework by preventing legitimate victims from coming forward for fear of not being believed, or even being prosecuted, having reported a crime.

In researching this issue, Haws (1997) has prepared a brief but detailed account of his failed attempt to find a legitimate and accurate study supporting the claim that only 2% of reported rapes are false reports:

> If you talk to sexual assault counselors, you'll most likely hear the low figure: that 2 percent of all accusations of sexual assault reported to law enforcement across the country are later found to be false, which, the counselors say, is the same rate as for other crimes. Of all the numbers out there, this has been cited most often, appearing in publications from *The Boston Globe* to the *Houston Chronicle, The Christian Science Monitor,* the *Minneapolis Star Tribune, Newsweek,* and *Editor and Publisher.*
>
> Sometimes the figure is attributed to a particular source, but that's still no guarantee the numbers can't be challenged. Marcia L. Roth, the author of the 1996 op-ed article in the *Louisville Courier-Journal,* attributed the 2 percent rate to the 1993 book *Rape, the Misunderstood Crime,* by Julie Allison and Lawrence Wrightsman. But Allison and Wrightsman weren't so unequivocal. Noting that the frequency of false rape reports is difficult to assess, they didn't do their own study; instead they looked at a synthesis of research findings from a 1979 book, *Understanding the Rape Victim,* by Sedelle Katz and Mary Ann Mazur. Katz and Mazur, it turns out, had reviewed studies dating back to 1956 that showed the frequency of unfounded and false rape reports ranging from a low of 1 percent to a high of 25 percent. Allison and Wrightsman simply chose the study that showed 2 percent.
>
> Another named source for the 2 percent figure has been *Against Our Will,* the groundbreaking book on sexual violence by Susan Brownmiller published in 1975. She was reporting on the phenomenon that in New York City, the rate of false accusations dropped "dramatically" to 2 percent as soon as the police began using policewomen instead of men to interview complainants.
>
> Sometimes the 2 percent figure appears without any attribution. It simply floats out there, as in a 1994 article in the *Houston Chronicle* that cites a women's center official as the source for the false-rape-report figure of "between 2 and 3 percent." Period. And sometimes the attribution is vague but credible-sounding, like "federal statistics" or "the FBI." In 1992, *The Boston Globe* reported that a rape counselor stated the 2 percent rate for false reporting of rapes is the same as for false reports of other crimes—"according to the FBI."
>
> But the FBI has been saying since 1991 that the annual rate for the false reporting of forcible sexual assault across the country has been

a consistent 8 percent (through 1995, the most recent year available). That's four times higher than the average of the false-reporting rates of the other crimes tracked by the FBI in its *Uniform Crime Report*. The agency's guidelines define a report as false when an investigation determines that no offense occurred. A complainant's failure or refusal to cooperate in the investigation does not, by itself, lead to a finding of false report.

The writings of Susan Brownmiller, published three decades ago, stand out on this issue. In her work, *Against Our Will* (1975, 435), she argues:

> A decade ago the FBI's *Uniform Crime Reports* noted that 20 percent of all rapes reported to the police "were determined by investigation to be unfounded." By 1973 the figure had dropped to 15 percent, while rape remained, in the FBI's words, "the most underreported crime." A 15 percent figure for false accusations is undeniably high, yet when New York City instituted a special sex crimes analysis squad and put police *women* (instead of men) in charge of interviewing complainants, the number of false charges in New York dropped dramatically to 2 percent, a figure that corresponded exactly to the rate of false reports for other crimes.

Firstly, the statistic cited appears specific to New York City, so its use as a number representing national trends is inappropriate. Secondly, to support the 2% statistic provided, Brownmiller (1975, 373) references the remarks of Lawrence H. Cook, appellate division justice, before the Association of the Bar of the City of New York, January 16, 1974. In response to criticisms for using this non–peer reviewed remark at a public meeting as the basis for professional arguments and opinions, she wrote this brief response some twenty years later (Brownmiller 1995):

> The cite from the New York City Rape Analysis Squad was reported by Judge Lawrence Cooke to the NY Bar Association in 1974. Cooke was a leading appellate justice at that time. Cooke, the Bar Association, and the NYC Rape Analysis Squad were impeccable sources. The information was fresh and exciting. It had appeared nowhere else. The person who attempted to discount it in the post you reproduced denigrated New York State's leading appellate justice, a city agency, and me.

Ultimately, we are left to conclude that there is no published study or data to support any claim that the national false rape allegation rate is or was ever around 2%, even from those who originally cited that number. Rather, it comes primarily from a judge giving a speech to some attorneys 30 years ago whose source has, to date, not been validated.

Unfortunately, the 2% figure has found its way into legitimate research and texts on the subject, inappropriately offered as a national average or as the basis for refuting that false reports happen at all. For example, an otherwise excellent text on the subject of police culture and sexual assault referred to false reports of sexual assault as a "myth" (Gregory and Lees 1999, 90):

> Behind the mutual recriminations about the handling of rape and sexual assault cases, the dominant discourse on male and female sexuality, shared by most police officers, lawyers, magistrates, judges and juries, gives rise to the myth of false allegations and to misunderstandings around the notion of consent.

Consider also the otherwise even-handed discussion in Anderson (2004, 984–986), which concludes with a fair assessment of the current state of the science:

> To be sure, there are personality disorders that might lead a man or woman to lie in any number of outrageous ways, including lodging a false report of a crime. There is, however, no specific empirical research connecting any of these personality disorders with false complaints of rape to the police. In fact, there is no good empirical data on false rape complaints either historically or currently. A debate over the number of false complaints nevertheless continues.
>
> One side of the debate maintains that only two percent of rape complaints made to the police are false. In her popular 1975 book on rape, *Against Our Will,* Susan Brownmiller wrote, "when New York City instituted a special sex crimes analysis squad and put police-women (instead of men) in charge of interviewing complainants, the number of false charges in New York dropped dramatically to 2 percent, a figure that corresponded exactly to the rate of false reports for other violent crimes." Over time and perhaps through repetition, this two percent false rate has come to constitute the "conventional scholarly wisdom" on the matter. The United States Justice Department appears to agree, stating that "[f]alse accusations of sexual assault are estimated to occur at the low rate of two percent—similar to the rate of false accusations for other violent crimes."
>
> The other side of the debate claims that eight percent or more of rape complaints made to the police are false, a percentage disproportionate to other crimes. The F.B.I. *Uniform Crime Reports* have in the past indicated that, overall, about eight percent of forcible rape complaints reported to police are "unfounded." The term "unfounded" is misleading, however, because it does not mean "false." Rather, police may code a case "unfounded" when they conclude that it is unverifiable, not serious, or not prosecutable. Various factors can

increase a city's percentage of "unfounded" rape complaints, such as police incompetence, bias, or insensitivity to rape victims. As the Department of Justice found, police may think a rape claim is false or unfounded if the victim had a prior relationship with the attacker, used drugs or alcohol at the time of the attack, lacked visible signs of injury, delayed notifying police, did not have a rape exam, blames herself for the rape, or did not immediately conceive of the assault as a rape.

Thus, neither side's numbers in the debate over the rate of false complaints of rape lodged with the police appear to be supported by the kind of empirical evidence upon which one might feel confident. As a scientific matter, the frequency of false rape complaints to police or other legal authorities remains unknown.

It is true that good data on the subject is not available, and good empirical studies have yet to be performed. However, what can be stated with certainty is that the oft-cited 2% has no basis in reality, and is not reflective of national crime trends. It is time that we move forward and away from the citation of this figure to newer, more reliable data. Consider the following meta-analysis of available research to date.

McDowell

Charles P. McDowell, a supervisory special agent serving with the U.S. Air Force, studied false reports extensively. Although his study is unpublished, McDowell examined 1,218 cases that were initially reported as rapes. He found that 460 rape allegations were proven, 212 rape allegations were disproved, and 546 rape allegations were unresolved. The total percentage of false reports for all reported rapes was 17.41%, or 212 out of 1,218. The total false report rate for all resolved rape allegations was 31.55%, or 212 out of 672 (McDowell 1985).

Kanin

Eugene Kanin of Purdue University in Indiana conducted one of the few published studies on false reports. Kanin studied all rapes (n = 109) occurring in an unnamed midwestern city with a population of 70,000 from 1978 to 1987. Kanin found a 41% false report rate (1994). It should be noted that in Kanin's study a false report could only be identified by virtue of a confession from the alleged victim. In the same paper, Kanin also discussed the results of an unpublished study he conducted in 1988, which examined all forcible rape complaints during a three-year period on two midwestern college campuses. The false report rate in that study was 50% (1994).

What these numbers combine to suggest is that the rate of false reporting for rape varies from city to city, from state to state, and from region to region. As those of us who work cases know from experience, it can be very high. However, depending on how one approaches the phenomenon to collect and report data, and who is cited as a reference, the numbers can be made to paint a variety of pictures. We strongly urge further research of the matter by those controlling the data rather than burying it, which has too often been the case. The FBI's national average, which includes only reporting police agencies, suggests a false report rate of around 8%. Given other contextual support for higher rates of false reporting throughout the country (see footnote 4), this should be viewed as the most conservative estimate— the lowest possible estimate. It is by no means considered the limit.

Red Flags

When faced with an allegation of sexual assault an investigator at times walks a fine line between being supportive of a victim and trying to determine if the allegation of sexual assault is a false report. Sex crimes investigators are fully aware that false allegations of sexual assault are common. There are several collections of red flags for false allegations. These flags must be used in a measured manner, as a truthful person can easily raise some red flags.

It is also important to keep in mind that complainants may be telling the complete truth; may be holding back information for a variety of reasons; or may even be misrepresenting only parts of their actual attack. Simply because one has determined that a complainant has lied in one area does not necessarily mean that he or she has lied in all areas, or that an attack did not take place. For example, a victim could report a rape and a review of the alleged crime scene might determine that the report is not corroborated by the condition or evidence at that scene. It could be that the report is unfounded, but it could also be that the victim (for whatever reason) is reluctant to place himself or herself at the true crime scene. It is important to sort out inconsistencies early in the investigation either to identify a false report, or to salvage the prosecution of an actual criminal.

Dietz and Hazelwood

During testimony at the Tawana Brawley grand jury, Dr. Park Elliot Dietz, a forensic psychiatrist, proposed twenty false report red flags that he had developed along with retired Supervisory Special Agent Roy Hazelwood of the Federal Bureau of Investigation (*Court TV* 1997). While under oath, Dietz specifically mentioned the existence of false report red flags and stated that, based on his own research and consultation with Hazelwood, there are 20 characteristics that have appeared in false allegation cases. These are provided below, with commentary as appropriate:

1. *The story tends to be bizarre or sensational.* It is hard to assess this as given. Surely an unusual account will require explanation, but finding something unusual or "bizarre" is subjective to experience. Also, the fact that an account is sensational may or may not be helpful. The fact that some sensational cases are false reports may in fact skew our perception.

It may be that sensational false reports are the exception, but they are the ones that the media reports on. It may be that nonsensational cases are more numerous but receive less media attention.

2. *The pseudo-victim injures himself or herself, sometimes seriously, or simulates injury for the purpose of gaining support.* This cue is difficult to interpret, as it implies the investigator is aware that the injury is self-inflicted or carries secondary gain. If we are that far along, we would submit that we have no further need for additional red flags—we should already be scrutinizing the issue.

3. *The pseudo-victim presents in such a way that people believe no one would do this to himself or herself.* This, also, is difficult to interpret. This may appear obvious until one is presented with a real case. Perhaps a better admonition would be never to assume that people would not go to great lengths to accomplish something when sufficiently motivated. All portions of the complainants account should be tested to determine whether or not he or she could have been responsible. If the answer is yes, then reality must not be dismissed or explained away.

4. *The pseudo-victim does not initially report the incident to police.* The question begged here is what constitutes a reasonable delay? Does a delay constitute a victim calling a friend before calling 911, or is it a delay if a victim reports the crime three months later? This is a highly subjective criterion that requires more explanation to be useful as a potential indicator. Also, delays in reporting are common in legitimate reports. This criterion has such limited specificity as to border on worthless, especially when relied heavily upon to declare a report false. Perhaps it would be more useful to look for unexplained or unexplainable delays. The unexplained and unexplainable are always a red flag to the alert investigator.

5. *A stranger is accused.* Many false reporters will actually name or even provide detailed descriptions of a suspect in their complaint. This may not constitute the majority of false report cases, but there have been far too many to agree that accusing a stranger is a red flag. It begs serious study before more can be inferred from its mere occurrence.

6. *The pseudo-victim claims that overwhelming force was used, or that he or she resisted greatly, or that there were multiple assailants.* Taken out of context, it is hard to imagine how this is helpful. One might argue that it must be taken in context, but there is nothing to indicate this. One might question the credibility of an account where five assailants assaulted a victim who reported heroic resistance in the absence of any injuries, but this particular red flag does not indicate that and remains uncomfortably vague.

7. *The account is either overly detailed or very vague.* Although "very vague" would likely be easily noted, it is not clear at what point "very vague" morphs into "vague" or even "limited detail." Also, the determination of "overly detailed" would seem to be in the eye of the beholder. While the intent of this red flag seems justified, there is little to allow one to operationalize this criterion. If a complainant avoids giving details that can be verified, that would be a more useful red flag.

8. *The pseudo-victim reports having his or her eyes closed during the attack or was unconscious, or passed out, or has no memory of what happened, or was drugged, and so cannot provide details.* This would serve to avoid giving details that could be followed up on. However, it is only a red flag if the context is sufficient. If these circumstances are reported when the victim has been caught in an inconsistency, or after other scrupulous details have been provided, then there is reason for doubt. This will give investigators something to confirm or refute through the evidence they collected (it is hoped) and preserved during the initial phases of the investigation.

9. *The pseudo-victim is indifferent to his or her injuries.* Apparent indifference to injuries is subjective (per investigator) and may or may not be related to a false report.

10. *The expected laboratory findings are absent.* This needs to be fleshed out further. Certainly if the victim claims that something occurred and laboratory analysis can confirm it—and fails to—then this is a red flag. However, it may only serve to prove that the victim has a poor memory of events.

11. *The pseudo-victim is vague about the location of the assault, or there is no evidence at the scene to corroborate the complaint.* Being vague about the location of the assault may or may not be a red flag. This would depend on whether the circumstances of the complaint permitted victim memory. For example, a victim that has suffered a head injury, lack of oxygen, been drugged, or used alcohol prior to the alleged attack might be vague about many details. However, absence of corroborating evidence is always a red flag to the alert investigator—unless an absence of evidence is not unexpected.

12. *Damage to the clothing is inconsistent with the injuries.* This would be a useful red flag regarding the truthfulness of statements about injuries but not necessarily proof of a false report.

13. *There are escalating personal problems in the life of the pseudo-victim.* It is hard to assess the significance of this red flag in an individual case, as "escalating personal problems" may conceivably place one at greater risk for assault.

14. *The pseudo-victim has been exposed in the past to accounts of similar things.* It may be hard to apply this, as any American adult or adolescent with access to a television and the Internet would likely meet this criterion. But it is not unreasonable to keep this in mind, as people can model their behavior and report based on either false reports they are aware of, or actual rapes that they have known about. What would be needed is evidence that the complainant could have been exposed to the material (i.e., that it happened prior to the complaint and was widely report), along with evidence that the complaint is sufficiently similar.

15. *The pseudo-victim's post-assault behavior is inconsistent with the allegations.* The post-assault behaviors need to be spelled out. Are Dietz and Hazelwood referring to the victim laughing, becoming hysterical, crying, and/or not crying at inappropriate moments? Are they referring to the victim going to a party a day or two after the alleged assault? Are they referring to having sexual intercourse the same night as a violent and painful rape was reported? Without some kind of detail and elucidation, this red flag would be difficult to apply to an actual case. This could be important, but can be very subjective and open to misinterpretation. The "gutsy" return to "normalcy" of a rape victim could, or a quick flight back into health could be seen as lack of injury and possible "evidence" of a false report.

16. *The pseudo-victim is uncooperative with the investigation.* This is generally important, absent some explaining variable. But it must be kept in mind that rape victims are entitled to react the way they react, and do not necessarily fit into a mold we expect, including cooperation with law enforcement. If the victim has perceived disinterest or other emotions on the part of investigators, he or she might be less cooperative than expected. Also, there are different levels of cooperation that may be perceived as uncooperative, when in fact they are simply a reflection of other variables unseen or misperceived by the investigator.

17. *When the pseudo-victim talks to the authorities, he or she tends to steer the conversation away from the specific to the unprovable.* This may be a useful red flag, so long as it is consistent and not a feature of shame or poor memory. This is also similar to a previous red flag (No. 7).

18. *There is writing on the body of the pseudo-victim.* While this occurred in the Tawana Brawley case, it has occurred infrequently in our case experience. If it can be determined through crime reconstruction or wound pattern analysis whether the victim could have made the injury, then this has value to the investigation. If it cannot, merely the existence of such evidence would seem to indicate little. This, too, is a behavior that begs serious study before more can be inferred from its mere occurrence.

19. *There is a history of making other false allegations.* One must be careful
    with this criterion, but it is clearly something that cannot be ignored.
    It is potentially a significant red flag, as long as prior allegations were
    accurately determined to be unfounded. A useful discussion of this issue
    is provided in Epstein (2006, 657–658):

> In order to be relevant in a criminal proceeding, a false accusation
> must connote one of three phenomena: a report of forced sexual
> contact where there was no sexual conduct at all; a claim of forced
> contact where the actual encounter was consensual; or an accusation
> of a particular person when the complainant knows that her assailant
> was someone else. The second guideline should set standards for
> admissibility. For impeachment purposes, the requirement of "good
> faith" in posing the question is the requisite standard. As to the
> admission of false accusation proof as substantive non-character "plan"
> or "doctrine of chance" evidence, the governing standard must be that
> used for all "other acts" evidence—whether there is some evidence
> that would permit the jury to find that a false accusation had occurred,
> i.e., "such evidence should be admitted if there is sufficient evidence
> to support a finding by the jury that the defendant committed the
> similar act." The last guideline should prevent undue prejudice and
> the harms meant to be protected by Rape Shield Laws. Litigation of a
> pre-trial motion in limine by the prosecution to ascertain the intended
> use of "false accusation" evidence will ensure that only proper proof is
> introduced and proper questioning occurs.

Readers are encouraged to give thought to this red flag, and consideration to
the admonitions provided.

20. *There is a history of extensive medical care.* As listed, without commentary
    from Dietz and Hazelwood as to what this means, this may not be as
    helpful as one might suspect. For example, a history of mental illness
    may provide evidence that the victim is out of touch with reality, or it
    may make the victim more vulnerable to assault.

Some of these red flags have investigative value under the right conditions.
However, many of them are much too vague and subjective to be of use on
their own. We would suggest that the inconsistencies of each case be evaluated
in its context, and that the more general red flags be redefined with an eye to
greater clarity of context before being applied in actual casework.

Brown, Crowley, Peck, and Slaughter

Brown, Crowley, Peck, and Slaughter (1997) conducted research to address the
issue of genital injury in female sexual assault victims. This study examined
311 rape victims who entered San Louis Obispo General Hospital's emergency

room in California between January of 1985 and December of 1993. The study also examined a control group of 75 women, from the same location and time period, who had engaged in consensual intercourse. Of those 75 women, 48 had initially been evaluated as victims of rape but later admitted that their encounters had been consensual. Though not conducted to address the issue of false reports specifically, this study ultimately revealed a 13.37% rate of false rape reporters. This study, it should be remembered, involved victims and alleged victims that presented to an emergency room.

REVIEW OF VICTIM REPORT

The interview with an alleged victim of sexual assault is perhaps the most vital part of a sex crime investigator's effort to establish the facts of a case. Unfortunately, it is common for even seasoned investigators to accept an alleged victim's statement or story without question or suspicion. This uncritical aspect may arise out of a fear of disturbing the alleged victim, being viewed as politically incorrect by victim advocates and colleagues, or lack of knowledge about the investigation of potential false reports. As explained in Donnelly (2007, 898):

> Victim advocates almost always consider accusers to be "victims" even before it is known that a crime has been committed. They also react in horror any time expert investigators suggest that false allegations of sexual assault are common and distinguishable from truthful ones.

An uncritical aspect may also arise out of a common problem that inhabits much of police culture: investigative apathy.[6] Too many investigators will go to great lengths to explain away factual inconsistencies in an alleged victim's story if it suits them. Inconsistencies that have been explained away in this manner, rather than actually investigated, should be treated as suspect. Whatever the case, there is no legitimate reason to avoid a detailed, frame-by-frame examination of the logic and rationale in any victim's statement. Regardless of the consequences, every alleged victim's statement must be examined thoroughly. If there are breaks in the logic, they must be explained.

---

[6]It is important to note that there are other considerations motivating investigators, forensic examiners, and researchers away from the identification and study of false reports. Aside from apathy, an overall political environment that sanctions such identifications and investigations can promulgate a fearful investigative mindset. This fear of political reprisal routinely provides for the failure to correctly identify and investigate false reports to their fullest conclusion. As discussed in Palmer and Thornhill (2000), "To some feminists, the concept of false rape allegation itself constitutes discriminatory harassment." It is not unreasonable in such an environment for investigators and forensic examiners to be concerned that the investigation of a false report, and even the consideration of false reporting as a viable case theory, will result in negative consequences from colleagues, superiors, the media, victim advocates, and the general public.

False Report Interview Strategy

The literature review just provided demonstrates two things. Firstly, investigators and forensic examiners are very likely to encounter a false report if they work sex crimes. Secondly, due to the dearth of literature and the limited investigative experience behind it, investigators and forensic examiners will often be unprepared when this happens.

False reporters may report their allegations to the police in the same way that real victims do. The interviewer will want to treat the potential false report case the same as any other, up until the point of the second part of the formal interview, the frame-by-frame analysis. This is where the interviewer should confront the alleged victim with any contradictions between his or her statement and the physical evidence. Any contradiction in the victim's statement needs to be explained by the victim, not the interviewer. The interviewer should never accept contradictory statements in the victim's statement because the victim was upset or experiencing trauma. These contradictions must be explained logically.

At some point during the interview, the interviewer may be convinced that the false reporter is lying. In this case, it is recommended that the investigator inform the false reporter that he or she is now a suspect in a criminal investigation, and then read the Miranda warnings. Failing to do so could be problematic for any future prosecution.

The BAFRI

As suggested by the dearth of research in the area of false rape allegations, and the lack of professional awareness and willingness to investigate such instances, the need for tools to assess potential false reports is not being met or even pursued. Baeza (Baeza and Turvey, 2002) offered the BAFRI as one tool to assess false reports.

The Baeza False Report Index (BAFRI)

The following is a list of false report red flags created by Detective John J. Baeza (retired). Every investigator, victimologist, criminologist, criminal profiler, and attorney should be aware of this index when examining or investigating any case that involves an alleged sex crime.

[7] The value of this list is its identification of areas that require further investigative attention, that is, red flags. They can and will exist in legitimate cases, but when these elements are present, they must be examined, understood, and explained.

One or more of the circumstantial red flags described in this index has surfaced in most, if not all, of the false reports investigated by Baeza and Turvey (2002),[7] but they caution investigators against relying blindly on them or placing undue weight on a limited number. These red flags are listed below, with commentary:

1. *A female victim has demanded to speak with a female officer or investigator.*
   (This excludes those cases in which a male officer or investigator

has acted inappropriately towards the female). As indicated by the disqualifier in parentheses, this must be assessed from the perspective of the victim.

2. *A female victim's husband, boyfriend, or other intimate partner has forced her to report the alleged crime, rather than having reported the crime of her own volition.* This is a major red flag, especially when the allegation provides an alibi for an otherwise unexplainable delay in returning home.

3. *A victim's parents have forced him or her to report the alleged crime, rather than having reported the crime of his or her own volition.* This is essentially a corollary of the previous flag.

4. *A victim, most often under age (less than 18 years old), has returned home after his or her curfew.* Again, this is a major red flag, especially when the complaint provides an alibi for an otherwise unexplainable delay in returning home.

5. *A victim states that he or she was abducted at a busy intersection (or some other very public location) during the day, and there are no witnesses to the incident.*

6. *A victim states that he or she was attacked by a masked offender in the middle of the day on a busy street.* Although at first glance this red flag appears similar to Number 5, it actually highlights an important issue—that of paradoxical offender behavior. Descriptions of offender behavior that seem to defy common sense (the mask would seem to draw attention to the offender) should raise some level of suspicion.

7. *A victim is in a drug rehabilitation program and is out past curfew.* This is another alibi flag. Most chemical dependency residential programs have curfews and will discharge residents who do not return by a certain time. Claiming a rape will explain the absence.

8. *A pregnant female victim is forced by a parent or guardian to report the crime to police.*

9. *A victim cannot describe the suspect nor provide details of the crime.* As with the red flag described in the section on Dietz and Hazelwood, the utility of this red flag will depend on the level of vagueness and the overall context.

10. *A victim has previously been charged with falsely reporting an incident.* As previously discussed, one needs to look for a pattern of lying or false representations. This red flag must be taken in context.

11. *A victim has previously reported a similar crime to the police.* The investigators must keep in mind that it is not uncommon for victims to have been assaulted previously—especially if they are medium- or high-exposure victims (see discussions in Chapters 5 and 6).

12. *A victim focuses on relocating to a new home or apartment during the investigation.*

13. *A victim focuses on initiating a lawsuit or on monetary gain during the investigation.*

14. *A victim displays "TV" behavior when initiating a complaint, mimicking the way that stereotypical victims act on television and in film (hysterical, demand female officer, catatonic, etc.).* This may be hard to assess, as the "normal" response to a sexual assault can span the spectrum of behaviors. That said, the basic admonition is well heeded.

15. *A victim cries at crucial points in the interview to avoid answering key questions.* This can be an important flag. The behavior to focus on is avoidance of giving details that can be corroborated, not the crying per se.

16. *A victim has a long psychiatric history.* As discussed previously, this may be a red flag for a false accusation, but it may also be an exposure factor for victimization. Not to be taken out of context.

At this point it must be made absolutely clear that this index (or any other collection of red flags) should be used as a guide only. The items are not foolproof indicators that the victim is falsely reporting a crime. To the sex crimes investigator or forensic examiner, these red flags suggest only the possibility that the allegations may be false and that further investigation is needed.

One of the authors of this chapter (McGrath 2000) suggests conceptualizing the assessment of a false report as a three-pronged approach, reviewing behavioral, linguistic, and physical evidence in an attempt to determine the credibility of the allegation.[8] Behavioral red flags would include the presentation of the victim and how cooperative she or he was, among other things. Some examples (McGrath 2000) are:

- Any behavior that functions to interfere with the investigation
- Initiation of a report, or pressure to report, by someone other than the victim, unless the victim is unable to report or is too young to represent him- or herself
- Complainant unable to say where the assault occurred (unless some other aspect of the crime would reasonably preclude knowing where it occurred)
- Vague description of assailant when descriptions of other facets of crime are more detailed
- Interest of complainant more directed to a goal other than the reporting of the crime (e.g., change in housing, disability payments, attention, lawsuit, etc.)
- Report of rape serves to provide an alibi

Linguistic assessment would be related to any statements made by the victim and/or suspects that can be examined to help determine credibility and identify areas that warrant further exploration. A properly performed statement analysis can be more helpful than a polygraph examination.[9] It should be noted that statement analysis is actually a form of behavioral analysis. Since there are multiple ways of saying the same thing, choosing how to say or write

[8]It should be kept in mind that determining the credibility of a witness (which is what the complainant may eventually be) should be an important step in any criminal investigation.

[9]It should be noted that we are not endorsing the polygraph, just commenting on it, as polygraph exams are often used in investigations.

something is a behavior that can be analyzed. The pronouns that are used, changes in words denoting certain things or people, and certain wordings, can suggest to the investigator areas that require further explication. A detailed discussion of statement analysis is beyond the scope of this chapter.

Physical evidence is often overlooked in investigations on two levels. First, in terms of recognizing and collecting it and, second, in ensuring that the description of a crime (either by a victim or as a result of a confession) matches—to a reasonable extent—the evidence found at the crime scene or as a result of forensic testing. Examples of issues related to physical evidence that should raise concern are (McGrath 2000):

- Crime scene reconstruction is at odds with story of victim.
- Injuries sustained by victim are consistent with known patterns of self-inflicted injuries, or there is a lack of defensive wounds when a significant struggle is reported.
- Damage to clothing is not consistent with either the account of the assault ("He grabbed my collar and yanked me toward him," yet shirt or blouse is neatly ironed) or wounds.
- Lack of injury to victim when account implies significant force was used.

There is no substitute for a thorough investigation. Some red flags are more helpful than others, and some (e.g., delayed reporting) are so unreliable as to be more misleading than useful. We are not aware of any published studies wherein red flags for false allegations have been statistically analyzed for discriminative value, either alone or in groups. Such research may make it easier to assess unfounded or false allegations, although ultimately the final call will remain with the law enforcement investigator.

MOTIVATIONS FOR FALSE REPORTS

As with any list of potential motives for human behavior, there is often no clear delineation, and sometimes motives overlap. Human behavior in general is multidetermined. Some of the more common motivations leading to a false report are provided below. This is not intended to be an exhaustive list.

Revenge

Revenge is the act of inflicting harm on others in return for harm suffered at their hands, direction, or by their complicity. This includes situations where the reporter is angry at the accused and expresses that anger through a false report. Typically, a prior relationship with the accused is involved. It often occurs in child custody cases and in subordinate relationships. It may also be used as a punishment for perceived infidelity.

Need for Attention

This category may include those who are said to be "crying out for help" as well as those with some degree of personality disorder or mental illness. It can include those who want attention from friends, relatives, spouses, or even wish the attention of the media.

Medical Treatment

Often this motivation is in play when the reporter makes a false complaint to obtain drugs or treatment related to pregnancy, AIDS, or sexually transmitted diseases. For example, one of the authors of this chapter (Turvey) worked a rape case where the victim claimed to have been attacked by a widely publicized serial rapist. She was an apparent prostitute and represented a general deviation in the victim preference for that particular serial offender. The details of her account were unverifiable, and the alleged assault took place in a location where no corroborating evidence was found. Several months later, she also spontaneously reported being "raped" by possibly the same offender. She reported that this rape occurred prior to the rape she initially reported. However, she stated that the first rape turned from an act of violence into what can only be described as a consensual romantic encounter. The complainant had a history of multiple abortions, and she requested "treatment for morning after pill" during the sexual assault exam, despite no internal ejaculation being reported. These factors and many others led Turvey to strongly suspect that both complaints were in fact false reports.

Profit

Profit refers to emotional, material, or financial gain. This may include the filing of a lawsuit by the reporter as well as the desire for new and better housing. For example, crime victims can reap financial reward by suing property owners (and their insurance companies) in what are referred to as premises liability lawsuits. In such a lawsuit, the victim argues that his or her attack could have been foreseen by the property owner and was therefore preventable. Property owners and in some cases landlords are subsequently held financially responsible for criminal attacks on their property, when judgments favor the victim. Judgments in such cases can range into the millions of dollars, which is a powerful financial incentive to make a false report.

Failure of Customer to Pay or Adequately Compensate a Sex Worker

These cases involve prostitutes or other sex/erotic-related workers such as escorts, strippers, or dancers. They may not have received payment or may have been somehow wronged by their customer. They may allege that they were sexually assaulted, raped, or otherwise violated, as a way of retaliating.

Ironically, when sex workers are actually raped they are unlikely to report it. This can be for a variety of reasons, including that they consider such attacks part of the cost of doing business; they doubt that they will be believed because of the nature of their work; or because law enforcement officers are regular nonpaying customers, and they don't need the attention that an investigation will bring.

However, sex workers may report a rape if they perceive a continued threat, and if they perceive that law enforcement will do something about it—as in the recent case of a prostitute in Pomona, California, who reported being raped by a police officer within an hour of being attacked. In that case, it turned out to be a man wearing a security guard uniform with a security badge who was pretending to be a police officer in order to coerce sex from those he felt would not report the crime out of fear. He was arrested while picking up another prostitute.

Explanation for Loss of Virginity, Pregnancy, or Sexually Transmitted Disease

The loss of virginity, an unwanted or unexpected pregnancy, or sexually transmitted disease may be explained away by some with a false complaint of rape. This may be related to infidelity, or it may be related to cultural or family expectations regarding sexual activity. Although this is more commonly found in juveniles, the same reasoning may motivate adults as well.

Alibi for Inappropriate Absence

This is a common motivation for juveniles and adults alike. The false reporter may be so desperate for an alibi to explain his or her absence that he or she will claim that an abduction or rape has occurred. This is common among those living in group homes or in treatment programs while under conditions of parole or release, where the consequences for failing to return prior to curfew can be severe. It may also be used by teenagers out past curfew, or by an adult to conceal infidelity.

New Housing

A desire for new housing can often motivate individuals to falsely report a rape to authorities. This is especially common in areas where rent-controlled housing is offered by the government. There are long waiting lists to get into the most desirable housing projects. Some residents believe that a way to jump to the front of this list is to claim that a rape or other attack occurred inside their current apartment. It may also be used as a way to get moved to more desirable housing within the same building, as keeping victims of rape in the same unit may be viewed as inappropriate or cruel.

Child Custody

Child custody battles are among the most heated and divisive legal disputes that can occur. When character and parental fitness are at issue, an allegation of sexual assault can be very strategic. These false reports can, and sometimes do, include allegations of rape or sexual abuse of one of the children, made by one side or the other, in an attempt to gain custody of the child in question. Some have merit; some don't. The purpose of an investigation is to find out which is the case. It is hoped that this will take place before things get to a jury.

Attempt to Veil a Reoccurrence of Drug or Alcohol Use

This category includes individuals who have abstained from the use of drugs or alcohol for some period of time and then suddenly relapse, making it necessary for them to develop an excuse for their behavior. They may claim that they were raped and forced to ingest drugs or alcohol against their will. Or, alternately, they may claim that they returned to using drugs or alcohol to deal with the pain of the incident.

Change of Heart after a Consensual Sexual Encounter

This is common in juvenile dating situations in which one of the parties of a consensual sexual encounter later feels guilty, angry, or vexed. In order to conceal or explain this behavior to him- or herself or to others and parental figures, he or she falsely claims to have been raped. This less commonly involves adults who are trying to explain evidence of sexual behavior to a boyfriend, girlfriend or spouse.

It will be helpful to present one high-profile false report case, as it highlights several things: first, that the false reporter usually suffers no legal consequences; second, that the falsely accused suffer greatly; third, that allegations of rape can become political; and finally, that collusion between government agencies (the prosecutor and the laboratory that did the DNA testing) can work to conceal or at least further false accusations.

CASE EXAMPLE: DUKE UNIVERSITY LACROSSE TEAM CASE

Duke University lacrosse team players Reade Seligmann, David Evans, and Collin Finnerty were charged with first-degree kidnapping and first-degree sexual offense after an off-campus team party in March 2006. Ultimately dismissed as false, with the North Carolina attorney general declaring the accused were "innocent" (CNN 2007), the allegations in this case made national news, increased racial tensions, and spanned multiple motives on the part of the accuser, from alleged mental instability, to avoiding criminal charges, to profit, and to revenge.

According to the complaint, Crystal Gail Mangum accused members of the Duke lacrosse team of dragging her into a bathroom at one of their parties, raping her, and shouting racial slurs during an off-campus party in March of 2006. However, none of this came to light until after she was arrested the same night for public intoxication. And only days after making the complaint she bragged to coworkers about the possibility of filing civil actions against those involved.

This case had almost every problem imaginable, and in the absence of public attention it is possible that the accused players, ultimately cleared of all charges, could have been jailed for a very long time. Consider the context: the accuser was a stripper with a criminal history, an alleged mental health history, and a history of unfounded claims of being gang raped. A vocal segment of the African-American community was rallying and demanding swift justice. Racial tensions were, in some circles, rising. The prosecutor was running for reelection, conspiring with forensic personnel to conceal evidence, and openly attacking the defendants in the press. And Duke University was put in the unenviable position of punishing its lacrosse coach and players for crimes that it turns out did not occur.

FIGURE 8.3

"Exotic dancer" Crystal Gail Mangum. This is a prisoner intake photo from June 2002, when Mangum was arrested by the Durham County Sheriff's Office for charges related to motor vehicle theft.

The following is a timeline of significant events:

- March 13, 2006 — Duke University lacrosse players throw a party at an off-campus house, hiring two strippers.
- March 14 — One of the dancers tells the police she was forced into a bathroom by three men and beaten, raped, and sodomized.
- March 23 — Forty-six of 47 team members comply with the judge's order to provide DNA. The sole black member is not tested because the accuser said her attackers were white.
- March 28 — Duke University suspends the lacrosse team from playing.
- March 29 — District Attorney Mike Nifong refers to members of the lacrosse team as "a bunch of hooligans" in the press.
- April 4 — The accuser identifies her attackers in a photo lineup.
- April 5 — Lacrosse coach Mike Pressler is forced to resign. Duke President Richard Brodhead cancels the rest of the season.
- April 10 — Defense attorneys announce DNA tests fail to connect any of the players to the accuser.
- April 17 — Grand jury indicts Reade Seligmann and Collin Finnerty on rape and other charges.
- April 25 — Granville County authorities confirm the accuser told police 10 years ago that three men raped her when she was 14. None of the men was charged.

- May 15 — Grand jury indicts team co-captain David Evans on rape charges. He calls the allegations "fantastic lies."
- June 5 — Duke University president says team can resume play in 2007 under close monitoring.
- Nov. 7 — DA Mike Nifong wins the election to continue as district attorney.
- Dec. 15 — Forensic scientist Brian Meehan, Lab Director of DNA Security, Inc., in an agreement with Nifong, omitted from his report that genetic material from several men—none of them Duke team members—was found in accuser's underwear and body.[10]
- Dec. 22 — Nifong drops the rape charges, saying the woman is no longer certain whether she was penetrated. The players still face charges of kidnapping and sexual offense.
- Dec. 28 — North Carolina Bar files ethics charges against Nifong, accusing him of making misleading and inflammatory comments to the media about the athletes. (He is also later accused of withholding evidence and lying to the court.)
- Jan. 3, 2007 — Duke invites Seligmann and Finnerty to return to school. (They have not returned.) The accuser gives birth. Both sides later say she was not impregnated at the party.
- Jan. 12 — Nifong asks to withdraw from the case because of ethics charges.
- Jan. 13 — The North Carolina attorney general's office begins reviewing the case, not only by going over the case to date, but by conducting an independent investigation, including interviewing witnesses.
- Apr. 10 — The North Carolina attorney general reports his office's findings. The investigation raised such discrepancies to what the complainant claimed versus the actual evidence that, "Based on the significant inconsistencies between the evidence and the various accounts given by the accusing witness, we believe these three individuals are innocent of these charges" (CNN 2007).

The attorney general's office investigation was thorough, as noted in the office's April 2007 public statement that included the following (Cooper 2007):

> During the past 12 weeks, our lawyers and investigators have reviewed the remaining allegations of sexual assault and kidnapping that resulted from a party on March 13, 2006, in Durham, North Carolina. We carefully reviewed the evidence, collected by the Durham County prosecutor's office and the Durham Police Department.

---

[10]To be perfectly clear, Brian Meehan, Lab Director of DNA Security, Inc., made a conscious decision to assist DA Mike Nifong with the job of hiding exculpatory DNA results in this case (Neff, Niolet, and Blythe 2007). For a crime lab of any kind to make an examination of evidence for which there is no report detailing items examined, tests performed, and results achieved is at the least forensically unacceptable and professionally unethical.

We've also conducted our own interviews and evidence gathering. Our attorneys and [State Bureau of Investigation] agents have interviewed numerous people who were at the party, DNA and other experts, the Durham County district attorney, Durham police officers, defense attorneys, and the accusing witness on several occasions. We have reviewed statements given over the year, photographs, records, and other evidence.

The result of our review and investigation shows clearly that there is insufficient evidence to proceed on any of the charges. Today we are filing notices of dismissal for all charges against Reade Seligmann, Collin Finnerty, and David Evans. The result is that these cases are over, and no more criminal proceedings will occur.

We believe that these cases were the result of a tragic rush to accuse and a failure to verify serious allegations. Based on the significant inconsistencies between the evidence and the various accounts given by the accusing witness, we believe these three individuals are innocent of these charges.

Now, we approached this case with the understanding that rape and sexual assault victims often have some inconsistencies in their account of a traumatic event. However, in this case, the inconsistencies were so significant and so contrary to the evidence that we have no credible evidence that an attack occurred in that house on that night.

Now, the prosecuting witness in this case responded to our questions and offered information. She did want to move forward with the prosecution. However, the contradictions in her many versions of what occurred and the conflicts between what she said occurred and other evidence like photographs and phone records, could not be rectified.

Our investigation shows that the eyewitness identification procedures were faulty and unreliable. No DNA confirms the accuser's story. No other witness confirms her story. Other evidence contradicts her story. She contradicts herself....

Now, in this case, with the weight of the state behind him, the Durham district attorney pushed forward unchecked. There were many points in this case where caution would have served justice better than bravado, and in the rush to condemn a community and a state, lost the ability to see clearly....

This case shows the enormous consequences of over-reaching by a prosecutor. What has been learned here is that the internal checks on a criminal charge—sworn statements, reasonable grounds, proper suspect photo lineups, and accurate and fair discovery—all are critically important.

Therefore, I propose a law that the North Carolina Supreme Court have the authority to remove a case from a prosecutor in limited circumstances. This would give the courts a new tool to deal with a prosecutor who needs to step away from a case where justice demands.

FIGURE 8.4

Reade Seligmann, Collin Finnerty, and David Evans, already cleared of any charges, attend a press conference subsequent to Mike Nifong's disbarment.

In June 2007, Mike Nifong, the prosecutor in the Duke University lacrosse team rape case, was disbarred for unethical conduct related to his actions in that attempted prosecution. The chairman of the disciplinary committee blamed Nifong's "political ambition," a "self-serving agenda," and "self-deception."

FIGURE 8.5

A defrocked Mike Nifong listens to the verdict of the North Carolina Bar Association's Ethics Committee. "We are in unanimous agreement that there is no discipline short of disbarment that would be appropriate in this case," said F. Lane Williamson, the committee's chairman. The three-member panel found Nifong guilty of fraud, dishonesty, deceit, or misrepresentation; of making false statements of material fact before a judge; of making false statements of material fact before bar investigators; and of lying about withholding exculpatory DNA evidence.

The attorneys for each of the exonerated Duke lacrosse team players have promised civil action in an attempt to make their clients whole.

CONCLUSION

False reports are a problem for all of the professional communities that encounter them, and they are more frequent than those with pro-victim political or social agendas would have us believe. The hostility with which inquiry into false reporting has been met has resulted in a standstill with respect to scientific research. As a result, we have no good or even current data on the subject—we only know that lower estimates are continually disproved.

False reporters span all ages, all walks of life, and are capable of staging both injuries and evidence to support their claims. A thorough investigation of the evidence has traditionally been the best way to reveal the false reporter, who is more likely to confess when confronted with logical inconsistencies in his or her statements and behavior. Unfortunately, law enforcement resources are drained away from actual victims by such cases. Innocent citizens are exposed to the possibility of false accusations and damage to their personal and professional lives. Legitimate victims of sexual assault are exposed to the possibility of encountering overtaxed law enforcement resources that are inadequate to the task of investigating their cases thoroughly or competently. Building owners, private companies, and insurance companies are exposed to the threat of costly liability lawsuits. As stated in Gross (1924, 14):[11]

> Not only must the self-made victim be exposed, but innocent people who may be suspected must be protected.

Furthermore, research relating to sexual assault, which is often used as the basis for law-enforcement resource and budget allocations, not to mention expert forensic testimony, is necessarily biased or otherwise compromised when such cases go unidentified. This is a problem in both the criminal and civil realms. Hence, the need for more and better research in this area cannot be emphasized too strongly. Nor can the need for objectivity, thorough investigations of each complaint, and strict adherence to the forensic evidence.

SUMMARY

There are many reasons for false reports. False reports may be made for financial gain, to garner sympathy, for revenge, for crime concealment, to excuse other behavior, and so on. When recognized, it is common for the false reporter to suffer no legal consequences for filing a false report. Despite the many case studies that can be offered, professional literature on the subject remains scarce, as there have been very few scientific studies conducted to date

[11]This sentiment is echoed today by former Manhattan Sex Crimes Prosecutor Linda Fairstein, who states, "False reports of rape do occur.... [and] have made it difficult for legitimate victims to be taken seriously.... For all prosecutors ... it is critical to acknowledge that false accusations of rape are made." (cited in Sarnoff, 1997).

to ascertain false report rates or percentages. The literature that does offer rates and percentages is often unreliable, misrepresented, or inaccurate, as can be seen with the elusive sources for the 2% false report statistic for sexual assault. The actual rates that have been garnered through research vary between 8% and 50% for sexual assault.

When faced with an allegation, investigators walk a fine line between being supportive and compassionate and trying to determine if the allegation is factual. Several red flags have been offered by various authors as an aid to determine which reports are false. If specific and objective, red flags may have investigative value under the right conditions; however, it is important that each case be evaluated in context to determine whether the red flags apply. These should be used with caution, as a truthful person can easily raise some red flags while an actual false reporter may show none at all.

Unfortunately, it is not uncommon for even experienced investigators to accept an alleged victim's statement without critical thought or suspicion. This acceptance may be the result of fear of disturbing the alleged victim, or being viewed as politically incorrect by victim advocates and colleagues, or of a lack of knowledge about the investigation of potential false reports.

Questions

1. True or False: There is a dearth of professional literature on the subject of false reports.
2. True or False: Only 2% of sexual assaults are false reports.
3. Describe why it is important to identify when false reports are being made, in terms of its effects on the legal system, alleged victims, and alleged offenders.
4. Name and describe two red flags proposed by the BAFRI.
5. Red flags must be neither _____ nor _____ in order to be of assistance to investigations.
6. Name and describe four general motivations for making a false allegation.
7. True or False: It is common for the false reporter to suffer no legal consequences for having made a false report.

REFERENCES

Abshire, R. 2007. "Arrest warrants issued for Terrell cousins after hoax." *Dallas Morning News*, March 22. www.dallasnews.com/sharedcontent/dws/dn/latestnews/stories/032207dnmetterrellfound.3291295.html.

Anderson, M. 2004. "The Legacy of the Prompt Complaint Requirement, Corroboration Requirement, and Cautionary Instructions on Campus Sexual Assault." *Boston University Law Review* 84 (October): 945–1022.

Aiken, M., A. Burgess, and R. Hazelwood. 1995. "False Rape Allegations." In *Practical Aspects of Rape Investigation: A Multidisciplinary Approach*, edited by A. Burgess and R. Hazelwood. Boca Raton, FL: CRC Press.

Baeza, J., and B. Turvey. 2002. "False Reports." In *Criminal Profiling: An Introduction to Behavioral Evidence Analysis,* 2nd ed., edited by B. Turvey. London: Academic Press.

Block, A.P. 1990. "Rape Trauma Syndrome as Scientific Expert Testimony." *Archives of Sexual Behavior* 19, no. 4: 309–323.

Brown, C., S. Crowley, R. Peck, and L. Slaughter. 1997. "Patterns of Genital Injury in Female Sexual Assault Victims." *American Journal of Obstetrics and Gynecology* 176, March: 609–616.

Brownmiller, S. 1975. *Against Our Will: Men, Women, and Rape.* New York: Fawcett Columbine.

———. Personal e-mail communication to David R. Throop of the Men's Issues Page, June 27, 1995. http://www.menweb.org/throop/falsereport/commentary/brownback.html.

Bryden, D.P., and S. Lengnick. 1997. "Rape in the Criminal Justice System." *Journal of Criminal Law and Criminology* 87, Summer: 1194–1384.

Burgess, A.W., and R.R. Hazelwood, eds. 2001. *Practical Aspects of Rape Investigation: A Multidisciplinary Approach,* 3rd ed. Boca Raton, FL: CRC Press.

Burgess, A.W., R.R. Hazelwood, and A.G. Burgess. 2001. "False Rape Allegations." In *Practical Aspects of Rape Investigation: A Multidisciplinary Approach,* 3rd ed., edited by Burgess A.G. and R.R. Hazelwood. Boca Raton, FL: CRC Press.

Burgess, A.W., and L.L. Holmstrom. 1974. "Rape Trauma Syndrome." *American Journal of Psychiatry* 131, September: 981–986.

CBS News. 2005. "Wilbanks: What she was thinking," June 22. http://www.cbsnews.com/stories/2005/06/22/national/main703401.shtml.

CNN. 2004a. "Police: Student says she was abducted at knifepoint," April 1. http://www.cnn.com/2004/US/Midwest/03/31/missing.student/index.html?iref=newssearch.

———. 2004b. "Student who faked abduction given probation," April 1. http://www.cnn.com/2004/LAW/07/01/missing.student.sentence/index.html?iref=newssearch.

———. 2005. "Charges not ruled out for runaway bride," May 2. http://www.cnn.com/2005/US/05/01/wilbanks.found/index.html.

———. 2007. "N.C. attorney general: Duke players 'innocent,'" April 11. http://www.cnn.com/2007/LAW/04/11/cooper.transcript/index.html.

Cooper, R. 2007. Press Release. North Carolina Attorney General's Office, April 11.

Court TV. 1997. "Report of the grand jury concerning the Tawana Brawley investigation." Online Legal Documents. http://www.courttv.com/legaldocs/newsmakers/tawana/part3.html#sexual.

Donnelly, E. 2007. "Constructing the Co-Ed Military." *Duke Journal of Gender Law and Policy* no. 14, May: 815–952.

Dunleavy, S. 1999. "Cybersex victim's kin: She's a liar." *New York Post,* July 26.

Dunleavy, S. Cybersex victim's kin: She's a liar. New York Post, July 26, 1999. Inquirer Staff, Timoney commends rape-squad reforms. Philadelphia Inquirer, December 13, 2000.

Epstein, J. 2006. "True Lies: The Constitutional and Evidentiary Bases for Admitting Prior False Accusation Evidence in Sexual Assault Prosecutions." *Quinnipiac Law Review* 24: 609–658.

Gregory, J., and S. Lees. 1999. *Policing Sexual Assault.* New York: Routledge.

Gross, H. 1924. *Criminal Investigation,* 3rd ed. London: Sweet and Maxwell.

Haws, D. 1997. "The Elusive Numbers on False Rape." *Columbia Journalism Review* November/December: http://www.cjr.org/year/97/6/rape.asp.

Herman, J.L. 1990. "Sex Offenders: A Feminist Perspective." In *Handbook of Sexual Assault: Issues, Theories, and Treatment of the Offender,* edited by W.L. Marshall, D.R. Laws, H.E. Barbaree, 177–193. New York: Plenum Press.

Inquirer Staff. 2000. "Timoney Commends Rape-Squad Reforms." *Philadelphia Inquirer,* December 13.

Johnson, B.E., D.L. Kuck, and P.R. Schander. 1997. "Rape Myth Acceptance and Sociodemographic Characteristics: A Multidimensional Analysis." *Sex Roles: A Journal of Research* no. 36, June: 693–708.

Kanin, E. 1994. "False Rape Allegations." *Archives of Sexual Behavior* 23, no. 1: 81–92.

MacDonald, J. 1973. "False Accusations of Rape." *Medical Aspects of Human Sexuality* no. 7, May: 170–194.

Martin, P. 2005. "The Sacrifice of a Parent: An Analysis of Parental Rights Related to False Allegations of Child Sexual Abuse." *Thomas M. Cooley Journal of Practical and Clinical Law* (Hilary Term), 7: 251–283.

McDowell, C. 1985. *Chicago Lawyer,* June. http://www.coeffic.demon.co.uk/descrim.htm.

McGrath, M. 2000. "False Allegations of Rape and the Criminal Profiler." *The Journal of Behavioral Profiling* 1, no. 3.

———. 2005. "*People v. Oliver Jovanovic:* From Cybersex to Sexual Assault Allegations." Appendix in *Rape Investigation Handbook,* by J. Savino and B. Turvey. London: Academic Press.

Neff, J., B. Niolet, and A. Blythe. 2006. "Head of DNA lab says he and Nifong agreed not to report results." *Charlotte News-Observer,* Dec. 8.

Palmer, C., and R. Thornhill. 2000. *A History of Rape.* Cambridge: MIT Press.

Radford, B. 2005. "Police, psychics search for 'abducted' runaway bride." *Skeptical Inquirer* 294, July 1: 7.

Rosario, R. 2004. "Happy ending may obscure disturbing reality." *Pioneer Press,* April 2. http://www.twincities.com/mld/twincities/news/8334507.htm.

Sarnoff, S. (1997). "Assessing the Costs of False Allegations of Child Abuse: A Prescriptive" Institute for Psychological Therapies Journal, vol. 9; url: http://www.ipt-forensics.com/journal/volume9/j9_3_2.htm.

Spilbor, J.M. 2003. "What If Kobe Bryant Has Been Falsely Accused? Why the Law of Acquaintance and Date Rape Should Seriously Penalize False Reports." *Findlaw's Writ,* August 11. http://writ.news.findlaw.com/commentary/20030811_spilbor.html.

CHAPTER 9

Intimate Violence

Brent E. Turvey

KEY TERMS

- *Domestic homicide:* occurs when one family member, household member, or intimate kills another.
- *Domestic violence:* a general term that may be used to describe physical aggression between family members, household members, or intimates.
- *Intimate Terrorism:* a type of intimate personal violence where violence is one tactic in a larger pattern of power and control. It involves more frequent per-couple incidents, more severe violence, and results in more serious injury.
- *Intimate violence:* a particular type of domestic violence that occurs when a current or former intimate relationship partner becomes physically violent towards the other.
- *Situational Couple Violence:* occurs in the context of a specific disagreement that spirals into a violent incident. It is an isolated reaction to conflict and does not involve a larger pattern of power and control.
- *Violent Resistance:* situations where a female victim defends herself against her aggressive male partner.

CONTENTS

Domestic violence is a general term that may be used to describe physical aggression between family members, household members, or intimates. Accordingly, intimate violence is a particular type of domestic violence that occurs when a current or former intimate relationship partner becomes physically violent towards the other. It does not necessarily involve people that live together, but those involved must be or have been involved in a deep personal relationship of some kind. Often it is a sexual or romantic relationship, though it can involve nonsexual relationships. In cases of intimate violence, barring mental disorder or defect, the motivation is almost exclusively about power, anger/revenge, profit, or some combination of these.

299

This chapter will discuss the dynamics of abuse in intimate relationships. It will also discuss some of the major risk factors associated with intimate violence, dispelling certain myths along the way. The chapter will close with a focus on law enforcement–involved intimate homicide, using this particular subtype to provide a contrast with the many others that the victimologist may encounter. Case examples and research findings will be adduced as needed.

THE DYNAMICS OF INTIMATE VIOLENCE

The dynamics of intimate violence—the way it begins, expresses, and evolves—are complex. Yet they are driven by a sense of overall powerlessness experienced on the part of the aggressor. This powerlessness is expressed by the assertion of power and control over the victim. As explained in Burke (2007, 555): "Outside the realm of criminal law, social scientists almost universally describe domestic violence as an ongoing pattern of conduct motivated by the batterer's desire for power and control over the victim." Burke then goes on to explain more precisely why domestic violence is different from other forms of interpersonal violence, with respect to qualitative and quantitative features (567–569):

A. Quantitative Factors: Frequency and Duration

Compared to assaults between strangers or nonintimate acquaintances, violence between intimates is more likely to involve repeated assaults over a period of time, rather than a one-time incident of violence. One quantitative aspect of domestic violence is its frequency. One expert estimates that sixty-three percent of men who assault their wives repeat the behavior. That estimate is consistent with the results of the National Violence Against Women Survey, which found that more than sixty-five percent of the women who reported being physically assaulted by an intimate partner said they were victimized multiple times by that same person. Nearly twenty percent of the assaulted women recalled ten or more incidents, and the average number of assaults by the same partner was nearly seven. Domestic violence is quantitatively distinct from nonintimate violence not only in its frequency, but also in its duration. The same survey found that nearly seventy percent of women who had been assaulted by an intimate partner reported that their victimization lasted more than one year. For more than a quarter of the women, the victimization occurred over more than five years, and the average duration of the violence was four and a half years. Indeed, even the language used to describe the experience of domestic violence reflects its frequent and prolonged character. We say that a woman who has been assaulted by her husband is "battered" or "beaten," or has been subjected to "domestic violence," suggesting a general status or a continued phenomenon. In contrast, when a person has been assaulted by a stranger or casual acquaintance, we say he has been "attacked" or "assaulted," or has gotten into a "fight," suggesting a one-time act of violence, not violence more generally.

B. Qualitative Factors: Power and Control

The frequency and duration of domestic violence distinguish it quantitatively from other examples of criminal violence, but they also give rise to a qualitative distinction. Social scientists universally speak of domestic violence in terms that transcend the physical injuries from individual incidents of assault. Instead, they speak of domestic violence as a pattern of conduct that uses physical battering as just one method of inflicting emotional trauma.

Although social scientists caution that there is no singular profile of a domestic abuser's psychology, they commonly use a framework of power and control to explain the coercive nature of domestic violence, emphasizing that the intended harm goes beyond physical injury. Empirical evidence supports the theory that domestic violence is often driven by a desire to control. For example, men who are jealous, controlling, or verbally abusive are statistically more likely to assault, rape, or stalk their partners. Many domestic violence offenders suffer from low self-esteem and little self-control, and may physically retaliate against exercises of independence by their intimate partners.

In a discussion of the contradictions found in domestic violence research, specifically regarding the issue of male versus female victims,[1] Ver Steegh (2005, 1382–1384) refers to a domestic violence typology that may be useful:

Disquieting inconsistencies [in domestic violence research], as well as major contradictions, are either ignored or become the subject of rancorous cross-professional debate. For example, for the past twenty-five years, researchers have engaged in an intense debate concerning how often assaults occur and whether men and women are equally violent. The controversy stems from the contradictory findings of

---

[1] There is a great deal of literature on the subject of female victims of domestic abuse. I agree that women are far more often the victims of domestic abuse. Rennison (2003) found that 85% of intimate-partner violence victims were, in fact, women. However, I also agree that men may become victims as well—especially in cases that involve female substance abuse or mental disturbance, to say nothing of male homosexual relationships. This will be discussed further. Bearing that in mind, the generic term *victims* is far more appropriate for use in objective victimology.

various studies. Epidemiological "family conflict" studies show higher overall assault rates with nearly equal rates of assault by men and women. In contrast, so-called "crime" studies and police call data show lower overall annual assault rates and much higher rates of assault by men than by women.

The "family conflict" studies have been criticized by service providers and some feminist scholars who challenge the methodology of the studies, particularly the use of reliance on the Conflict Tactics Scale. These critics believe that the studies focus too heavily on specific acts of aggression and too little on resulting injury and the context of the behavior. "However, both groups of researchers agree that women are ten times as likely as men to be injured as a result of domestic violence." Differences also stem from definitional issues. The family conflict researchers define domestic violence narrowly in terms of physical assault, while service providers and clinical researchers define it broadly to include all types of maltreatment.

In the final analysis, despite the high level of acrimony, these studies may not actually contradict each other. As Murray Straus explains, researchers may in fact be observing and measuring different phenomena. He asserts that both groups of researchers are correct. They are merely studying different populations experiencing different types of violence. He speculates that, "these two types of violence probably have different etiologies and probably require different types of intervention."

Researcher Michael P. Johnson has taken the process of integrating competing studies to its conclusion by developing a comprehensive typology that accounts for contradictory research and connects contrasting perspectives. Based on his analysis of the "family conflict" and the "feminist" studies discussed above, he concludes that women's advocates and service providers are primarily observing one type of domestic violence, Intimate Terrorism, while family conflict researchers are predominantly measuring another type of violence, Situational Couple Violence.

The Johnson Typology of Intimate Personal Violence (IPV) provides four discrete categories that are meant to take an offender's use of threats, economic control, privilege and punishment, children, isolation, emotional abuse, and sexual control into account. These are *Intimate Terrorism* (IT), *Violent Resistance* (VR), *Situational Couple Violence* (SCV), and *Mutual Violent Control* (MVC). They are determined based on offender motivation and the overall pattern of offense behavior. According to Johnson (2006, 1009–1010):

"intimate terrorism," refers to relationships in which only one of
the spouses is violent and controlling. The other spouse is either
nonviolent or has used violence but is not controlling . . . [Then there
are] cases in which the focal spouse is violent but not controlling, and
his or her partner is violent and controlling. I call it violent resistance,
and it is almost entirely a woman's type of violence in this sample
of heterosexual relationships. Of course, that is because in these
marriages almost all of the intimate terrorism is perpetrated by men,
and in some cases the wives do respond with violence, although rarely
are they also controlling . . . "situational couple violence," [refers to]
individual noncontrolling violence in a dyadic context in which neither
of the spouses is violent and controlling . . . "mutual violent control,"
refers to controlling violence in a relationship in which both spouses
are violent and controlling.

Ver Steegh (2005) actually provides a more useful discussion of the Johnson
IPV Typology for our purposes. Of *Intimate Terrorism,* she writes (1387–1390):

1. Intimate Terrorism
   a. The Johnson Typology: Intimate Terrorism

Intimate Terrorism (IT) is the type of violence observed in battered
women's shelters and measured by crime and clinical studies. In
Intimate Terrorism, violence is one tactic in a larger pattern of power
and control. Control is exerted by making threats, wielding economic
control, applying privilege and punishment, manipulating and
threatening children, isolating the victim, and inflicting emotional
and sexual abuse. As compared with other types of violence, Intimate
Terrorism involves more frequent per couple incidents, more severe
violence, and results in more serious injury. This type of violence is
quite likely to escalate over time.

Intimate Terrorism is nearly always perpetrated by men upon
women, and female victims are more likely to suffer from Post
Traumatic Stress Syndrome (PTSD), depression, and poor health.
These women actively seek formal help and are likely to leave
the abuser. Intimate Terrorism accounts for somewhere between
eleven percent and thirty-five percent of domestic violence
situations.

. . .

i. Victims of Intimate Terrorism

While most research regarding victims of domestic violence does not
explicitly distinguish between Intimate Terrorism and Situational
Couple Violence, much of the research seems focused on female

victims of Intimate Terrorism. The most commonly held view of "battered women" is based on "the traumatization model" which includes themes such as "learned helplessness" and "battered women's syndrome." Some women who are victims of Intimate Terrorism suffer from Post Traumatic Stress Disorder as a result of the abuse. Victims experience painful and serious physical injuries, as well as depression, PTSD, suicide attempts, and substance abuse. Victimization is also related to difficulty maintaining employment and a permanent residence.

However, contrary to popular belief, many victims of domestic violence leave the violent relationship. In fact, Richard Gelles reports that women who experience the most frequent and severe violence (arguably victims of Intimate Terrorism) are more likely to leave. This is consistent with research demonstrating victims' use of a "vast array of personal strategies and help resources." For example, in one study, researcher Lee Bowker found that women used seven personal strategies (such as talking to or avoiding their partner, hiding or running away, threatening to call police or file for divorce, or fighting back physically) to end the abuse, after which they accessed informal and formal resources (including police, clergy, physicians, and lawyers). Victims, therefore, are not necessarily passive but may be active survivors of abuse.

Of *Situational Couple Violence,* Ver Steegh writes (2005, 1394–1396):

2. Situational Couple Violence
   a. The Johnson Typology: Situational Couple Violence

Situational Couple Violence (SCV) occurs in the context of a specific disagreement that spirals into a violent incident; it is an isolated reaction to conflict and does not involve a larger pattern of power and control. Situational Couple Violence generally involves fewer per couple incidents than Intimate Terrorism, and the violence is generally less severe and less likely to result in injury. It is important to note, however, that Situational Couple Violence is not simply a milder form of Intimate Terrorism. Situational Couple Violence can involve severe violence; however, the violence is not part of a larger pattern of control.

Situational Couple Violence is the type of domestic violence measured in the epidemiological "family conflict" studies, and it is initiated nearly equally by men and women. However, there is evidence that men and women are differently motivated and that women suffer more injury and negative consequences resulting from the violence. These consequences include higher levels of depression, low self-esteem, and substance abuse. This type of violence usually does not escalate and may in fact de-escalate or stop altogether. Situational Couple Violence is the most common form of domestic violence accounting for an estimated fifty-one percent of cases.

i. Victims of Situational Couple Violence

There is a common assumption that all victims of domestic violence should want to leave their relationships. Obviously, many should and do leave, including some victims of Situational Couple Violence. However, others want to live safely in their current relationships, seeking only an end to the violence. As compared to victims of Intimate Terrorism, victims of Situational Couple Violence are more likely to voluntarily choose to work on the relationship rather than leave it. Campbell, Rose, Kub, and Nedd suggest that victims engage in "a process of achieving nonviolence," which includes negotiating with the partner and implementing strategies to end the violence; this research is likely to apply to victims of Situational Couple Violence. Similarly, Campbell, Miller, Cardwell, and Belknap found that after two and one-half years, only twenty-five percent of battered women were still being abused. Forty-seven percent were in a relationship with no violence (half were in new relationships and half in the same relationship, but violence free for one year), and twenty percent had left the abuser but not entered into another relationship. One might speculate that victims in relationships that became free of violence for at least one year were more likely to have been victims of Situational Couple Violence.

Relatively fewer services are available to victims who choose to stay in their relationships. However, these couples could benefit from monitoring and enhancement of their conflict resolution skills. Such support would also be beneficial to Situational Couple Violence victims who decide to leave the relationship. Thought should also be given to the reality that some of the victims of Situational Couple Violence are men. Even though female victims of Situational Couple Violence are more likely to experience injury and other detrimental effects than are male victims, some male victims might seek supportive services.

Of *Violent Resistance* Ver Steegh (2005, 1398) writes:

> iv. Violent Resistance
>
> Violent Resistance involves situations where a female victim defends herself against her aggressive male partner. In one study, researchers found that victims who resist violence, either physically or verbally, were twice as likely to be injured.
>
> While some perpetrators of Situational Couple Violence are female, they must be carefully distinguished from women who are violent resisters of Intimate Terrorism. Confusing a woman defending herself from Intimate Terrorism with a woman perpetrator of Situational Couple Violence could be a deadly mistake for her and her children. A woman resisting Intimate Terrorism (and her children) needs immediate protection, not anger management techniques. The possibility of such a mistake illustrates a danger inherent in the creation and use of typologies. At the same time, "a monolithic etiological model of marital aggression is inadequate to capture the diversity of relationship and individual dynamics in physically aggressive marriages."

Ver Steegh's discussion of the Johnson IPV Typology thus ends with an important caveat about the limitations of any typology. General categories can be a useful theoretical lens at the outset of any victimology, but they are invariably limited for meaningful application in a particular case. This is because individual cases may involve multiple categories of violence at different times. Also, there are many specific dynamic variables to consider that a general typology will not anticipate—such as drugs, alcohol, or mental illness, to name but a few. Therefore, it is important for victimologists to understand how individual relationship dynamics can be perceived and communicated, to investigate and grasp what precisely motivates them, and to assess the subsequent risk and actual exposure involved. According to Mills (1999), a good way to consistently describe the different kinds of abuse dynamics that can occur in a relationship is via the behavior-motivational typology, here presented. The cautionary note is that, as with any behavioral motivational typology, the categories are not exclusive. The following has been adapted from Mills (1999), with the gender-specific term *woman* replaced with the generic term *victim*:

1. *Rejection.* This includes criticizing, punishing, or judging the victim, refusing to help the person, and routinely discounting the victim's opinion.
2. *Degradation.* This includes verbally abusing and physically humiliating the victim.
3. *Terrorization.* This involves threatening to harm the victim or the victim's loved ones and punishing the victim by playing on his or her fears. It can

include behaviors like setting unrealistic expectations with threat of loss and harm if they are not met.

4. *Social isolation*. This involves preventing the victim from engaging in normal social activities and other interactions with people.
5. *Missocialization*. This involves corrupting the victim by encouraging the victim to engage in criminal or delinquent behavior.
6. *Exploitation*. This involves using the victim to support the abuser and his or her abusive lifestyle.
7. *Emotional unresponsiveness*. This includes showing detachment and lack of involvement with the victim and interacting only if absolutely necessary. It also includes failure to express affection, caring, and love toward the victim.
8. *Close confinement*. This includes restricting the victim's movement, even to the point of imprisonment.

RISK AND EXPOSURE

It is generally well known that drugs and alcohol play a significant role in domestic violence. Some studies have shown that as many as 92% of domestic batterers used alcohol or drugs before domestic assaults (Brookoff et al. 1997), and that the use of alcohol or drugs is one of the most significant risk factors for domestic violence (Bennet et al. 1994). Whatever the current or local numbers surrounding the reader, it is enough to know that the association between substance abuse and domestic violence makes itself clear in criminal casework to the point of exhaustion. It is, however, a mistake to assume that this association is necessarily causal. In some cases, substance abuse may be symptomatic of other issues (i.e., as a self-medicating or coping mechanism for a mental defect or disorder) as opposed to being the explicit reason for subsequent violence.

Less well known is the fact that many domestic abuse and neglect deaths fail to be counted as domestic homicides. For example, a study conducted by Johnson, Lutz, and Websdale (2000) revealed that, in Florida, the Florida Department of Law Enforcement (FDLE) itemized 230 domestic homicides for 1994. Researchers went on to discover that there were actually 319 domestic homicides, roughly a third more than had been officially counted. In 1995, the FDLE list itemized 195 domestic homicides, but the final total was 295. One of the other reasons cited for this consistent misclassification was the fact that the law enforcement agencies did not code boyfriend/girlfriend homicides as domestic when the two people did not live together. Consequently, as bad as the problem of intimate homicide appears when one examines the statistics, it is actually much worse.

According to the research presented in Johnson, Lutz, and Websdale (2000), there are a number of circumstances that increase one's risk of domestic homicide (written from the perspective of female victims). The high-risk factors are as follows:

1. Prior history of domestic violence
   - Escalation of violence
   - Past homicide attempts; choking
   - Rape and sexual violence
   - Violence toward pets
   - Violence during pregnancy
2. Escaping violent relationships
   - Marital estrangement
3. Obsessive-possessiveness
   - Extreme jealousy
   - Stalking
   - Obsessiveness about the relationship
   - Suicide attempts or threats
4. Prior police involvement
5. Prior criminal history of the perpetrator
6. Threats to kill
7. Alcohol/drug problems
8. Protection orders
9. Acute perceptions of betrayal
10. Child custody disputes
    - Past attempts to kill or abduct children
    - Severe abuse of children
    - Sexual abuse of children
11. Mental illness of perpetrator (paranoia, schizophrenia, depression)
    - Severe abuse as child
12. Hostage-taking
13. Children are hers not his
14. Change in circumstances
    - Unemployment
15. Her fear!

Depending on the facts and the victim's perceptions in the particular case, whether the research is deemed to suggest a greater degree of risk or a risk of death is far less important to the court than is the court's per se heightened vigilance when confronted with any number of these factors.

Victimologists must look for and consider these factors in the preparation of *any* victimology. The existence of any one or more of these factors (aside from 13 and 14) should be enough to place a person in the medium- to high-exposure category for potentially being the victim of violence, if not homicide. Sources of information that can have a direct bearing on these factors include medical records, court records, mental health records, phone records, e-mail records, prescriptions on hand, personal toxicology, and personal diaries. Failure to gather this kind of information in this or any case leaves the analyst in the dark with respect to the actual risks and exposures of a particular victim.

DOMESTIC HOMICIDE

Domestic homicide occurs when one family member, household member, or intimate kills another. It is often the result of accumulated as opposed to situational rage, and therefore it is often the culmination of long-term fighting, abuse, or betrayal. It also frequently occurs in association with drug and alcohol use. Subsequently, it can involve some of the more violent and aberrant behaviors that investigators will encounter.

It is well known that domestic homicide is a regular occurrence in the United States, to say nothing of the rest of the world. In the United States alone, more than three women are murdered by an intimate partner every day (BJS 2003). According to FBI statistics, domestic homicide is more than twice as likely to involve the killing of a female victim (BJS 1996) and regularly results in the death of more than one person at the hands of the offender, as well as the offender's own death.[2]

With intimate homicides, it is particularly vital to establish the context of the violent behavior. Given that exposure to domestic violence and abuse increases the risk of domestic homicide, those risk factors must be considered as well. As Wilson (2005) observes, these include the age of the woman, being a mother of children not related to the male aggressor, and making threats to leave or actually leaving the male. She also notes with respect to domestic homicide, "there does seem to be a tendency for men who kill their female intimates to do so when the women are in their child-bearing years." Wilson goes on to discuss the issue of threats to leave or actual departure as a major precipitating event, citing some fairly alarming research (307–309):

> Perhaps the largest single trigger for male violence is a woman's threat or attempt to leave her partner. Ironically, where domestic violence is already a problem, the very act that is undertaken in order to assure survival often ends up activating a dose of lethal violence.

> The evidence that women are at a particularly high risk of violence of homicide when they are poised to leave or recently have left a relationship is overwhelming. Three quarters of homicide victims and eighty-five percent of victims of severe (but non-fatal) abuse had tried to leave the relationship within the past year. In situations where abuse is ongoing, leaving can end the violence, but when it does not, the abuse often becomes more extreme.

---

[2]According to a Florida study conducted in 1994 (Task Force 1997), 38% of domestic homicides involve multiple victims, usually combining a spouse homicide and suicide or child homicide. According to a San Francisco study, from 1995 to 1996, 43% of the male murderers in domestic homicides killed themselves after killing the woman (Hallinan 1997).

According to one report, an attempt to leave was the precipitating [causal] factor in forty-five percent of femicides. In another study by Brewer and Paulsen, while female-initiated separation was a motivating factor in fifty-six percent of the cases of wife-killing, this trend was not found in situations where men initiated the separation. In a study of 293 women killed by intimates in North Carolina from 1991 to 1993, Beth Moracco and her colleagues at the University of North Carolina School for Public Health found that forty-two percent had been killed after they threatened to separate, tried to separate, or had recently separated from their partners.

Women are at particularly high risk in the two months after the separation. The proximity in time of the deadly attack to the separation is not a coincidence. In cases in which the husband's abuse does turn deadly, it is often clear that the event that precipitated the lethal attack was her departure. In the aftermath of uxoricide, it is often noted that husbands did precisely what they threatened to do, and husbands often admit that their spouse's desertion was the cause of the deadly violence. Hence, there is rarely any question as to what motivated the murder—in these cases, the women who died were attempting to leave their killers.

Just as lethal assaults increase when a wife threatens to leave, so do non-lethal assaults. As Wilson and Daly point out, "[a] credible threat of violent death can very effectively control people, and the . . . evidence on risks to estranged wives suggests that such threats by husbands are often sincere." This remark underscores the proprietary aspect of this type of violence. In fact, sexual jealousy and fear of desertion both elicit similar aggressive reactions. Clearly, killing a wife is not utilitarian if the goal is to assure access for future procreation. Ironically, what motivates this type of homicide is clearly not a desire to be free of the woman. Were that the case, presumably the man would allow her to leave. Instead, Wilson, Johnson, and Daily propose that uxoricide occurs when male proprietariness gets carried to an extreme. In many cases, the male may have used the threat of lethal violence in the past in a less counterproductive way to successfully prevent his wife from leaving. Proprietary uxoricide may occur in cases where men use more force than intended, attempting to intimidate their wives into staying. Equally likely, however, is the possibility that the man was simply carrying out a promise he made the woman before she left, adopting the attitude, "If I can't have her, then no one shall."

In such cases, homicide can be a proprietary expression. Arguably, this may be associated with historical or cultural views of certain groups of people as property, reinforced by criminal law that has been drafted and interpreted accordingly. As will be discussed in Chapter 14, regarding offender perspectives, related practices and traditions have been used to rationalize horrific acts of sexual violence.

PREGNANCY AS A RISK FACTOR

The previous section begs the question of pregnancy as a risk factor. In recent years, there has been considerable media coverage of intimate homicides involving pregnant women. Headlines, copy, and pundits have repeatedly and incorrectly affirmed that homicide is *the* leading cause or *a* leading cause of death for pregnant women. Much of the related reporting has been biased, inflammatory, or just plain uninformed. This circumstance has been made worse by reporters and criminal profilers citing incorrect or nonexistent data and research to support their particular view.

The actual study at the heart of these numbers, published in the *American Journal of Public Health* (Chang et al. 2005), reports that 31% of all pregnancy-related deaths that were also injury-related deaths between 1991 and 1999 were the result of homicide. Specifically, they found that homicide was not the leading cause of death for pregnant women, as many in the media have been eagerly reporting:

> For the years 1991 through 1999, 7342 deaths were reported to the PMSS [Pregnancy Mortality Surveillance System]. A majority of the reported deaths (n = 4200 [57.2%]) were pregnancy-related (e.g., they occurred during or within 1 year of pregnancy and were causally related to pregnancy).[3] A total of 1993 deaths (27.1%) were pregnancy associated and injury related.

> The remaining 1149 (15.7%) deaths included those that were pregnancy associated but not caused by injuries or pregnancy complications and those that were not pregnancy associated (e.g., the time interval between the end of pregnancy and maternal death exceeded 1 year).

> Of all pregnancy-associated injury deaths (n = 1993), 617 (31.0%) women died as a result of homicide, ranking homicide as the second leading cause of total reported injury deaths among pregnant women and postpartum women, following deaths caused by motor vehicle accidents (44.1%). The rest of the pregnancy-associated injury deaths were attributed to unintentional injuries (12.7%), suicide (10.3%), and other (2.0%). . . .

---

[3]See J. Chang, L.D. Elam-Evans, C.J. Berg, et al., "Pregnancy Related Mortality Surveillance: United States, 1991–1999," *MMWR Surveillance Summary* (2003), 52: 1–8.

When interpreting this report's finding that homicide is the second leading cause of injury related death among pregnant and postpartum women, it is important to note that our findings regarding homicides involving pregnant and postpartum women are similar to national statistics on homicide among all women of reproductive age (regardless of whether they are pregnant or not).

According to the study, there were 4,200 pregnancy-related deaths between 1991 and 1999; these were deaths that occurred during or within 1 year of pregnancy and were causally related to pregnancy. Note that 1,993 (47.5%) of these pregnancy-related deaths were also injury related; 613 (14.6%) of pregnancy-related deaths were the result of homicide. So homicide is not in fact the leading cause of death among pregnant women, nor is it even the leading cause of death among all pregnancy-associated injury deaths. This matters because certain "experts" have no difficulty going on television and stating the opposite—and the media is quick to repeat it, and the public is very quick to believe.

Certainly, any victim's pregnancy is a potential motive for any violence that might be suffered. It must be considered when preparing a victimology. However, as with all factors, it must be considered in its particular context, and its value must not be overstated simply because it makes a good sound bite. This is one of those areas where experts can do the most good by educating themselves so that they may subsequently educate the public in an honest and informed fashion when asked to do so.

ORDERS OF PROTECTION AND "SEPARATION ASSAULT"

One of the risk or exposure factors not mentioned previously is the issuance of a protective order by the court, barring the offender from contact with the victim. The issue of "Orders of Protection" or "Restraining Orders" is deceptively complex. On the face of things, it seems reasonable that all victims of domestic violence should want or should have protection orders in place, both to notify law enforcement of their situation and to provide a solid foundation for law enforcement or legal actions in the future. However, as explained in Tarr (2007, 388–390):

Not all women should get an Order for Protection. As a threshold matter, women do not easily define themselves as "victims of domestic violence" because, as with many social ills in our society, denial serves as a psychological means of surviving. For decades, social service providers, religious leaders and the justice system ignored domestic violence or blamed the victim, resulting in a disincentive to self-identify.

A woman may decide that she should NOT get an Order for Protection to escape a physically dangerous situation because the period when a woman decides to leave is the time she is most vulnerable. Martha Mahoney coined the term "separation assault" to capture this moment of extreme danger. Women in these situations may appear to be clueless to outsiders, but they are often able to read when the violence is going to escalate and thus know when the time is right to escape. Getting an Order for Protection is only getting a piece of paper, a court order that says to "stay away"; it does not give the woman a personal bodyguard. In most jurisdictions, the police will serve the perpetrator and assist the victim at the moment that the perpetrator is required to move out of any shared premises or pick up personal property. However, after that, it is a piece of paper and only the beginning of the story.

If a batterer is accustomed to flouting the law, the Order may be useless. One of my clients had an Order for Protection and her estranged husband came to her home and shot her. In less extreme cases, the batterer will try to test the boundaries of the Order, and often harassment on the phone and in person at the workplace is part of the game. At what point does she call the police to have him arrested for violating the order? Would an employer assess her as being hysterical or whiney for calling the police over what is viewed as a "trivial matter," or suggest that she has been too passive for waiting too long to call?

Depending on the jurisdiction, the police may or may not arrest the batterer when he violates the Order, and each time he gets away without consequence, he feels more empowered. Many jurisdictions have "mandatory arrest" laws that require arrest if the officer has probable cause to believe a violation has taken place. Although it may be a means of asserting some strength for the victim, the arrest can cause economic and emotional discord for children. Research indicates that despite the arrests, only a small portion of domestic violence cases are prosecuted; thus, some locales have adopted "no drop" policies that range from eliminating all prosecutorial discretion so that all cases are prosecuted, to less rigid assumptions of prosecution.

A key element in the "no drop" policies is the elimination of the victim's participation in the decision to prosecute, though she may be subpoenaed to testify regardless of the consequences. Therefore, the employer who sees an Order for Protection and subsequent invocation of the criminal justice system as a means of gaining a reliable employee is ignoring the reality of what may come in terms of lost time on the job and emotional turmoil in the employee's life. Even if arrested, even if prosecuted, even if tried, and even if convicted, there is a high likelihood that the perpetrator will not serve time, will not be physically removed from the vicinity of the victim, or will not even be deterred by the process.

The decision to get a protection order is an individual one. In some instances, it is a reasonable precaution that will have a specific and reliable result. For others, it may be irrelevant or actually make matters worse. Therefore, the failure to seek and receive a protection order is not in itself evidence that a complainant feels safe. In fact, precisely the opposite may be true.

THE PERFECT VICTIM: INTIMATE VIOLENCE BY LAW ENFORCEMENT[4]

Most law enforcement officers have been trained to understand that domestic violence is a serious crime that can result in serious injury or death.[5] They have also likely been trained to understand that domestic violence happens regardless of socioeconomic status, race, ethnicity, age, education, employment status, or marital status. Furthermore, they have likely been trained or experienced that domestic batterers use emotional, psychological, economic, and physical abuse as a way of controlling their intimate partners. In extreme cases, this control is far-reaching, involving such things as screening the victim's phone calls, alienating family members, forbidding long-time friends from visiting the residence, preventing the development of new friends, and constantly monitoring the victim's conversations and whereabouts. Even in the absence of formal training, certainly most law enforcement officers have responded to a domestic violence call and handed a domestic violence informational pamphlet to a victim that contains at least some of these facts. This knowledge and training may be ignored, however, when the accused is one of their own.

The Numbers and "Professional Courtesy"

Research has shown that police families are more likely to experience domestic violence than others. This may be due to the nature of the work and the personality of those who are attracted to it. According to one source, citing two different studies (Davidow and Teichroeb 2003):

---

[4]Portions of this section were previously published in Turvey (2003).

[5]In 1993, 2,289 men and women were killed by an intimate partner. This toll accounted for 32.2% of all murders committed during that year. In the year 2000, the total number of men and women killed by an intimate partner dropped to 1,687. However, this new toll accounted for 37.2% of all murders committed during that year (Rennison 2003). The numbers dropped, but the proportions increased. Subsequently, intimate partner homicides remain a significant issue for law enforcement, currently filling more than a third of the national homicide caseload.

Police officers may be more prone to mistreating their families than others, partly because some attracted to such work are more authoritarian and liable to misuse their training, experts say. Although more in-depth research is needed, two informal studies report rates of physical violence in law-enforcement homes of up to 40 percent. One study was done by Arizona State University family-studies professor Leanor Boulin Johnson in the late 1980s, while the other was published in the *Police Studies* journal in 1992.

According to another source (Brannan 2003):

Domestic violence is 2 to 4 times more common in police families than in the general population. In two separate studies, 40% of police officers self-report that they have used violence against their domestic partners within the last year. In the general population, it's estimated that domestic violence occurs in about 10% of families.

Other estimates suggest that as many as 15% of U.S. families experience domestic violence ("Facts" 2003). This figure remains less than half of the self-reported numbers for law enforcement families.

Law enforcement officers are trained to take control of any situation in conflict and remain in control as the undisputed authority until that conflict has been resolved. Any challenge or perceived challenge to that authority necessitates a response, and the use of force, or violence, is one available option. For a particular percentage of officers, the temptation to use force to resolve every conflict, on and off the job, is regularly indulged.

Despite the increased occurrence of domestic violence within the ranks, it has too often been the practice of police officers to ignore their training and experience when dealing with other officers of the law. That is to say, for some law enforcement officers and supervisors, the first instinct is to protect their brother officers, preserve the departmental image, or work to limit the liability of the city government, rather than investigating or supporting domestic violence allegations against one of their own.

This is often done under the guise of extending what is referred to in law enforcement as "professional courtesy," whereby laws are selectively enforced when fellow officers may have broken them. In this way, one officer is preserved from having to go up against another. Also in this way, conflict is avoided within and between departments. According to Captain Dottie Davis, Director of the Fort Wayne, Indiana, police academy and a specialist in police abuse (Davidow and Teichroeb 2003):

"Rather than protecting our own, we need to do a better job of weeding them out . . . Most (departments) would rather keep their heads in the sand."

Anne O'Dell, a retired San Diego Police Sergeant and domestic violence coordinator, suggests that police departments have ignored the problem of domestic violence within the ranks because (Kauffman 2003):

> "There's still that belief [within law enforcement] that our own guys would not do that. Our own guys are the good guys. This is a guy who backs me up. This is a guy I trust with my life. Certainly he isn't doing this. SHE must be the problem."

Another possibility includes the fear of being ostracized by the law enforcement community as an informer or a whistleblower. Those that inform cannot be trusted, and trust is essential between officers expected to protect each other in potentially life-threatening circumstances. Either of these can be enough to keep an officer from thinking objectively and performing his or her sworn duty.

The Culture of Victim Fear

The immediate consequences of ignoring or failing to thoroughly investigate police-involved domestic violence allegations are incurred primarily by the victim. Being a victim of domestic violence is bad enough, with its damaging effects on one's sense of personal safety, emotional and financial security, and self-worth. It can take a lot of time and a lot of mistakes before a victim of domestic violence has the emotional strength to call 911 for help. Then there is the shame, the social stigma, and the self-doubt. But victims of domestic violence can overcome these issues. As found in one study of 389 women of intimate violence in Chicago (Johnson, Leone, and Cohan 2007, 436):

> Women who experience partner violence of any kind are not passive victims but rather actively cope with the violence. In fact, 81% of all women in this study sought some form of help. The more potent finding, however, is that violence type predicted different help-seeking patterns. Women subjected to [Intimate Terrorism] rely more heavily on social institutions, whereas [Situational Couple Violence] victims rely more on friends or neighbors.

The study goes on to explain (438):

> [T]he help-seeking differences between IT and SCV victims are apparent and likely reflect differences in victims' needs. The fundamental implication of these findings is that the dominating context that defines IT combined with the more severe physical violence and consequences forces its victims to seek help from multiple social institutions at a higher rate than victims of SCV.

Victims of domestic violence by a police officer face not only traditional barriers but others as well. The biggest hurdle for this particular victim population—

one that permeates their fears—is what has been referred to within the law enforcement community as the "Brotherhood in Blue" (Davidow and Teichroeb 2003):

> Police officers can be among the most sophisticated, manipulative batterers, armed with an insider's knowledge of the legal system.
>
> They know how to restrain and intimidate without leaving marks, experts say. They undermine the credibility of their victims, portraying them as mentally unstable and vindictive. They call 911 first and claim to be the victim. They know what to say on the witness stand.
>
> Fellow officers may gather incomplete evidence at the scene by failing to take photos or witness statements, or by writing up an incident as "mutual combat" rather than determining the primary aggressor, said [Captain Dottie] Davis, the Indiana expert.
>
> "They can control the investigation the whole way through the system," she said.
>
> And they can often count on other officers to back them up. Victims of abusive cops say the "Brotherhood in Blue" is one more reason to be afraid.

First, the victim may not feel safe because his or her abuser has, at the very least, a government-issued firearm. The existence of that firearm represents an extreme choice that may be made by the abuser at any time. The victim must live with the constant fear that her abuser may make that choice at any time. She may even live with threats involving the firearm, whether direct or veiled.

Second, the victim may not feel safe because the abuser has a police badge and all of the authority that comes with it. Law enforcement officers have a tremendous amount of power, authority, discretion, and influence. They also have greater ability and resources to track people down. There are few places to run that a law enforcement officer cannot find given enough time and motivation. The fear of suffering the full weight of this authority and ability is daunting to even the most law-abiding citizen.

Third, the victim may not feel safe calling the police because the abuser *is* the police, and may have relationships with potential responding officers (i.e., friend, colleague, supervisor, etc.). If such a relationship does not exist at the outset, general law enforcement comradery may develop quickly once the abuser's badge is shown. The abuser, after all, speaks the language and knows how to handle fellow officers. The abuser may even be extended "professional courtesy." In the worst cases, other law enforcement officers may pose a threat to victim safety because of their willingness and ability to assist the abuser with intimidating, harassing, and monitoring the victim.

Fourth, the victim may not feel safe going to a domestic violence shelter because her abuser likely knows where all of the shelters are; it will not be a protected sanctuary at an unknown location. Additionally, the abuser may have relationships with those working at the shelters, professional or otherwise. If not, again, the abuser can easily cultivate such a relationship.

Fifth, the victim runs the risk of not being believed by anyone, including law enforcement responders, victims' advocates, and the prosecutor's office, because she is accusing a law enforcement officer. It will be the victim's word against the word of someone who testifies in court, under oath, on a regular basis. Further still, from an administrative or supervisory point of view, if the officer's word is no good, then all of his cases are compromised. If the victim's word is no good, then none of the law enforcement officer's cases are compromised. The choice for some may be that simple.

Sixth, the victim may fear that mandatory arrest laws for domestic violence cases, and the office of the prosecutor, will not protect her should she decide to call 911 and seek to press charges. Mandatory arrest laws exist to prevent law enforcement from making subjective determinations regarding arrest during a domestic violence call. They are meant to prevent police apathy, abuser likeability, personal relationships, and other personal bias from influencing the decision to arrest. Ultimately, they are meant to prevent the primary aggressor in such cases from further injuring or killing the victim after law enforcement has departed the residence. Many states have these kinds of laws. However, the reality is that individual departments maintain broad discretion, and can find reasons not to arrest if they work hard enough and refrain from investigating too thoroughly. As discussed in Durant (2003):

> Changes in law . . . do not necessarily change officers' behavior; studies and anecdotal reports suggest that many officers still do not arrest in response to a report of domestic violence. . . .

> Although most states now mandate or encourage arrest when there is probable cause that a domestic violence incident has occurred, police still retain discretion to determine, under a mandatory regime, when probable cause exists and, under a pro-arrest regime, whether or not to arrest at all.

The decision not to arrest, despite mandatory arrest laws, may have something to do with the issues already discussed. However, it may also have to do with law enforcement perceiving a lack of support from prosecutors. The local district attorney may not prosecute domestic violence crimes against police officers with the same zeal for justice as others. According to one study (Brannan 2003):

> In San Diego, a national model in domestic violence prosecution, the City Attorney typically prosecutes 92% of referred domestic violence cases, but only 42% of cases where the batterer is a cop.

When a prosecutor cannot or will not put a case on, this often goes right back to the quality of the investigation that was performed. A case that has not been properly investigated and assembled by law enforcement in the first place should not be accepted by the prosecutor's office, as it will invite an alert jury to acquit. In such ways, law enforcement has tremendous influence over whether a case can be brought to trial, whether the district attorney is willing or not.

In this culture of fear, it is not difficult to appreciate that victims of domestic violence by law enforcement intimates must overcome significant barriers to ask for any kind of help. It is also easy to appreciate their silence once these fears are realized, by a failure to investigate or a failure to protect. In this fashion, those who are meant to help victims become what they were intended to shield, and are subsequently unworthy of service.

Tacit Approval

The victim's fears are not unreasonable, nor are they unjustified. Firstly, the motive for officer misconduct in such cases is self-evident. Many officers value their career above all else. Consider that merely an allegation of abuse is serious. Before there is even an investigation it can temporarily cost an officer his current assignment or worse—his badge and gun—the symbols of law enforcement authority, culture, and identity.

Secondly, the failure to investigate or protect is not isolated to the actions of one officer engaged in abusive conduct and another officer willing to extend "professional courtesy" by ignoring department policy and the law. The problem is systemic and cannot survive without at least the tacit approval of law enforcement administrators and prosecutors. For example, one independent investigation revealed that over a five-year period 41 officers in King County and Pierce County, Washington, were accused of assaulting, stalking, threatening, or harassing their wives, girlfriends, or children. However, only half of those officers faced charges (Davidow and Teichroeb 2003). This same investigation found further evidence of disparity between domestic violence complaints that involved police officers and those that did not, including police departments that were (Davidow and Teichroeb 2003):

- Creating a double standard by not immediately arresting officers accused of domestic violence. Ordinary citizens facing such allegations are routinely jailed.
- Putting victims at greater risk by not taking away the officers' guns. During the investigation, officers suspected of abuse should be taken off patrol and not allowed to carry weapons, according to model policies drafted by national experts.
- Failing to conduct thorough internal investigations of the incidents—or, in some cases, not bothering with any review. That's how officers escape disciplinary action, experts say.

- Rarely determining there was wrongdoing in domestic violence complaints against officers, and meting out minimal discipline in the vast majority of those cases.
- Lacking specific policies on how to deal with officers accused of abuse.

Also of great concern was the fact that only one of these cases resulted in a conviction. The patrol officer in that case had made harassing phone calls to his former wife. However, he kept his badge, gun, and authority despite earning a criminal conviction (Davidow and Teichroeb 2003). That a criminal conviction against a police officer does not result in immediate termination is unfathomable. Then King County Sheriff Dave Reichert stated (Davidow and Teichroeb 2003), "domestic violence is a 'firing offense' for any officer, regardless of whether the accused is found guilty in the courts."

I agree, as the hypocrisy of a convict charged with protecting the citizenry, armed with a badge and a gun, is of the worst sort. But not every law enforcement agency agrees. This was inadvertently revealed at the turn of the century, on the cusp of a new federal law prohibiting those convicted of certain domestic violence crimes from carrying a firearm (Rodriquez 2000):

> A new federal law that makes it illegal for anyone convicted of domestic violence to carry a gun is threatening the jobs of dozens of police officers around the country.
>
> Officers in Texas, Colorado, California, Minnesota and Michigan have been re-assigned or put on administrative leave as a result of their past arrests. The numbers are growing, and those affected are claiming the law is unfair and even unconstitutional.

It should go without saying that a criminal is unfit for police service. As argued by Dallas Police Chief Ben Click (Rodriquez 2000), "I don't want people on this police department that don't have the maturity or self-control that is necessary to do this job." Therefore, the retention of such an officer speaks to a negligent administrator, and a disregard for the safety of the community.

This is where law enforcement management and leadership play the greatest role. Their example and their absolute intolerance of any acts of domestic violence by subordinate officers can create the right environment for reducing its existence. This kind of management and leadership is not common, and requires unflinching links in the chain of accountability.

In my experience, there is a chain of accountability for law enforcement that breaks down at the same point in many cities, providing for law enforcement officers and agencies to act almost independently of any external supervision or review. A supervisor, usually a sergeant, reviews the work (the reports) of each officer or investigator. Sergeants report to lieutenants. In larger departments, lieutenants may report to captains or even precinct commanders. They in turn report to chiefs of police. The communication disconnect tends to occur where sworn law enforcement administrators report (or fail to report) to civilian law enforcement administrators. Chiefs of police (or the equivalent form of law enforcement administrator) are supposed to report to a city manager or to an elected city assembly, counsel, or commission of some kind. In other words, law enforcement oversight is ultimately the responsibility of an appointed civilian administrator or an elected body of civilians. That is how the law is written, but that is not how it works in practice.

In practice, sworn law enforcement administrators do not necessarily discuss the day-to-day operations of the police department, let alone internal investigations, with civilian law enforcement administrators. In fact, they may rarely meet to discuss anything with them at all. Or when they do meet, it is to discuss the police department budget or topical public safety issues. In any case, there is not necessarily any oversight regarding the investigation or discipline of law enforcement personnel; allegations of police misconduct are handled internally and may not ever be passed up to civilian law enforcement administrators for explanation or review. This practice may be mandated by official policy. Or it may be a result of the very real consideration that law enforcement officers are inherently intimidating to civilians, and those civilians are sometimes less willing to hold them accountable, even when it is their job. Regardless, the net result is that sworn law enforcement administrators may have little if any oversight, and subsequently may suffer very little real accountability.

Given the existence of this disconnect in communication between sworn and civilian law enforcement administrators, it is clear how domestic violence complaints against officers may occur yet remain obscured from view. However, it is also clear that for this to continue requires civilian law enforcement administrators who are unwilling or unable to supervise their sworn employees.

If an investigation into police-involved domestic violence does occur, the facts as they are revealed may expose the municipality to greater and greater liability. There may have been a concealed or uninvestigated history of domestic violence, harassment, or threats by the officer involved, or within the ranks of the department. This could involve failure to investigate, witness tampering, collusion, evidence destruction, false reporting, abuses of office, and other criminal and administrative misconduct. Some of those in positions of authority may even have been aware of these and other circumstances, and ignored or helped to actively conceal them.[6]

---

[6]These are only some of the possibilities. A deceptive police officer is a liability from a casework standpoint, because law enforcement duties regularly require sworn courtroom testimony. In some cases, the outcome of a hearing or a trial will hinge on the character and reliability of an officer. If he has any history of deception in his casework, it diminishes his credibility. It would be foolish to put such an officer on the witness stand. Consequently, it is not uncommon for various levels of misconduct to go undocumented, ignored, or to receive an application of whitewash—for purely political reasons.

Case Example: Intimate Murder-Suicide—The Shooting Death of Crystal Brame

FIGURE 9.1
David Brame, chief of police in Tacoma, Washington, attends a press conference in early 2003.

In February, 2003, Crystal Brame of Tacoma, Washington, filed for divorce from her husband of 12 years, Tacoma Police Chief David Brame. In divorce papers filed with the report, she alleged a history of physical and emotional abuse, including death threats. Subsequently, local newspapers reported on the divorce and her allegations. Human resource officials recommended suspending Chief Brame, taking away his badge and gun. Ray Corpuz, the city administrator, ignored that advice and stated that the city should not investigate the case because it was a "private matter." Both the mayor of Tacoma and its city administrator were in agreement, as reported to the press on April 26, 2003.

That same day, just after 3:00 p.m., Crystal Brame and David Brame met by chance at a parking lot in Gig Harbor. He had picked their two children up from daycare earlier and they were with him in his car. An altercation ensued during which he shot Crystal Brame in the head with his service weapon, and then turned it on himself. He died later that day, and she died the next week on May 3.

RED FLAGS

FIGURE 9.2
David Brame's police-issued Glock handgun was recovered at the scene.

Quite a number of red flags went up regarding Chief Brame prior to the murder-suicide in which he killed his estranged wife. Had those in positions in law enforcement administration responded to one or more of them, David Brame may have been neutralized in some fashion, and Crystal Brame may not have been killed or victimized at all. Consider the following:

- In 1981, two police psychologists recommended that David Brame not be hired as a police officer by the city of Tacoma. He was reported to have failed the behavioral portion of one evaluation, in which the psychologist determined that "It appears Mr. Brame is a marginal police officer applicant and the prognosis for his developing into an above average officer is judged poor at this time." It was also determined that David Brame had a "tendency to exaggerate his potential to the point of being deceptive" (Barker and Skolnik 2003).

- In 1989, while working as a patrol officer, David Brame was accused of raping a woman he had dated once 15 months previously. According to sworn testimony by retired Captain David Olsen, who had investigated the rape claim, "both he and another detective believed Brame was guilty of raping the woman" (Barker and Skolnik 2003). According to reports (*Estate of Crystal Brame v. City of Tacoma, et al.* 2003), Brame confessed to detectives who then handed the case file over to their chief for review. Then-Chief Ray Fjetland determined that the allegation could not be sustained because of witness reluctance and the passage of time.

- According to reports (*Estate of Crystal Brame v. City of Tacoma, et al.* 2003), David Brame was accused of sexual harassment towards fellow Tacoma police officers and "alleged promises of promotion in exchange for sex."

- In his application for the chief's position in December 2001, David Brame gave references that should have raised red flags and disqualified him for the position. According to published reports (Hagey and Modeen 2003):

  The job references David Brame supplied when he was a candidate for Tacoma's police chief in December 2001 should have been enough, on their own, to eliminate him as a finalist for the post, human resources specialists in and outside the city say.

  Nearly half his references—six of 13 people—could not be reached for comment by human resources officials. Three of those who did speak made vague references to something in Brame's past that would embarrass him or the city if made public.

  And several key people who logically would have been listed as references—including two former police chiefs, his current boss and two peers—were omitted.

  Human resources officials contacted some of those people—including Brame's then-boss, Chief James Hairston, and two assistant chiefs— but they flatly refused to talk about Brame.

  "That would have been a huge red flag," said Dawn MacNab, principal with Waldron and Co., a Seattle firm that specializes in executive job searches for government agencies and nonprofit organizations.

Mary Brown, assistant director of Tacoma's human resources department, identified these red flags to Tacoma city manager Ray Corpuz in a written note and followed that up with a verbal briefing (Hagey and Modeen 2003). Rather than investigate these issues further, Corpuz ultimately hired Brame to become chief of police.

- According to documents filed in the Brames' divorce case, there was a history of domestic violence. They report that ("Police chief" 2003), "Crystal accused her husband of pointing his gun at her, trying to choke her in November and saying he 'could snap my neck if he wanted to.'"

- According to reports, Crystal Brame disclosed David Brame's violent and aberrant behavior to her family after they were divorced in February of 2003. This included that he had "choked her four times the previous year, shoved her in a closet and pointed a gun at her head. Each time he would send her flowers to apologize. She also told her psychologist that David Brame was pressing her to have group sex" (Teichroeb 2003).

The Administrative Response

The response of police administrators in this case included initial public support for Chief Brame, then the issuance of misleading public statements about who knew what, and when. It also included officers being placed on leave, and at least one resignation:

- David Brame's close friend and second in command, Catherine Woodard, took command of the Tacoma PD after the murder-suicide. When it was learned that she had accompanied him to divorce-related hearings and to help retrieve his children while in uniform, further intimidating Crystal Brame, she was placed on paid administrative leave by city administrator Ray Corpuz pending an investigation into "possible criminal misconduct."

- During her four days as acting chief of police, Catherine Woodward placed officer Patrick Frantz, president of police union Local 6, on paid administrative leave pending an investigation into a threatening e-mail he allegedly sent to the journalist that had first reported on the Brame divorce.

- City administrator Ray Corpuz subsequently placed himself on paid administrative leave, and then announced he would resign after the Brame investigation concluded.

The estate of Crystal Brame subsequently filed a lawsuit against the city of Tacoma for $75 million, seeking financial damages for the "harassment, domestic violence against, and, ultimately, the fatal shooting of Crystal Brame" (*Brame v. City of Tacoma et al.* 2003). In 2005, Crystal Brame-Judson's family settled for $12 million and the promise of certain reforms regarding better domestic violence training for law enforcement, domestic violence legislation, and increased oversight in relation to complaints against police officers.

SUMMARY

Domestic violence is more than physical injuries from individual incidents of assault. It is a pattern of conduct that uses physical battering as just one method of inflicting emotional trauma. In this chapter the Johnson Typology of Intimate Personal Violence was discussed, which provides four categories that are meant to take an offender's use of threats, economic control, privilege and punishment, children, isolation, emotional abuse, and sexual control into account. Moreover, the Mills behavior motivation typology was presented, which discusses eight types of abuse dynamics, including rejection, degradation, terrorization, social isolation, missocialization, exploitation, emotional unresponsiveness, and close confinement, that often happen in Intimate Violence situations.

The risk factors for domestic homicide were discussed, including pregnancy, attempting to leave the relationship, and so on. Further, issues with reporting and presenting statistics of domestic homicide and violence were discussed in some detail, with a focus on the media's misrepresentation of research surrounding pregnant women becoming victims. The problems with protective orders and the culture of secrecy within law enforcement were also examined in some detail.

It should now be clear that the ways intimate violence begins, expresses, and evolves are quite complex. They are often driven by an overall sense of powerlessness experienced on the part of the aggressor, and may present in various ways depending on the context of the situation, the people involved, and any precipitating factors.

Questions

1. True or False: Violence between intimates is less likely to involve repeated assaults over a period of a time as opposed to a one-time incident of violence.
2. According to the Johnson typology, what type of intimate personal violence is most often observed in battered women's shelters and measured by crime and clinical studies?
3. True or False: Situational Couple Violence is a milder form of Intimate Terrorism.
4. Situational Couple Violence is the most _____ (common/uncommon) form of domestic violence, accounting for an estimated 51% of cases.
5. Name and describe three of the different types of abuse dynamics discussed in Mills (1999).
6. What is one of the most significant risk factors for domestic violence?
7. What are some of the most significant risk factors for domestic homicide?

REFERENCES

Barker, J., and S. Skolnik. 2003. "Tacoma police knew Brame had been accused of rape." *Seattle Post-Intelligencer*, May 10. http://seattlepi.nwsource.com/local/121446 tacoma10.html.

BJS (Bureau of Justice Statistics). Crime Data Brief. 2003. Intimate Partner Violence, 1993–2001, February.

Bowker, L.H. 1993. "A Battered Woman's Problems Are Social, Not Psychological." In *Current Controversies on Family Violence*, edited by Donileen R. Loseke, Richard J. Gelles and Mary M. Cavanaugh. London: Sage Publication.

Boulin-Johnson, L. 1991. On the Frontlines: Police Stress and Family Well-Being (paper presented at a hearing before the Select Committee on Children, Youth, and Families, U.S. House of Representatives, 102nd Congress).

Brewer, V.E., and D.J. Paulsen. 1999. A Comparison of U.S. and Canadian Findings on Uxoricide Risk for Women With Children Sired by Previous Partners, 3 Homicide Stud. 317.

Brookoff, D., O'Brien, K., Cook, C.S., Thompson, T.D., and C. Williams. 1997. "Characteristics of Participants in Domestic Violence." *Journal of the American Medical Association* 277, no. 17: 1369–1373.

Bureau of Justice Statistics (BJS) Crime Data Brief. 2003. Intimate Partner Violence, 1993–2001, February.

Burke, A. 2007. "Domestic Violence as a Crime of Pattern and Intent: An Alternative Reconceptualization." *George Washington Law Review* 75, April: 552–612.

Brannan, T. 2003. "Domestic Violence in Police Families." *Purple Berets*, June, http://www.purpleberets.org/violence_police_families.html.

Campbell, J., Rose, L., Kub, J., and D. Nedd. 1998. "Voices of Strength and Resistance: A Contextual and Longitudinal Analysis of Women's Responses to Battering," *Journal of Interpersonal Violence*, Vol. 13, No. 6, 743–762.

Campbell, J.C., Miller, P., Cardwell, M.M., and R.A. Belknap. 1994. "Relationship status of battered women over time." *Journal of Family Violence*, 9(2), 99–111.

Chang, J., C. Berg, L. Saltzman, and J. Herndon. 2005. "Homicide: A Leading Cause of Injury Deaths among Pregnant and Postpartum Women in the United States, 1991–1999." *American Journal of Public Health* 95, no. 3: 471–477.

Davidow, J., and R. Teichroeb. 2003. "Cops who abuse their wives rarely pay the price." *Seattle Post-Intelligencer*, July 23. http://seattlepi.nwsource.com/local/131879_cops23.html.

Durant, C. 2003. "When to Arrest: What Influences Police Determination to Arrest When There Is a Report of Domestic Violence?" *Southern California Review of Law and Women's Studies*, 12, Spring: 301–340.

Estate of Crystal Brame v. City of Tacoma et al. 2003. "Claim for Damages and Offer for Settlement." August 22.

"Facts about domestic violence." 2003. *Seattle Post-Intelligencer*, July 23. http://seattlepi.nwsource.com/local/131932_dvfacts23.html.

Ferraro, K.J. 1997. "Battered Women: Strategies for Survival" in Albert P. Cardarelli (ed.) Violence Between Intimate Partners, Upper Saddle River, NJ: Allyn & Bacon.

Gelles, R. 1997. Intimate Violence in Families, Third edition. London: Sage Publication.

Goode, E. 2000. When Women Find Love Is Fatal, N.Y. Times, Feb. 15, p. F1.

Hagey, J., and M. Modeen. 2003. "References should have eliminated Brame, officials say." *Tacoma News Tribune*, May 11. http://dwb.thenewstribune.com/news/projects/ david_brame/police/story/3856110p-3455288c.html.

Hallinan, T. 1997. "Domestic Terror: Family and Domestic Violence Homicide Cases in San Francisco 1993–1994." San Francisco Family Violence Project, San Francisco District Attorney's Office, March 31.

Johnson, M. 2006. "Conflict and Control: Gender Symmetry and Asymmetry in Domestic Violence." *Violence Against Women* 12, no, 11: 1003–1018.

Johnson, M., J. Leone, and C. Cohan. 2007. "Victim Help Seeking: Differences between Intimate Terrorism and Situational Couple Violence." *Family Relations* 56, December: 427–439.

Johnson, J., V. Lutz, and N. Websdale. 2000. "Death by Intimacy: Risk Factors for Domestic Violence." *Pace Law Review* 20, Spring: 1101–1134.

Kauffman, H. 2003. "Husband, Cop and Enemy." *CBS News*, July 21. http://www .cbsnews.com/stories/2003/07/21/earlyshow/living/main564202.shtml

Mills, L. 1999. "Killing Her Softly: Intimate Abuse and the Violence of State Intervention." *Harvard Law Review* 1132, December: 550–613.

Murray A. Straus 1999. "The Controversy Over Domestic Violence By Women," in Ximena B. Arrias and Stuart Oskamp, eds., Violence in Intimate Relationships, Thousand Oaks, CA: Sage Publications.

Neidig, P.H., Russell, H.E., and Seng, A.F. 1992. Interspousal aggression in law enforcement families: A preliminary investigation. *Police Studies*, 15 (1), 30–38.

"Police chief had sought help for stress." 2003. *CNN*, April 28. http://www.cnn .com/2003/US/West/04/27/police.shooting.ap/.

Rennison, C. 2003. "Intimate Partner Violence, 1993–2001." U.S. Department of Justice, Bureau of Justice Statistics, February.

Rodriquez, R. 2000. "Some police say domestic violence law a threat to their jobs." *CNN*, January 6.

Tarr, N. 2007. "Employment and Economic Security for Victims of Domestic Abuse." *Southern California Review of Law and Social Justice* 16, Spring: 371–427.

Teichroeb, R. 2003. "Why rein in the police? 5-year-old David Brame Jr. knows." *Seattle Post-Intelligencer,* July 25. http://seattlepi.nwsource.com/local/132287_dvbrame25 .html.

Task Force. 1997. "Florida Governor's Task Force on Domestic and Sexual Violence." *Florida Mortality Review Project*, Table 12: 45.

Turvey, B. 2003. "The Reality of Police-Involved Domestic Violence: Lessons for Law Enforcement Administrators." *Illinois Law Enforcement Executive Forum* 3, no. 5: 51–64.

Ver Steegh, N. 2005. "Differentiating Types of Domestic Violence: Implications For Child Custody," *Louisiana Law Review*, Vol. 65, Summer, pp. 1379–1429.

Wilson, M.J. 2005. "An Evolutionary Perspective on Male Domestic Violence: Practical and Policy Implications." *American Journal of Criminal Law*, 32, Summer: 291–323.

Wilson, M. and Daly, M. 1996. Male Sexual Proprietariness and Violence Against Wives, *Current Directions in Psychological Science*, 5, 1, pp. 2–7.

Wilson, M., Johnson, H., and Daly, M. 1995. Lethal and Nonlethal Violence Against Wives, *Canadian Journal of Criminology* 37, 3, pp. 331–361.

CHAPTER 10

Victims of Stalking

Wayne Petherick

KEY TERMS

Domestic violence: actual or threatened psychological, physical, or sexual violence within a family environment. It is often viewed within the bounds of an existing sexual or emotional relationship.

Erotomania: a condition in which sufferers harbor a delusion that they are loved by another.

Obsessive relational intrusion: (also referred to as *the incompetent suitor*) similar to stalking but involves a narrower set of behaviors, including the repeated invasion of one's privacy by another person who desires or presumes an intimate relationship with the victim.

Stalking: a repeated pattern of intrusion and harassment by one person against another, which is generally viewed as threatening towards the victim.

CONTENTS

Stalking involves a repeated pattern of intrusion and harassment by (most typically) one person against another. It has serious physical and psychological implications for victims and presents problems to investigators, because it involves dynamics and behavior that are poorly understood (Petherick 2008). This includes, but is by no means limited to, motivations, effects on the victim, appropriate responses, and outcomes from intervention. The actual methods employed by stalkers are similarly many and varied, ranging from covert surveillance, letter writing, telephony, and in extreme forms, assault, sexual assault, and homicide.

Individual victims will respond to the variety of intrusions in different ways. Some will simply accommodate the behavior into existing belief structures (this is what I deserve), while others will tolerate it to the point that they develop a variety of psychological symptoms arising from chronic anxiety and stress, while still others will become proactive in their attempts to resolve the situation. There can be no doubt that the range of responses will be as numerous as the victims themselves. It is the purpose of this chapter to examine the victims of stalking and to provide some theoretical and practical understanding of the offense.

Although the impact of stalking on victims should be apparent, it is worthwhile to restate the obvious before going any further. As Pathé and Mullen explain (2002, 1):

> The victim is central to stalking. Stalking has been criminalized because of its impact upon its victims. In many jurisdictions the crime of stalking is dependent on the behavior creating fear in the target. The reaction of the victim becomes central to the definition of the crime rather than, as is customary, the criminal intentions of the offender. Thus stalking becomes a victim-defined crime.

WHAT IS STALKING?

Stalking is a crime of considerable social impact, the import of which cannot be overstated. It emerged in the 1980s as a focus of media attention (Emerson, Ferris, and Brooks-Gardner 1998), catalyzed by the homicide of actress Rebecca Shaeffer in 1989. Others have called it the "crime of the 90s" (Goode 1995), with many jurisdictions proscribing the conduct in that decade or shortly thereafter. (California was the first U.S. state in 1990, with others following suit within 3 years; see Hargreaves 2000.) In Australia, Queensland was the first jurisdiction to implement legislation, and as in the United States, other states soon followed. The United Kingdom provides cover for victims under the Protection from Harassment Act, introduced in 1997.

While components of the offense differ, sometimes substantially, there is some uniformity in the way stalking is defined and described. For example, California's Penal Code Section 646.9 originally described a "credible threat," later stating that the offender only need put the victim "in reasonable fear for his or her safety." Section 359B of the Queensland Criminal Code identifies a number of behaviors that constitute the act, and states that they:

> (i) would cause the stalked person apprehension or fear, reasonably arising in all the circumstances, of violence to, or against property of, the stalked person or another person; or

> (ii) causes detriment, reasonably arising in all the circumstances, to the stalked person or another person.

This piece of legislation includes the "reasonable person" test, which is a common threshold standard from which the impact of stalking can be measured. This test ensures that the victim's reactions are not merely idiosyncratic responses to low levels of intrusion and that any reasonable person in the same set of circumstances would measure his or her experience in the same way.

Another important consideration, one that plays a pivotal role in most offense types, is the intent of the offender. Most of the United States require that the offender intended to cause fear in the victim, with some considering the fear requirement met if the victim is reasonably frightened (National Institute of Justice 1996). Queensland's Criminal Code also requires that the conduct be intentionally directed at a person (the "stalked person"). In the Australian state of New South Wales, stalking is considered an offense when the offender intends to cause the victim to fear personal injury (Department of Justice and the Attorney General 2003). In this jurisdiction, the intent requirement is intertwined with the reasonable person test. That is, if it could be known that the behavior would cause another person fear, then the intent element is met. This is discussed in part by Goode (1995, 28):

> Most American versions seemed to require that the harasser perform various types of conduct variously described, with an intent that the victim be intimidated or terrorized. There was a [great] deal of debate about the need for and specification of this requirement in the American literature, but it fitted well with Australian common law traditions which provide, in the most general of terms, that a serious offense ought to require proof of criminal intent. It also had the advantage of appropriately limiting the scope of the crime. What does it matter that the harasser is engaged in a labor dispute, a fraud investigation, investigative journalism and the like? If he or she harasses the victim with an intent to cause serious harm or intimidation, that should surely be criminal.

> It appeared that the best way to limit the scope of the offense to the targeted group was to require proof of an intention to cause serious fear, harm, or apprehension.

Other researchers have identified a similar constellation of behaviors but opt instead for the term obsessive relational intrusion, or ORI. While stalking ostensibly involves a vast array of harassing behaviors, ORI describes a much more narrow intrusion. Cupach and Spitzberg (1998, 234–235) define it as the "repeated and unwanted pursuit and invasion of one's sense of physical or symbolic privacy by another person, either stranger or acquaintance, who desires and/or presumes an intimate relationship." In this way, it differs from stalking only in a subtle fashion, limited to instances where the intrusion comes about in an attempt to establish a romantic relationship. It is therefore similar to what Mullen, Pathé, and Purcell (2000) call the *incompetent suitor*.

Spitzberg and Cupach (2001, 99) suggest that while there is some overlap between stalking and ORI, the two should be considered to be different, for the following reasons:

> First, to be considered stalking, behavior must be threatening, whereas some ORI behavior may be viewed as harassing, annoying, frustrating, or aggravating, but not necessarily threatening.... Second, to be considered stalking, behavior does not need to be in the pursuit of intimacy, whereas ORI behavior pursues intimacy by definition.

It should be noted however, that the fear requirement is not a component of stalking per se. Rather, it is a feature of a given set of laws in a given jurisdiction. It is my experience that the behavior of many stalkers is in no way, shape, or form *intended* to cause the victim fear or harm. The easiest examples include the former partner who goes too far in trying to reclaim a lost love, or of the potential suitor in showing his or her affections. Indeed, if one thinks about these two examples in particular, inducing fear in the victim may be counterproductive in establishing or reestablishing a relationship (except in those instances in which a person enters into a relationship for fear of what may happen if he or she doesn't).

As such ORIs are perhaps best thought of as describing the context of particular subtypes of stalking, rather than being a separate type of fixated pursuit, as Spitzberg and Cupach have described it. What is confusing here, is that although stalking and ORI are identified as being different acts, Spitzberg and Cupach (2001, 99) suggest that each is a nondiscrete element of the other:

> Thus, although stalking and ORI are technically distinct concepts, the majority of stalking cases consist of obsessive relational intrusion, and many if not most of ORI cases can be considered forms of stalking, even if they might not meet strict legal tests as such in a court of law.

The distinction between stalking and ORI may subsequently be redundant.

VICTIMS OF STALKING

The variety of features of victims and the factors that lead to their victimization mean that victims come in all shapes and sizes, from all ethnic, racial, cultural, socioeconomic, relationship, and other backgrounds. Some stalkers know their victims and others do not; some mean their victims harm, and some do not. The vast majority of victims is not celebrities, though this group is more likely to attract media attention than any other. This leads to a greater perception of stalking among celebrities than there is in reality, not to mention enhancing the fear of violence among victims. As discussed by Monaghan (1998, 17):

If you are being stalked, Hollywood myths aren't likely to throw light on your situation.

You are, after all, unlikely to be a celebrity. You're even less likely to be that other common object of stalking in the movies, the woman about to be attacked by a stranger with a kitchen knife.

Such attacks do occur. But, although they are fodder for the tabloids, research shows they are uncommon in real life.

The misapprehension of stalking is "substantial," says J. Reid Meloy, an associate clinical professor of psychiatry at the University of California at San Diego's School of Medicine. "It is fed by the commercial media, which focus on the more lurid, violent cases."

Dr. Meloy and a growing number of researchers are working to correct such misunderstanding. "Research in this area is very vibrant now," he says.

Public attention to stalking has been galvanized in recent years by cases involving such celebrities as David Letterman and Madonna. As a result of such high-profile incidents, California passed the nation's first anti-stalking law in 1990. Within four years—as the problem of domestic abuse also drew more attention—all of the other states had followed suit.[1]

The following section will detail some victim groups that have received specific attention in the literature and have been the focus of research endeavors to ascertain what, if anything, may make them prone to becoming victims of this serious and prevalent crime.

Domestic Violence and Stalking

Perhaps the most obvious context for stalking is that of domestic violence. The break up of an intimate relationship can leave both partners with a sense of abandonment, anxiety, longing, and/or hatred, which may result in a strong desire for reconciliation, revilement, or revenge. An intimate relationship already involves deep and often enduring emotional feelings, many of which resurface or increase at the dissolution of the relationship. Because of this, stalking within the context of domestic violence is among the most worthy areas of study.

---

[1] It should be noted that, despite the often-cited link between celebrity stalking and the introduction of the first stalking laws in the United States, "anti-stalking" legislation was actually introduced owing to an increasing number of domestic homicides that followed stalking by former intimates. For a thorough discussion, see Lemon (1994) and Watson (1998).

Domestic violence is considered to be actual or threatened psychological, physical, or sexual violence within a family environment (Baldry 2002). Baldry further suggests that domestic violence can be defined as occurring within a marriage, de facto relationship, divorce, separation, past de facto relationships, and dating relationships. For the purpose of this chapter, domestic violence is considered to be physical, psychological, or sexual violence that occurs within the bounds of an existing sexual or emotional relationship. This would exclude those situations where the victim and the offender are only acquaintances, friends, or otherwise casually related.

For example, here is an account of stalking involving prior intimates (Duncan 2001, 29–30):

> A mid 40-year-old, black male from a southern state was referred by the court system for an evaluation of his competency to stand trial and responsibility at the time of the instant offense. His charge was that of a firearms violation. His offense involved his approaching his ex-girlfriend at her place of employment and attempting to shoot her at point blank range while she sat in her car. Fortunately, his firearm malfunctioned and no one was physically hurt. This event occurred in front of many witnesses who noted that the perpetrator then entered his own car and drove off. He was later apprehended, being significantly intoxicated at the time. A closer look at this case revealed the victim, approximately one year prior to the assault, had received several pleading letters from the defendant shortly after she had broken off their relationship. After she continued to be dissuaded by the defendant's pleading, the victim started receiving anonymous letters of a threatening nature. More so, the victim's neighbors received letters supposedly written by the victim, which described them in a very denigrating manner. Some time later, the victim found her car vandalized. The morning before the firearm's violation and assault, the victim's car tires were slashed. Unfortunately, little else is known about the defendant's psychosocial development or the victim's relationship with the defendant.
>
> During an interview with the defendant, he denied authoring any of the anonymous letters or vandalizing the victim's car. He stated he would never do such a thing because he was still in love with her. He claimed he did not remember any portion of the assault because he was intoxicated. A review of his background showed the defendant to be well educated with a college degree. However, he was chronically underemployed. He was divorced several years prior to the assault in question. His history also showed a chronic problem with alcohol including several prior treatment efforts to curb his alcohol

consumption. He reported his drinking had significantly increased during the months leading up to the offense in question. Other than drunk driving violations, his previous convictions centered around domestic violence in a previous relationship.

The National Violence Against Women survey (Tjaden and Thoennes 1998) found that 59% of female victims were stalked by a current or former partner. Although approximately half of these were stalked while the relationship was still ongoing, other research (Budd, Mattinson, and Myhill 2000) found that the prevalence of stalking was lowest for those who were married (1.2%); those who were single, separated, divorced, or cohabiting were all more likely to be victims than those who were married. What's more, other research (McClennan 1996) has found that stalking involving intimates is more likely to endure than that involving strangers, with Mullen, Pathé, Purcell, and Stuart (1999) also finding that rejected ex-partners were more likely to assault their victims.

Turning from victims to the law, Currie (2000, 1) conducted a survey of magistrates in the Australian state of Queensland regarding their views of stalking and domestic violence:

> Magistrates were asked to engage with the issue of stalking as it related to domestic violence…their opinion was canvassed on two issues: how well the Domestic Violence legislation dovetailed with the stalking provisions of the Queensland Criminal Code; and how comfortable they were making domestic violence orders when the harassment complained of included, for example, making phone calls, driving past, or the constant sending of flowers, etc.

This survey was conducted on 96 magistrates and acting magistrates with a response rate of 40% with 9 of the 12 female magistrates responding, and 28 of the 84 male magistrates responding. The survey questionnaire asked two questions directly relevant to stalking, with the first being "how well does the domestic violence (Family Protection) Act, 1989, dovetail with the stalking provisions of the Criminal Code?" and "are you comfortable making orders when the harassment complained of is, for example, the constant sending of flowers/letters, making phone calls, driving past, etc?" For the first question, 60% of the sample as a whole stated that the legislation worked well together, with 10% of the sample stating that the legislation did not work well together (the rest either did not respond or felt that their experience was too limited to make the call). For the second question, 65% of the sample said they were comfortable approving orders when the harassment was not physical in nature, and 12.5% said they were not comfortable approving orders. Currie summarizes by suggesting that, while most magistrates categorize stalking as actionable by a protection order, some may have difficulty constructing it that way or being satisfied that the behavior has occurred. Of concern is the result that at least two magistrates believe that some "victims" make allegations of nonphysical violence to end a relationship rather than to get legitimate protection. This discussion will be advanced further in the section on false reports.

The Stalking of Mental Health Workers and Other Professionals

Those who work with malfunctioning populations may, at times, come to the attention of stalkers. This may be owing to simple opportunity; for the individual predisposed to developing fixations on another, the professional may simply be in the wrong situation at the wrong time. For erotomanic individuals whose targets are usually of an elevated social status, the professional may easily become the target of their delusions. In other instances, for the stalker who is simply seeking someone who shows him or her care and attention, the therapeutic relationship provides the milieu for these feelings of intimacy to arise. Here follows an example reported by the Associated Press (2008):

> A Sheboygan woman accused of stalking her psychologist and then confessing to him in hopes of getting more attention has been committed for mental health supervision.
>
> Thirty-one-year-old Nicole Hencke was found not guilty of felony stalking by reason of mental disease or defect.
>
> A criminal complaint accuses her of stalking the psychologist, slashing his tires, leaving nails in his driveway and repeatedly peering through the windows of his house in the middle of the night.
>
> Hencke was committed by Circuit Court Judge Gary Langhoff, who placed her under the supervision of the State Department of Mental Health and Family Services for 18 months. He ordered the state agency to present a plan within 21 days summarizing her needs for supervision and treatment and describing who will provide them.

Psychologists and psychiatrists may be the most obvious professionals to be put into these situations. However, criminologists, police officers, nurses, or just about any other professional may come to the attention of the stalker during their involvement with a given case. For example, I was the subject of several after-hours telephone calls from a stalker during an intervention. The purpose of these calls was not to scare or intimidate me, but for the stalker to describe his role in the grand scheme of things (or to mitigate his role), and by giving his side of the story. Although I was not necessarily concerned, the intrusion into my home was unsettling.

The stalking of mental health workers by clients is a significant professional problem, and one that new members of the profession should be attuned to. Galeazzi, Elkins, and Curci (2005, 137) provide some general commentary on this issue:

It is advisable that mental health professionals maintain high levels of attention to the maintenance of boundaries in working with patients; avoid confusion between personal and professional involvement; take seriously prodromal features that possibly herald the initiation of stalking, such as requests for personal details by patients; and report stalking incidents in team meetings or supervision (for professionals working in private practice). On a policy level, the issue of harassment and stalking by patients needs to be addressed, taking into consideration the fact that even very inexperienced professionals such as residents are also at risk.

Because of the associated risks, this subject has been the focus of considerable study, resulting in an increase in knowledge about how often it happens, and what the consequences of the attention may be.

Romans, Hays, and White (1996) recruited participants across the United States from a member pool of the International Association of Counseling Services, Inc. Representing an overall response rate of 53%, a total of 178 usable questionnaires were returned. Ten of these respondents reported being stalked by a current or former client, with 9 reporting only one intrusion, and one reporting 3 intrusions. Interestingly, of the 10 who reported being stalked, 6 were male and 4 were female, suggesting that, for this sample at least, males are at greater risk of being stalked. This is especially noteworthy, owing to the fact that there were far more females (n = 115) than males (n = 59) in the sample. Perhaps of greater interest is that 14 respondents claimed that family members or someone else close to them had been stalked by a former client. Seventeen further noted that they had supervised junior members of staff who had been stalked by former clients.

The variety of psychological maladies that may lead a client to stalk his or her clinician is many and varied, ranging from delusional and psychotic disorders to personality disorders. These include erotomania, which has been the subject of a fairly extensive research review, and among the personality disorders (PD), borderline PD. This latter condition may particularly become a problem if the clinician tries to sever therapeutic ties with the client.

Erotomania is a condition in which the sufferer harbors a delusion that he or she is loved by another (see Mullen 1997; Mullen, Pathé, and Purcell 2000). This other is usually a person of higher social status with whom the stalker is not associated. Because it is a mental disorder, erotomanics may be likely to come into contact with a variety of mental health workers who may become the subject of their delusions, with the target not having to do anything in particular to warrant the attraction.[2]

---

[2]Erotomanics may experience *delusions of reference*, in which innocent gestures such as brushing aside one's hair, shuffling papers, or scratching one's nose may be seen as a "come on."

Leong and Silva (1992, 11–12) discuss the appropriate course of action for the mental health worker who comes to the erotomanic's attention:

> If a physician discovers that he or she is the erotomanic target of a patient, an attempt at psychiatric intervention is indicated. If the patient has a psychiatrist (or psychotherapist), the care giver should be contacted. Otherwise, an attempt should be made to refer the patient for psychiatric evaluation. Even if the patient is actively involved in psychiatric treatment, results have not been particularly encouraging. For patients with schizophrenia or a delusional disorder, the only effective treatment has been neuroleptic medication. Even this has not always been successful in diminishing or eliminating erotomanic delusions. If the patient is not involved in psychiatric treatment and continues to present as a behavioral problem, more drastic measures must be implemented. The first is to obtain a restraining order to allow legal action if the erotomanic patient continues to interfere with the physician's professional or personal life. Although there is some risk that a restraining order may exacerbate the erotomanic behavior, this may happen without any intervention by the target. If the delusional patient disregards the restraining order, intermediate-term involuntary commitment can be attempted, as in the case of this patient. Because treatment may not be successful, involuntary commitment may be the only effective method to separate the delusional person from the target.
>
> Obtaining immediate-term involuntary commitment is the best our society can do in dealing with erotomanic behavior. Long-term or indefinite commitment is possible only if a person continues to pose a statutorily defined level of danger. Because many persons in such an adversarial setting could hide their erotomanic beliefs and act in accordance with hospital rules, long-term commitment is not likely to occur. The hope is that the delusional person will be sufficiently discouraged by immediate-term involuntary commitment to discontinue any further involvement with the erotomanic target. Unfortunately, our present system cannot always prevent a tragedy from occurring. Wholesale preventive detention of erotomanic persons is not legally or ethically justifiable, unless all, including physicians, are willing to forego constitutional guarantees. While physicians can take measures to protect themselves, such as home and office security measures, security-conscious travel, restricting access to the home address, and the use of self defense weapons, these precautions may appear overly draconian.

Aside from the sometimes intense inconvenience (for want of a better term) that may accompany stalking, another important consideration is the risk of violence to the therapist or those around him or her (perhaps including other clients who stalkers might feel are eating away at "their time"). Meloy, Davis, and Lovette (2001) looked into the risk factors for violence among stalkers and found that an Axis II diagnosis was present in 13 of 59 cases (22%) and that an Axis II diagnosis was present in 24 of 59 (41%) cases where there was a history of violence. While the Axis I diagnosis was marginally lower (13 with a history of violence versus 15 with no history of violence), the presence of a history of violence among those diagnosed with an Axis II disorder was double (present in 12 cases of nonviolence versus 24 cases with a history of violence).

College and University Students

As a special population, college and university students are also at an elevated risk of stalking owing to a variety of factors:

1. Students, both male and female, may experience their first "adult" relationship.
2. Students, both male and female, may experience a variety of sexual relationships.
3. Students, both male and female, may experience their first prolonged separation from the comfort and support of familial and social networks.

Lee (1998, 17) suggests that it may be the university environment itself, rather than any feature of the victim or offender:

> It may be common for a male student to begin stalking a female student if he develops a "crush" on her, but he is too shy to ask for a date. Rather than waiting to run into her by chance on campus, he may prefer to catch calculated glimpses of his beloved and find out tidbits about her life and habits. He may even involve his friends in his detective work, expanding the number of people who may learn to enjoy stalking as an absorbing pastime.[3]

In 1997, Fremouw, Westrup, and Pennypacker conducted the first epidemiological study to determine the prevalence of stalking victimization among students. To do so, they collected data on a sample of 294 students, with a follow-up study conducted on another 299. The first study included 165 females and 129 males, with a mean age of 19.1 and 19.2, respectively. The second study included 153 females and 146 males, again with a mean age of 19.2 and 19.1, respectively.

---

[3]As an aside, it is not known to what degree stalking is a conditioned response such as this suggests, so this may be an overly simplistic characterization of the genesis of stalking.

Of the results in Study 1, 44 of the 165 females (26.6%) and 17 of the 129 males (14.7%) reported having been stalked. Study 2, with a refined survey, found that 35.2% of females and 18.4% of males had been stalked.

In a large-scale study exploring the sexual victimization of college women, Fisher, Cullen, and Turner (2000) found that 13.1% (n = 581) of students in the sample had been stalked since the start of the school year (with a response rate of 156.5 per 1,000). As with many studies, the specific results are a function of the definition used, which we will turn to at the end of this section. Of the respondents in Fisher, Cullen, and Turner (2000), four in five knew their stalkers, most of whom were ex-boyfriends, followed by classmates, acquaintances, friends, and lastly, coworkers. Roughly one-third of the respondents were stalked only off campus, with the rest being stalked only on campus or a combination of both.

LeBlanc et al. (2001) were also interested in the level of victimization in college samples by surveying students at the Worcester Polytechnic Institute (WPI). The survey was sent to a randomly selected group of 600 students and 142 staff, with 172 students (71 males and 101 females) and 13 staff responding to the survey. Owing to the low response rate among staff, they were not considered further. Three (4%) of the male respondents reported being stalked, while 21 (12%) of the female students responded similarly, suggesting similar levels of victimization as those studies already detailed.

To put these results into perspective, let's consider the general prevalence of stalking in the community. One of the first studies to delve into this problem was conducted under the auspices of the National Institute of Justice (see Tjaden 1997). This survey found that stalking affects about 1 million women and 400,000 men annually in the United States, with approximately 8% of women and 2% of men being stalked at some time in their life. Most victims are women (80%) who know their stalkers (79%), with 87% of stalkers being men.

Later, Basile et al. (2006) provided national prevalence estimates, again in the United States. This study of 9,684 interviews (4,877 women and 4,807 men), showed that of those aged 18 and above, 4.5% reported being stalked in a way they perceived as threatening. Approximately 7% of women were stalked, with about 2% of men being victimized, findings that are in line with the original NIJ study nearly a decade before. These results have been tabulated by study with reference to these two community baseline studies to illustrate the elevated level of victimization in college samples.

What Table 10.1 shows is that stalking among college students is considerably higher than its prevalence in the community. This perhaps highlights the elevated risk of victimization of students, and it is likely that this risk comes from the nexus of factors associated with being a university student.

Table 10.1 Comparison of Prevalence between Non-College and College Stalking Victims

Study	Sample size	Prevalence	Difference (Tjaden)	Difference (Basile et al.)
Fremouw et al.	294 (299 phase 2)	Female = 44 (26%) Male = 17 (14.7%)	Female = +18% Male = +12.7%	Female = +19% Male = +12.7%
Fisher et al.	581	Female = 76 (13.1%)	Female = +5.1%	Female = +6.1%
LeBlanc et al.	172	Female = 21 (12%) Male = 3 (4%)	Female = +4% Male = +2%	Female = +5% Male = +2%

Celebrity Victims

Celebrities, although by no means comprising the largest group of stalking victims, have attracted more than their fair share of attention and are perhaps the most instrumental in bringing awareness of stalking victimization to the fore. These statements from the Office of Justice Programs (1997, 2) highlight this fact:

> Although celebrity stalking cases such as Madonna's and David Letterman's have been largely responsible for raising the national consciousness regarding this crime, the vast majority of stalking victims are not public figures. Stalking affects people in all walks of life, crossing racial, social, religious, ethnic, and economic boundaries. Even cyberspace has been contaminated with this crime.

There is a dearth of research and literature on celebrity stalking, despite the frequency with which it is discussed in the literature as catalyzing the legislation. The murder of actress Rebecca Schaeffer is discussed over and over again, with reference to this crime as being solely responsible for California Penal Code 646.9 (the first state in the United States to introduce stalking legislation; see Holmes 2001; Schlesinger 2006).

Holmes (2001, 23) classifies celebrity stalkers in his typology based on the motivation and anticipated gain. Owing to its short length, we here reproduce the discussion in its entirety:

> The celebrity stalker is one who stalks someone typically in the entertainment profession: recording artist, actor or actress, or athlete (football, baseball, tennis, etc.). Although this victim is well known on an interpersonal level, for example a famous TV star, the target is personally unknown. For example Robert Bardo mailed Rebecca Schaeffer love letters 2 years before he killed her. At one time he traveled by bus from Arizona to Hollywood to personally deliver flowers and a giant teddy bear. Refused admittance to the studio, he obtained her address. Bardo wrote his sister months before and confessed a love for Schaeffer.

The victim is selected carefully by the celebrity stalker. The motivation is personal; the anticipated gain is psychological. As with the case of Bardo, violence is often fatal. Sometimes it is not. This is illustrated by the case of Arthur Jackson's knife-wielding assault on Theresa Saldana. A delivery man just happened to come upon the attack and wrestled the knife away from Jackson only after he repeatedly stabbed Saldana. His intent was to kill; the interdiction of a stranger circumvented his intent. With the celebrity stalker, there is no personal affinity, no lines of bloodship, and of course, no sexual motivation.

Hargreaves (2000) similarly provides a general discussion on the issue of celebrity stalkers. Here, it is noted that the motivation is an obsessional attraction to the celebrity, and actions of the stalker include sending letters and gifts, attempted contact by telephone, visits to appearance venues, and surveillance. It is further noted that the behavior is often linked to erotomania, and that research on the subject has focused on the characteristics of threatening and inappropriate letters to high-profile victims and members of Congress (undoubtedly, a reference to the studies of Dietz et al.). It is suggested that the results of the studies into celebrity stalking have limited applicability to noncelebrities.

Mullen, Pathé, and Purcell (2000) suggest that celebrity stalkers are remarkable for their lack of intimacy. Some harbor a delusional belief that they are loved by the victim (as is the case with erotomania), while others know that their love is not reciprocated but may believe that it will be, given time (as would be the case with reassurance-oriented behavior [see Turvey 2008] or in the Mullen, Pathé, and Purcell classification, intimacy seekers). Importantly, they note that violence occurs infrequently although these cases tend to be reported more frequently, overinflating the perception of how often this actually occurs. This overinflation has also been echoed by Schlesinger (2006), who states that only a small number of stalkers become violent, and that fewer kill. On the media, Mullen, Pathé, and Purcell note (56):

> The media can promote stalking of public figures by its reporting of these cases, glamorizing them and fulfilling the stalker's dreams of a relationship of sorts with their victim. The attention accorded to these individuals, especially those who ultimately become assassins, may fulfill one of the stalker's objectives: to achieve fame, or at least notoriety, their behavior culminating in the biggest and most important of their life.

The following example from *Cosmopolitan* discusses the stalking of Deborah Gibson by an obsessed fan (Lewittes 1998, 202):

> Last May 24th at 11.15 p.m., singer/actress Deborah Gibson walked out of the Palace Theatre in New York City like she always did after starring as Belle in Broadway's Beauty and the Beast. But this time, waiting for the former teen singing sensation was 29-year-old stalker

Michael Falkner. Gibson, 28, immediately recognized Falkner, a Debbie Gibson International Fan Club member whom she had met on numerous occasions. But now she feared for her safety, because Falkner had crossed the line from fervent fan to frightening stalker. In the preceding months, Falkner sent Gibson 50 menacing e-mails, addressed to her fan club. Gibson says the letters "threatened sexual violence."

Fighting off Fright

Although Falkner alerted Gibson's office that he'd be at the theatre, according to court papers, Gibson was still very much "alarmed" and "in fear of physical injury" when she saw the college student from Eau Claire, Wisconsin, lurking outside the New York City Theatre. But because of Falkner's advance notice, police were poised to arrest him. At press time, Falkner had been charged with 10 counts of harassment and up to one year in prison. Gibson has now joined the ranks of celebrities like Steven Spielberg, Howard Stern, and Rosie Perez, all of whom have been terrified targets of stalkers in recent months.

Falkner reportedly traveled to New York to confront Gibson personally because he was fuming that the squeaky-clean singer took part last May in "Broadway Bares," an AIDS charity event that featured stars performing mock stripteases. Falkner strongly disapproved of her racy role. "This is classic star-stalker behavior," says Glen Skoler, Ph.D., whose research and writing appear in *The Psychology of Stalking* (Academic Press, 1998). Skoler explains that "the individual first idealizes a star like Gibson as virginal—a Madonna—but something will trigger them to view the star as a whore who needs punishing or rescuing.

Unfortunately, Falkner isn't the singer's first stalker nor the first she's had arrested. On September 14, 1989, at the Blossom Music Centre near Cuyahoga Falls, Ohio, Gibson-obsessed fan Robert Pelfrey, then 37, was arrested before entering a concert with a trunkful of weapons. The father of four was later found guilty and served six years for threatening Gibson's life. He's since been released but has not tried to contact the former object of his obsession. At first, Pelfrey sent love letters to the teen recording star's office, and then, says Gibson, he began angrily writing, "If I can't have you all to myself, I'll have to kill you" and warned her that he'd be at that particular concert.

This example illustrates the fear that being a victim of stalking can evoke in a celebrity, as well as showing some typical features of celebrity stalking. For example, Falkner was a member of Gibson's fan club, in the same way that Robert John Bardo was a member of Rebecca Schaeffer's fan club (the case that catalyzed stalking laws in California).

THE EFFECT OF STALKING ON VICTIMS

As noted at the outset of this chapter, the effects on victims of stalking will be as varied as the victims themselves. This is largely due to the differences in individual coping styles, the severity of the harassment, the influences of prior relationships, the intent of the stalker. There are undoubtedly other factors, however.

In an effort to better understand and measure the effect of stalking on victims, national projects have been undertaken in the United States (see Tjaden 1997), in the United Kingdom (see Budd and Mattinson 1998), and in Australia (McLennan 1996; Mullen, Pathé, and Purcell 2000). Tjaden (1997) found that of the 16,000 people interviewed (8,000 men and 8,000 women), victims experienced the social and psychological aftermath long after the pursuit had ended. Approximately one-third of victims report seeking psychological treatment, one-fifth lost time from work, and 7% never returned to work. About 20% of victims attribute the end of the stalking to their having moved away (in itself a very stressful act). Budd and Mattinson (1998) found that 92% of the victims were annoyed or irritated, while three-quarters of the sample (from a total sample of nearly 10,000 people) found the stalking distressing or upsetting. Seventy-one percent said that they had changed their behavior in at least one of three ways. In Australia, it was found that one million females had been stalked at some time in their lives[4] and that 165,700 had been stalked in the 12 months prior to the survey (McLennan 1996). In other Australian research, Mullen, Pathé, and Purcell (2000) found that the psychological responses to stalking often paralleled those of domestic violence victims, and that of 100 stalking victims, all but 6 made major life changes, with 53% changing employment and 39% moving residences. An increase in anxiety was noted in 83% of cases, and intrusive recollections and flashbacks were reported in 55% of cases (Pathé and Mullen 1997).

Blauuw, Winkel, and Arensman (2000) conducted a study of 246 people where the stalking occurred for a period of more than one month. Results suggest that victims exhibit a wide range of effects that in all cases exceed prevalence in the general community. A finding worthy of consideration is that the symptoms exhibited by this group were more consistent with a psychiatric outpatient sample than a sample from the general population. On the *Somatic Symptoms* scale, stalking victims scored 11.2 (general population scores were 6.6 with a psychiatric sample being 11.7); *Anxiety and Insomnia* was 12.8 for the victims (6.6 and 12.6, respectively, for the other groups); *Social Dysfunction* scores were 10.5 (6.9 and 11.9, respectively); and *Severe Depression* scores were 7.3 (1.6 and 9.5, respectively).

---

[4]This study has received some criticism, because it only examined females and used too broad a definition, among other issues (see Mullen, Pathé, and Purcell, 2000).

These results collectively suggest that stalking is a crime of considerable physical and physiological impact in which there may be direct threats to physical safety as well as enduring emotional and social consequences. Owing to this, there is a need to define investigative techniques and strategies that can be brought to bear in stalking cases with the end goal of ceasing the behavior at the earliest possible time. I will discuss some techniques that I have found useful in the following sections.

FALSE REPORTS

While distasteful to certain fraternities, the concept of the false stalking victim, indeed the false victim of any crime, must be discussed in an open, honest, and nonjudgmental way by anyone seriously interested in understanding any crime where false reports may be offered. This is for a variety of reasons. First, for the investigative community, false reports are time consuming, sapping precious resources away from crime control and legitimate victims. Second, for the mental health community, the identification of false reporters may aid in identifying their treatment needs, but perhaps more importantly, weed them out from support groups where they again divert scarce resources away from legitimate victims and others in need. Last, from a research point of view, the ability to study false reporting cases is crucial because the reality is we know so little about them.

Thus far, false reporting stalking victims have not been the subject of extensive studies. Those handful of articles written on the subject have typically relied on small samples sizes of proven false reporters (proving a false report can be exceptionally difficult) or with a larger number of false reporters who are not proven but assumed through inter-rater coding.

Mohandie, Hatcher, and Raymond (1998) were among the first to write on the subject of false reporting victims. They suggest, from an examination of the Los Angeles police department's databases, that false reports occur in about 1 in 50 cases, or about 2%, with a false report being identified if the "victim" confessed it and the investigators determined the case was false. Just as important as these estimates of the prevalence of false reporting, Mohandie and colleagues offer five ways in which false reports impact the criminal justice system (226–227):

1. The time and energy devoted in investigating false claims takes away valuable, and increasingly scarce, resources from genuine crimes and victims.
2. Unsolved and frequently high-profile cases involving these kinds of serious allegations can result in negative publicity and political problems for the investigating agencies, as well as any other organizations involved in the false claim.

3. Innocent people can be wrongly accused, and in extreme situations this can result in wrongful imprisonment.
4. Civil litigation at the initiation of the victim and/or the wrongfully accused can be costly.
5. Desperate and troubled individuals who may benefit from mental health assistance go untreated or enter the health care system and are treated as "legitimate" victims.

Pathé, Mullen, and Purcell (1999) were perhaps the first to systematically study the issue of falsely reporting victims through the comparison of the features of 12 false reporters to 100 legitimate cases. Their basis for rejecting a case as legitimate was on the "basis of the claims being clearly, and repeatedly, at odds with the available objective information" (170). Their results suggest that false reporters exhibit a variety of paranoid illnesses, among other psychiatric diagnoses. No differences were found in age, gender, or social class between the false and legitimate victims; however, none of the fictitious victims was in a stable relationship at the time of the offense, false victims claim a shorter duration of victimization, and they were also more likely to utilize psychiatric services than legitimate victims.

In addition to the findings of these basic differences between false and legitimate reporters, Pathé and colleagues propose a number of types of pseudo-victims. The first involves a stalker who preempts the victim's coming complaint by accusing the victim. The second involves reporters with serious mental disorders, while the third involves prior stalking victims who have become hypersensitive to potential victimization. The fourth and fifth types show some crossover, being factitious victims and malingerers.

By looking at a general sample of 357 respondents in the United Kingdom, Sheridan and Blauuw (2004) adopted an inter-rater approach to determining which of these cases were false victims. The false reporting rate among this sample was 11.5%.

Taking a similar approach to Pathé, Mullen, and Purcell (1999), Petherick (2008) sought to identify the difference between a proven sample of false reporters and the general literature on the characteristics of stalking victims. This approach was seen to be favorable for several reasons. There may be differences in the homogeneity of both legitimate and false reporters depending on the background and qualifications of the expert involved. Put another way, a psychiatrist may see a different group from a general practitioner, who may see a different group from a criminologist, who may again see a different group from those who present to police. So, comparing the real and false cases may be relevant to the groups that individual usually deals with, but it may not tell you how any group of false reporters differs from stalkers *in general*. It is also seen to be favorable to the approach taken by Sheridan and Blauuw (2004) because, regardless of the degree of agreement among coders, it is still possible to be duped by a credible false reporter. It is also possible to classify a real case as false depending on the amount of evidence available, the presentation style of the victim, and any peripheral psychopathology that may influence his or her credibility (e.g., a generally paranoid person may come across as oversensitive). I have seen real cases written off as false, and false cases followed through as real. I would suggest, therefore, that a case not be classified as false until it is unequivocally proven so, rather than relying on the gut-feeling or intuition of the individual assessing a given case.

The following section is taken from Petherick (2008, 466–472) and reproduced nearly in its entirety:

> The author has worked on a number of both legitimate and false complaints. For the purpose of this study, only those false reports which have been proven (and not those which are simply suspected) will be examined on a variety of different features. These include the reporter's age, sex, occupation, marital status, whether they have identified a suspect, motivation of the victim and the stalker, whether the stalker engaged in break and enter or surveillance, if the victim had physical evidence, if they reported the case to the police, or involved others in any way. While these cases are not of actual victimization, the term victim and stalker will still be employed because this is the context in which the cases were reported.

> While the sample size is relatively small (N = 8) the features of the cases are instructive on a number of fronts. First of all, by comparing them to the data on legitimate reports some significant differences between false and legitimate complaints emerge. These will be outlined shortly.

> Few individuals or organizations are dedicated to the investigation of stalking, and some of these may not be interested in vetting the false claims from the genuine. Further, it is unlikely that any one person or group will have access to a large amount of data on this issue unless they are working on a considerable volume of cases. If we adopt Mohandie, Hatcher and Raymond's (1998) position that 2% of all stalking cases are falsely reported, even someone working on 1,000 cases per year would only see around 20 false reports. This number of cases is unrealistic and not likely to be encountered. Lastly, suspecting a case as false is vastly different than proving it unequivocally, so even those reports whose veracity is questionable are excluded from this analysis. The cases included in the study are all from the author's files and constitute only proven false claims.

Of the eight cases reviewed, only two were males, suggesting that false reporting is more common among females. However, legitimate victimization is also more common among females (McLennan 1996; Sheridan, Davies, and Boon 2001; Dussuyer 2002; Purcell, Pathé, and Mullen 2002), and so there may be some concordance between gender and crime selection in false reporters. The ages ranged from the late 20s to 82 years of age, with the most common period being in the third or fourth decade of life (two were in their late 20s and four were in their 30s when the reports were made). Research has indicated that while stalkers are generally older than the average criminal (Zona, Sharma, and Lane 1993; Mullen and Pathé 1994; Harmon, Rosner, and Owens 1995; Meloy 1998), victims are typically younger than average, from the late teens to late 20s (McLennan 1996; Tjaden and Thoennes 1999). The results of this sample indicate that false reporting victims are generally older than typical stalking victims.

The false reporters were predominantly unemployed (50%) or not otherwise gainfully engaged (25%) (one was retired and one was on a disability pension). One-quarter of the subjects were employed, with one having a very unstable prior work history. This suggests that the amount of disposable time one has is linked to lodging a false report. Interestingly, of the eight cases, five were classified as delusional/factitious (cases 3–7), all of whom were unemployed except for one who was on a pension. Of the other cases, two were classified as profit or personal gain with one being employed (case 1) and another being unemployed (case 2) while a third was classified as a mistaken belief (case 8) and was on a disability pension. In the profit/personal gain cases, one was intended to split a husband and wife up when the victim fell in love with the husband following an affair. In the second case, the reports constituted an attempt by the victim to get relocation in her Housing Commission situation owing to the alleged danger she was in. Sheridan, Davies, and Boon (2001) report that in one survey of 95 victims, only 6 were unemployed, and Purcell, Pathé, and Mullen (2002) found that 76% of their approximately 2700 respondents were employed at the time of the stalking. Sheridan, Davies, and Boon (2001) likewise found that only 1.4% of victims in another study were unemployed. This sample has a considerably higher rate of unemployment among those claiming to be stalking victims.

Another interesting feature from the data is the fact that all except one were single at the time of the reporting (1, 2 and 4–8). The one case that was in a relationship (de facto) proved interesting because her partner helped perpetuate the belief she was being stalked. While not a causative factor, both admitted to smoking a large amount of marijuana and many of the reports of the stalking she provided were originally reported to her by him. This relationship dissolved when he left town unexpectedly, and she booked herself into a private psychiatric facility. This coupled with the issue of free time suggests that the lack of gainful employment and/or a stable relationship are critical factors in the development of false reporters.

In all cases except one, the victims claimed to know their stalker. In the one exception, the victim claimed she had no idea who was harassing her. While the figures differ somewhat between studies, there is general agreement that most victims know their stalkers. For instance, Tjaden (1997) commenting on one National Institute of Justice survey found that only 21% of stalkers were strangers (therefore, 79% knew their stalker). Purcell, Pathé, and Mullen (2002) found that 57% of stalking victims knew their pursuer. Wallis (1996) found that a stranger stalked only 32% of victims. These studies indicate therefore that the stalker-victim relationship may not be a discriminating feature between false and legitimate reports.

While the longest claimed pursuit lasted 36 months before the victim sought help, all other cases saw a much shorter alleged duration. The shortest was 2 months and the second longest was 6 months. The most common duration was three to four months prior to reporting. Other studies have noted that most stalking episodes last one year or less (Tjaden 1997), last between four weeks and 20 years with the median being 12 months (Mullen, Pathé, Purcell, and Stuart 1999) and 1.5 years (Tjaden and Thoennes 1997). Many stalking victims report that they do not seek help immediately, instead waiting until they feel they can no longer cope with the pursuit. Many classify a single inconsequential act as the "straw that broke the camel's back." One victim sheds light on this reluctance to report:

> I thought I could cope. I thought I could handle it. Sure, the constant calls were annoying, but they were also a little flattering. At first anyway. One day I ran into a good friend and she said it had been nine months since she had seen me. It hadn't seemed that long but doing the math I realized it had been. I hadn't been to the movies, gone to clubs, gone to coffee shops, just hung out in ages. I had hardly been out of the house at all. I realized I had become a hermit because of this and it all got too much, thinking about it all at once. At the time I didn't want help, this was my problem, it was personal. I realize now that I need help or this may never stop.

When questioned as to the motive of their stalker, the majority of reporters ascribed revenge as their pursuer's motivation (5 out of 8 cases), with 3 of the 8 citing control as the central issue motivating the stalker. Anecdotal experience in working with legitimate victims suggests that the majority of stalking victims will respond that they simply do not know what is motivating their pursuer, with others providing motivations that are not quantifiable ("he/she is just sick"). With regards to the false victim's motivation, most cases were classified as delusional with 5 out of the 8 meeting the criteria. Two cases were classified as profit or personal gain and only one as mistaken belief. With a larger sample, it is anticipated that more of the motivations discussed elsewhere in this sample would come to the fore.

With regards to whether the alleged stalker had broken into their property, 5 of the 8 claimed that they had. Many of these cases possessed interesting features. In one it was primarily this claim that led to the categorization of this case as a false report. The stalker was reported to have climbed five stories of sheer brick, broken in through a triple locked window which also had a dowel in the window track, watched the victim while she slept and then left the same way they had come in, replacing the dowel in the track from outside of the triple locked window. In the second case, the false victim claimed the stalker could assume invisibility and come and go at their leisure. During the telephone interview the victim went quiet and whispered into the phone "he is here with me now, and has just touched my foot under the table!" In all cases where the victim claimed not to have endured break-ins, it was alleged the offender had undertaken a comprehensive regimen of surveillance, both covert and overt, on their property, vehicles and person.

A comprehensive survey of the available literature uncovered very few studies in which respondents claimed to be victims of electronic surveillance, though this is a common claim among false reporters. In this sample, 5 out of the 8 (62%) claimed to have endured some form of electronic bugging including video surveillance. In one example, the victim would not even speak on her home telephone because she claimed that not only was her phone bugged, but that the stalker had planted listening devices in every room of her house. In another case (case 7) the victim claimed that the stalker had developed an elaborate network of over 200 contacts that monitored her every move through the use of mobile phones and handheld computers equipped with cameras and Internet access. In the one study found, Sheridan, Davies, and Boon (2001) report that only 13% of respondents cite any form of electronic surveillance (in this study only the bugging of the victims home was noted). This is in stark contrast to the 62% noted herein.

Only one of the cases (case 1) actually had any form of physical evidence with which to bolster their claim of victimization. In this case, all of the material was manufactured by the victim for personal gain. The lengths this person had gone through should be applauded, and she presented much more information than many legitimate victims will collect during any given victimization.

Half of the cases reported their victimization to the police (cases 1, 2, 6 and 7). Three of these four cases were classified as delusional/factitious, which may account for the relatively high rate of complaints made to the police, given these individuals have a steadfast belief in the existence and threat of the stalker. In the one exception out of the four (case 2) the report was made to police because without a formal complaint, the government housing agency would not consider relocating her on the grounds of there being a preeminent threat. As the purpose was to secure an upgrade to her supplied living conditions, she had little choice in whether the case was reported, and this case was classified as personal gain or profit. In case 1, the false victim made every attempt to avoid contact with the police.

When working with a number of stalking cases, despite individual personality and behavior eccentricities, one becomes used to victim responses and develops an insight into the reporting style of the victim. To the seasoned investigator, any deviation from this may be indicative of a false report and sometimes suspicions are aroused from the first contact with the alleged victim. Mohandie, Hatcher, and Raymond (1998) have identified these as *initial attributions* and *victim presentation*. In this sample, only one victim (case 1) provided a reporting style consistent with typical victim behavior. This was also the case that involved the manufactured physical evidence, and perhaps as she had spent considerable time putting this material together, was better able to pass herself off as a victim.

Though Pathé, Mullen, and Purcell (1999) found that false reporting victims were not more likely to enlist the help of friends, family, police, or lawyers, only two cases in the current sample attempted to bring their situation to light without the help of others. The majority of cases (6 of 8) brought in some form of assistance, which ranged from hiring private security to conduct surveillance or an investigation, other consultants, criminologists, security experts or victims of crime groups. During this call for assistance, case 2 attempted to solicit sex from a member of the security team, case 4 almost made a career out of taking part in student surveys on stalking in the hope of seeking help, case 5 made many inquiries of private security but was eventually put off by the cost, and case 6 made several trips a week to a local victim support group.

The sample is admittedly small, but there are inherent difficulties with securing larger sample sizes of known false reports in stalking, some of which have been discussed. There is a definite need for improvement of knowledge in this area, and a great need to conduct more research. Distilling the cases into their elements has proven useful in assessing other false reports, and hopefully this small study contributes to knowledge in this area.

SUMMARY

The repeated and potentially threatening harassment of one person by another is referred to as stalking. It was recognized as a legal problem in California in 1990 and in the Australian state of Queensland only a few years later. Stalking victims come in a variety of forms, from strangers to lovers, and celebrities to psychologists. The impact of victimization on any one person, however, is relatively uniform. Stalking victims generally experience the full range of psychological conditions, from those paralleling post-traumatic stress disorder to general anxiety and hypervigilance.

Stalking is a crime of considerable social impact and occurs with far greater prevalence than other types such as homicide, though in some cases it can lead to murder or sexual assault. As this chapter has shown, there is also a link between stalking and domestic violence. Only through an understanding of the victim in a stalking case can we truly come to appreciate the whole nature of the offense and be better equipped to deal with it.

Questions

1. What is the "reasonable person" test?
2. What is the difference between stalking and obsessive relational intrusion?
3. True or False: National projects in various countries have found that victims of stalking experience the social and psychological aftermath long after stalking has ended.
4. Name three ways that false reporting harms the criminal justice system.
5. Of the eight cases of stalking false reporters reviewed herein, what were three common characteristics of the false reporter?
6. True or False: Stalking involving intimates is more likely to endure than that involving strangers.
7. Name two reasons why college and university students are at an elevated risk for becoming the victims of stalking.

REFERENCES

Associated Press. 2008. "Wis. woman confesses to stalking psychologist in the hopes of getting more attention." http://www.wsaw.com/home/headlines/16105912.html. Accessed on 21 March 2008.

Baldry, A.C. 2002. "From Domestic Violence to Stalking: The Infinite Cycle of Violence." In *Stalking and Psychosexual Obsession: Psychological Perspectives for Prevention, Policing and Treatment*, edited by J. Boon and L. Sheridan. West Sussex: John Wiley, pp. 83–104.

Basile, K.C., M.H. Swahn, J. Chen, and L.E. Saltzman. 2006. "Stalking in the United States: Recent National Prevalence Estimates." *American Journal of Preventative Medicine* 31, no. 2: 172–175.

Blauuw, E., F.W. Winkel, and E. Arensman. 2000. "The Toll of Stalking: The Relationship between Features of Stalking and Psychopathology of Victims." Paper presented at the Stalking: Criminal Justice Responses Conference, December 7–8. Sydney: Australian Institute of Criminology.

Budd, T., and J. Mattinson. 1998. "Stalking: Findings from the 1998 British Crime Survey." *Home Office Research: Development and Statistics Directorate*. http://www.homeoffice.gov.uk/rds/pdfs/r129.pdf.

Budd, T., J. Mattinson, and A. Myhill. 2000. "The Extent and Nature of Stalking: Findings from the British Crime Survey." *Home Office Research: Development and Statistics Directorate: Home Office Research Study 210*, http://www.homeoffice.gov.uk/rds/pdfs/r129.pdf.

California Penal Code. Section 646.9: Stalking.

Cupach, W.R., and B.H. Spitzberg. 1998. "Obsessive Relational Intrusion and Stalking." In *The Dark Side of Close Relationships*, edited by B.H. Spitzberg and W.R. Cupach. New Jersey: Lawrence Erlbaum, pp. 233–263.

Currie, S. 2000. "Stalking and Domestic Violence: Views of Queensland Magistrates." Paper presented at the Stalking: Criminal Justice Responses Conference convened by the Australian Institute of Criminology, December 7–8. Sydney, Australia.

Department of Justice and the Attorney General. 2003. "The Offense of Stalking: Discussion Paper." http://www.justice.qld.gov.au/ourlaws/papers/stalking.htm.

Dietz, P.E., D.B. Matthews, C. Van Duyne, D.A. Martell, C.D.H. Parry, T. Stewart, J. Warren, and J.D. Crowder. 1991. "Threatening and Otherwise Inappropriate Letters Sent to Hollywood Celebrities." *Journal of Forensic Sciences* 36, no. 1: 185–209.

Deitz, P.E., D.B. Matthews, D.A. Martell, T.M. Stewart, D.R. Hrouda, and J. Warren. 1991. "Threatening and Otherwise Inappropriate Letters to Members of the United States Congress." *Journal of Forensic Sciences* 36, no. 5: 1445–1468.

Duncan, S.A. 2001. "Stalking: A Case in Review." *The Forensic Examiner*, September–October: 28–30.

Dussuyer, I. 2002. "Is Stalking Legislation Effective in Protecting Victims?" Paper presented at the Stalking: Criminal Justice Responses Conference convened by the Australian Institute of Criminology, December 7–8. Sydney, Australia.

Emerson, R.M., K.O. Ferris, and C. Brooks-Gardner. 1998. "On Being Stalked." *Social Problems* 45, no. 3: 289–314.

Fisher, B.S., F.T. Cullen, and M.G. Turner. 2000. "The Sexual Victimization of College Women." National Institute of Justice Bureau of Justice Statistics Research Report, December.

Fremouw, W.J., D. Westrup, and J. Pennypacker. 1997. "Stalking on Campus: The Prevalence and Strategies for Coping with Stalking." *Journal of Forensic Sciences* 42, no. 4: 666–669.

Galeazzi, G.M., K. Elkins, and P. Curci. 2005. "The Stalking of Mental Health Professionals by Patients." *Psychiatry Services* 56, no. 2: 137–138.

Goode, M. 1995. "Stalking: Crime of the 90s?" *Criminal Law Journal* 19, no. 1: 21–31.

Hargreaves, J. 2000. "Stalking." *Encyclopedia of Forensic Science*. London: Academic Press, pp. 1350–1356.

Harmon, R., R. Rosner, and H. Owens. 1995. "Obsessional Harassment and Erotomania, in a Criminal Court Population." *Journal of Forensic Sciences* 40, no. 40: 188–196.

Holmes, R.M. 2001. "Criminal Stalking: An Analysis of the Various Typologies of Stalking." In *Stalking Crimes and Victim Protection: Prevention, Intervention, Threat Assessment and Case Management*, edited by J.A. Davis. Boca Raton, FL: CRC Press, pp. 19–30.

LeBlanc, J.L., G.J. Levesque, J.B. Richardson, and L.H. Berka. 2001. "Survey of Stalking at WPI." *Journal of Forensic Sciences* 46, no. 2: 367–369.

Lee, R.K. 1998. "Romantic and Electronic Stalking in a College Context." *William and Mary Journal of Women and the Law*, Spring, 4: 373–446.

Lemon, N.K.D. 1994. "Domestic violence and stalking: A comment on the model anti-stalking code proposed by the National Institute of Justice." http://www.bwjp.org/documents/stalking.htm.

Leong, G.B., and A. Silva. 1992. "The Physician as Erotomanic Object." *The Western Journal of Medicine* 156, no. 1: 77–78.

Lewittes, M. 1998. "A Male Fan Turned Psycho Stalker." *Cosmopolitan* 225, no. 3: 202–204.

McLennan, W. 1996. "Women's Safety in Australia." Canberra: Australian Bureau of Statistics. ABS Catalogue Number 4128.0.

Meloy, J.R. 1998. "The Psychology of Stalking." In *The Psychology of Stalking: Clinical and Forensic Perspectives*, edited by J.R. Meloy. London: Academic Press, pp. 2–21.

———, B. Davis, and J. Lovette. 2001. "Risk Factors for Violence among Stalkers." *Journal of Threat Assessment* 1, no. 1: 3–16.

Mohandie, K., C. Hatcher, and D. Raymond. 1998. "False Victimisation Syndromes in Stalking." In *The Psychology of Stalking: Clinical and Forensic Perspectives*, edited by J.R. Meloy. London: Academic Press.

Monaghan, P. 1998. "Beyond the Hollywood Myths: Researchers Examine Stalkers and Their Victims." *Higher Education Chronicle* 44, no. 26: A17–A20.

Mullen, P. 1997. "Erotomanias: Pathologies of Love and Stalking." *Directions in Mental Health Counseling* 7, no. 3: 3–15.

———, and M. Pathé. 1994. "Stalking and the Pathologies of Love." *Australian and New Zealand Journal of Psychiatry* 28, no. 28: 469–477.

———, M. Pathé, R. Purcell, R., and G. Stuart. 1999. "Study of Stalkers." *The American Journal of Psychiatry* 156, no. 8:

———, M. Pathé, and R. Purcell. 2000. *Stalkers and Their Victims*. Oxford: Oxford University Press.

National Institute of Justice. 1996. "Domestic Violence, Stalking, and Antistalking Legislation: An Annual Report to Congress under the Violence Against Women Act." April. http://www.ncjrs.gov/pdffiles/stlkbook.pdf.

Office of Justice Programs. 1997. "Domestic Violence and Stalking: The Second Annual Report to Congress under the Violence Against Women Act." Violence Against Women Grants Office. Washington: U.S. Department of Justice.

Pathé, M., and P. Mullen. 1997. "The Impact of Stalkers on Their Victims." *British Journal of Psychiatry* 170, no. 170: 12–17.

———. 2002. "Victims of Stalking." In *Stalking and Psychosexual Obsession: Psychological Perspectives for Prevention, Policing and Treatment,* edited by J. Boon and L. Sheridan. West Sussex: Wiley, pp. 1–22.

———, and R. Purcell. 1999. "Stalking: False Claims of Victimisation." *British Journal of Psychiatry* 174, no. 174: 170–172.

———. 2008. "Stalking." In *Criminal Profiling: An Introduction to Behavioral Evidence Analysis,* 2nd ed., edited by B.E. Turvey. Boston: Academic Press, pp. 449–482.

Purcell, R., M. Pathé, and E. Mullen. 2002. "The Prevalence and Nature of Stalking in the Australian Community." *Australian and New Zealand Journal of Psychiatry* 36, no. 36: 114–120.

Queensland Criminal Code Act. 1899. Section 359: Unlawful Stalking.

Romans, J.S.C., J.R. Hays, and T.K. White. 1996. "Stalking and Related Behaviors Experiences by Counseling Center Staff Members from Current or Former Clients." *Professional Psychology: Research and Practice* 27, no. 6: 595–599.

Schlesinger, L. 2006. "Celebrity Stalking, Homicide, and Suicide: A Psychological Autopsy." *International Journal of Offender Therapy and Comparative Criminology* 50, no. 1: 39–46.

Sheridan, L., G.M. Davies, and J. Boon. 2001. "Stalking: Perceptions and Prevalence." *Journal of Interpersonal Violence* 16, no. 2: 151–167.

Sheridan, L., and E. Blauuw. 2004. "Characteristics of False Stalking Reports." *Criminal Justice and Behavior* 31, no. 1: 55–72.

Spitzberg, B.H., and W.R. Cupach. 2001. "Paradoxes of Pursuit: Toward a Relational Model of Stalking-Related Phenomenon." In *Stalking Crimes and Victim Protection: Prevention, Intervention, Threat Assessment and Case Management,* edited by J.R. Davis. Boca Raton, FL: CRC Press, pp. 97–136.

Tjaden, P. 1997. "The Crime of Stalking: How Big Is the Problem?" *National Institute of Justice Research Preview,* November:

———, and N. Thoennes. 1998. "Stalking in America: Findings from the National Violence Against Women Survey." *National Institute of Justice and the Centres for Disease Control and Prevention: Research in Brief,* April.

———, and N. Thoennes. 1999. "Prevalence and Incidence of Violence Against Women: Findings from the National Violence Against Women Survey." *The Criminologist* 24, no. 3: 1–19.

Turvey, B.E. 2008. *Criminal profiling: An Introduction to Behavioral Evidence Analysis,* 3rd. ed. Boston: Academic Press.

Wallis, M. 1996. "Outlawing Stalkers." *Policing Today UK* 24, no. 2: 25–29.

Watson, J. 1998. "First Anti-Stalking Law in County." Letter to the League of Women Voters, May 13. http://www.smartvoter.org/1998jun/ca/or/vote/watson_j/paper1.html.

Zona, M.A., K.K. Sharma, and J.C. Lane. 1993. "A Comparative Study of Erotomanic and Obsessional Subjects in a Forensic Sample." *Journal of the Forensic Sciences* 38, no. 4: 894–903.

CHAPTER 11

Workplace Violence

Wayne Petherick and Brent E. Turvey

KEY TERMS

- *Anger-retaliatory motives:* crime scene behaviors that indicate a great deal of rage, either toward a specific person, group, or institution, or a symbol of any of these.
- *Collateral victims:* those who are attacked and injured unintentionally, because of their proximity to a primary or secondary target within a given environment.
- *Idiographic victim study:* the study of the concrete; examining individual victims and their actual qualities.
- *Intent:* the specific aim that guides behavior.
- *Motive:* the emotional, psychological, and material needs that impel and are satisfied by behavior.
- *Nomothetic victim study:* the examination of grouped victim data, as opposed to individual victim case information.
- *Primary target:* one who is of the greatest importance to the offender; dictates the location and timing of any attack.
- *Profit motives:* motives that service material or personal gain. These can be found in all types of homicides, robberies, burglaries, muggings, arsons, bombings, kidnappings, most forms of white-collar crime, and so on.
- *Secondary target:* one who is of lesser importance to the offender.
- *Victim selection:* the process used by an offender to choose his or her intended victim or victims.
- *Workplace violence:* violence or the threat of violence against workers.

CONTENTS

Workplace violence is defined by one authority as "violence or the threat of violence against workers" (OSHA 2002, 1). Because of sensational coverage by the popular media, the public perception of the frequency of different incarnations of workplace-related violence, such as homicide, is likely to be greatly distorted.[1] Watching the evening news, it is not difficult to understand why. In our present culture, where sexuality, violence, and fear are valuable retail commodities, the workplace is routinely characterized with one or more of these when given airtime or column space. Stories without such marketable traits are seldom featured.

This problem and others are encapsulated in a summary of cause-and-effect issues regarding workplace violence, prepared by Riley (2003, 2–3):

> While incidents of workplace violence do not appear to be on the rise, society is paying greater attention to the problem. Increasing awareness of workplace violence is due, in part, to the media's sensationalism of acts of violence in the workplace. However, the significant toll exerted by workplace violence cannot be understated, and the statistics are alarming. One out of every four employees will be a victim of workplace violence during their life. One out of every six violent crimes occurs in the workplace. As an occupational hazard, homicide is the second leading cause of death, accounting for one sixth of all occupational fatalities. Every year 1,000 people are murdered in the workplace; another 1.5 to 2 million people are victims of assault, rape, or robbery. Offenders use various means to disrupt the workplace. For example, every day 16,400 threats are made, 723 workers are attacked and 43,800 workers are harassed.
>
> Workplace violence also has a ripple effect, affecting not only the targeted victim, but everyone associated with the workplace. Violence in the workplace may inflict irreparable psychological harm. One report concludes that "negative publicity drives customers away, valued employees leave the company and new hires are harder to attract." Workplace violence also imposes substantial financial costs. Experts estimate the total economic loss to be around $4.2 billion a year. Given the frequency and severity of workplace violence, it is not surprising that for the last three years, workplace violence has been employers' greatest concern.

As professionals, forensic victimologists are required to have insight into the actual nature and occurrence of a particular type of crime before offering

---

[1]This is owing to the *availability heuristic*. As explained in Chapter 2, this is in play when judgments are made based on what one can remember rather than on complete or actual information. We use it for judging the commonality, frequency, or likelihood of events when assessing subjects about which we have very little actual knowledge.

related interpretations and opinions. We need to know more than what is being reported on the nightly news or in the crime section of the daily paper. And we need real tools with which to approach and analyze the evidence that presents in casework. Unfortunately, there is no shortage of "professionals" operating in precisely the opposite fashion.

The goals of this chapter are twofold: to dispel any myths regarding workplace violence perpetuated by the media and to provide forensic victimologists with the terminology and theoretical lenses with which to perceive workplace violence more objectively.

NOMOTHETICALLY SPEAKING: THE AGGREGATE

As discussed in Chapter 3, **nomothetic victim study** is the examination of grouped victim data, as opposed to individual victim case information. Such study is useful in theory generation and also in providing context. However, it is not often useful for rendering final conclusions about the evidence of a particular case. With that in mind, it is necessary to review the nomothetic basics regarding workplace violence.

In the United States, workplace violence accounts for about 18% of all violent crime that occurs in a given year (Duhart 2001). The least victimized (safest) profession tends to be that of college or university instructor; the most victimized (high risk) is law enforcement (Duhart 2001).

In the United States, there are on average about 900 incidents of workplace-related homicide every year. There are also 36,500 incidents of workplace-related rape/sexual assault, and 70,100 incidents of workplace-related robbery—out of an average of 1,744,300 total reported incidents. Therefore, taken as a whole, rape/sexual assault, robbery, and homicide tend to account for about 6% of all reported workplace-related violent crime victimization. The remaining majority (approximately 94%) tends to fall into one of two categories: aggravated assault (325,000 incidents/year) and simple assault (1,311,700 incidents/year) (Duhart 2001).

With respect to nomothetic crime victim characteristics of nonhomicide workplace violence victims, Duhart (2001) provides the following summarized information (2–8):

> Males were victimized more than females for both workplace violent crime and violent crime overall during 1993–99. The violent crime victimization rate for working or on duty males was 56% higher than the female rate (15 versus 10 per 1,000 in the workplace). Overall, 18% of violent crimes were workplace victimizations; 22% of all male and 15% of all female violent crimes were committed while the victim was working or on duty.

Although NCVS data have consistently shown that blacks experience violent crime at rates higher than whites and persons of other races, violent *workplace* crime rates were highest among whites. While working or on duty, whites experienced 13 workplace victimizations per 1,000 in the workforce, a rate 25% higher than the black rate (10 per 1,000 in the workforce) and 59% higher than the rate among persons of "other" races. The black workplace victimization rate was similar to that of Hispanics (10 per 1,000 in the workforce) and slightly higher than the rate for persons of "other" races.

Persons age 20–34 experienced workplace violence at a rate higher than any other age group considered. Workers age 12–19 and 35–49 experienced workplace crime at similar rates (12 per 1,000 in the workforce).

Workplace victimization rates for never married and divorced or separated persons were similar, and both were higher than the rates for married or widowed persons.

Type of crime and gender

Except for rape and sexual assault, males experienced all categories of workplace violent crime at higher rates and percentages than did females. About two-thirds of all robberies, aggravated assaults, and simple assaults in the workplace were committed against males. The rates of victimization (per 1,000 in the workforce) for these crimes were at least 54% higher for males when compared to those for females.

Type of crime and race

Whites experienced more than four-fifths of all rapes and sexual assaults (88%), robberies (81%), aggravated assaults (86%), and simple assaults (89%) occurring in the workplace.

Per capita rates of aggravated assault in the workplace were similar for all racial categories. The rate of workplace simple assault for whites was higher than that for blacks and persons of other races. Blacks and whites were robbed while working or on duty at similar rates (1 per 1,000 in the workforce).

Average annual rate of victimization in the workplace, by occupation, 1993–99

Occupation was measured by categorizing the victim's reported job at the time of the victimization into broad occupational fields...

Persons employed in law enforcement were victimized while at work or on duty at the highest rate of all occupations examined—followed by persons working in the mental health field. Retail sales workers were victimized in the workplace at a somewhat higher rate (20 per 1,000 in the workforce) than those employed in the teaching, transportation, or medical field.

Among the occupational groups examined, police officers accounted for 11% of all workplace victimizations and were victimized while at work or on duty at a rate higher than all other occupations examined (261 per 1,000), while college or university teachers were victimized the least (2 per 1,000).

The workplace violent crime victimization rate for nurses was not significantly different from that for physicians; however, nurses experienced workplace crime at a rate 72% higher than medical technicians and at more than twice the rate of other medical field workers (22 versus 13 and 9, respectively).

Professional (social worker/psychiatrist) and custodial care provider in the mental health care field were victimized while working or on duty at similar rates (68 and 69 per 1,000, respectively)—but at rates more than 3 times those in the medical field.

Except for junior high school teachers, the workplace victimization rate for persons employed in special education facilities was highest among teachers. Elementary school teachers experienced workplace violence at a rate lower than that for junior high and high school teachers (17 versus 54 and 38 per 1,000 in the workforce, respectively). Junior high school teachers' workplace violent crime rate was somewhat higher than that of high school teachers.

Private security workers' workplace violent crime rate was the lowest of all law enforcement workers (87 per 1,000 private security workers). Within the retail sales field, bartenders were victimized while working at a rate similar to that of gas station attendants and somewhat higher than that of convenience store workers. Within the transportation field, taxi cab drivers were victimized while working or on duty at the highest rate.

Assault, by occupation

Simple and aggravated assaults accounted for 94% of all workplace violent victimizations. There were 4 simple assaults for every aggravated assault occurring while the victim was at work or on duty. The rate at which persons in law enforcement experienced aggravated assault (29 per 1,000 in the workforce) was more than 3 times the rate for all other occupational fields. The workplace aggravated assault rate among mental health workers was somewhat higher than the rate among retail sales employees and significantly higher than the rate for the medical, teaching, transportation, or other fields.

Mental health workers experienced simple assault at rates higher than all other occupational fields except law enforcement; persons working in the law enforcement field experienced simple assault at a rate at least twice that of all other occupational fields.

Robbery, by occupation

Almost 4 of every 10 robberies occurring while the victim was at work or on duty were committed against persons in the retail sales or transportation field. Transportation workers were robbed at a higher rate than any other occupational field reported (3 per 1,000 in the workplace).

Characteristics of victimization

Time of victimization

Overall, more workplace crimes occurred between noon and 6 p.m. than in any other 6-hour period of the day.

About 55% of all workplace crimes occurring against employees in the law enforcement field were committed at night. Law enforcement was the only field experiencing more workplace crime at night (between 6 p.m. and 6 a.m.) than during the day (between 6 a.m. and 6 p.m.). Retail sales workers experienced workplace crime at similar percentages regardless of the time of their shift.

Victims' reaction to attack

More than three-quarters of all workplace violent crime victims did not physically resist (no resistance, unarmed confrontation, and nonconfrontational tactics during the attack). Three percent of workplace violence victims defended themselves by threatening or attacking their assailant with a firearm or other weapon.

Law enforcement officers victimized while working or on duty were more likely to threaten or attack their assailant with a weapon or firearm than any other victims of workplace violence (9% of all workplace crimes committed against them).

Victim's injury

Twelve percent of all workplace violence victims sustained injuries from the incident. Of those injuries sustained from workplace violence incidents, about 10 out of 11 were minor injuries. Fifty-three percent of all injured victims were not treated or did not receive medical care for injuries sustained, while 26% received treatment from a medical office, clinic, or hospital.

Weapon use

Armed assailants committed a fifth of all workplace crimes. Armed assailants were more likely to use a firearm than a knife or other weapon such as rocks, clubs, bottles, or other objects (8% versus 6%, respectively).

Transportation workers were victimized on the job by offenders with a weapon at a percentage somewhat higher (32%) than any other occupational field....

Workplace violence victims were more likely to be victimized by a stranger than by someone they knew. In more than half of all workplace victimizations, a stranger was the perpetrator. About 1% of all workplace crime was committed by a current or former boyfriend, girlfriend, or spouse—an intimate—of the victim.

Workers in the mental health field and teachers were the only occupations more likely to be victimized by someone they knew than by a stranger. Law enforcement employees were victimized by a stranger more than any other occupation; about three-quarters of all law enforcement victimizations were committed by a stranger.

Specific to nomothetic data from homicide victims, Duhart (2001) also provides the following data (10):

Characteristics of victims of homicide in the workplace

Males accounted for four-fifths of all workplace homicide victims. Persons between ages 25 and 44 were the victims of more than half of all workplace homicides. Whites experienced more workplace homicides than blacks or persons of other races between 1993 and 1999.

Homicide victim/offender association

During 1993–99, 84% of all workplace homicides were committed by offenders who were strangers to the victim, primarily during robberies or attempted robberies. Coworkers or former coworkers committed a higher percentage of homicides in the workplace when compared to customers or clients (7% versus 4% of all workplace homicides, respectively). The number of work-related homicides committed by a husband over the 7-year period was 40 times the number committed by a wife (122 versus 3, respectively).

Personal acquaintances such as boyfriends or other acquaintances committed similar percentages of work-related homicides (1%).

Characteristics of incidents of workplace homicide

Most workplace homicides were committed with guns. Shooting accounted for more than 80% of all workplace homicides. Of all 4-hour periods in the day, the highest percentage of work-related homicides occurred between 8 p.m. and midnight, accounting for more than a fifth of all workplace homicides.

Further discussion of this issue in Matejkovic (2004) reveals that despite some reports to the contrary, homicide is not the leading cause of death in the workplace—unless you are a female (309):

> Homicides are the second leading cause of death in the workplace generally. According to the National Institute for Occupational Safety and Health (NIOSH), homicide is the leading cause of death for females in the workplace, accounting for 40% of all female workplace deaths. Twenty-five percent of female victims were assaulted by people known to them, and 16% of women workplace homicides are a result of domestic violence. In nearly two-thirds of workplace assaults, women were the victims.

This echoes Riley (2003), as cited at the beginning of the chapter.

All of these contextual victim statistics are interesting and even important for developing case theories and establishing risk or exposure factors in some instances. However, one must bear in mind that grouped and averaged victim data is also abstract. It does not represent particular victims that exist in the real world. It represents possibility, not actuality. This limitation is important to understand and must be incorporated into subsequent findings regarding case-specific interpretations.

Domestic Violence

As suggested in Chapter 9, domestic violence in its many incarnations is perhaps one of the greatest threats to public health in the United States. It can bruise, crush, and ultimately destroy the physical, mental, and economical well-being of any of its victims. It creates unsafe homes, unsafe communities, and unsafe work environments. None among these is immune. As explained in Tarr (2007, 376–377):

> The issue of domestic violence is relevant in the employment context because its consequences impact every aspect of the victim's life. Domestic violence can cause victims to be absent or late for work, interfere with their ability to perform on the job, result in termination of their employment, or force them to quit their jobs to escape the violence. Their abusers stalk them at work, make harassing phone calls to their place of employment, prevent them from going to work because of abuse or other interfering behavior, and call supervisors to get the victims in trouble. At the most extreme, victims of domestic violence are murdered by their abusive partners.

The victimologist may be confronted with cases where domestic abuse is suspected but not yet confirmed. There are circumstances highly indicative of domestic abuse, and some may be apparent to those in the workplace. Questions to ask coworkers include:

1. Does the victim report being threatened or injured by a domestic partner?
2. Does the victim show feelings of fear and social withdrawal?
3. Does the victim evidence bruises or physical complaints that have been the result of an assault?
4. Does the victim engage in intermittent crying or outbursts of anger while talking with a domestic partner at the workplace, either on the telephone or in person?
5. Does the victim suffer from frequent or prolonged periods of depression, irritability, anxiety, and apathetic withdrawal?
6. Does the victim suffer from a lack of concentration?
7. Does the victim suffer from increased absenteeism or reduced productivity?
8. Does the victim's spouse or partner make disruptive visits to the workplace?
9. Does the victim's spouse or partner call the workplace repeatedly to check up on him or her?
10. Does the victim's spouse or partner become hostile with or threaten to harm anyone at the workplace?

Given the persistence of these types of circumstances, domestic violence also creates particular challenges for employers with respect to employee safety and any related liability (Matejkovic 2004, 311–312):

> While workplace violence from any source is obviously a concern for employers, the issues presented when acts of domestic violence spill into the workplace are particularly thorny, as employers face exposure to liability claims based upon a variety of sources and theories. It is apparent that when domestic violence spills into the workplace, the victims include not only the individuals involved, but also the victim's employer, which must deal with the adverse publicity and often claims made by the individual victims, and too often innocent bystanders, including coworkers, who also may suffer injuries in any violent act.

What this means is that some employers may feel compelled to act in a way that protects their businesses and other employees at the expense of a domestic violence victim who brings danger to the doorstep. Kennedy (2005, 1777) provides a reasonable discussion of workplace violence in general as it relates to employer liability:

> Employers can sometimes find themselves liable in tort for those instances of workplace violence which were "substantially certain"

to befall their employees and where no preventive action was taken to protect these employees. Causes of action such as negligent hiring, negligent retention, negligent supervision, and negligent entrustment have been successfully brought against employers by injured employees who are not barred by workers compensation laws from bringing suit. To avoid such litigation, to prevent other financial losses, and to fulfill their moral duty to their employees, many employers are adopting "zero tolerance" policies toward aggressive behavior on the part of their employees. Security surveys are being conducted to identify threats to employee safety. Employee Assistance Programs are becoming responsive to victimization prevention needs, and company leaders are forming threat assessment teams to evaluate developing situations that may prove a threat to employee safety.

Of course, not every employer has the foresight or the economic means to respond proactively to workplace violence, let alone attend to the needs of specific employees.

Many employers see victims of domestic violence as a liability and act accordingly. In some cases, at-risk employees may simply be terminated. In others, where the employee enjoys protection from arbitrary termination, they may simply start building a file—actively soliciting complaints and documenting absences and errors. The smallest issue becomes another immovable stone as the employee-victim is walled off from the rest of the workplace until his or her termination becomes inevitable.

Even when the victim or employer does everything right, however, there remains the possibility of tragedy.

Case Example: Cindy Bischof

Consider the case of 43-year-old real estate broker Cindy Bischof, in Elmhurst, Illinois. She was shot to death in the parking lot of her workplace, Darwin Realty, by a former boyfriend. He then shot himself. As explained in Twohy and Ford (2008):

Cindy Bischof thought her breakup with a longtime boyfriend would go smoothly after he agreed to move out of her house. But Michael Giroux quickly turned hostile, writing up a plan to destroy her home and following through with it.

Terrified after Giroux, 60, spray-painted every wall and piece of furniture in her Arlington Heights home last

FIGURE 11.1

Cindy L. Bischof was a successful real estate agent and had won a number of awards for her work. She did everything she could to keep her coworkers safe by confronting the problem with her ex-boyfriend head on and following the law. He was, in the end, undeterred.

spring, the 43-year-old real estate broker moved swiftly to secure a protective order from a Cook County judge that prohibited him from contacting her.

When [Giroux] violated the order on two occasions, including an attempt to hang himself on her patio, she didn't hesitate to press charges that landed him in jail for two months followed by home confinement.

To relatives and prosecutors, it appeared that Bischof was taking all the necessary steps to stay safe and that the legal system was delivering protection.

But after Giroux was released from home confinement this month, he showed up at Bischof's office in Elmhurst armed with a .38-caliber revolver. When she tried to get into her car, he shot her repeatedly then turned the gun on himself....

A woman's risk of being seriously injured or killed by an intimate partner increases when she breaks off the relationship. In certain cases, a protective court order is not enough and the only viable option is for a woman to either enter a shelter or relocate, experts say....

Research has identified danger signs—such as suicide attempts and losing interest in work, both of which Giroux displayed—that point to an increased likelihood of murder....

But as Giroux demonstrated, some people are not deterred by aggressive prosecution....

Today, the Illinois Domestic Violence Act is seen as one of the strongest laws of its kind in the country, said Dawn Dalton, executive director of the Chicago Metropolitan Battered Women's Network. Still, victims and their advocates see flaws in the legal system. If someone violates an order of protection, the person is supposed to face legal consequences, in some cases jail.

But some police officers, prosecutors and judges can be dismissive of violations, allowing harassment, stalking and other abusive behavior to continue, said Jennifer Greene, director of legal advocacy at Family Rescue, an organization that helps victims of domestic abuse in Cook County.

That was not the case with Bischof, who secured a two-year order of protection against Giroux last June after he vandalized her house. After pleading guilty to vandalism, he was ordered to serve time in Cook County Jail and underwent a psychiatric evaluation.

When Bischof reported that he had called and threatened to kill her family during the 4th of July weekend, he was charged with violating the protection order. Police re-arrested him in early September after he showed up at Bischof's house and placed a rope around his neck in an apparent suicide attempt, records show.

The judge set bond at $75,000 and ordered Giroux to undergo another mental health evaluation.

He pleaded guilty in November to violating the order of protection and was sentenced to 63 days in jail followed by 60 days of home confinement and two years of intensive probation.

For several months, Bischof heard nothing from Giroux and thought the danger might have passed, said her mother, Barbara Bischof.

In a brief voice-mail message about 10 days before the slaying, he apologized for everything he had done. It seemed harmless, so Bischof didn't report it, her mother said.

But Giroux's behavior mirrored warning signs of a harasser bent on violence, according to advocates and legal authorities.

Studies of women killed by an intimate partner have identified common traits among the perpetrators. Among them: access to a gun, previous threat with a weapon, estrangement from the partner, stalking, forced sex, abuse during pregnancy, drug abuse and unemployment.

Giroux did not have a Firearm Owners Identification Card, which Illinois requires to buy guns. Elmhurst police say they are working with federal officials to determine how he got the pistol used to kill Bischof.

Giroux had financial troubles for years before he and Bischof started dating, and his fortunes seemed to decline during their three-year relationship, according to relatives and court records. Records show he was unemployed for at least part of the time and that he had declared bankruptcy in 2002.

"When individuals are unemployed or they start spiraling downward …then that's a huge, huge red flag," said Pam Paziotopoulos, a former head of the Cook County state's attorney's domestic violence division.

Quite different from the victim who stays with an abuser, enabling him to continue perpetuating abuse, Cindy Bischof actually confronted her ex-boyfriend's abuse and reported him to law enforcement when appropriate. She saw the danger, reported it, and tried to remove it from her life. Unfortunately, these actions along with other converging problems in his life caused him to fixate on her further and, ultimately, to seek her destruction along with his own.

IDIOGRAPHIC ANALYSIS

As explained in Chapter 3, **idiographic victim analysis** involves the study of the concrete: examining individual victims and their actual qualities. It focuses on specific cases and the unique traits or functioning of the individuals involved. In this section, we will discuss certain basic idiographic considerations with respect to workplace violence, and adduce illustrative examples as necessary.[2]

Targets

All offenders have particular victim or target criteria that satisfy their needs, no matter how general or specific. They may want to hit a thousand targets, or just one. They may want to destroy everything they hit, or inflict tactical damage. *Victim selection* refers to the process that is used by offenders to choose their intended victim or victims (Turvey 2008, 204). Depending on the tactical capabilities of the offender, this process may be passive or active.

Holmes and Holmes (2000) refer to this as *victim selectivity*. However, the term "selectivity" implies particular criteria that are actively sought by the offender. This describes only some offenders.

In some cases, as with Cindy Bischof, a particular victim will be the entire reason for the commission of an offense. In other cases, the victim can be a function of ease and opportunity—someone whom the offender can expediently acquire for his or her intended purposes. And in still other cases, the victim may be representative of a group. This all depends on the intent of the offender.

There are essentially three kinds of targets: primary, secondary, and collateral.

Primary Targets

A *primary target* is one that is of the greatest importance to the offender. It dictates the location and timing of any attack. Often, the offender will have planned out and intended to hit that victim at the risk of foregoing any or all other targets in the environment. In some cases, there will be more than one primary target.

In workplace violence cases, the primary target (victim) will be known to the offender; the connection between them will be personal. This remains true whether the primary target is a specific person, a specific cluster of persons, or the workplace itself.

---

[2]Law enforcement–oriented examples will be used more often than not in this chapter for two very specific reasons: first, law enforcement–related workplace violence is the most common, and therefore the most likely to be encountered by the forensic victimologist; and second, law enforcement investigators represent an overwhelming number of practicing victimologists.

Secondary Targets

A *secondary target* is one who is of lesser importance to the offender. It will not dictate the location and timing of an attack. However, it will be a conscious choice based on the availability within environmental and temporal constraints dictated by primary targets. Not all offenders will take the time to deliberate over the possibility of achieving secondary targets, and some offenders might have the intent but not the opportunity to acquire secondary targets.

In workplace violence cases, secondary targets will be representative of the primary target. Someone who is associated with them, immediately subordinate to them, or superior to them. Or something that they control or own. Instead of a supervisor, their secretary; instead of a coworker, their partner, friend, or intimate (if available); and instead of a person, their office, belongings, or vehicle.

Collateral Victims

A *collateral victim* is one who is attacked and injured unintentionally, because of his or her proximity to a primary or secondary target within a given environment. The victim's injury is completely uncalculated and incidental to the intended outcome. A collateral victim is in fact not a target. It is important to distinguish between secondary targets and collateral victims, the key difference being the intent of the offender.

In workplace violence cases, collateral victims will be hit because they are simply in the way. They are in the wrong place at the wrong time. The person who is hit by a bullet that comes through a wall; people killed in a fire set to damage a building; an explosion intended to blow up a person in a room that hits a gas main and takes out an entire city block.

Victim-Offender Relationship

In every case examined by a victimologist, the relationship between the victim and the offender should be established. However, before we dive in and commence sorting, let us take a moment and embrace the cautionary offered in Kennedy (2005, 1776):

> Because the circumstances and targets of workplace violence vary widely, so, too, will the motivations of various perpetrators. Due to the wide range of workplace violence incident types, no single etiological theory will generalize broadly enough to be universally applicable.

The importance of these words will become clear as we discuss specific examples subsequent to the typology.

According to Loveless (2001, 4), there are essentially four types of workplace violence offenders with respect to their relationship to the workplace itself:

Criminal Intent (e.g., stranger theft); *Customer/Client* or *Worker-on-Worker* (e.g., coworker, former employee); and the *Personal Relationship* (e.g., intimate, spouse, friend, or relative of an employee):

| *Criminal Intent (Type I):* The perpetrator has no legitimate relationship to the business or its employees, and is usually committing a crime in conjunction with the violence. These crimes can include robbery, shoplifting, and trespassing. The vast majority of workplace homicides (85%) fall into this category.

Customer/Client (Type II): The perpetrator has a legitimate relationship with the business and becomes violent while being served by the business. This category includes customers, clients, patients, students, inmates, and any other group for which the business provides services. It is believed that a large proportion of customer/client incidents occur in the health care industry, in settings such as nursing homes or psychiatric facilities; the victims are often patient caregivers. Police officers, prison staff, flight attendants, and teachers are some other examples of workers who may be exposed to this kind of workplace violence.

Worker-on-Worker (Type III): The perpetrator is an employee or past employee of the business who attacks or threatens another employee(s) or past employee(s) in the workplace. Worker-on-worker fatalities account for approximately 7% of all workplace violence homicides.

Personal Relationship (Type IV): The perpetrator usually does not have a relationship with the business but has a personal relationship with the intended victim. This category includes victims of domestic violence assaulted or threatened while at work.

There is the suggestion that these are discrete relationship types, with each useful as a broad descriptive category for a particular case. However, as with most nomothetic classification systems, this does not bear out in actual case-work. In application, these categories are oversimplified, and a single incident may contain more that one relationship, especially when multiple victims are involved.

To illustrate victim-offender relationships in an applied fashion, the following actual case examples are provided with discussion.

Case Example: Customer/Client and Worker-on-Worker

Consider the case of Michael Burgess, sheriff in Custer County, Oklahoma, since 1994. He surrendered to agents of the Oklahoma Bureau of Investigation in April of 2008, facing 35 felony charges, including multiple counts of rape, forcible oral sodomy, bribery by a public official, and perjury. As detailed in Schoetz (2008):

> The charges were announced by James Boring, a district attorney in Texas County, Okla., who took control of the Burgess investigation in May 2007 after prosecutors in Custer County cited a conflict of interest in the case and the state attorney general requested Boring's involvement.
>
> Information presented in court documents filed in Custer County District Court Wednesday signed by Boring and an agent for the Oklahoma State Bureau of Investigation lay out a pattern of alleged criminal behavior from 2005 to 2007. Burgess allegedly used his power as sheriff repeatedly to pressure a female employee, inmates and members of his county's drug court program to pleasure him in exchange for special treatment.
>
> Burgess offered his official resignation Wednesday, effective immediately. He was released on $50,000 bond under the condition that he has no direct or indirect contact with any of the prosecution's 33 witnesses....
>
> The documents paint a predatory profile of a sheriff who authorities say would force inmates under his supervision to perform oral, vaginal and anal sex in his office, his official sheriff's vehicle, local motels and hotels, a truck stop, and houses belonging to inmates and friends.
>
> The four women named in the court documents who were either inmates or members of the county's drug program all were promised some type of leniency or preferential treatment in return for their sexual favors.
>
> The alleged sexual liaisons took place between February 2006 and April 2007, according to court documents. One of the women even traveled with the sheriff to Oklahoma City in April 2006 to take part in a "legislative" initiative relating to drug court programs across the state.
>
> "During the night of their stay at the Biltmore Hotel, Sheriff [Burgess] directed and required that [the woman] stay with him at the hotel rather than go with other participants and their counselor for dinner," according to the probable cause affidavit for the sheriff's arrest. "Sheriff [Burgess] took [the woman] to his room at the Biltmore Hotel where he engaged in multiple acts of sexual intercourse with [the woman] during the night."
>
> On May 21, 2007, however, that same woman failed a drug test that was required as part of her release from jail. "When she failed the

drug screen, she disclosed that she had been having sex with Sheriff [Burgess] and that he had promised her that he would protect her and keep her from going back to jail," the documents stated.

In the hours after the woman told of her sexual history with the sheriff, authorities say Burgess contacted the woman's cousin, a female who was also part of the drug court program and asked her to remove any DNA evidence, such as a condom, from the woman's house that might incriminate him. Burgess allegedly promised to have her brother released from jail in exchange for helping cover up the sexual tryst. It was the statement by the woman who failed the drug test that triggered the state's involvement.

Another allegation involves a former sheriff's office employee who accused Burgess of inappropriately touching her at a restaurant, in a courtroom and while she tried on her sheriff's office uniform.

A federal lawsuit was filed in October after Boring's investigation began. In the suit, 12 former inmates alleged that the sheriff's employees had them engage in wet T-shirt contests and offered cigarettes to women who exposed their breasts.

Burgess, a former police officer and state government investigator, was appointed sheriff in 1994 when his predecessor died. He was elected to the position in 1996 and re-elected in 2000 and 2004....

The daily population at Custer County Detention and Law Enforcement Center is about 80 inmates, according the sheriff's office Web site. The sheriff oversaw a staff that included an undersheriff, 10 deputies, 11 jailors, seven dispatchers and an administrative assistant.

If true, the allegations in this case represent workplace violence of a sexual nature by the sheriff towards a coworker (Type III) who is also a subordinate. This because he is alleged to have touched her inappropriately on multiple occasions in work-related contexts, and because he is her supervisor. There is also very little argument to be made that unwanted sexual contact is not also coercive in the context provided.

This case reveals that perhaps special subcategories of the Type III relationship are warranted, given that when victim and offender are not equals at work this can alter any subsequent relationship dynamic: Type IIIa, Supervisor to Subordinate; Type IIIb, Subordinate to Supervisor; and Type IIIc, Workplace Neutrals. Any descriptors will do, so long as the power relationship is made clear, especially in cases involving sexual violence.

This case also represents a *Customer/Client (Type II)* relationship. There can be no question that, if true, these allegations amount to numerous instances of coerced sex acts and sexual performance inflicted against prisoners in the sheriff's custody. The citizens within that sheriff's jurisdiction are his "customers," as they pay for his services, even when they are being detained by lawful arrest.

Again, this relationship type as defined does not make the power structure or relationship of victim and offender all that clear when applied to a specific case. In fact it seems to assume that the violence is one way—originating from the client or customer. As such, special subcategories of the Type II relationship are warranted to delineate the origin of the violence, and whether or not the "client" is actually a ward of some kind.

Case Example: Customer/Client, Worker-on-Worker, and Possible Criminal Intent

The case of police officer Jay Dailey in Duluth, Georgia, brings attention to the "always armed; always on-duty" policy that is a common law enforcement practice in the United States—requiring off-duty officers to carry their weapons. It makes every place that police officers goes in the community, whether on duty or off, an extension of their workplace.

The facts in the case are not generally disputed, however, some of the circumstances are still being investigated as of this writing. In February of 2008, Officer Dailey assaulted a female motorist and damaged her vehicle after feigning injury to gain her trust, then he opened fire on a responding officer. The known facts are provided in Simmons (2008):

> Fulton officer Paul Phillips returned only four rounds, said Gwinnett County police Detective Shelly Millsap, who testified in a preliminary hearing.
>
> The shootout left Dailey and Phillips wounded on a two-lane road and culminated a bizarre series of events in the small town of Sugar Hill. Dailey's memory appeared disjointed when detectives questioned him at the hospital, Millsap said. Dailey allegedly admitted he had been drinking, remembered wrecking his car and thought he recalled shooting a police officer. "He made a motion as if pulling a trigger and said his finger was tired," Millsap said.
>
> When he was arrested, Dailey had a handgun tucked into the rear of his waistband and another stashed in his front pocket.
>
> Detectives eventually pieced together what happened that day after talking to the victims and witnesses. Millsap, the only witness at the preliminary hearing, gave this account of the shootout on Level Creek Road:
>
> Dailey was off-duty when he flagged down a female motorist, who said she'd never met him before. He slumped over and grabbed his stomach,

claiming he was injured. The officer wore jeans, a green knit shirt and a bulletproof vest and flashed a police badge.

When the woman started to call 911 on her cell phone, Dailey grew agitated and sprayed her with pepper spray. He reached through the car window, struggled with her over the phone and threatened to kill her, saying "you're ruining my life now."

Dailey is also accused of pointing a gun at two passing motorists. One of the motorists continued down the street and signaled to Phillips, a Fulton officer who was off-duty and driving home from a part-time job. Phillips wore a uniform and drove a marked patrol car.

When Philips got out of the car, Dailey allegedly drew his gun. Phillips raised his hand to say "hold on" and was shot by Dailey.

After the two officers exchanged gunfire, Phillips retreated to his car for cover. Dailey came around to the driver's side and fired several more shots at Phillips, two of which pierced the windshield of the patrol car. Phillips told detectives that Dailey was still pulling the trigger after he ran out of bullets. Other police arrived and arrested Dailey.

Both officers were injured. Phillips, 37, is still recovering from a gunshot wound to the arm at Gwinnett Medical Center. Dailey was shot in the hand and wore a bandage in court on Tuesday. Dailey appeared fidgety and wiped away tears at several times during the testimony. . . .

Duluth police spokesman Maj. Don Woodruff said Dailey was fired last week. He has until Feb. 15 to appeal.

As of this writing, Dailey is waiting to stand trial on charges related to this incident.

In this case, there are multiple attacks on multiple victims with multiple weapons by a single and admittedly intoxicated police officer.

At the outset, this case may involve a *Criminal Intent (Type I)* relationship. In order to determine this, we need to know precisely what officer Dailey intended to accomplish by stopping the female motorist. We do know that it resulted in her being assaulted with pepper spray, and her car window was broken after his arm got stuck in it. What we do not know is why he wrecked his own car, the injuries he sustained prior to the shooting, and whether there were any influences on his state of mind other than alcohol. Did he intend to steal or "commandeer" her vehicle? Did he intend to sexually assault her? Was his request for help legitimate in his mind at the time? These are all possibilities, some of which are consistent with a criminal-intent relationship. Also, and to be very clear, the possibility of this being a legitimate car-stop gone wrong is removed by the fact that Dailey did not have a vehicle of his own, was not on duty, and opened fire on a fellow officer.

FIGURE 11.2
The scene of the shooting between officers Jay Dailey and Paul Phillips after responders arrived. Officer Phillip's marked vehicle is on the right, door still open.

FIGURE 11.3
Former Duluth police officer Jay Dailey sits in court, still wearing bandages over an injured hand. He is seated next to his attorney, Theresa Hood.

This case certainly involves a *Customer/Client (Type II)* relationship, as the citizen who was attacked is a client of law enforcement. Again, a mechanism for identifying the power disparity here is needed, as this relationship is not on par with someone buying a pack of cigarettes and being pepper sprayed by the clerk.

This case also certainly involves a *Worker-on-Worker (Type III)* relationship, as one of the victims was also employed as a police officer, with equitable firepower and authority, although they worked for different agencies and had no prior relationship.

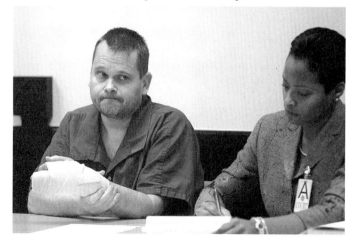

MOTIVATIONAL EVENTS AND CIRCUMSTANCES

A great deal has been written about the particular motivations of individuals who have perpetrated acts of workplace violence—much of it sensational, generalized, and wrong. Moreover, what is referred to as a motivation is often a description of the progression of events and circumstances that led to violence. An example would be stating that a given employee was fired, or in a dispute with his supervisor, and then "went postal"—arriving at work with a firearm and shooting everyone who showed up, starting with the supervisor. The actual motive in such a case would be anger or revenge.

As explained in Petherick and Turvey (2008, 276), *motive* is "the emotional, psychological, and material needs that impel and are satisfied by behavior," while *intent* is "the specific aim that guides behavior." The available motives for workplace violence are no different than for any other type of violence. They include the service of profit, anger, power, and sadism, with no bright yellow line between them.

Also, bear in mind that motive is relative. What might enrage one person in his or her set of personal circumstances (and toxicology) might just as easily be ignored by someone else; what precisely constitutes a lot of money (an amount worth killing or stealing for), is often a function of individual wealth; and what is unacceptable violent behavior in one employment setting is par for the course in another.

Case Example: In Custody Assault, Anger Motivated

As explained in Turvey (2008, 285), *anger-retaliatory* motives are "evidence by crime scene behaviors that indicate a great deal of rage, either toward a specific person, group, institution, or a symbol of either. These types of behaviors are commonly evidenced in stranger-to-stranger sexual assaults, domestic homicides, work-related homicides, and cases involving political or religious terrorists."

Consider the 2007 case of a former police officer, now a part-time jail officer, in Homer, Alaska. A prisoner that was in the process of being taken into custody spat in his face at the police station while a state trooper was attempting to remove the prisoner's handcuffs. The jail officer responded by choking the still cuffed prisoner with his bare hands and ramming him into the wall. The state trooper was knocked to the ground. The details, taken directly from the Alaska Bureau of Investigation's report on the incident, are provided in Armstrong (2008):

> During processing of a prisoner arrested last May, an Alaska State Trooper and two Homer Police officers had to separate a jail guard from the prisoner, an Alaska State Trooper investigator wrote in a report released last week by the Alaska Department of Public Safety. The trooper report said the guard choked the prisoner while he was being booked on a charge of disorderly conduct and resisting arrest at the Homer Jail.

> Homer Police Chief Mark Robl confirmed the incident happened, but, citing department policy, declined to identify the jail officer or the suspect or say if any disciplinary action was taken against the jailer.

The city of Homer conducted its own internal investigation and determined the jailer violated the Homer Police Use of Force Policy. Serious disciplinary action was taken against the jailer, said Homer City Manager Walt Wrede, but he did not specify the action....

Investigator Mark Granda of the Alaska Bureau of Investigations, the author of the report, forwarded the case to the Alaska Office of Special Prosecutions and Appeals for review of a charge of assault in the third degree, a class C felony. No charges were returned against the guard. Robl said the jail officer still works as a guard for Homer Police.

The trooper report said the city suspended the jailer the night of the incident and while troopers did their investigation.

The incident came to the attention of the Homer News when an anonymous caller last month reported the alleged assault. The Department of Public Safety provided the Homer News with a redacted copy of its report after the paper filed an Open Records Request. The report identifies Granda, Trooper Derek Loop, the arresting officer, and Robl, but no other parties were named.

In the trooper report, Robl describes the jail guard as a former Homer Police officer with 22 years experience who retired in 1999. The officer has been working as a part-time jail guard since 2007....

Based on interviews with the trooper who arrested the suspect, the suspect, another trooper at the jail, a dispatcher, a Homer Police officer, a police sergeant and the jail officer, ABI Investigator Granda gives this account:

At about 12:55 a.m. on May 28, Trooper Derek Loop took an Anchor Point man to the Homer Jail after arresting him for disorderly conduct and resisting arrest. The report identified Loop as the arresting officer, but did not name other police or troopers involved. Troopers arrested the man while investigating a 911 call and hang up made from his Anchor Point home. Troopers found no emergency, but when the man became belligerent, they arrested him.

The disorderly conduct charge was later dismissed, and the Anchor Point man pleaded no contest to resisting arrest and served 10 days in jail.

Loop told Granda he dropped off the suspect in the police booking room and left the room. While he stood in the hallway outside the booking room, a dispatcher on duty told him to get into the booking room. Loop went into the room and saw the jailer with both hands around the suspect's neck. He said the suspect's neck and face were turning red. Loop said the suspect blew and spat in the jailer's face, and the jailer said, "Nobody does that to me."

A police officer told Granda a similar story. He said the jailer had both arms straightened out and pushed against the suspect's throat. He said the suspect was still handcuffed. He said this was the first time he saw the jailer act like that. After thinking about the incident, he said he felt the jailer's use of force was inappropriate.

Another trooper at the jail said he had just finished booking another person for a driving under the influence charge. He heard from the jailer that Loop was bringing in a suspect who would take several people to handle. The trooper recognized the suspect from earlier arrests for domestic violence assault, resisting arrest and eluding police. He helped the jailer book the suspect.

The trooper said the suspect mouthed off when he was brought into the booking area. He said the jailer took off the right handcuff, but couldn't get the left handcuff off because of a piece of metal stuck in the keyhole. The trooper used a Leatherman tool to remove the metal. He was still working on the handcuff when the jailer grabbed the suspect's neck with both hands and shoved him against the wall. The jailer, the trooper and the suspect were all standing.

The trooper said he either stepped away or was pushed, and then yelled to the jailer, "Let him go, let him go." He said the suspect did not fight back, that he turned a dark purple-blue color, made a raspy sound and his tongue stuck out of his mouth. The suspect was put on a bench and handcuffed to a rail on the wall above it.

The trooper later called the Kenai District Attorney's office about the incident and was advised to report the incident to his supervisor.

A police officer at the station that night came into the booking room after the alleged assault. He told Granda he called a trooper sergeant about the incident.

Granda's report noted the booking room had videotape cameras, but no one had put a tape in the camera and recorded the incident. Police and troopers also did not have audio tape recorders running during the incident, although they turned on the recorders after the incident.

In an interview with Granda, the jailer said he did not feel he did anything wrong. He said when the trooper had trouble with the left handcuff, he kept a hold on the handcuffs so the suspect wouldn't use the handcuffs as a weapon. The suspect tried to pull his hand away from the jailer. When the suspect blew in his face, the jailer said he pushed him away at arm's length. After the suspect spat on him, the jailer said he reached up with his left hand to hold the suspect's neck and pushed him against the wall.

Robl told Granda Homer has a Use of Force policy that prohibits choke holds. Robl said when the jailer started working, he read the police department's jail and department policy manuals and signed a statement that he read the jail policy. Robl said the jailer was supposed to have sent Robl an e-mail saying he'd reviewed the department policy manual, but Robl could not find a copy of that e-mail.

The jailer told Granda he had reviewed the police department's policy and jail policy manual. He said he knows choke holds are not allowed, but said he did not do a choke hold on the suspect. The jailer defined a choke hold as getting behind the suspect and putting his neck between your arm and chest. The jailer told Granda he believed the suspect assaulted him and his use of force was justified.

The jailer told Granda he used force against the suspect because he spat in his face. "My intent was not to be spit on again and to make sure he didn't get loose," the jailer told Granda.

In this case the assault of the suspect in custody by the jail officer was viewed by all as a violation of the Homer Police Department's use of force policies. However, the incident did not come to light until reported by a witness from an outside agency. Additionally, the incident details and suspect information were withheld from the public by the Homer Police Department, to say nothing of the lack of an arrest. This is precisely the opposite of what happens when regular citizens admit to the commission of a crime.

It should also be noted that the jail officer was not terminated for committing the prisoner assault when officers throughout Alaska have been fired for precisely the same conduct, and even far less. The Homer Police Department has consequently exposed itself to incredible liability with respect to the foreseeable future incidents. They have also sent a clear message to the community that it will work hard to protect its own, and to keep police crime and misconduct in house. There are fewer practices more corrosive to the public's trust of law enforcement.

With respect to motive, the jail officer felt he had been disrespected and responded to a nonlethal gesture with potentially lethal force. Such context, intent, and subsequent over-the-top responses are the very essence of anger-retaliatory behavior. The jail officer became instantly enraged by the suspect's actions, wanted to teach him a lesson, and did.

Case Example: Debt, Divorce, and Termination, Profit and Anger Motivated

As explained in Petherick and Turvey (2008, 289), *profit* motives are "those that service material or personal gain. These can be found in all types of homicides, robberies, burglaries, muggings, arsons, bombings, kidnappings, and most forms of white-collar crime, to name just a few. Profit-motivated behaviors are the exceptions that prove the rule . . . as they do not necessarily satisfy psychological or emotional needs (unless material gain is associated with a psychological need or even compulsion)."

Consider the 2007 case of 38-year-old Anthony LaCalamita, an auditor with Gordon Advisers PC, an accounting firm in Troy, Michigan. In the space of a month, all of his problems converged and his life essentially collapsed. This culminated in a workplace shooting incident that took the life of one coworker and wounded two others. As explained in Snell (2007):

> [LaCalamita] had been losing money in his real estate investments. Three weeks ago, he and his wife separated. Last week, he was fired from his job as an auditor at a Troy accounting firm.
>
> On Monday morning, according to police and witnesses, LaCalamita burst into the offices of his former employer and opened fire with a shotgun, killing one employee and wounding two others.
>
> By Monday night, he was in the custody of the Troy Police Department.
>
> Troubles for LaCalamita, 38, started mounting in 2006 when he began unloading properties at a loss in one of the country's worst housing markets. In one transaction, he sold a Plymouth home in October for $100,000 less than he owed on the mortgage, property records show.
>
> He also owed more than $100,000 on two loans obtained last year for a multi-unit building in Detroit.
>
> The deals were partially offset in February 2006 when he sold a Garden City home for $32,000 more than the amount he paid a year earlier, property records show. . . . The real estate losses followed a few profitable investments. From 2004 to 2005, LaCalamita made about $140,000 profit selling three homes in Livonia and Canton Township.
>
> Police: Couple separated
>
> Three weeks ago, LaCalamita and wife Michele separated, police said.
>
> He moved to Troy into the Kirts Village apartments, a two-story brick building with mustard-colored siding located east of Crooks, where police tape blocked the entrance Monday night as officers combed for

clues. His wife apparently is living in Novi's Whispering Meadows subdivision, in a $263,000 tan-brick home with manicured hedges purchased a year ago.

According to testimony from one of the victims, LaCalamita was fired for not putting in the required time and effort at his job. After his termination, he went to a shooting range for practice, and then purchased a shotgun, as detailed in Brasier (2008):

> Three days before he went on a shooting spree at the Troy office building where he had been fired, Anthony LaCalamita went target practicing at a local gun range, using a Remington shotgun, the kind of gun he then bought and used to shoot three of his former colleagues.

> "He was a normal customer, a nice guy, nothing out of the ordinary," said Roy Jihad, manager of Target Sports, a Royal Oak gun shop and range told jurors in the second day of LaCalamita's murder trial. LaCalamita arrived at the gun shop on April 6, 2007, the morning after he was fired from Gordon Advisers PC, asking to buy a gun.

> He paid $48 for a half hour of target practice in the range at the back of the building, located on Woodward, then purchased a Remington shot gun, and four boxes of ammunition. He also apparently lied on the application to purchase the gun, saying he had never been committed to a mental hospital. Records show he was twice admitted after suicide attempts.

On the day of the shooting, LaCalamita appeared to have specific targets in mind when he entered his former place of employment. As explained in Aguilar (2007):

> Ninety minutes after reporting to work, Jean Larson heard what turned out to be deadly gunfire inside her office building—then "all hell broke loose."

> Police say Anthony LaCalamita III, an accounting firm employee fired from his job last week, returned Monday to the building where he previously worked and shot three people, killing one. Two of the victims were apparently targeted, police said.

> "We heard pop, pop, pop," smelled gunpowder and heard coworkers yelling, said Larson, 48, a staff accountant for G&C, a subsidiary of Gordon Advisors. "I heard one employee screaming, 'He's got a gun. He's got a gun.' ... It was a panic. No one knew what to do. No one knew where to go."

> The gunman then left the office complex and headed north, where he was spotted hours later by a motorist 50 miles north of Detroit. He was taken into custody after leading officers on a 30-mile highway chase that reached speeds up to 120 mph.

LaCalamita, 38, said nothing after officers surrounded him, Genesee County Sheriff Robert J. Pickell said. Officers subdued him and found a 12-gauge pump-action shotgun and three live shells in the vehicle, the sheriff said.

Madeline Kafoury, 63, was killed, the company said.

LaCalamita was being held on charges of fleeing and eluding police. Police investigators met Tuesday with Oakland County prosecutors to decide charges in the shootings, and LaCalamita was to be arraigned Wednesday, Troy Police Lt. Gerry Scherlinck said....

"We are especially devastated by the death of Madeline Kafoury and our hearts go out to her family. Maddie was revered by clients, employees and owners alike," the statement said. Larson said Kafoury was well-known and well-liked. She said Kafoury retired last year after tax season ended, but returned part-time this year after her successor quit.

Scherlinck identified the other victims as a 47-year-old man and a 48-year-old man. He said the men were in management positions, and the gunman may have also been seeking another man who wasn't at the office at the time. "It appears that he was especially targeting those two males," Scherlinck said.

Frank DeArmas, whose wife works part-time in the office, said two partners in the firm, Paul Riva, 47, of Sterling Heights, and Alan Steinberg, 48, of Bruce Township, were still being treated Tuesday at a local hospital....

Witnesses told police that when the gunman walked into the office on the building's second floor around 10 a.m. Monday, he looked as if he was trying to hide something, Craft said.

Police couldn't say how many shots were fired.

After briefly assembling in the employee lunchroom, some employees opted to hole up inside individual offices. Larson joined two female coworkers, barricading the locked door with chairs, turning off the lights and silencing their cell phones.

Beneath a desk, the three curled up and kept quiet. "I was just so scared," Larson said. "I just kept thinking, 'this can't be happening.'"

In this case, there is not one specific event or circumstance that can be considered the sole reason for the shootings. Certainly LaCalamita externalized more blame to his supervisors, but without the other combined financial and personal losses, his employment might not have been an issue. Add to these proximate circumstances the pathological debt and mental health issues related to prior suicide attempts and the tipping point was apparently reached. Given the high-speed chase that followed the shooting, one is left to wonder where LaCalamita was headed and how much more planning was actually involved—if any.

As of this writing, the trial of Anthony LaCalamita continues, although the question of guilt is not an issue.

FIGURE 11.4
Anthony LaCalamita, 38, is arrested and given a gun shot residue test after eluding police on the day of the shooting.

FIGURE 11.5
A shackled Anthony LaCalamita hangs his head as a sheriff's deputy in court assists him.

SUMMARY

Workplace violence takes many forms, affecting employees and employers alike. However, some professions are more susceptible than others. Moreover, the power dynamics between individuals involved are not always equitable. This needs to be investigated and established in every case.

It would be a mistake to conclude that there is one lens (e.g., typology, classification system) through which to view a particular case involving workplace violence. This type of violence is characterized by the same behaviors and motivations evident in other forms of violent crime—because it involves most of them—therefore, one approach won't cover it.

The greatest mistake that a victimologist can make when analyzing these kinds of cases is to apply nomothetic workplace victim research as a conclusive absolute when it is in fact an abstract theory. Each offender chooses his or her own targets. Each offender incurs his or her own collaterals. Each offender has his or her own motivations and underlying circumstances. It is the job of the forensic victimologist to investigate these and render them out.

Questions

1. True or False: Homicide is the second leading cause of death, accounting for one-sixth of all occupational fatalities.
2. How is nomothetic research useful in developing forensic victimologies?
3. What is the occupation most at risk of violent crime?
4. What are three of the questions that should be asked of coworkers to determine if domestic violence is occurring in the life of an employee?
5. Explain the difference between motive and intent.

REFERENCES

Aguilar, D. "Police: 'Purpose' behind Mich. office shooting" USA Today, April 10, 2007; http://www.usatoday.com/news/nation/2007-04-10-office-shooting_N.htm.

Armstrong, M. 2008. "Homer jail guard investigated: Jailer choked suspect, report says; no charges filed." *Homer News*, April 24. http://www.homernews.com/stories/042408/news_1_003.shtml.

Brasier, L.L. 2008. "LaCalamita practiced at gun range before rampage, owner testifies." *Detroit Free Press*, April 22. http://www.freep.com/apps/pbcs.dll/article?AID=/20080422/NEWS03/80422041/1005/news.

Duhart, D. 2001. "Violence in the Workplace, 1993–99." *Bureau of Justice Statistics*, Special Report, NCJ 190076, December. Washington, DC.

Holmes, R., and S. Holmes. 2000. *Mass Murder in the United States*. Upper Saddle River, NJ: Prentice Hall.

Kennedy, D. 2005. "Workplace Violence." In *Encyclopedia of Criminology*, Vol. III, edited by J. Miller and R. Wright, 1775–1777. New York: Routledge.

Loveless, L. 2001. "Workplace Violence: A Report to the Nation." Injury Prevention Research Center, the University of Iowa, February. Iowa City, IA. http://www.public-health.uiowa.edu/IPRC/NATION.pdf.

Matejkovic, J. 2004. "Which Suit Would You Like? The Employer's Dilemma in Dealing with Domestic Violence." *Capital University Law Review* 33, Winter: 309–346.

OSHA. 2002. "Workplace Violence: OSHA Fact Sheet." Washington, DC: U.S. Department of Labor, Occupational Safety and Health Administration.

Petherick, W.A. 2006. *Serial Crime: Theoretical and Practical Issues in Behavioral Profiling*, Boston: Academic Press.

Petherick, W., and B. Turvey. 2008. "Victimology." In *Criminal Profiling: An Introduction to Behavioral Evidence Analysis*, 3rd ed., edited by B. Turvey. San Diego: Elsevier Science.

———. 2008. "Criminal motivation." In *Criminal Profiling: An Introduction to Behavioral Evidence Analysis*, 3rd ed., edited by B. Turvey. San Diego: Elsevier Science.

Riley, K. 2003. "Employer TROs Are All the Rage: A New Approach to Workplace Violence." *Nevada Law Journal* 4, Fall: 1–34.

Schoetz, D. 2008. "Sheriff embroiled in inmate sex scandal." *ABCNews.com*, April 18. http://abcnews.go.com/print?id=4674575.

Simmons, A. 2008. "Duluth cop admits drinking before shooting another cop." *The Atlanta Journal-Constitution*, February 12. http://www.ajc.com/metro/content/metro/gwinnett/stories/2008/02/12/dailey_0213.html.

Snell, R. 2007. "How auditor's life unraveled." *The Detroit News*, April 10. http://www.detnews.com/apps/pbcs.dll/article?AID=/20070410/METRO/704100359.

Tarr, N. 2007. "Employment and Economic Security for Victims of Domestic Abuse." *Southern California Review of Law and Social Justice* 16, Spring: 371–427.

Turvey, B. 2008. *Criminal Profiling: An Introduction to Behavioral Evidence Analysis*, 3rd ed. Boston: Elsevier Science.

Twohey, M., and L. Ford. 2008. "The law didn't save her." *Chicago Tribune*, March 16. www.chicagotribune.com/news/chi-domestic-violence_bd16mar16,0,6195124.story.

CHAPTER 12

School Shootings

Wayne Petherick and Brent E. Turvey

KEY TERMS

- *Collateral victims:* those who are attacked and injured unintentionally because of their proximity to a primary or secondary target within a given environment.
- *Familial problems:* problems that might expose a student to violent behavior or cause him or her to act violently, such as exposure to or suffering as a victim of family violence.
- *Internal problems:* problems that might expose a student to violent behavior or cause them to act violently, such as chemical, biological, or psychological problems.
- *Peer relationship problems:* problems that might expose students to violent behavior or cause them to act violently, such as lack of parental guidance, support, and attachment, and a subsequent inability to resist or cope with peers.
- *Primary targets:* those that are of greatest importance to the offender; they dictate the location and timing of the attack.
- *School shootings:* a particular form of workplace violence that occurs when anyone enters a campus and begins firing a weapon, such as a rifle, shotgun, or handgun.
- *Secondary targets:* those that are of lesser importance to the offender; they will not dictate the location and timing of an attack.
- *Social and environmental factors:* those that might expose a student to violent behavior or cause him or her to act violently, such as routine exposure to violence as a component of fantasy or entertainment.

CONTENTS

As with any attack that occurs at an educational facility—to include grade schools, colleges, and universities—*school shootings* are a particular form of workplace violence. The relationships are fairly straightforward in this regard. Instructors, administrators, and support staff are employed and work on site, and students are the "clients." Violent attacks may occur between or within any of these groups or their relationships.[1]

A *school shooting* occurs when anyone enters a campus and begins firing a weapon, such as a rifle, shotgun, or handgun. The specific target is irrelevant to this definition. Only the location and the use of a firearm are relevent. There is no one profile to describe the school shooter, no checklist of red flags that will predict his or her behavior, and no preferred victim type—though this is exactly what many nomothetically derived profiles, checklists, and victimologies would have us believe.

The goals of this chapter are to dispel any myths regarding school shootings perpetuated by sensational media coverage of such incidents, and to provide forensic victimologists with the terminology and theoretical lenses through which to perceive school shootings more objectively.

NOMOTHETICALLY SPEAKING: THE AGGREGATE

There is wide agreement amongst researchers that no consistent school shooter profile exists. However, according to one study, there are some interesting themes that emerge in such cases, if one only considers incidents with student offenders. As described in Angel (2001, 486–487):

> All of these cases involved students bringing firearms to their schools and killing and wounding multiple victims. I will refer to these as "the school shooter cases." All the multiple shot, multiple victim school shooters have been white male adolescents who went to school with firearms and the intent to kill, and then killed. In a shockingly large percentage of these cases, they killed or wounded girls that they claimed to have "loved." Girls they harassed and stalked. Girls they believed had rejected them. Girls they killed in juvenile separation attacks.
>
> The pattern to all of the school shooter cases is that the killers were white boys who saw themselves as rejected by a girl or woman and/ or who had their "manhood" threatened by bullying and, often, by being called gay. They all had access to firearms—rifles, shot guns, and

---

[1]Chapter 11 noted that university lecturers are among the lowest risk groups for workplace violence; however, despite the infrequency of their being victims, such incidents do exist and need to be discussed.

pistols. All of the school shooters left clear indicators that they were about to commit mass violence. An extremely high number of them attempted, threatened, or actually committed suicide or died during or after their attacks.

This research was not as directed towards illuminating the characteristics of school shooter attacks by students as it was on finding a relationship between violence and gender stereotypes—which it did. It also draws deeply from the well of school shooter archetypes, namely, the lovelorn and bullied white male adolescent. This is not to say that this isn't a persistent theme, but rather that the weakness of any generalization is that it tends to be a generalization.

The findings reported in Vossekuil et al. (2002), however, are more detailed. This study was conducted by the U.S. Secret Service in conjunction with the Department of Education. Researchers (8) "identified 37 incidents of targeted school violence involving 41 attackers that occurred in the United States from 1974, the year in which the earliest incident identified took place, through June 2000, when data collection for the study was completed."

Again, a specific profile did not emerge in this study. Tendencies surfaced; predispositions became evident. However, the only concrete and universal trait shared by school shooters in the study is the fact that 100% of them were male. With respect to incident characteristics, they found that (15–16):

> In almost three-quarters of the incidents, the attacker killed one or more students, faculty or others at the school (73 percent, n = 2716). In the remaining incidents, the attackers used a weapon to injure at least one person at school (24 percent, n = 9). In one incident, a student killed his family and then held his class hostage with a weapon.

- More than one-half of the attacks occurred during the school day (59 percent, n = 22), with fewer occurring before school (22 percent, n = 8) or after school (16 percent, n = 6).
- Almost all of the attackers were current students at the school where they carried out their attacks (95 percent, n = 39). Only two attackers were former students of the school where they carried out their attacks at the time of those attacks (5 percent, n = 2).
- All of the incidents of targeted school violence examined in the Safe School Initiative were committed by boys or young men (100 percent, n = 41).
- In most of the incidents, the attackers carried out the attack alone (81 percent, n = 30). In four of the incidents, the attacker engaged in the attack on his own but had assistance in planning the attack (11 percent, n = 4). In three incidents, two or more attackers carried out the attack together (8 percent, n = 3).

- Most attackers used some type of gun as their primary weapon, with over half of the attackers using handguns (61 percent, n = 25), and nearly half of them using rifles or shotguns (49 percent, n = 20). [FN18] Three-quarters of the attackers used only one weapon (76 percent, n = 31) to harm their victims, although almost half of the attackers had more than one weapon with them at the time of the attack (46 percent, n = 19).

With respect to victim and targeting characteristics, Vossekuil et al. found that planning and forethought were typical (16):

> Perpetrators of incidents of targeted school violence chose a range of targets for their attacks, including fellow students, faculty and staff, and the school itself. These incidents were usually planned in advance and for most part included intent to harm a specific, preselected target, whether or not the attacker's execution of the incident, in fact, resulted in harm to the target ....

- In over half of the incidents (54 percent, n = 22), the attacker had selected at least one school administrator, faculty member or staff member as a target. Students were chosen as targets in fewer than half of the incidents (41 percent, n = 15).
- In nearly half of the incidents, the attackers were known to have chosen more than one target prior to their attack (44 percent, n = 16).
- Most attackers had a grievance against at least one of their targets prior to the attack (73 percent, n = 30).
- In almost half of the incidents (46 percent, n = 17), individuals who were targeted prior to the attack also became victims (i.e., individuals actually harmed in the attack). However, other individuals at the school, who were not identified as original targets of the attack, were injured or killed as well.

> Among these non-targeted individuals, over half were other students (57 percent, n = 21) and over one-third (39 percent, n = 16) were school administrators, faculty or staff.

Ultimately, Vossekuil et al. rendered 10 key findings from their study that beg further investigation and research, most of which will frontload any effort with an overwhelming sense of helplessness and despair (31):

> The 10 key findings that the authors believe may have implications for the development of strategies to address the problem of targeted school violence are as follows:

- Incidents of targeted violence at school rarely are sudden, impulsive acts.
- Prior to most incidents, other people knew about the attacker's idea and/or plan to attack.

- Most attackers did not threaten their targets directly prior to advancing the attack.
- There is no accurate or useful profile of students who engaged in targeted school violence.
- Most attackers engaged in some behavior prior to the incident that caused others concern or indicated a need for help.
- Most attackers had difficulty coping with significant losses or personal failures. Moreover, many had considered or attempted suicide.
- Many attackers felt bullied, persecuted, or injured by others prior to the attack.
- Most attackers had access to and had used weapons prior to the attack.
- In many cases, other students were involved in some capacity.
- Despite prompt law enforcement responses, most shooting incidents were stopped by means other than law enforcement intervention.

In line with the above research of Vossekuil et al., a number of checklists are available for the purpose of identifying potential school shooters. They are essentially an aggregate of previous high-profile incidents, offering a snapshot of common characteristics. Interestingly, most also identify the problem with the predictive validity of the checklist, suggest it is a starting point only. This is a caution that we wholly endorse. Consider the following from the National School Safety Center (1998):

> The National School Safety Center offers the following checklist derived from tracking school-associated violent deaths in the United States from July 1992 to the present.... After studying common characteristics of youngsters who have caused such deaths, NSSC has identified the following behaviors, which could indicate a youth's potential for harming him/herself or others.
>
> Accounts of these tragic incidents repeatedly indicate that in most cases, a troubled youth has demonstrated or has talked to others about problems with bullying and feelings of isolation, anger, depression and frustration. While there is no foolproof system for identifying potentially dangerous students who may harm themselves and/or others, this checklist provides a starting point.
>
> These characteristics should serve to alert school administrators, teachers and support staff to address needs of troubled students through meetings with parents, provision of school counseling, guidance and mentoring services, as well as referrals to appropriate community health/social services and law enforcement personnel. Further, such behavior should also provide an early warning signal that

safe school plans and crisis prevention/intervention procedures must be in place to protect the health and safety of all school students and staff members so that schools remain safe havens for learning.

- Has a history of tantrums and uncontrollable angry outbursts.
- Characteristically resorts to name calling, cursing or abusive language.
- Habitually makes violent threats when angry.
- Has previously brought a weapon to school.
- Has a background of serious disciplinary problems at school and in the community.
- Has a background of drug, alcohol or other substance abuse or dependency.
- Is on the fringe of his/her peer group with few or no close friends.
- Is preoccupied with weapons, explosives or other incendiary devices.
- Has previously been truant, suspended or expelled from school.
- Displays cruelty to animals.
- Has little or no supervision and support from parents or a caring adult.
- Has witnessed or been a victim of abuse or neglect in the home.
- Has been bullied and/or bullies or intimidates peers or younger children.
- Tends to blame others for difficulties and problems s/he causes her/himself.
- Consistently prefers TV shows, movies or music expressing violent themes and acts.
- Prefers reading materials dealing with violent themes, rituals and abuse.
- Reflects anger, frustration and the dark side of life in school essays or writing projects.
- Is involved with a gang or an antisocial group on the fringe of peer acceptance.
- Is often depressed and/or has significant mood swings.
- Has threatened or attempted suicide.

Unfortunately, many of these characteristics may not become known until after a full examination of the background characteristics of the offender has been conducted. They may assist with determining why the incident occurred, but reveal little about how to identify troubled or at-risk persons. Also, many of these characteristics are quite prevalent in student groups across the board; specifically, teenage angst, largely reflected herein, does not necessarily reflect violent and destructive tendencies.

In a move away from these limited reports, psychological assessment tools are meant to provide a more rigorous and empirically sound approach to risk assessment. However, research in the area has cast a somewhat gloomy light on the efficacy of these models as well. Let's consider three of the more common tools for this purpose: the PCL-R, the VRAG, and the Static-99.

Freedman (2001) provides a fairly critical commentary on the use of the PCL-R as a tool for predicting the propensity to commit violence, as well as being incorporated into other risk-assessment tools such as the VRAG. Rightly stated within this critique is that the uncritical reliance on such tools promotes the unjustified incarcerations of people who would not otherwise have posed a risk, perhaps because of the propensity of mental health professionals to favor assessments of risk over none, resulting in a large number of false positives.

This problem has been canvassed by Ogloff and Davis (2005, 311), with their second critique relating directly to the use of such checklists as described above:

> It was found, perhaps not surprisingly, that psychiatrists, psychologists, and release decision-makers tended to make conservative decisions that suggested that people were at risk for dangerousness or violence when, in fact, they were not....

> At least three problems led to false positive errors made in predicting risk for violence. First, research had not identified empirically supported risk factors associated with violence. As such, many myths existed about the factors that indicated that one was at risk for being violent. The so-called "triad" is a good example. For many years it was incorrectly believed that if one child had been prone to encopresis, fire setting, and harming animals as a child, one would be at risk for violence.

> Second, in addition to failing to identify the correct factors that increased one's level of risk for violence, even when some valid factors were identified, it was difficult for clinicians to systematically assess them or to understand how they went together. For example, if we know that mental illness and substance abuse are two risk factors, what would we consider one's level of risk to be if one had a mental illness but not a substance abuse problem (or vice versa), or if one had both a mental illness and substance abuse problem contemporaneously?

> Finally, and perhaps most insidious, is the fact that the base rate for violence in many populations is generally so low that it is difficult to accurately predict whether one will be violent in the future.

These concerns can be easily juxtaposed with those of Freedman (2001, 91), especially points two and three above, regarding the use of the PCL-R for violence prediction:

The research that has been conducted thus far shows that the use of the PCL-R to predict violent behavior involves substantial and unacceptable rates of error. Although the PCL-R has been used to differentiate between psychopaths and non-psychopaths, the more important concern is within-group statistics. As discussed previously, because the research has artificially increased the number of people claimed to score high by lowering the cutting scores, the proper analysis of the reliability and validity of the instrument must start with intragroup assessment of the high-scoring group.

The evidence of intragroup statistics indicates poor prediction capacity concerning violence. The rate of false-positives associated with use of the PCL-R, although often unreported in favor of inter-group data, is strikingly consistent and very high, worse than a coin toss in predictive validity.

The VRAG, or Violence Risk Appraisal Guide, and the Static-99 are another two, and among the most popular two, Actuarial Risk Assessment Instruments (ARAIs). Both have also been severely criticized by Litwack (2001) and Hart, Michie, and Cooke (2007). The study by Litwack will not be chronicled further here. Suffice it to say that it is a very comprehensive meta-analysis of the literature surrounding risk assessment and a must-read for any student or practitioner with more than a passing interest in the area.

Hart and colleagues examined the efficacy of both the VRAG and the Static-99. For the VRAG, the precision of the instrument was assessed for violent recidivism over a 10-year period. For the Static-99, the precision of the instrument was assessed for sexually violent recidivism over a 15-year period. For each instrument, a 95% confidence interval was employed to determine the accuracy of prediction. Without needing to dig deeper into the results of the study, the point can be well made simply by quoting the discussion section (63 below). However, the reader is advised to consult the paper for a full and complete discussion of their findings.

Our analyses indicated that two popular ARAIs used in risk assessment have poor precision. The margins of error for risk estimates made when using the tests were substantial, even at the group level. At the individual level, the margins of error were so high as to render the test results virtually meaningless. Our findings are consistent with Bohr's conclusion that predicting the future is very difficult.

Our findings will likely come as no surprise to many people. The difficulties in predicting the outcomes for groups versus individuals—whether in the context of games of chance or of violence risk assessments—are intuitively obvious.

By now, the point should be fairly clear: the nomothetic average may apply, or it may not; there may be factors in an individual's background that contribute to his or her violence risk, and there may not. Until the full analysis of a case has been undertaken, the existence of these factors may never be known—often long after the trigger has been pulled. Additionally, the use of commonly accepted tools, such as ARAIs, is fraught with peril: their ability to predict group behavior may be possible, but their ability to predict the behavior of the individual is questionable. The average can predict the average, and little else.

Case Example: Louisiana Technical College

On February 8, 2008, at 8:35 a.m., Latina Williams, 23, killed herself and two other students in a second-floor classroom at Louisiana Technical College in Baton Rouge, Louisiana. She fired six shots from a .357-caliber revolver into Karsheika Graves, 21, and Taneshia Butler, 26. Then she reloaded and shot herself in the head (Smith and Vetter 2008).

The 911 call details were published in Smith (2008):

> Calls started pouring into 911 dispatch after shots rang out inside Louisiana Technical College on Feb. 8. The Baton Rouge Police Department released tapes of the calls Friday....

> "Has anybody been shot?" dispatch asked the first caller, who dialed 911 at 8:35 a.m.

> "I don't know, I'm in the office right now. I heard a shooting in the hallway and I hear screaming," she said.

> Less than two minutes later, a woman called from an upstairs nursing classroom, near the shooting. "We're locked in the room and we've turned the light off," the woman said.

> She added that she did not know who the shooter was, but heard shouts of, "Get down, hurry, run," from the hallway.

> A minute later, a sister of someone inside the school called 911 to relay her sister's message at 8:38 a.m.

> "I was calling to report a shooting at LTC. My sister just called me and told me that they are shooting inside the building," she says calmly.

> A particularly harried caller phoned at 8:40 a.m., after police had arrived at the scene.

> "Come on help!" she screams as dispatch answers.

> "Yes? Can I help you?" the dispatcher replies.

> "The school!" she says.

> "Where? Which school?" the dispatcher asks.

"She shot several times! I don't know who was shot or how many shots, times," the caller replies, out of breath.

The caller said she ran out of the building to get her phone after the shots rang out.

Dispatchers helped assure those who were locked down in classrooms before police reached them. One caller phoned at 8:41 a.m. from the second floor near the crime scene, saying that the school is under lockdown.

"They have police on scene and they have EMS up there, OK?" the dispatcher assured the caller.

The final caller in the tapes had barricaded herself in a bathroom at the school. "Are they gonna let us know when it's safe to come out of the bathroom at Louisiana Technical College?" she asked.

Janes (2008), quoting directly from public statements made by the Baton Rouge police, provides insight into Williams' state of mind prior to the attack. They are reminiscent of reported findings from the white male school shooter population:

Latina Williams had been living in a car and showing signs of paranoia before she went to a New Orleans pawnshop where she bought the .357-caliber revolver she used the next day to fatally shoot two classmates and then herself, police said Monday.

Williams, 23, kept the weapon concealed in her purse as she opened fire Friday at her Louisiana Technical College nursing classmates before stopping to reload, Baton Rouge Police Department spokesman Sgt. Don Kelly said.

Don't worry, I'm not mad at y'all, Williams told those in the classroom before turning the gun on herself, witnesses said.

Police believe that shortly before the morning onslaught Williams anonymously called a crisis counselor, indicating she planned to take her own life, Kelly said. The alarmed counselor contacted authorities to tell them about the nameless call around the time Williams was opening fire inside her classroom....

Williams had no permanent residence and was apparently living out of her car, Kelly said in a written release. She was estranged from her family in Mississippi and had sparingly spoken with them in the past two years....

Kelly also said Latina Williams had displayed signs of paranoia, though he declined to elaborate further on her mental state....

The day before the shooting, Williams purchased a .357-caliber revolver and a box of ammunition from a New Orleans pawn shop, Kelly said. He would not release the name of the pawn shop, but he did say some of the money used in the purchase came from the sale of some of Williams's possessions.

Police will complete their investigation sometime next week, Kelly said.

Investigators have not found any connection between Williams and her victims, Graves and Butler, to explain why or if they were targeted, Kelly said. Authorities have not been able to determine if Williams left a suicide note.

At a memorial service Sunday night, classmates of Graves and Butler said they did not believe the shooting was provoked, only that their proximity to Williams when she entered the classroom led to their deaths.

Possible red flags

Williams's homelessness, estrangement from her family, paranoid behavior and the call to the counselor were all indicators of a risk for violence, said Kathy Seifert, a Maryland-based psychologist with an expertise in youth and family violence....

"You can look at these risk factors and can see there's going to be a bad outcome if there is no treatment," said Seifert, who has written the book *How Children Become Violent* and said she is researching another about women and violence.

Seifert said there were basic similarities between Williams and Cho Seung-Hui, the gunman who opened fire in a Virginia Tech building and murdered 32 people before killing himself.

Cho kept to himself, did not interact with other students and had a psychiatric problem that had not been addressed when he moved from secondary school to college.

Williams's classmates said she stuck to herself and ate alone at lunch. In a class photo, Williams is barely visible, hiding her face behind other students.

Seifert said Williams homelessness was likely one of the stressors that could have contributed to the violence that ended her life and took two others.

"Anybody can come unglued if the stressors they are under exceeds their resources," Seifert said. "She had risk factors for violence, suicide. It could have been mental breakdown. When you see somebody with all these risk factors, there is a need to assess this person so the inevitable outcome doesn't happen."

This example shatters major inviolate findings in published nomothetic school shooting research—the offender was not only black, but she was also a female. Another issue is Williams' connection with the two victims and how they were targeted. If indeed no personal connection is evident, then the context becomes all-important. Her primary target may have been herself, and she may have simply wanted everyone to see and to remember her destruction.

More interesting than her race and sex (these barriers were bound to be broken) is the issue of her overall comportment. The absence of outward rage (other than the big gun and the killing) and the reported apologetic nature of Williams' demeanor are not evident in the literature to date. In fact, quite the opposite. School shooters are known for their angry or vacant expressions; their ruthless and purposeful victim selection; and their recriminating taunts towards victims. No matter how you approach it, using the existing literature as a guide to the Williams' case only leads to becoming immediately lost.

Given this example, the cautionary from the Chapter 11 remains relevant and bears repeating. Contextual data is interesting, and even important for developing case theories and establishing risk or exposure factors in some instances. However, grouped and averaged victim data is also abstract. It does not represent particular victims that exist in the real world. It represents possibility, not actuality. And that possibility is limited by what has been recognized and studied. In actual casework, one is bound to encounter circumstances that have not been previously documented, let alone studied. This limitation is important to understand, and must be incorporated into subsequent findings regarding case-specific interpretations.

To be clear—it is fair to say that we won't really know what is present in a case until it is established by the evidence. Prediction is often inaccurate, and therefore rarely responsible. Nomothetic information is useful for forming possible theories and avenues of investigation, but these theories need to be tested against the real-world circumstances of a particular case. Then, and only then, can the full universe of the case be known and the nomothetic theories that exist be established as relevant to *this* victim, *this* offender, and *this* crime.

IDIOGRAPHIC ANALYSIS

In this section, we will discuss certain basic idiographic considerations with respect to school shootings and adduce illustrative examples as necessary.

Targets

As explained in Chapter 11, all offenders have particular victim or target criteria that satisfy their needs—no matter how general or specific. There are essentially three kinds of targets: primary, secondary, and collateral.

Primary Targets

A *primary target* is someone who is of the greatest importance to the offender. He or she dictates the location and timing of any attack. Often, the offender will have planned out and intend to hit that victim at the risk of foregoing any or all other targets in the environment. In some cases, there will be more than one primary target.

In school shootings, the student shooter may target a classmate that has made fun of him or her in the past, a romantic interest that has left him or her feeling scorned (whether this is real or perceived), a teacher who gave an unfavorable mark, or an administrator who gave an unfavorable punishment. The student may also target the school in general, seeking the greatest destruction and body count in his or her efforts.

Secondary Targets

A *secondary target* is someone who is of lesser importance to the offender. It will not dictate the location and timing of an attack. However, it will be a conscious choice based on the availability within environmental and temporal constraints dictated by primary targets. Not all offenders will take the time to deliberate over the possibility of achieving secondary targets.

In school shootings, secondary targets will be representative of the primary target, someone or something that is associated with them. Instead of a teacher, the principal; instead of a classmate, their friends or intimates (if available); and instead of the principal, his or her office, belongings, or vehicle.

Collateral Victims

A *collateral victim* is someone who is attacked and injured unintentionally, because of his or her proximity to a primary or secondary target within a given environment. The injury of collateral victims is completely uncalculated and incidental to the intended outcome. A collateral victim is in fact not a target. It is important to distinguish between secondary targets and collateral victims— the key difference being the intent of the attacker.

In school shootings, collateral victims will be hit because they are in the way. They are in the wrong place at the wrong time. The student who is hit by a bullet that comes through a wall; the teacher hit by a shotgun blast meant for the student standing beside him or her; or the principal who is shot while trying to get a primary target to safety. Many collateral victims are simply in the field of fire.

EXPOSURE FACTORS

Rather than try to create a new breed of criminal in which to cast the school shooter, we take the approach that a step back is necessary. Because school shootings can originate from other forms of school violence, we recommend a general approach to understand school shootings. Lintott (2004) breaks down the general factors that influence school violence of all kinds into four general areas: internal problems, familial problems, peer relationship problems, and social/ environmental factors.

Internal Problems

Students with *internal problems* that may expose them to violent behavior or cause them to act violently include those with chemical, biological, or psychological problems. This is explained thoroughly in Lintott (2004, 556–557):

> Some students may have disabilities so severe that they need an intensely therapeutic environment, one that is not practical in a traditional school setting. Not every student, however, that has a mild chemical imbalance needs to be removed from a public school setting....

> One problem associated with student violence is a neurological chemical imbalance. When a student feels threatened, the body produces noradrenaline, the "alarm hormone" that produces the instinct to fight or flee. At the same time, high amounts of stress may decrease seretonin, the "feel-good hormone," which reduces the effects of noradrenaline. This chemical imbalance may create a stressful situation where a child is more likely to interpret neutral behavior as aggressive and react violently. Thus, some students may be chemically prone to violence, making it difficult for schools to anticipate and understand the student's violent reactions and to respond appropriately.

> Other problems associated with student violence and biological disorders are hyperactivity and attention deficit disorder. These students lack problem-solving capabilities and have difficulty controlling their emotions. Students with these problems may not be able to distinguish between non-violent situations and those conflicts that could result in violence. While some of this behavior may be curbed by medication, not all children have adequate healthcare. Furthermore, some parents refuse to medicate their children because the medication causes a change in the child's personality, or the parents do not want the stigma of having a "medicated child." This problem may be compounded if the student has an improper diet. Studies have shown that a diet high in sugar may increase aggressive behavior. It is the complexity of factors in dealing with these students that requires a school system to expend a great deal of attention to behavior and aggression.

Students with learning disabilities are also more likely to be involved in violence. Learning-disabled children experience daily failure and frustration, leading to a negative self-image that is often reinforced by teachers and peers. This negative self-image may result in an attempt to gain recognition through delinquent behavior, some of which may be in the form of aggressive actions. Therefore, violent reactions to conflict may be a natural reaction to an internal, medical disability.

Familial Problems

Students with *familial problems* that may expose them to violent behavior or cause them to act violently include those who have been exposed to or suffered as a victim of family violence. As explained in Lintott (2004, 557–558):

> A predominant theme is that family violence in the home is often associated with student violence. Researchers have proposed that a child who is a victim of family violence may be responding to this traumatic experience through disruptive or violent classroom behavior. This is due to the abused child's heightened levels of anxiety even when in a non-abusive environment, and they "express their anger and hurt through antisocial behaviors." This trend in violent behavior has been observed increasingly in very young students.
>
> Another problem associated with school violence is parental acceptance of violent responses to conflict. When the child is taught to solve conflict with violence by his family, but is taught to resolve the conflict nonviolently by the school, the child becomes confused. This student needs constant affirmation that there are non-violent ways to deal with conflicts, and that these are appropriate while in school. Without a significant support system, however, practitioners find that it is unlikely that the student will reject the violent influence of his family or guardians.

Peer Relationship Problems

Students with *peer relationship problems* that may expose them to violent behavior or cause them to act violently include those who do not have parental guidance, support, and attachment, and subsequently are unable to resist or cope with their peers. As explained in Lintott (2004, 558–559):

> Students' relationships with peers are very important in predicting school performance and delinquent behavior. Students who do not have "parental support and attachment are less equipped to deal with school demands and the resulting frustration of school failure." These students are "more vulnerable to the temptations and pressures they experience from their peers, and many youth turn to disruptive and delinquent behavior in schools."

A compounding problem affecting peer relationships in urban schools today is the presence of gangs. Twenty-nine percent of urban students reported that street gangs were present in their schools. These gangs can range from national organizations involved in organized crime, to cliques of students who have "gang signs" or "gang colors," but may not be considered a "gang" under all definitions. These groups can provide its members a sense of identity and belonging, increasing that member's self-esteem. Unfortunately, this makes those students who are doing poorly in school and not involved in school activities the most likely students to join gangs. Violence among gangs can stem from issues such as status, reputation, or "turf," and a substantial amount of gang violence can permeate into school. When violence is gang related, traditional mechanisms that a school uses to curb violence may not have an impact. In these situations, the pressure from the gang to commit violence may overwhelm the influence of a school to dissuade violence.

Social and Environmental Factors

Students with *social and environmental factors* that may expose them to violent behavior or cause them to act violently include those who are routinely exposed to violence as a component of fantasy or entertainment. However, such factors are not enough to impel anyone towards an act of violence. It is commonly understood that most people who watch violent movies, play violent video games, or listen to music with violent lyrics do not commit violent crime. There must be something else present. As explained in Lintott (2004, 559):

> Many practitioners today feel that the increase in school violence can be attributed to increased violence in popular culture. Media outlets such as television and the Internet are commonly blamed for the increase of school violence. According to the American Psychological Association, "children watch an average of 8,000 murders and 100,000 other violent acts on television before finishing elementary school."...

> While the extent to which violent images can encourage actual violence is beyond the scope of this note, it is important to note that this violent environment may affect those students who are more prone to violence due to other factors.

> Finally ... violence may be increased in our schools because of administrators' responses to school violence. One study found that excessive discipline for misbehaving students often increases violent behavior in students. In 1984, the National School Boards Association warned that "traditional approaches—such as punishment, removing troublemakers, and similar measures—often harden delinquent behavior patterns, alienate troubled youths from the schools, and foster distrust."

We include these general factors as influencing school violence because it is necessary to appreciate the extent to which the school shooter may in fact be born of victimization. Many, pushed down by successive failures, an inability to cope, and lack of support, are simply coming back over the top with a response that they believe is acceptable. Many (and certainly not all) believe that they have been victimized and are fighting back.

MOTIVATIONAL EVENTS AND CIRCUMSTANCES

The motivations for school shootings have traditionally focused on anger, retaliation, and rage. School shooters are, in this regard, perceived as a form of urban terrorist. This is an oversimplification that comes from our first response to the notion of a school shooting: we aren't safe; our children aren't safe; and our communities are not safe. We are filled with terror, and we are not wrong to feel terrorized.

However, that may not have been the intent of a given school shooter. It is true enough that it is the intent for some. But not all are primarily angry; not all want a high body count; and not all are interested in evoking terror. Some just want what they want, and then they don't want anything else ever again.

Case Examples

Consider the following cases, all of which go against the published research. The first involves an Asian male with narcissistic motives that evoking terror (and the accompanying air-time) will satisfy. The second involves a nonstudent shooter with an obvious sexual motive who chose victims beyond the media's immediate reach.

Case Example: Virginia Tech

Because of available cell phone and Internet technology and the competitive nature of the 24-hour news cycle, the relationship between violent crime and the media is rapidly approaching a critical mass. Victims and offenders alike are communicating directly with news outlets before, during, and after the commission of crimes. It's a matter of narcissism, supply, and demand. Certain offenders want to be seen, the media outlets want to make money, and the public wants to see offenders commit crime as well as any related victim suffering.

In April of 2007, 23-year-old Virginia Tech student Cho Seung-Hui, a senior and English major, committed a mass homicide with the highest body count (32 dead, many others wounded) in the history of U.S. school shootings. Though his background and mental state are similar to many school shooters, his Asian descent is not (Flannery 2008, 287–289):

> Seung Hui Cho was an angry and disturbed college student. During
> his tenure at Virginia Tech, Cho showed himself to be a loner who was
> withdrawn from those around him. Cho was also the type of person

who had had suicidal and homicidal ideations as early as the eighth grade and who stabbed at the carpet in a female student's room in the presence of his college suitemates. In addition, Cho also took inappropriate pictures of his female college classmates from a camera under his desk, wrote poetry that was all about violence, and thus was individually counseled, and identified as a Virginia Tech student with problems. In response to being asked to cease his conduct, Cho e-mailed a suitemate stating that "I might as well kill myself now." ...

Virginia Tech conducted an assessment and pre-screen interview of Cho at 8:15 p.m. on December 13, 2005. A licensed clinical social worker for New River Valley Community Services Board (CSB) interviewed Cho and a police officer, as well as Cho's roommate and his suitemate. The social worker found that Cho was "mentally ill," was an imminent danger to himself or others, and was not willing to be treated voluntarily. She recommended involuntary hospitalization and indicated that the CSB could assist with treatment. The social worker then located a psychiatric bed, as required by state law, at St. Albans Behavioral Health Center at the Carilion New River Valley Medical Center. When Cho was admitted to this hospital overnight, he denied that he was violent but admitted that he did have access to a firearm.

The hearing concerning Cho's psychological condition was held on December 14, 2005 before Special Justice Paul M. Barnett of the Montgomery County General District Court. The Justice considered various source materials and heard from Cho himself. He concluded that Cho "presents an imminent danger to himself as a result of mental illness" and ordered "O-P [outpatient treatment]—to follow all recommended treatments."

After these events, the warning signs kept piling up. Cho subsequently wrote a paper for his creative writing class about "a young man who hated the students at his school and planned to kill them and himself," saying, among other things, "I hate my life . . . This is it . . . This is when you die with me." Another professor alerted a dean about Cho's distressing conduct but nothing happened, not even the counseling that the professor recommended.

Numerous precursors and warning signs were evident. And everyone knew that he was getting worse, from the courts to the counselors. But nothing happened. Details of the shootings, and a timeline, are provided in Flannery (2008, 292–294):

On April 16, 2007, at about 7:15 a.m. at the West Ambler Johnston residential hall, Cho shot and killed Emily Hilscher and Ryan

Christopher Clark. The police responded to the scene, but no one was taken into custody. At 9:26 a.m., two hours and fifteen minutes after the first shooting, the Virginia Tech Administration sent an e-mail to staff, faculty and students about the first shooting.

About two-and-a-half hours after the first shooting, and about ten minutes after the e-mail was circulated, Cho started shooting in Room 206 in Norris Hall, killing nine and wounding three of the thirteen students in that room. Cho then went across the hall and entered Room 207, a German class. Cho shot the teacher, as well as the students near the front of the classroom, and then started walking down the aisle shooting other students.

Cho then left the classroom and walked into the hallway. In the meantime, students in Room 205 heard gunshots and barricaded the door. Cho fired through the door.

As the tragic event unfolded further, in Room 211, the teacher asked a student to call 911 on her cell phone.

The students shoved a desk in front of the door but Cho pushed past it. Cho then walked down the row of desks shooting people. The student with the cell phone was shot in the leg. Another student picked up the cell phone and begged the police to hurry. Cho heard her speak and shot her, grazing her head twice. She played dead while holding the phone under her head with the line open.

Three of the students pretended to be dead and managed to survive. Meanwhile, police outside tried but failed to shoot open the locks that Cho affixed to the three doors at Norris Hall.

Cho then went back to Room 207, the German class, where two injured students and two that were not injured managed to hold the door shut with their feet and hands. In response, Cho returned to the French class and opened fire on the students there again.

At about 9:45 a.m., five minutes into the siege, a janitor saw Cho loading his gun and thus was able to escape....

Cho also tried to enter Room 204, where an engineering professor braced his body against the door, taking Cho's shots himself and losing his life, while saving many students who had time to escape through the window.

Tragically, two students did not escape the carnage and were shot by Cho....

Cho then returned to Room 206 to shoot the survivors. At that time, the police finally used a shotgun to break the locks and stormed the second floor.

At 9:50 a.m., the administration sent a second e-mail warning the campus: "A gunman is loose on campus. Stay in buildings until further notice. Stay away from all windows." Four loudspeakers blasted this same message.

At 9:51 a.m., Cho shot himself in the head.

In keeping with the new relationship between the media and mass murder, and the narcissism at work behind this particular crime, Cho Seung-Hui mailed photographs, video, and writings to *NBC News* that chronicled his motives and state of mind. NBC aired it, and the public consumed it without hesitation.

As per Cho's intent, international mass media coverage and infamy followed. This was all much to the distress of the victims, their families, and the Virginia Tech community in general.

Case Example: Monash University, Australia, University Shooting

There is a belief among Australians, as well as citizens of other nations, that Australia is somehow insulated from extreme forms of violence. Given incidents receive wide media coverage but ultimately tend to be written off as entirely the province of the United States. However, this is not necessarily going to remain the case, as the potential for extreme violence exists in Australian culture.

In 1997 in Australia, Martin Bryant opened fire in the historic Tasmanian town of Port Arthur, killing 35 and wounding a further 37. This case remains the worst homicidal shooting spree in history, and most certainly the worst act of violence in Australia. And it reminds us that countries with a typically low level of violent crime are not immune to the worst-case scenarios.

On October 1, 2002, Australians were again reminded of the very real problem of extreme acts of violence when Huan Yun Xiang opened fire in an econometrics tutorial at Monash University in the Australian state of Victoria, killing two and wounding four others. Murphy, Ketchell, and Heasley (2002) provide the following:

Two students were dead and a third was left fighting for his life late yesterday after a disgruntled commerce student opened fire with two handguns in a Monash University tutorial.

The gunman, believed to be a fourth year honors student, walked into the sixth-floor econometrics tutorial about 11.20 a.m., carrying two small hand pistols. He opened fire, killing two Asian students in their 20s instantly.

A 30-year-old man was airlifted to the Alfred Hospital suffering abdominal injuries and was last night in a critical condition in the Alfred Hospital.

Four other students, all suffering gunshot wounds, were taken to hospital. A woman was shot in the jaw and others suffered multiple wounds, including one man in his 20s who underwent surgery at St Vincent's Hospital to reattach a finger shot off in the attack.

Thanh Huynh, sister of Lee Huynh, one of the victims, said the attack was indiscriminate.

"He was in a tutorial room ... I think there was meant to be a presentation by the gunman today," she told Channel Nine. "I said 'What happened?' and he said the guy, the gunman, just went berserk and started shooting everyone and he was unfortunately one of the ones that got shot in the legs."

Witnesses said the gunman was wrestled to the floor and disarmed by a lecturer and at least one other student.

"The people on the floor at the time were just unbelievable. They definitely saved lives. One of the men in the class managed to disarm the gunman, secure the weapons, and treat two of the patients," said Paul Howells, the first paramedic to arrive at the scene. "Credit should also be given to the attending ambulance officers, who did a superb job. The death toll could have been much worse."

The gunman was arrested at the scene and showed no resistance to police. Last night he was being questioned by homicide squad detectives with the help of an interpreter.

Victoria Police Superintendent Trevor Parks confirmed the gunman was a student in the class, but would not confirm his name. He said the tutor and a student were believed to have wrestled the gunman to the floor, immobilizing him while others called the police. He said there were fewer than 10 key witnesses.

"If the gunman hadn't been subdued at the time it would have been a major disaster."

He described the alleged gunman as an Asian male in his mid-30s. He said the wounded suffered gunshots to legs, arms, backs and shoulders, with up to four of the victims being shot more than once.

Fellow students said the gunman came to Australia about four years ago from China to study commerce. He had few friends and struggled with English.

"He would often become frustrated in tutorials because no one could understand him," a university classmate said.

Students at Monash said scenes in the 11-story building were chaotic immediately after the shooting, with students jostling onto crowded escalators to escape. At one stage, some thought the gunman was loose in the student union, opposite the Menzies building.

"We were very concerned about the lack of effective communication," said student newspaper editor Jesse Macneal-Brown. "It was some time before everybody knew what was going on."

A transcript from the ABC television program *Lateline* provides further information following interviews with students and commentary regarding the gunman (Carbonell 2002):

Melbourne's Monash University is reviewing its security after a fatal shooting earlier today. Two people were killed and five wounded when an economics student opened fire in his classroom.

A teacher and another student tackled the man preventing any further carnage. He is now being questioned by police.

Rachel Carbonell reports.

RACHEL CARBONELL, REPORTER: Pandemonium erupted when the gunman opened fire on the sixth floor of this building.

POLICEMAN: Move to the other side, please. Just clear well away from this area.

RACHEL CARBONELL: Two students in their early 20s died at the scene.

STUDENT #1: Everyone was pretty scared because we heard screaming and then like five minutes later we saw the police helicopter here.

STUDENT #2: I saw two people on the floor. One of them was being cradled by someone else and there were blood patches on the floor and stuff.

STUDENT #3: I saw two bodies being brought out on stretchers. The first guy looked like he had a wound to the stomach and then the second guy looked injured. He was lucid, though, and he looked like he was alright.

STUDENT #4: The world is an increasingly hostile and crazy place. It's ridiculous. It's coming so close to home now.

RACHEL CARBONELL: The university says there were approximately 2,000 people inside the building at the time of the shooting. Fearing for their lives, some fled the building.

Others barricaded themselves inside.

Police say the tragedy could have been much worse if a student and teacher hadn't subdued the man.

SUPERINTENDENT TREVOR PARKS, VICTORIA POLICE: If they hadn't acted quickly and overpowered that gunman, who knows where it would have gone.

RACHEL CARBONELL: Emergency services say the scene was confusing and it was difficult to remove the wounded.

DAVID HOWELL, METROPOLITAN AMBULANCE SERVICE: Well, pandemonium—there was a lot of milling around.

People couldn't get in, they needed to get their equipment in and they needed to make sure the area was safe.

RACHEL CARBONELL: As the injured were being taken to hospital, in the background a man arrested at the scene was being led away by police for questioning.

Of the five injured, two are in a serious condition.

Politicians moved quickly to express sympathy for the families of those hurt and shock that another tragedy has hit Australians so soon after the Bali bombings.

SIMON CREAN, OPPOSITION LEADER: Our thoughts, of course, more. Speaker, go out to the survivors and ensuring that they have a speedy...

JOHN HOWARD, AUSTRALIAN PM: The loss of life there in such violent circumstances is always a matter of regret, especially so when it is young.

RACHEL CARBONELL: The university has set up telephone hotlines for those wanting information on the welfare of their loved ones and is offering counseling to staff and students.

Initial investigations into the case revealed a student who was largely alienated from his fellow colleagues, having few friends, and struggling with English. According to the report by Murphy, Ketchell, and Heasley (2002) and others, Xiang would often become frustrated in tutorials because no one could understand him.

Interestingly, despite strict gun control laws brought about by the Bryant shootings in Tasmania, Xiang was a registered gun owner and used licensed pistols in this shooting. He was also Asian, not the white male typical of school shooter profiles.

At trial, Xiang was found not guilty of murder and attempted murder, as explained in Topsfield (2004):

> A commerce student who killed two classmates, wounded four others and shot a lecturer during a bloody rampage at Monash University, was yesterday found not guilty of murder and attempted murder because of mental impairment.
>
> A Supreme Court jury delivered its verdict after a two-day trial in which both the defense and prosecution agreed that Huan Yun "Allen" Xiang was suffering from a paranoid delusional disorder when he opened fire on his econometrics tutorial on October 21, 2002.
>
> The tragedy precipitated a $118 million national handgun buyback. Tougher laws for obtaining and keeping a gun were also introduced last year after it emerged that in the six months before the shooting rampage Xiang became a licensed gun owner and amassed an arsenal of seven firearms.
>
> Justice Bernard Teague yesterday ordered Xiang, 38, to be detained for up to 25 years.
>
> He said Xiang should go into the custody of the Thomas Embling Hospital, a high-security hospital for people with mental illness, but "regrettably" a bed was not available for several weeks.
>
> "It is getting to the stage where politicians will have to consider that we are housing in prison too many people suffering from mental illness," Justice Teague said.
>
> Students William Wu and Steven Chan, both 26, were killed in the shooting rampage.
>
> Lecturer Lee Gordon-Brown—who was lauded as a hero for restraining Xiang before police arrived, despite being severely wounded—was shot in the arm and the leg.
>
> Xiang pleaded not guilty to two counts of murder and five counts of attempted murder because of mental impairment.
>
> Outside court, Dr. Gordon-Brown's parents, Oxley and Joan Gordon-Brown, expressed relief that the trial was over.
>
> "I just hope the experts got it right and he (Xiang) is not smarter than them," Mr. Gordon-Brown said.

He spoke of his pride in his son, who had returned to lecturing within weeks of the tragedy. "He still has a bullet in him. He'll remember it for the rest of his life," Mr. Gordon-Brown said.

Acting Vice-Chancellor of Monash University Alan Lindsay said yesterday's verdict would provide a degree of closure to this tragic chapter for the university community.

"Nothing will replace Steven Chan and William Wu, two exceptionally bright Monash honors students whose lives were cut short," Professor Lindsay said.

At 11.15 a.m. on October 21, 2002, Xiang, who was described as an excellent student, was sitting quietly reading a newspaper at the back of a lecture room on the sixth floor of the university's Robert Menzies building.

As the class of 12 students began to revise for an exam, sharp bangs were heard and students began screaming and diving to the floor in panic.

Xiang was seen standing on a desk with his arms outstretched pointing a black object and yelling: "You never understand me."

In court, forensic psychiatrist Dr. Douglas Bell said Xiang believed his victims were plotting to destroy him academically and have him killed. He said Xiang described student William Wu as the "Godfather" of Monash University and believed he was the representative of all evil across the world.

"He saw it as his responsibility to do what he could to get rid of the William Wus of the world and then to kill himself," Dr. Bell said.

The psychiatrist said paranoid delusional disorder was difficult to diagnose and, despite his mental illness, Xiang was able to continue operating at a high level academically.

Students and staff at the university could not have known Xiang was severely mentally ill or predicted the terrible tragedy that unfolded, Dr. Bell said.

Xiang will be remanded in custody until a bed becomes available at the Thomas Embling Hospital in two to three weeks.

Case Example: Nickel Mines—Amish School Shooting

As we have made clear throughout this text, it is a mistake to practice as though prior case experience will allow us to generalize accurately regarding present offenses. Not every school shooting is the work of a disenfranchised white student with an ax to grind against a particular student or school. Nor is technology always present. Nor is every school shooting about present anger or wrongs. Sometimes the shooter is an outsider; sometimes technology is literally absent; and sometimes the motive comes from the past. Consider the case of Charles Carl Roberts IV. On October 2, 2006, he defied all school shooter archetypes to date (Holusha 2006):

> A lone gunman walked into a one-room schoolhouse in a largely Amish community in southeastern Pennsylvania today and shot as many as 10 girls, killing three immediately before turning the gun on himself and dying at the scene, according to the state police.
>
> The school is just outside Nickel Mines, a tiny village about 55 miles west of Philadelphia.
>
> The man, identified as Charles Carl Roberts IV, 32, who lived in the area, was evidently nursing a long-ago grievance expressed in notes left for his wife and children, said Jeffrey Miller, commissioner of the state police.
>
> He said the gunman lined the girls against the blackboard, bound their feet and shot them execution-style in the head. "He split them up, males and females," Commissioner Miller said. "He let the males go, some of the adults go. He bound the females at the blackboard, and apparently executed them."
>
> Three of the girls were dead at the scene in Nickel Mines, Pa., and seven others were rushed to nearby hospitals, some of them severely wounded. An earlier Associated Press report quoted a local coroner as saying there were six people dead, but the coroner later said he was unsure.
>
> The A.P. said.... "There was some issue in the past" that had left the gunman with a desire to harm female students, Commissioner Miller said. He said that the murders were premeditated and that the gunman had called his wife—without telling her he was holding hostages in a school—that he would not be coming home.
>
> Commissioner Miller said Mr. Roberts called his wife from a cell phone, saying he was "acting out in revenge for something that happened 20 years ago." "It seems as though he wanted to attack young, female victims," he said, according to The Associated Press.
>
> The gunman released about 16 boys in the class, a pregnant teacher's aide and three women with small children before the shooting began,

Commissioner Miller said. The principal teacher escaped at that time and ran to a nearby property to call 911.

The gunman, who was not Amish, evidently chose the small, private Amish school in Lancaster County about 55 miles west of Philadelphia because the security would be lax, Commissioner Miller said. He said when police tried to talk to the gunman over loudspeakers to begin negotiations, Mr. Roberts made a cellphone call from inside the building threatening to start shooting unless police pulled back.

He was armed with an automatic pistol and a shotgun and had barricaded the doors to the school with structural lumber to slow down the police, who tried to charge in once the shooting started.

Police said the gunman worked as a truck driver who collected milk from nearby farms for processing and sale. Police said he walked his own children to a nearby bus stop before borrowing a relative's pick-up truck and heading for the Amish school.

Commissioner Miller of the State Police said the gunman was not wanted for any crimes and apparently did not have a criminal record.

Far from being revenge-oriented, as suggested by some, the motive behind the Amish schoolhouse takeover appears to be a sex crime that ended in suicide. This is detailed in Knight (2006):

"He wasn't agitated, he wasn't screaming, he was just taking control," said Commissioner Jeffrey Miller, of the Pennsylvania Police, as he recounted the last moments of Charles Carl Roberts IV, a milk lorry driver, who shot ten Amish schoolgirls at close range yesterday morning.

In the first insight into the possible motives of Roberts, a respected and well-liked father of three, Mr. Miller said that the gunman had called his wife, Marie, on a mobile phone soon after taking the schoolgirls hostage and said he had attacked two young relatives as a 12-year-old.

"I'm not coming home, the police are here," he is reported to have said before directing her to suicide notes in which Roberts said he had been assailed by dreams of assaulting young people again.

Police said today that Roberts had panicked when ten state troopers surrounded the one-room Georgetown Amish School in the tiny village of Nickel Mines, Pennsylvania, and started "executing" the schoolgirls rather than following what appeared to be a plan "to victimize them in many ways."

Three girls died instantly when Roberts shot them in the back of the head and two more succumbed to their injuries overnight. Five others remain in hospital after being shot in the head and back. All of the victims were students. The dead girls were named today as Naomi Rose Edersol, 7, Anna Mae Stolzfus, 12, Marian Fischer, 13, and sisters Lina and Mary Liz Miller, aged 7 and 8.

Roberts then killed himself as police broke through the windows of the school. Officers had to free the dead and wounded from wires that bound their ankles.

Roberts had nailed close the side door of the school and blocked the main entrance with a piece of wood and desks. As well as equipping himself with 600 rounds of ammunition and a change of clothes, he also brought plastic handcuffs, planks of wood mounted with ten pairs of hooks, apparently to restrain his victims, and KY jelly, a sexual lubricant.

At a news conference this afternoon, Mr. Miller said that rambling suicide notes left for Roberts's wife, Marie, and his three children, suggested that the gunman, a home-schooled Christian, acted out of grief for a daughter who died nine years ago and as a furious reaction to his alleged attack on two relatives as young as 3 when he was just 12 years old.

Mr. Miller said that Roberts's confession had come as a complete surprise to his wife and that interviews with his family, although ongoing, had yet to corroborate any wrongdoing. "They have no knowledge of any molestation of family members or anyone else," he said.

Although it is unclear what, if any, crime Roberts committed as a young boy, his assault, America's third fatal school shooting incident in the last week, was meticulously planned. Mr. Miller said today that Roberts parked his milk lorry outside the Nickel Mines Auction House, just yards from the school, after every shift and that the unprotected building represented "a target of opportunity."

Based on his phone call and suicide letters, investigators believed he wanted to attack girls of a certain age rather than members of the Amish community.

Police discovered a checklist and receipts that showed Roberts was buying equipment for the attack up to six days ago. A handwritten list in a notebook read: "Tape. Eyebolts. Tools. Nails. Hoes. KY. Bullets. Guns. Binoculars. Earplugs. Batteries. Flashlight. Candle. Wood."

Study of this case should make clear, again, that nomothetic data does not universally apply to specific cases, and can mislead the victimologist; motivations and relationships must be investigated rather than assumed for the purposes of analysis.

SUMMARY

School shootings are a particular form of workplace violence that defy profiles and predictions. Despite sensational coverage by the popular media, they vary with respect to victim-offender relationships, victim targeting, and offender motivation. The archetypical angry white male student shooter image is slowly eroding, and other races and genders are emerging. Rather than seeing school shooters as an isolated construct, it may be more useful to view them within the overall context of school violence—as both a cause and consequence—in order that a more informed analysis of individual cases may be possible.

Questions

1. True or False: There is a checklist of red flags that may be used to help predict who will become a school shooter.
2. Incidents of targeted violence at school _____ (rarely/usually) are sudden impulsive acts.
3. Name five characteristics often displayed in potentially dangerous students.
4. What are the motivations for school shootings?
5. Explain the difference between secondary targets and collateral victims.

REFERENCES

Angel, M. 2001. "The School Shooters: Surprise! Boys Are Far More Violent Than Girls and Gender Stereotypes Underlie School Violence." *Ohio Northern University Law Review* 27, no. : 485–516.

Carbonell, R. 2002. "Two killed in university shooting." *ABC Lateline,* October 21.

Daniel, P. and Coriell, K. 1992. Suspension and Expulsion in America's Public Schools: Has Unfairness Resulted From a Narrowing of Due Process? *HAMLINE Journal of Public Law & Policy,* 13, 1: 1–11.

Flannery, J. 2008. "Students Died at Virginia Tech because Our Government Failed to Act!" *George Mason University Civil Rights Law Journal* 18, Spring: 285–3044.

Freedman, D. 2001. "False Prediction of Future Dangerousness: Error Rates and Psychopathy Checklist—Revised." *Journal of the American Academy of Psychiatry and Law* 29, no. 1: 89–95.

Hart, S.D., C. Michie, and D.J. Cooke. 2007. "Precision of Actuarial Risk Assessment Instruments." *British Journal of Psychiatry* 190, no. 49: 60–65.

Holusha, J. 2006. "Students killed by gunman at Amish schoolhouse." *New York Times,* October 2.

Janes, J. 2008. "Killer acted paranoid: Woman lived in car, believed suicidal before shootings." *The Baton Rouge Advocate*, April 12.

Knight, S. 2006. "Amish school shooter's sex crime secret." *The Age*, October 4.

Lintott. J. 2004. "Teaching and Learning in the Face of School Violence." *Georgetown Journal on Poverty Law and Policy* 11, Fall: 553–580.

Litwack, T.R. 2001. Actuarial versus Clinical Assessments of Dangerousness." *Psychology, Public Policy, and Law* 7, no. 2: 409–443.

Murphy, P., M. Ketchell, and A. Heasley. 2002. "Two die as gunman attacks his own class." *Sydney Morning Herald*, October 22.

Ogloff, J.P.R., and M. Davis. 2005. "Assessing Risk for Violence in the Australian Context." In *Issues in Australian Crime and Criminal Justice*, edited by D. Chappell and P. Wilson, . Sydney: LexisNexis/Butterworth.

Smith, S. 2008. "First 911 caller asked: 'Anybody been shot?'" *The Baton Rouge Advocate*, April 5.

Smith, S., and K. Vetter. 2008. "911 tapes reveal chaos at LTC/Woman killed 2, self in February shootings." *The Baton Rouge Advocate*, April 5.

Stephens, R. (1998). "Checklist of Characteristics of Youth Who Have Caused School-Associated Violent Deaths" National School Safety Center," Westlake Village, CA; http://www.schoolsafety.us/Checklist-of-Characteristics-of-Youth-Who-Have-Caused-School-Associated-Violent-Deaths-p-7.html.

Topsfield, J. 2004. "Monash gunman not guilty." *The Age*, June 18.

Vossekuil, B., R. Fein, M. Reddy, R. Borum, and W. Modzeleski. 2002. *The Final Report and Findings of the Safe School Initiative: Implications for the Prevention of School Attacks in the United States*. Washington, DC: U.S. Secret Service and U.S. Department of Education, May.

CHAPTER 13

Stranger Violence

Wayne Petherick and Brent E. Turvey

KEY TERMS

• *Availability heuristic:* judging the commonality, frequency, or likelihood of events; when used, people answer a question of probability by asking whether examples come readily to mind.

• *Collateral victims:* those who are attacked and injured unintentionally because of their proximity to a primary or secondary target within a given environment.

• *Convenience offenders:* those who select victims who can easily learn their identity, the locations they frequent, and the circumstances that will be more likely to result in their later identification and apprehension.

• *Displaced anger:* anger directed at someone or something other than the original instigator of that feeling; it is directed at a representative or proxy.

• *Homicide:* death at the hands of another, regardless of intent.

• *Precautionary offenders:* those who select victims whom they do not know, locations they do not frequent, and circumstances that will be less likely to result in their later identification and apprehension.

• *Primary targets:* those who are of greatest importance to the offender; they dictate the location and timing of the attack.

• *Secondary targets:* those who are of lesser importance to the offender; they will not dictate the location and timing of an attack.

• *Stranger violence:* when an offender attacks a victim whom he or she does not know; someone who is not part of the family, not a friend or coworker, and not an acquaintance of any kind.

CONTENTS

A stranger is someone who is unknown or foreign. *Stranger violence* occurs when an offender attacks a victim whom he or she does not know; someone who is not part of the family, not a friend or coworker, and not an acquaintance of any kind. Though generally less common than violence suffered at the hands of friends, family, and acquaintances, stranger violence enjoys a great deal more of our attention.

As we will examine, this begins with the media. News, film, television, mystery novels, and true crime books provide a constant deluge of stories and imagery depicting the perils of stranger crime. The general public cannot help but be limited by what is available from these sources.

But it is not just the public who are at risk of bias and preconception; investigators have their own limiting influences. Consider, for instance, when victims are unable to identify their attacker, either because they did not see the attacker, cannot recall what they saw, or died as a result of the attack. In part because of the *availability heuristic*, in part because of investigative politics, and in part because of preconceived bias, it is preferable for some investigators to advance and maintain only those case theories that do not implicate a victim's friends or family. They may do this by not considering and adequately working to eliminate those in the victim's home as suspects out of a misplaced belief that a stranger crime is the first, best, or most expedient theory.

Similar influences can take hold over criminologists. Given that a majority of crime researchers lack direct access to specific case data beyond media accounts, too many are left to study its coverage. As with the public, they may fall prey to specific types of sensationalized imagery that, in the absence of inoculatory case experience, may infect their methods and findings. This is to say nothing of their emotions, which can also be infectious.

It is far more interesting, and marketable, for the criminologist to study strangers who lurk in dark alleys than it is to study the extent to which friends and family members victimize each other. After all, if the greatest danger comes from inside our homes and the narrow circle of friends we draw around ourselves, then we can never truly be safe; that which we cling to for protection and for comfort is also our greatest liability. Examining how truly horrible the situation is only makes it more horrible. As Collins (2007, 133) explains there is a resulting dissonance between perception and reality with respect to stranger crime:

> In 2002, approximately 65 percent of all murder victims under the age of 13 were killed by a family member. Yet these crimes are not ordinarily the ones that capture public attention; instead, we reserve our greatest outrage for those relatively rare cases where a child is murdered or sexually molested by a sexual-predator stranger. As a result, we have

a tremendous mismatch between perception and reality: we think we are tough on crimes committed against children by passing statutes like Megan's Law, but in practice, we are overlooking the reality that children face the most danger from family members rather than from strangers. As one reporter for the Washington Post recently wrote "People think child homicide is big news, like Adam Walsh or JonBenet Ramsey[,] . . . but they're wrong. Six or seven infants, toddlers or children under the age of 10 are killed by adults in the District [of Columbia] each year, about 1,500 across the country. Most of them, if they make the news at all, are dispatched with paragraphs as short as their lives." Equally troubling, these cases often do not result in a perpetrator being held accountable by the criminal justice system, particularly when that perpetrator is a parent.

Further still, Collins (2007, 134) argues that culturally we have romanticized family relationships—specifically parent-child relationships—to the point of denial about what is going on in our homes right in front of us:

[W]e struggle with holding some parents accountable for the harm they do to their children, because of our tendency to romanticize the parent-child relationship. This romanticization phenomenon has several core components. First, we continue to believe that love, not law, is sufficient to protect our children, even in situations where love is clearly not enough. In other words, we engage in denial; we want to believe that parents will do the right thing by their children without the intervention of the criminal justice system. As a result, we tend to focus on therapeutic approaches to address violence committed against children, without grappling sufficiently with difficult questions about whether the criminal justice system can also play an appropriate role. In contrast, reformers working in the spousal-abuse area have been far more willing to consider utilizing a criminal approach. The second component is minimization: when violence does occur, we tend to downplay it. This phenomenon is reflected both in statutes that treat intrafamilial and extrafamilial offenders differently and in the difficulties prosecutors face in securing criminal convictions against parents.

These cultural tendencies and professional failings have had specific consequences across the criminal justice spectra, as discussed in Dawson (2006, 1418–1419):

The degree of intimacy that exists between victims and defendants has traditionally been seen as a major explanatory variable in determining criminal justice outcomes in cases of violent crime. Typically, it is argued that intimate violence and, in particular, violence between intimate partners, is treated more leniently by the courts than crimes between those who share more distant relationships. Even though numerous legislative and policy changes have occurred in recent decades to respond to intimate violence, it is still commonly assumed that these acts are treated more leniently than non-intimate violence by criminal justice actors. This belief has persisted despite the lack of consistent empirical support for an association between intimacy and law. As a result, one might argue, as Hagan and O'Donnel have with respect to gender and sentencing, that the perceived criminal justice leniency toward intimate violence has become part of conventional criminological and sociological wisdom. In other words, it may be that sociologists and citizens alike assume that those who victimize intimates are less cold-blooded, less rational, less dangerous, and, in sum, less blameworthy, for example, than those who victimize non-intimates. These assumptions may also lead one to believe that defendants who victimize intimates are, and should be, treated more leniently by the courts than those who share more distant relationships with their victims. This may also explain the lack of systematic and empirical research that has focused on the association between intimacy and law, compared to the abundance of research that has examined the effect of other variables on criminal justice outcomes such as gender, race and age.

Enter here the forensic victimologist, who in order to study the victim competently must also examine his or her friends and family in a manner that is guaranteed to upset pretty much everyone when problems are found to exist. And they do invariably exist, whether in the form of a hairline fracture in the structural supports of a home, or a smoking crater where the home once was. As a result of these existent problems, even when unrelated to the crime at hand, victims' families tend not to embrace scrutiny that might require the airing of dirty laundry. Investigators tend not to appreciate victim scrutiny because they have to deal with victim families on a personal and political level. The courts tend not to appreciate victim scrutiny because they must appear to lean in favor of the victim, whether they do or not. Forensic victimologists must walk within these worlds and yet be apart from them, insulated from criticism by objectivity, scientific methodology, and an accelerated understanding of how and why their role is necessary to the investigation of fact.

One way to develop such insulation is through a greater appreciation of stranger violence as a reality in many unsolved cases that can cause legitimate public fear. However, because of the prevalence of intimate violence, forensic victimologists must be fearless in their efforts to help to eliminate friends and family first. This can only be accomplished with thorough investigative and forensic efforts.

The goals of this chapter, then, are to dispel the prevailing myths and rhetoric connected with stranger violence that are perpetuated by sensational media coverage of such incidents, and to provide forensic victimologists with the terminology and theoretical lenses through which to perceive stranger violence more objectively.

MEDIA DISTORTION OF PUBLIC PERCEPTION

Most people do not work in the criminal justice system and consequently do not have direct, unfiltered access to actual accounts of crime. Even those that do tend to know only what occurs within their allotted bandwidth—with respect to a specific region, jurisdiction, and occupation. Unless one works cases in multiple regions of varying social contrast, overall perceptions about crime and related trends come primarily from one source: the media.

There is a specific relationship between the media and public fear. People fear the unknown. They tend to shy away from unfamiliar environments and individuals. They tend to embrace the emotional safety of the usual, the customary, and the routine.

Those in the media are fully aware of what frightens the public, but they are also aware of something else. Fear from a distance is a form of entertainment. The more fear a story evokes in the viewership or readership, the more marketable the story. This becomes more important when we consider that fear of stranger crime, specifically, represents the ultimate fear of the unknown.

Media outlets are businesses. They are also less and less concerned with delivering accurate information to consumers—especially in the news. Newspapers and newscasts are about delivering market share to advertisers and turning a profit. As explained in Buckler (2005, 2–3), they do so based on various criteria unrelated to rendering a fair or balanced perspective regarding crime and criminals:

> Communication scholars and criminologists have provided theoretical commentary about the particular factors that influenced journalist and news editor assessment of the newsworthiness of crime stories based on market-driven criteria. Chermak (1995) argued that the staff of news organizations assessed newsworthiness of a crime occurrence on the basis of five criteria: (a) the violent or heinous nature of the offense, (b) demographic factors of the victim and offender (age, race, gender, income, and socioeconomic status), (c) characteristics of the incident producers (the news agency), (d) the uniqueness of the event, and (e) event salience (e.g., is the offense a local event?). Prichard and Hughes (1997) similarly argued that the important determinants of news organization assessment of

newsworthiness included such factors as how unusual the criminal event was relative to characteristics of more typically occurring offenses, the qualities of the parties involved, and the extent to which the behavior violated formally and informally established cultural norms and expectations.

Practicing journalists have also acknowledged that there are certain criteria that are used to judge the marketability of crime news events. One such set of criteria was recognized by Pat Doyle in 1976 and has been referred to as the "Doyle criteria,"* (Johnstone, Hawkins, and Michener 1994). The pursuit of stories that are marketable is best conceptualized as an organizational pressure that is placed upon journalists and news editors that influences their decisions in how they cover the news. In this regard, journalists and news editors, in making their news coverage decisions, act as agents of the news organization and vicariously make day-to-day decisions that support the market-driven approach of the news organization.

*[Buckler's note:] In a 1976 interview of Pat Doyle of the *New York Daily News*, he described four elements of a human interest story that Johnstone et al. (1994) have referred to as the "Doyle criteria." According to Doyle, a human interest story is one that either (a) involves a socially "prominent" or "respectable" citizen who is involved as either an offender or as a victim; (b) the victim is an innocent or an overmatched target; (c) the murder was either shocking or brutal, involved multiple victims and/or offenders, or in which a particularly brutal method of killing was employed; or (d) the narrative generates mystery, suspense, or drama.

What this tells us is that the more extreme elements in a story, the more violent, and the more sensational, the more likely it is that the media will fixate on it. This is because it will be entertaining, consequently more people will watch it, and thus more ad revenue may be commanded from advertisers. The extreme case or circumstance is therefore the media norm. This also tells us that if we rely on the news as our primary source regarding general perceptions of crime, we are literally being sold a bill of goods. Our perception of crime becomes a reflection of the extreme rather than the usual.

Fear is a form of entertainment for many—sometimes healthy and sometimes not. Fear of stranger violence, however, is the ultimate fear of the unknown. Our resulting preoccupation with it has created a media marketplace rich with memorable examples to populate our availability heuristics. The result is a distorted perception that affects the way crime is reported, investigated, studied, adjudicated, and reported all over again.

NOMOTHETICALLY SPEAKING: THE AGGREGATE

Because the media damages our perspective of crime so thoroughly and on such a regular basis, it is vital that we ground ourselves with some actual data. As for previous chapters, the warning regarding nomothetic study remains: group data tells us about groups, not individuals.

Homicide

Homicide refers to death at the hands of another, regardless of intent. There are many different kinds of homicide, although they are commonly grouped for study. According to Catalano (2006, 2), there were 16,140 murders (intentional killings) and non-negligent manslaughters (unintentional killings) in the United States that were reported to the FBI in 2004 (most recent data available):

- Most murder victims were male (78%).
- When the race of the murder victim was known, about half were white (49.8%), almost half were black (47.6%), and about 2.6% were of another race.
- When information on the victim-offender relationship was available, 77% of the offenders were known to the victim, while 23% were a stranger to the victim.
- Firearms were used in the majority of murders (70%).
- Offenders were most often male (90%) and age 18 or older (92%).
- Homicide is generally intraracial.
- Arguments were the most often cited circumstance leading to murder (44%).
- Homicides occurred in connection with another felony (such as rape, robbery, or arson) in 23% of incidents.

This data indicates that strangers currently account for less than a quarter of all homicides. It also gives strong support to the theory that men are the most likely to kill, and that women are the least likely to be killed. However, this is a theory only and must be demonstrated before being offered as a conclusion when examining a particular case.

Consider the spate of stranger killings that occurred in the United Kingdom during 2007 (Cohen 2007, 12):

> A crowd of 40 teenagers armed with baseball bats, bricks and chains was swarming around some youngsters—but it was what they were shouting that struck fear into her heart. "At first," says Mrs. [Seniz] Yersever, 40, [of Beckenham, south London] who owns a fastfood outlet with her husband, "I couldn't make it out, but then I realised it wasn't words they were yelling. They were making primitive animal

FIGURE 13.1

In June of 2007, Ben Hitchcock, 16, was stabbed to death in south London by a street gang.

noises, like apes, egging each other on, and it was like nothing I'd ever heard." Minutes later, Ben Hitchcock, 16, a schoolboy who had just completed his GCSEs, lay dying, a knife plunged into his back, while the gang—who were total strangers according to Ben's friends—fled towards Lewisham.

What confused Mrs. Yersever, a mother of three, when she ran to help was that Ben had not been robbed or mugged.

Nor, it appears, was he a member of a gang. He was just a middle-class boy having fun on a Saturday night caught in a Lord of the Flies–type attack by a marauding mob.

The tragic killing of Ben was one of four in London over the weekend. While each death has a unique narrative, what is most chilling is the casual manner with which they occurred.

Annaka Pinto, 17, was shot dead after a petty row with a girl in the Swan pub in Tottenham. Mikey Brown, 23, was stabbed to death during an argument at The Works nightclub in Kingston. Carlos Moreno, 23, a chef, was killed—seemingly in a random drive-by shooting—while sitting on his moped outside a friend's house in Acton.

Ken Hong, 38, a father of three from Streatham, died from the injuries he sustained earlier in the week when he tried to stop his car being stolen, and the driver accelerated, throwing him from the bonnet....

This year, it seems, we are witnessing a new phenomenon—the rise of casual death. Forget mugging, theft, gang rivalry, family feuds, or revenge as motives. A trivial tiff, it seems, can be sufficient motive.

Are we only waking up to this phenomenon because teenage violence appears to have burst its banks, spilling out of inner city ghettoes and into leafy middle-class suburbs like Beckenham and Kingston? Camila Batmanghelidjh, 42, founder of Kids Company, a charity that attempts to rehabilitate disaffected children, says we are witnessing a frightening new paradigm. "Compared to when we started Kids Company 10 years ago, when they were damaged but 'fixable,' we are seeing children who have grown up as victims of so much violence and neglect, it feels like their soul has been killed off.

"When you talk to them, there is no joy left. They feel their life is worthless, so there is no way they can see value in somebody's else's life. Consequently, it's no big deal to kill somebody. Do the killers of Ben Hitchcock feel any remorse? Are they mortified by what they've done? Definitely not.

"They know it's wrong to stab you in the face, or empty a gun into your belly, but they just don't care." The Kids Company founder reveals that in parts of south London people are seeing increasing cases of torture between teenagers which are seldom reported. "One 15-year-old girl had a shotgun put in her mouth by another teenager and was told to go on the game and sell drugs, or else.

"There are many heartbreaking cases—I could go on and on," she said.

How did it come to this? According to youth workers, although the burgeoning gap between the rich and the poor is cited, the problem is more about allocating resources. . . .

A London University study investigating three social service departments found that of 7,165 referrals made for child protection in one south London borough, only 215 children were put on the child protection register.

A lack of financial resources causes social services to keep raising the bar, with catastrophic results.

"For example, a 16-year-old girl was being sexually abused by her stepfather, but when social services interrogated him, he said it was only physical abuse and that it was part of their culture. So they sent this girl home," explains Ms. Batmanghelidjh. "What happened next was predictable: she ran away and was taken in by a drug dealer and started recruiting her own gang. Could she end up stabbing someone over something as trivial as that which led to the death of Sian Simpson? Absolutely."

What is to be done? Matt Calvert, 33, founder of Prospex, a north London charity targeting disengaged teenagers, says there are no quick fixes. "The way to influence disaffected young people is to build up a relationship one-on-one, and that takes time and money," he said. "Most of the kids I see are illiterate so when there's a disagreement, they don't know how to express themselves verbally, and they immediately resort to fighting. Unless we teach them another way to sort out altercations, there'll be more blood on the pavement."

But yesterday the view from Mrs. Yersever's bedroom window was evidence there is still a painfully long way to go. All day school children made their way to the makeshift memorial of bouquets against the garden wall to pay their respects to their friend Ben.

The coverage here, while perhaps factually accurate, certainly intends to paint a picture that evokes public fear. While it may be true that stranger homicides in London experienced an increase during this period, they are still generally less common than intimate homicides. However, the reporter did acknowledge the frequent connection between intimate violence and stranger violence, and that is something useful.

When questioned about the increase in stranger violence and homicides at the end of 2006, police in the United Kingdom offered their own theories, which foreshadowed (if not contextualized) future media coverage. Kennedy (2006, 14) explains, with specific case examples:

> Fighting was to blame for more of the random killings in the West Country than knives and guns, according to prosecutors.
>
> Roger Coe-Salazar, the chief Crown prosecutor for Devon and Cornwall, studied the recent increase in homicides carried out by strangers, and found that residents appeared to be in most danger of being killed by local young men than drug gangs or other violent criminals.
>
> There have been 26 random killings in the region in the past five years, more than in Merseyside, causing retired officers to return to work and the force's serious crimes investigations team to be tripled in size in an attempt to solve the murders.
>
> Mr. Coe-Salazar, a former defense barrister, and his team have achieved a 100 percent conviction rate for the killers, all of whom were men. Most were involved in street fights, though three cases involved sex attacks and two of them involved robbery.
>
> Mr. Coe-Salazar said: Most of these stranger murders tend to be petty crime got out of hand—silly fights, bungled amateur burglaries and just stupid behavior that has just gone too far. I sound like some old uncle—I'm just in my forties—I just get a feeling there is a lack of respect. There's also a growing excuse culture, that it's always somebody else's fault where somebody has gone off the rails.
>
> "There's a need to blame the Government and State for creating the problem rather than people taking ownership of their own lives."
>
> Only two people in the area had died at the hands of strangers in the final three years of the last century....
>
> The victims of the most notorious murderers were Graham and Carol Fisher. Lee Firkins, 31, and his brother Robert, 33, from Somerset, seeing themselves as the new Kray twins, terrorized locals on a robbing spree around Cornwall. The Fishers were about to settle down to tea in

front of the television at home in Wadebridge when the balaclava-clad brothers burst in, then shot and battered them to death.

In response to questions from *The Times,* the Crown Prosecution Service analyzed the area's stranger killings. While the most high-profile random murders have involved visitors to the peninsula such as the Firkins brothers, prosecutors discovered that most of the killers were locals.

There is no sign of a knife culture to blame. Nor were these the results of drug gangsters fighting over turf. Mr. Coe-Salazar said that knives had been used in a number of the cases, as had sawn-off shotguns and fist fighting, in equal measure.

The first of the killings was in 2001, when the naked body of Dawn Bresland was discovered in an alley in Plymouth. Described by friends as a fun-loving divorcee nicknamed "Dallas Dawn," she had been strangled by a convicted rapist using her handbag strap.

Two of the killings, in separate towns, involved young men using their cars to murder strangers. Neil Pearson was fatally hit in Plymouth by a driver high on alcohol, cannabis and a heroin substitute, who decided to mount the pavement and run over him "for fun." Philip Cousins, 33, a pedestrian in a narrow road in Crediton, found himself blocking the path of a motorist who had drunk a large quantity of wine. The driver accelerated at Mr. Cousins, knocked him down, drove over him forwards and in reverse, and dragged his body 35 yards. Mr. Cousins suffered 32 injuries, including a broken skull, broken ribs and two tire marks from his groin to his head.

Alan Allanson was killed for gate-crashing a party in Torquay. The host, a man with 34 previous convictions including some for serious violence, murdered him within half an hour of his arrival, kicking him so viciously that his nose bone was severed from his skull.

Charlotte Pinkney, 16, disappeared after being driven from a party in Ilfracombe by a 24-year-old scaffolder who wanted to have sex with her. He was convicted of murdering her although no body has been found.

Alicia Eborne, 18, was killed when she was the lone passenger on a bus in Plymouth and refused the driver's sexual advances.

Flo Seccombe, 71, was sleeping rough in a bus station in Plymouth when a 17-year-old mentally disturbed boy, who was high on alcohol, cannabis and amphetamines, stabbed her in the neck.

Patrick Parkes remonstrated with a 23-year-old man in Fowey who threw a glass; the killer punched him fatally to the ground and was convicted of manslaughter.

Alan Edge was killed in Falmouth by a man in a drunken rage, also convicted of manslaughter.

Matthew Stiling, a football club captain, was stabbed through the heart with a sword in the street after an argument in a Sidmouth club.

George Jenkin, 83, was battered to death by two young burglars using a 25-lb. rock at his home in Penzance.

The Metropolitan police dealt with 57 stranger killings in the first four years of Labour's rule, a toll that almost doubled to 101 cases over the next four years, when the total number of homicides across the capital was falling.

Note that these homicides are fairly representative of the type that can occur in Australia, Canada, the United Kingdom, and the United States. A distinct similarity is the persistence of drugs and alcohol. However, a significant difference is that, in the United States, firearms are more often involved.

Consider a snapshot from one region in the United States during the same time period, provided from police reports collected in Bruder (2007, 10):

The 10 people who died by homicide in Clackamas County in 2006 ranged in age from 19 months to 85 years old.

The youngest was crushed under a chair by his 4-year-old sister while their father slept nearby. The oldest, a woman suffering from advanced Parkinson's disease, was shot by her husband, who then killed himself.

Police believed most of the victims knew their killers but said one man was killed by a stranger who hit him with a car and stabbed him as he was on his way home from a Milwaukie bar. Clackamas County sheriff's detectives consider two of the homicides unsolved. They are still searching for the killers of Meghan Flynn Kohl, the 21-year-old daughter of a Washington County Circuit Court judge, and Andrew William Corpe, 44, a transient. Last year, officers shot and killed four people. This year, no one was fatally shot by police....

*Marrissa Lynne Boros, 24, was fatally shot by her boyfriend during a Jan. 11 altercation in her Clackamas home. Police responding to an anonymous call found Boros dead in her home in the 7600 block of Southeast Overland Street, and her two boys, ages 4 and 5, unattended. Her boyfriend, Keith James Bryant, 27, an ex-convict with an extensive and violent criminal history, was arrested in Portland a few hours later on a parole violation.

In December, Bryant pleaded guilty to killing Boros. Bryant was also convicted of attempted murder and assault with a firearm

in other incidents that included shooting at a Milwaukie man.
He received consecutive sentences totaling at least 22½ years
in prison.

*Juan Gabriel Perez Solis, 36, was fatally shot by his wife on Jan. 19 at
their Milwaukie home.

Prosecutors did not bring charges against Rose Perez, 50, after a seven-
month investigation suggested Juan Perez was beating her with a stick
when she shot him in the chest with a rifle.

Responding to a call from a neighbor, Milwaukie police found Juan
Perez dead in the kitchen of the couple's home in the 10900 block of
Southeast Myrtle Street. He was holding a wooden stick, and Rose
Perez's hair was intertwined in his fingers as though he'd pulled it from
her head, prosecutors said.

Rose Perez told investigators that she and her husband had been
arguing because he said he was going to move in with their daughter-
in-law, who she said was pregnant with Juan Perez's child.

*Tyler Scott Watson, 42, of Gladstone was killed on March 27 by
a homeless friend who was staying at his apartment in the
200 block of West Arlington Street. Jason Arthur Brown, 37, gouged
him with a knife near his Adam's apple, slashed his scalp and
strangled him with a stereo cord. Brown pleaded guilty to murder
in May and was sentenced to life in prison with possibility of parole
after 25 years.

Brown and Watson lived across the street from each other in Gladstone
as children and reestablished their friendship in 1997, said Watson's
brother, Timothy. Brown was homeless and had a criminal record that
included convictions for first-degree burglary, drunken driving and
assault. Tyler Watson would let Brown sleep on the couch of his one-
bedroom apartment for stretches of time, Timothy Watson said, and
sometimes Brown refused to leave....

*Timmie Laurel Stumpf, 55, and her husband, Craig Stephen Stumpf,
60, were found dead in their home in the Charbonneau district of
Wilsonville on April 7, after friends and relatives failed in attempts to
contact them. Both had been stabbed several times.

Police soon arrested Timmie Stumpf's son, Joseph Ray O'Neil, 26, of
Southeast Portland in connection with the killings. O'Neil has been
charged with two counts of aggravated murder and is being held
without bail in the Clackamas County Jail.

A trial date has not yet been set. O'Neil, described by police as a drifter, also has been accused of menacing his former girlfriend and stabbing her dog.

*Meghan Flynn Kohl, 21, was found dead at home July 21 by two roommates who shared her Gladstone apartment in the 200 block of West Arlington Street. An autopsy confirmed that she died of homicidal violence, but police did not specify how she was killed. She lived in the same small apartment complex where Tyler Scott Watson had been murdered four months earlier. Kohl was the daughter of Washington County Circuit Judge Thomas W. Kohl....

*Beverly Liberto, 85, a Clackamas woman suffering from advanced Parkinson's disease, was fatally shot Aug. 21 by her husband, Anthony Liberto, 91, who then killed himself, according to police.

Before the shootings, Anthony Liberto had spoken with his wife's in-home caregiver and was despondent at the prospect of his wife entering a nursing home, said Detective Jim Strovink, spokesman for the Clackamas County Sheriff's Office.

Parkinson's disease left Beverly Liberto unable to feed or care for herself. She had been admitted to a care facility earlier this year, Strovink said, but after 10 hours Anthony Liberto took her home. After his wife's caregiver left about 4 p.m., Anthony Liberto tidied their house in a manufactured-home park off Southeast 122nd Avenue, Strovink said. He left a note, then shot his wife with a handgun, activated her medical alert bracelet, and shot himself.

*Anthony Vaughn, who was 19 months old, died Sept. 9 when his sister crushed him under a chair in the family's Milwaukie apartment. Investigators determined that Anthony died after his 4-year-old sister repeatedly jumped on the footrest of a recliner, collapsing the boy's chest and cutting off circulation to the heart....

*Andrew William Corpe, 44, was found shot to death Oct. 20 in Johnson Creek near Southeast Johnson Creek Boulevard and Bell Avenue. A passing bicyclist discovered his body floating in the creek, which runs along the popular Springwater Corridor Trail.

Corpe was a transient who had been arrested 24 times in Oregon, according to the Clackamas County Sheriff's Office. The arrests include accusations of burglary, theft, assaulting a public safety officer and driving under the influence of intoxicants. . . .

*Darrell Wyant, 64, of Milwaukie was fatally stabbed while walking home from a bar early Dec. 3. Hours after the incident, Jeremy C.

Metelak, 27, also of Milwaukie, turned himself in to authorities. He was later charged with aggravated murder, felony hit and run, and possession of methamphetamine.

Investigators said Metelak was outside his house at about 3 a.m. when Darrell Wyant, who had just left Bo's Pub on Southeast McLoughlin Boulevard, walked past. The two men, who apparently did not know each other, got into an argument before Metelak drove into Wyant on Southeast Hull Avenue and then stabbed him, police said.

Note how intimate homicides contextualize the infrequency of stranger homicides in this region, and how this leads to decreased solvability. This phenomenon is consistent with overall findings evident in Turvey (2006, 45):

This preliminary review of rape and murder clearance rates, in combination with investigative realities and solvability factors, strongly suggests that investigative and forensic skill, ability and attentiveness are not being brought to bear in the majority of these cases. As a result, the vast majority of cases are being cleared because the victim-offender relationship is already known, and the investigation may focus on developing that presumed connection. In other words, criminal investigation is at this point reactive.

This gets back to an issue raised at the beginning of this chapter: investigative bias and presumption related to the victim-offender relationship. Intimate homicides are the easiest to solve because they do not involve criminal investigation with respect to suspect development—the responsible party is often standing over the body, weapon in hand. However, a theory of intimate homicide may in some cases be politically inexpedient—the family may be wealthy or influential; the investigator may be or become emotionally involved with the family; or public sentiment may hamper efforts to investigate intimate suspects. Whatever the case, investigators must refrain from following the path of least effort and least resistance in their casework. It is not their job to make friends. Rather they must investigate the evidence, following it scrupulously to its actual end.

Nonhomicidal Violent Crime

In the United States, the most recent figures available for reported crime provide that there were a total of 5,173,710 violent crimes committed in 2005. Violent crime statistics include reported rapes, robberies, and assaults. Of those violent crimes, almost 46% of them were committed by strangers (a total of 2,369,150 incidents) (Catalano 2006). This would make it appear fair and accurate to state that stranger crime is less common than nonstranger crime, on average. However, closer inspection of the data suggests that such a statement actually leaves a false impression.

Table 13.1   Victim and offender relationship, 2005

Relationship with victim	Violent crime		Rape/sexual assault		Robbery		Aggravated assault		Simple assault	
	Number	Percent	Number	Percent	Number	Percent	Number	Percent	Number	Percent
Male victims										
Total	3,028,370	100%	15,130	100%*	452,760	100%	665,600	100%	1,894,880	100%
Nonstranger	1,295,870	43%	0	0%*	104,900	23%	282,240	42%	908,740	48%
Intimate	78,180	3	0	0*	14,520	3*	7,460	1*	56,200	3
Other relative	138,390	5	0	0*	9,560	2*	36,920	6	91,910	5
Friend/acquaintance	1,079,310	36	0	0*	80,830	18	237,860	36	760,620	40
Stranger	1,637,700	54%	15,130	100%*	333,390	74%	356,750	54%	932,430	49%
Relationship unknown	94,810	3%	0	0%*	14,470	3%*	26,620	4%	53,720	3%
Female victims										
Total	2,145,340	100%	176,540	100%	172,090	100%	386,660	100%	1,410,050	100%
Nonstranger	1,382,640	64%	128,440	73%	85,150	50%	240,580	62%	928,470	66%
Intimate	389,100	18	49,980	28%	15,480	9*	47,980	12	275,660	20
Other relative	162,760	8	11,880	7*	2,560	2*	35,240	9*	113070	8
Friend/acquaintance	830,790	39	66,580	38	67,100	39	157,370	41	539,740	38
Stranger	731,450	34%	45,050	26%	81,860	48%	141,080	37%	463,460	33%
Relationship unknown	31,240	2%*	3,050	2%*	5,080	3%*	5,00	1%*	18,120	1%*

Note: Percentages may not total to 100% because of rounding.
*Based on 10 or fewer sample cases.

Table 9, from Catalano (2006, 9).

According to Catalano (2006), 3,028,360 violent crimes were committed against males and 2,145,340 were committed against females (see Table 13.1). This means that males were victims of violent crime a third more often than females. Moreover, males were victimized by strangers 54% of the time (a total of 1,637,700 incidents). By contrast, females were victimized by strangers only 34% of the time (a total of 731,450 incidents). As explained further in Catalano (2006, 10):

> Victim-offender relationship
>
> Historically, females have been most often victimized by someone they knew, while males were more likely to be victimized by a stranger. This finding continued during 2005 (Table 9). Of those offenders victimizing females, 18% were described as intimates and 34% as strangers. In contrast, of those offenders victimizing males, 3% were described as intimates and 54% as strangers. Women reported being raped or sexually assaulted by a friend or acquaintance in 38% of such victimizations.

This means that stranger crime is more common than nonstranger crime among male victims. It also means that females are at less risk of stranger crime than males, and less likely to be the victim of a stranger crime in general. Again, the reliability of such theories must be demonstrated before being offered conclusively when examining a particular case.

Unfortunately, these stranger crime numbers just aren't getting through to the public, from which our professional castes are drawn. The perception remains among the uninitiated that stranger violence is the greater likelihood and subsequent threat. Consider the perspective offered in Gruenberg (2008):

> In my nine years of working with survivors of sexual assault in the Boulder area as well as the Roaring Fork Valley, I have found that society as a whole has a very conflicted and often ill-informed view of both the crime and the nature of the victim. Ask the average individual to describe the mental picture that they have of what a "rape" looks like and you will invariably be painted the picture of an unknown male assailant hiding behind a Dumpster in a dark alley [who] attacks a female victim. The sexual acts are then forcibly attained through physical violence possibly including the use of a weapon. This is what I refer to as one of the myths of rape.

> The truth, however, is that most women are sexually assaulted by someone whom they know: a boyfriend, a date, a husband, a parent or family member, a friend, a teacher or coach. The sobering statistic is that 80 percent of sexual assault victims know their assailant.[1] In addition, most sexual assaults include no physical force. Instead the perpetrator utilizes threats, intimidation, manipulation, verbal and emotional pressure, an imbalance of power and control, and of course

[1] This is actually not consistent with the recent national percentage of nonstranger sexual assaults, provided in Catalano (2006) at 64%. However, Gruenberg may have been speaking locally or experientially.

substances that can affect a victim's ability to give consent, the most pervasive and accessible being alcohol.

Consistent with Dawson (2006), who was cited previously, consequences within the criminal justice system related to this misinformed view are further discussed in Hessick (2007, 345–346):

> The specter of violence at the hands of a stranger dominates the modern construction of crime. Despite the higher rate of non-stranger violence, respondents to a recent poll indicated a belief that they were significantly more likely to be shot or badly hurt by a stranger than hit by their spouse or partner. Criminal law commentators have long remarked that violent crimes committed by strangers are more likely to lead to an arrest, result in a conviction, and garner a longer sentence than comparable crimes committed by family or acquaintances. Well-publicized studies of capital sentencing decisions have consistently demonstrated that offenders who murder strangers are significantly more likely to receive the death penalty than offenders who murder people they already know. The idea that crimes between strangers are more serious than crimes between those who already know each other has been repeated so often that it has become the conventional wisdom in criminal law.

It is consequently the burden of the forensic victimologist to use this information in at least three ways: first, as a shield to the barrage of stranger crime imagery that can soften the availability heuristic; second, as a contextual case note, to help structure the initial viability of case theories; and third, as an educational mandate, to help fight the battle against ignorance that persists in investigative and forensic contexts.

Case Example: Paul C. Aud

Consider the case of 34-year-old Paul C. Aud in Fitchburg, Wisconsin, as detailed in DeFour (2008):

> A Fitchburg man who attacked a stranger in the stairwell of her apartment building in 2006 was sentenced Friday to seven years and six months in prison.
>
> Dane County Circuit Judge John Markson also placed Paul C. Aud, 34, on nine years and six months of extended supervision after prison. Markson found Aud guilty of second degree attempted sexual assault and substantial battery in November.
>
> The parallels with recent unsolved homicides in Madison, apparently committed by strangers in the victims' homes, made Aud's sentencing

that much more emotional. "It's people like you we have to be protected from," the victim's father said while angrily reading a victim impact statement. "Time and time again these kids are getting murdered, attacked, robbed. Enough. We have to stop and show people this is an example."

The victim's father may have been referring to Joel Marino, who was stabbed in his home Jan. 28, and Brittany Zimmerman, who was fatally attacked in her home April 2, and Kelly Nolan, who disappeared June 23 and was found dead in the town of Dunn in July.

Mike Verveer, a 4th District alderman and assistant district attorney, said the Aud crime was "the beginning of what has been a fairly tense time in terms of Downtown public safety for students." A spate of muggings that targeted students at bar time and another case where two women were kidnapped and sexually assaulted also has contributed to the unease.

"Madison is experiencing more big-city crime than when I was a freshman," said Verveer, about 39. "(But) crime statistics show that we are a relatively safe city. . . . Of course, that means nothing to the victim."

During his statement Friday, Aud, with his parents and two siblings looking on, apologized to the victim and her family. "I'm aware that violence has increased over the past several years Downtown and on the UW campus, and I am ashamed that I was a part of that," Aud said. . . .

The victim's mother, voice quivering at times, described how the incident had forever changed her daughter. She was afraid to be alone, afraid to sleep, afraid to eat and had attempted suicide twice since the attack, she said.

The victim, a 20-year-old UW-Madison student at the time of the attack, described how she still suffered from chronic back pain, sleep deprivation, eating disorders, addiction to alcohol and prescription pills and had dropped out of school three times, causing her to lose a scholarship. . . .

During the hearing, Aud was portrayed as having had steady employment, a supportive family, and a long-term girlfriend but also a history of alcoholism and "dark sexual fantasies."

. . . Markson agreed with arguments made by Assistant District Attorney Lana Mades that Aud failed to demonstrate reform, as was apparent last August when, while released on $9,000 bail awaiting trial, he was charged with exposing himself to two women. Since then he has served nearly 170 days in jail. The charge of lewd and lascivious conduct was dropped on the condition that the incident be considered in the sentence.

"What I see is a Jekyll and Hyde situation," Markson said. "Only you know what motivated you that night—and I'm not sure you do."

Mades asked for a sentence of 14 years in prison and nine years, six months of extended supervision for the two crimes. Aud was sentenced for an Aug. 23, 2006, incident that occurred in the stairwell of a Langdon Street apartment building.

Investigators were able to match DNA evidence from a cigarette Aud smoked during a Sept. 7, 2006, police interview with samples taken from a pair of sunglasses that he dropped during the attack.

During the trial, Aud testified that the attack was motivated by drunken anger. He said he drank a pint of vodka and a bottle of wine that day before following the woman into her apartment building and beating her.

He denied sexually assaulting the woman, who testified that he punched her repeatedly in the head, pulled her by her hair down a flight of stairs, then pulled her legs apart and tried to undo his zipper as he kneeled between her legs. He fled when she repeatedly kicked him, she said.

Note how in this case the prevalence of other stranger crimes in the public consciousness impacted the victim, her family, the judge's sentence, and the rapist's apology. While the rape created a very real fear for the victim and her family, the media emphasis on reporting stranger crime cannot be overlooked.

IDIOGRAPHIC ANALYSIS

In this section, we will discuss certain basic idiographic considerations with respect to stranger violence, and adduce illustrative examples as necessary.

Targets

Every offender has particular victim or target criteria that satisfy his or her needs, no matter how general or specific. As with intimate crime, there are essentially three kinds of targets: primary, secondary, and collateral. However, a general question is raised at the outset: why target a stranger?

The first reason implies a level of planning and forethought that is simply not present in the vast majority of crime: *to avoid detection*. This is a particular feature of unimpaired serial offenders:[2] those who select victims whom they don't know, locations they don't frequent, and circumstances that will be less likely to result in their later identification and apprehension. These may be referred to generally as *precautionary offenders*. Their victims are the product of a conscious set of criteria, no matter how indefinite. They are chosen because they satisfy a need, and the offender takes time to seek them out where they may be found.

The second reason is precisely the opposite of the first, requires little or no planning and forethought, and is also the most common: *opportunity*. This is a particular feature of impaired and inexperienced offenders: those who select victims who can easily learn their identity, locations they frequent, and circumstances that will be more likely to result in their later identification and apprehension. These may be referred to generally as *convenience offenders*. Their victims are not the product of reflection and care but rather of proximity. They are chosen simply because they are within easy reach and involve little effort to acquire.

Primary Targets

A *primary target* is someone who is of the greatest importance to the offender, and who dictates the location and timing of any attack. Often, the offender will have planned out and intended to hit that victim at the risk of foregoing any or all other targets in the environment. In some cases, there will be more than one primary target.

In cases of stranger violence, offenders may target a person whom they meet at a bar; a jogger running in a public park; or a home in a conveniently located neighborhood. Their targeting of primary victims is dictated by what they want from them, and whether the attack is planned or unplanned. If planned, they go where their preferred victim type may be found; if unplanned, they target those in their immediate environment.

Secondary Targets

A *secondary target* is someone who is of lesser importance to the offender; he or she will not dictate the location and timing of an attack. However, a secondary target will be a conscious choice based on the availability within the environmental and temporal constraints dictated by primary targets. Not all offenders will take the time to deliberate over the possibility of achieving secondary targets.

---

[2]The term *unimpaired* refers to those who are not under the influence of drugs, alcohol, intense mood swings, or the delusions that can accompany mental illness.

In cases of stranger violence, secondary targets will often be those who are incidentally discovered with the primary target. They are targets of intentional opportunity. Examples include an unknown roommate found with an intended rape victim who is then also raped; people standing in line at the bank who are forced to give up valuables by bank robbers; someone who witnesses a crime and is eliminated on the spot to prevent his or her testimony; or freinds who attempt to defend a victim being assaulted in a pub fight.

Collateral Victims

A *collateral victim* is someone who is attacked and injured unintentionally because of his or her proximity to a primary or secondary target within a given environment. His or her injury is completely uncalculated and incidental to the intended outcome. A collateral victim is, in fact, not a target. It is important to distinguish between secondary targets and collateral victims, the key difference being the intent of the attacker.

In cases of stranger violence, collateral victims will be hit because they are in the way. They are in the wrong place at the wrong time. However, collateral stranger victims are unique, because they may be harmed in the course of non-stranger violence. Examples include a child left in a car seat by a parent forced from a vehicle in a carjacking; a bystander killed by stray gunfire related to a nonstranger shooting; a bomb intended for one mailbox that is accidentally placed and goes off in another.

Case Example: Mt. Nelson, Australia

Consider the case of a the 36-year-old Mt. Nelson man, fixing a lawnmower at his home just before noon in November of 2007. As explained in Smith (2007, 9):

> Police said a stranger appeared in the man's yard and the two men argued briefly before the resident was stabbed.
>
> He was stabbed in the abdomen and arm, although police are still unsure what type of weapon was used.
>
> The attacker fled the scene and the injured man called an ambulance. Ambulance staff alerted police. The injured man was taken to the Royal Hobart Hospital for treatment and while his injuries were serious they were not life-threatening.
>
> Uniform police and Hobart CIB searched the yard of the white weatherboard home and surrounding areas yesterday afternoon, looking for the perpetrator and any clues that would explain why he made the seemingly random attack....
>
> Sergeant Gerry King said police did not believe the victim knew his attacker. "From what we understand the 36-year-old male was

working in the backyard when he was approached by another person," Sgt. King said.

"They had a short argument and the other male stabbed or slashed the resident with a sharp weapon.

"As far as we can tell, they are strangers. At this stage, no relationship between the victim and offender has been established."

He reassured residents of Mt. Nelson and the wider Hobart community that the incident was isolated—although he admitted the attack was strange. "It is a bit strange but unfortunately some bizarre things do happen from time to time," he said. "Residents shouldn't worry, attacks of this type are very unusual."

The circumstances of this crime are similar to an incident of so-called "water rage" that occurred in Sydney only a month prior—resulting in homicide. As explained in Jones (2007):

Ken Proctor suffered a massive heart attack on Wednesday after he was allegedly punched in the head by a stranger, who then kicked him as he lay on the ground.

He died a short time later in hospital.

Police will allege the attack occurred as the 66-year-old watered the garden of his Sylvania home, and began as an argument about water use. Mr. Proctor had been complying with Sydney's water restrictions at the time of the attack.

Todd Munter, 36, also of Sylvania, in Sydney's south, has been charged with murder and remains in custody following a court appearance yesterday. Today, Mr. Proctor's widow Lyn was close to tears as she told how her husband usually watered in the mornings, but had gone out into the garden that afternoon at her request "I said to him 'The roses are going to die, it was a hot day, can you do it this afternoon,'" Mrs. Proctor told the Seven Network. "I keep thinking I shouldn't have asked him to do that."

Further details are available in Squires (2007):

Australia has suffered its first "water rage" death as the country confronts its seventh year of crippling drought.

Strict water restrictions have already provoked countless neighborhood feuds, but this is the first time someone has lost his life over the increasingly precious resource. Ken Proctor, 66, was watering his lawn with a hose in a Sydney suburb when a passerby, Todd Munter, 36, made a remark about him wasting water.

Proctor then reportedly turned the hose on Mr. Munter, drenching him and provoking a fight. The younger man allegedly attacked him, pushing him to the ground while kicking and punching him. Proctor suffered a massive heart attack and died in hospital. Mr. Munter was tackled by two passersby, including an off-duty policeman.

The incident happened around 5:30 p.m. on Wednesday, meaning the victim was complying with the city's tough water conservation regulations, which limit hose use to Wednesdays and Sundays before 10 a.m. and after 4 p.m.

According to court records, Munter was chronically depressed, and also heavily medicated with painkillers similar to morphine (because of ongoing back problems) at the time of the attack.

Both cases are excellent examples of stranger violence resulting from a statistically typical source—an argument—with the sensational feature of "water rage" or "hose rage." Continued coverage of "water rage" incidents might lead the public to believe that such incidents are more common than they actually are. In fact, even in the world of stranger crime, it's still more dangerous to go to the pub.

MOTIVATIONAL EVENTS AND CIRCUMSTANCES

The motivations involved with stranger violence differ from those related to intimate violence only in that they tend to be intrinsic rather than extrinsic. That is to say, the motives in stranger violence tend to come from within the offender, without deliberation about, or ongoing reinforcement by, the eventual stranger victim. The offender brings the need for violent expression with him or her to the circumstance. The victims are selected because they can satisfy the motive at reduced risk, or **because they are convenient** when the motive engages.

For example, if a person gets angry with someone he just met, to the point of violence, that emotion reflects more about the problems that exist in his own life. His anger is likely to be *displaced*—a result of his particular history and circumstances[3]—whereas violence between two people who know each other is more likely to be cumulative, with a mutual history of interactions to feed the flames. Additionally, drugs, alcohol, or mental illness may cause, enable, or lead to a mood or misunderstanding that results in a physical altercation. Again, these are intrinsic circumstances that have less to do with the ultimate victim than the attacker.

---

[3]*Displaced anger* is anger directed at someone or something other than the original instigator of that feeling; it is directed at a representative or proxy.

Consider the data from a study of Australian homicides conducted by Davies and Mouzos (2007, 28):

> In terms of motive, one-third of stranger homicides were attributed to an alcohol-related (17%) or other argument (16%). Twenty-two percent of deaths resulted from an argument or altercation about money or drugs, including acquiring money for drugs. A further 13 percent occurred as a result of the offender seeking revenge for some perceived wrongdoing.
>
> Almost two out of five stranger homicides (n = 35; 38%) occurred during the course of another crime, usually a robbery (n = 17) or some other property offence, including theft, break and enter or arson (n = 7). Seven stranger homicides occurred during the course of a sexual assault; all involving female victims (n = 8). One of these cases involved a real estate agent who was lured by the offender to a vacant house (case no. 093/06). In another case, the female victim died after a serious assault in bushes on the side of the road (case no. 256/06).

While the percentages vary between the United States, the United Kingdom, Canada, and Australia, the motives and circumstances are not at all dissimilar.

Case Example: Adam Lane

Adam Leroy Lane was a 43-year-old truck driver from North Carolina. The facts and circumstances surrounding his crimes suggest that he would be best referred to as a precautionary offender with a power motivation, with respect to his reasons for targeting stranger victims.

On July 30, 2007, Lane broke into the home of Jean and Kevin McDonough. He was dressed in black, wore a mask and gloves, and carried a choke wire and a belt with Chinese throwing stars. Once inside the home, he attempted to rape their 15-year-old daughter at knife-point, As described in Ellement (2007):

FIGURE 13.2
Adam Leroy Lane being led by authorities to his arraignment.

> The girl screamed, and her parents came running. The mother fought with Lane, who slashed her hands, police said. The father put Lane in a headlock, and the girl called 911.
>
> Once New Jersey authorities learned of the case, they charged Lane with killing 38-year-old Monica Massaro less than 24 hours before he

allegedly attacked the Chelmsford family. In both cases, authorities in both states said, Lane drove into a truck stop and then drifted into neighboring towns, searching for victims.

Details relating to the homicides are provided in Hepp (2007):

> The truck driver charged with murdering a New Jersey woman and trying to rape a Massachusetts teenager is now being investigated by authorities in Pennsylvania as a possible suspect in the stabbing death of one woman and the slashing of another.
>
> In each of the four cases the victim was attacked late at night, while at home but not behind locked doors, and was stabbed, cut, or threatened with a knife.
>
> Police in Pennsylvania confirmed Friday they are investigating Adam Leroy Lane in connection with the July 13 stabbing death of Darlene Ewalt in a Harrisburg suburb, and the wounding of a woman in her home near York on July 17.
>
> The attacks occurred about two weeks before Lane, a 43-year-old trucker from Jonesboro, N.C., is accused of killing 38-year-old Monica Massaro in her Hunterdon County home. Investigators have said Lane parked his rig at a truck stop just off Interstate 78 in the early morning of July 29 and walked the streets of Bloomsbury trying several doors before finding the door to Massaro's Main Street duplex unlocked. She was found the following day, stabbed repeatedly in the head, neck and chest.
>
> Lane then drove to the Boston suburb of Chelmsford, where police said he parked his rig at an Interstate highway truck stop and walked to a nearby residential area. Again finding an unlocked door, Lane entered a home just before 4 a.m. on July 30 and tried to rape a 15-year-old girl at knifepoint before her father grabbed him and held him for police, authorities said.

Lane ultimately pleaded guilty in the McDonough case to home invasion, armed assault in a dwelling, assault with intent to commit murder, and assault and battery with a dangerous weapon. He was subsequently sentenced in Lowell Superior Court to 25 to 30 years in prison. As of this writing, the investigation into Lane's involvement with other crimes in other states is ongoing.

SUMMARY

Stranger violence is a very real concern with motives and means similar to those found in nonstranger violence. However, motives in stranger violence tend to be intrinsic to the offender, and victim targeting tends to be more dependent upon offender planning with respect to precautionary intent. Despite the fact that there are fewer stranger crimes than not, the media reports them with greater frequency. This creates a false impression in the minds of the public, and can also have a negative impact on the criminal justice system.

In unsolved cases, determining whether a victim suffered his or her attack at the hands of a stranger is a crucial yet too often political consideration. It dictates the nature and extent of investigative direction, and the ultimate suspect pool. Forensic victimologists must remain objective in their analysis despite these pressures, and be willing to follow the evidence to its actual rather than expeditious end.

Questions

1. True or False: It is generally more common that violence is suffered at the hands of friends, family, and acquaintances, and stranger violence enjoys a great deal less of our attention.

2. Why do investigators often not appreciate victim scrutiny?

3. Where do overall perceptions about crime and related trends come from?

4. What criteria are used to determine the newsworthiness of a crime occurrence according to Doyle (1976)?

5. According to FBI statistics from 2004, what portion of homicides were perpetrated by strangers?

6. True or False: For female victims, stranger crime is less common than nonstranger crime on average.

7. How do the motivations involved with stranger violence differ from those related to intimate violence?

REFERENCES

Bruder, J. 2007. "Motives and circumstances of 2006 homicides vary widely." *The Oregonian*, January 4.

Buckler, 2005. "Assessing the Newsworthiness of Homicide Events: An Analysis of Coverage in the *Houston Chronicle*." *Journal of Criminal Justice and Popular Culture* 12, no. 1: 1–25.

Catalano, S. 2006. *National Crime Victimization Survey: Criminal Victimization, 2005.* Washington, DC: U.S. Department of Justice, Office of Justice Programs, Bureau of Justice Statistics Bulletin, NCJ 214644, September.

Chermak, S. 1995. Victims in the news: Crime and the American news media. Boulder, CO: Westview Press.

Cohen, D. 2007. "Wrong place, wrong time: The rise of casual killings: Witnesses tell of murder in their suburban street, another dead teenager, another random attack." *The Evening Standard*, London, UK, June 26.

Collins, J. 2007. "Lady Madonna, Children at Your Feet: The Criminal Justice System's Romanticization of the Parent-Child Relationship." *Iowa Law Review* 93, November: 131–184.

Davies, M., and J. Mouzos. 2007. "Homicide in Australia: 2005–06 National Homicide Monitoring Program Annual Report." Canberra: Australian Institute of Criminology, Research and Public Policy Series, No. 77.

Dawson, M. 2006. "Intimacy and Violence: Exploring the Role of Victim-Defendant Relationship in Criminal Law." *Journal of Criminal Law and Criminology* 96, Summer: 1417–1449.

DeFour, M. 2008. "Fitchburg man sentenced in attack on Madison woman." *The Wisconsin State Journal*, April 26.

Ellement, J. 2007. "Victims face alleged intruder in court: Trucker is held without bail." *The Boston Globe*, September 13. http://www.boston.com/news/local/articles/2007/09/13/victims_face_alleged_intruder_in_court.

Gruenberg, J. 2008. "Exposing the myths of rape." *The Aspen Times*, April 13. http://www.aspentimes.com/article/20080413/COLUMN/471926728/0/FRONTPAGE.

Hepp, R. 2007. "Suspect in Hunterdon murder investigated in two Pa. attacks." *New Jersey Star-Ledger*, September 1. http://www.nj.com/news/index.ssf/2007/09/suspect_in_hunterdon_murder_in.html.

Hessick, C. 2007. "Violence between Lovers, Strangers, and Friends." *Washington University Law Review* 85, : 343–407.

Johnstone, J.W.C., Hawkins, D.F., and Michener, A. 1994. Homicide reporting in Chicago dailies. *Journalism Quarterly*, 71, 860–872

Jones, G. 2007. "Grandfather Ken Proctor dies after hose rage." *Sydney Herald-Sun*, November 2. http://www.news.com.au/heraldsun/story/0,21985,22688624-662,00.html.

Kennedy, D. 2006. "Tragic toll of fights and petty crime that cost lives; killed by strangers." *The Times UK*, December 27.

Prichard, D., and Hughes, K. 1997. Patterns of deviance in crime news. *Journal of Communication*, 47, 49–67.

Squires, N. 2007. "Amid drought, Australia has first 'water rage' death." *The New York Daily Telegraph*, November 2. http://www2.nysun.com/article/65747.

Smith, L. 2007. "Man stabbed while fixing lawnmower: Attack baffles police." *Mercury Abstracts*, Hobart, Australia, November 30.

Turvey, B.E. 2006. "Beneath the Numbers: Rape and Homicide Clearance Rates in the United States." *Journal of Behavioral Profiling* 6, no. 1: 36–47.

CHAPTER 14

Sexual Offenders and Their Victims

Angela N. Torres and Angela van der Walt[1]

KEY TERMS

Child molestation: any sexual contact with a child or adolescent below the age of consent.

Child pornography: any picture or video depicting a child in a sexual manner.

Date rape: nonviolent rape between acquaintances that is not accompanied by any assault or battery except for the unwanted sexual touching and overpowerment inherent in a nonconsensual sexual act.

Exhibitionism: in a criminal context, noncontact sexual assault where offenders expose themselves to others.

Fetish: when an individual becomes sexually aroused by an object.

Fixed-victim profile selection: where offenders have specific characteristics they are attracted to and wait to come across people who possess these qualities.

Gang rape: two or more males having sex with a nonconsenting female or male.

Grooming/Victim set-up: what a sex offender does in order to commit the sexual assault and to reduce the chance of being caught.

Hebephilia: recurrent, intense, sexual arousal and behaviors involving postpubescent adolescents.

Noncontact sexual assault: any sexual crime where the perpetrator does not physically touch the victim.

Opportunistic victim selection: choosing victims based on their access and availability.

Partner rape: forcing of sex on another person with whom someone is in a significant relationship, such as a wife, girlfriend, boyfriend, or fiancée.

Pedophilia: a recurrent, intense, sexually arousing fantasy, sexual urge, or behavior involving prepubescent children.

Planful victim selection: where time is taken to select victims and plan how the sexual assault will be accomplished.

Rapist: anyone who has physical sexual contact with a nonconsenting individual.

CONTENTS

[1]Angela van der Walt, PsyD, has worked in sex-offender therapy for several years, in both group and individual contexts. Angela Torres, PhD, has interviewed many sexual offenders in the context of a lengthy sex-offender–risk research study. Both authors have conducted sexual-offender risk assessment evaluations. This chapter is subsequently a blend of the authors' scholarly research and direct experience working with sex offenders.

445

Sexual offender: a heterogeneous term to describe anyone who has been convicted of a sex crime of any type.

Sexual offense: any time a person forces a sexual act upon another without his or her consent.

Sodomy: any sexual act that does not involve a penis penetrating a vagina. It can include behaviors such as manual stimulation of a partner, oral sex, anal sex, and the use of sexual toys.

Statutory rape: crimes of sex between a person who is below the legal age of consent with someone who is above the legal age to consent. Legally, the term refers to acts that are both consensual and nonconsensual. The age of consent differs depending on jurisdiction.

Voyeurism: when a person becomes sexually aroused by watching the private activity of others, especially when it involves nudity or sexual behavior. Perpetrators are commonly referred to as "peeping Toms."

[2]It is understood that sexual offenders can be male or female, and victims can be of either sex; however, throughout this chapter, offenders will be referred to as male, while victims will be referred to as female, unless otherwise noted.

[3]See Griffin and West (2006, 143): "Sex offenders are treated as the outcasts of our communities. They are stigmatized and exiled by the community, law enforcement, media, other offenders, and professionals in the field of sex research, psychology, and criminology. They are demonized through general discussion, crime reports, research focus, and paper titles."

[4]See Fenton (2001, 45): "These predators can operate in any social classification or situation." See also Nagayama-Hall (1996, 3): "Often the perpetrators are pillars of society, including clergy, police, teachers, and physicians."

Sexual offenses are considered among the most heinous crimes that can be committed by one person against another. Frequently conjured images of the sexual offender include the stranger rapist who lies in wait, ready to spring out and abduct the weak, the young, or the innocent.[2] They also include the trolling child molester who kidnaps victims from public parks or as they walk home alone from school—perhaps with the aid of candy or tales of a lost puppy. These and other traditional images of sexual offenders, regularly depicted in books, films, and television, are as frightening as they are lasting. They color how people feel about and react to sex offenders in general, and how professionals treat them in specific.[3] However, it is often the case that these stereotypes are the exception instead of the rule. As explained in Peters-Baker (1998, 629), there is no one definitive profile:

> What is your image of a sex offender? Is he the dirty old man reading erotica material in the back of the bookstore, a stranger in dark clothing lurking behind the bushes, a respected priest, a decorated scout leader? The truth about sex offenders is that each of these individuals fits the profile of a sex offender.

Whatever we believe, the reality is that sexual offenders are not just socially displaced strangers—they are more commonly our teachers, our bankers, our fathers, our sisters, our children, and our friends.[4]

The purpose of this chapter is to move readers towards a deeper understanding of sexual offenders and their victims—beyond the stereotypical and purely theoretical. First, we will outline what sexual offending is, and the legal history of managing, containing, and punishing sexual offenders. Then, typologies of sexual offenders will be described. Typologies are useful because different types of sexual offenders have different victim populations, with different levels of risk for sexual offending in the future. Next, we will share some of the justifications sexual offenders commonly use to explain their behavior. Rationales for sexually offending are often a blend of denial, manipulation, and bizarre cognitive distortions. Finally, we will review different victim types and what sexual offenders seek in victims of sexual assault.

A BRIEF LEGAL AND CULTURAL HISTORY OF SEXUAL OFFENDING

The contemporary view is that whenever someone forces a sexual act upon another without his or her consent, such an act is a sexual offense. The person who forced the act is a sexual offender, and the person forced into the act is a victim of a sexual assault. However, this has not always been the case.

Sex Crimes as Property Crimes

Interestingly, it is property law that has shaped and defined who can be a victim of a criminal sexual act. Historically, children, slaves, animals, and other similarly classed groups have been considered the property of white, land-owning men.[5] Until fairly recently, women in particular were viewed as the property of their fathers and subsequently of their husbands after marriage. Such beliefs are the basis for modern marriage traditions, such as the father "giving away the bride" at her wedding. In a legal sense, this often exempted husbands from being charged with rape related to any sexual acts they committed with their wives, whether she agreed to them or not. As provided in Woolley (2007, 275–277):

> Under traditional property theories, women were considered the property of their husbands, or fathers if unmarried. First, the concept of marital rape was a legal nullity analogous to the inability to steal what one already owns. "The rape of a married woman by her husband himself was not a transgression at all because a man was allowed to treat his chattel as he deemed appropriate." Thus women who were forced to have sex in their marriage did not even have the option of seeking criminal prosecution.

---

[5]As one example, consider Pokorak (2006, 1): "For most of this nation's history, raping a Black woman was simply not a crime. First, laws prevented the prosecution of any offender for the rape of a slave woman. At the same time, the rape of a White woman by a Black man was treated with especial violence. The Thirteenth and Fourteenth Amendments were proposed and ratified as vehicles to ensure the equal protection of the laws. After their enactment, although the de jure prohibition on prosecuting the rape of Black women ended, de facto barriers to prosecution remained."

Second, the marital rape exemption was defended under the assertion that a husband and wife acted in concert and the wife had no separate rights apart from her husband. The husband was legally responsible for his wife's conduct. . . . This doctrine of coverture gave husbands physical and legal control over their wives. Once married, women lacked legal standing apart from their husbands to enter into contracts, own their own property, or defend themselves in court. Consequently, a husband would be unlikely to go to court on behalf of his wife to allege he had raped her.

The third justification for the marital rape exemption is that the courts and police are often reluctant to pierce the veil of privacy regarding sexual matters as they are seen as at the heart of marital and familial relations. Kapila Juthani, a scholar and researcher on police treatment of domestic violence, argued that domestic violence is "largely unacknowledged by the public or legal system due in part to the lingering beliefs that the husband and wife become legally one upon marriage . . . the law did not reach domestic violence largely because it occurred in the private sphere."

. . .

The fourth (and perhaps most popular) justification for the marital rape exemption was the notion that a woman's marriage vows provided ongoing consent to her husband's sexual demands.

Even though major legal progress had already been achieved with fashioning rights for children, slaves, and animals, it was not until 1993 that marital rape became illegal in all fifty of the United States (Woolley 2007).[6]

Marriage and Sexual Control

Despite a long history of arranged marriages and marriages of convenience,[7] modern Western law and culture tend towards the belief that people may choose their sexual and marriage partners freely. However, in Western and non-Western cultures alike there are those who seek to maintain control over the sexuality of women.[8] In such cases, the institution of marriage is or provides a mechanism for sexual control. It can be seen in the tradition of fathers arranging marriages between their daughters and sons in order to

---

[6]According to Woolley (2007, 269): "Although marital rape has been a pervasive socio-cultural problem for centuries, most activity involving the recognition, criminalization, and reform of marital rape laws has occurred in the past few decades."

[7]See generally Adams (2007), Jackson (2007), and Torgoley (2006).

[8]Adams (2007) provides an international (non-U.S.) overview of historical and contemporary intimate violence against women to include sexual assault. It describes how men control women, physically, sexually, and financially—with the legal protection of male-dominated courts that often purport to know better on paper.

capitalize political power, for financial well-being, to formulate alliances, and to move up the social hierarchy.[9] Or it can be more violent, involving control over female sexuality with long-standing traditions such as "honor killings,"[10] female circumcision,[11] and forced prostitution. As explained in Jackson (2007, 897), this last form of sexual control is still suffered by women all over the world, irrespective of culture or religion:

> In China, decades of abortion and infanticide favoring male children has left fewer women available for marriage, impelling "bride trafficking" where men purchase women and girls outright for purposes of forced marriage. In the United States, one small study of forty women in prostitution found that

---

[9]In many cultures, contemporary attitudes regarding arranged marriages still reflect the historical tradition of sexual control and ownership rather than the letter of any written law. Recently this has proven to be true in the United States with the case of polygamist Warren S. Jeffs, the president of the Fundamentalist Church of Jesus Christ of Latter Day Saints. In 2007, he was tried and convicted for sex crimes related to his performance of forced child bride marriages in Utah—originally evading arrest with the assistance of local law enforcement (Turvey 2008, xxxi). While a rarity in the United States, arranged marriages are still common in other cultures. For example, consider the issue of dowry deaths —a major social problem in the Indian subcontinent. A dowry is money or property brought by a bride (or her family) to pay the bride's future husband to marry her. Dowry deaths involve the killing of a bride by her husband or his family for failure to provide sufficient dowry—reflecting the view of marriage as a property-oriented or financial transaction. With a long history, the dowry institution and related violence persist, as explained in Bhave (2007, 292–293):

> In 1961, India enacted the Dowry Prohibition Act, its most important legislation aimed at curbing the problems dowry provokes. The Indian Parliament later amended its national penal code in 1983, and again in 1986, to proscribe the offense of dowry death. The government's attempt to cure the problem through criminal legislation, however, has been futile. While some courts have upheld dowry death convictions, the government generally has not enforced the criminal laws and has failed to investigate potential dowry deaths properly. Further, the Indian Supreme Court ruled recently that India's penal code does not permit courts to compel dowry death perpetrators to pay compensation as a form of criminal punishment to their victims.

[10]So-called "honor killings" often take place in Muslim cultures. A common scenario involves a family that perceives a loss of honor due to some type of "sexual immodesty" by a female family member. She is then killed by a family member as a way of reinstating honor in the eyes of the community. In some instances, a woman who has been raped is then murdered by her family for bringing shame upon them as a victim of rape. As explained in Asamoah-Wade (2000, 21): "Hundreds of women are killed around the world every year on the basis of accusations of infidelity. These murders can occur as a result of mere suspicions of infidelity, a woman's attempt to marry a man of her choice, or as a result of promiscuous behavior."

[11]Female circumcision, also known as *female genital mutilation* (FGM), is the practice, mostly occurring in Africa, of removing the clitoris and/or outer genitalia of a young girl. This is often done without anesthesia by family members or community leaders with crude materials and no medical training. It is done out of religious practice and as a cultural milestone in a young woman's life. As described in Collopy (2007, 470–471):

> FGM is a series of procedures involving the removal of all or part of the external genitalia. The procedure is performed on approximately two million females each year in Africa, Asia, and the Middle East. An estimated total of 80 to 110 million women and girls already have undergone FGM. The procedure is "extremely painful . . . It permanently disfigures the female genitalia [and] exposes the girl or woman to the risk of serious, potentially life-threatening complications . . . [including,] among others, bleeding, infection, urine retention, stress, shock, psychological trauma, and damage to the urethra and anus." It is "a form of 'sexual oppression' that is 'based on the manipulation of women's sexuality in order to assure male dominance and exploitation.'" For these reasons, the United Nations, Amnesty International, and other international human rights organizations condemn FGM as a human rights violation. Many countries, including the United States, have criminalized FGM.

almost 30 percent of the U.S.-born women were prostituted by husbands or boyfriends. Across the world, husbands use physical abuse to extract sexual and domestic services from their wives, even prostituting them for profit or selling them outright to brothels or agents.

Brokers conduct some of this marriage-based slave trade in public; for example, one Taiwanese publication recently advertised nearly thirty Vietnamese women for sale as brides at a price of about $6,000 apiece.

Thus, even where there are now laws on the books to prevent the sexual control of wives and daughters, overt cultural attitudes and practices that maintain women as a sexual commodity or property can still be found.

Sex Crimes and the Age of Consent

In contrast to those who seek to achieve or maintain sexual control over women, we have found that many men became entangled in "statutory rape" charges. These are crimes of "consensual" sex between a person (most often the female) who is below the legal age of consent with someone (most often the male) who is of legal age of consent to sex. As explained in Oglebsy (2007, 1069–1071):

> The crime of statutory rape appears in substance as far back in time as the 4,000-year-old Code of Hammurabi, which provided that a man be seized and slain if he raped a betrothed virgin, whom the law considered to be an innocent victim. It was not until 1275 A.D. that the Statutes of Westminster established the first known English definition of the offense of statutory rape, making it illegal to "ravish" a female under the age of twelve years; English law lowered the age at which a female could legally consent to sexual relations to ten years old in 1576 A.D.

> In the early years of the development of the American system, statutory rape laws were absorbed into the legal landscape via the English common law. American case law has even specifically held that the definitive English statute from 1576 was part of the common law originally imported into the United States. This trend in American case law signifies basic agreement with the legislative purpose and intent behind the original English statutes. Such agreement has allowed the courts to interpret American statutory rape laws by relying upon long-standing historical reasoning to bolster the majority trend of classifying statutory rape as a strict liability crime with no availability of affirmative defenses, such as mistake of age of one's sexual partner. Because of this method of judicial interpretation, such strict liability criminal statutes continue to thrive in the modern era, causing unfair, unjust, and possibly even unconstitutional outcomes in statutory rape prosecutions around the country today.

English and Teare (2001, 830–831) go further, explaining:

> "Statutory rape" itself is a somewhat imprecise term, and not one
> that usually appears in state criminal codes. It is often loosely used
> to describe sex between adults and minors, even in circumstances
> when that description does not correspond to any specific legal crime
> or classification. . . . From a legal perspective, the concept of statutory
> rape (rather than the term itself) usually refers to sexual intercourse
> that involves at least one minor and is prohibited in a state's criminal
> code because the minor is below what is commonly referred to as the
> "age of consent." Thus, legally the term may be used to cover both
> consensual and nonconsensual acts.

Consider, for example, that the age of consent for sexual behaviors in the state
of California is 18 years old (California Penal Code, Section 261-269). As a
strict matter of law, a 16-year-old female who is dating her 19-year-old boyfriend and then has sex with him is the victim of sexual assault—no matter
what the circumstances. Many citizens of California would not consider her a
victim, or the young man a sexual offender. However, it is the law that defines
who is and is not the victim of sexual assault, and the law varies widely from
state to state.

Additionally, each state defines what is appropriate for the prosecution in such
cases. As a practical matter, many district attorneys choose not to prosecute
some statutory rape cases based on a variety of factors, including age difference.
For example, some states will not prosecute if the "victim" is 15 or older (even
though the law states consent is an older age), or unless the "perpetrator" is in a
position of trust such as a teacher or coach.[12] In Texas, for example, the act is not
prosecuted unless there is a significant age difference, as explained in Gardiner,
Glosser, and Fishman (2004, 110).

> Children less than 14 years of age are unable to consent to sexual
> acts regardless of the age of the defendant. Sexual acts with children
> less than 17 years of age and at least 14 years of age are illegal if the
> defendant is more than 3 years older than the victim.

So the issue of whether or not someone is a sexual offender may not only be
a function of the age of the victim, but the laws of state where the victim lives
and the attitudes of the local prosecutor.

---

[12]In Minnesota, sexual acts with someone under 16 years of age can be illegal if the victim is 13 years of age or less.
However, sexual abuse is defined in the statute "to only include those acts perpetrated by a person responsible for the
child's care, someone living in the same house as the child or related to the child, or someone in a position of authority"
(Gardiner, Glosser, and Fishman 2004, 67–68).

Sodomy Decriminalized

The law not only defines who can be a "victim" of sexual assault, but also which specific sexual behaviors can be criminalized, even between consenting adults. The clearest examples of this are so-called "anti-sodomy laws." Sodomy may be defined as any sexual act that does not involve a penis penetrating a vagina. It can include behaviors such as manual stimulation of a partner (e.g., mutual masturbation), oral sex, anal sex, and the use of sexual toys (e.g., vibrators, dildos). Anti-sodomy laws originally served to punish people for engaging in sexual behavior for the sake of pleasure only, that is, sexual behavior that does not lead to the potential conception of a child. More recently, sodomy laws were used to criminalize acts between consenting gay and lesbian people. As explained in Hough (2004, 105–106):

> References to sodomy can be traced back to biblical times. Historically, the definition of sodomy has often been confusing, but the courts have almost always defined sodomy as an act done by men. In fact, in the late twentieth century, courts and theorists found sodomy between women to be a legal impossibility. Today sodomy is defined as "oral or anal copulation between humans, especially those of the same sex."
>
> Sodomy is an example of a private act that does not harm the actors or others, but has been prohibited on the basis of moral arguments. Sodomy laws were not originally created to regulate homosexual sex; in fact, they were originally applied to almost all sexual activity outside of marital procreative sex. These laws did not classify people as homosexual and were not applied to gay and lesbian people as a class. It was only when society began to recognize homosexuals as an identifiable group of people and began to identify homosexual people with sodomitical acts that sodomy laws were targeted toward a specific group in society.
>
> In colonial times, laws against sodomy were often not directed at homosexual conduct, but were focused on sexual acts between men and children, men raping women, or men engaging in bestiality. These laws were created on the grounds that sodomy was immoral and unchristian.
>
> It has only been in recent history that sodomy has been attached to a certain type of person, rather than just to a particular sexual activity. In today's society, sodomy laws have defined the place of gay people in American society. Even in cases where sodomy is referred to in a gender-neutral way, the assumption is that it refers to homosexual acts only, not to sodomy in other contexts. The existence of sodomy laws has limited homosexuals to a second-class position in society, whether or not the laws have actually been enforced. This second-class status

is reflected in derogatory synonyms for sodomy such as: unnatural offense, abominable and detestable crime against nature, and buggery. Until the Supreme Court's landmark decision in *Lawrence v. Texas*, states were allowed to prohibit sodomy and prosecute homosexual couples who engaged in consensual sexual acts.

Sodomy was essentially decriminalized by the U.S. Supreme Court in *Lawrence v. Texas*, 539 U.S. 558 (2003).[13] Like some statutory rape cases, the impetus for prosecuting sodomy as a crime was related to a moral imperative rather than actual harm suffered by a coerced victim. These and related issues become important when considering the different types of sex offenders that inhabit the penal system.

SEX OFFENDER TYPES

The term *sex offender* refers generally to anyone who has been convicted of a sex crime. The heterogeneity of what we call sexual offending makes the term almost meaningless and even misleading. Consider, for example, that both the man convicted for indecent exposure while peeing on the side of the road and the sadistic rapist may be categorized as sex offenders. We need to be careful when we use this term, and when we are interpreting its use by others.

As already mentioned, sexual offending crosses the barriers of gender, race, socioeconomic status, age, religion, and sexual orientation.[14] There is no typical offender, and no typical victim. Subsequently, no one is immune to the devastating impact that sex crimes can inflict, and most of us know someone who is a victim of sexual assault.

Again, for the purposes of this chapter, we are going to focus the majority of our attention on adult male sex offenders. This subset contains the highest number of perpetrators and is the most routinely researched group of sex offenders. It also makes up the majority of our research.

---

[13]Even though Justice Clarence Thomas (*Lawrence v. Texas* 2003) dissented with the majority decision in *Lawrence* on the strict face of the law, he wrote that the anti-sodomy laws in Texas were "uncommonly silly," and "[p]unishing someone for expressing his sexual preference through noncommercial consensual conduct with another adult does not appear to be a worthy way to expend valuable law enforcement resources."

[14]As explained in Baerga-Buffler and Johnson (2006, 14):

Pedophiles, rapists, child molesters, child traffickers, and Internet child pornographers are all classified as sex offenders. The reality is that sex offenders are not a homogeneous group. On the contrary, they are a very heterogeneous group who come from all walks of life, professions, and lifestyles. They range from the "dirty old man hiding in alley ways," to the highly educated professor, law enforcement officer, and teacher. Physically, sex offenders are indistinguishable from you or me—which is essentially why it is critical for probation and pretrial services officers to be aware of who these sex offenders are and, just as important, the potential risk they pose to the community.

Sexual offenders often commit multiple assaults ranging across a variety of sexually deviant behavior before they are identified in the criminal justice system (English 1998). Abel and Rouleau (1990) collected self-reports from convicted sex offenders and found that 51% had sexually abused victims from multiple age groups, 20% had abused both male and female victims, and 23% of offenders convicted of abusing family members had also molested children outside the family. Additionally, they found that sexually deviant behavior often begins early in life, for some as early as 10 years of age (Abel and Rouleau 1990). This suggests that the sexually deviant behavior of these offenders is likely integrated and ingrained into their lifestyle (English 1998).

As a whole, male sex offenders are more dissimilar than similar.[15] However, some similarities appear to exist. Based on our collective experiences, male sex offenders commonly have inappropriate anger management skills, increased levels of anxiety, and a higher prevalence of mood disregulation. They are also likely to display antisocial behavior, such as making verbal and physical threats; perpetrating violence towards self, others, and property; engaging in inappropriate behavior; having a lack of consideration for others; and instigating confrontation with others. Their cognitions (mental processes and understandings) often follow themes of criminal and sexual deviance as well as paranoia towards others. Adult male sex offenders tend to have difficulty regulating impulses, most apparently their sexual impulses. They have a propensity to complain about others, blame others, refuse to engage in therapeutic services, and often refuse medications. Sexual offenders also often have histories of substance abuse or dependence. In addition, they tend to have difficulty establishing and sustaining relationships. Our experience as therapists is consistent with research cited in Fabian (2005, 130–131):

> researchers found that sexual recidivists were likely to have poor social supports, attitudes tolerant of sexual assault, antisocial lifestyles, poor self-management strategies, and difficulties cooperating with supervision. The recidivists showed increased anger and subjective distress just before reoffending. Sex offenders are more likely to sexually reoffend

---

[15]Interestingly, according to Baker (1997, 577):

Numerous studies have also found that men who rape are "normal" to the extent that psychologists fail to find evidence of abnormality. Male levels of sexual aggression do not correlate with elevated scores on the Psychopathic Deviate scale. One well-cited study found that 35 percent of college men indicated a likelihood to rape if they were sure that they could get away with it. Psychologists working with rapists in prison report that the incident of mental illness among rapists varies from only 2 to 20 percent. Researchers have consistently failed to find significant psychological differences between the rapist and nonrapist populations. There is simply no evidence, save the rape itself, suggesting that all or even most rapists are objectively depraved.

if they experience sexual energy aroused by many circumstances, including negative affect, and if they feel deprived or frustrated when they are unable to pacify their sexual urges. They often experience stress, depression, loneliness, fear of intimacy and rejection, often leading to feelings of hostility and anger. Sex offenders may deal with these affective states through deviant sexual fantasy and masturbatory practices. Ultimately, these factors may impede their ability to control their urge to engage in offending behaviors.

Hanson and Harris developed the Sex Offender Need Assessment Rating (SONAR), a method for measuring change in risk levels. The authors note that sex offenders may have problems with emotional or sexual regulation, general self-regulation and impulse control problems, such as using drugs, quitting jobs or school, and having multiple short-term sexual relationships.

As previously discussed, criminal sexual acts are defined by a conviction in a court of law as opposed to the persistence of some discernable mental ill-ness.[16] Criminal sexual acts are consequently many and varied across each jurisdiction—to include anything from prostitution to pedophilia to voyeurism. Individual sex crimes can involve varying levels of violence, manipulation, and/or seduction. For the purposes of this shorter treatment, we have chosen to focus our discussion on the more common forms of sex crimes that we encounter in our forensic assessments: child molestation, rape, and noncontact sexual assault.

Child Molestation

This category covers a wide range of criminal acts from incest to pedophilia. These sex offenders are those who have sexual contact with any child or adolescent below the age of consent. Offenders may be strangers, acquaintances, or family members. Child molesters make up the largest portion of convicted sex offenders (Lindsay et al. 2004).

More often than not, the sexual abuse of children occurs in their own homes (Marshall, Serran, and Cortoni 2000). These children are often abused by someone within their immediate or extended family. This can take the form of incest, a biological relative having sexual contact with a child, or a stepparent,

---

[16]This remains true unless there is some underlying psychopathology, such as pedophilia or sadism, which is uncommon. However, as explained in Prentky et al. (2006, 366): "Although pedophilia, unquestionably, is a diagnosis that, in appropriate cases, can satisfy the required elements for a mental disorder, the universal application of the diagnosis of pedophilia for all child molesters fails to differentiate among them, producing one highly heterogeneous group, all classified as pedophiles."

stepsibling, or pseudo-parent.[17] These children are often chosen because of the perpetrators' access and opportunity to be alone with them. They are extremely vulnerable and have limited resources to report the abuse. Owing to the ease with which they are accessed by known offenders, child victims often suffer longstanding abuse that becomes increasingly intrusive. These types of offenses have an enormous impact on their victims, as the psychological damage and confusion caused by being harmed by a person who is supposed to care for you is difficult to comprehend and overcome.

According to the *Diagnostic and Statistical Manual of Mental Disorders*, 4th Edition, Text Revision (DSM-IV-TR 2000,), *pedophilia* is a recurrent, intense, sexually arousing fantasy, sexual urge, or behavior involving prepubescent children. Pedophiles can be either of the exclusive type, only sexually aroused by prepubescent children, or nonexclusive type, aroused by both adults and prepubescent children. Their sexual arousal can be toward girls, boys, or both. Pedophilia becomes a criminal act when the arousal is acted upon. For example, one pedophile was a missionary on the African continent, who sexually abused hundreds of African boys during his 40-plus years of missionary service. His sexual abuse never came to light until he returned to the United States and sexually abused his grandsons. It is likely that due to his high status within the community he worked in overseas, his sexual molestation was never reported.

Many pedophiles seek out positions of trust to get near children, such as working at a swimming pool or dating a woman with young children. A position of trust is one where an adult is in a care-giving role with a child or adolescent. A case example illustrating this involved a teenage boy who started a babysitting business. He promoted his babysitting services with the clear intention of seeking sexual contact with children. Once he gained access to these children, he began showing them pornography, touching them inappropriately, and becoming physically and emotionally abusive toward them. Due to the nature and severity of his offenses, he was tried and sentenced as an adult.

Hebephilia involves recurrent, intense, sexual arousal and behaviors involving postpubescent adolescents. Just like pedophiles, hebephiles can be of an exclusive or a nonexclusive type. These individuals seek out sexual relationships with postpubescent adolescent boys and/or girls who are still under the age of consent. A famous line from the movie *Dazed and Confused* perfectly depicts a hebephile: "I keep getting older, but they stay the same age" (referring to high school girls). These offenses can take the form of statutory rape (which will be discussed in further detail in the next section, on rape), position of trust hebephilia, or stranger hebephilia.

---

[17]A pseudo-parent is a nonbiological, nonlegal parental figure.

A position of trust would include a teacher, coach, stepparent, or religious leader who engages in sexual contact with an adolescent under the age of 18. Due to the nature of his role with the adolescent, such a caregiver can be prosecuted for sexual assault even if the adolescent is above the age of consent but under the age of 18. A stranger hebephile attempts to seduce adolescents below the age of consent. Since the introduction of the Internet, this has frequently occurred online. An adult will seek out minors in chat rooms or other Internet locations with the intention of soliciting sexual contact. Due to the frequency of this, many law enforcement agencies have set up "sting" operations online using officers or volunteers of legal age posing as those beneath the age of consent. Although this is common knowledge, thanks to the popularity of shows such as NBC's *To Catch a Predator*, they continue to make arrests on a regular basis.

Rape

The second subgroup of our discussion are **rapists**—those who have physical sexual contact with a nonconsenting individual. These offenders include stranger rapists, date rapists, gang rapists, statutory rapists, and partner rapists.

Stranger rapists are the least common yet the most feared sexual predators. These individuals are the stalkers, the guys in the bushes, the repairmen you let into the house, and the thieves who happen to find a woman home alone. These rapists can be planful, carefully selecting their victims, or they can be opportunistic, happening upon a vulnerable woman during the course of another crime. Some rapists will have a certain victim preference, such as women with straight blond hair of medium build, while more opportunistic rapists may only care that the victim is a woman. The commonality among these perpetrators is that they are unknown to the victim. In fact, they often thrive off the anonymity they have and the fear they instill in their victims. In this respect, rape is actually a form of terrorism.

Baker (2004, 179) defines *date rape* as "'nonviolent' rape between acquaintances . . . that is not accompanied by any assault or battery except the battery implicit in unwanted sexual touching and the assault implicit in the ability of someone bigger and stronger to overpower someone smaller and weaker." These rapists are often familiar with their victims. Their victims often consent to spending time with them and sometimes consent to some sexual contact. However, when the victim decides to stop the sexual contact, or turns down a proposal for sexual contact and the offender continues to have sexual contact, it becomes rape.[18] These rapists often deflect responsibility for the assault, claiming it was consensual or that they were unable to stop. Date rapists also tend to have multiple victims and are at times encouraged by their male peers. As explained in Baker (2004, 180):

[18]Date rape is often one of the most difficult types of sexual offenses to prosecute, because it becomes a "he said, she said" type of scenario. Such cases are particularly difficult to prosecute when the victim initially consents to a sexual act or when the victim and/or perpetrator is intoxicated. Alcohol and drug use by the victim can make her question if a rape took place or fear that she will not be believed. This may also contribute to not reporting the rape.

Date rape happens, in large part, because some men want or need sex so much that the question of consent becomes irrelevant. These men need sex so much because, for them, the greater the number of sexual encounters they have, the more they demonstrate their masculinity to other men. Their desire for sex exists completely apart from its consensual nature, and it is integrally linked to the cultural construct of masculinity.

A common example would be a 20-year-old female college student attending a fraternity party. The female becomes intoxicated and agrees to go to a bedroom with a frat boy. They begin having sexual contact, and then the female attempts to end the contact. She is met with pleading, coercion, force, or violence, as the perpetrator continues to have intercourse with her.

Gang rape, although infrequent, is on the rise (Ullman 1999). This offense consists of two or more males having sex with a nonconsenting female or male. These rapists often instigate additional men to participate in the act and cheer them on, as if it is a game. This was accurately depicted in the movie *The Accused*, starring Jodie Foster. Her character, Sarah Tobias, went out to a bar and became intoxicated. She was dancing and flirting with several men when two of them began to rape her. This occurred in the presence of many other patrons who only hooted and hollered while she was assaulted.

Gang rape is also found in association with street gang activities (e.g., the Crips or Bloods). Many female gang members, for example, are initiated into the gang by having sex with multiple male gang members.[19] However, sex with multiple simultaneous partners can also be a rite of passage for some groups of males, whether organized as a gang or not. As described in Baker (2004, 186–188):

> For these men, sex is often a means of gaining the esteem of their peers. 'Scoring' is seen as an individual accomplishment for which one earns prestige. Many young men are eager to have sex because they want to think of themselves and to have others think of them as men worthy of esteem.

> Sometimes these esteem systems are explicit. The infamous Spur Posse gang of adolescent boys in Southern California devised a game in which each boy got a point for every girl (most of them were between 13 and 16 years old) he had sex with. The winner was he who had the most points. Arguably, the Spur Posse story got so much attention in the press and in the rape literature not because it was so outrageous, but because the Posse point system made so perfectly explicit that which we know happens every day anyway. Anyone familiar with locker room or fraternity banter knows that an affirmative answer to the question 'did you score?' entitles one to the respect of one's peers. . . .

---

[19]The process of being initiated into a gang through gang rape is called being "sexed in."

Peer support also explains numerous gang rape stories with which we are now, sadly, familiar. Consider the comments of Nathan McCall when he joined the 'train' his gang was running on a 13 year old girl: "All the fellas were there and everybody was anxious to show everybody else how cool and worldly he was." Or consider the behavior of the men who stood by and cheered as their friends raped a woman at a bar in New Bedford, Massachusetts, a scene depicted in the movie *The Accused*. The more they "performed," the more praise they received from their peers.

A horrific gang rape offense that has remained vivid to us involved a 13-year-old girl. She grew up in the inner city, and like many others, she was fascinated by the gang lifestyle. She decided to join a gang and was told she would have to pull a "train"[20] with seven gang members as her initiation into the gang. She agreed and had sex with seven men in an abandoned house. One of the gang members found a metal pipe and convinced the girl to masturbate with it while the members watched. As she was masturbating with the pipe, another member kicked the pipe inside her. When she pulled it out, tissue from her body was stuck to the pipe. The gang members fled from the house, leaving her there alone. She was found later that night crawling out of the house. In order to save this young girl's life, doctors were forced to perform a hysterectomy on her.

As already discussed, *statutory rapists* are defined differently by each state. Each state has identified an age of consent: the age in which a teenager is legally allowed to give consent to sexual contact with an adult. If an adult has intercourse with a postpubescent teenager below the legally defined age of consent, he (or she) can be criminally charged with a sex crime. Some states have set the age of consent at 15, while others hold it at 18. Some state laws maintain that in order for adults to be charged with rape, they must be 10 years older than the victim, while others identify anyone over the age of 18 as potential offenders. This grouping of rapists tends to be the most controversial, as societal opinions regarding statutory rape being a criminal act varies. It was not that long ago that men routinely married 12- or 13-year-old girls, and in some cultures around the world this continues to be an acceptable way of life. However, in the United States, our laws clearly state that teenagers are not able to give consent for sex until they reach a certain age.

Partner rape is the forcing of sex on another person with whom one is in a significant relationship, such as a wife, girlfriend, boyfriend, or fiancée. Partner rape often occurs within the context of other forms of domestic violence, such

---

[20]A "train" is when a person, often a woman, has sex with several men, one right after the other without any rest or break between sexual acts.

as physical or emotional abuse. This is one of the most difficult crimes to prosecute, as it is extremely difficult for a victim to report and prove the sex was not consenting beyond a reasonable doubt.

Included within the subcategory of rapists are the deviant sexual acts that most communities condemn. Some of these acts include fetishes, while others are identified as unacceptable sexual behaviors in society. A *fetish* is when an individual becomes sexually aroused by an object (DSM-IV-TR 2000,). For example, *necrophilia* is having sexual contact with dead people. Another fetish is *zoophilia*, having sexual contact with animals, which is sometimes referred to as *bestiality*. Other more common fetishes include arousal by a specific part of a body or clothing typically worn by someone, such as feet or underwear.

Unacceptable sexual behavior in society is any sexual act that the overwhelming majority of society would describe as deplorable and intolerable. An example would be *frottage*, the act of touching a stranger's breast, buttock, or genital area without their consent. Another example of an unacceptable sexual behavior is illustrated in the following offense. A Caucasian male portrayed himself as an African-American female online and lured men to his home. He set up a scenario where the men come into his home, go into the bathroom, blindfold themselves, and get into the shower. When the men arrive at his home, they see photos of an African-American woman, for the perpetrator's wife happens to be African American. The men assume this is the woman they are about to have a sexual encounter with at the house. Once these men got into the shower, the perpetrator performed oral sex on them. Since these men have obviously not consented to have sex with a male partner, this sexual act constitutes a crime.

Often victims of rape are blamed for the assaults they endure. They hear, "If only you had not been wearing that short skirt"; "You should never have let him into your home"; "A wife is supposed to satisfy her husband's sexual needs"; "How did you get yourself into that situation"; and "You must have been asking for it." Although more and more rapists are now being held responsible for their offenses, blaming the victim still occurs. The victims of rape are sometimes physically injured, and they are always emotionally scarred.

Noncontact Sexual Assault

Noncontact sexual assault is any sexual crime where the perpetrator does not physically touch the victim. These crimes consist of anything from looking at child pornography to peeping on someone changing through a window. The commission of these acts is for the sexual gratification of the perpetrator.

As mentioned above, fetishes with nonconsenting individuals can become sexual offenses. A noncontact sexual assault fetish includes crimes such as the theft of another's underwear. A specific example involved a young man who lived in an apartment building with public laundry facilities. When women in the building washed their clothing, he would sneak over, steal their underwear, and masturbate with the underwear.

Another noncontact sexual assault is exhibitionism. *Exhibitionists* are offenders who expose themselves to others, typically a stranger and usually in a public place. These offenses could involve anything from a "trench coat flasher" to a male wearing short shorts that allows for his penis to be partially exposed. In the case of the "trench coat flasher," surprise on the victim's face is not interpreted as disgust or shock at the act; instead, it is sometimes interpreted by the offender as surprise about the enormous size of his penis. These perpetrators tend to commit the largest number of offenses. It is not unusual for these sex offenders to report more than 500 past offenses. A woman in her 50s once confided that she had hired an interior house painter and returned home to find him painting her home in the nude. This is a clear, yet unusual, example of an exhibitionist.

Public masturbation is also considered a noncontact sexual offense. Just as one would imagine, these individuals masturbate in public places. A common modus operandi for these perpetrators is to masturbate in their cars where others can easily see them, such as at a park or a parking lot. These individuals are aroused by the possibility that others will see them masturbating. One sexual offender stated that he would drive around town in his pickup truck until he saw a woman or small group of women walking. He would see the women and begin masturbating. He would then open the truck door to expose himself masturbating to the victims. He said that most of the time it resulted in a shocked expression and some choice comments from the women. He also claimed that sometimes a woman would come to the truck and perform oral sex on him once she saw him masturbate; however, the truthfulness of his claims is very suspect.

The next subcategory is *voyeurism*. These sex offenders are commonly referred to as "peeping Toms." Voyeuristic offenses consist of a variety of offenses. Some of the most common include perpetrators looking through windows with the hope of seeing people in various states of undress; taking pictures of others in bathrooms; and viewing others in dressing rooms without their knowledge. A specific example involved a manager at a health club. He drilled holes into the women's locker room so he could view women changing and showering. These offenders often escalate in risk level, as barely avoiding detection is part of their arousal.

Another set of noncontact sexual offenders are those responsible for sexual harassment. This can include sexually explicit phone callers and Internet communicators. These individuals will call or e-mail strangers or people they know and make sexually inappropriate comments. A second type of sexual harasser makes sexual comments or gestures to another during face-to-face contact. This can occur in the workplace, or any other public domain.

Child pornography is an additional noncontact sexual offense. This includes any picture or video depicting a child in a sexual manner. Child pornography has been difficult to define, as it can include fully clothed children positioned in provocative poses. Professionals often state, "I know it when I see it," when asked to define what constitutes child pornography. However, a picture of a child in a bathing suit can be a sweet memory of a fun summer day for one person, and used by another for sexual gratification. It is illegal to produce, view, or sell sexual images of children. Child pornography has increased significantly since the introduction of the Internet, as it has become much easier to access and exchange these images. It is also a criminal offense to show a child pictures or videos of adult pornography. An offender who distributed and possessed volumes of child pornography stated that his distribution crime was not egregious because he never touched a child. He failed to recognize or admit that a child at some point was assaulted for the pornography, and his purchases propagated this sexual abuse.

OFFENDER JUSTIFICATIONS FOR SEX OFFENDING

Sex offenders must overcome their knowledge that sexual abuse is both wrong and criminal in order to commit a sexual assault. They come up with a variety of ways to justify their sexually abusive behaviors and make it acceptable to themselves. The following sections will present the most common justifications for sex offending.

"I'm a victim of sex abuse"

Childhood sexual abuse is a devastating problem throughout the world (Beitchman et al. 1992). Of the great many children who become victims of sexual abuse, the majority neither abuses nor neglects their own or other children (Herman 1992). However, of the subset that does go on to commit sexual abuse on children, many have experienced sexual abuse during their own childhoods (Marshall, Serran, and Cortoni 2000). Studies differ in the statistics they offer regarding male sexual offenders who have themselves been victims of childhood sexual abuse. Ryan (1989) found that as many as 70% to 80% of adult sex offenders were themselves victims, while Simons, Wurtele, and Heil (2002) reported that 25% to 70% of all adult male sexual perpetrators report a history of childhood sexual abuse. While the statistics show discrepancies in the number of convicted sexual offenders who have been victims, the conclusions are consistent: a statistically large portion of convicted sexual offenders have been perpetrated against sexually as children.

The reason why some children who are sexually abused grow up to become perpetrators while others do not is unclear. Several possible theories have been developed to try to answer this question (Bagley, Wood, and Young 1994). They include: the child develops an impulse to overcome victimization by identifying with the perpetrator; the child's arousal becomes fixated on the sexual abuse; the child develops addicted sexual behaviors; the child develops cognitive distortions that prevent the development of empathy; the child becomes victim to intergeneration transmission of deviant behaviors; the child develops a pattern of violent offending of which sexual abuse becomes a part; and the child has socially learned sexually abusive behaviors. Of these competing theories, none has been successful at breaking this cycle (Bagley, Wood, and Young 1994).

Even though it is a fact that many sex offenders are victims of childhood sexual abuse, using this as a justification to abuse other children is unacceptable. These offenders, more than others, know firsthand the devastating impact that sexual abuse has on a child. This is a commonly used yet disgusting example of an offender's justification of sexual abuse.

"She was asking for it"

Common justifications that fall under this category are offenders who say, "She came onto me," or that the victim "wanted it," or that the victim was sexually precocious. Some adult males will state that the victim was the sexual aggressor and actually enticed them into a sexual act. Most disturbingly, we hear this justification used by child molesters. For example, an adult male convicted of sexual assault against a minor told one of us that the 3-year-old female victim "came onto him" and was the sexual aggressor in the scenario. A little child who sits on the lap of an adult, wears short shorts, or runs around naked after a bath is interpreted as flirting by child molesters who use this excuse. Child victims of offenders who use this excuse are sometimes viewed by the offenders as sexually precocious and old beyond their years in regard to sexual matters.

In terms of acquaintance rape, the justification used was "she wanted it." This is not a misperception of sexual cues; rather, these offenders use this justification as a means of forcing sex on their victim.

"I am not a bad guy"

We have confronted many offenders who felt they were not a "bad guy," and instead were doing the victim a service or favor. For instance, a common justification is that the offender was "teaching" the victim about sex. Offenders who molest children often use this rationale. The sexual offenders see themselves as teachers and mentors for the sexual development of their child victims. Some of the offenders we spoke to stated that the children were going to learn about sex anyway and should learn from someone who was "caring" and could tutor them.

A sexual offender one of us interviewed used another version of the "I'm a good guy" rationale. He told about how he and his friend discovered a man and woman in their car. The offenders took the young couple and beat the male almost to death. Then they took turns repeatedly raping the woman. Afterwards, they forced her to walk through the field with them, naked and beaten. When the three of them reached a barbed wire fence, the friend of the offender relaying the tale wanted to force the young woman to crawl through the barbed wire as another way to humiliate and torture her. However, the offender being interviewed stated he thought that was "too much." Because he was a "nice guy," he took the effort to pick her up and throw her over the fence. It mattered to him to be seen as a "good guy" even in a scenario where he described raping and terrorizing a young woman and almost murdering a young man.

Another way offenders minimize their sexual offenses is by highlighting all the good that they have done in other areas of their life. The pedophile mentioned earlier, who molested hundreds of young boys while a missionary in Africa, justified his offenses because of all the other good he was contributing to the community in which he was offending.

A rare instance of this is the delusional romantic. Some sexual offenders will use the excuse that the sex took place within the context of a romantic relationship. The most famous example of this is the teacher-student sexual relationships. A young adult female becomes enamored with a young teenage boy, believing that she is in a romantic relationship with him even though he is a child. A more extreme version of this is the rapist who kisses the victim, demanding that she tell him that she loves him or likes what he is doing to her.

"We were just having a little fun"

Another common justification we have heard is that the offense was not a crime or not as horrible as the victim said. The rapist will say that he and the victim were having "a little fun" or that he vaginally raped the victim but will deny beating or anally raping the victim. A variation of this justification is that the rape did not hurt the victim rapist. Some rapists will tell the victim that they will not hurt her. Then the offender will command the victim to take her clothes off and rape her. He did not see the act of rape as being as "harmful" as beating her.

"I'm addicted to sex"

Stating that sex is an addiction is another justification for sexual offending that we have heard. Rapists and other sexual offenders will state that sex is an addiction, likening their offending to heroin dependence or alcoholism. By saying that sexual offending is like an addiction, the offender tries to minimize the context and blame a "disease" instead of taking responsibility for his behavior.

"I was drunk"; "I was on drugs"

Another common excuse we hear as offenders attempt to minimize their responsibility for a sexual offense was alcohol or drug use. Offenders will often use this excuse, as if they can be absolved from all responsibility. However, when you ask them about the hours or days precipitating the offense, the offenders' use of alcohol and drugs is somewhat calculated. For example, one child molester said he was not fully responsible for his actions because he was drunk at the time of his numerous offenses, elaborating that he would never have committed the offenses if he were sober. However, after questioning, it was clear that the offender intentionally became intoxicated before he was placed into a situation where he would be alone with children: he would drink before he babysat his grandchildren. This was his way of "allowing" himself to engage in this behavior.

Another similar excuse for behavior is that pornography is the reason they offend. Most famously, serial killer Ted Bundy provided the excuse that pornography caused him to rape and murder. Again, the offender uses pornography as a means of excusing his sexual violence.

"I was just bored and curious"

An interesting justification we heard from those who viewed, produced, and distributed child pornography was that they viewed the pornography out of curiosity. One offender, who was convicted of *possession of child pornography*, informed one of us that he had the child pornography not because it was sexually arousing to him, but because he was drawn to the "rarity" of it. He likened childhood pornography to rare B-side tracks by musicians, and to Hungarian folklore. Another offender who was convicted of *possession and distribution of child pornography* stated that he was not aroused by the child pornography; rather, he knew that child pornography was rare and marketable to a certain set of people. He said he distributed child pornography to make money to support his drug habit.

A similar justification is that the offender engaged in criminally deviant sexual acts because he became "bored with vanilla sex."

VICTIM SELECTION

In our experience, the majority of sex offenders can be categorized into three subtypes related to how they select their victims. The first is *opportunistic*. These perpetrators choose their victims based on access and availability. An example would be a babysitter who becomes sexually aroused and molests the child he or she is babysitting, not because of an attraction to the child, but because the child is there.

The second type of sex offender is *planful*. These offenders take time to choose who their victim will be and plan out how they will accomplish the sexual assault. For instance, this type of sex offender could be a stalker who carefully selects a woman, learns her schedule and common travel routes, and sets up a situation to rape her.

The final type is a sex offender with a *fixed victim* profile. These offenders have very specific qualities they are attracted to and wait to come across people who posses these characteristics. An example is a pedophile who only molests blond-haired, blue-eyed, outgoing, five-year-old girls.

During our interviews with various sexual offenders, offenders have shared what they looked for in their adult and child victims. Child molesters look for children who are less likely to tell another adult that they are being abused due to low self-esteem, poor parent-child relationships, and their own desire for attention, even if it's negative attention. They look for children who do not have a lot of parental involvement. Distracted, poor, single mothers with children whom the mothers perceive to be in need of a father figure for their children are often targets of child molesters. Some will engage in "romantic" relationships with these women in order to have access to the children.

Other offenders will enter into positions of trust such as a coach. They will offer to bring the child to and from practices and games, and offer extra attention with coaching. The parents will often feel thankful for this other adult's interest in their child and their ability to give attention and provide certain things for their children. It is not until the child reveals the abuse to the parent that the abuse comes to light. Sometimes this does not happen until many years after the abuse. Even though the child does not like the sexual abuse, he or she is often confused and enjoys the attention and gifts. It is often after the child "ages out" of the preferred victim age or body characteristics the pedophile desires that the abuse ceases. When the child is no longer abused or receives other types of "attention," the child then reports the abuse. Children with a strong sense of self, strong familial ties, parental involvement, and resources such as transportation and money, are less likely to be victims of abuse.

Many adults have been victims of some type of sexual assault. Because there are so many types of sexual offenders, it's difficult to name a specific adult victim profile. For example, opportunistic rapists may choose victims who appear to be unaware of their surroundings, have poor self-esteem, be under the influence of alcohol or drugs, or be alone. Another interesting phenomenon we observed in our work with perpetrators and victims of sexual assault is that people who have been victimized before are sometimes victimized again.

Grooming/Victim Set-Up

Grooming or victim set-up refers to what a sex offender does in order to commit the sexual assault and to reduce the chance of being caught. A common way this is accomplished is through quid pro quo or indebting. A sex offender may do something for the victim in order for the victim to feel obligated to do something for the perpetrator. An example would be a stepfather lying to the child's mother to keep the child from getting in trouble and then using this against the child. "If you don't give me a blow job, I will tell your mother that you are failing your math class."

Another frequently used grooming technique is flattery. A sex offender may compliment a child with poor self-esteem in order to coax her into having sexual contact. For instance, a sex offender may tell an emotionally abused child that she is smart, pretty, and special. These may be the only positive remarks she has ever received, and it feels good. The perpetrator will then use this as reinforcement for the child having sexual contact with him.

Physical or emotional abuse is another way to set up a victim while protecting the offender. When a person is harmed, he or she will become fearful of the person causing the harm. The perpetrator is then able to control the victim. In this manner a sex offender may threaten the victim with physical harm if he or she does not participate in the sexual contact or may use violence within the commission of the sexual assault. When a victim is fearful of the offender, it is much more difficult for him or her to report the sex abuse.

A fourth grooming behavior is *inoculation*, which is when an offender sets up the circumstances so another caregiver is unalarmed when a child presents with alarming behavior. An example that comes to mind involved divorced parents with joint custody of a child. Prior to the father beginning to sexually abuse his 3-year-old daughter, he began making complaints to the mother that the child was scratching and rubbing herself. He accused the mother of not properly cleaning the daughter's vaginal area. Soon thereafter, he began sexually assaulting the child. He believed that if the child complained, the mother would think it was an ongoing problem for her daughter and would not suspect the father was sexually abusing the child.

The use of substances can be used either as a way to break down the barriers of a victim or an excuse for sexually abusive behaviors. An offender may give a potential victim alcohol or Rohypnol (date rape drug) to intoxicate and reduce the chance of resistance from a victim. In addition, if a victim does not remember or only vaguely remembers, it becomes more difficult for her to report the assault. Offenders may also drink or use drugs as a way not to be held responsible for their abusive behavior. They have often made statements to their victims such as, "I would never hurt you, but the alcohol made me do it." This also increases the likelihood that the victim will not report the sexual assault.

As already mentioned earlier in this chapter, religious figures often hold a position of trust and access with respect to various victim populations. Additionally, religion itself has also been used as a way to groom or set up victims. Perpetrators have been known to tell their victims, "God said it was okay," or "God wants me to teach you this." The perpetrators who use this technique often have some type of religious role with the victim, whether it be a formal teaching position or a parent instructing the child's religious development.

Preying on the naïve or friendly nature of a child, or the vulnerable, is a common grooming technique for sex offenders. This is how many stranger perpetrators lure their victims into cars, their homes, or other secluded areas. An offender may tell a child that her mother has been in a car accident and he is supposed to take her to a hospital in order to get the child in the car with him. Another example would be an offender asking a mentally retarded woman to help him find his lost puppy.

Another frequently used grooming technique is *pornography*. Offenders use pornography as a way to normalize sexual activity. Some perpetrators will intentionally display pornography, and then attempt to make it accidental and embarrassing when the victim sees it. They often will use it as a progression toward a hands-on sexual assault. If the child does not tell about viewing the pornography, the offender will watch it with the child, then ask the child if he wants to try what was viewed, and so on. This has been a very effective way for perpetrators to set up their victims.

The last method to groom and set up a victim that we will discuss is taking on a position of trust. Priests, teachers, coaches, foster parents, babysitters, and other care-giving positions exist with inherent power over numerous potential victims. It is not only difficult for others to believe that these caring people would harm a child, it is also hard for a child to recognize the perpetration as abuse. It is common for pedophiles or hebephiles to obtain positions of trust as a way to be near children and adolescents. They use their position to build further trust in the children and adults with whom they work. Only after this trust has been developed will these offenders abuse their victims. A case that illustrates this involved a Christian youth leader who volunteered his time to the community. He gained the trust of the children and their parents. He then chose the most vulnerable children to abuse; those with poor self-esteem and little parental supervision. After the first accusations were made, many of the parents came to the defense of the youth leader. It was not until after he admitted the sexual abuse that they acknowledged he was a sex offender.

SUMMARY

The popular portrayal of the sexual offender often includes the creepy stranger waiting in a dark parking lot, or the scheming child molester using a puppy to lure innocent children. However, the frightening reality is that a sexual offender is more likely to be a person of trust from among your family, friends, or community.

The sexual behaviors that have been criminalized, as well as who may be considered a victim of a sexual crime, have been shaped by many factors. These factors include property law, religion, and culture. A myriad of different sexual behaviors may be categorized as sexual offenses. They range from the relatively benign, in the case of public urination, to the horrific serial sadistic rapist. Just as varied as their behaviors, sexual offenders are an extremely heterogeneous group. Therefore, the term "sexual offender" is fairly useless as a construct. Instead, describing offenders by their type of offense (e.g., rapist, child molester, exhibitionist, etc.) is more useful to understand victim selection and management of these offenders. There are some commonalities between sexual offenders, including poor anger management, anxiety, mood deregulation, antisocial behavior, and poor impulse control.

Sex offender attitudes towards their victims appear to have been shaped by the same influences just described—property law, religion, and culture. This may be found in the kind of value they place on women that exists beneath the surface of their justifications and rationalizations for offending. In our collective experience as researchers and therapists, we have found that many different sexual offenders use similar justifications when discussing their offenses. These include but are not limited to: "I was a victim of sexual abuse"; "She was asking for it"; "I'm not a bad guy"; "We were just having a little fun"; "I'm addicted to sex"; "I was drunk/on drugs"; and "I was bored or curious." There are also different types of victim selection: some offenders are more opportunistic, while others are more planful in their behaviors or have a fixed victim profile. Offenders will use similar techniques to gain access to victims, often through the process of grooming. These methods include indebting, flattery, abuse, inoculation, substance abuse, religion, preying, pornography, and exploiting positions of trust.

Questions

1. True or False: Sexual offenders often commit multiple assaults ranging across a variety of sexually deviant behaviors before they are identified in the criminal justice system.
2. True or False: Sodomy is a term used to refer to anal sex.
3. Child molesters make up the _____ (largest/smallest) portion of sex offenders.
4. Name and describe the two types of pedophilia.
5. True or False: Stranger rape is the most common type of rape.
6. True or False: The frequency of gang rape is increasing.
7. A statistically _____ (large/small) portion of convicted sexual offenders were the victims of sexual assault as children.

REFERENCES

Abel, G.G., and J.L. Rouleau. 1990. "The Nature and Extent of Sexual Assault." In *Handbook of Sexual Assault: Issues, Theories and Treatment of the Offender*, edited by W.L. Marshall, D.R. Laws, and H.E. Barbaree, 9–20. New York: Plenum Press.

Adams, R. 2007 "Violence against Women and International Law: The Fundamental Right to State Protection from Domestic Violence." *New York International Law Review* 20, Winter 20: 57–129.

Asamoah-Wade, Y. 2000. "Women's Human Rights and 'Honor Killings' in Islamic Cultures." *Buffalo Women's Law Journal* 8, no. : 21–23.

Bagley, C., M. Wood, and L. Young. 1994. "Victim to Abuser: Mental Health and Behavioral Sequels of Child Sexual Abuse in a Community Survey of Young Adult Males." *Child Abuse and Neglect* 188, no. : 683–697.

Baker, K. 1997. "Once a Rapist? Motivational Evidence and Relevancy in Rape Law." *Harvard Law Review* 110, January: 563–624.

Baker, K. 2004. "Sex, Rape, and Shame." *DePaul Journal of Health Care Law* 8, Fall: 179–236.

Baerga-Buffler, M., and J. Johnson. 2006. "Sex Offender Management in the Federal Probation and Pretrial Services System." *Federal Probation* 70, June: 13–17.

Beitchman, J.H., K.J. Zucker, J.E. Hood, G.A. daCosta, D. Akman, and E. Cassavia. 1992. "A Review of the Long-Term Effects of Child Sexual Abuse." *Child Abuse and Neglect* 16, no. : 101–118.

Bhave, S. 2007. "Deterring Dowry Deaths in India: Applying Tort Law to Reverse the Economic Incentives That Fuel the Dowry Market." *Suffolk University Law Review* 40, no. : 291–313.

Collopy, D. 2007. "Incorporating a Hardship Factor in Asylum Claims Based on Female Genital Mutilation: A Legislative Solution to Protect the Best Interests of Children." *Georgetown Immigration Law Journal* 21, Spring: 469–503.

DSM-IV-TR. 2000. *Diagnostic and Statistical Manual of Mental Disorders.* 4th ed. Text Revised. Washington, DC: American Psychiatric Association.

English, K. 1998. "The Containment Approach: An Aggressive Strategy for the Community Management of Adult Sex Offenders." *Psychology, Public Policy, and Law* 4, no. 1/2: 218–235.

English, A., and C. Teare. 2001. "Statutory Rape Enforcement and Child Abuse Reporting: Effects on Health Care Access for Adolescents." *DePaul Law Review* 50, Spring: 827–864.

Fabian, J. 2005. "The Risky Business of Conducting Risk Assessments for Those Already Civilly Committed as Sexually Violent Predators." *William Mitchell Law Review* 32, no. : 81–159.

Fenton, Z. 2001. "Faith in Justice: Fiduciaries, Malpractice and Sexual Abuse by Clergy." *Michigan Journal of Gender and Law* 8, no. : 45–96.

Gardiner, K., A. Glosser, and M. Fishman. 2004. "Statutory Rape: A Guide to State Laws and Reporting Requirements." Office of the Assistant Secretary for Planning and Evaluation, U.S. Department of Health and Human Services, December 15. http://www.lewin.com/Lewin_Publications/Human_Services/StateLawsReport.htm.

Griffin, M., and D. West. 2006. "The Lowest of the Low? Addressing the Disparity between Community View, Public Policy, and Treatment Effectiveness for Sex Offenders." *Law and Psychology Review* 30, Spring: 149–163.

Herman, J.L. 1992. *Trauma and Recovery.* Revised Edition. New York: Basic Books.

Hough, N.A. 2004. "Sodomy and prostitution: Laws protecting the 'fabric of society'" Pierce Law Review, Vol. 3, December, pp. 101–124.

Jackson, S. 2007 "Marriages of Convenience: International Marriage Brokers, Mail-Order Brides, and Domestic Servitude." *University of Toledo Law Review* 38, Spring: 895–922.

Lawrence and Garner v. Texas. 2003. Supreme Court of the United States, No. 02–102 (539 U.S. 558), Decided June 26, 2003.

Lindsay, W.R., L. Murphy, G. Smith, D. Murphy, Z. Edwards, C. Chittock, A. Grieve, and S.J. Young. 2004. "The Dynamic Risk Assessment and Management System: An Assessment of Immediate Risk of Violence for Individuals with Offending and Challenging Behavior." *Journal of Applied Research in Intellectual Disabilities* 17, no. : 267–274.

Marshall, W.L., G.A. Serran, and F.A. Cortoni. 2000. "Childhood Attachments, Sexual Abuse, and Their Relationship to Adult Coping in Child Molesters." *Sexual Abuse: A Journal of Research and Treatment* 12, no. 1: 17–26.

Nagayama-Hall, G. 1996 *Theory-Based Assessment, Treatment, and Prevention of Sexual Aggression.* New York: Oxford University Press.

Peters-Baker, J. 1998. "Challenging Traditional Notions of Managing Sex Offenders: Prognosis Is Lifetime Management." *UMKC Law Review* 66, Spring: 629–679.

Pokorak, J. 2006. "Rape as a Badge of Slavery: The Legal History of, and Remedies for, Prosecutorial Race-of-Victim Charging Disparities." *Nevada Law Journal* 7, Fall: 1–54.

Prentky, R., E. Janus, H. Barbaree, B. Schwartz, and M. Kafka. 2006. "Sexually Violent Predators in the Courtroom." *Psychology, Public Policy, and Law* 12, November: 357–386.

Ryan, G. 1989. "Victim to Victimizer: Rethinking Victim Treatment." *Journal of Interpersonal Violence* 4, no. 3: 325–341.

Simons, D., S.K. Wurtele, and P. Heil. 2002. "Childhood Victimization and Lack of Empathy as Predictors of Sexual Offending against Women and Children." *Journal of Interpersonal Violence* 17, no. 12: 1291–1307.

Torgoley, S. 2006. "Trafficking and Forced Prostitution: A Manifestation of Modern Slavery." *Tulane Journal of International and Comparative Law* 14, Spring: 553–578.

Turvey, B. 2008 *Criminal Profiling.* 3rd ed. Boston: Elsevier Science.

Ullman, S.E. 1999. "A Comparison of Gang and Individual Rape Incidents." *Violence Victims* 14, no. 2: 123–133.

Woolley, M. 2007 "Marital Rape: A Unique Blend of Domestic Violence and Non-Marital Rape Issues." *Hastings Women's Law Journal* 18, Summer: 269–293.

CHAPTER 15

Victimology at Trial

Claire Ferguson and Brent E. Turvey

KEY TERMS

Cognitive psychology: the psychological science that studies cognition, the mental processes that are believed to underlie behavior.

Exclusionary rules: used in a court of law to ensure that evidence deemed relevant and admissible is not confusing, misleading, or otherwise a distraction from the task at hand.

Observer effects: errors of apprehension, recording, recall, computation, or interpretation that result from some state or trait of the observer. They are subconscious influences affecting all forensic examiners, making it more difficult for him or her to remain objective and honest and avoid advocacy.

Privilege: rules of privilege can result in the court being denied access to information about the victim that would generally be considered relevant.

Rape shield laws: laws designed to protect victims from humiliation and harassment in the courtroom by limiting the introduction of evidence pertaining to a victim's sexual history.

Relevance: any victim information that is deemed relevant may be admissible in court, where relevance refers to whether or not the victim information serves to prove or disprove a fact in question.

Victim impact statements: accounts by victims or their families designed to inform the judge, jury, and parole boards of the impact the crime has had on their lives.

Victimology—that is, information about the victim, his or her background, actions, and injuries—is a regular feature of civil and criminal trials. In cases involving victim death, evidence about the victim may be presented by fact witnesses, such as family members and investigators, or by expert witnesses, such as medical examiners, mental health experts, and other qualified professionals. In cases that involve a living victim, the victim may testify to these things in person along with corroboration from family members or medical and mental health professionals. It is fair to say that in a criminal matter, without evidence and testimony related to the victim, there can be no charges, no arrest, and no trial.

This chapter will discuss the purpose of victimology, and victimologists, in court proceedings. The first part will review the victim's role at trial, as well as admissibility issues related to victim information. The second part will discuss issues related to forensic examiners that might give victimology evidence, such as expert admissibility and bias. We will conclude with a discussion of the different types of forensic examiners that traditionally give victimology evidence at trial, and why each may be considered relevant.

THE VICTIM AT TRIAL

According to the U.S. Bureau of Justice Statistics (Reaves 2006), the vast majority of cases brought against criminal defendants never go to trial.[1] There are a number of circumstances that can cause this result. Sometimes the prosecutor finds there is a lack of evidence to proceed; sometimes the judge finds there is a lack of evidence to proceed; sometimes the accused pleads guilty and a trial is unnecessary; and sometimes the accused makes a deal, pleading guilty to lesser charges for a reduced sentence.

In each case that is dropped on a prosecutor's desk, he or she must determine which of these courses to pursue: to go to court or take another path. When there is less evidence, or less certainty as to guilt, taking a case to trial is referred to as "rolling the dice," for it is difficult on even the best days to predict what juries will do. The decision to go to trial is by no means final. As a case moves forward and new information is revealed, the decision to prosecute, drop, or plea the case may be revisited, even mid-trial.

Victimology, for the purpose of presenting victims, the harm and loss they suffered, their present character, and their background, can play a key role in this decision-making process. However, forget everything that films and television have portrayed about police and prosecutors working hand in hand with victims or their families. Such involvement is not the norm. The tenuous and sometimes misleading relationship between victims of crime and the prosecution is characterized in Pokorak (2007, 697–699):

> Each lawyer, judge and second year law student understands that the prosecution's "client" is the state. The core roles of the prosecutor are to represent the interests of the government and the interests of

---

[1] As explained in Reaves (2006, 7), who studied the conviction data related to violent felons in large urban cities: "Eighty-eight percent of violent felons were convicted through a guilty plea and 12% at trial."

citizens as a whole. In its most blunt incarnation, the specific victim of a crime is relevant to a prosecutor only as a witness and a symbol of the threat a defendant poses to society. Because of this professional distance from individual victims, chief prosecutors in most jurisdictions are elected, and the chief prosecutors in the federal system are appointed by the President in power.

This representational and political aspect of the prosecutor's role, however, is in part responsible for the confusion about the prosecutor's duty to individual victims. While arguing for voter support in the political arena, most prosecutorial candidates prefer to speechify about representing victims rather than talk about representing a political subdivision. It is simply much more powerful to talk about vindicating a specific victim's harm than to more accurately discuss the abstract harm to the society as a whole. Likewise, it is easier to display pictures of an individual's wounds than to try to describe the damage done to a community.

Add to this political reality the very important movement by victims to seek respect and dignity in the courts—particularly the criminal courts. Victims have seen judges as too indifferent to their concerns, defendants as too powerful in the balance of power inside the courts, and prosecutors as too insensitive to their needs. Currently, the victim's movement attempts to educate judges and limit defendants' rights, while supporting prosecutors and increased budgets for their offices.

This latter alliance is not surprising, as victims have generally seen the prosecutor as the most directly accessible player in the criminal justice system. However, this alliance of convenience is now starting to fray as victims are beginning to understand that their real interests are too often subjugated to the prosecutor's legal and ethical duties as imposed by the role of public prosecution.

Perhaps the largest reason for the reassessment of this relationship of convenience is the conflicted way prosecutors relate to victims. Although they portray themselves as the champions of victims, prosecutors are too often forced to be the primary messengers, if not agents, of victim disappointment in the criminal justice system. For example, when cases fall apart and are dismissed, it is the prosecutor who is responsible for dealing with the victim. If a victim's legal interests diverge from that of the prosecutor, her special status as complaining witness is often abandoned, and she is then treated as a "mere witness." Any time victims provide exculpatory information regarding the crime, prosecutors are legally and ethically bound to disclose that information to the defendant. Whenever a victim's presence is needed at a hearing, either to supply testimony or for simple emotional impact, prosecutors generally issue a subpoena to guarantee her presence. And, though a victim may be consulted when a prosecutor assesses the correct plea to offer, her opinion is often necessarily second to the prosecutor's independent case assessment. In short, it is the very powers granted to the prosecution because of its unique public purpose that give rise to the conflicts with individual victims.

These scenarios pose difficult challenges that are a constant reality in the most scrupulous public prosecution offices. The problems caused by these situations are exacerbated when victims are led to believe, either overtly or by compassionate promises, that the prosecutor represents them—that the prosecutor is their personal attorney in the upcoming criminal proceedings. Although, as mentioned above, this message may be generally suggested in the political contests for election, the direct representation concept is thoroughly reinforced by statutory obligations of prosecutors vis-a-vis victims in pre-trial proceedings and sentencing hearings. Additionally, victims cannot be faulted in their well-founded belief that the prosecutor is their personal attorney in light of the words and common practices of police, victim witness advocates, and paralegals who are employed by prosecutorial offices.

In short, victims soon find their role at trial is not one of partnership with the prosecutor but one of performance for the judge and jury. They must either perform the role of victim to gain sympathy, or that of pure fact witness to make a particular record of events. Sometimes, in fact much of the time, they will be asked to do both. For many victims this means a simple change in their normal mode of dress or demeanor; for others, it means attempting to with-hold certain kinds of details about their personal life to maintain credibility; and for still others, it means trying to keep the court from learning that they smoked marijuana to calm down before going under oath. And that's when the facts are on their side.

The general role of victims in legal proceedings is described bluntly from the perspective of a public defender in Gruber (2003, 654–657):

> The role of the victim in the legal process starts at the beginning of a criminal case. Prosecutors generally take into consideration whether or not the victim desires to "press charges," although they do not do so in every case and in fact cannot in some arenas like domestic violence. Prosecutors, as a matter of course, take the victim's wishes into consideration during the plea negotiation process. For example, as a public defender, I often encountered rejections of plea suggestions on the ground that "the victim would never accept such a plea

agreement." Indeed, some jurisdictions require prosecutors to consult the victim during plea bargaining.

Turning to the trial phase of the prosecution, the victim participates in the trial most importantly as an essential witness. Victims' rights advocates have successfully persuaded legislatures to exempt victims from rules that prohibit testifying witnesses from observing the trial. Indeed, some victims' rights advocates argue that the victim (or victim's family) should have an absolute right to testify during the guilt as well as sentencing phase of a trial, even if the testimony has little probative value and tends to prejudice the defendant.

Ultimately, from the view of the prosecution, the role of the victims is to help establish that the theory of the crime is correct. They are meant to assist in demonstrating that events unfolded in a particular way causing a particular type of harm. Also, and sometimes unfairly, victims (and their various proxies) must establish that they are being truthful or that they did not contribute to the harm that was caused. The more any victim fails at these tasks, the more difficult it is to secure a conviction at the ceiling of the charges made by the prosecution. The victim's place, then, is to "watch from the sidelines and testify when called upon" without losing the case through bad character or bad conduct (Simmons 2007, footnote 315).

Once a conviction has been secured, the victim or the victim's family may take on a more emotional role during the penalty phase of the trial; they may be allowed to provide a Victim Impact Statement. This will be discussed at the end of the next section.

EVIDENTIARY AND ADMISSIBILITY ISSUES

The question of whether or not a certain piece of evidence or information should be admissible in any court is really a question of: "Should the fact finder be exposed to [this information or evidence], and thus permitted to take [this information or evidence] into account in arriving at a verdict" (Roberts and Zuckerman 2004, 96). It is the role of the judge to act as a filter for the information that both prosecution and defense hope to use in support of their version of events. Put simply, the judge does this by determining what is relevant to the specific issues at hand and what is not.

Theoretically, any victim information that is deemed relevant and does not fall under any of the *exclusionary rules*[2] present in most legal systems is admissible in court. When proposing a working definition for what is meant by the term *relevant*, Keane (2006, 22) suggests that "the relevant fact need only make the matter requiring proof more (or less) probable." That is, a piece of evidence or information may be deemed sufficiently relevant by the presiding judge if that judge believes that a fact at issue will be proved or disproved to be more or less

[2]An *exclusionary rule* is one that forbids the use or introduction of a particular type of evidence at trial.

probable based on that piece of evidence. Roberts and Zuckerman (2004, 98) explain relevance simply as "*x* is relevant to *y* for our purposes if *x* contributes towards proving or disproving *y*." The judge has wide discretion in determining whether or not certain information and evidence will be relevant to the jury. Issues with this discretion will be addressed presently.

As already mentioned, there are certain rules that judges must adhere to that theoretically exclude certain types of evidence in every case (Keane 2006; Roberts and Zuckerman 2004; Murphy 2008). These are called *exclusionary rules,* and they are designed to ensure that evidence that is deemed relevant is not also confusing, misleading, or otherwise a distraction from the task at hand (Keane 2006; Roberts and Zuckerman 2004). There are many exclusionary rules that may be argued for various types of evidence, however, the one most relevant to this discussion of forensic victimology is the rule pertaining to privilege.

According to Roberts and Zuckerman (2004, 97): "Rules of privilege protect relationships founded on mutual reliance and confidentiality, such as the bond of trust between husband and wife, or between the client and legal advisor, at the cost of depriving the fact-finder of relevant information." Rules of privilege can result in the trier being denied access to pertinent information relating to the victim. For example, it is recognized that doctors, mental health professionals, spouses, legal professionals, and victims themselves may be privy to important victimological evidence that is crucial to the case. However, these individuals may be exempt from giving evidence of certain facts, or from giving evidence at all based on these privileges.

One precedent-setting case taken from the Supreme Court of Canada provides a useful example. In 1991, Bishop Hubert O'Connor was charged with several sexual assaults, the most recent of which allegedly occurred 24 years prior to the charges being filed (Fitz-James 1996). The following excerpt is taken directly from the judgment made by the Supreme Court of Canada (*R v. O'Connor* 1995, 2–3):

> The accused was charged with a number of sexual offenses. Defense counsel obtained a pre-trial order requiring that the Crown disclose the complainants' entire medical, counseling and school records and that the complainants authorize production of such records.... The trial judge made it clear that he was to be provided promptly with therapy records relating to all four complainants.... The accused later applied for a judicial stay of proceedings based on nondisclosure of several items.... [The Crown council] submitted that uninhibited disclosure of medical and therapeutic records would revictimize the victims, and suggested that the disclosure order exhibited gender bias. The trial judge dismissed the application for a stay, finding that the failure to disclose certain medical records had been an oversight. In light of the

difficulties encountered during discovery, Crown counsel then agreed to waive any privilege with respect to the contents of the Crown's file and to prepare a binder in relation to each of the complainants containing all information in the Crown's possession relating to each of them. On the second day of the trial, counsel for the accused made another application for a judicial stay of proceedings based largely on the fact that the Crown was still unable to guarantee to the accused that full disclosure had been made. The trial judge stayed proceedings on all four counts. He noted the constant intervention required by the court to ensure full compliance with the disclosure order and found that the Crown's earlier conduct had created "an aura" that had pervaded and ultimately destroyed the case.

Put simply, the Crown attorney in this case was unable or unwilling to produce the victim information that she was ordered to disclose. The charges against Bishop O'Connor were subsequently dismissed. The Crown was not without appeal, however, and the Supreme Court eventually found that the Crown was right in its attempts to protect the rights and privacy of the complainants involved. This despite the fact that opposing counsel maintained such information was pertinent to O'Connor's defense. As a result, the Supreme Court developed a series of rules that must be followed in order to determine which medical and psychiatric records of a complainant may be disclosed to the court. These guidelines (as adapted from Fitz-James 1996) state:

> When balancing the fair trial rights of the accused with the complainants right to privacy, the judge must take into account: whether the records are necessary to make full answer and defense; the probative nature of the record; the extent and nature of the reasonable expectation of privacy vested in the records; whether the production of the record is based on any discriminatory belief or bias; and the potential prejudice to the complainant's dignity, privacy or security that would be occasioned by the production of the records.

> Only after carefully considering each factor can the judge release the records fully to the accused.

It is important to think carefully about these guidelines. In so doing, it may become apparent that there is still much subjective interpretation required. The judge must develop an opinion as to whether the record will be necessary for the accused to make a full defense, and more importantly, whether disclosing the record is based on any discriminatory belief or bias. Not only this, but the use of these guidelines hinges on the fact that the defense is assumed to be aware already of what will be found in the records, as he or she is expected to convince the judge that the record is necessary to make a defense. One is left wondering whether such records may be of more use before the trial, in preparing the defense. For example, if the accused is of the position that the complainant has made a false allegation against him or her, and further believes that his or her psychiatric records will indicate a propensity towards false statements, impaired psychological functioning, or perhaps even provide exculpatory statements made to the mental health professional, it will be very difficult for the defense to prove that such information exists in these records if he or she has not seen them. Basically, the records are needed to prove that the records are needed. Herein lies the problem for the accused.

When addressing the question of which victim information will be admissible in court, it is important to remember that regardless of country or jurisdiction, adversarial systems in general provide that judges maintain a large amount of discretion (Murphy 2008). In criminal cases, it is the duty of the judge to ensure that the accused receives a fair trial. In order to fulfill this duty the judge maintains the power to exclude any evidence he or she sees fit based on a balance between its *probative*[3] value and any foreseeable prejudice. As explained in Murphy (2008, 47): "the judge should consider the probative value of the evidence, the likely extent of the unfair prejudice, and the circumstances of the trial as a whole, and in a necessarily subjective manner, do what appears necessary in those circumstances to secure a fair trial."

Unfortunately, this level of consideration does not always occur, as cognitive research has found that judges are just as prone to bias and error as anyone else. For example, as Guthrie (2007, 455–456) writes:

> good judges, who make up the vast majority of the trial bench, are prone to predictable blinders that can lead them to misjudge.

> To say that judges misjudge is to say simply that they are human, and that their decision making, though often quite good and arguably better than that of many other expert and novice decision makers, is subject to error. The problem with flawed judicial decisions—in contrast to the bad decisions the rest of us make—is that they shape the lives of untold numbers of disputants.

Additionally, as Guthrie, Rachlinski, and Wistrich (2007, 43) write, judges tend to make decisions based on intuitive systems of cognition rather than deliberate ones:[4]

> We believe that most judges attempt to "reach their decisions utilizing facts, evidence, and highly constrained legal criteria, while putting aside personal biases, attitudes, emotions, and

---

[3]*Probative* refers to evidence that tends to prove or disprove a particular fact that is relevant at trial.

[4]As explained in Guthrie, Rachlinski, and Wistrich (2007, footnote 28), "the term *deliberate system* is meant to encompass all processes that require effort, that is, attention and deliberation."

other individuating factors." Despite their best efforts, however, judges, like everyone else, have two cognitive systems for making judgments—the intuitive and the deliberative—and the intuitive system appears to have a powerful effect on judges' decision making. The intuitive approach might work well in some cases, but it can lead to erroneous and unjust outcomes in others. The justice system should take what steps it can to increase the likelihood that judges will decide cases in a predominately deliberative, rather than a predominately intuitive, way.

This empirical reality may begin to explain why the admissibility of victimological evidence varies so greatly within states, counties, and even courthouses. When intuition (i.e., instinct informed by subconscious reasoning) is at the helm, we are at the mercy of our subconscious biases and prejudices.

SHIELD LAWS

Shield laws come in a variety of forms, but rape shield laws will be the focus of the current discussion, for they are most commonly at issue with respect to forensic victimology.

Originally, rape shield laws were developed as a way to protect victims from fear of humiliation and harassment in the courtroom regarding their sexual history. In the simplest definition, shield laws are meant to do just that: to *shield* the victim from being further victimized by the system (Berger 1977). As explained in Flowe et al. (2007, 159–160):

> The legal system has historically treated claims of rape with skepticism. Many states, for example, once had cautionary instructions to the jury warning of women's propensity to make false charges of rape. Moreover, evidence of promiscuity was routinely admitted at trial to undermine the credibility of a complainant and to demonstrate to the jury that in all likelihood she consented on the occasion in question (Anderson 2002). Since the 1970s, however, all state legislatures have passed changes in rape statutes. One major change was the enactment of so-called rape shield laws, which limit the introduction of evidence at trial concerning the complainant's sexual history. Congress (Fed. R. Evid. 412), the military (Mil. R. Evid. 412), and all of the states (Miller 1997) have implemented rape shield laws. Similar to federal and military rape shield laws, almost half of the states generally exclude all sexual history evidence unless it (1) relates to the complainant's sexual conduct with the defendant, or (2) provides information regarding pregnancy, disease, or the source of semen. In the remaining states, sexual history evidence is generally allowed for proving consent, for

impeaching the complainant's credibility, or when a trial judge agrees that it is relevant (Anderson 2002, for a historical review of the chastity requirement in rape law, and Price 1996, for a review of rape shield laws by state). Rape shield provisions attempt to balance protecting the complainant from potentially capricious invasions of privacy, and the defendant's rights to confront and cross-examine witnesses about potentially probative information (Galvin 1986; Herman 1976–1977; Lowery 1992; Price 1996). As such, sexual history evidence can still be admitted despite rape shield provisions if the defendant is able to successfully demonstrate that it is relevant in establishing his innocence.

In the past, accused rapists could mount a fairly convincing argument for consent if they were able to prove that a female complainant had a history of sexual promiscuity—or any sexual activity at all, for that matter. This was based on traditionally held notions that (adapted from Berger 1977, 54):

- Women who do not value chastity are immoral and therefore cannot be trusted as witnesses; and
- Women who have had consensual sex previously are more likely to agree to have sex again, and therefore proving past sexual experience lends to consent.

Rape shield laws were designed to prevent the defense from simply arguing that a victim did not value chastity and would therefore consent to the advances of the accused just so long as the defense could demonstrate she had some sort of sexual history. According to Berger (1977, 54) shield laws were not only designed to alleviate revictimization in the courtroom but "in line with these goals they encourage the victim to report the assault and assist in bringing the offender to justice by testifying against him in court. In so far as the laws in fact increase the number of prosecutions, they support the government's aim of deterring would-be rapists as well as its interest in going after actual suspects." These goals are undoubtedly good ones and it would be difficult to find anyone who would not support compassion towards actual victims.

However, there are problems. First, these laws have further endorsed the notion that rape victims should be unequivocally believed and supported, regardless of any weaknesses in the evidence against the accused. Moreover, a lack of this pro-victim attitude is often perceived as politically incorrect or unnecessarily cold. After all, who would lie about being the victim of something so heinous as a rape, and what kind of monster would doubt the story? Finally, rape shield laws have the potential to make it easier for prosecutors to make their case, especially when there is victim history that might be relevant to the facts at hand. As explained in Pokorak (2007, 726–728):

the rape shield laws that were enacted to exclude extraneous and irrelevant evidence of past sexual activity by the victim are universally seen as protecting that victim from inappropriate attacks on her character at trial and before a jury. Indeed, the federal rape shield rule was specifically enacted to protect the privacy of victims. The federal rape shield evidentiary rule bans the trial use of any evidence of prior sexual conduct or sexual predisposition on the part of the victim unless that evidence fits into specifically listed exceptions.

There are basically four different types of rape shield statutes: the federal model, the "Michigan" model, full discretion for the trial court, and the "consent and credibility" test. Each of these models focuses on the exclusion of evidence that directly implicates the victim's most private and personal information—her past sexual conduct. The fact that exclusion of this evidence makes the prosecutor's case easier to prove is secondary to the statutory intent of keeping rape victims free from vicious intrusion.

As is evident from the discussion in Chapter 8, on false reporting, as well as the Preface, there are many who are motivated for various reasons to feign victimization. The endorsement of blind victim advocacy through shield laws may assist false reporters to slip through the cracks of the justice system, simply because no one wants to challenge a rape victim out of fear of political repercussions. It is undoubtedly important to encourage victims of rape to come forward and to testify against their attackers in a court of law, however, this encouragement cannot come at the cost of a loss of freedom for the falsely accused.

What we are arguing is not that the defense should be allowed to bring forward any information that may indicate a victim is not of good character. Rather, that there not be a blanket statute barring relevant evidence from being admitted. We maintain that in all cases it is necessary to objectively collect, examine, and question victim information. First it guides the investigation, and then it informs subsequent court proceedings. Surely this may be done with compassion, without personally attacking the victim, and without blindly accepting everything he or she says.

Ultimately, we agree that nothing about the victim should be put to the jury without much consideration. However, demonstrably relevant facts and information should not be barred from the courtroom, regardless of what effect this may have on the victim. Defendants must be given the opportunity to defend themselves, and not be deprived of information that may explain or otherwise contextualize the evidence against them.

VICTIM IMPACT STATEMENTS

Victim impact statements (VIS) are accounts by victims or their family members designed to inform the judge, jury, and/or parole boards of the impact that the crime has had on their lives. This can take the form of physical, financial, psychological, and emotional harm. VIS are presented to the court prior to sentencing but after a conviction has been made, or during parole hearings. They allow victims to explicitly detail in their own words how the convicted criminal's actions have affected their lives (Wallace 1998).

Living victims of crime have reported suffering from post-traumatic stress disorder, depression, sleep disturbances, feelings of alienation and helplessness, fear, anger, and lack of control (Williams 1999). Moreover, families living in the wake of a violent or unexpected death may suffer emotionally and financially. These consequences of crime are not always clear in the courtroom for a variety of reasons, or they may not be given a clear face during the trial. Subsequently, some courts recognize the explicit need for the trier to be made aware of these affects. A useful discussion is provided in Myers and Greene (2004, 492–493):

> Victim impact statements are presented to jurors, judges, or parole officers. They generally concern the impact of the defendant's crime on the victim (i.e., primary victim) or, in the case of a capital crime, the victim's surviving relatives (i.e., related victim). Although the particulars of VIS may vary from one jurisdiction to another, they typically contain information that (a) identifies the offender, (b) indicates financial losses suffered by the victim, (c) lists physical injuries suffered by the victim including seriousness and permanence, (d) describes changes to the victim's personal welfare or familial relationships, (e) identifies requests for psychological services initiated by the victim or the victim's surviving family, and (f) contains other information related to the impact of the offense on the victim or the victim's family (*Booth v. Maryland* 1987, 2531).
>
> The current practice of allowing the introduction of VIS during sentencing is the result of a slow evolution in the role of the victim in judicial proceedings. Leaders of various victims' rights organizations have called for greater involvement by victims in the criminal justice process. This concern for victims' rights was initiated in the 1940s and intensified in the 1970s. It coincided with increasing acceptance of conservative views regarding the "crime control" model of criminal justice that emphasizes efficiency over due process concerns (Henderson 1985). Heightened attention to the role of crime victims in judicial proceedings is probably driven by multiple factors: public dissatisfaction with the treatment of victims by the criminal justice

system, prosecutors' beliefs about the benefits of cooperation from victims in securing convictions, and politicians' desires to portray themselves as tough on criminals and sympathetic toward victims.

Those who advocate the use of VIS during sentencing cite numerous advantages including psychological benefits to the victim and fairer sentencing decisions (Kilpatrick and Otto 1987). Providing the jury with information about the harm suffered by victims is believed to enhance the chances that sentencing will be consistent with the principle of proportionality (Erez 1990). Additionally, proponents argue that fairness requires that victims have the same opportunities as perpetrators to speak before the jury and share their personal qualities and character traits (Erez 1994; Sumner 1987). The use of VIS may also promote improved attitudes among victims with regard to the criminal justice process (Kelly 1984) and could result in a greater willingness on the part of victims to participate in the prosecution of crimes.

To sum up the perceived benefits of VIS: they can give a face and a voice to those who have suffered a loss; they can be empowering and potentially healing; and they may even promote a positive environment for victim cooperation at trial (as opposed to victim hostility and mistrust towards the prosecutor and the court, which are all too common).

VIS: Admissibility

Some courts have been alert enough to recognize that VIS are often used not as a form of relevant victim expression and empowerment but rather as a tool for the prosecutor to introduce irrelevant and inflammatory details to play on the emotions of jurors or other triers of fact. Hence, there have been significant reinterpretations of the legitimate role that VIS may play at trial, starting with *Booth v. Maryland* (1987). A history of VIS admissibility in the United States is provided in Kuhn (2006, 254–259):

> In *Booth* [*v. Maryland* 1987], the United States Supreme Court invalidated a Maryland statute that required consideration of victim impact statements during the sentencing phase of capital murder trials. The Court found that the statute violated the Eighth Amendment. In 1983, John Booth and an accomplice robbed and murdered an elderly couple in the couple's West Baltimore home. Booth was the couple's neighbor, and he knew that they would be able to identify him to police so he "bound and gagged [them] and then stabbed [them] repeatedly in the chest with a kitchen knife."
>
> The victim impact evidence in Booth's trial was comprised of information gathered from the victims' children and grandchildren. That evidence did not compare the value of the defendant's and victims' lives, but did

describe the emotional trauma suffered by the victims' family, as well as the victims' personal characteristics. For example, the jury was told that the victims' daughter suffered from a lack of sleep, withdrawal, distrust, and could no longer look at kitchen knives or watch violent movies without being reminded of her parents' murders. The victims' son reported that he suffered from lack of sleep and depression. He also characterized his parents as loving parents and grandparents, "amazing people who attended the senior citizens' center and made many devout friends. . . ." and said that "[t]heir funeral was the largest in the history of the . . . [f]uneral [h]ome." The victims' granddaughter explained how the murders ruined a family wedding that took place days after the killings.

The family members also offered their "opinions and characterizations of the crimes." For example, the victims' son stated that he believed that his parents were "butchered like animals." Additionally, the victims' daughter stated that she would never be able to forgive the defendant and that she believed such a murderer could never "be rehabilitated."

The Supreme Court's majority opinion, delivered by Justice Powell, held that the statements detailing the family's grief caused by the murders "serve[d] no other purpose than to inflame the jury and divert it from deciding the case on the relevant evidence concerning the crime and the defendant." The Court reasoned that admitting such "emotionally charged opinions as to what conclusions the jury should draw" is contrary to the "reasoned decision-making" required in capital cases. Justice Powell's opinion also held that victim impact evidence presenting the family's emotional distress and the victims' characteristics was not appropriate for a capital sentencing hearing. The Court explained that such evidence may be completely unrelated to the defendant's "blameworthiness," and that it may result in a sentence based on factors unknown to, nor considered by the defendant when he made the decision to kill. The Court also cited inequality in different families' abilities to be "articulate and persuasive" resulting in a possible variation in the effect of victim impact evidence from case to case. The Court also could not justify allowing a sentencing decision to turn on whether a victim was a "sterling member of the community," or one of "questionable character." Powell also cited the difficulty the defense would have in rebutting this type of victim impact evidence without shifting the focus away from the defendant and onto a "mini-trial" of the victim's character. This type of "mini-trial" would distract the jury from determining the appropriateness of the death penalty in light of the defendant's background and the circumstances of the crime. The Court did state, however, that there might be times during a capital trial when information that would have been used as victim impact evidence may be relevant. For example, similar types of evidence might be admitted to illustrate the circumstances of the crime or to rebut arguments offered by the defense.

In [*South Carolina v.*] *Gathers* [1989], the Supreme Court did not overturn *Booth,* but held that its opinion in *Booth* did not preclude the admissibility of all information common to victim impact evidence if the information "relate[d] directly to the circumstances of the crime." *Gathers* involved the brutal murder of Richard Haynes, who referred to himself as "Reverend Minister" and considered himself a preacher. Haynes was a thirty-one-year-old man who had a history of mental illness and typically carried with him religious articles including two Bibles, rosary beads, religious tracts, and a plastic angel. Haynes's mother testified that he often preached to others about his religious beliefs. One evening, Demetrius Gathers and three companions approached Haynes, who had been sitting alone on a park bench. Gathers tried to strike up a conversation with Haynes, but Haynes snubbed this attempt. Gathers and his friends then severely beat Haynes and smashed a bottle over his head. Then, Gathers beat Haynes with an umbrella and forced the umbrella into his anus. At some point later in the night, Gathers returned to the scene and stabbed Haynes to death.

The prosecutor used victim impact evidence during his closing statement, which, in part, described the religious items Haynes carried that Gathers found when rifling through Haynes's pockets. The prosecutor proposed that Gathers saw a voter registration card, and a religious tract called the "Game Guy's Prayer" before murdering Haynes. The prosecutor read aloud the "Game Guy's Prayer" during the closing argument. The Supreme Court affirmed the South Carolina Supreme Court in finding that the prosecutor's "'extensive comments to the jury regarding the victim's character were unnecessary for an understanding of the circumstances of the crime'. . . ." Justice Brennan, writing for the Court, declared that "[the defendant's] punishment must be tailored to his personal responsibility and moral guilt."

In *Payne* [*v. Tennessee* 1991], Charisse Christopher and her two toddlers, Lacie and Nicholas, were stabbed repeatedly in their home by Pervis Tyrone Payne. The mother and one child bled to death, while the other child, who had been viciously stabbed and left for dead, survived. The prosecution used victim impact evidence in its closing argument to relay to the jury the effect that the murders had on the surviving child who witnessed his mother's and sister's slayings. During the sentencing phase of the trial, Charisse's mother testified that, "[Nicholas] cries for his mom. He doesn't seem to understand why she doesn't come home. And he cries for his sister Lacie. He comes to me many times during the week, and asks me, Grandmama, do you miss my Lacie[?] . . . I'm worried about my Lacie." The prosecutor also commented on the effect the crimes had on Nicholas:

> But we know that Nicholas was alive. And Nicholas was in the same room. Nicholas was still conscious. His eyes were open. . . . He was able to follow [the paramedics'] directions. He was able to hold his intestines in as he was carried to the ambulance. So he knew what happened to his mother and baby sister. . . . But there is something that you can do for Nicholas. Somewhere down the road Nicholas is going to grow up, hopefully. He's going to want to know what happened. And he is going to know what happened to his baby sister and his mother. He is going to want to know what type of justice was done. . . . With your verdict, you will provide the answer.

The Supreme Court revisited the issue of victim impact statements and held that the Eighth Amendment is not a bar to the use of victim impact evidence in the sentencing phase of a capital trial if a state chooses to permit the admission of such evidence. The Court decided that a state might introduce evidence during the sentencing phase about the specific harm caused by the defendant, so that the jury can assess the defendant's moral culpability and blameworthiness. Additionally, a state may introduce information about the victim and the impact of the murder on the victim's family, so that the jury can decide whether to impose the death penalty. The Court did state, however, that if evidence "is so unduly prejudicial that it renders the trial fundamentally unfair, [then] . . . the Fourteenth Amendment provides a mechanism for relief."

In *Payne*, the Supreme Court did not explicitly rule on the constitutionality of victim impact statements that compare the value of the life of the defendant to the value of the life of the victim. The Court did address the issue of juries potentially finding that defendants whose victims contributed to their communities deserve punishment more than those whose victims are regarded as "less worthy." The Court asserted, however, that victim impact evidence is not generally offered to "encourage comparative judgments of this kind." Instead, the Court stressed that victim impact evidence is designed to display to the jury a victim's "uniqueness as an individual human being," leaving it to the jury to decide what the resultant loss to the community might be.

The issue of VIS has also been a feature of the Canadian legal system. In 1988, the Canadian government made three significant reforms involving victims of crimes, one of which was the introduction of victim impact statements (VIS) as a consideration when determining sentencing. Furthering this reform were several amendments to the Criminal Code, including an explicit statement that one of the fundamental purposes of sentencing is to serve the interests of victims (Section 718, 1995) and to permit victims to deliver their VIS orally in open court if so desired (Section 722, 1999) (Policy Centre for Victims Issues 2001).

Similar opportunities for victims and their family to given written or verbal statements to the court prior to sentencing are provided in other Western countries as well, including Australia and the United Kingdom.

VIS: The Debate

As already suggested, the use of VIS has led to many debates between victim and offender advocates. It is believed by some that victim participation will lead to dignity for victims, regaining of some control, and greater satisfaction in the justice system (Kilpatrick and Otto 1987). Advocates of offender rights hold that the allowance of victim input into sentencing will undermine the objective nature of a judge's ruling, allowing a source of inconsistency that has no place in a court of law (Grabosky 1987). Generally, the debate about the use of VIS centers around the notion that sentences may be increased when victim input is admitted; that the process of composing VIS may or may not be therapeutic in and of itself; and that victims may feel more or less satisfaction with the legal system depending on how their statements are used.

Psychologists studying the issue from an empirical and cognitive standpoint have made it clear that while victims need to have a voice in the justice system, VIS as they are currently used can have an improper and inflammatory effect on jurors. Consequently, they hold that reform is necessary to make the process more evenhanded. As explained in Myers and Greene (2004, 511):

> So what *is* the proper role of VIS in capital trials, and should their use be prohibited or welcomed? One might argue, based on the body of empirical research that we recounted, that jurors are *improperly* affected by VIS. Support for this notion comes from studies showing that mock jurors' sentencing sentiments are influenced by the extent to which victims' survivors have suffered, the social value of the victim, and the highly emotional content of the VIS—issues that have little *legal* relevance to the sentencing decision. Others might argue, though, that VIS are indeed relevant to the ultimate judgment precisely because jurors pay attention to them and are affected by them. This notion, more commonsensical than legal (see, e.g., Finkel 1995), leads to the conclusion that VIS may provide legitimate and, indeed, desired input to the sentencer.

Can we reconcile these opposing perspectives? Probably not without giving a great deal more thought to the disjunction between legal standards that define capital sentencing (inconsistent and haphazardly drawn as they are across jurisdictions) and jurors' notions of what is important and useful information for them to have when sentencing a capital offender.

But even without that undertaking, we feel strongly that victim impact evidence that distracts jurors' attention from considerations that are clearly relevant to the sentencing decision—namely, the circumstances of the crime and the background and character of the defendant—should be disallowed or limited. We acknowledge that the determination of when VIS are useful to jurors and when they distract may be impossible to know ahead of time. That is, judges are probably ill-equipped to forecast how juries would make use of victim impact evidence. But we already have some examples of situations in which judges have limited or regulated the extent of the VIS. We think that these were the proper decisions.

We agree not only that VIS reforms and limits are necessary to maintain an objective stream of information directed towards the trier of fact, but also that the forensic victimologists should refrain from reliance on such information if they encounter it in their examinations. Information compiled by investigators for investigative and forensic purposes is significantly different from that compiled by the victim or the victim's family to achieve an emotional impact. As will be explained further in the next section, the forensic victimologist must make threshold determinations about all evidence.

EXPERT TESTIMONY

When victimologists testify at trial, they do so as expert witnesses. In the United States, under Article VII, Rule 702 of the Federal Rules of Evidence (FRE), the court may permit a witness qualified as an expert to provide an opinion regarding "scientific, technical, or other specialized knowledge" if such testimony "will assist the trier of fact." The two key criteria for admission of expert testimony under FRE 702 are a qualified witness and helpful testimony. However, some courts go further in their assessment of expert testimony, applying either the *Frye* test or the *Daubert* test to determine admissibility. As explained in Saks et al. (2004, 4): "Under virtually all evidence codes, trial courts must evaluate the admissibility of proffered expert testimony. The manner in which they accomplish this task, however, varies greatly among jurisdictions." The different admissibility issues are explained in Cooley (2006, 522–525):

> In *Frye v. United States* [293 F. 1013 (D.C. Cir. 1923)], the Court of Appeals for the District of Columbia affirmed the exclusion of a

psychologist's finding, based on blood pressure measurements, that the defendant was being truthful when he denied committing a murder. The *Frye* Court required a showing that the psychologist's novel scientific test for deception be generally accepted by the relevant scientific community.

. . . Although many courts throughout the United States embraced *Frye*'s general acceptance standard [see *United States v. Addison*, 498 F. 2d. 741 (D.C. Cir. 1974); *Reed v. State,* 391 A.2d 364 (Md. 1978); and *People v. Kelly,* 549 P.2d 1240 (Cal. 1976)], it still had numerous admitted shortcomings (Giannelli 1980). In 1975, the Federal Rules of Evidence were signed into law. Rule 702 revolutionized expert testimony by sweeping away the restrictive doctrine that curtailed expert testimony under the common law. Rule 702 employed a "helpfulness" test that departed from the common law's more strict standard requiring an expert's testimony to be "beyond the ken" of an ordinary trier of fact.

. . . Legal scholars and courts characterized this rule as a "relevancy test" (Giannelli 1994). As applied, this test often meant that once a court qualified a witness, so too was his or her technique automatically qualified (Giannelli and Imwinkelried 1999). Ironically, neither the advisory committee's commentary nor Rule 702 mentioned *Frye*. The failure to clarify whether Rule 702 superseded *Frye* produced confusion among federal (and even state courts) during the 1970s and 1980s.

In *Daubert v. Merrell Dow Pharmaceuticals, Inc.* (509 U.S. 579, 1993), the Supreme Court held that Rule 702 superceded *Frye. Daubert* stressed that trial judges were obligated to utilize their "gatekeeping" capacities when screening expert testimony to make certain that it is "not only relevant, but reliable" (509 U.S. 589). In carrying out their gatekeeping responsibilities, the Supreme Court instructed trial judges to assess not merely whether a technique or theory was generally accepted but also whether it was testable, falsifiable, and whether it possessed an identifiable error rate and had undergone the rigors of peer review (509 U.S. 589).

. . . *Daubert,* nevertheless, left open the question of whether "technical" and "specialized knowledge," the two other forms of expert testimony identified in Rule 702, fell within the parameters of *Daubert*'s reliability standard.

In *Kumho Tire Co. v. Carmichael* (526 U.S. 137, 1999), the Supreme Court held that *Daubert* "applies not only to testimony based on 'scientific' knowledge, but also to testimony based on 'technical' and 'other specialized' knowledge" (526 U.S. 141). The Supreme Court believed it would be an administrative nightmare if trial judges were required to apply different admissibility standards to areas of knowledge where "there is no clear line that divides . . . one from the other" (526 U.S. 148). *Kumho Tire* put forth another significant, although less overt, principle that the decision must focus on the "task at hand" and not the standard reliability of a generally and broadly defined vicinity of expertise (Risinger 2000).

Rule 702 was amended in 2000. The amendment codified the Supreme Court's decisions in *Daubert, Kumho Tire*, and *General Electric Co. v. Joiner* (522 U.S. 136, 1997, holding that abuse of discretion is the proper standard of review for district court evidentiary rulings). Rule 702 now reads:

> If scientific, technical, or other specialized knowledge will assist the trier of fact to understand the evidence or to determine a fact in issue, a witness qualified as an expert by knowledge, skill, experience, training, or education, may testify thereto in the form of an opinion or otherwise, if (1) the testimony is based upon sufficient facts or data, (2) the testimony is the product of reliable principles and methods, and (3) the witness has applied the principles and methods reliably to the facts of the case.

Like *Daubert* and its progeny, newly amended FRE 702 forces courts to question the empirical underpinnings of all expert testimony and to exclude those opinions that are "connected to existing data only by the *ipse dixit* of the expert" (*General Elec. Co. v. Joiner*, 522 U.S. 136, 146, 1997). Since *Daubert* was handed down, courts and legal observers have expressed trepidations that *Daubert*'s emphasis on empirical testability, scientific falsifiability, and error rates poses serious trouble for the forensic sciences.

It must be pointed out that *Frye, Daubert,* and *Kumho* are legal guidelines for admissibility, not scientific standards for reliability. This means that judges are free to use any or all of the guidelines of either when assessing expertise and determining expert admissibility. It also means that they are free to ignore them as well. As explained in Blinka (2006, 221–222):

> trial judges are granted enormously broad discretion in determining whether the trier of fact may profit from expert assistance and, if so, the precise form and content of that assistance. The witness's qualifications present the range of possible assistance from which the judge will select, a discretionary determination guided by the limited gatekeeping function. The options may range from total exclusion (this witness has nothing to add) to exposition or opinion testimony.

Moreover, because these are legal standards and not scientific ones, and they are imposed inconsistently on forensic experts by the court, more than a few forensic scientists have expressed dissent over some of the prongs of *Daubert*. For informed discussions of these issues, see Thornton (1994) and Chisum and Turvey (2006).

The Role of Experts

As a general rule, opinions are not allowed from witnesses giving evidence in court; they are allowed to speak only regarding what they have perceived with their senses, not what they make of or believe about their perceptions. The reason for this general rule is to protect the court from opinions masquerading as fact. That is, if all witnesses were allowed to give their opinions openly, the judge and jury may be tempted to simply accept said opinions rather than drawing their own conclusions based on the facts of the case (Keane 2006).

There are a few exceptions to this general rule. One such exception is expert testimony, which is the allowance for appropriately qualified experts to give their opinion on a matter that would otherwise remain confusing or elusive to the court. That is, expert opinion evidence is admitted when a subject comes into question during the proceedings that the court does not have the specialized knowledge required to make an informed decision about (Keane 2006; Murphy 2008). Put simply by Keane (2006, 553): "the opinion evidence of an expert is only admissible on a matter calling for expertise."

Despite the fact that expert opinion evidence is routinely allowed into court, the goals of the general rule prohibiting opinions remain. Subsequently, measures are taken to ensure that the triers of fact are not usurped by expert testimony, and that they come to their own conclusions based on all the facts of the case. Ensuring this objectivity is theoretically done in many ways. It is generally a question of education, training, and experience; whether or not the sum of one or more of these has made the witness competent enough to give expert evidence. Demonstrable expertise may come in the form of peer-reviewed research and publications, advanced training, organizational memberships, educational qualifications such as degrees and diplomas, or it may be wholly experiential (Roberts and Zuckerman 2004). It is, however, important to recognize this as an area of discretion on the part of the judge, where virtually anyone having more than common knowledge on a subject could be deemed an expert depending on the case.

The role of the expert within the court seems fairly straightforward, theoretically speaking. Experts are meant to educate the court regarding their areas of specialized knowledge: to provide not only the results of any examinations performed but what they mean. In theory, experts are meant to remain objective and balanced regardless of the fact that one side or the other may be paying for their time. According to the provisions (of Rule 35.3 of Civil Procedure Rules of 1998) made in British Law (Murphy 2008, 366):

> 1) It is the duty of an expert to help the court on the matters within his expertise
> 2) This function overrides any obligation to the person from whom he has received instructions or by whom he is paid. . . .

> The requirement of objectivity suggests that the expert should avoid assuming the role of an advocate, and must be candid and revealing: the extent to which any questions that may be raised fall outside his sphere of expertise; the extent to which any opinion he expresses is controversial; any materials which may contradict his opinion; and the extent to which the data provided to him restrict his ability to render more than a provisional opinion. The expert should also cooperate in limiting as far as possible the ambit of disagreement between the experts on different sides of the case.

Along with this British statute, there are similar rules guiding the presentation of expert testimony in other countries. By and large, expert witnesses are expected to be honest, avoid advocacy, and remain objective. For some, this is clearly understood and routinely accomplished. For others, it is not. Apart from overt instances of conscious forensic fraud[5] on the part of duplicitous examiners who fabricate evidence, credentials, or findings, there are also subconscious influences pressing the victimologist. These are referred to as *observer effects*, ignorance of which can be detrimental to any forensic examination.

Observer Effects

Victimologists have tremendous authority and an immense responsibility. If their examinations are distorted in any fashion, the results can be catastrophic for everyone concerned—from the investigation to the courtroom. Consequently, observer effects should be of particular concern to victimologists. This is because so much of their role involves the selective recognition, documentation, and interpretation of physical and behavioral evidence. Add to this the fact that victimological evidence is often charged with emotional and political content.

Taylor (in Roberts and Zuckerman 2004, 297) explains eloquently that

> it is often quite surprising to see with what facility and to what an extent [expert witnesses'] views can be made to correspond with

---

[5]See generally Turvey (2003).

the wishes or the interests of the parties who call them. They do not, indeed, willfully misrepresent what they think, but their judgments become so warped by regarding the subject in one point of view, that, even when conscientiously disposed, they are incapable of forming an independent opinion.

This is a reference to what cognitive psychologists have termed *observer effects*. As Risinger and colleagues (2002, 9) explained in their groundbreaking article on observer effects in forensic science, many different forms of observer effects can bias the forensic examiner: "At the most general level, observer effects are errors of apprehension, recording, recall, computation, or interpretation that result from some trait or state of the observer."

These covert biases are more concerning than deliberate fraud and misconduct because they are often misperceived, or even thought of as beneficial, and therefore tend to go undetected. Consequently, in order to blunt their impact, scientists and researchers must be aware that these influences exist and can indeed significantly influence their analyses. Once conceded, they can be studied and understood; once understood, they can be addressed and even mitigated. The vast majority of scientific disciplines accepts the need to blunt examiner bias and observer effects as a given, and this is reflected in their published research. Put simply, "[s]ensitivity to the problems of observer effects has become integral to the modern scientific method" (Risinger et al. 2002, 6).

One of the contextual issues influencing observer effects specific to victimology is the very term *victim*. As should be clear from the previous chapters, this word is used inconsistently and can be highly politicized. It also tends to carry with it certain assumptions. First, it implies that there has indeed been harm, when this may actually be a matter that has yet to be determined in court. Subsequently, the objective victimologist will prefer to use the term "alleged victim" or "complainant" in such circumstances. Second, according to Williams (2004), the word *victim* tends to suggest positive characteristics, for example (adapted from Williams 2004, 101):

- The individuals are blameless of the crime;
- They are deserving of sympathy and should be absolved;
- They deserve compensation;
- They have a right to expect that their transgressor be fully punished;
- They are good people;
- They are honest;
- They are morally superior;
- Their view of the crime and what should be done about it should be given precedence over the views of others, even professionals in the system.

These endowments are problematic in that they can influence the interpretation of the physical and behavioral evidence. Clearly such views are not conducive to the search for objective facts and knowledge within the justice system. Any of the professionals involved in victim-related behavioral interpretations holding one or more of the above assumptions as inviolate, consciously or subconsciously, might be swayed to gloss over or outright ignore unfavorable victim information. As explained in Petherick and Turvey (2008, 44–45):

> As cognitive psychologists have repeatedly documented, tested, and illustrated, "[T]he scientific observer [is] an imperfectly calibrated instrument" (Rosenthal 1966, 3). Their imperfections stem from the fact that subtle forms of bias, whether conscious or unconscious, can easily contaminate their seemingly objective undertakings. Observer effects are present when the results of a forensic examination are distorted by the context and mental state of the forensic examiner, to include the examiner's subconscious expectations and desires.
>
> Identifying and curtailing this kind of bias is a considerable task when one takes into account the forensic community's affiliation with both law enforcement and the prosecution. Specifically, this association has fashioned an atmosphere in which an unsettling number of forensic professionals have all but abandoned objectivity and have become completely partial to the prosecution's objectives, goals, and philosophies. They may even go so far as to regard this association as virtuous and heroic, and they may believe any alternative philosophy to be a manifestation of something that is morally bankrupt. So strong is the influence of this association between forensic evidence examination and law enforcement that some forensic examiners have even deliberately fabricated evidence, or testified falsely, so that the prosecution might prove its case; however, this is the extreme end of the spectrum.
>
> It is fair to say that the majority of practitioners in the forensic community routinely acknowledge the existence of overt forms of conscious bias. That is, they generally recognize and condemn forensic ignorance, forensic fraud, and evidence fabricators when it is dragged into the light and exposed for all to see. Moreover, the forensic community seems to realize that to effectively serve the criminal justice system, they must immediately eliminate individuals, procedures, or circumstances that call into question examiner objectivity and neutrality (although this may be called into question in some specific cases, when forensic science organizations essentially fail in their duty to regulate membership and protect inept and unethical examiners).

Although the forensic community is somewhat attenuated to the potential for extreme forms of outright fraud and overt bias, it tends to be wholly unaware when it comes to understanding and accepting that well-documented forms of covert bias can taint even the most impartial scientific examinations. This is disheartening for the simple reason that covert and subconscious biases represent a far greater threat to the forensic community than do the small percentage of overtly biased, dishonest, or fraudulent forensic examiners.

To grasp the elusive yet powerful nature of subconscious bias requires a brief lesson in cognitive psychology. *Cognitive psychology* is the psychological science that studies cognition, the mental processes that are believed to underlie behavior. The following is a well-established principle of cognitive psychology: An individual's desires and expectations can influence his or her perceptions, observations, and interpretations of events. In other words, the results of one's observations are dependent on at least two things: (1) the object or circumstance being observed and (2) the person's state of mind.

Ultimately, any conscious or subconscious assumption of the victim as an inherently good and honest person (or conversely as an inherently bad and duplicitous person) can effect the context under which related evidence is viewed—bringing bias and prejudice into the decision-making process. This may hinder the ability of victimologists to remain impartial and unemotional in their analysis. It may also lead to the presentation of inaccurate victim evidence before the judge, jury, and community, causing an unwarranted verdict or sentence.

To be clear, improper bias may arise from the political and cultural endowments of the definition of the term *victim*, not from accurate victim information itself. It is accepted that accurate information, whether for or against victim reliability, will actually bias the examiner towards the facts. This is the desired outcome of any forensic victimology.

When information about the victim is presented in court there are many motivations behind it—and not all of them are oriented towards the establishment of fact. These hinge on who is offering the information, whom they work for, and what they believe. All of this influences what is at stake for them, be it their reputation, either personally or professionally; their relationship with the victim or accused; or their personal, political, or professional goals.

Another contextual issue influencing observer effects specific to victimology is the emotion involved. Learning about the victim, and the harm he or she suffered, can be intensely emotional. It can leave the judge, jury, and community with a sense of shock, anger, sympathy, or sadness. Certainly the victimologist is not immune to similar responses. When information comes directly from a victim during an interview or on the witness stand, the impact may be greater. Heightened sensitivity in this regard can create examiner expectation that is yet another form of observer effects, as explained in Risinger et al. (2002, 24–26):

> There also is an extensive literature on "need-determined perception," that is, how an emotionally heightened or "hot" motivational state, as distinct from a "cool" cognitive expectation, affects what the observer perceives. If even the mildest of expectations can affect perception, then it is not surprising to find that where an observer has strong motivation to see something, perhaps a motivation springing from hope or anger, reinforced by role-defined desires, that something has an increased likelihood of being "seen." And to be sure, scientists and their assistants may have strong hopes about what it is that they will "merely observe" . . .
>
> Many individuals have attitudes toward what they are observing and harbor a preference for one outcome over another. Other observers, perhaps less committed to the data and more committed to the uses to which an observation will be put, might be even more susceptible to observer effects. Here, research on the effects of the perceived role of the observer becomes relevant once again. Research on need-determined perception shows that in general the world appears different to people who have a desire to see it in different ways, and how different the world appears is related to the intensity of that desire.
>
> . . . observer effects may occur at any of several stages of observation, from the initial observation to the conclusions drawn about what was observed. The errors at each of these stages may be described as follows:
>
> - Errors of Apprehending (errors that occur at the stage of initial perception);
> - Errors of Recording (errors that creep in at the stage where what is observed is recorded, assuming a record beyond memory is even made);
> - Errors of Memory (errors that are induced by both desires and the need for schematic consistency, and that escalate over time when memory is relied on);
> - Errors of Computation (errors that occur when correct observations accurately recorded or remembered are transformed into incorrect results when calculations are performed on them); and
> - Errors of Interpretation (errors that occur when examiners draw incorrect conclusions from the data).
>
> In the case of errors of interpretation, the criteria for the "true" values of the underlying observations are often so vague, ephemeral, and

submerged in the interpretation, that one often cannot discover the inaccuracy in the interpretative conclusion. Interestingly, this most error prone circumstance corresponds to the realm of the expert testifying in a legal proceeding: the expert's "opinion." It is exactly where stimuli are most on the border of accurate perception and classification that conditions most favor errors of interpretation. The more ambiguous and ill-defined the stimulus and the more frustrated or motivated the observer, the more likely one or more observer effects will occur, resulting in an inaccurate result.

When it comes to emotion, it is difficult if not impossible to disregard the way we feel. Even in the most strong-willed individuals, our true feelings may subtly or grossly influence the way we behave and communicate; the way we collect and examine evidence; and the interpretations that can result. Despite strong emotions, it is imperative that the greatest effort be made to weigh all the information available, check whether theories are supported or refuted, and remain objective in seeking and explaining the truth. Recognizing that it can be a problem is the first and most important step, as this opens the door to seeking a remedy.

It is also clear that emotions can affect the way that evidence is collected, presented, and viewed in court. In fact, those charged with presenting the evidence may purposely offer emotional evidence as a way to advocate for their position—to sway a judge or jury when the evidence alone does not take them far enough. This is where the forensic victimologist has great value in cooling such zealous interpretations, as an objective foil.

THE ROLE OF FORENSIC VICTIMOLOGY

In cases where victims' actions, history, or demeanor is relevant to legal proceedings, a victimologist may be asked to examine victim-oriented behavioral evidence and contextualize it before the trier of fact. This is the *forensic* aspect of forensic victimology.[6] As has been discussed, the rules of admissibility vary from state to state, court to court, and judge to judge, as admissibility of victimology evidence is made by the court on an individual basis, and based on a sometimes-unique interpretation of the law.

The question arises, then, as to the role of victimology—and the victimologist—in this venue. In general, forensic victimologists should conduct themselves as both scientists and educators. It is their role to provide a cooling effect

---

[6] The single feature that distinguishes forensic victimologists from all others in the field is the expectation that they may be asked to provide expert testimony regarding their findings in a court of law. If a victimologist conducts examinations and renders findings without this expectation hanging over his or her work, it is not being done in a forensic context, and subsequent conclusions may not be prepared with the same standards of confidence or certainty.

to the often-heated issues surrounding victim-oriented behavioral evidence. They must examine the evidence impartially, through the lens of the scientific method, and render conclusions related to victimology in accordance with their findings. When necessary, they must be able to explain their findings to the court and show how they achieved them.

For the small percentage of cases that do go to trial, there is an unavoidable vulnerability to the accumulation of errors, improper motivations, and the zeal of advocates on either side of the courtroom. This is particularly true of information related to the victim. As described in previous chapters, victimological information can be compiled ineptly, reported inaccurately, or provided in a biased manner—and that is when it is collected at all. The misinformation that follows may combine during court proceedings to have a tremendous impact. Bad information can create a snowball effect: errors and omissions in the original information provided to the police can lead to errors in the investigation; these can lead to problems in the case assembled against the accused; which can lead to mistakes in the charges handed down and how the case is brought by the prosecution; leading to false perceptions by the judge, jury, and media. All of these can have influence over whether or not a defendant is convicted and how he or she is sentenced.

Generally speaking, one purpose of forensic victimology is to help prevent this snowball effect from happening. Victimological information should be gathered objectively and consistently, and then used to describe or evaluate victims and their circumstances so that judges and juries are privy to information that may be relevant to their decisions. In this context, direct questions must be asked: Was the victim using drugs; Does the victim have a history of falsely reporting crime; What was the extent of the victim's physical injuries; Was the victim conscious during the attack; Does the victim have a history of taking rides from strangers or letting strangers into the home; Does the victim lock the door at night? The judge, who determines what is legally admissible, decides the issue of relevance for these and similarly themed questions. Then, as already discussed, the judge makes a ruling: sometimes everything about a victim is admissible, sometimes nothing, and sometimes the court "splits the baby" by admitting a percentage of victim information.

The more accurate and complete the victim information provided, the clearer the context of the crime. This is an investigative axiom. During an investigation, everything about the victim must be learned and documented, with nothing treated as trivial. Unfortunately, there is a tendency on the part of some investigators to avoid gathering some or all of the victimology, to deprive the court of contextual information that might sway the findings against prevailing case theories. The court should view this practice with dismay, as informed decisions about what to admit and what to keep out cannot be made in the absence of a complete investigative effort and record.

As already discussed in this chapter, presenting victimological information in court involves a different standard from the investigative effort. Investigative victimology gathers everything; the court decides admissibility based on that record in the context of the collective issues in a case. Typically, victimological evidence must serve a particular purpose related to a legal issue to be admissible. For example, victimological information may demonstrate that a crime has actually occurred, or that the elements of this case meet the definition of the charges brought against the accused. Information about the victim will undoubtedly contextualize the crime and help to reconstruct exactly what took place and in what order. Information about the victim may also allow the judge and jury to better understand who the victim is or was, why he or she was targeted, how he or she was acquired and harmed, and most importantly by whom. On the other hand, if there is a specific reason to doubt the victim's credibility or the accuracy of particular statements, victimology may be introduced at trial to bring this to light. These are just some of the many possible scenarios, but the theme remains clear: to be admissible in court, victimology must be relevant to a factual matter or legal question, and not simply part of a smear campaign.

LEGAL VS. SCIENTIFIC SUFFICIENCY

At this point we need to put ourselves back on track and distinguish between legal and scientific sufficiency of evidence. The standards for a given judge in a given courtroom in a given state are important, because they dictate what the victimologist may testify to in a particular case. However, these legal standards have no hold over a victimologist's methods and science. In other words, what is sufficiently reliable for legal purposes may not be sufficiently reliable for inclusion in a victimology. It is the victimologist's responsibility to know the difference, in order to make it clear to the court when necessary.

As Thornton explains (1994, 476):

> Although there is a forensic science profession in the United States, and although many of us spend much of our time in courts of law, we have for the most part been passive spectators to the court decisions that deal with the admissibility of scientific evidence. In one sense, this is as it should be. It is the job of the law, and not of science, to determine how science is to be used in the courts. But in another sense, our passivity has served both ourselves and the legal system poorly. It is the job of science, and not of law, to determine what is good science and what is not.

And as Thornton further notes (1994, 483):

> Every scientist understands that there are courts of law. By and large, they are accorded respect. I am not as certain that every lawyer understands that there are courts of science as well. They are not as

easily identified because they do not exist in a particular point in space, nor is there one man or woman in a black robe that symbolizes the court, nor a marble anteroom outside smelling of urine and industrial strength disinfectant. Courts of science are constructs of the mind, which bring clarity and coherency to scientific and technical matters. They are built not of marble, but from the scientific method. Every scientist is expected to serve as his or her own presiding judge, and if a costume is necessary, it is a white lab coat instead of a black robe. But these courts have certain rules also, just as courts of law. And the scientist who declines to practice his or her profession by the rules of science will soon find that he or she has earned only the derision of his or her colleagues, and eventually finds that he or she cannot continue to practice at all.

A threshold evidentiary and admissibility issue is whether statements made by the victim, or about the victim, are of sufficient quality to be used in a court proceeding. Consider the case of James Sherman, a police officer in Newport News, Virginia, on trial for sexually abusing a teenage girl. As explained in Zielinski (2008):

> Attorneys for James Sherman presented 10 motions to Williamsburg-James City County Circuit Judge Samuel Powell Tuesday. Sherman, 40, is charged with aggravated sexual battery and indecent liberties with a child in connection with the abuse of the teen at a James City County apartment between July 2005 and July 2006.
>
> Sherman's attorney Marc Messier said that the girl testified in a deposition that the allegations she made against Sherman were false, but then testified at the preliminary hearing that he had in fact touched her inappropriately on multiple occasions. He said it is inadmissible to use perjured testimony to secure a criminal conviction, and that the victim's testimony should be suppressed.
>
> "I don't know that anybody can know which to believe at this point," Messier said. "The fact is, we have perjury." Williamsburg-James City County Commonwealth's Attorney Nate Green admitted that the girl had lied under oath, but said prosecutors believe her statement at the preliminary hearing was true and that her testimony at trial would not be perjury.
>
> Powell took the motion under advisement Tuesday so that he could read relevant case law dealing with the issue.

Is the victim a reliable source of information in this case, and is her testimony admissible? These are two very separate questions. For the court, both answers are a matter of law, admissibility, and precedent. After much research, answers and interpretations of the law may be clear to murky depending on the jurist and jurisdiction.

For the forensic victimologist, however, the law is not a factor, and the second question is irrelevant to a victimological analysis. The issues for the forensic victimologist with any evidence are *sufficiency* and *reliability*. Is the evidence provided in a victim's statement or testimony of sufficient quantity and quality (reliability) to form the basis of forensic conclusions? Here, the answer is clearly no. The question is not whether the victim was lying under oath, but when. In circumstances where the victim's statements cannot be trusted, for whatever reason, the forensic victimologist has a duty to warn, or advise, that any findings based solely on the word of the victim may not rise to the level of reliability required for purposes of forensic analysis and subsequent expert testimony. While contradictory or inherently dubious victim statements may have investigative utility, they are not reliable enough to stand on their own for the purpose of forensic behavioral analysis. Such a finding may be of great value in a legal proceeding, especially if the statement is deemed admissible.

EXPERT VICTIMOLOGISTS

As discussed throughout this text, and explained at the beginning of this chapter, victimology comes in at trial as evidence through a number of professional and expert witnesses. Though certainly not an exclusive list, the following are common examples.

Forensic Pathologists

In cases involving violent or unexpected death, a medical examiner or coroner will examine a decedent's body to determine the nature in which he or she interacted with his or her environment in such a manner as to cause death. Using a blend of medical and forensic knowledge, forensic pathologists assign a nondiagnostic but forensic determination as to the manner of death, whether it be natural, accidental, suicide, homicide, or undetermined. In making such determinations, the three most important things are *history*, *history*, and *history*. As stated clearly and succinctly in the National Institute of Justice manual *Death Investigation: A Guide for the Scene Investigator* (NIJ 1999, 39):

> Establishing a decedent profile includes documenting a discovery[7] history and circumstances surrounding the discovery. The basic profile will dictate subsequent levels of investigation, jurisdiction, and authority. The focus (breadth/depth) of further investigation is dependent on this information.

---

[7]*Discovery* refers to documents and other evidence that must by disclosed by one side of a legal dispute to the other as a strict matter of law.

Information about a victim's history and lifestyle is therefore gathered as part of a competent medicolegal investigation and then incorporated into forensic findings. Subsequently, forensic pathologists regularly offer testimony about victim event history (based on injuries), medical history, and lifestyle in order to support their conclusions regarding the cause and manner of death. In fact, in every homicide trial that involves a body (only a few will not), the medical examiner will be there to testify about the victim and his or her demise.

Medical Professionals

In cases that involve actual or potential nonlethal victim injury, such as rape, assault, and attempted homicide, the victim will be taken to an emergency room or clinic and examined by staff. Typically, this includes paramedics, emergency room physicians, nurses, and sexual assault nurse examiners. Each of these medical professionals must take a complete victim history and write a report that covers the nature of the examinations, findings, and any medical care provided. They may even document the victim's injuries or lack thereof with charts or photographs. At trial, medical professionals may be called on by the prosecution or defense to explain what they did, what they didn't do, what they found, and what it means.

Toxicologists

A forensic toxicologist examines the victim's biological fluids, hair, and organs to determine the presence or absence of drugs and their metabolites; chemicals such as ethanol and other volatile substances; carbon monoxide and other gases; metals; and other toxic chemicals. The forensic toxicologist then evaluates the role of these elements in causing death or modifying behavior. Samples are taken from the victim subsequent to an autopsy or as part of a medical examination, in accordance with agency-specific protocols and the law. At trial, a forensic toxicologist may testify as to whether certain drugs or chemicals were present in the victim, at what levels, and what those levels mean in the case at hand. For example, if there is alcohol, was the victim legally drunk or necessarily impaired? Was there poison in the victim's system, and how long did it take to accumulate? If there were drugs present, were they consistent with therapeutic levels of prescription medication, or overdose levels of illicit narcotics? And how long had the victim been taking or abusing the drugs found in his or her system?

In cases involving victim death, toxicology is standard except when inept forensic examiners fail to request it. However, in nondeath cases, many police investigators will actively work to prevent this kind of examination from being performed. This is because the presence of alcohol or other drugs in the victim's system at the time of the crime may be used to accurately suggest a lack of victim reliability. Victim toxicology should be standard in all criminal cases. It's absence may suggest bias, ignorance, or budgetary constraints.

Mental Health Professionals

Victims of crime may have a history of mental health issues prior to an attack, or they may develop mental health issues subsequently. Also, the court may request a mental health evaluation of the victim. In any case, the victim may be seeing a psychologist, psychiatrist, counselor, or some other mental health professional. His or her mental health issues and any related treatment might have a direct bearing on the case at hand. Testimony from mental health professionals can include everything from the victim's general state of mind and awareness; to details regarding uncharged acts involving intimates; to the precise nature of the psychological and emotional harm that an attack may have caused. As already discussed in Chapter 7, "Psychological Aspects of Victimology," this may also involve testimony regarding any number of victim syndromes. For an example of examiner bias as it relates to forensic medical professionals and the purposeful concealment of victim mental health history, see the Preface.

Profilers

Victimology is an essential component in the criminal profiling process (Turvey 2008). Consequently, criminal profilers may be called upon to perform examinations that incorporate victimology into their findings for investigative and forensic purposes. This may be to assist with crime analysis, case linkage, motivational analysis, or simply to offer an opinion regarding the victim's risk or exposure to various kinds of harm or loss.

SUMMARY

In a criminal trial, the prosecutor serves the interests of the state and not the victim. The role of the victim at trial is therefore not necessarily one of partnership with the prosecutor, but rather one of performance for the judge and jury. Victims serve to help establish certain elements of the crime through their evidence of injury and any related testimony. However, once a guilty verdict has been achieved, the victim or his or her family may have some influence over sentencing through the delivery of victim impact statements.

Victim information and related professional attitudes can influence the presentation and admissibility of evidence. Forensic victimology may serve a very important role in the legal process with respect to cooling the emotional content that victim information brings to the legal process through objective examination and interpretation. However, the court, for various reasons relating to admissibility, may curtail victim information and any related expert testimony. Moreover, experts and judges alike are prone to bias in their cognitive functioning, conscious and subconscious alike. In working towards scientific objectivity to blunt subconscious bias, forensic victimologists must understand that they serve a scientific standard of evidentiary reliability and not a legal one, regardless of what the court decides will be presented before the jury.

Questions

1. Describe three pieces of information that victim impact statements usually contain.
2. Define *relevance* as it pertains to victimological information
3. What are some of the problems with rape shield laws?
4. What are two tests used to determine the admissibility of expert testimony in court? Describe the differences between them.
5. True or False: *Frye, Daubert,* and *Kumho* can be considered scientific standards as well as legal guidelines for admissibility.
6. Name and describe three errors that lead to observer effects
7. True or False: What is sufficiently reliable for legal purposes is usually sufficiently reliable for inclusion in a victimology.
8. Name and describe two common examples of expert witnesses in victimology.

REFERENCES

Anderson, M. 2002. From chastity requirement to sexuality license: Sexual consent and a new rape shield law. *George Washington Law Review,* 70, 51–165.

Berger, V. 1977. "Man's Trial, Women's Tribulation: Rape Cases in the Courtroom." *Columbia Law Review* 7, no. : 1–103.

Blinka, D. 2006. "Expert Testimony and the Relevancy Rule in the Age of Daubert." *Marquette Law Review* 902, Winter: 173–226.

Booth v. Maryland. 1987. 482 U.S. 496.

Chisum, W.J., and B. Turvey. 2006. *Crime Reconstruction.* Boston: Elsevier Science.

Cooley, C. 2006. "Reconstructionists in a Post-Daubert and Post-DNA Courtroom." In *Crime Reconstruction,* edited by W.J. Chisum and B. Turvey, . Boston: Elsevier Science.

Erez, E. 1990. Victim participation in sentencing: Rhetoric and reality. *Journal of Criminal Justice,* 18, 19–31.

Erez, E. 1994. Victim participation in sentencing: And the debate goes on. *International Review of Victimology,* 3, 17–32.

Finkel, N. 1995. *Commonsense justice: Jurors' notions of the law.* Cambridge, MA: Harvard University Press.

Fitz-James, M. 1996. "What to Do if Your Records Are Subpoenaed." *Medical Post* 32, no. 5: 50.

Flowe, H., E. Ebbesen, and A. Putcha-Bhagavatula. 2007. "Rape Shield Laws and Sexual Behavior Evidence: Effects of Consent Level and Women's Sexual History on Rape Allegations." *Law and Human Behavior* 31, no. 2: 159–175.

Galvin, H.R. 1986. Shielding rape victims in the state and federal courts: A proposal for the 2nd decade. *Minnesota Law Review,* 70, 763–916.

Giannelli, P.C. 1980. "The Admissibility of Novel Scientific Evidence: Frye v. United States, A Half-Century Later," *Colum. L. Rev.,* 80, 1197–1243.

Giannelli, P.C. 1994. "Daubert: Interpreting the Federal Rules of Evidence," *Cardozo L. Rev.,* 15, 1999.

Grabosky, P. 1987. "Victims." In *The Criminal Justice System,* edited by J. Bastan, M. Richardson, C. Reynolds, and G. Zdenkowski, . Syndey: Pluto Press.

Gruber, A. 2003. "Victim Wrongs: The Case for a General Criminal Defense Based on Wrongful Victim Behavior in an Era of Victims' Rights." *Temple Law Review* 76, Winter: 645–738.

Guthrie, C. 2007. "Misjudging." *Nevada Law Journal* 7, Spring: 420–456.

Guthrie, C., J. Rachlinski, and A. Wistrich. 2007. "Blinking on the Bench: How Judges Decide Cases." *Cornell Law Review* 93, November: 1–43.

Herman, L. (1976–77). What's wrong with rape reform laws? The Civil Liberties Law Review, 60–73.

Keane, A. 2006. *The Modern Law of Evidence.* 6th ed. London: Oxford University Press.

Kelly, D.P. 1984. Victims' perceptions of criminal justice. *Pepperdine Law Review,* 11, 15–22.

Kilpatrick, D., and R. Otto. 1987. "Constitutionally Guaranteed Participation in *Criminal* Justice Proceedings for Victims: Potential Effects of Psychological Functioning." *Wayne Law Review* 34, no. 1: 7–28.

Kuhn, P. 2006. "Victim Impact Statements in Capital Sentencing and *Humphries v. Ozmint:* Do 'Worthless' Defendants Pay a Higher Price." *New England Journal on Criminal and Civil Confinement* 32, Summer: 251–278.

Lowery, D. 1992. The sixth amendment, the preclusionary sanction, and rape shield laws: Michigan vs. Lucas, 111 S. Ct. 1743 (1991). *Cincinnati Law Review,* 61, 297–329.

Miller, N. 1997. Review of state sexual assault laws, 1997. Alexandria, V.A.: *Institute of Law and Justice.*

Murphy, P. 2008. *Murphy on Evidence.* 10th ed. New York: Oxford University Press.

Myers and Green. 2004. "The Prejudicial nature of Victim Impact Statements" *Psychology, Public Policy, and Law,* Vol. 10; 492–511.

NIJ (National Institute of Justice). 1999. *Death Investigation: A Guide for the Scene Investigator.* Research Report NCJ 167568. Washington, DC: NIJ.

Payne v. Tennessee, 111 S. Ct. 2597 (1991).

Petherick, W., and B. Turvey. 2008. "Criminal Profiling, the Scientific Method, and Logic." In *Criminal Profiling: An Introduction to Behavioral Evidence Analysis.* 3rd ed., edited by B. Turvey, . Boston: Elsevier Science.

Pokorak, J. 2007. "Rape Victims and Prosecutors: The Inevitable Ethical Conflict of De Facto Client/Attorney Relationships." *South Texas Law Review* 48, Spring: 695–732.

Policy Centre for Victims Issues. 2001. *Victims of Crime Research Series: The Role of the Victim in the Criminal Process a Literature Review: 1989 to 1999.* Department of Justice, Canada, Research and Statistics Division. http://www.justice.gc.ca/en/ps/rs/rep/2000/victims_role.html.

Policy Centre for Victims Issues. 2002. *Victims of Crime Research Series: Summary Report on Victim Impact Focus Groups.* Department of Justice, Canada, Research and Statistics Division. http://www.justice.gc.ca /en/ps /rs/rep/2000/victims_sum.html.

Price, J.M. 1996. Constitutional law-Sex, lies, and rape shield statutes: The constitutionality of interpreting rape shield statutes to exclude evidence relating to the victim's motive to fabricate. *Western New England Law Review,* 18, 541–576.

Reaves, B. 2006. "Violent Felons in Large Urban Counties." Washington, DC: Bureau of Justice Statistics, NCJ 205289, July.

Regina v. O'Connor. 1995. 4 S.C.R. 411, Court of Appeal for British Columbia, 1995: February 1; 1995: December 14.

Risinger, M. 2000. "Defining the 'Task at Hand': Non-Science Forensic Science after Kumho Tire Co. v. Carmichael," *Wash. & Lee. L. Rev.,* 57, 767.

Risinger, D.M., M. Saks, W. Thompson, and R. Rosenthal. 2002. "The Daubert/ Kumho Implications of Observer Effects in Forensic Science: Hidden Problems of Expectation and Suggestion." *California Law Review* 90, no. 1: 1–56.

Roberts, P., and A. Zuckerman. 2004. *Criminal Evidence.* New York: Oxford University Press.

Rosenthal, R. 1966. Experimenter Effects in Behavioral Research, New York: Appleton-Century-Crofts.

Saks, M., D. Faigman, D. Kaye, and D. Sanders. 2004. "Admissibility of Scientific Evidence." In *Annotated Scientific Evidence Reference Manual,* edited by M. Saks, D. Faigman, D. Kaye, and D. Sanders, . St. Paul, MN: West Publishing.

Simmons, R. 2007. "Private Criminal Justice." *Wake Forest Law Review* 47, Winter: 911–990.

South Carolina v. Gathers, 490 U.S. 805 (1989).

Sumner, C.J. 1987. Victim participation in the criminal justice system. *Australian and New Zealand Journal of Criminology,* 20, 195–217.

Thornton, J. 1994. 'Courts of Law v. Courts of Science: A Forensic Scientist's Reaction to Daubert." *Shepard's Expert and Scientific Quarterly* 1, no. 3: 475–485.

Turvey, B. 2003. "Forensic Frauds: A Study of 42 Cases." *Journal of Behavioral Profiling* 4, no. 1: .

Turvey, B., ed. 2008. *Criminal Profiling: An Introduction to Behavioral Evidence Analysis.* 3rd ed. Boston: Elsevier Science.

United States Federal Rules of Evidence (FRE) Article VII, Rule 702.

Wallace, H. 1998. *Victimology: Legal, Psychological and Social Perspectives.* Upper Saddle River, NJ: Allyn and Bacon.

Williams, B. 1999. *Working with Victims of Crime: Policies, Politics, and Practices.* London: Athenaeum Press.

Williams, K. 2004. *Textbook on Criminology.* New York: Oxford University Press.

Zielinski, D. 2008. "Victim in sexual abuse trial commits perjury." *DailyPress.com,* January 23. http://www.dailypress.com/news/local/williamsburg/dp-news_sherman_0123jan23,0,6314781.story.

CHAPTER 16

Wrongful Convictions: Victims of the Criminal Justice System

Brent E. Turvey

KEY TERMS

Forensic expert: a professional that has been qualified by the court to give opinion-oriented testimony in relation to their area of education, training, or experience.

Legal truth: the current disposition of the court, or law on a particular matter.

Miscarriage of justice: a general term used to describe the inequity which occurs when a victim or offender does not receive fair treatment by the justice system, often resulting in a legal outcome that is not in their favor.

Scientific fact: something that is not in dispute, having been established by scientific examination and testing.

Wrongful conviction: a particular miscarriage of justice in which a defendant is found legally guilty in court, by a judge or jury, despite being factually innocent of the crime.

CONTENTS

In this textbook we have discussed victims that suffer at the hands of friends, family members, coworkers, and strangers. The intended role of the criminal justice system in these instances is that of impartial arbitrator—to decide who did what, if the law has been broken, and then determine a fair punishment. Law enforcement is meant to investigate the facts; forensic examiners are meant to analyze evidence and explain its meaning in court; prosecutors are meant to seek justice; defense attorneys are meant to defend their clients; and judges are meant to impartially render the law in order to preserve the rights of all parties.

However, as several of the examples in previous chapters have already demonstrated, the criminal justice system is not always experienced as a level course of events for those involved. It cannot be ignored that sometimes those who control various segments of the justice system are unjust. A defendant can become a victim of their bias, corruption, ignorance, error, and indifference. When this occurs, it is referred to as a *miscarriage of justice*. As explained in Naughton

(2005, 165), current definitions of what precisely constitutes a miscarriage are both legalistic and retrospective:

> One of the defining features of the study of miscarriages of justice is that whatever allegations of wrongful criminal conviction there may be, a miscarriage of justice cannot be said to have occurred unless, and until, the appeal courts quash a criminal conviction. For instance, the Birmingham Six (Mullin 1986)—perhaps one of the most notable cases in recent times—had two unsuccessful appeals before they successfully overturned their criminal convictions and were officially acknowledged as miscarriage-of-justice victims. This renders the study of miscarriages of justice inherently legalistic and retrospective. "Legalistic," as miscarriages of justice are wholly determined by the rules and procedures of the appeal courts—if those rules and procedures change, then the way in which miscarriages of justice are defined and quantified will also change. "Retrospective," as there is no way of knowing about how many wrongful convictions will be overturned in the future or how many are in the process of being overturned. They remain "alleged" miscarriages of justice until they pass the test and achieve a successful appeal.

This passage is useful, but Naughton ignores the reality that miscarriages of justice take many forms. Specifically, they do not require a conviction in order to inflict harm upon a factually innocent suspect or defendant. Nor are they inflicted upon only the factually innocent. They can be caused by investigative apathy; false and erroneous testimony; evidence tampering; forensic error; forensic fraud; ineffective assistance of defense counsel (incompetent lawyering); prosecutorial misconduct; jury misconduct; judicial misconduct; and overall ignorance of the law. Any of these and more can result in a miscarriage of justice, such as a wrongful arrest, wrongful detention, malicious prosecution, sentencing error, wrongful acquittal, or even wrongful conviction. The question is not whether these defendants are victims of the system, but rather how much harm is inflicted, and whether the miscarriage is recognized and remedied. Consequently, the notion that miscarriages are confined only to wrongful convictions—which are the focus of this chapter—is misplaced.

A *wrongful conviction* is a particular miscarriage of justice in which a defendant is found legally guilty in court, by a judge or jury (also known as the trier of fact), despite being factually innocent of the crime.

Wrongful convictions can happen intentionally, at the hands of one or more individuals working in concert or individually, who are looking to subvert justice. In some cases, this will involve a primary victim, implicating a specific factually innocent defendant. In other cases, it will involve actively concealing the truth, leaving the remaining facts to implicate whomever they will.

However, wrongful convictions can also occur despite the best intentions of everyone involved, due to unintended and unforeseen failures in one or more parts of the process. In these cases, justice is not intentionally sabotaged, but the factually innocent defendant becomes a collateral victim of the original crime.

The goals of this chapter, then, are to dispel prevailing myths and rhetoric connected with the nature and causes of miscarriages in general, wrongful convictions in specific, and to bring those harmed by the criminal justice system to their rightful place at the criminal justice table—as victims of crime. It is also meant to educate the forensic victimologist regarding the consequences of his or her efforts and eventual testimony. As such, it is best treated as a primer to the issues presented, most of which demand far more in-depth coverage.

A HISTORICAL PERSPECTIVE

That wrongful convictions can and do occur is not a revelation only recently made possible by modern scientific advances in suspect identification. Historically, courts of law—even when tempered by juries and adversarial systems—have made errors. It is safe to say, in fact, that wrongful convictions have been with each and every court that has taken up the task of judging guilt or innocence.

FIGURE 16.1

Guido Reni's *Joseph and Potiphar's Wife*, 1631.

The Bible

Consider the biblical example of Joseph and Potiphar's wife, memorialized here in Guido Reni's oil on canvas rendering from about 1631 A.D. The story goes (Genesis 39:7–20) that Joseph, a slave, had repeatedly rebuffed the sexual advances of his master's wife. She was, unfortunately, persistent and not to be denied. On one occasion, she was able to get hold of Joseph's garment as he tried to leave the house, and he ran out without it.

Angered by his refusals, she staged her bedroom with his garment, to appear as though Joseph had raped her. She then reported Joseph's "crime" to the men of her household, who in turn informed her husband. Her husband,

Potiphar, was also a captain of Pharaoh's guard. Needless to say, Joseph went right to prison for a crime that he did not commit, as Potiphar was not likely to doubt his wife.

This example, though distant and unsubstantiated, is representative of a particular source of wrongful convictions still found in courtrooms today—the false witness. That it exists in a text written thousands of years ago, likely as a cautionary tale, is significant.

The Three Perrys

There is a tendency to view wrongful convictions as a modern revelation, with DNA providing the certainty needed to demonstrate actual innocence when circumstances permit. However, the literature makes it clear that such thinking ignores a well-documented history of both wrongful convictions and executions. Consider the case of the three Perrys in England, as detailed in Smith (2005, 1189–1192):

> By some accounts, legal observers only discovered the problem of wrongful execution in the past two decades, when the increased availability and accuracy of DNA testing brought the problem of wrongful conviction—and the even more shocking prospect of wrongful execution— to public attention. In truth, wrongful execution cast a specter over Anglo-American criminal justice administration from the seventeenth through the early nineteenth centuries. During this period, English and American legal commentators confronted the sobering possibility not only that persons might be executed wrongfully, but that they undeniably had been—at times for committing offenses that had never occurred at all....
>
> On August 16, 1660, William Harrison, the steward of Lady Campden, left his home in Gloucestershire, England, for a nearby town to collect some rents. By eight or nine o'clock that night, the seventy-year-old Harrison still had not returned from his rounds. Harrison's wife sent her servant, a fourteen-year-old boy named John Perry, to look for her husband—but to no avail. The following morning, Harrison's son Edward took up the search. After meeting up with the servant boy John, Edward discovered his father's hat and collar near a road in a "hackt," "cut," and "bloody" state. Although the townspeople of Campden "haste[en]d...in multitudes to search for...[Harrison's] body," they managed to turn up nothing.
>
> Suspicion soon fell upon John, who was brought before a justice of the peace (JP) the following day. The boy claimed that, on the night of Harrison's disappearance, he had begun his search in earnest but had been "afraid to go forwards" because of the "dark" and, instead, had returned to rest in his master's "hen-roost." At around midnight,

John had ventured forth once again but had "lost his way" in a "great mist" and "so lay the rest of the night under a hedge." When he awoke the next day, he went to a neighboring town, spoke to some people there, and later met up with Edward. Four other persons who appeared before the JP corroborated John's story. Nonetheless, the JP committed John to custody.

Once confined, the young boy began to talk. He claimed to some of his interlocutors that a "tinker" had killed Harrison, to others that "a gentleman's servant…had robbed and murdered him," and to "others again…that [Harrison] was murdered, and hid in a bean-rick." As these stories proliferated, John was once again brought before the JP, a week after his initial commitment. This time, he told a more chilling story. He now claimed that his mother, Joan, and brother, Richard, had lain in wait for Harrison on the night of Harrison's disappearance, strangled him, and robbed him of his money bags. John also claimed to have heard his mother and brother discuss throwing Harrison's body "into the great sink"—a bog near a local mill. Additional searches, however, failed to turn up Harrison's body.

When the JP interrogated Joan and Richard, both denied any wrongdoing. But at the next meeting of the Gloucestershire assizes in September 1660, a pair of indictments were brought against the three Perrys: the first, for breaking into Harrison's house the previous year, a crime in which John—in his apparent mania to confess—had also implicated the whole family; and the second, for robbing and murdering Harrison on the night of his disappearance. The Perrys pleaded guilty to the first charge, begged for a pardon, and received it. The presiding judge refused to send the second charge to the jury because the body of Harrison still had not been found.

Unfortunately, the Perrys' troubles did not end—for John continued to talk. Not only did he persist in swearing that his mother and brother had killed Harrison, but he now claimed that the two had "attempted to poison him in…jail, so that he durst neither eat nor drink with them." At the Gloucestershire assizes in Spring 1661, a second indictment for murder was brought against the three Perrys. Suddenly John—apparently coming to his senses—insisted that, at the time of his previous confessions, he was "mad, and knew not what he said." Joan and Robert, for their part, desperately continued to protest their innocence. Although Harrison's body still had not been found—in "the great sink" or anywhere else—a new assize judge, Sir Robert Hyde, permitted the case to go to a jury. The jury duly pronounced all three members of the family guilty and Joan, Richard, and John Perry were promptly hanged and gibbeted on Broadway Hill near Campden.

So ended the lives of the three Perrys. But two years after their executions, a "wondrous" event occurred: William Harrison returned to Gloucestershire, claiming to have been attacked on the night of his disappearance by an unknown man on horseback, pressed to serve on a sailing ship, sold into slavery in Turkey, and ultimately spirited back to England by way of Lisbon.

This example is also representative of a particular source of wrongful convictions that persists in the modern justice system—the false confession.

The Boorn Brothers

The United States is not immune from a similar history. Consider the case of the Boorn brothers, as detailed in Smith (2005, 1205–1206):

In 1812, Russell Colvin, a local eccentric prone to wandering, disappeared from his home in Manchester, Vermont. His brothers-in-law, Jesse and Stephen Boorn, were suspected of Colvin's disappearance, but the body of Colvin, the supposed victim, could not be found. After seven years had passed, and long after initial suspicion had dissipated from the brothers, a relative of the two suspects claimed to have experienced a dream in which Colvin had appeared to him.

Interest in Colvin's disappearance and presumed murder revived and, during the course of a renewed investigation, a dog uncovered some bones believed to be those of Colvin. Upon the basis of this new "evidence," which seemed, by the "scientific" standards of the day, to demonstrate conclusively that Colvin had been killed, Jesse Boorn was imprisoned. Thereafter, a convicted forger in an adjacent cell claimed to the authorities that Jesse had confessed. When confronted with his alleged jailhouse statement, Jesse placed the blame on his brother Stephen, who had relocated to New York and was apparently believed by Jesse to be outside the jurisdiction of the Vermont courts. Tracked down and arrested in New York, Stephen ultimately confessed to killing Colvin in self-defense, likely concluding— quite sensibly—that the decision of Jesse to accuse him of Colvin's killing rendered his prospects for acquittal rather dim. Instead, both brothers were tried, convicted, and sentenced to death. Although the Vermont legislature commuted Jesse's sentence to life imprisonment, it declined to respite the sentence of Stephen—seemingly, the more culpable of the two.

Supporters of the condemned man then undertook a concerted effort to find Colvin, placing advertisements in regional newspapers containing descriptions of the man they believed to be merely missing, and not dead. Shortly before Stephen Boorn was to have been executed, Colvin miraculously re-emerged after a resident of New York City had read the description of Colvin in a local newspaper and notified the Boorns' representatives that a man fitting Colvin's description was living in New Jersey. Colvin's "triumphant" return to Vermont secured the release of both of his erstwhile "killers."

This example is also representative of a particular source of wrongful convictions that persists in the modern justice system—the jailhouse informant.

Gary Dotson

In modern history, the first person to be exonerated of a criminal conviction with DNA evidence was Gary Dotson, in the 1980s. In 1979, Dotson had been wrongly convicted and incarcerated for a rape that never happened. Details are taken from Connors et al. (1996, 52–53):

Gary Dotson (Chicago, Illinois)

Factual background. On the evening of July 9, 1977, the complainant was walking home from work when two men forced her into the back seat of a car and raped her. She also testified that one of the men tried to write words on her stomach using a broken beer bottle. She was then pushed from the car onto the street.

In July 1979 Gary Dotson was convicted of aggravated kidnapping and rape.

He was sentenced to not less than 25 and not more than 50 years.

Prosecutor's evidence at trial. The prosecution's case included the following evidence:

- A composite sketch of the defendant, which the complainant helped with, was prepared by the police.
- The victim identified Dotson from a police mug book.
- Dotson was identified by the victim from a police lineup.
- The State's expert serologist testified that the semen on the victim's undergarment came from a type B secretor and that the defendant was a

type B secretor. (It was later reported that the State's serologist failed to disclose that the victim was also a type B secretor.)[1]

- Testimony was presented that a pubic hair removed from the victim's underwear was similar to the defendant's and dissimilar to the victim's.

Postconviction challenges. In March 1985 the victim recanted her testimony.

She said she had fabricated the rape to hide a legitimate sexual encounter with her boyfriend. Dotson contended that the victim's recantation of testimony constituted grounds to vacate the original sentence. At the hearing on Dotson's motion for a new trial, the same judge from the original trial refused to order a new trial. His reasoning was that the complainant was more believable in her original testimony than in her recantation.

The governor accepted authority for the case and held a session of the Illinois Prisoner Review Board. The governor stated that he did not believe the victim's recantation and refused to pardon Dotson. On May 12, 1985, however, the governor commuted Dotson's sentence to the 6 years he had already served, pending good behavior. In 1987 the governor revoked Dotson's parole after Dotson was accused by his wife of assaulting her. The Appellate Court of Illinois affirmed Dotson's conviction on November 12, 1987 (516 N.E.2d 718). On Christmas Eve 1987 the governor granted Dotson a "last chance parole." Two days later, Dotson was arrested in a barroom fight, and his parole was revoked. In 1988 Dotson's new attorney had DNA tests conducted that were not available at the time of the alleged rape.

DNA results. A sample of semen from the victim's underwear was sent to Dr. Alec Jeffreys in England for RFLP analysis. The sample was badly degraded, however, and results were inconclusive. Samples were then sent to Forensic Science Associates in Richmond, California. The lab performed PCR DQ alpha tests that showed that the semen on the victim's undergarments could not have come from Dotson but could have come from the victim's boyfriend.

---

[1]As explained in the commentary by Rowe (1996, xvi–xvii):

> the forensic serologist who testified against Gary Dotson failed to disclose that, because the alleged victim was also a type B secretor, the fraction of the male population that could have contributed the semen found on the vaginal swabs exceeded 60 percent, making the serological evidence in the case probative of very little. In this instance, the prosecution's expert witness failed to volunteer potentially exculpatory information but did not actually lie under oath.

The failure of forensic experts to be forthcoming about the limits of inclusionary evidence, by clearly and accurately explaining the context of statistical probabilities, remains a problem to this day—particularly in the field of DNA.

Conclusion. The chief judge of the Cook County Criminal Court ruled that Dotson was entitled to a new trial. The State attorney's office, however, decided not to prosecute based on the victim's lack of credibility and the DNA test results. Dotson's conviction was overturned on August 14, 1989, after he had served a total of 8 years.

Since Dotson's exoneration, the number of convicted defendants freed because of DNA has steadily increased as testing methods have become more able and sensitive.

NOMOTHETICALLY SPEAKING: THE AGGREGATE

There are more than a few criminal justice practitioners who cling to the notion that wrongful convictions in the modern criminal justice system are either rare and therefore irrelevent, or the acceptable cost of a free society. Not suprisingly, such opinions tend to come from those with a vested professional interest in the absolute certainty of legal convictions, namely law enforcement investigators, state employed forensic practitioners, prosecutors, and judges.[2] As explained in Bernhard (2004, 716):

> Bias against those who have been accused and reluctance to accept the possibility of mistake color prosecutorial attitudes...Even when DNA evidence clearly exonerates, prosecutors have trouble admitting that they convicted the wrong person.

Risinger (2007) refers to some of those with such extremist views as *Paleyites* (763–768):

> Paleyites, whom I have named after the early exponent of this position, the 18th-century proto-utilitarian the Rev. William Paley, believe that, even though it is wrong to convict an innocent person, such convictions not only are inevitable in a human system, but represent the necessary social price of maintaining sufficient criminal law enforcement to provide an appropriate level of security for the public in general. Hence, one should not be moved by the prospect of wrongful conviction to take actions that would reduce such convictions, no matter how common, at the cost of reducing convictions of the guilty to a dysfunctional level. Paleyites tend to be conservative, in the sense that any changes to

---

[2]Many in the judiciary are former prosecutors, and some judges come to the profession with a particular background and mindset. Some are able to overcome this; others are not. In any case, judges are paid to deliver a fair and balanced interpretation of the law, without prejudice to the defendant. However, if they allow injustices in their court by act or omission, this reflects poorly on their judgment, for lack of a better word. Consequently, they have a vested interest in keeping secure any decisions and convictions that have been attained in their courtroom. Admitting to a miscarriage may undercut this interest.

current ways of conducting the criminal justice process, proposed for their supposed effect on protecting the innocent, will be presumed so counterproductive in their effect on convicting the guilty that they will be opposed. . . .

Traditionally, a certain stripe of Paleyite has also denied that wrongful convictions happen at all, or, that if they happen, they happen so rarely that worrying about them is like worrying about being struck by a meteorite. The reasons assigned for this assumed near-perfection in regard to false-positive error have generally been the numerous layers of filtration involved in the pre-trial system, and the general fairness of the adversary trial itself, with its formal requirement that the prosecution prove guilt beyond a reasonable doubt.

Such a position is very difficult to take in the era of DNA exonerations. As explained by another legal scholar (Uphoff 2006, 838):

The growing number of DNA exonerations and the attendant publicity surrounding these cases and other wrongful convictions sound an increasingly loud [and] discordant note in the normal chorus of praise for the American criminal justice system.

However, the most recent sudy of wrongful convictions offers perhaps the best overall insight, noting that over 208 postconviction DNA exonerations have occurred in cases of rape and homicide since 1989 (Garrett 2008, 56–57):

Postconviction DNA testing changed the landscape of criminal justice in the United States. Actors in the criminal system long doubted whether courts ever wrongly convicted people; for example, Judge Learned Hand famously called "the ghost of the innocent man convicted . . . an unreal dream." With the benefit of DNA testing, we now know our courts have convicted innocent people and have even sentenced some to death. This has happened, as Justice Souter recently noted, "in numbers never imagined before the development of DNA tests." Since 1989, when postconviction DNA testing was first performed, 208 people have been exonerated by postconviction DNA testing in the United States.

Exoneration cases have altered the way judges, lawyers, legislators, the public, and scholars perceive the criminal system's accuracy.

Even as this textbook goes to press, DNA exonerations continue. The most recent, in Texas, has led to calls for criminal prosecution of those prosecutors who withhold evidence at trial. This currently does not happen except under extreme circumstances, such as the Duke LaCrosse case (see Chapter 8). As detailed in Emily and McGonigle (2008):

Wrongful convictions, nearly half of them involving prosecutorial misconduct, have cost Texas taxpayers $8.6 million in compensation since 2001, according to state comptroller records obtained by *The Dallas Morning News.* Dallas County accounts for about one-third of that.

[Dallas County District Attorney] Mr. [Craig] Watkins said that he was still pondering what kind of punishment unethical prosecutors deserve but that the worst offenders might deserve prison time. He said he also was considering the launch of a campaign to mandate disbarment for any prosecutor found to have intentionally withheld evidence from the defense.

Such ideas could not be more at odds with the win-at-all-costs philosophy that was the hallmark of legendarily hard-line Dallas County District Attorney Henry Wade and, to a lesser extent, of subsequent administrations.

"Most prosecutors would say, 'No, no, no,'" said Bennett Gershman, a Pace University law professor who studies prosecutorial misconduct.

It is rare for a prosecutor to advocate strict penalties for misconduct— even when it's intentional, said Mr. Gershman, a former New York prosecutor. "I couldn't give you five cases in the last 40 years of criminal charges against prosecutors," he said.

State Sen. Rodney Ellis, chief author of the Texas law that created the compensation system for wrongfully convicted inmates, said he, too, would support criminalizing the intentional withholding of evidence by prosecutors. No criminal charge exists in Texas for a prosecutor who intentionally commits a "Brady violation."

That term refers to the 1963 U.S. Supreme Court ruling in *Brady vs. Maryland,* which held that prosecutors violate defendants' constitutional rights if they intentionally or accidentally withhold evidence favorable to the defense....

Of the 45 wrongful-conviction cases for which the state has paid compensation, at least 22 of them involved prosecutors withholding evidence from the defense: 19 in the infamous Tulia drug convictions and three of Dallas County's DNA exonerations. The remainder of the payouts involved exculpatory DNA evidence or other flaws.

"I think there is a growing realization that we are clearly at a tipping point in Texas," Mr. Ellis said. "And people of conscience have got to be willing to look at it and see what we can do to make the system work better." ...

Mr. Ellis said the total amount paid so far confirms his suspicion that wrongful convictions are far more common in Texas than people realize. Taxpayers should expect to pay "considerably" more as the number of exonerations rises.

Texas already accounts for 14 percent of the estimated 216 DNA-based exonerations around the nation. Dallas County, with 17 exonerations from genetic testing, tops every other local jurisdiction in the U.S. since 2001.

In the most recent exoneration last week, prosecutors originally pursued a murder case against James Lee Woodard but did not tell the defense that three men were with the victim just before she was raped and killed in 1980. Two of the men were later convicted of sexual assault in separate cases.

Mr. Woodard spent 27 years and four months in prison—longer than anyone in the country exonerated by DNA.

Accordingly, I agree that the sheer and continuously mounting volume of overturned convictions has made positions of denial appear not just untenable and naïve, but too often belligerently ignorant.

RESEARCH

The question persists: How often does the court get it wrong? Where is the data to answer this question? First of all, there is no centralized database from which to draw these numbers. Each of the U.S. states, even each individual county, keeps and maintains data regarding wrongful convictions (or fails to do so) in their own way. Second of all, the available numbers are limited to capital cases and some rape cases where DNA evidence has been preserved, and where the judiciary has permitted postconviction review. This means the available data is a narrow sample of the total cases. Having said all that, the available numbers are not encouraging.

Rape-Homicide Exoneration Rate in the United States

One study determined that the minimum factually wrongful conviction rate (exoneration rate) for rape-homicide alone, in the 1980s, was about 5% (Risinger 2007, 780):

Whatever the depth (or shallowness) of one's emotional or moral response to a 3–5% factual innocence error rate in a significant set of real-world capital cases, it is hard to characterize it as de minimis, or to fairly say that it represents a "remote" possibility of conviction of the innocent. Paleyites often depend on the tenability of such assertions either to make themselves feel better, or to convince the general mass of people that there is no systemic problem of wrongful conviction to be considered, or both. . . .

In addition, Paleyites will find little to comfort them regarding claims that such exonerations are demonstrations of "the system working," or that reversals through the ordinary appellate process take care of the problem of wrongful conviction.

This is consistent with the findings of another study conducted by *Chicago Tribune* reporters Ken Armstrong and Maurice Possley. In 1999, they produced a five-part series reporting on their national study of approximately 11,000 court rulings over 36 years. They found 381 defendants who had their homicide convictions reversed due to prosecutorial misconduct alone (Joy 2006, footnote 2).

Wrongful Convictions in the United States: 1989–2003

A more inclusive study of exonerations in the United States from 1989 through 2003 (Gross et al. 2005, 524) provides better detail:

Overall, we found 340 exonerations, 327 men and 13 women; 144 of them were cleared by DNA evidence, 196 by other means. With a handful of exceptions, they had been in prison for years. More than half had served terms of 10 years or more; 80% had been imprisoned for at least 5 years. As a group, they had spent more than 3400 years in prison for crimes for which they should never have been convicted—an average of more than 10 years each.

Rather than offering a total percentage estimate of wrongful convictions for the timeframe examined, Gross et al. concluded that for a number of reasons such a task is not feasible, offering an estimate of knowns instead. They also explain where the holes are in the data, and to some extent why (551):

We can't come close to estimating the number of false convictions that occur in the United States, but the accumulating mass of exonerations gives us a glimpse of what we're missing. We have located 340 exonerations from 1989 through 2003, not counting hundreds of additional exonerated defendants in the Tulia and Rampart scandals and other mass exonerations, or more than seventy convicted childcare sex abuse defendants. Almost all the individual exonerations that we know about are clustered in two crimes, rape and murder. They are surrounded by widening circles of categories of cases with false convictions that have not been detected: rape convictions that have not been reexamined with DNA evidence; robberies, for which DNA identification is useless; murder cases that are ignored because the defendants were not sentenced to death; assault and drug convictions that are forgotten entirely. Any plausible guess at the total number of miscarriages of justice in America in the last 15 years must be in the thousands, perhaps tens of thousands.

Based on my own casework and research, this estimate of the total number of wrongful convictions in the United States appears conservative.

Death Penalty Miscarriage Rate in the United States: 1973–1995

Even more disturbing is the known miscarriage or error rate for cases of the most serious nature, where one would expect the best efforts to be made by all involved. This was established by the first study of its kind, conducted on 4,578 state capital (death penalty) cases between 1973 and 1995 (Liebman et al. 2000, 1846–1850):

Six years in the making, our central findings thus far are these:

- Between 1973 and 1995, approximately 5,760 death sentences were imposed in the United States. Only 313 (5.4%; one in 19) of those resulted in an execution during the period.

- Of the 5,760 death sentences imposed in the study period, 4,578 (79%) were finally reviewed on "direct appeal" by a state high court. Of those, 1,885 (41%) were thrown out on the basis of "serious error" (error that substantially undermines the reliability of the outcome).

- Most of the remainder of the death sentences were then inspected by state postconviction courts. Although incomplete, our data (reported in *A Broken System*) reveal that state postconviction review is an important source of review in some states, including Florida, Georgia, Indiana, Maryland, Mississippi, and North Carolina. In Maryland, for example, at least 52% of capital judgments reviewed in state postconviction proceedings during the study period were overturned due to serious error; the same was true for at least 25% of the capital judgments that were similarly reviewed in Indiana, and at least 20% of those reviewed in Mississippi.

- Of the death sentences that survived state direct and postconviction review, 599 were finally reviewed on a first habeas corpus petition during the 23-year study period. Of those 599, 237 (40%) were overturned due to serious error.

- The "overall success rate" of capital judgments undergoing judicial inspection, and its converse, the "overall error-rate," are crucial factors in assessing the efficiency of our capital punishment system.

The "overall success rate" is the proportion of capital judgments that underwent, and passed, the three-stage judicial inspection process during the study period. The "overall error rate" is the frequency with which capital judgments that underwent full inspection were overturned at one of the three stages due to serious error. Nationally, over the entire 1973–1995 period, the overall error-rate in our capital punishment system was 68%.

- Because "serious error" is error that substantially undermines the reliability of the guilt finding or death sentence imposed at trial, each instance of that error warrants public concern. The most common errors found at the state post-conviction stage (where our data are most complete) are (1) egregiously incompetent defense lawyering (accounting for 37% of the state postconviction reversals), and (2) prosecutorial suppression of evidence that the defendant is innocent or does not deserve the death penalty (accounting for another 16%—or 19%, when all forms of law enforcement misconduct are considered). These two violations count as "serious," and thus warrant reversal, only when there is a "reasonable probability" that, but for the responsible lawyer's miscues, the outcome of the trial would have been different.

The result of very high rates of serious, reversible error among capital convictions and sentences, and very low rates of capital reconviction and resentencing, is the severe attrition of capital judgments. This means that in the most serious cases, those where the death penalty was imposed, the court's sentence was overturned approximately 68% of the time because it was wrong—either because of actual innocence or the identification of some other miscarriage of justice causing the sentence to be reduced or vacated entirely.

CAUSAL FACTORS

As stated at the beginning of this chapter, there are multiple potential origins for any wrongful conviction. As described in Garrett (2008, 60), based on a study of 200 postconviction DNA exonerations, eyewitness identification and false or misleading forensic evidence top the list:[3]

---

[3]In describing a study of DNA exonerations published by the Innocence Project, Joy (2006, footnote 38) ranks the causes of wrongful convictions with similar results:

> After mistaken identification, the other most common factors leading to wrongful convictions in the first 70 DNA exonerations were: serology inclusion (40 cases), police misconduct (38 cases), prosecutorial misconduct (34 cases), defective or fraudulent science (26 cases), bad defense lawyering (23 cases), microscopic hair comparison matches (21 cases), false witness testimony (17 cases), informants or jailhouse snitches (16 cases), and false confessions (15 cases).

All were convicted of rape or murder, and all but the nine who pleaded guilty were convicted after a trial. A few predictable types of unreliable or false evidence supported these convictions. The vast majority of the exonerees (79%) were convicted based on eyewitness testimony; we now know that all of these eyewitnesses were incorrect. Fifty-seven percent were convicted based on forensic evidence, chiefly serological analysis and microscopic hair comparison. Eighteen percent were convicted based on informant testimony, and 16% of exonerees falsely confessed.

Though not a complete list, causal factors in wrongful convictions tend to include one or more of the following:

1. Incorrect eyewitness identification
2. Misrepresented evidence
3. Misunderstood evidence
4. False confessions
5. False testimony from "jailhouse" informants
6. Ineffective or incompetent defense counsel
7. Prosecutorial misconduct

For the purposes of this text, we will confine our discussion to the top contributors: incorrect eyewitness identification, and false or misleading forensic evidence. However, the examples adduced will bear on other causes.

INCORRECT EYEWITNESS IDENTIFICATION

Eyewitness identifications occur when witnesses to a crime or crime-related event provide a report to authorities that they recognize a person, or their physical features, such that they can unequivocally name them, or accurately "recognize" them, at a later time. Either the eyewitness knows the person, has regular contact with him or her, or recalls the accused to such a level of detail to be able to point them out to authorities in public, pick them out of a physical lineup, or pick them out of a photo lineup.

There are a myriad of studies that have explored the strengths and weaknesses of eyewitness identification. At the end of the day, it all comes down to the artfulness of pattern recognition and the tenuousness of human memory. Basically, sometimes eyewitnesses are wrong, which is the leading cause of wrongful convictions. As explained in Fradella (2006, 4):

> There is no truly accurate way to know how frequently mistaken identifications result in wrongful convictions. But, decades of research on the topic have consistently found that mistaken identification is the leading cause of wrongful convictions. In fact, it is so common that it practically rivals the sum of all other errors that

lead to wrongful conviction. For example, between seventy-five and eighty-five percent of the convictions overturned by DNA evidence have involved a mistaken eyewitness. This is likely due to the fact, as the Supreme Court has observed, that "despite its inherent unreliability, much eyewitness identification evidence has a powerful impact on juries. . . . All evidence points rather strikingly to the conclusion that there is almost nothing more convincing than a live human being who takes the stand, points a finger at the defendant, and says, 'That's the one!'" Yet, studies have repeatedly shown a roughly forty percent rate of mistaken identifications. In spite of this, nearly 80,000 suspects are targeted every year based on an eyewitness identification.

The problems with eyewitness identifications, from a legal or forensic and cognitive perspective, are described in Overbeck (2005, 1895–1904), who provides a tour of the confounding variables:

> Few kinds of evidence are as compelling, or as damning, as eyewitness testimony: A human being, frequently a victim, takes the stand, looks at the defendant, and says, "He did it." Eyewitness testimony is a staple element of criminal cases. In 1999, eyewitness identifications led to 75,000 prosecutions in the United States. . . .
>
> From a jury's perspective, eyewitness testimony is one of the most persuasive forms of evidence. Nevertheless, psychological studies have indicated that even the most sincere eyewitnesses are frequently inaccurate. Various factors, such as the passage of time, the introduction of new information, and the identification procedures used by the police, can influence the accuracy of eyewitness accounts. Many jurors are unaware of the weaknesses of eyewitness testimony, and thus routinely overcredit it, which can lead to wrongful convictions.
>
> A. Juror Reliance on Eyewitnesses
> Eyewitness testimony can be extremely persuasive in the courtroom, particularly in criminal trials. In an experimental setting, the introduction of eyewitness testimony has been shown to increase conviction rates dramatically. In mock trials conducted by Elizabeth Loftus, jurors were four times more likely to convict when they heard eyewitness testimony than when they did not. Even when a defense attorney attacked the witness's credibility on cross-examination, conviction rates remained very high.
>
> This study indicates that jurors place substantial weight on eyewitness identification. In fact, jurors place more weight on eyewitness testimony than on many other types of evidence, including fingerprint evidence.

Therefore, it is of paramount importance that witnesses are accurate, or at least that jurors are able to detect when they are inaccurate. ~~Unfortunately, neither occurs often.~~

B. Eyewitnesses Are Frequently Inaccurate

Lawyers and judges have long been concerned with eyewitness accuracy. In an oft-cited passage from *United States v. Wade,* the Supreme Court noted that "the vagaries of eyewitness identification are well-known; the annals of criminal law are rife with instances of mistaken identification." Since the 1970s, a growing body of psychological research has been available to add to the debate. Some of the major psychological findings are outlined below.

1. Accuracy of Memories Over Time

One factor that can influence eyewitness accuracy is the simple passage of time. Memory does not diminish at a uniform rate. Rather, we forget at a rapid rate immediately following an event, and the rate of forgetting then diminishes over time. This is called the "forgetting curve." Thus, even if an eyewitness testifies shortly after an event, her memory may already be substantially diminished.

Furthermore, what happens in the time between the observation and the recall of an event can influence, and even change, a person's memory of it. Witnesses frequently encounter new information after they experience an event. This information can come from other witnesses, investigators, attorneys, or any number of other sources. Post-event information can enhance or compromise a witness's memory. For example, suggesting a fact, such as the presence of a stop sign at the scene of an accident, greatly increases a witness's chances of remembering it, whether it was there or not.

If witnesses encounter additional information that conflicts with their memory of an event, and therefore cannot be easily assimilated into the existing memory, they will compromise between the new information and the information they remember, creating a new memory. Sometimes compromise is impossible, such as when a witness sees a stop sign but is later told it was a yield sign. Witnesses will then frequently "adjust" their memories to be consistent with the subsequent information, rather than with what they originally perceived.

2. Stress, Violence, and Weapon Focus

Stress can affect a witness's original perception of an event as well as her subsequent recall of the event. Stress and other forms of emotional provocation can improve perception to some extent, but when stress levels get too high, they can impair a witness's ability to assess the situation accurately. Violence is one major factor that causes stress for eyewitnesses of crimes, particularly victims. Researchers have found that both men and women recall violent events with much less accuracy than nonviolent ones. The presence of a weapon further undermines a witness's ability to remember events. Witnesses focus on the weapon more frequently and for longer periods than other objects in the scene. This phenomenon is called "weapon focus." As a result of weapon focus, witnesses spend less time focusing on other details of the crime, including the appearance of the assailant. This may result in less accurate eyewitness identifications.

3. Witness Confidence

Common sense may suggest that the more confident a witness is, the more likely it is that her memory is accurate. However, psychological research has shown little or no correlation between eyewitness confidence and accuracy. In some studies, researchers asked eyewitnesses how confident they were in their ability to make a positive identification before viewing a lineup. This pre-identification confidence proved to be a poor predictor of the witnesses' actual ability to identify the correct suspect in the lineup. Other studies asked eyewitnesses about their confidence levels after they had viewed a lineup and made an identification. The correlation between post-identification confidence and accuracy was only slightly higher than that for pre-identification confidence. Some studies have shown no relationship at all between confidence and accuracy, and some even suggest a negative correlation—that witnesses can be more confident when they are inaccurate than when they are accurate.

In addition, witness confidence is subject to outside influences. Witnesses who are questioned repeatedly become more confident in their accounts, regardless of accuracy. Those who are told they have identified the "correct" suspect also become more confident. Similarly, briefing eyewitnesses about cross-examination—including the likelihood that opposing counsel will attempt to discredit them—increases eyewitness confidence, accuracy notwithstanding. Furthermore, if a witness believes that she is not the only eyewitness, information about another witness's identification can have a dramatic effect on her confidence.

Taken together, this research indicates that although juries often consider eyewitness confidence in weighing credibility, confidence is an unreliable indicator of accuracy, and can be influenced by factors bearing no relation to the accuracy of a witness's identification.

4. Unconscious Transference

The phenomenon of unconscious transference occurs when a witness has seen an individual in one situation, and then incorrectly recalls seeing that person in a second situation. For example, a person in a lineup may look familiar to the witness, and the witness may unconsciously interpret this familiarity as stemming from the crime. The familiar person may, however, only have been an innocent bystander, someone the witness saw just prior to the crime, or even someone the witness saw at an entirely different time from the crime. An illustration of this point from an early study involved a railroad ticket agent who identified a sailor as the person who held him up at gunpoint. The sailor had an airtight alibi. It turned out that the sailor was stationed at a base near the railroad, and the ticket agent had sold him tickets on several prior occasions. The ticket agent recognized his face, and remembered him as the perpetrator. This could happen in any eyewitness identification situation, but is particularly likely in situations where witnesses view more than one photo array or lineup. An eyewitness may see someone for the first time in an initial lineup, but if that same person is present in a second lineup, the witness could "unconsciously transfer his or her visualization of the subject . . . and incorrectly identify the subject in the second lineup."

5. Cross-Racial Identifications

People are generally better at recognizing the faces of people who are the same race as they are. Witnesses identify same-race faces correctly more often, and falsely identify them less often. There is substantial psychological research to support the existence of this phenomenon, but there is little indication of why this is the case. One theory is that people have more experience with their own race, and therefore are better able to recognize same-race faces than different-race faces. However, numerous studies have shown that witnesses with substantial exposure to another race were no better at recognizing different-race faces. Another theory is that racial prejudice may influence eyewitness identification of different-race faces, but psychological research has found that racial attitudes have no impact on accuracy. Regardless of the cause, reduced accuracy in cross-race identifications is highly relevant in any trial involving an eyewitness of a different race than the defendant.

C. Juries Do Not Know That Eyewitnesses Are Inaccurate

Perhaps most importantly, psychological studies also illustrate that most people do not have a good understanding of the factors that influence the accuracy of eyewitness identifications. A number of studies have focused on potential jurors' understanding—or misunderstanding—of these factors. These studies, conducted across different populations, indicate that potential jurors generally do not understand the influence these factors have. For example, only slightly more than half of the Americans surveyed were aware that people have more difficulty identifying people of other races than people of their own race. Potential jurors are similarly unaware that viewing a person's picture in a photo array will increase the chances of picking that person out of a lineup. Furthermore, many people surveyed grossly overestimated a witness's ability to retain memories. These results offer a glimpse into lay misperception about eyewitness accuracy.

Rather than focusing on awareness of various factors, many recent studies seek to evaluate how well jurors actually judge eyewitness accuracy. In these studies, mock jurors read descriptions of prior eyewitness identification studies and are asked to predict the accuracy of the resulting eyewitness identifications. For example, the mock jurors are told that in the prior study, the witnesses observed a "crime" and later made an eyewitness identification. The mock jurors are also told about any variables involved, for instance, that some of the witnesses would see a perpetrator of their own race, and that some would see a perpetrator of a different race, or that some witnesses had seen the perpetrator appear in prior lineups. The mock jurors then predict the accuracy of the eyewitness identifications, based on the witness' particular conditions. Across several studies, the mock jurors repeatedly predicted a higher level of accuracy than the witnesses had actually demonstrated in the previous experiments. These prediction studies indicate that jurors consistently overestimate the accuracy of eyewitness identifications. Given the relationship between faulty eyewitness identifications and false convictions, educating juries about the weaknesses of eyewitness testimony is extremely important.

Based on these considerations, it is not unreasonable to argue that providing any forensic interpretations on eyewitness testimony alone is a substandard practice—requiring an assumption of accuracy and reliability that is not warranted. Eyewitness statements should be considered as part of a forensic analysis only when they can at least in part be corroborated by the established facts, or a reconstruction of the physical evidence.

Case Example: A Perfect Storm of Causal Factors

Consider the case of Ronald Williamson out of Ada, Oklahoma. The following account is taken from the court record (*Williamson v. Ward* 1997):

> The murder occurred in 1982 in the small town of Ada, Oklahoma. The victim, 21-year-old Debra Sue Carter, was found dead in her apartment. The door had been broken open and the crime scene showed signs of a struggle. The police found a washcloth forced into Ms. Carter's mouth

and a ligature around her neck. The police concluded that Ms. Carter had been sexually assaulted, and suffocated. The police recovered latent fingerprints, hair, and body fluids from the scene, and found a bloody fingerprint on the wall of the bedroom in which the body was located. The only latent prints identified were those of the victim and an Ada police detective who investigated the crime. In a 1983 report, a state fingerprint expert concluded that the bloody print did not match that of the victim or of Mr. Williamson, who was a suspect by that time.

Ms. Carter had worked at the Coachlight Club. The murder took place after she left the Club in the early morning hours of December 8, 1982. Mr. Williamson was known to frequent the Club with Dennis Fritz, and one witness placed Mr. Williamson at the Club the night of the murder. Mr. Williamson was first interviewed by the authorities in March 1983. He denied any involvement and agreed to provide hair and saliva samples. His mother stated that he was home by 10:00 p.m. the night of the murder. Mr. Williamson was interviewed several additional times in 1983 by both the Ada police and agents from the Oklahoma State Bureau of Investigation (OSBI), and he took two inconclusive polygraph examinations. He continued to assert that he knew nothing about the crime.

From October 1984 through January 1985, Mr. Williamson was incarcerated in the Pontotoc County Jail on an unrelated bad-check charge. In August 1985, Charles W. Amos of the Mental Health Services of Southern Oklahoma determined that Mr. Williamson was not competent to stand trial on this charge, and in September the state district judge in that case ruled him incompetent and sent him to Eastern State Hospital. In October, Dr. R.D. Garcia, Chief Forensic Psychiatrist at Eastern State Hospital, issued an opinion stating that Mr. Williamson was competent and returned him for trial. In February 1986, Terri Holland, who had been incarcerated in the Pontotoc County Jail while Mr. Williamson was held there a year earlier, informed the District Attorney that she had heard Mr. Williamson confess to the murder when they were in jail together. On May 1, 1987, the victim's body was exhumed and another set of her fingerprints was obtained. The state fingerprint expert then changed his opinion and concluded that the bloody print found on the bedroom matched that of the victim. Mr. Williamson was arrested on May 8. On May 9, after being held in the Pontotoc County Jail for twenty-four hours, Mr. Williamson gave a statement to Agent Gary Rogers of the OSBI describing a dream in which he had committed the murder. Mr. Williamson also related the contents of a similar dream to a Pontotoc County jailor on May 22.

Neither of these statements was recorded. In September 1987, another man, Ricky Jo Simmons, confessed to killing Ms. Carter in a statement that was videotaped by police. Mr. Williamson was tried and convicted in April 1988.

Details regarding Williamson's defense, trial, and last-hour exoneration are taken from Uphoff (2006, 763–764):

> Ronald Williamson was one indigent defendant who had no choice but to go to trial with an attorney who was woefully unprepared to do so. His attorney, W.B. Ward, was a sole practitioner appointed to defend Williamson in a capital murder case. His appointed co-counsel withdrew shortly before trial so Ward tried the case alone. He did not receive any investigative or expert services and was paid a total of $3,200 for his efforts. Ward explained to the trial judge that he had to make a living and could not spend any more time than was necessary on this case. Unfortunately, the time Ward spent investigating Williamson's case was far from adequate. Despite being aware of some of Williamson's psychiatric history, Ward failed to investigate his mental condition. Had he done so, he would have discovered that Williamson had a long history of mental illness that left him delusional with a distorted perception of reality. Although Williamson's dream confession to the police was a major part of the prosecution's case, Ward failed to challenge it and the jury never learned of Williamson's mental condition. Nor did the jury learn that another man, Ricky Simmons, confessed to the crime. Based on [Williamson's] dream confession, the testimony of a jailhouse informant, and some questionable hair comparison testimony, the jury convicted Williamson at trial and sentenced him to death.
>
> Five days before Williamson was to be executed, the federal district court issued a stay and subsequently overturned his conviction. Based on counsel's inept performance, the Tenth Circuit Court of Appeals agreed that Williamson's conviction should be reversed and ordered a new trial. While he was awaiting retrial, Williamson's DNA was tested and he was cleared of any involvement in the murder.

This case involved a false confession inferred from a dream (not the first such case by any stretch), a jailhouse informant, misleading scientific testimony, ineffective defense counsel, and concealment of potentially exculpatory evidence from the jury—namely, the actual confession of Ricky Simmons. It also highlights the failure of the court system to provide adequate funding in a capital murder case, for defense counsel or private forensic experts. As such, it underscores the reality that causal factors can surround a case and attack it from all directions. This weighs more in favor of an overall systemic influence on the initial wrongful conviction and death sentence than merely a series of honest mistakes.

FORENSIC EXPERTS AND WRONGFUL CONVICTIONS

As careful students will note from chasing down the references at the end of this chapter, much has been written on the subject of wrongful convictions. Its history, extent, causes, victims, and costs are much debated in literature. Yet very little in the way of conciliatory writing or coverage actually comes from those in the forensic community who have participated in wrongful convictions, nor have those in the forensic community engaged in significant self-reflection on the subject.

More disturbing, there is a portion of the forensic community that does not dwell on its role in the courtroom, as though this is strictly a place of laws, lawyers, and lawyering where they have no say about what is said or done. We see it in forensic examiners who have heard of but not actually read *Brady v. Maryland* (1963)—with no understanding of what they must disclose; we see it in forensic examiners who consider it the responsibility of attorneys to ask them the right questions in order to unlock favorable testimony—with no perceived duty to prevent false impressions being left in the minds of jurors about the limitations of their findings; we see it in forensic examiners who are illiterate with respect to the laws of evidence and professional ethical standards that bind them when giving expert testimony; we see it in forensic examiners who cling to unreal claims of forensic infallibility, despite being unable to define the scientific method or how they applied it to their findings when asked under oath. Such indifference to the rule of science and law is nothing short of contempt towards the criminal justice system and one's role in it. Such indifference is the hallmark of faulty forensic science in wrongful convictions.

A quote that bears repeating from Chapter 15, Thornton (1994, 483) provides a warning meant primarily for those forensic examiners who do not understand their role in court, or that the mandates of science require a great deal more than the court may want or require:

> Every scientist understands that there are courts of law. By and large, they are accorded respect. I am not as certain that every lawyer understands that there are courts of science as well. They are not as easily identified because they do not exist in a particular point in space, nor is there one man or woman in a black robe that symbolizes the court, nor a marble anteroom outside smelling of urine and industrial strength disinfectant. Courts of science are constructs of the mind which bring clarity and coherency to scientific and technical matters. They are built not of marble, but from the scientific method. Every scientist is expected to serve as his or her own presiding judge, and if a costume is necessary, it is a white lab coat instead of a black robe. But these courts have certain rules also, just as courts of law. And the scientist who declines to practice his or her profession by the rules of

science will soon find that he or she has earned only the derision of his or her colleagues, and eventually finds that he or she cannot continue to practice at all.

A scientist who cannot practice successfully in the courts of science has no business in the courts of law. Forensic victimologists, like any other forensic examiner, have a duty to know and practice within the bounds of the law, as well as within scientific standards. This requires knowing both.

SCIENTIFIC FACT VS. LEGAL TRUTH

Despite the position of some jurists, the superior court (also known as the trial court) is not the final arbiter of fact. Rather, it determines legal truth—until the next legal cycle. Any position to the contrary ignores the reality of the appellate court, which can reverse superior court decisions, and state supreme courts, which can reverse the appellate court. It also ignores the aforementioned advent of DNA exonerations, proving every day that many in the United States are found legally guilty in court while being factually innocent of the crime.

In this way, we cleave scientific fact from legal truth. As we have learned, legal truth is a function of the prevailing judgments in a given court that are susceptible to review, revision, and even reversal. It is a matter of law, which is dynamic. Scientific fact is determined using the scientific method and exists in a sphere independent of the court. No legal finding can change a scientific fact, it can only rule on its admissibility. However the opposite occurs on a regular basis.

A fairly useful discussion regarding the intersection of law and science is provided in Thornton (1983, 86–88), as well as a reminder regarding the abuse of scientific testimony:

> Law and science on occasion have conflicting goals, each having developed in response to different social and intellectual needs. The goal of law is the just resolution of human conflict, while the goal of science traditionally has been cast, although perhaps too smugly, as the search for "truth." Certainly there is nothing intrinsically dichotomous in the pursuit of these goals; the court or jury strives in good faith to determine the truth in a given situation as a way to resolve conflicts. But proof is viewed somewhat differently by law and science, as is the application of logic and the perception of societal values.
>
> Numerous writers have commented on these differences, including Glanville Williams in his *Proof of Guilt* (1958): "The principles of [the legal system] are not the product of scientific observation, but

embody a system of values. These values do not necessarily have to be changed with the march of knowledge of the material world...The rule conferring upon an accused the right not to be questioned...may be a good or a bad rule, [but it] has certainly not been made better or worse by the invention of printing or the aeroplane."...

How, then, do these differences between law and science lead to abuse of forensic science? They do simply because all the players want to win and are likely to use any ethical means at their disposal to do so. The attorneys in a case are aligned with only one side, and it is entirely appropriate under the adversary system for them to advocate a particular point of view, even without full and fair disclosure of all relevant facts. Subject only to the rules of evidence, the rules of procedure, and the Code of Professional Responsibility, attorneys are free to manipulate scientific evidence to maximize the opportunity for their side to prevail. Not only is behavior of this sort countenanced by the law, it is the ethical responsibility of counsel to attempt to do so.

With this in mind, forensic examiners must not only anticipate but rather expect that their findings and related testimony will be, at best, misrepresented by attorneys making arguments on both sides once they have left the witness stand. It is consequently their duty to report findings and testify in such a manner as to prevent this from happening whenever possible.

FAULTY FORENSICS

The defining quality of forensic experts is the possibility that they will be called upon to present their findings, under penalty of perjury, in a court of law. Subsequently, they will be asked to explain to the court what those findings mean and how they came to them. Those experts whose work does not bring them into court are not forensic in nature. As provided in Thornton (1997, 3):

The single feature that distinguishes forensic scientists from any other scientist is the certain expectation that they will appear in court and testify to their findings and offer an opinion as to the significance of those findings. The forensic scientist will testify not only to what things are, but to what things mean. Forensic science is science exercised on behalf of the law in the just resolution of conflict.

The unique role of the forensic expert is that of educator to attorneys, judges, and juries. The trust extended to them by the court under these circumstances is not trivial. Results of their examinations and any related opinions can greatly influence the outcome of a trial. In civil matters, reputations and fortunes may be lost or won. In criminal matters, nothing less than the life and liberty of the accused is at stake. A convincing forensic expert with favorable findings or opinions can be terribly compelling to a judge or jury, and thus tip the scales for either side.

The majority of forensic scientists and other forensic experts takes their court responsibilities seriously, and the quality of their work reflects integrity to the evidence. Of course, flaws and fallibility are arguably an integral facet of human nature and thus every human endeavor. They are to be expected, admitted, and addressed. However, my own ongoing research continues to uncover a steady stream of forensic experts willing to provide sworn expert testimony or reports to the court that contain deceptive or misleading findings and opinions. Separate from error born of accident and human fallibility, these are instances of forensic fraud. As described in Thompson (2000):

> In addition to honest mistakes born of incompetence and overwork, there are continuously uncovered examples of fraud: the lab analyst, believing that the verdict justifies the means, willing to lie on the stand or fake test results.

Forensic fraud is not a matter to be taken lightly. As discussed in Saks (2001), it is a breach of both professional ethics and the law:

> Where a proffered expert knows himself or herself to be a quack or otherwise to be offering false testimony, the situation is like that of any other witness who is perpetrating a fraud on the court. Such acts are illegal as well as unethical.

A fraudulent expert of any kind is certainly unreliable, and certainly not to be extended the trust and confidence of the court. Such an expert betrays the trust of the client, the court, and the public, as well as contributes directly to the victimization of the innocent. But we must remember that fraudulent experts are more than just liars, and more than just unreliable; they are also criminal. If forensic fraud is suspected and then demonstrated, a number of consequences can result—dependent, sadly, almost entirely on the amount of media attention that ensues:

1. The public and professional trust in the forensic community involved is severely damaged, and negative views reinforced.
2. If employed by a government or private agency, the fraudulent expert may be sanctioned by removal to research or nonforensic investigative duties. He or she may even be terminated, though this is not always the case.
3. The fraudulent expert's entire case history may be scrutinized for potential errors at the expense of his or her employer and the court.
4. The fraudulent expert may be criminally prosecuted by the legal community he or she has defrauded and suffer fines or even jail time.

5. The fraudulent expert or his or her employer may be exposed to civil liability.

6. Criminal convictions or sentences involving the expert's testimony may be reversed at great expense of time and resources to everyone concerned.

7. The fraudulent expert is typically not able to testify in court once the crime comes to light. However, a few have delayed this consequence by simply moving to a new state or a new agency, fleeing from allegations of misconduct.

As described, the consequences of forensic fraud for all concerned are weighty, to say nothing of the potential contributions to wrongful convictions. As a result, those with authority within forensic communities (institutions, agencies, and organizations) continue to downplay instances of demonstrable forensic fraud as isolated events rather than a significant problem. Such actions certainly seem biased towards protecting the forensic professions from criticism, although this may not be the most accurate interpretation.[4]

Consider the findings published in Cooley (2007, 390–395):

> Contrary to what many forensic examiners profess, there is an unmistakable correlation between overturned convictions and erroneous and/or fraudulent forensic science. To date, there have been 204 convictions thrown out or overturned because postconviction DNA tests either conclusively exonerated a previously convicted person or cast such serious doubts on the State's case [that] the State moved to have the defendant released and all charges dismissed. While a number of these flawed convictions stem from eyewitness misidentifications, false confessions, jailhouse snitches, and incompetent defense counsel, there is a discernible association between these cases and defective and/or fraudulent forensic science.

In many of these cases, forensic examiners, particularly hair analysts, offered opinions that were later proved wrong by new DNA tests. Besides hair misidentifications, convictions have been vacated or overturned due to misidentified fingerprints; fabricated fingerprints; misleading testimony; misinterpreted firearms evidence; miscalculated DNA statistics; forensic fraud; misinterpreted drug evidence; misidentified bite marks; faulty blood testing; misinterpreted burn patterns; misidentified earprints; misidentified handwriting; and erroneous autopsy conclusions. More significantly, courts have vacated death sentences

---

[4]The only published research of forensic fraud (Turvey 2003) found that in 34 (81%) of 42 total cases, forensic fraud was committed on behalf of the prosecution, and most often by law enforcement crime lab personnel. This would suggest that bias is more associated with employment by the police or prosecution.

and capital convictions because of botched autopsies; misleading testimony; misidentified boot prints; erroneous burn pattern interpretations; misidentified hair evidence; misidentified bite marks; forensic fraud; and erroneous firearms identifications. Additionally, innocent people have been wrongly accused of serious offenses like murder, rape, and train bombings because of misidentified fingerprints; misidentified firearms; misidentified shoe prints; misidentified bite marks; erroneously interpreted burn patterns; and misinterpreted autopsy results. Likewise, there are several cases currently pending in state post-conviction or federal habeas corpus that not only raise significant questions regarding the defendant's guilt and/or death sentence, but the forensic evidence used to secure the conviction, death sentence, or both. Finally, there is evidence that suggests erroneous or unsubstantiated forensic science played a role in an innocent person's execution.

While many of these errors can and will be labeled as honest human errors, this does not diminish the fact that an unacceptable number of errors could have been avoided had the forensic science community: (1) been properly funded; (2) conducted adequate research; and (3) properly trained its examiners. Besides being emotionally and psychologically devastating for the wrongly accused or convicted person and the victims, wrongful accusations and convictions are economically disastrous, because they typically generate extensive litigation resulting in large financial settlements.

These findings are echoed more recently by research published in Garrett (2008, 81–86):

> Forensic evidence was the second leading type of evidence supporting these erroneous convictions. In many cases, little more than flimsy forensic evidence supported the conviction. Some had more than one type introduced. One hundred and thirteen cases (57%) involved introduction of forensic evidence at trial, with serological analysis of blood or semen the most common (79 cases), followed by expert comparison of hair evidence (43 cases), soil comparison (5 cases), DNA tests (3 cases), bite mark evidence (3 cases), fingerprint evidence (2 cases), dog scent identification (2 cases), spectrographic voice evidence (1 case), shoe prints (1 case), and fiber comparison (1 case).

> The forensic evidence was often fairly central to the prosecution's case even though it may have been known to have limited probative power at the time of trial. For example, exonerations in cases involving serology may not show misconduct, but rather either the limitations of old-fashioned serology as compared with more advanced DNA testing technology or unintentional error in conducting such testing. Serological testing sorts individuals into just a handful of different blood types, typically using the A, B, and H antigens,

each shared by high percentages of the population; for example, approximately 40% of the population possesses only the H antigen, making them the O type. In contrast, DNA testing can provide random match probabilities greater than all humans who have ever lived (for example, one in 100 trillion).

Despite its relative lack of probative power, serological evidence was often all that law enforcement could use at the time of the investigation. In this group of cases, which chiefly consist of rape convictions in the pre–DNA era, serological evidence was the most common type of forensic evidence introduced at trial, and it typically involved analysis of materials from a rape kit prepared after an assault. Serological evidence was usually not the only evidence at trial—though in one case the serological evidence was the central evidence at trial and in another case serology and hair evidence were the central evidence at trial. In 46 of the exonerees' cases (23%), there was an eyewitness identification added to the serological evidence. In four cases, the serology was added to a confession. In three more it was added to alleged self-inculpatory remarks. In two cases, the serological evidence was added to informant testimony. Thus, despite its typical lack of probative power, serological evidence often bolstered other evidence at trial.

Many, and perhaps most, cases, however, appear to have involved not merely use of evidence with limited probative value, but the improper use of then-existing forensic science. To a surprising extent, the forensic testimony at trial was improper based on science at the time. A preliminary review of serological testimony during these exonerees' trials disclosed that more than half involved improper testimony by forensic examiners.

The second most common type of evidence in these cases, visual hair comparison testimony, is notoriously unreliable. Absent any data regarding probabilities that hair or fiber may match visually, experts can make only a subjective assessment whether two hairs or two fibers are "consistent" and share similarities. Forty-three cases (22%) involved false visual hair or fiber comparison. Hair evidence was used in forty-two cases. In some cases that visual hair comparison evidence was particularly central to the prosecution's case. Calvin Scott spent 20 years behind bars based largely on hair comparison evidence alone, in a case where the victim did not get a good look at her attacker and could not identify Scott. In eleven cases, visual hair comparison testimony was added to eyewitness testimony as evidence of identity. In five cases, hair comparison testimony and an informant were presented at trial.

Just as with the serological cases, a preliminary review suggests that microscopic hair comparison testimony at trial often distorted or misstated the forensic evidence to inflate its probative significance. Errors were due not merely to the underlying unreliability of visual hair comparison, but were at a minimum compounded by improper and misleading testimony regarding comparisons conducted. Most commonly, state experts mischaracterized their results by purporting to "match" hairs or constructing the probability of such a match, rather than merely visually comparing hairs and either observing certain similarities or excluding any common source. For example, in the case of Paul D. Kordonowy, convicted of rape where the victim did not see her assailant, the conviction rested on forensic evidence. Montana Forensic Science Laboratory specialist Arnold Melnikoff did not correctly explain the lack of probative power of hair comparison. Instead, he testified that he could distinguish head hairs in 99 of 100 cases, telling the jury that Kordonowy's hair and blood type matched those found at the scene. In fact, an enzyme in the blood sample did not match Kordonowy, nor did the hairs, and yet Melnikoff's testimony contributed to Kordonowy's wrongful imprisonment for 13 years. Melnikoff was later fired, but not before he falsified testimony in at least one other case. In the case of Jimmy Ray Bromgard, Melnikoff used made-up probabilities that he then improperly multiplied as follows: "[T]he odds were one in one hundred that two people would have head hair or pubic hair so similar that they could not be distinguished by microscopic comparison and the odds of both head and pubic hair from two people being indistinguishable would be about one in ten thousand."...

Each of three cases in which faulty DNA evidence was introduced at trial involved experts who offered misleading testimony and mischaracterized their own laboratory reports. Two cases involved improper analysis and testimony that resulted in false inclusions. In one case, that of Gilbert Alejandro, the criminalist claimed a DNA match even though neither he nor anyone else had even conducted the DNA testing.

Bite mark evidence, also notoriously unreliable, was relied on in three cases, in one providing the only evidence of guilt in a capital case. The forensic evidence was rarely challenged with any success on appeal or postconviction, though six exonerees obtained reversals based on challenges to forensic evidence at trial. None of the 113 persons who were convicted based on forensic evidence raised a fabrication of evidence claim under the Due Process Clause. However, some exonerees raised state evidence law claims (15), ineffective assistance claims (11), or prosecutorial misconduct claims (2) to challenge the forensic evidence introduced at trial. These figures represent a total of 25 exonerees, or 32% of the 77 cases with written decisions involving convictions based on forensic evidence. One reason for the dearth of challenges to forensic evidence may be that indigent defendants could not afford to hire a forensic expert. Indigent defendants frequently fail to receive funding for such independent experts. Thus, until the DNA testing was done, these exonerees may simply have been unable to show that the forensic evidence at trial was false or unreliable.

The above paints an extremely disparaging picture of the forensic community. This includes consideration of forensic practitioners who refuse to concede or address flawed or fraudulent science, those in the criminal justice system who have all but lost faith in forensic experts, and those who count on the willingness of forensic examiners to be exploited. Until these issues are put on the table for serious discussion and specific remedies are brought to bear, those in the forensic community can and will be measured by the weakest links among them with respect to competence and ethics.

FIGURE 16.2

The body of Peggy Hettrick, 37, was found in a field. She had been stabbed to death.

Case Example: Timothy Masters

Consider the case of Timothy L. Masters from Ft. Collins, Colorado, convicted for the 1987 murder of 37-year-old Peggy Hettrick—a crime Masters would have had to commit when he was 15 years old. The following is taken entirely from the court record in *Colorado v. Masters* (2001):

Late one night in 1987, as the victim walked along a road near a field adjacent to defendant's home, she was subjected to an apparent surprise attack and was stabbed in the back by a person wielding a knife with a five-inch blade. She was dragged more than a hundred feet into the open field and was found by a passerby the next morning. When found, the body had been partially disrobed and had been sexually mutilated with a very sharp instrument, possibly a scalpel. Scratches were evident on one side of her face, and a pool of blood surrounded her body.

During the investigation that morning, police contacted defendant's father at home. Since defendant's bedroom faced the field, and the victim's body could be seen from his bedroom window, the police contacted the 15-year-old defendant at his high school concerning the possibility that he had seen the body on his way to school. When the police detective first spoke to defendant and asked him if he knew why the detective was there, defendant nodded and stated that "it had been bothering him" and that he thought he had seen a body as he was walking to catch the bus. He explained that he did not report it because he believed the body to be a mannequin.

Because of his failure immediately to report the victim's body, defendant became a suspect. A consensual search of defendant's bedroom revealed a large collection of survival knives with long blades, one containing a scalpel in its handle, a fillet knife, a machete, and a ninja sword, as well as a suitcase containing pornographic depictions of female anatomy and a large number of drawings and narratives.

These latter written materials had been created by defendant and depicted surprise attacks, gruesome death scenes, and scenes of violence and sex. Some of the drawings depicted persons with scratches across their cheeks with pools of blood surrounding them, and there were scenes of torture, cutting of body parts, and depictions of survival knives with long blades.

A consensual search of defendant's locker and backpack revealed additional drawings and narratives, including two maps of the field and surrounding area and a drawing of a body being dragged by another person.

The murder had taken place almost exactly four years following the death of defendant's mother. Both the victim and the mother had wavy red hair. Defendant did not know the victim, but admitted that he might have seen her around the neighborhood; they lived in the same area and shopped at the same Albertson's supermarket.

During an interrogation following a *Miranda* advisement and waiver, a detective stated to defendant that stabbing someone with a serrated edged knife would cause a lot of damage. Defendant replied, "Yeah, but it would be tough to pull it back out."

Defendant also had stated that the victim was wearing pink shoes. The victim's socks were in fact pink but could not be seen at the crime scene because of the positioning of the body and the arrangement of the clothing.

The detective asked defendant if he had any suggestions concerning investigation of the case, and defendant said to check the ditch under a particular bridge. Six months later, a survival knife with a serrated edge was found in the ditch very close to the bridge. The coroner opined at trial that the serration on that knife could account for the irregularity in the stab wound in the victim's back that he had observed upon autopsy.

The police investigation did not find any blood matching the victim's on any of defendant's clothing or property. Also, there was no fiber evidence that would link defendant to the murder, and there was no property of the victim or any severed body parts found in defendant's possession. As a result, no charges were filed, and the murder remained unsolved.

Ten years later, the police department consulted a forensic psychologist with expertise in the area of "sexual homicides." The psychologist reviewed the drawings and narratives that defendant had produced, together with the other evidence in the case, and prepared reports containing his opinion. He opined that defendant had killed the victim and, by doing so, had symbolically killed his own mother.

Based on this and the other evidence, defendant was arrested and charged with first degree murder in 1998. The police obtained a search warrant and seized additional drawings and narratives defendant had created following the crime.

By a motion *in limine,* defendant sought to bar the psychologist's testimony and to preclude admission of the drawings and narratives under CRE 404(b). At a hearing on the motion, the psychologist testified at length regarding research in the area of sexual homicide. The psychologist stated that a sexual homicide, *i.e.,* one in which there is sexual activity by the perpetrator, is generally preceded by a triggering event in the emotional life of the perpetrator. He explained that fantasy is the motivation behind sexual homicides and that a perpetrator's fantasies become a rehearsal for his commission of the crime. He described in detail five different categories of such fantasies and opined how defendant's drawings and narratives fit into each of the five categories.

He opined that the materials reflected a preference for surprise attack, rather than a ruse or seduction; that the materials exhibited "piquerism," *i.e.,* stabbing and slicing as the means of sexually penetrating the victim's body, as demonstrated by defendant's preoccupation with knives and cutting; that the victim resembled defendant's mother in age and hair color, and the killing occurred almost exactly four years after the defendant's mother had died; that the victim was a stranger or, at most, a casual acquaintance; and that defendant perceived himself as a warrior character without empathy or feeling who engaged, through fictional narratives and pictures, in a variety of killings.

The court admitted the drawings and narratives under CRE 404(b), but limited the expert's testimony. The court permitted the psychologist to testify about the concept of sexual homicide and the associated concepts of triggering events, fantasy, and rehearsal fantasy, and allowed him to describe evidence that fit its characteristics. The expert, however, was precluded from giving an opinion that this was a sexual homicide, that defendant fit the characteristics of a sexual homicide perpetrator, that defendant committed the crime, or that any drawing or narrative was evidence that defendant had committed this crime. He was also permitted to testify hypothetically concerning the type of event that might be a trigger for a sexual homicide and to give an opinion that a drawing or narrative defendant had created was an example of one of the categories noted.

Among the other testimony presented at trial was that of the defendant's high school teacher and a counselor, who were permitted to testify concerning an incident at school that had happened approximately one month before the victim's murder. The prosecution theorized that this incident was a triggering event for the murder.

According to the court record, the expert hired by the prosecution in this case was Dr. J. Reid Meloy. As explained in Campbell (2008):

> Meloy came onto the case in late 1997 after famed FBI criminal profiler Roy Hazelwood recommended him to Fort Collins Police Det. Jim Broderick. Broderick, now a lieutenant, needed professional validity for his theory that Masters' voluminous drawings and short stories not only provided the motive for the brutal 1987 stabbing murder and sexual mutilation of Peggy Hettrick, but the evidence as well.
>
> Meloy seemed happy to oblige. Broderick provided him with crime scene videotapes, police interviews with Masters, police reports, photographs, maps and transcripts. He sent him more than 2,000 pages of Masters' productions. When all was said and done, Meloy was paid more than $52,700 for his work on the case.
>
> ... Meloy was interviewed for a 2000 documentary about the case that appeared on the A&E Network's "Cold Case Files." The show is an uncritical ode to how Meloy, Broderick, Gilmore and Blair joined forces to crack the case using something akin to mentalism.
>
> "After spending six months on the case, I felt I understood the motivations for this homicide and that I had become convinced that Timothy Masters was the individual that had committed this homicide," Meloy said on the show.
>
> For Meloy, Masters' drawings represented a "fantasy rehearsal" for the crime, especially a doodle on Masters' math homework of a

knife-wielding hand cutting a diamond shape that Meloy interpreted as a vagina, "which may have been a rehearsal of the genital mutilation," as he wrote in his first report to Broderick.

Equally damning in Meloy's interpretation was a picture Masters drew the day after he saw Hettrick's body. It depicted one figure dragging another, which was apparently wounded or dead, from behind. The wounded figure was riddled with arrows and blood seemed to flow from its back.

The figure's heels dug furrows in the ground similar to furrows found where Hettrick's body was dumped.

Entirely discounting the presence of the arrows—which had nothing whatsoever to do with the murder—Meloy wrote in his report that this picture represented the crime as it actually happened.

"This is not a drawing of the crime scene as seen by Tim Masters on the morning of Feb. 11 as he went to school," Meloy wrote. "This is an accurate and vivid drawing of the homicide as it is occurring. It is unlikely that Tim Masters could have inferred such criminal behavior by just viewing the corpse, unless he was an experienced forensic investigator. It is much more likely, in my opinion, that he was drawing the crime to rekindle his memory of the sexual homicide he committed the day before."

Although these two depictions were the most critical in bolstering the prosecution's case, Meloy told the A&E interviewer that the sheer volume of Masters' productions also implicated him.

"Lt. Broderick provided me with approximately 2,200 pages of drawings and narratives produced by this young man before and immediately after the homicide," he said on the TV show. "This is a voluminous amount of material. In my 18 years of doing this kind of work I have never seen such voluminous productions by a suspect in a sexual homicide. And that tells us he was preoccupied with sexual violence, with violence, with sexually sadistic images, with images of domination and degradation of women, and he was also fascinated by knives."

Jolene Blair also commented about this on the show. "It wasn't just the fact that he had these drawings...but the number, the sheer number we found," she said. "What we needed to do is demonstrate that this wasn't just a passing fancy of this kid, this was complete obsession with death, specifically the death of a woman, and try to draw parallels between the drawings and our crime scene."

In court, the jury was bombarded with Masters' scary pictures that were shown on a large video monitor while Meloy pointed out features of them that he testified showed pairing of sex and violence; evidence of "picquerism," the sadistic pleasure derived from stabbing; degradation of women; and fascination with weapons and death.

In his first report to Broderick, Meloy wrote that Masters killed Hettrick because he felt abandoned by his mother, who died unexpectedly almost exactly four years to the day before the murder. He opined that her death, an "emotionally distant" relationship with his father who spent a lot of time away from home while on active duty in the Navy, the departure of his sister from their home to join the U.S. Army, and his retreat into a fantasy world combined to create a boiling kettle of latent violence just waiting to erupt.

"A retreat into such a compensatory narcissistic fantasy world, replete with sexuality and violence, works for awhile, but at a great cost," Meloy wrote. "The unexpressed rage continues, depression may ensue, and anger toward women as sources of both pain (abandonment) and erotic stimulation builds."

Peggy Hettrick's random appearance on the road near Masters' house as she walked home from a Fort Collins tavern—according to the prosecution's theory of events—proved the tragic tipping point for this troubled person, in Meloy's view.

"Sexual homicide represents the solution, particularly in the form it took in this case: If I kill a woman, she cannot abandon me; if I desexualize her (genital mutilation) she cannot stimulate me," [Meloy] wrote. "These are not conscious thoughts for Tim Masters, but likely represent the unconscious beliefs that drove his behavior the night of Feb. 11, 1987, when he killed and sexually mutilated Peggy Hettrick, a victim of choice and opportunity. Ms. Hettrick represented all Women (sic) to Tim Masters."

On March 26, 1999, a Larimer County jury convicted Masters of first-degree murder and he was sentenced to life in prison. Two subsequent appeals failed. However, in 2008, DNA testing exonerated him of the crime. As explained in Hughes (2008):

special prosecutors appointed to review that case concluded that DNA found on Hettrick's body matches someone else, and excludes the now-deceased Dr. Richard Hammond, another potential suspect.

"It is our belief as special prosecutors in this case that the new evidence meets the constitutional requirements of Rule 35C. That requires a vacation of the original conviction and sentence and entitles Mr. Masters to a new trial," said Adams County District Attorney Don Quick at a hastily called Denver press conference Friday.

Legal observers said it was unlikely that Masters would be tried again in the case.

Quick was appointed as an outside prosecutor because Masters' bid for a new trial centered on accusations that Fort Collins police and Larimer County prosecutors withheld evidence during his case. The two prosecutors in the original case are now Larimer County judges, and the lead police investigator, Lt. Jim Broderick, now runs the police department's Internal Affairs unit.

Several years ago, a new defense team took up Masters' cause and recently submitted DNA evidence found on Hettrick's clothing for independent analysis in the Netherlands.

On Jan. 15, defense lawyers turned over the profile gleaned from that DNA to prosecutors, who compared it with a partial sample they had developed. The Dutch [DNA] profilers are expected to be at Tuesday's court hearing.

On Friday, after several hours of discussion with officials from the Colorado Bureau of Investigation, Quick decided the new evidence entitled Masters to a new trial—and demanded further investigation.

FIGURE 16.3

Timothy Masters, convicted in no small part by his drawings, was freed from prison after his sentence was vacated. He was released on January 22, 2008.

The Masters' case is far from over, however, as those involved are now under close scrutiny. Among other wrongdoings, the defense team has accused the prosecution of withholding reports and opinions of experts with contrary opinions, withholding Dr. Meloy's report, and failing to investigate alternate suspects. As explained in Pilsner (2008):

[The 19th Judicial District Attorney's Office in Weld County] has spent the past few months reviewing Fort Collins Police Lt. Jim Broderick and his actions while investigating Masters for the 1986 murder of Peggy Hettrick. . . .

Broderick faces allegations that he lied while under oath on the stand, illegally taped a conversation between Masters and his father and failed to turn over some of the documents that could have assisted in Masters' defense.

The prosecutors in the Masters' case, Terry Gilmore and Jolene Blair, also are being investigated by the state Supreme Court's Office of Attorney Regulation for any misconduct they might have committed during Masters' prosecution. As of this writing, these individuals remain under investigation for their actions in the Masters' case.

SUMMARY

Wrongful convictions are not rare. Nor are they a recent historical phenomenon. Known wrongful conviction rates since the 1980s make clear that they actually exist at a volume and frequency that can no longer be denied, ignored, or defended. Although the lead cause is faulty eyewitness identification, forensic error and fraud are closing the gap at second place. Most often, such errors favor the prosecution. Consequently, forensic victimologists are warned to adopt a scientific mandate with practice standards that embrace objectivity and reliability, and to refrain from reports, testimony, or conduct that contribute to furthering the problem—if they wish to be worthy of any trust afforded by the criminal justice system.

Questions

1. True or False: Wrongful convictions can occur despite the best intentions of everyone involved.
2. True or False: False convictions did not take place before the advent of DNA technology.
3. What are some factors that may lead to false convictions?
4. According to the most recent research, since 1989 _____ people have been exonerated of rape and homicide by DNA evidence.
5. Explain the differences between scientific fact and legal truth.
6. What is a Brady violation?
7. What is the leading cause of wrongful convictions?
8. What are three factors that can influence the accuracy of eyewitness testimony?
9. What are some of the consequences of forensic fraud?
10. True or False: Visual hair comparison is notoriously unreliable.

REFERENCES

Bernhard, A. 2004. "Justice Still Fails: A Review of Recent Efforts to Compensate Individuals Who Have Been Unjustly Convicted and Later Exonerated." *Drake Law Review* 52, Summer: 703–738.

Brady v. Maryland. 1963. U.S. Supreme Court, No. 490 373 U.S. 83. Decided May 13.

Campbell, G. 2008. "The Tim Masters case: Chasing Reid Meloy." *Fort Collins Now*, February 1. http://www.fortcollinsnow.com/article/20080201/NEWS/297958975.

Colorado v. Masters. 2001. Colorado Court of Appeals, Div. IV. No. 99CA0896, 33 P.3d 1191. Denied March 22.

Connors, E., T. Lundregan, N. Miller, and T. McEwen. 1996. *Convicted by Juries, Exonerated by Science: Case Studies in the Use of DNA Evidence to Establish Innocence after Trial.* Washington, DC: National Institute of Justice, Office of Justice Programs, U.S. Department of Justice, NCJ 161258, June.

Cooley, C. 2007. "Forensic Science and Capital Punishment Reform: An 'Intellectually Honest' Assessment." *George Mason University Civil Rights Law Journal* 17, Spring: 299–422.

Emily, J., and S. McGonigle. 2008. "Dallas County district attorney wants unethical prosecutors punished." *The Dallas Morning News*, May 4.

Fradella, H. 2006. "Why Judges Should Admit Expert Testimony on the Unreliability of Eyewitness Testimony." *Federal Courts Law Review* 3, June: 1–46.

Joy, P. 2006. "The Relationship between Prosecutorial Misconduct and Wrongful Convictions: Shaping Remedies for a Broken System." *Wisconsin Law Review* 84: 399–429.

Garrett, B. 2008. "Judging Innocence." *Columbia Law Review* 108, January: 55–142.

Gross, S., K. Jacoby, D. Matheson, N. Montgomery, and S. Patil. 2005. "Exonerations in the United States, 1989 through 2003." *Journal of Criminal Law and Criminology* 95, Winter: 523–559.

Hughes, T. 2008. "Masters to go free: Prosecutor moves to vacate conviction after DNA linked to former boyfriend." *The Fort Collins Coloradoan*, January 19. http://www.coloradoan.com/apps/pbcs.dll/article?AID=/20080119/NEWS01/801190361/1002/CUSTOMERSERVICE02.

Liebman, J.S., Fagan, J., and West, V.A. "Broken System: Error Rates in Capital Cases 1973–1995" available at www.thejusticeproject.org.

Liebman, J., S. Rifkind, V. West, and J. Lloyd. 2000. "Capital Attrition: Error Rates in Capital Cases, 1973–1995." *Texas Law Review* 78, June: 1839–1865

Mullin, C. 1986. Error of Judgement: The Truth About the Birmingham Bombs. London: Chatto & Windus Ltd.

Naughton, M. 2005. "Redefining Miscarriages of Justice." *British Journal of Criminology* 45, March: 165–179.

Overbeck, J. 2005. "Beyond Admissibility: A Practical Look at the Use of Eyewitness Expert Testimony in the Federal Courts." *New York University Law Review* 80, December: 1895–1920.

Pilsner, J. 2008. "Review continues into actions of lead Masters investigator." *The Reporter–Herald*, May 3.

Risinger, D.M. 2007. "Innocents Convicted: An Empirically Justified Factual Wrongful Conviction Rate." *Journal of Criminal Law and Criminology* 97, Spring: 761–804.

Rowe, W. 1996. "Commentary by Walter F. Rowe." In *Convicted by Juries, Exonerated by Science: Case Studies in the Use of DNA Evidence to Establish Innocence after Trial*, edited by E. Connors, T. Lundregan, N. Miller, and T. McEwen. Washington, DC: National Institute of Justice, Office of Justice Programs, U.S. Department of Justice, NCJ 161258, June.

Saks, M. 2001. "Scientific Evidence and the Ethical Obligations of Attorneys." *Cleveland State Law Review* 49, no. 3: 421–438.

Smith, B. 2005. "The History of Wrongful Execution." *Hastings Law Journal* 56, June: 1185–1233.

Thompson, C. 2000. "Crime bomb: Police crime labs are churning out tainted evidence—And nobody's doing anything about it." *SFBG.com*, November 22.

Thornton, J. 1983. "Uses and Abuses of Forensic Science." In *Science and Law: An Essential Alliance*, edited by W. Thomas, 79–90. Boulder, CO: Westview Press.

Thornton, J. 1994. "Courts of Law v. Courts of Science: A Forensic Scientist's Reaction to Daubert." *Shepard's Expert and Scientific Quarterly* 1, no. 3: 475–485.

Thornton, J.I. 1997. "The General Assumptions and Rationale of Forensic Identification." In *Modern Scientific Evidence: The Law and Science of Expert Testimony*, Vol. 2, edited by D. Faigman, D. Kaye, M. Saks, and J. Sanders, . St. Paul, MN: West Publishing Co.

Turvey, B. 2003. "Forensic Frauds: A Study of 42 Cases." *Journal of Behavioral Profiling* 4, no. 1: .

Uphoff, R. 2006. "Convicting the Innocent: Aberration or Systemic Problem?" *Wisconsin Law Review* , no. : 739–842.

Williams, G. 1958. The Proof of Guilt: A Study of the English Criminal Trial, London: Stevens & Sons, Ltd.

Williamson v. Ward. 1997. United States Court of Appeals, Tenth Circuit, No. 95–7141, April 10. 110 F.3d 1508, 97 CJ C.A.R. 516.

Index